THE VIEW FROM KING STREET

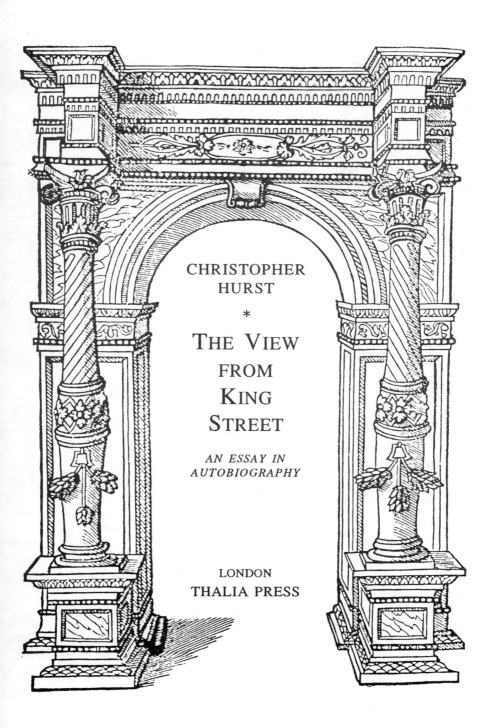

CHRISTOPHER
HURST

*

THE VIEW
FROM
KING
STREET

*AN ESSAY IN
AUTOBIOGRAPHY*

LONDON
THALIA PRESS

First published in the United Kingdom
in an edition of 500 copies
by Thalia Press, and distributed by
C. Hurst & Co. (Publishers) Ltd.,
38 King Street, London WC2E 8JZ
© C. Hurst & Co. (Publishers) Ltd., 1997
All rights reserved.
Typeset by Print Line, New Delhi, and
printed in India
ISBN 1-85065-325-9

*The 'arch' used to decorate the title-page
is from a Yiddish translation of the Pentateuch,
Prophets and Hagiographia published by the
Yehoash Publishing Co., New York, in 1941.*

Apology to the Reader

In 1967 I founded a publishing house called C. Hurst & Co. which at the time of writing is still in business, and I embarked on this book with the thought that a few people, if given the opportunity, might not be averse to reading about my activities in connection with this firm and with publishing generally. My trade has given me a kind of life which I can recommend to others, so there is a missionary element in the wish to write about it.

Autobiographers, even the most serious and single-minded, usually write a chapter, or half of one, at the beginning about their early lives, parents and influences. Whether or not anyone will be interested apart from family and close friends, the writer regards it as an allowable indulgence, and the reader is free to skip it before coming on to the 'important' part. Perhaps it is also window-dressing, to prove that the writer is human as well as important and successful. I have gone rather further than this, because I had hardly begun when a far stronger urge came over me than the original one: this was to write at length and in detail about myself.

I am not writing about my life because I think it has an objective claim on the attention of the public or any section of it. There are neither aristocrats nor proletarians in my traceable lineage, so I cannot write about life in a castle or in a back-to-back, either of which might have genuine curiosity value. My father was a physician of note, and in certain medical circles his is still a conjurable name more than fifty years after his death. But this is not the same as having a parent who was a well-known politician or showbusiness personality – a celebrity – or merely a socialite. Such people attract others of their kind like wasps round a jampot. There were certainly great names among my father's patients, but I hardly met any of them. And although I went to school at Eton, very few of my friends or even acquaintances there were the sons of notable people, or later became notable themselves. The drift of my work also largely precludes my meeting the great or the notorious – unlike some of my publishing colleagues.

So what excuse do I have for offering this book to the public? Some years ago I read C.G. Jung's statement: 'Encounters with people of so many different kinds and on so many different levels have been for me incomparably more important than fragmentary conversation with celebrities. The finest and most significant conversations of my life were anonymous.'* I have met fewer celebrities than Jung, and certainly fewer than George Weidenfeld whose fascinating *Remembering My Good Friends* (1995) is the most recent publishing memoir I have read, and was therefore afraid that if I used those words as an epigraph it might be taken as an oblique form of name-dropping. But I subscribe to them, and call them in aid to justify this enterprise. And I hope not to be accused of hubris for saying that I also find justification in what E.H. Gombrich wrote of 'The Water-Seller of Seville' by Velazquez: 'No one who stands before this picture feels inclined to ask whether the objects represented are beautiful or ugly, or whether the scene it represents is important or trivial.'** Everyone's life is sacred and worth writing about; so here too there is a missionary element to this book, as well as an exhibitionistic one. I would like to encourage people who may have lived muddled, unfulfilled and even sordid lives – or all three – to write about them.

There is the story of the Tsar of Russia who, on a tour in the latter part of the 19th century, was told of a very old man in the village he was visiting who as a child had seen Napoleon. The Tsar commanded that the old man be brought into his presence, and then asked him what he remembered about the French Emperor. 'All I remember', said the old man, 'is that he had a long white beard.' Even verifiable encounters with the great can fall victim to the long white beard syndrome. Encounters with the obscure present fewer dangers.

I am grateful to Andre Deutsch, Leopold Ullstein, John Bunting, Derick Mirfin, Stella Heiden, Colin Haycraft, David Hale, Hubert Schaafsma and my cousin Betty Nicholson for information they have given me which has been useful in writing the book, and I cannot thank Ravi Dayal and Tom Treadwell enough for reading a substantial part of the manuscript and giving me the trenchant advice I sought from them. My thanks to the Liberal International, my cousin Mary D'Aprano and Christopher Maclehose for the loan of photographs. No single dedication is possible, but first and foremost it is to my wife Rachel, with love and gratitude; also to my children Andrew, Josephine, Daniel and Martin; my step-children (past and present) Christopher Anthony, Kate and Dan; my sisters Pam and Rosemary and their progeny; Michael Dwyer; and several more.

March 1997   C. H.

---

* *Memories, Dreams, Reflections*, Flamingo edition (Fontana), p. 168.
** *The Story of Art*, 3rd edn, Phaidon Press, 1950, p. 306.

Contents

Book II. The Road to King Street and the View therefrom

Illustrations

❧

ix

Frederick A. Praeger

Miss Ogilvy and Daniel Hurst

Gustav Nachtigal and Humphrey Fisher

Group including President Jayewardene of Sri Lanka at book
    launching, Colombo, 1981

The author and Eduardo de Laiglesia, Madrid, 1993

Michael Dwyer

Between pages 322 *and* 323

Title page and pp. 10-11 of A.A. Balkema's catalogue of publications,
Amsterdam, 1942-5

Book I
The Pre-history of
a Publisher

Home

When you are driving down the A30 and have passed Staines, Egham and Holloway College, you come to a right turn at Virginia Water down a narrower road that leads to Ascot. In the angle of that turning, between the waterside and the road, George IV assembled a collection of Roman columns and other antique masonry to give the semblance of an authentic ruin, enhanced by overhanging trees and a little rocky waterfall some distance behind. I would only see this sight on the rare occasions when travelling the other way, en route for London with my parents and two sisters. Fortunately the car had to slow down as the corner was turned, giving me time to drink it in. I loved the 'ruin', having never seen a real one, and the waterfall, however, pitiful in size and strength, could claim relationship to Niagara and even the newly-discovered Angel Fall in Venezuela, said to be a mile high (it is actually less). I had a 'craze' for both waterfalls and ruins, and questioned my parents about ones they had seen, and found that my father had walked *behind* Niagara as a young man along a passage that later fell in, and my mother had seen Pompeii and Herculaneum.

In the Great West Road, nearer London, there were some motor-car showrooms where the latest aerodynamic American sedans were displayed, such as the Chrysler, Packard, Lincoln Zephyr and Cord. Here our car was travelling at speed, but the thrill of this gleaming futuristic vision was no less for being brief. By the time we reached Virginia Water again on the way home it would be dark.

Turning that corner in the direction of Ascot today, I immediately feel that the scenery is familiar. It is the edge of Windsor Forest, and the trees are big and dense. At the edge of Ascot village there is a smaller road to the right skirting the eastern side of the racecourse. Where the course turns, there is a crossroads, and from there you can either turn right to Windsor, passing 'The Squirrel' and a few royal estate cottages bearing the rare monogram 'E.R. 1936', crossing the cattle-grid into the Great Park itself and then into the town; or you turn left along a straight road hugging the northern side of the racecourse, with a series of substantial late Victorian villas, set well back in their gardens, on your right. About half a mile along this road, just before a turning called Kennel Ride, is Heath

End. There my family lived between 1921 and the end of December
1939.

Heath End is divided from the road all along the frontage by
a high hedge with a gap in the centre containing a single wrought-iron
gate, which I never saw opened. This was in direct line to the
centre of the house, and in between was a concentric rose garden
with a raised octagonal pond in the centre. Water-lilies grew in the
pond and just below the surface of the water was a network of
bars. Once I was walking round the octagonal parapet when a piece
of stone broke away under my feet and I fell in. During the moment
while I was falling I saw in an upper window the face of our
between-maid Betty, looking out. Because of the bars I got out quickly
and ran into the house. Betty's face had disappeared, but she did
not give any sort of alarm. The iron gate was a gift from my father
to my mother, and it is possible to see in its pattern numerous
juxtapositions of the letter C. This made our close neighbour Mrs
Lennox say to my mother soon after we left Ascot that each time
she passed the gate, the repeated C would say to her 'Cooie, Cooie,
Cooie', my mother's pet name. My father also installed a leaden
replica of Donatello's 'Boy with a Dolphin' in the middle of the
pond: water spouted from the dolphin's mouth if a tap near the
house was turned.

Heath End is the only house which has ever truly meant home
to me, and I remember every inch of it. Although I went to a
boarding school in 1938 and we often had long holidays abroad,
I was never unhappy there, and when we had to leave it after the
beginning of the war, the wrench was painful. I was 'brave' at
the time of our move but, one night some months later, did cry
uncontrollably when I thought about Heath End on going to bed.
When I told my mother the reason for my distress, she sympathised.
The garden, like the house, had a satisfyingly enclosing and nurturing
quality.

The front door was at the back of the house, and before it lay
a gravel expanse, with (as you looked outwards) the 'service' wing
on the right, and a similar wing containing some of our rooms on
the left. Straight ahead, through a break in a yew hedge, you entered
an avenue with a herbaceous border on each side, backed with con-
tinuations of the yew hedge. A sundial stood in the centre half way
down, and at the end, near the back of the property, was a curved
wooden seat. Beyond the yew hedge on the left was our garden,
consisting mainly of lawn, and beyond the hedge on the right was
the kitchen garden, with the gardener's cottage and adjoining greenhouse
at the far end, and close to it the back wall of the garage with

the chauffeur's flat above it. About the edges of the lawn were many rhododendron bushes, one big enough to walk through, and along the west boundary were some tall wellingtonias, which were common in the vicinity; the sun went down behind them and thus they were associated with bed-time. A cedar tree, which we could climb, was in the middle of the lawn near the front of the garden. This was a private world invisible from outside except through the iron gate.

The windows at Heath End were of generous size and had mullions and rectangular leaded lights; the doors had brass handles of Art Nouveau inspiration. The corridors that ran through much of the width of the house upstairs and downstairs were long enough for playing games and riding my tricycle; the one upstairs had an enticing alcove above the front door, containing a long seat. The least used room in the house was a ballroom which was only used twice for that purpose within my memory – we called it the playroom, and it had a frieze painted by one of my father's patients who was a daughter of the Duke of Wellington (I assumed him to be the Iron Duke), portraying several varieties of animal, all consisting of a family with a mother and father, two 'big' children and one tiny one representing myself (maliciously drawing attention to this innocent device was one of numerous ways my sister Rosemary found of getting a rise out of me). A nice big hall occupied the centre of the house from front to back, and contained the oval desk where my father worked and deep armchairs seldom used except for me to 'work out' with somersaults and leaps off the arms into the cushions. It was also where I stood on a wooden chair to help my father into his overcoat when he was about to out.

The dining-room was painted dark green, and with its large tables and sideboards, Turkey carpet, German grandfather clock and oil paintings was, of all the rooms, the most suggestive of Forsytian solidity. It contained a landscape-shaped portrait of my father as a young man sitting on a sofa, painted by Sir Hubert von Herkomer (1849-1914), a grateful patient, and given to him as a wedding present. A conventional 'society'-type portrait of my mother, done by P.A. de Laszlo in 1919 at a cost of £400, hung in the pale green drawing-room; the cut-glass chandelier and wall sconces in that room particularly enchanted me. All of it was probably much smaller than it appears in my memory.

I was born in my parents' double bed at Heath End on 24 December 1929. Of my two sisters Pam was seven and Rosemary not quite five. All of us were healthy, although Pam had a milder form of my father's asthma. Of the two Rosemary was the more robust physically and in personality, although Pam was sensitive and intelligent; for years she was the one with whom I got on, whereas there was hardly any let-up in the warfare between myself and Rosemary. My mother was thirty-five when I was born (my father was fifty), and although she did not appear delicate she was lacking in energy and stayed in bed every morning till late, not out of idleness or wantonness but because my father insisted on it. She never came with the rest of us on our not very strenuous walks between church and lunch on Sundays.

My father did not mix locally, or have friends outside his profession. He was an eminent physician,[*] and was perhaps peculiar in being single-mindedly absorbed in his work. He would go to London every week to do his ward rounds at Guy's Hospital of which he was senior physician throughout the 1930s, and once a year, as well as sharing a portion of our family holidays with us, he would travel to the continent (and once across the Atlantic) with the Medical Pilgrims, a group of distinguished provincial physicians which he founded for the purpose of visiting medical centres abroad. On most days he would drive the five miles to the gastro-enterological clinic which he and a younger colleague, John Venables, founded soon after the Great War with financial help from Venables's rich uncle Ralph Machin, and which became a centre of excellence for this branch of medicine. It was the focus of his private practice, and was housed in a mansion on the edge of Windsor Forest called New Lodge, built in a scholarly Gothic style for a Belgian ambassador called Van der Weyer (the entwined letters 'VW' were to be found in profusion throughout the house). My parents were of the generation that saw no charm in this kind of architecture, and thought it a great joke that Queen Victoria, on visiting the ambassador to view his creation, declared it to be *'un vrai bijou'*. (Having seen the house again in recent years, I agree with the Queen; it is very fine.) I was fascinated that it had its own generator, which chugged away in an outbuilding, and a tall tower to the top of which I was once taken by the butler, Fisher.

In between his visits to London and New Lodge, my father wrote ceaselessly – case-notes about his patients or his own papers for publication. He found a little time for clay modelling and drawing, and offered me the reward of a few postage stamps if I would pose for him. With a pencil he could capture a good likeness, and he

[*] See *Dictionary of National Biography, 1941-1950*; H.C. Cameron, *Mr. Guy's Hospital*, Longmans, 1954, pp. 309-11; *Guy's Hospital Reports*, vol. 89 (vol. 19, 4th series), no. 4, 1939; *Guy's Gazette*, 30 June 1979 (centenary appreciation by W.N. Mann); and his own *A Twentieth-Century Physician*, Edward Arnold, 1949.

taught me the rudiments of drawing. For me it was a misfortune that his energy and ability or desire to communicate with me were curbed by asthma and deafness and the two-generation age-gap between us. A bright time was when we all gathered in the drawing-room after he had returned home from New Lodge, especially in winter with the fire alight. A glass of milk and a sponge finger, which he would dunk in the milk, were brought to him on a salver by the parlour-maid wearing her black and white evening uniform. Often he would fall asleep in his chair. If we were lucky we might get a game with him – of racing demon or a simple affair of writing down as many geographical names as possible beginning with a single letter within a limited time – or I might have some music on the piano with my mother. My father, though not musical, liked listening to me play. Music had been deeply embedded in his family for three generations before his but had passed him and his siblings by altogether.

My father had been a passable swimmer and skier as a young man, and indeed broke his nose – it was permanently crooked so that he looked quite different in the mirror – playing cricket on the sands at Scarborough as a boy. But all this ceased long before my time. I never saw him swim, run, or throw or kick a ball. Under an undiminished head of smooth black hair his sallow-skinned face was drawn, with sunken cheeks, his thin shoulders were hunched, and he walked with a stick. Rarely, a beautiful smile would appear but his laugh was silent; there was no spontaneous fun which we could share, or any easy give and take with any of us; nor could he take any sort of joke against himself. One had to shout for him to hear, and any sudden exertion or shock could make him short of breath: he would then restore his strength the quick way by injecting adrenalin into his thigh through his trouser-leg. It must be partly a lack of feeling in myself, but also partly the quasi-medical atmosphere that pervaded almost our whole existence, that made me react to his suffering by withdrawing rather than going towards him. To this day other people's chest disorders fill me with dread; I would never have made a doctor. It is an irony of fate that a generation earlier, as a vital young bachelor uncle, he charmed his young nephews and nieces with jokes and games.

I have to say too that my father made only the most minimal direct contribution to my intellectual development. He was uninterested in literature, history or any abstract philosophical or religious questions: or at least he was no longer interested in them because, sick as he was, he must have been all too aware that his available time was shrinking while his work relentlessly increased. What little I

learned at home about these things – and it was very little – came
from my mother, who admitted that she was under-educated, and
balked at any serious intellectual inquiry, or discussion of what constituted
religious truth, for fear of her stock of received ideas being upset.
Almost the only time I heard my father enunciate a general principle
with some wit was when I asked him what 'short-sighted' meant
if the eyesight was not being referred to. He said that if he were
to have a swimming pool built in the garden and a band to play
there every afternoon, that would be short-sighted.

My parents were both interested in current international affairs
(but not in national politics), which in the 1930s no educated person
could ignore. This had important consequences for me. A short-term
one was what I did well in general knowledge tests at school; later
it helped to determine my *métier*. The lack of intellectual stimulus
at home must have been a part-cause of the constant trouble I got
into at Eton for not being interested in more than a fraction of
the syllabus.

However, while my father's mind remained closed to me, he freely
revealed his body – calling me into the bathroom to talk to him while
he took his cold bath, in which he made funny faces and sounds
that made me laugh, and handing me a towel to dry his feet afterwards.
This activity gave me an advantage over my sisters to whom it
was naturally barred.

My mother had an Irish name – Cushla – but no Irish blood. She
was the youngest child – there were three daughters and a son – of
Frederick Riddiford (1850-1900), a sheep farmer of Palmerston North
in the North Island of New Zealand, who died painfully after being
thrown from his horse while hunting and then trodden on by it.
His wife Alice McGregor, daughter of Scottish migrants who claimed
descent from Rob Roy, was the only one of my grandparents whose
life-span intersected with mine but we never met. Frederick's parents
Daniel and Harriot emigrated from southern England in 1839, and
he was their second son. The eldest son Edward (1842-1911), who
became known by his Maori sobriquet 'King', acquired enormous
wealth. First he inherited all his father's prime sheep runs, and then
shrewdly expanded his patrimony; dying just before the Great War,
he left his three surviving sons with incomes of approximately £50,000
each. He was notoriously mean and ruthless; before his late marriage
he sired a parallel family by a Maori woman, in whose arms he
is said to have died; and his wife Aunt Nellie, who outlived him
long enough to visit us at Ascot in my time, is recorded in the
Encyclopaedia of New Zealand as saying that her husband would
not have noticed if she had dropped dead beside him. Just as there

are few doctors in England who have not heard of Sir Arthur Hurst, even half a century after his death, so most New Zealanders have heard of the Riddifords, if only as a clan of land-grabbers, whose glory has gradually waned since the time of King. Frederick's offspring were, relatively, the 'poor Riddifords' and, as the only continuing male line besides King's, the cadet branch. An old cousin of my mother's, looking at a faded photograph of Frederick in our house, said to me 'He was tough'. I learned later that he refused to work with King and thus possibly share in his riches; so he was tough morally as well as physically.

As a young girl my mother loved King's youngest son Lionel and dreamed of marrying him when she grew up, but he died young. She left her school in New Zealand early to travel to Europe with her mother, who was seeking a cure for incipient blindness at clinics and watering places, and her next sister Alys, spending short periods at international schools in France and Switzerland. A friend at the French establishment was Cicely Courtneidge who played truant to go to the Parisian theatres and with whom she kept in irregular contact over the years. An abiding memory of a different sort was of the German girls in the school celebrating the anniversary of the German victory over the French at Sedan less than forty years earlier by standing up together in the dining-room and toasting their beloved fatherland with the exclamation 'Hoch!'. She had a brief taste of high life in England. At Henley regatta her party were walking along directly behind the royal party, and Edward VII, clearly tipped off by one of his companions, turned round and stared straight at her; and she went to the Christ Church ball, being punted down the Cherwell to Oxford from Woodeaton, several miles upstream, where her partner's father was the squarson.

Her beauty determined her fate. As the only remaining unmarried daughter, she arrived with her mother at a hotel in Caux, above the Lake of Geneva, just before Christmas 1911, still some months short of her eighteenth birthday. My father, a bachelor of thirty-two now settled into a routine of taking winter holidays in the Alps where the light air relieved his asthma and he could bobsleigh, was already there, and spotted the two women as they came into the hotel dining-room on the evening of their arrival. According to his version of the affair, he immediately fell in love and decided that Cooie would be his wife. In a love-letter he wrote some months later, after she had rejected his proposal of marriage, he told her that he had despaired of ever meeting a girl who would truly attract him, and that his family and friends had given him up as lacking a heart. Now, finally, he knew what he wanted and was going to get it.

Not being in love with my father or ready for marriage – as she freely admitted to me after his death – and with her adult life barely begun, my mother at first resisted him. The differences in age and background seemed not to worry her, and I was never given the feeling by this essentially unselfish woman that she felt her youth and freedom had been taken from her before the natural time. But one definite reason she gave for rejecting his suit was his lack of religious belief, shared by all his siblings, about which he could not dissemble. He kept the promise she extracted from him never to mention this to any children they might have, but it could not escape our notice that he never came to church with us; and once when visiting me at school without my mother and unable to escape our Sunday morning service, he winked at me during the blessing. He gave the impression of regarding religious belief and especially its professional exponents with benign amusement. Yet he was sufficiently tolerant, when one of his colleagues wanted to prevent his son from training for the priesthood, to take the son's part.

There was speculation in his family on why they did not produce any children for the first ten years of their marriage. At first it was assumed to have something to do with my mother's youth and innocence, later that my father's involvement with X-rays was making him sterile. A fantasy of mine from early childhood was that there were earlier offspring whose existence for some reason was kept secret from us children, and who might suddenly appear. It has never entirely gone away.

My parents had a harmonious marriage – one of convenience in the highest sense. The fuel that kept it going was my father's exclusive devotion to his bewitching, much younger bride who, in spite of her educational and intellectual deficiencies, was intelligent, serious and well brought up, spoke French adequately, was musical and had an unerring and unpriggish moral sense which he, virtuous man as he was, did not share. She was not trained to look after herself, and when she was suddenly left a widow at the age of fifty, her disorientation was severe and grew steadily worse. Her inherent moral toughness turned to obstinacy.

The most interesting episode in her life, and possibly in his too, was towards the end of the Great War. After serving in Lemnos and Salonika during the Gallipoli campaign and other hospital appointments at home, he was ordered by the War Office to set up a hospital for treating war neuroses. In his unfinished autobiography *A Twentieth Century Physician* there is almost nothing about it but it is well documented in medical literature, most accessibly in his best-known book *Medical Diseases of the War* (Edward Arnold, 1st edn 1916) of which he dedicated the second edition (1918) 'to my wife, to whose patience and skill many stammering, aphasic and deaf soldiers owe so much'.* That was no empty compliment. At Seale Hayne Military Hospital (the building was a commandeered agricultural college in South Devon), using the techniques of hypnotism and 'persuasion', he and his hand-picked team of medical colleagues restored shellshocked soldiers to the command of their faculties. Team-work under my father's dynamic leadership was the essence, and a side-result was a flood of publications.** The same recipe – a talented team, observation, publication – was reproduced at New Lodge Clinic. He was a gastro-enterologist who had strayed into a field on the borders between neurology and psychiatry, and after the war he continued to practise it for a time (he and Freud might have lived on separate planets: he found Freud's emphasis on sex repugnant). But having thought this work supremely worthwhile when his patients were wounded soldiers, he became disillusioned when they were well-off civilians. I once came upon a scribbled chart he had made of his professional earnings, and they were higher in 1920 than in any year except 1937.

My mother told me how the two of them, on a short break from Seale Hayne, were in Piccadilly walking behind a young soldier in 'hospital blue' uniform, bent and shuffling like an old man. My father remarked casually that this was not an 'organic' disorder but a 'functional' one caused by shellshock. She overcame his reluctant to speak to the man, and eventually they took him to their suite at the Ritz. Within an hour he was not merely walking but running along the hotel corridor. He had thought he was permanently crippled.

Our household was a very peaceful place. The pace of life was

---

* The book reappeared in 1940 with the modified title *Medical Diseases of War*, and by 1944 had gone through four editions. The dedication to my mother appears slightly altered. In the Second World War my father was hardly ever called on to deal with war neuroses, but in 1940 a young army captain, Richard Annand, was sent to see him at our house – he had been deafened by an explosion close to him during the B.E.F.'s retreat to the Channel, when he also won the V.C., and it was thought that my father could help if anyone could. I was enlisted to play tunes on the piano that he was supposed to know to see if he recognised them, but his deafness proved to be 'organic' and thus incurable. I felt awed to be in the presence of this hero, and was impressed too by the supportive and loving behaviour of his wife. (I caught sight of them circling the floor together at a dance in their native North Yorkshire ten years later and this aspect of their relationship seemed unchanged.)

** Notably *Seale Hayne Neurological Studies*, edited by him, of which six issues were published between 1918 and 1920 by Oxford University Press.

unhurried and orderly. Nothing happened to cause fear or anxiety, and everyone was kind and polite. We went away for holidays in the winter and summer, there were rare visits to the pantomime, the circus and the Aldershot Tattoo, twice we visited London for great events of national rejoicing, and there was a little excitement each year during the week of Ascot Races – 'Ascot Week' – when my parents might entertain some of their handful of non-medical friends or a New Zealand relation. Although my two sisters and I shared in this life equally, the fact that they were older and female meant that their private worlds and mine remained apart: we had our enmities and alliances, but these were at arm's length.

Living in the house with us were a cook, a parlourmaid, a housemaid, a between-maid and – from early 1930 till the spring of 1935 – my beloved Nanny. Until they began school in 1933 at the ages of ten and eight, my sisters also had a governess. The servants had attic bedrooms at the top of the linoleum-covered back stairs (except for the parlourmaid who occupied the former butler's room with its own stair from her pantry), while Nanny slept with me and Rosemary in a large bedroom known as the night nursery, next to my parents' room. I didn't see much of the maids. I would harry Dorothy, the housemaid, and try to play with her ceiling broom, and brave the synthetic wrath of Florrie, the cook, to get into the kitchen: when I asked her what a gleaming new mixing machine was, she said 'It's a skedaddle', the message being lost on me because it seemed an appropriate name for a piece of machinery. From them I learned the hit songs of the day – 'Oh play to me, gipsy', 'The daring young man on the flying trapeze, who flies through the air with the greatest of ease', 'Twas on the isle of Capree that I found her', and 'Who's been polishing the sun, driving all the clouds awa-ay?'

Within the grounds lived the gardener Joseph Bravery and his wife Rhoda – an assistant gardener came in each day – and the chauffeur Charles Hitchcock and his wife Ella. Bravery and Hitchcock were both veterans of the Great War, but they had nothing else in common. Hitchcock was short of stature, but he had a military bearing, with a little pepper and salt moustache, and looked unaffectedly smart in his black double-breasted suit, white shirt and black tie, and his cap with its shiny peak. This was all part of the great pride he felt in his employment. Although the parlourmaid was responsible for the master's clothes, Hitchcock was truly my father's personal servant. They can have communicated little – with my father deaf and sitting in the back of the car, either immersed in his work or catching a nap – but they were bound to eachother by mutual respect. Inevitably he was thrilled when my father was knighted;

it enhanced his status with his peers, and nobody milady'd my mother with more relish. I spent many hours with him in the car being driven to school or waiting for my parents. He would occasionally sing – quite melodiously – but more often he told me about cars he had driven for past employers, and mentioned rare and defunct marques, like the Reo and the Hotchkiss. Very rarely I was taken up into his flat above the garage. While he had served in Palestine during the war (as a sergeant), Mrs Hitchcock had been to Egypt, and possessed two small pieces of stone, one polished and the other in the rough state, supposedly from the Pyramids. I was allowed to handle these treasures and to play on her harmonium, which she called an American organ. Once I asked Hitchcock to write in a new autograph book, but he excused himself, saying that he would get 'the wife' to do it as she was 'the scholar'. (He once also said that my father spoke good English but he did not; I found this perplexing because I understood him better than I did my father.) Mrs Hitchcock was dreadfully thin, and suffered from asthma and her nerves. It was sad that, relatively educated though she was, their only child, a son (Hitchcock boasted that all the boy's three names had belonged to English kings), was far from bright, whereas his two grown-up daughters by an earlier marriage were of the same good clay as Hitchcock himself. Unfortunately I was too incurious to ask him about his early life, of which I learned nothing.

We had a 'little car' – an Armstrong-Siddeley – and a 20/25 h.p. Rolls-Royce of 1933 vintage (the last year in which the 'RR' seal on the radiator was red). Sedate but well designed, with enormous headlamps and an encased spare wheel set into each of the two front mudguards, it was a vision of pomp and power, which both Hitchcock and I, each in our different ways, deeply enjoyed. It affected the opinion each of us had of ourselves and of the rest of the world. With his chamois leather he brought out the innermost lights in the black paintwork, and the grey upholstered interior was spotless too. Both cars had running-boards.

Our last ride with Hitchcock was at the very end of 1939 when he drove us to our new home in Oxford. (I saw the Rolls only once again – in a garage in Reading where it spent the war, to be sold immediately afterwards.) Thereafter he worked for a local car hire firm in Ascot, having found a new home in the chauffeur's flat at the Lennoxes' house near ours along the Windsor road. Visiting him once there in my late teens, I felt awkward as our old natural relationship had gone. Mrs Hitchcock's health had not improved, but she survived him, and each of us wrote the other a long letter about Hitchcock when he died in 1952.

Bravery, the gardener, was dark and had probably been good-looking as a younger man, but his face now had a saturnine air. His personality lacked the cheery openness and the solidity of Hitchcock's. But he was friendly to me: in the earliest days before I went to kindergarten, I often trailed along beside him as he plied the motor-mower, and rode in his wheelbarrow on top of the mound of newly cut grass. My mother was a devoted gardener – it was one area of life where she was completely free (my father's gardening was limited to trimming a pair of topiary birds known• as Swan and Edgar). Hitchcock once reported to my father that Bravery was selling produce from the kitchen garden to a dealer in Reading, whose van he had seen parked in the drive, and my father was angry – not with Bravery but with Hitchcock. He hated tale-bearing and would not investigate the story. Bravery and Hitchcock, in spite of being close neighbours for ten years, were never friends and addressed eachother as 'Mr Bravery' and 'Mr Hitchcock'. Bravery, in his own way, wore uniform; I never saw him without his baize apron and stained trilby hat.

Symmetrically, just as Bravery was the dark horse and Hitchcock the creature of light, so Mrs Bravery was as sunny and outgoing as Mrs Hitchcock was reserved and anxiety-ridden. She was short, broad and motherly – unfortunately they had no children. Although her speech was perfectly articulated, it was classic sharp-flavoured Cockney; I wish I could transliterate the second syllable of 'Tuppy' (the name of her black cat) as she pronounced it; and I can still hear her saying 'pretty flowers'. Sometime in the late '30s the Braverys bought a tandem bicycle, and the one time I saw them speeding along on it they were different people, free and not servants any more. Such a thing could not have been contemplated by the Hitchcocks – she was too frail, and it would have compromised his dignity. After the farewells on that sad day in December 1939 we never saw the Braverys again. They sent me a card on my twenty-first birthday eleven years later, but all it said was 'from R. and J. Bravery' – there was no address and no written message.

Florrie, the cook, once helped me to prepare a couple of jam tarts, one for Mrs Bravery and the other for Mrs Hitchcock. The finished articles were convincingly shapeless, but they looked and probably were good to eat, and I eagerly set forth, holding a plate in each hand, to deliver them. I reached Mrs Hitchcock safely, but as I tried to knock on Mrs Bravery's door, her tart slipped off the plate and fragmented on the ground. She consoled me in my grief.

Nanny – Gladys Mary Cullen – was born on 25 April 1906 in a small house near the Brayford pool in Lincoln, where she still lived, by herself, ninety years later. For five years and a few months she cared for me night and day and gave to that task all her abundant intelligence, love and moral goodness. I cannot say what we 'did' – once, in winter, we went away, just the two of us, to a boarding house in Worthing run by a Mrs Cooling, where the sight of the lamplighter passing in the street below and of the gas lamp in our room must be one of my earliest memories. At home one of our routines was to listen to Walford Davies's music programmes for children on the wireless in the drawing room; I never heard her play the piano or sing, but this was a way in which she could communicate her passionately felt love of music to me. If I was upset, I would race around the house looking for Nanny before burying my face in her white overall and releasing my emotions.

I will never know what my mother felt about my total attachment to Nanny. Such a thing could never have happened to her if she had married a New Zealand farmer, but no doubt the arrangement had the full blessing of my father, who must have thought the rough and tumble of looking after her children too great a strain. It had been the same with my sisters before me, but the relationship between me and my Nanny was demonstrably closer than that between Rosemary and hers, who was older and, in direct contrast to Gladys Gullen, a famous spanker. I loved my mother but differently: it was a more sanitised and formal relationship. She had no idea how to discipline children; once, after Nanny's time, when the reigning governess was out and my mother and I were in the dining-room together having lunch, I misbehaved in some way and refused to stop when she told me to. Instead of boxing my ears, she rang for the parlour-maid and asked her to remove me from the room, which, wearing her starched cap and apron, she did. Like other non-violent resisters, I went limp and was simply dragged across the floor. Blissful memories of my mother sitting on my bed and singing me old lullabies, and looking gorgeous when dressed up for a party, belong in a different compartment.

Nanny was compact and purposeful in body and mind. Much later I heard her natal speech – broad Lincolnshire – in the mouths of her siblings, but she spoke with a purity of vowel and consonant, with only a hint of the local intonation. (She has never ceased to say 'you was', which I have recently discovered is an archaic singular version of 'you were', and therefore not ungrammatical.) She was the eldest of five children of George Cullen, 'funeral carriage master', whose own father had been a drunken spendthrift, and his wife who came from a yeoman family called Ablewhite – her father was a farm bailiff in a village just outside Lincoln. At school she won a scholarship and meant to train as a teacher, but in the end decided to become a children's nurse in the hope – soon realised – that it would enable her to travel.

Her very first employment was as under-nurse to my sisters, and she told me nearly seventy years later of her excitement at sitting with my parents in the dining-car of a train headed for the Swiss Alps; it was her first foreign trip. She impressed my parents because some years later my mother wrote asking her to come back and look after me. Accordingly she took over from the 'monthly nurse' when I was a month old. By then she was not quite twenty-four, a balanced and psychologically healthy woman who – because of her modest yet clear ambitions and her 'plainness' – might not find it easy to meet a suitable marriage partner, and at the age when many women give birth to their first child. (As a nanny, too, she was socially isolated – too humble to sit downstairs with her employers and too superior to consort with the servants; thus she whiled away the evenings in the nursery, making do and mending, and reading. Once in a while my mother would come in and chat with her.) At eighty-four, just as I was about to leave her house after spending a day and a night there, she clasped me to her and said 'I want to thank you for all the joy you gave me when you was a little boy.' It was only surprising to hear her say these potent words outright – in the past she had remarked, more than once, 'You was always my baby'. The words penetrated me deeply and after I got home I wrote to her to say that I reciprocated them – that I was her child though not born of her body.

We had an earthy relationship such as I could never have had with my mother. I saw her happy – and cast down, as when she had one of her migraines and collapsed in a chair weeping. But that is incidental: she did for me what the Lord does in the 23rd Psalm, leading me beside the still waters and restoring my soul. Apart from the charade of a child's prayers and listening for God to answer, she only once tried to broach the subject of God. It was at the Hotel Regina in Wengen where we stayed when I was just five – her departure was only four months away. There was a little girl in the hotel called Meiti (pronounced 'mighty'), who liked to stand on a step, shouting '*voila! voila!*' and then '*oop!*' as she jumped off. These words temporarily became like a war-cry for us. Nanny and I were in our hotel bedroom and as we were looking out at the tree-covered mountainside across the valley, she brought the talk round to something *mighty*. I knew that she meant God, but with deliberate devilry said '*voila! voila! oop!*' and so put her off her stroke. She never returned to the subject. In Ascot she used to go to chapel – her family were Methodist – on Sunday evenings, and once (I only learned this much later) she preached at the Congregational church in Sunninghill on Onesimus the slave, the subject of Paul's letter to Philemon. The father of one of her subsequent charges was a scientist and a determined freethinker: coming into the nursery unexpectedly, he found his child being read a Bible story and gave Nanny a furious scolding.

I have a photograph taken by my mother of Nanny and myself standing in front of our magnolia tree during its brief period in bloom. I am trying to force a grin, but she looks bleak and as if she can scarcely see. A few minutes later I was waving from our front door as Hitchcock drove her away to the station. It was the early spring of 1935, and later the same day Miss Ina Reed arrived, ushering in a new order: she was a governess, not a nanny. Still today, I feel sad when I see a magnolia in bloom.

Many nannies, in the heyday of that genus, passed from family to family, playing their appointed role until, growing old, they retired to a home. This was not to be the destiny of Gladys Cullen. She did indeed go to another family after us, the Bartons. Early in 1993 she received a telephone call from Mrs Barton, with whom she had not spoken for about fifty-five years. Now very old herself, this lady explained that for the whole of the past day, for no clear reason, she had been thinking of Nanny continuously and at last, for her peace of mind, had decided to phone. They talked for more than an hour.

The day after war broke out in September 1939, she gave up her job in London and returned to Lincoln. She had been looking after the daughter of a Finnish diplomat, and her employer soon pleaded with her to return. She felt obliged to decline, and heard later that the little girl, together with her subsequent nanny, were killed by a direct hit on their London home during the Blitz.

The reason why she could not leave Lincoln was family obligation. Her two brothers, who worked with their ageing father in the funeral carriage business, joined the armed services, and her sisters were married. Now, as the only child of her parents who was 'free', she drove hearses and following cars for her father. The result was that when the brothers returned from the war and their father died, Gladys became a partner. The men maintained and drove the vehicles, while she did the office work from home and drove when needed.

Just once, in the late 1940s, Nanny returned to her earlier profession and went to look after the child of the British Consul-General in Houston, Texas, Mr Henderson. She did it in the teeth of pleas from her widowed mother not to go, but persisted. After her return she joined the Soroptimists, the women's equivalent of Rotary, and eventually became area president for the North Midlands. The business continued till the early 1980s, when the three partners all felt incapable of carrying on. They also could not get used to charging higher prices for their services, which had become necessary in the era of high inflation. The younger members of the family had other occupations, and so the business was wound up and the assets were sold. These consisted mainly of the vehicles. Two of them were Rolls-Royce Phantoms of the mid-1920s. One, which had belonged to the Duke of Rutland, they converted into a hearse (after the demise of the business an enthusiast converted it back to a saloon). The other, once the property of a county magnate called Le Marchant, was kept in its pristine state so that when the assizes were on, the judge would have a suitable conveyance to be driven to court in his robes. For years it was used for no other purpose and at one time the local press were calling for this relic of the past to be discarded, but suddenly in the 1970s it came back into fashion and was used several times every Saturday for weddings. When the vehicles were about to be sold, Nanny wrote to a former charge, Peter (Lord) Palumbo, whom she knew to be a fancier of vintage cars, but he courteously declined; small cars were his fancy.

Nanny once recounted to me a characteristic incident. She had been driving one of the following cars at a funeral, and afterwards an elderly female member of the bereaved family came up to her and said 'Miss Cullen, thank you for driving so nicely.' One might wonder how one can drive nicely, but of course Nanny would have been unable to drive in any other way. Higher praise was unnecessary, even if it could be found. Conversely, when in the old days she said she was *disappointed* by my behaviour, this was an extremely severe pronouncement.

In her working life she saw the number of undertakers in Lincoln dwindle from over forty, several of them small joiners' shops, to two, the Co-op and another multiple store. Some of the old ideals of service embodied by the Cullens had dwindled too. They had never been undertakers themselves, but they did keep, tucked away in their garage, a large coffin known as 'the shell' which they would take out when called by the police to collect a body – say, one found in the canal. It was a necessary task which the professional undertakers shunned. When she was eighty-seven, Nanny told me with asperity that she had just changed the instructions for the disposal of her body – the firm she had previously nominated no longer came up to acceptable standards.

It would be useless to try to quantify the influence this woman had on my life. Perhaps it is best summed up in Evelyn Waugh's reply when asked how he could subscribe to the Christian religion and yet be so nasty – that without it he would have been far worse.

Our part of Ascot was sober and dull. Most of our near neighbours were much older than my parents and lived, as we did, in large late Victorian houses with servants and well tended grounds. Right next door was a younger family, with a son of my age. The father manufactured a nationally known bathroom product, but the mother had gone away to live in an asylum. This was also the situation of another family who lived a mile or two away, of which the daughters were my sisters' closest friends. The father was a gentleman of leisure who caused a mild stir when a play he had written was staged in the West End. Their household was run by a stout, wrinkled Indian *ayah* – she was called 'Nanny' and wore a starched uniform, and it never occurred to me that she was not English.

The family we knew best were the Lennoxes, who lived a little way up the Windsor road from us in a house called Waverly. Early in 1940 we all went over to Ascot from our new home in Oxford to lunch with Lady Waddilove, the new tenant of Heath End. The door was opened by a butler and everything looked more opulent than before, but even I could see that taste was lacking. Afterwards we went on to the Lennoxes for tea, and although I had hardly ever seen Mr Lennox, a solicitor, I remember him vividly from this occasion, a dignified man with a white moustache and glasses, sitting in a small wing-chair. Mrs Lennox, as long as I knew her, looked thin and faded, also with glasses and with grey hair tied in a bun at the back, but was both distinguished-looking and effusive, with a ringing contralto voice and laugh. Their two elder children were grown up and married, an unmarried daughter lived at home and bred spaniels, and the youngest daughter, a little older than Pam, was irrepressibly friendly and nosey, with a bouncy hobbledoy manner, but acknowledged to be slightly odd; we knew her best since she often came visiting. But soon after our visit Mr Lennox died, and even before the undertakers arrived a bomb fell on Ascot heath and the ceiling of the room in which he lay dead shed its plaster all over his body. But this was nothing to the shock that awaited the family: unknown to them, he had run up debts. Mrs Lennox refused to go bankrupt and turned their home into a genteel boarding house – they only moved away to a smaller house in the country some years after the war, when the debts were paid off.

Several rich families lived within a mile or two of us at Ascot. There were the Ashers at Ascot Place, devout Jews, and I dimly recall a party there given for their grandchildren. Much more conspicuous were the Weigalls: Sir Archibald, a handsome old-fashioned dandy who had been governor of one of the states in Australia, and his Lady, sole heiress to the Maple furniture fortune. Her daughter had died under an anaesthetic, and therefore she refused surgery for a disabling condition of her own, and sped about in an electric wheelchair. She kept a private doctor and nurse in attendance at her house, Englemere, and had a fully equipped surgery, to which my mother was once rushed when she cut her finger on some glass during a charity fête in the garden (on the same occasion Lady Weigall's chair shot forward too abruptly on the rough ground, and a box of china fell off the back and was smashed). In Oxford during the war we had as house guests a succession of army doctors who provided my father with rich material for observation. One was totally absorbed in archaeology and talked of nothing else; was he at all interested in his actual profession? Another, a Scot, had what my father termed a 'long latent period' – he would make belated replies to what had been said a minute or two before, after the conversation had moved on. Yet another was regarded by both my parents as a poor sort of fellow – the reason being that he was once Lady Weigall's private doctor.

Probably even richer than the Weigalls were the Cunliffe-Owens, who lived at Sunningdale Park (scene of government negotiations in the 1970s resulting in the abortive power-sharing agreement for Northern Ireland). They were a convivial lot: my sisters and the Cunliffe-Owen girls were at the same school – St George's, Ascot – and so we were all invited there for a ball in 1938, and I was kitted out in an Eton suit. Probably it was a rather raffish affair, because one of the two things I remember about it was Jack Doyle, the boxer, singing 'Irish Eyes a-smiling' with sweat pouring down his face; the other was a young man popping my and other children's balloons with his cigarette as he and his partner circled the dance floor. Our hosts were not a happy family – the children's mother had died, and I was astounded to hear one of the daughters telling my sisters openly, in their house, how she hated her American stepmother.

'Ascot village' was a broad main road, with a few memorable shops – Mr Zaradi, the immaculately dressed little Greek tobacconist with his waxed moustache; a horse-faced woman who measured out in a brass weighing-scale her wonderful fudge, my mother's only acknowledged extravagance; the newsagent of vast girth, Miss Baines (if we heard a loud bang in the distance, we would say it was Miss Baines bursting); and an antique filling station selling a variety of brands of 'motor spirit' (Hitchcock's name for petrol – he referred to the hooter as a 'klaxon'), each pump with a different porcelain 'hat' – Shell, BP, Cleveland and so on. The Cleveland 'hat' was rectangular, and I had a series of nightmares in which a man called Cleveland would appear, with the petrol-pump's 'hat' in place of a head, accompanied by a woman named Figgis. The village was reached from our house by walking across the heath. On the side nearest to our house we would walk across the racecourse, but on the other side, close to the grandstands, a tunnel went under it, where our steps were answered by a rubbery echo. I approached the tunnel with fear because it was where I first beheld an unfortunate lady (she was a 'lady') who had some deformity of the cheekbones which caused her eyes to bulge hideously, and a wide gaping mouth. Somehow her cloche hat made her even more terrifying. At our first encounter I could not control myself and hid behind Nanny as she passed. Later the agony lessened – her red setter always trotted far out in front and warned of its mistress's approach.

My first taste of school came in the summer term of 1935, soon after Nanny left and Miss Reed – 'Reedum' – took her place. It was a little kindergarten with two classes, run by a Mrs Morrison in two rooms of her pleasant, spacious home. Her husband was a somnolent man-about-the-house, in ancient tweeds and with a pipe, who took no part in the proceedings. Socially it was mixed, but upper-middle-class children predominated – Mrs Morrison's own class. It took me a while to learn the lingo of school. The two classes occupied adjoining rooms on the ground floor, but when I was in the lower form I was always hearing about the upper form, and presumed that they had their lessons in the mysterious apartments upstairs and that I had not yet seen them. It was disappointing when I found that I already knew the entire company. Also the word 'breaking up', to signify the end of term, made me visualise all the children flying away from the school *en masse* in different directions. The teacher of the upper form was Miss Thomas, certainly well into middle age, and I remember her confused look when I immediately said 'Thomasina Tittlemouse' on first meeting her. Keeping my place was not something I yet knew about. For such a tiny establishment to employ a visiting French teacher who was really French must have been a rarity, even then. Mademoiselle Placide, dressed in black with white upswept hair and metal-rimmed, small-paned glasses, knew how to teach. When she intoned *'le nez'*, for example, we all, she included, touched the table round which we sat with our noses.

I was not tough and easily met my match in a girl called Peggy: we had a wrestling match in the garden and I ended on the ground with her sitting on top of me. Later the two of us had the star parts in the 'school play' consisting of the Mad Hatter's Tea Party. She was Alice and I the Mad Hatter, wearing an old top hat of Mr Morrison's. Looking into eachother's eyes as we bandied insults put in our mouths by Lewis Carroll, we (certainly I) felt a wave of professional comradeship. After this was over, the 'company' sang the then popular song 'Everything Stops for Tea' with appropriate gestures.

In 1937 several things happened to boost my self-regard. Most important of all, my father was knighted in the Coronation honours. My sisters and I always went into our parents' bedroom together to wish them good-morning, and I would put my father's slippers on his feet as he stuck each in turn out from under the bedclothes (on one April Fool's day, it was my mother's feet that appeared – he said that his had shrunk in the night). On this particular morning they told us the great news. I was sorry to learn that we did not thereby become 'honourable', but there seemed all the same to be plenty of reflected glory to bask in.

My father, Rosemary and I watched the Coronation procession from a stand overlooking Constitution Hill inside the garden of Buckingham Palace. (The last occasion of this kind, only two years before, was George V's Jubilee, and that time I had watched with Reedum from a bedroom window on the eighth floor of the Hotel Metropole in Northumberland Avenue – it was hot and we saw people being carried away on stretchers, but of the procession we could figure out very little.) This time it rained for most of the day – as we drove home in the evening, Hitchcock said 'It must have washed the King's heart away', and we sniggered in the back of the car at his good-hearted sententiousness. It came as an anti-climax when the Coronation coach passed with the King and Queen; somehow he seemed dull after the probably equally dull but (to me) much more kingly figure of George V and the dashing Edward VIII. I did get a *frisson* on seeing Queen Mary, but my best moment was when the carriage passed bearing the Sultan of Zanzibar in his turban and Emir Abdullah of Transjordan in his Arab robe and headgear. I knew them so well from my stamp collection that they were old friends. It must have been about this time that I dreamed that I was in my bed at home, and sitting beside it were George V and Queen Mary, who had come to visit me. George – already dead but still registering with me as the 'real' king – was handing me Penny Blacks.

Endless phalanxes of troops marched or rode past, and the Indian ones in their coloured tunics and turbans were the most splendid. One of that numberless band was Reedum's brother, who was in the Southern Rhodesian police. He visited his. sister one evening at our house, and she brought him up to my room so that I could actually meet face to face this thrilling figure of whom I had heard so much. Bronzed, handsome, moustachio'd and smiling, he did not disappoint. Even his name, Trevor, seemed the very summation of manliness. I have not said much about Reedum. Anyone who followed Nanny was going to be at a disadvantage, but I became quite attached to her. She was a good sort, robust and slightly mannish, with black hair done in 'earphones'; she could jump over the tennis net. No doubt she felt that I needed toughening up after the previous regime. Reedum left in the autumn of 1937 when I started going to a proper boys' school, called Earleywood, where I stayed all day and not just in the morning as at Mrs Morrison's. From now on there would be 'holiday governesses'.

Our nearest town, Windsor, was enveloped in Coronation fever and one day we all stood in a crowd and watched the King and Queen drive past within a few feet of us, followed by the Dukes of Gloucester and Kent; these last were not expected to look gracious or wave, and sat as still and expressionless as waxworks. The parade was fine, and so transfixed was I by the gloriously attired drum-major throwing his mace high in the air and catching it, that I found a cane at home and strutted along a secluded path in the garden, invisible from the house, trying to do likewise. My mother came upon me and we both laughed. When the spectacle in Windsor was over I said that I wanted to pee, and after much ado my father and I were taken to a urinal somewhere among the outer walls of the Castle, open to the sky, which was presumably used by guardsmen on duty. He embarrassed me by telling someone in some kind of authority that I wanted to 'pass water' (if it had been another doctor, he would have used the gentleman's slang phrase 'pump ship'). In this enclosure there were three gigantic adjoining pissoirs of brown earthenware, and I had to stand before the middle one dwarfed by my father on one side and his cicerone on the other. I had never been anywhere like this before, and although my bladder was full it refused to empty. This was the first manifestation of a syndrome which has dogged me since adolescence.

In the summer of 1937 I took final leave of Mrs Morrison and immediately went on an exciting holiday with my mother and a niece of hers from New Zealand, Rosalind Arkwright. The association of New Zealand with my mother – and its beautiful postage stamps of which my father had a nice collection – had already invested everything to do with the country, including its name, with a glow of romance, and Ros merely enhanced it. Her visit to the home country, during

which my mother presented her at court, was her twenty-first birthday
gift. If I had been the right age I would have fallen in love with
her: she had rich auburn hair and a fair skin, and her personality
was gentle but spirited. (The eldest of her three brothers, Francis,
had been a cadet at Dartmouth in the 1920s, and though cripplingly
shy had done well in the Navy. Our home became his, and he
was one of my godfathers. I have shadowy memories of him doing
hand-stands in our garden and running several paces up the trunk
of a sloping tree, but while on shore leave from his ship in Egypt,
he was concussed in a riding accident, and this, on top of heat-stroke
and, my mother believed, the accumulated strain of being away from
his parental home uninterruptedly for nine years, precipitated a mental
breakdown. His father came over to fetch him, and after he got
back he became violent and was shut away in a hospital, where
he stayed for the rest of a fairly long life. It only occurred to me
in my early teens that I had not heard about Francis for a long
time, and then I learned the truth.)

The holiday on which my mother, Ros and I went took the form
of a cruise on the small but luxurious P. & O. liner *The Viceroy
of India* (it was partly crewed by Lascars), visiting three Baltic cities:
Stockholm, Copenhagen and – the *pièce de résistance* – Danzig, now
Gdansk. Although nominally a free city in the 'Polish Corridor',
Danzig was thoroughly Nazified. Pictures of Hitler and swastika banners
were everywhere, and men greeted eachother in the street with the
Nazi salute. I remember nothing else apart from these few fleeting
visions and a mountainous cake covered in pink icing in a café
that we visited, where an old lady who seemed to me to resemble
Queen Victoria was sitting. When Ros and I met again more than
fifty years later, she mentioned an incident that had passed me by.
As we were about to go up the gangway on to the ship at the end
of our day in Danzig, a young man approached and asked if we would
take him with us. Alas, that story has no sequel that we know of.
Ros also remembered Hitchcock shaking hands as they parted at
Ascot station for the last time and saying that he would miss her.

During those years we usually spent the Christmas holiday at
a hotel in the Swiss Alps. We stayed twice at the Hôtel du Parc
in Villars-sur-Bex, less grand than the Palace Hotel nearby but very
comfortable. These trips rejuvenated my father, who joined us for
part of the time. The effect on my mother was the same in a more
moderate way; she skated a little and ski'd with us on the easy slopes.
This was the part of Switzerland where they first met in 1911.

I skated on the hotel's private rink, loving the scratchy music
that came from a loud-speaker outside the adjoining hut. There were

waltzes by Johann Strauss the younger, Lehar's 'Gold and Silver', Waldteufel's 'Les Patineurs', the 'White Horse Inn', the 'Stein Song' and many other entrancing pieces. I had not yet heard any classics, and this music filled the void. One morning the rink was cleared for Amy Johnson, the aviator, but the courtesy was misplaced because she could not skate and after a few uncertain steps fell heavily on her behind. Very different were Monsieur and Madame Brunet-Joli, the reigning world figure skating champions, who were at the hotel for a short visit. They would come to the rink about noon, and it was instantly and eagerly cleared for them. They of course had their own musical accompaniment and gave a display that can only be described in cliches. When they came into the dining-room for lunch, there was polite clapping, which they acknowledged gracefully.

The Hôtel du Parc had two resident musicians, Peter and Bert, who played the piano and drums at tea-time, and we were especially lucky because their favourite numbers were Irving Berlin's new hits 'Cheek to Cheek' and 'White Tie, Top Hat and Tails'. Tea-time was made even more delectable by 'Mont Blanc' patisseries, little tarts of short pastry filled with dry chestnut puree piped into long spaghetti-like strings and topped with whipped cream.

Like Sherlock Holmes, my father had a talent – in his case under-used – for disguise. As long as anyone could remember, he had won every fancy-dress competition he entered, and he did so again at this hotel – whether it was as Sir Harry Lauder or a postman I don't recall. He went to a party at his clinic, New Lodge, in 1936 blacked up, with a beard and wearing a topi, a cloak and puttees – as Haile Sellassie, then in the news. Nobody suspected who it really was, and one or two even believed it really was the Emperor himself, presumably come to be treated for a digestive disorder.

Returning from these Swiss journeys, we would put up for a couple of days at the Hôtel Continental in Paris, a place of high luxury. One afternoon we went to the theatre to see Grock, the clown. In adult life I have laughed even reading descriptions of his famous acts with musical instruments, especially a grand piano, but at the time I was bored and merely intrigued to see how much he seemed to amuse my father. Early in 1938 we went round the Paris Exposition between the Eiffel Tower and the Trocadero. Picasso's newly-painted 'Guernica' was on show in the pavilion of the Spanish republic, then losing the Civil War, but it was the last thing my parents would have wanted to see – a perversion of art from the country that had produced Velazquez. The pavilion I remember was the Soviet one, topped by giant idealised figures of a peasant and a factory worker.

Willingly to School

In the autumn of 1937 Earleywood preparatory school near Sunninghill was still new and small. There were barely thirty boys, all boarders, but there were three assistant masters and a mistress, two resident 'matrons' one medically trained and the other with domestic duties, and assorted humbler staff. The place was like a small country estate, with enclosed rough ground at the front and playing fields at the back with woods beyond.

Such a high staff-pupil ratio might have denoted an exclusive establishment for the scions of wealth and nobility, but many of the boarders were sons of clergy, then synonymous with genteel poverty. But the eyes of the proprietor and headmaster, Percy Aldrich-Blake ('A.B.'), were on higher things, which he could perhaps achieve quite soon if his poor pupils turned into good scholars – in my very first term a boy left to take up an Eton scholarship. In laying out the initial investment A.B. must have been helped by his recent marriage to a Miss Sandeman of the port family.

Mrs Aldrich-Blake was strikingly fine-looking, lively and pleasant, and much younger than her husband who was around forty, and we all wondered, not least my mother, how she ever came to ally herself with a man like A.B. This had nothing to do with his talents as a pedagogue, which were considerable, but everything to do with his aura. He was big and fleshy, and had glossy black hair and heavy eyebrows that met in the middle, so that a frown always seemed to accompany his oleagenous smile. He often dressed in plus-fours, and had some of the relaxations of a country gentleman, occasionally potting at rabbits or pigeons in the front field out of his study window, and sending his Clumber spaniel, Brutus, after them. His academic forte was coaching in Latin and Greek, and I had my first Latin lesson with him.

Apart from the individual classrooms, there was one large common schoolroom, around the walls of which were ranged all the boys' uniform wooden tuck-boxes, on which our names were painted in italics by a sign-writer. Here we would gather in a short break after lunch, sitting on our boxes, while A.B. gave out notices, read snippets of news from *The Times*, and lectured us on our behaviour. One unusual practice of the school was that every letter which a boy

either received from, or sent to, his parents had to be read by the
staff; this was the time when the censored incoming letters were
handed out. Once he made a particularly memorable observation.
One of the clergymen's sons, called Hardy, spoke with a strong
West Country burr, no doubt picked up from his father's rural
parishioners. A.B. said: 'You must all be careful how you speak.
Some of you do not speak well. I am thinking particularly of Hardy.'
The pieces of news he read out were of the order of a flying-boat
having got to Australia in record time, at which mutterings of 'Some
speed!' rippled round the room. Once I suddenly came awake as
he read: 'Sir Gerald Hurst has been appointed a country court judge.'
Everyone looked at me. This was my father's brother, as A.B. must
somehow have known. It may have been no more than an effort
by A.B. to be friendly, but it was probably part of his campaign
to ingratiate himself with my parents. The simple fact of my father
having been knighted made me especially important in A.B.'s eyes.
He was very anxious that I should stay at Earleywood for longer
than the current year, at the end of which I was going to move
to a school on the south coast recommended by my father's partner
John Venables, whose son had been there. He visited our house
to press his case, and on the annual sports day, without a by-your-leave,
he had 'Sir Arthur Hurst' printed on the programme among the posse
of four judges; my father had to excuse himself on grounds of in-
competence, but his name was there, which was the main thing.
The prizes were given away by an eccentric local lady called Mrs
King-George, whose only claim to distinction, admittedly a considerable
one, was her name.

When the end of the year came, I did leave – with real regret,
because I had done well and was rather popular with the other boys.
I had memorised a nonsense monologue and recited it to the entire
school as an impromptu farewell. If I had stayed there, I might
have done better academically and in sports than I did subsequently,
because A.B., as well as being a shameless snob, ran a hard and
vigorous regime, and I was malleable; also I am stimulated less
by competition than by the lack of it. In a small pool it is easy
to be a big fish, and I did not lack confidence, not to mention
cheek. Once, before I had thought what I was saying, I asked the
house matron whether she had ever been in a beauty contest. It
was the sort of remark I would have heard our maids making at
home. But this poor woman was ugly, and she sent me out of the
room. The medical matron, who was pretty, scolded me for answering
her 'OK chief'. I learned from an older boy two 'real' swear-words,
'bloody' and 'bugger', and duly repeated these to my father during

a walk we were taking near our house; Rosemary was there too. Immediately he whisked me off the path into the trees alongside and told me I must promise never to say them again. He occasionally said 'damn' and 'blast', but these were of a different order. If I had stayed at Earleywood – another big 'if' – I might perhaps have developed healthier habits of mind and body, but would have missed the peculiar benefits of my next school (where all forms of swearing were strictly forbidden, but where, unlike at Earleywood, it *was* permitted to have one's hands in one's pockets).

I have several peculiar memories of Earleywood. Once, idling and dreaming in the deep field during cricket practice, I suddenly saw a milkman walk out of the wood at the end of the field with a wooden yoke on his shoulders and a can hanging from each end of it – it was like a vision of Arcadia. The master who took us for 'Swedish drill' every morning (with the same movements and words of command as parade ground drill) and trained us to catch cricket balls was a young man of Scandinavian origin called Hansen-Raae. When one of our maids told me that she had met a master from my school at a local dance hall, and that he winked one eye rather often, I at once knew it was him; his large immobile face, fitfully lit up by flickers of amusement, must have been quite sexy. I didn't think about this again until, one day at lunch in the school dining-room, sitting as the youngest boy next to the medical matron, I noticed that she kept breaking into a smile – but it was directed over my shoulder and not at me. At last, unable to contain my curiosity, I followed her glance and saw Mr Hansen-Raae, at the opposite end of the next table, discreetly smiling back. Matron told me sharply to look to my front.

A routine service was held every morning in the school chapel, and at the end of it one day, as we sat in our places, A.B. came to the front and told us in his portentous way how important it was to wash our hands after going to the lavatory after breakfast (not only our hands, I reflected, because I once found, too late, that the lavatory seat was covered in shit). Being prone to embarrassment on this subject anyway, I felt mortified at hearing it discussed so publicly, and worse still in the chapel. This was all of a piece with my feelings about religious observance. I was intensely embarrassed by any open display of piety by anyone, but most of all by myself. From within me came a command that this was 'wet' and I must have nothing to do with it. For the next ten years, I had to attend some form of public worship twice a day during the school term, and remained totally impervious to it – except to good tunes and the rare inspiring sermon. I made it a point of honour to look bored and indifferent, and never to sing the hymns or follow the usual practice of closing one's eyes during the prayers. I had some comfort in knowing that in this my father and I were very much the same, though we never discussed it. I could never make out what my companious felt about God, Jesus and all the rest of it; was I alone in regarding the whole thing as an elaborate sham? It was a touchy subject, as I found out when I asked one of my best friends at my next school if his family were religious. He snapped back 'Of course', but I doubt if they were.

Percy Aldrich-Blake realised his ambition. During the war his school flourished and numbers increased. Among the newcomers were the sons of several eminent parents, including Field-Marshal Alexander, which would have made my father's knighthood seen rather small beer. Up till the 1960s the *Private Schools Yearbook* stated that Earleywood specialised in preparing boys for Eton and Wellington.

That summer my 'holiday governess' was a German Swiss girl of eighteen called Trudi Kubler. Her brother was a national swimming champion, and she did an impressive crawl herself – beefy, tanned and with banal good looks, she would have made a fine bathing belle. I could not yet swim, but was certainly not going to learn from Trudi. The reason for this was that I hated her; the feeling was instinctive and irrational. It had nothing to do with her admiration for Hitler; she always knew when he was going to broadcast, and eagerly tuned our wireless so that she could listen (such a foible being then regarded as regrettably misguided rather than wicked). That year we had an ill-favoured between-maid called Betty; objects disappeared from around the house, including my Jubilee and Coronation silver crown pieces, and it was rightly suspected that she was responsible: the police visited her family home which turned out to be a caravan. But before she was caught, the household got into a state of jitters, and no one more than Trudi. My bedroom (I now had my own, containing my favourite possessions – a set of hollow rubber models of Disney's Snow White and the Seven Dwarfs) was next to hers, and on two successive nights, while the house was in darkness, she called to me to go in to her – and then told me as she shuddered in bed that she had heard noises in the passage and was scared. That summer, in a unique access of gaiety, my parents threw a dance and a garden party on successive days, and I had a great time, especially during the garden party when Trudi tried with increasing desperation to get me to go inside the house away from the party, which was for grown-ups only, and I refused. Why should I, while I was having so much fun? Later she told me that she had spent the afternoon crying in her room, because I was so cruel. I had already lost any respect I ever had for her, and did not care.

Our running battle continued when we went for our summer holiday to Etretat on the Normandy coast (its cliff, pierced by a huge natural arch, appears in numerous Impressionist paintings). Again she accused me of cruelty as I was for ever giving her the slip. My parents' confidence in her remained unshaken till she was seen to be dosing herself with a patent medicine called 'Dr –'s Slimming Tea'. While my father might have hesitated, whatever his feelings, before suggesting that she should not listen to Hitler, he felt completely safe in doubting the efficacy and even the safety of the Slimming Tea. Her reply was long remembered: she had ordered it because (from his picture in the advertisement) 'Dr – looks so nice'. I suppose my father might have said *'Touché'*.

Then suddenly I could play truant no longer because my right hip started to hurt. It was tino-sinovitis, and when our boat reached Newhaven on the way home, Hitchcock, who was waiting with the car, was asked to carry me ashore. I could not remember ever having been so much as touched by him before, and the experience was strange – he was distinctly bristly. I must have refused to be carried by Trudi. (On the outward journey we crossed from Southampton to Cherbourg aboard the mighty *Normandie*, which sailed at 8 in the morning, so that we left home at 3. All I remember of it is the wake billowing out from the stern right to the horizon, and the vast gold-painted statue of Joan of Arc in one of the saloons; also it had bolder lines and was more streamlined than our own staid *Queen Mary*.

After we got home I had the ordeal of lying, face upwards, on my bed while my naked body was examined by the surgeon from Windsor, Gaymer Jones, whom I had only met before as the jovial host at a children's party. Like my father but with less taste, Gaymer did not mind showing the world his prosperity, which permeated his whole persona – gleaming bald head, huge horn-rimmed glasses and a well-fed, bellowing laugh. My mother gently observed that his house had the finest lace curtains in Windsor, and described the too numerous *objets* in the drawing-room as nicknacks. His Rolls-Royce was a size larger than my father's, and his chauffeur, Merkel, wore a Hollywood-style uniform that would have made Hitchcock wince. But this time, lying defenceless before him, I saw the man whose skill had earned him wealth and not the show-off. He asked me which side I slept on, and I answered that I had slept on whichever side it was 'for years'. 'Ah yes, years and years' said Gaymer Jones without batting an eyelid, and his unaccustomed shaft of irony went home. The sinovitis symptoms soon went away, and I was able to go to my new school on time. But Trudi had so infected me with her fears that I needed a night-light till the end of that summer holiday.

Interlude: Uncle Will

My Uncle Gerald recurs several times in this narrative, but not so Uncle Will, my father's eldest brother, of whom Gerald would only say that he was 'a terrible fellow'. In Bradford their mother, Fanny Hertz, put all her children to wetnurses, and legend has it that she discovered too late that Willy's was a prostitute. Convinced that he had sucked tainted milk which would permanently warp his character, she rejected him as soon as her perfect second child, Gerald, was born. He compensated throughout his life for the hurt this inflicted. In one early studio photograph of the three little boys wearing sailor suits, Willy, with his slightly crooked features, holds a horse-whip.

He was, ironically, the only one of the three who went to a public school – to keep him away from his brothers. But he only spent a term or two, successively, at Marlborough and Giggleswick before being packed off to a school in Alsace, of which he told the typical story that the form master placed a spitoon at the back of the classroom and spat into it, accurately, over the heads of the pupils. When my father was a studious freshman at Magdalen College, Oxford, Willy came to visit him wearing a straw boater with a Magdalen hatband; my father's friends said to him later that they had not known his brother was a Magdalen man, and he had to confess that he was not one. Willy married before the turn of the century and at first kept it a secret from the family; then his wife (Aunt Eda) ran away from him when their eldest child was a baby, but she returned and they stayed together for the rest of their lives. He described himself in *Who's Who* as a journalist, and this was indeed how he started off, in Montreal; but he soon founded and ran the Exclusive News Agency, a picture library with worldwide contacts and a pioneer in the field. It made him relatively rich and survived his death. He was never a commuter; when the business became too big to be carried on inside his capacious house in Roehampton, he built an office in the garden. In the early days he was twice bankrupt. My father, still unmarried and doing well, came to the rescue, but on one visit to their home he was chased out of the house by Willy, who shouted at him in the street: 'If you come near my wife again, I'll horse-whip you!' When Grandfather Hertz died in 1912 Gerald and Arthur were named as executors and Willy's legacy was held in trust. The resulting breach with Gerald – as the family's lawyer, doubtless responsible for this arrangement – was never healed, and Willy's four children grew up hardly knowing their cousins who lived only a few miles away.

By the time I knew Uncle Will, he and Aunt Eda seemed a dignified pair, but there was a hint of menace about him. He looked gross and not very benevolent – his heavy jaw was slightly slanted and his eyes too were not quite level. He loved to coat-trail with provocative opinions and improbable boasts, and because my mother refused to be fazed, he liked her and was thus disposed to be nice to us children. The day of my christening was particularly remembered by my sisters because he gave them some rubber beetles and spiders to put in our parents' bed; the maid then unknowingly put a hot-water bottle on top of them and they melted.

He earned fame among connoisseurs for his collection of Famille Rose china.* The pieces filled glass-fronted cabinets and were individually hung all over several walls of the house. Once a chord was struck on the piano (the women of the family were musical) and a plate fell off the wall and smashed. Will searched among the fragments till he found the broken metal wall-bracket and sued the supplier for compensation; my mother, unfairly, thought this an example of his dangerous character. Later he collected stamps – only those of the British Empire – and, as with the Famille Rose, there were no half-measures. It was a true philatelist's collection, meticulously mounted in twenty albums. Somehow, despite all this expense, he educated his children at well-known schools and maintained a home with all the physical comforts. But he cruelly taunted his younger daughter Daphne when she decided to enter a religious order, and once threw his younger son John out of the house, so that he came, when I was a small child, to take refuge with us. My mother commented to me that the children had turned out remarkably well, considering.

He and Aunt Eda arrived at our house one summer afternoon in a hired black limousine – neither of them could drive – and Uncle Will, confronting me in the garden, asked me pompously with a

---

* Many of the pieces illustrated in G.C. Williamson's *The Book of Famille Rose* (Methuen, 1927) were from his collection – described in the preface as 'wonderful'.

deadly-serious look to say who he was, adding that he had brought some stamps but would only give them to me if I answered correctly. Of course I knew who he was, but I was too nervous to speak and forfeited the stamps. My father wrote to him protesting that he had been too hard on me and I duly got some strange Chinese covers and a handsome letter.

Aunt Eda died of cancer early in 1941, and he was heartbroken, weeping continuously for days. But he did write to me at school and say that he hoped I would visit him during the holidays, when we would 'do stamps' together. But by then he too had died. Both his collections were sold at the bottom of the market. But over the years he had given my parents various lesser pieces and I still have a few of them.

Will worked tirelessly to succeed with the E.N.A., but it was not easy for him to see both his younger brothers, who had usurped his place from the nursery onwards, serve with distinction in the Great War while he remained a civilian, and later receive knighthoods. He could not decide whether to present a dignified or a raffish face to the world. Each year in the 1930s, he gave a stag dinner for his friends, at which false noses were *de rigueur* and roulette was played. I heard him say that he had taken parties of friends to *Me and My Girl*, the show that contained the 'Lambeth Walk', seventeen times (we saw it once). He had gone bald early, and wore a well-crafted toupée; I noticed the oddly straight hairline at the back of his neck, but was never told the reason for it while he lived. He gave himself a double-barrelled name, Martin-Hurst, and had our supposed family crest – a winged helmet – printed on his letterhead with a motto, *'Tout prest'*, that amused the family with its unintended reminder of his early financial tribulations. His great china collection enabled him to pose as a *grand seigneur*.

I was implicitly encouraged to regard Gerald and Arthur as my 'role-models', while Willy was complacently dismissed as a bogeyman. Yet I am closer in character to him than to the other two. The efficient intellect and unaffected goodness of Gerald and the genius of Arthur are remote from me. Willy was unsure of his identity, except when it came to running his business; then he knew exactly who he was.

St Ronan's

St Ronan's school, which was at West Worthing when I first went
there, has been the setting for a novel, *Hindsight* by Peter Dickinson
(1983),[*] and the headmaster W.B. ('Dick') Harris is sympathetically
portrayed by Evelyn Waugh in his autobiography *A Little Learning*.
When Waugh knew Dick Harris he was a young assistant housemaster
at Lancing, a few miles east along the coast from Worthing, and
about to join the army – it was 1916. In 1938 he was a vigorous
man just past fifty. Any attempt to describe him comes up against
the difficulty that there is little basis for comparison; I have never
known anyone else like him, and his school too, which he completely
dominated, was *sui generis*. About the only thing he had in common
with Aldrich-Blake was a remarkable pair of eyebrows, but instead
of being sinister, Dick's curled up above keen, laughing pale blue
eyes.

The school was founded in 1883 by a clergyman called Crick,
and he was succeeded in 1909 by Stanley Harris, then in his late
twenties, whose photographs show him as handsome in the mould
of the Christian hero of the time, manly, serious and gentle. He
was a brilliant athlete and reputed to have been an even more impressive
character than Dick, his younger brother. When Stanley died of cancer
in 1926, Dick took over and, so we were told, deliberately modelled
himself on the dead paragon. Their father had been governor of
Newfoundland, and Dick was at Westminster School and Pembroke
College, Cambridge, early in the century. In public he was unremittingly
outgoing and 'hearty', but it was all of a piece – with his clear vibrant
voice, a broad smile of unaffected warmth, and an ability to touch
and be touched that had nothing cloying about it. He was concerned
about our behaviour, of course, but had none of A.B.'s condescension

---

[*] Dickinson (born 1927) set the novel at Bicton, the grand country house to which the
school moved in 1940. He was one of the most intellectually gifted boys ever to pass
through it, and his family was *par excellence* a 'St Ronan's family' – two of his brothers,
and his cousins the Davidsons and a Butterwick, were all there. *Hindsight* was published
shortly before the school's centenary, when open house was held and many old boys, myself
included, foregathered. Dawn Vassar-Smith, wife and mother of the school's co-owners and
upholder of the old St Ronan's tradition, was still in a state of shock. I relayed this fact
to Peter Dickinson, who expressed surprise: hadn't they realised it was fiction?

and pomposity. Unlike the assistant masters who called us by our surnames only – as we did eachother – Dick used nicknames or variants of our first names ('Christo' in my case). There was no Mrs Dick Harris, but there was a school mother, cut out for the part, whose warmth and humanity made her the right match for Dick. This was Mrs Vassar-Smith ('Mrs Vass'), who had been a widow since shortly after the Great War, and had an only son, also called Dick, who later inherited a baronetcy from his uncle, as well as the school. It was rumoured, on dubious authority, that she and Stanley Harris would have married if he had not died.

The school was housed in a late Victorian red-brick barrack, specially built for it about a mile from the sea. Except for the 'private' section, it was spartan, with worn encaustic-tiled passages, linoleum in the classrooms, and high ceilings. On part of the first floor were small dormitories for the seniors – another part was a cavernous gym, also used for concerts, special lectures and school plays, with the masters' common room leading out of it – and on the top floor was a great dormitorium, divided up to a height of about five feet into wooden cubicles, for the smaller boys. The walls of the dining-room, the chapel and the main public or 'reading' room were variously covered with painted name-boards of 'old boys' and framed photographs of former cricket and football first elevens, heroes all.

As I made my first entrance to St Ronan's as a pupil, through the front door not normally used by the boys, I thought the look of the place was much the same as Earleywood's, without the rural setting – but the difference became clear when Mrs Vass took me in her arms and gave me a maternal kiss. She, Dick Harris and the head servant Jack gave the school the feeling of a family. There were only seventy-five boys, almost all – like Dick and Mrs Vass themselves – from secure middle-class families. Our fathers were doctors, regular officers in the armed services, civil servants, businessmen. Just a few belonged to what might be called the bourgeois aristocracy – sons or grandsons of prominent early twentieth-century public men, one of them a prime minister. Even fewer were *nouveaux riches*, though there were some. Hardly any had connections with the nobility.

Dick had a junior, though older partner R.S. Vinter, a mathematician who came to the school as a master in 1898. The boys always claimed that he was the best maths teacher in the south of England (why not in the whole of England?), and in truth I never met another so lucid and easy to follow. He was short, with hunched shoulders, and played the piano by ear. Like Dick he was a bachelor and, unlike the other masters, had his own quarters in the school, though we saw little of him because he was as quiet and retiring as Dick was outgoing and gregarious. The school's nursing sister, who was indiscreet if not also a fantasist, once told me that the two partners took their baths together (the boys' bathrooms contained three or four baths each), and when I showed surprise, added 'I don't suppose they stand and stare at eachother'. She also claimed that her brother was friendly with the Duke of Windsor.

Three of the assistant masters were middle-aged and had been at the school a long time. The senior of these was William Jevons ('Jevvy'), the only married one; to a junior he had a special aura because he taught Latin and, optionally, Greek only to the top three classes, to which one graduated after being in the school for at least two years. He had been at the school since 1912. Then there was the historian J.A. Hood, shy and prickly but with some *gravitas*, and E.F. Poole, teacher of junior maths and divinity, who had no *gravitas*. Both of them served in the Great War and came to the school in the early 1920s. There were three younger masters. The oldest of these, Sidney Postgate, was a fine linguist. There was a married man called Bromley, liked by everyone, who taught English and maths to the middle forms. And there was a keen and bright young bachelor, John Spens, who took the junior Latin; when we returned to school after the outbreak of war in September 1939, there was universal sadness when we found that he had already left to join up. The main burden of teaching the juniormost class, where I remained only for the winter term of 1938, fell on the headmaster's secretary, Anne Darlington. Thus the ratio of teachers to pupils was high. Two music teachers (Mr Wynn and Miss Dutton), a drawing master (Mr Morgan) and a man who played the chapel organ on Sunday mornings (Mr Leonard), came in from outside. Mr Wynn was my teacher, and a curious man; Miss Dutton, with straight grey hair cut in a fringe, ploddingly played Schubert marches in the gym, while the boys cavorted around. The lean, eager, bespectacled Mr Leonard is lit up by one glimpse, when he put his head round the door into the reading room one Sunday morning just before chapel and called out 'This morning we're having the Benedicite, boys!' Of course this was cheering news because we all liked singing the Benedicite, with its comic words and endless repetitions of 'Bless ye the Lord: Praise him and magnify him for ever', but it was the fact that he addressed us as 'boys' that stuck in the memory; this was something that our masters would not have done. It was a bit common.

The head servant, Jack – his real name was Hector Cripps – joined the staff as a bootboy aged thirteen during the Great War, and now he had a natural authority combined with a robustly handsome appearance. Under him were some three junior menservants who on rare occasions, like Sports Day, donned footmen's livery. We were strictly forbidden to talk with 'Jack's men', one of whom, Dick later told us, was of gentle birth but had a screw loose. The prohibition did not apply to Finch, Jack's deputy, a tall, shy, myopic albino, but it hardly needed to because he was a man of few words. Finch had one gift – he could run very fast, and year after year would romp home with his vast strides ahead of the field in the 'retainers' race' on Sports Day.

Vinter was a benign and solid if remote presence – he had tics, by which we could not help being amused. Hood was an unimaginative teacher, who set great store by facts and generally made a fascinating subject arid and dreary. He did however have a list of choice quotations which we were expected to memorise – such as the last words of Napoleon ('*Tête d'armée*') and Cecil Rhodes ('So much to do, so little done', which I only discovered years afterwards was itself a quotation from Tennyson), 'the pilot who weathered the storm' (said of Pitt the Younger) and Disraeli's 'I will sit down now but the time will come when you will hear me'. He had had a sadly confined life. While still at 'varsity', he fell off his bicycle and as he lay on the ground, conscious but unable to move or speak, heard the bystanders say that he was dead. As a result, he once confided to me, he had been unable to go to the Bar, for which he had been intended. Short, stocky and with pince-nez, he was apt to say in class that he did not want to find fault – and one brave contemporary of mine, Bill Shelley (who later changed his name to Benyon on inheriting a large estate, and became a Conservative M.P.), called his bluff and said that finding fault was exactly what he did do. After a hideous silence, Hood spluttered that he would report this insolence to Mr Harris, but he never did. 'The colonel', as we called him, had the air of a gentleman and a scholar, and Mrs Vass later told me she believed it was because of his private means and not his accident that he never did anything more demanding with his life.

Poole's main interests were not academic. After the school moved to Devon in 1940, he almost single-handedly set up the cricket pitches, and he became an assiduous member of the local Home Guard (Jack was an air-raid warden). By nature a good and gentle man though not a gentleman, Poole may have had a sense of intellectual and social inferiority to his colleagues and even to older boys who had grown out of his orbit – he only taught the bottom classes; I once saw him lash out furiously at a senior prefect who had been cocky. He had a grizzled moustache and glasses that made his eyes look larger than they were. When I read *Decline and Fall*, Captain Grimes reminded me of Poole, though the similarity was in fact slight; Poole had the air of someone without a home who might have had an adventurous past, but was incapable of deception. However he was known for his tall stories, especially a legendary one about how, in the trenches, he had his hair parted by a bullet. Leaving aside whether it was true or not, I thought, because I had not heard him tell it myself, that it was the invention of some clever and mischievous boy – until, on my first grown-up visit to the school, I arrived from the station to find all the staff sitting round the table in the private dining-room having tea. At the very moment when I entered, Poole was finishing his classic story.

Postgate was a complex man. He had 'finely chiselled' features and slightly prominent teeth, and was a brilliant teacher of French. He could easily have held a post at a public school, but there may have been reasons why Dick – who addressed him as Sidney – offered him a berth at St Ronan's. There are stories of boys being ambushed when alone in the school changing room by a homosexual master, and one of my most level-headed contemporaries told us that this happened to him when Postgate, while chatting to him in a friendly way, slipped a hand down inside his shorts and touched his 'thing'. It was done in a moment, and they laughed and went on talking. It never occurred to us that there was anything sinister about it. (But if he had been reported to Dick, what then?) When the war had been going on for a couple of years, Postgate, who was about forty, left to join up. Soon after this, we heard that he was getting married, and were invited by Dick to contribute to a wedding present. Later he let fall that the marriage plan had fallen through – but the gift had not been returned.

My first friend at the school was McMurtrie, a feeble, pale boy with a mop of curly ginger hair. He had a vampirish mother who had been 'on the stage' and kept white rats as pets (which resulted unfairly in his being nicknamed 'Rat'). She sent him – her treasured only child – a postcard every day with a few words on it scrawled in green ink. But it was soon clear that he needed me more than I needed him, and I drifted into the .more amusing company of another new boy, Nigel Colborn. I vaguely understood that he had divorced parents. We used to stick together on school walks and made endless silly jokes. We also sat next to eachother at meals, and agreed that our favourite pudding was jam or treacle tart. This led to a new series of jokes which included the rhyme *'Je suis*, I am – a tart of jam. *Tu es*, thou art – a treacle tart.' Innocently I repeated this several times when I got home for the holidays;

and somehow it reached the ears of my father – who, being deaf, generally didn't hear our childish prattle. He got entirely the wrong idea of why I was saying 'tart' so often, and told me sternly that it was not a nice word – he couldn't explain why, but I had to promise to stop saying it forthwith. What could possibly not be nice about jam tarts?

Colborn was not only jokey; he was compulsively naughty and got into ever-deepening trouble. Once the unfortunate drawing master, no disciplinarian, had to drag him bodily from his class to avoid total chaos. At the end of our first year, Dick tried to tame him with a 'public whacking', after 'private' ones had yielded no result. This meant that Colborn was caned in Dick's study while the whole school was assembled in the nearest classroom to hear the strokes; then poor Colborn had to come out of the study and walk past the open door. My friend by this time was getting hardened, and sly – I once caught him alone in our classroom with his hand inside my locker. Eventually he left to 'go to Kenya', and we only met again at a school reunion in 1948 to celebrate Vinter's fiftieth anniversary at the school. From being chubby and, in the early days, merry he had become lean and soft-spoken. Amazing that he should return to the scene of so much misery, yet probably Vinter had been kind to him. Nigel had forgotten me, or so he said. In the late 1960s he had a regular acting part in a long-running serial on TV, and I impressed my small children by telling them that we had been chums at school.

The case of Nigel Colborn was exceptional; Dick's authority was such that he hardly ever had to use the cane. It is hard to explain that he ruled almost entirely through love. Out of doors during the daytime breaks and in the evening before bedtime in the reading room, he would come among us and be immediately surrounded, jostled, slapped on the shoulder and bombarded with banter. It sounds hardly believable in a conventionally run school, but it had become an institution, and helped to civilise us. The consequence was that we were on the whole nice to eachother, and unafraid of the other grown-ups around the place; although we could not take the same liberties with the assistant masters as we took with Dick, some of the culture of joking and badinage spilled over on to them. When first seen by outsiders who had only known chilly, condescending masters who crushed spontaneous individual expression, Dick's regime – as I found out years later from an Eton friend who taught at St Ronan's for a term and could not abide it – might appear subversive of all good order and discipline. Of course it was a character test too, and for some, like Colborn, it failed. Dick could at once spot the introvert, or the one who, as he once wrote in my report, was 'more interested in things than folk'. He cultivated each one of us.

It was characteristic of Vinter that his only major intervention during the year took place in the dark – on Guy Fawkes' night, which he organised entirely himself. As the bonfire blazed on the playing field, his stooped figure could be seen darting to and fro as he let off the fireworks. I only saw this famous event once, in 1938, because by the next November it was already war-time and we had the black-out. When the 'grub shop' opened on Saturday afternoons, it was he who stood, largely hidden, behind the hatch and doled out pennyworths of chocolate, liquorice and sherbet. And in the winter terms he made rare appearances in the dormitories – just after lights-out when the room was dimly lit by the dying fire in the grate – distributing curious sweets known as 'jubjubs'. They were rubbery and tasteless, but the time-honoured ritual was exciting.

At the end of the Christmas term in 1938 there was a school concert in the gym – I played Schumann's 'Merry Peasant' – and the school play, organised by Jevvy and his wife: this consisted of a scene or two from *A Midsummer Night's Dream*, followed by a monologue in which a talented boy called Bill Hawdon played a Frenchman, wearing a top hat and a false beard, and speaking broken English. On the last day of term, snow was thick on the ground as we gathered in the courtyard at the back of the school before walking together to the station with Dick to catch the London train. All the staff, teaching and domestic, watched from the windows, and as we moved off they waved and we responded with a loud hurrah. A few minutes earlier I had seen a tiny incident which a stroke of fate implanted in my memory for ever. I was collecting my coat from the changing-room when I saw the feeble McMurtrie approach Bill Hawdon, who was leaving us that term to become a naval cadet at Dartmouth. He said 'Goodbye Bill'. By so doing he transcended the school convention that little boys like us did not call the big boys by their first names. 'Goodbye Mac', Bill replied jovially, giving McMurtrie a warm handshake. That was all. Then, two months later, in the bleak depths of the Easter term, we heard that Bill Hawdon had died at Dartmouth after being given a routine innoculation against scarlet fever. A few months after that, a brass memorial plate appeared on the chapel wall and an appreciation by Dick in the school magazine; Dick also had a framed photograph of Bill in his cadet's uniform on his desk – it was said that he had been especially fond of him, but everyone had liked him. Of course we were all stunned, but this was my first initiation into the mystery of death, and I brooded on it for a long time. A very early memory

I have is of standing looking out of an upstairs window in our house at Ascot towards a dense clump of rhododendron, with a dovecote in front of it, with white doves. I suddenly realised at that moment that there is no beginning or end of time. It made me feel that we were hanging in a void. Now, what could one make of Hawdon's bright and promising life so senselessly cut off?

And what of myself during that one year at St Ronan's before the war started? I was quite carefree, and did passably well at school 'work' though poorly at sport. My parents' valetudinarianism easily crossed the boundary into the school lives of my sisters and myself. Instinct, as well as memories of their own schooldays, should have told them that being different from the common herd at school is not conducive to happiness. Yet at Earleywood I had been the only day boy, coming to and fro with Hitchcock or Miss Reed every morning and evening, and when I first arrived at St Ronan's my mother installed herself at Warne's Hotel on the Worthing seafront and I stayed there with her every night for my first two weeks. Then, after I was left alone (I never felt in the least homesick), the school was instructed to put me to bed for three days if I showed any sign of a cold. When summer came, I could not go with the rest of the school to the local swimming bath for fear of infection (this was actually a relief because I still could not swim). At home a handkerchief that fell on the floor was immediately seized and put in the wash. My mother always fussed if she thought she was sitting in a through-draught and asked somebody, usually me, to close a door or a window.

My father, though harried by his asthma, never spared himself physically, but he turned my mother into the next thing to a permanent 'invalid'. She never got up before mid-day, and when we were out walking and came to a seat, she would sit down on it 'for a wee while', having inspected it to see that it bore no trace of damp. In my teens I was with her in the small orchard at our house outside Oxford, when she picked up an apple off the ground and took a bite out of it. I was so dumbfounded that I had the surrealistic thought that she was someone else in disguise.

Fortunately my father did not often need to use his medical skills on us. When he felt my neck glands with his bony fingers, and especially once when he ordered me to drop my trousers so that he could examine a sore on my behind, my whole body rebelled. But for the rest, the country's best medics were glad to remove the tonsils or freeze off the warts of Arthur Hurst's children.

Gastro-enterology was my father's speciality (being deaf, he would have been hampered in dealing with the heart or lungs), and in

1909 he published his book *Constipation and Allied Intestinal Disorders* (Oxford).* (When I first heard this title, the war was on, and I assumed that these were the disorders of our brave Allies – the French, Norwegians, Czechs and so on – whose national anthems were played on the BBC Home Service after the News on Sunday nights. Those of our German enemies obviously did not bear thinking about.) Hence he was a connoisseur of stools. Doubtless mine came under his scrutiny from time to time, but an indelible memory is of a Sunday morning walk in Windsor Forest, when our beloved corgi, Sandy, interrupted his scampering about on either side of our path to defaecate. My father, noticing this, immediately strode through the bracken to inspect the turds – I can still see his tweed overcoat, hat, stick and spectacles and his habitual air of intense concentration.

Our parents' obsession with physical health was expressed through prohibitions; we were never exhorted to go in for vigorous sports or body-building. None of us suffered worse from this than my elder sister Pam. Having inherited my father's chest weakness in a milder form, she was marked out as 'delicate'. She did not go to school at all till the age of ten, and then only as a day-girl to a posh local school (St George's, Ascot) – different from the rest as usual. Then she was sent to the fashionable St George's English School at Clarens near the Lake of Geneva where the daughter of Marlene Dietrich and several minor German princesses were fellow-pupils. Its strength lay more in the purity of the air than any academic rigour – or concern for culture, as was shown when my father, hearing that the treasures of the Prado were on show in Geneva after being evacuated from Madrid because of the Spanish Civil War, wrote to the headmistress asking if Pam could be allowed to see them; the answer came back that such a departure from routine was not possible. The bigger war cut short her school career in Switzerland, where she was happy, and after a term or two at a day school in Oxford, she took a secretarial course (one result of which was that I learned to type on her typewriter) and eventually joined the W.A.A.F. and so won liberation. But the old dead hand even touched her service career. She applied for a posting overseas, but when

---

* With a subject so universal in its application, one could quote endlessly from his writings on it for the sake of interest and amusement. Two gobbets can suffice here: 'Inefficient defaecation may be due to (1) habitual disregard of the call of defaecation, (2) inefficiency of the voluntary muscles which normally take part in defaecation, (3) the assumption of an unsuitable posture during the act, (4) weakness of the defaecation reflex, and (5) hysteria.' 'The Emperor Claudius made an effort to overcome the popular opinion that to allow the escape of wind is an offence against decent manners by issuing an edict, which made it lawful for any Roman *"flatum crepitumque ventris in convivio emittere"*.'

the medical records of the applicants were being sifted, her name was spotted by J.J. Conybeare, a Guy's physician who had become a senior R.A.F. medical officer. Confident that her parents would disapprove of their delicate daughter being exposed to dangerous foreign climes, he vetoed her application.

My sinovitis struck again in the Easter term, and I had the pleasure of going home early, but on arriving back at school for the summer term, I was still considered in a delicate state, and not allowed to run about out of doors. Instead an ancient wheelchair was produced, and the school carpenter made a board on which to rest my game-leg. My peers vied with eachother to wheel me around at high speed. The last trace of sinovitis soon departed, and never came back. But the stigma of being 'not very strong' lingered.

A famous ritual occurrence at the school was 'Arundel Day'. It was a day-long outing during working time in the summer term to the park of Arundel Castle a few miles away, and was announced only on the actual morning after chapel. Plans for the normal round of classes and games were cancelled, we piled into motor coaches with all the staff, and off we went. Lunch, on trestle tables in the open, included strawberries and cream, and there were games like rounders. But we also wandered through the park and generally did as we liked. This was my only Arundel Day because by the next year the war was on in earnest, and we had left Sussex. Sports Day that year was memorable for me because Sir Adrian Boult, the conductor, gave away the prizes. He and Dick had been school contemporaries and in his speech he said that Dick was always the centre of merriment and laughter.

That summer term I and a number of other boys, all aged nine or ten, started a game of coming together in various more remote places in the school grounds during break-times and looking at eachother's 'private parts'; the signal for doing this was a blast on a blade of grass. The official school phrase for any such behaviour was 'vulgarity', so we called ourselves the Vulgar Club. Probably the total number of such assignations did not exceed three or four, and it was near the end of a long term – soon, as we all went our separate ways, it would be forgotten. But at the beginning of the next term, we discovered that the little exploit had reached the ears of Dick through one of our number telling his parents. Each of us was summoned in turn to Dick's study, and made to sit on a stool beside the fireplace facing him as he glared down with his back to the window. He said to me that he was sure I would not want my father to know about it. I agreed. Then, as a condition of this not happening, he put me on my honour to report to him any instance of 'vulgarity' that I came upon in the school. I promised, and having so effortlessly got me on to his side he told me I could go, which I did feeling a shade bigger and more grown up than when I went in. He was trusting me – so did I ever live up to the promise he had extracted? I have to say that I twice reported a companion, one a special friend – for reasons of the utmost triviality. Later in my time at St Ronan's I did one or two things with other boys that were not so infantile and which I never thought of reporting, yet by some mysterious chain of information Dick seemed aware of them when we had our final talk before I left the school in 1943. But I have wondered what Dick thought when I went sneaking to him: was this encouragement of 'grassing' a devilishly cunning test of character – which I thereby failed? Did he really care about such tiny offences, or did he believe that good citizens should nark on each other? Why, likewise, did he cane poor Colborn publicly with the whole school assembled next door to gloat?

And by what strange quirk did he encourage a strange annual ritual, the 'rag'? This followed our Christmas supper, a splendid feast even when the war was on: the crowning moment came when the servants, led by Jack, filed into the dining-room holding platters with huge flaming puddings, to be greeted by cheers. As soon as 'For what we have received....' had been said, all the boys except the smallest would rush to the biggest classroom, which had been cleared of desks, remove their sweaters, and engage in a general wrestling bout. In my first term, I found the sight of the writhing bodies through the frosted glass of the classroom door, and the shouts and thuds, terrifying. When I later experienced it, it was less so: because of our very disparate stages of growth, it was easy for anyone seeking an easy victory to tumble someone smaller. Not surprisingly a lot of boys felt, or actually were, sick afterwards. Why did Mrs Vass allow it?

I had two special friends that summer term in 1939. One, David S., was a lithe, curly-haired boy with an exceptionally dark tan (being pale myself, I envied him), an only child whose father had an engineering business in the Isle of Wight and owned a small yacht; he was already an experienced sailor. He was shy, introverted and short-tempered, yet somehow grown-up beyond his age. The death of Bill Hawdon struck a sombre note for him; his parents had had a son who also died at Dartmouth at the age of thirteen (what sort of regime did they have there?), and he himself was only conceived after that disaster. The other friend was a lanky, ungainly fellow who, if that was possible, had even less aptitude for sport than I did. One of his nicknames was 'the Prof', because his father was a professor and, more important, he had a serious interest in science, and understood the principles of radio, electricity and the internal combustion engine. He read scientific literature and drew diagrams for fun. He shone in none of the subjects in the school curriculum, until in his last year he suddenly turned in Greek and Latin proses that won the praise of Jevvy.

The link between us started by chance. On school walks a master walked at the back of the crocodile flanked by two boys – reluctant companions if he was dull, like Hood, or eager ones augmented by others if, like John Spens, he could tell a good yarn. Once the Prof and I happened to be paired together, and I started telling him an adventure story – probably the same one I had heard being told by Spens, which the Prof had missed. I could not finish my story by the time the walk ended, so we met again in the next break and carried on with another instalment. Our story-telling began while we were still at Worthing, but did not really get into its stride until we moved to Devon, where the conditions for it were perfect, and. we had plenty of inspiration. By then the palm for telling good stories had passed to the Prof; he invented both a plot and a range of characters, and when it came round to my turn, I could only produce variations on his great theme. The setting was the school's new abode, a baronial hall in a magnificent park. Neither of us had ever seen such a place before, and invention could not have produced a better one. The hero was the unlikely figure of Mr Smith, one of our wartime replacement masters who was of military age but physically unfit for service (he surprised us all by singing 'A Wandering Minstrel, I' in a good tenor voice at our school concert). The villain was Pavlovsky – modelled on no-one we knew, whose secret weapon was a squadron of miniature aircraft called 'Hornets', radio-controlled and able to relay television pictures back to a screen in Pavlovsky's lair, and armed with little bombs, torpedoes and machine-guns with which they would attack the forces of good, led by Smith, that were headquartered in our school. This was no later than 1940-1, and although it would require no great knowledge or power of invention to think of all this today, it seems that the Prof was looking with uncanny accuracy far into the future. Anyway, the stories took on a life of their own and we could hardly wait until, matter-of-factly, we would meet for another episode. Perhaps it was unavoidable that sooner or later the fascination would wear off. The Pavlovsky-Smith seam was worked to exhaustion, and our new stories were not as good as the original ones. One day I ate the serpent's apple when I persuaded the Prof to let me start a wonderful new story before he had finished his current one; the sacrifice I thus exacted proved vain because my new story consisted of only one good idea and soon petered out. Finally an external assault killed off the whole thing, and our friendship with it.

The last holiday-time of peace started in a quite unexpected way. Within a day or two of my arriving home, our family was joined by a new member – a fourteen-year-old German boy called Thomas Naegele. Like ourselves (my sisters and I), he was half-Jewish; unlike us, he looked it. I had never heard my father refer to the fact that he was entirely Jewish by blood, that all his four grandparents were immigrants from Germany, and that up till 1916 his surname was Hertz. Yet without his help I had somehow become aware at least of the name-change by the time I was about seven. There was a moment of truth when all of us, including the governess, were on our way to Switzerland sitting in a train compartment, which one stranger, a middle-aged lady, shared with us. Suddenly I voiced a thought which, apropos of nothing, had just bubbled to the surface: 'Daddy', I said, helpfully raising my voice so that he could hear, 'why did you change your name?' Perhaps a modern family would have collapsed with laughter, but not ours: with a ghastly congested look on his face, my father edged his way along the seat towards me and, gasping for breath, said that he would tell me why some other time. He then got up and went down the train corridor to the lavatory to inject himself with adrenalin, thinking about me heaven knows what terrible thoughts. Yet the reason for the change was only that any sort of German name or connection had been felt to be undesirable for an English family in the Great War, much more than in the Second World War when to have a German-Jewish name like ours was almost a mark of honour. Added to this were my Uncle Gerald's political ambitions – he was already a Conservative parliamentary candidate before 1914. My father, his two brothers and their two uncles had thought at one point of adopting their wives' surnames, but in the end settled for the English name that sounded most like the old one, although 'Hurst' is an archaic word for a wood. If they had wanted an accurate translation of Hertz – a Germanisation of Naphthali, whose tribal motto was 'the *hind* let loose that giveth goodly words' (Genesis 49:21) – we should have called ourselves Hart. My father and Uncle Gerald both believed deeply that they were moving with the tide of history: the royal family changed its name, Guelph, to Windsor at the same time. The difference between Arthur and Gerald was that Gerald took a historian's interest in our family's past whereas Arthur was indifferent if not actually hostile to it. He seemed more curious about my mother's family, the Riddifords, even inventing a Crusader ancestor for them called Sir Guy Ris-de-Veau (French for sweetbreads).

But my father had fellow-feeling with his German Jewish medical confreres who were being persecuted by the Nazis, and in this summer of 1939 let it be known that we would provide hospitality for the son of a Jewish doctor during the school holidays. It was Thomas's mother who was the Jewish doctor; his father was a non-Jewish artist of marked individuality and independence, who still enjoys considerable posthumous fame in his native region of Germany.* Thomas had sampled English life in the raw as a boarder at Brighton College. And he was already skilled in drawing – especially in cartoon style – and graphics. For me, belatedly, it was like having a brother and, despite our difference in age, he played along and we had a lot of fun. My mother's pleas not to 'romp' fell on deaf ears. Once again (and for the last time, though we didn't yet know it) a governess was hired – Miss Wilson, whom we rebelled against on sight and whose efforts to interest us in her pet activity, theatricals, we doggedly thwarted. What made it worse was that she was a New Zealander – we felt she let that great country down. Soon we went off to Swanage, and spent days playing tennis and around the swimming pool, until our holiday was cut short by great events in the outside world. Hitchcock drove down to fetch us on 2 September, the day after the invasion of Poland, and the next morning at 11 o'clock we listened to Neville Chamberlain on the wireless saying that we were at war and that 'The right will prevail'. We still went to church after this, and my mother whispered the news to the pew-opener who passed it to the vicar who announced it to the congregation.

The only reason why it was Thomas whom we had to stay with us at all was a wonderfully characteristic one. The 'son of a Jewish doctor' we were offered first was seventeen years old, and because my sister Pam was also at that dangerous age, my mother turned him down for fear that the two of them would get up to some

---

* Reinhold Naegele's work occupies a gallery to itself in the town museum of Murrhardt, near Stuttgart, and his grave in the churchyard there is a *tour de force* by Thomas, himself an artist. On the one occasion that I met Reinhold, in New York, he gave me an etching of railway lines he had done in 1914. It is a conventional but fine piece of work which gives me pleasure whenever I look at it. In his later career he developed a strain of fantasy, and I will always regret not accepting an offer Thomas made me in the 1950s of a coloured lithograph by Reinhold showing a cross-section through a crowded urban neighbourhood, in which every householder was sitting on the lavatory. It was too strong meat for me then, but years later, when I had outgrown youthful prudery, I realised the beauty of the conception and asked Thomas if he still had a copy, but it had become a collector's item and was unobtainable.

hanky-panky. Rosemary was fourteen, and therefore Thomas, also being of that innocent age, was thought safe. This tale, like Goldsmith's *Elegy on the Death of a Mad Dog*, ended in the opposite way to what anyone, least of all my parents, could have expected. Thirteen years later, in New York, Thomas and Rosemary were married. Pam, in an established pattern, was the loser.

When we arrived home from Swanage, six children from two London working-class families were already billeted in the house – part of the earliest wave of 'evacuees'. The Turner family were well-grown and healthy and wore good clothes, but their companions the Munceys were puny. We did not see much of them because they ate in the kitchen, and played and slept in the maids' part of the house, and for my part I was concerned to spend as much of the time we had left before the end of the holiday with Thomas. Typically, Rosemary was the most friendly of us towards the evacuees.

Of course we were all fitted out with gasmasks, and on the very day that war was declared there was an air raid warning and we all sat on the floor in a dark passage at the back of the house. It was soon over, and had been a false alarm; perhaps nothing serious was going to happen and 'it would all be over by Christmas'. To relieve the extra strain on the household, our staff of four indoor servants was increased to five – with the arrival of the sister of the incumbent tweenie. The two, both in their mid-teens, sang in close harmony together, and the strains of their favourite song – 'Toodle-lumma-lumma, toodle-lumma-lumma, toodle-i-a, Any um-ber-ellas, any um-ber-ellas to mend today' – rang through the house.

Our only direct contact with the poor before this had happened a year or two earlier through a scheme at my sisters' school. Every girl was encouraged to correspond with a pen-friend in the East End of London, known as a 'sunbeam'. Of my sisters only Rosemary took it seriously, and one Sunday in summer her 'sunbeam' Louisa Wilson, Louisa's mother, a big brother and two sisters came down from Stepney for the day. We had lunch in the garden, and I have a photograph of us all, posing rather awkwardly, as a record of the occasion. In it one sees Mrs Wilson, a large woman with ancient clothes and a far-away look. What it doesn't reveal is that she had only one eye, and the empty eye-socket was uncovered. She and my mother exchanged a few short letters before and after the visit, and in each of Mrs Wilson's she ended by saying that she hoped my mother was not offended.

When we returned to St Ronan's at the end of September, we were all excited about the war. The campaign in far-away Poland was over, but things were moving around us on a satisfyingly large scale, and we waited for developments rather like spectators at a football match rooting for their side to win the first goal. As well as the lamented John Spens, a boy had already gone off to join his parents in India. Our music master, Mr Wynn, had left too. He was much too old to fight, but I would not be surprised if intelligence was his *métier*. He was a rich-and-strange specimen to find in a place like Worthing, and he told rich tales – for example, that he played before the German Kaiser, who presented him with a ring. It was probably this claim that drew from me the ill-judged boast that I had played to an earl's daughter, no less – an elderly patient of my father's who had become a family friend. This trivial event had made an impression on me for two reasons: the first being that we were not on social terms with any other members of the nobility, and the second that I was – and remain – susceptible to old hereditary titles, quarterings and the grand houses that are their proper setting. So was my father: he knew who was who (a good number of them had been his patients), and once, in the interval of a Priestley play, he commented only on the solecism of referring to a character as (say) 'Lady Brown' when she should have been 'Lady Mary Brown', or vice versa. I confess to an extensive knowledge of the wider ramifications of the British royal house, and more than a slight acquaintance with the courtesy titles and family names of the higher aristocracy – something so little spoken of that I have the impression, possibly mistaken, that this is an aberration I share with few other people. The whole area is made no less diverting because it is so hedged about with hypocrisy. Who will admit to being a snob? To return to Mr Wynn, he unsportingly reported my remark to Dick, who in turn mentioned it in a letter accompanying my end-of-term report. My father, who could not treat any disciplinary matter lightly, sat me down in our hotel suite in Switzerland and lectured me on how careful I had to be about such things 'now that Daddy has a knighthood'.

Anyway, Mr Wynn was gone and now in complete contrast we had Mrs Scott. She was the mother of two boys in the school, the elder of whom, during my first year, was the resident piano-player, able to pick up any popular tune by ear with all the internal harmonies in place (and usually standing rather than sitting at the keyboard). Amazingly Mrs Scott taught me, with no more than a few deft hints, how to improve my technique as a bar-room player, thus hastening the day when I would take over the office vacated by her son. All of us wondered how such a sweet woman could have married Mr Scott, for we had not only lost the much-liked John Spens as our junior Latin master, but in a double deprivation, got Mr Scott in his place. He was a stout, hideously ugly, late-middle-aged fellow, with a pouting under-lip like the spout of a jug, who tended to wear pink shirts and bow-ties, in our eyes the ultimate in pansiness. He spoke pompously and elaborately, and his sarcastic brand of humour went right over the heads of philistine small boys. One remark of his, in answer to a question from the class – 'I know almost everything, but not that' – might have struck an older audience as moderately amusing. He quickly stamped on a time-honoured custom – that if a boy put up his hand in class and asked 'Please-sir-can-I-go-round-the-corner?', the master would automatically agree. Not Mr Scott. Early in his tenure, he would reply 'Yes you can go' but when the boy reached the door he would call 'Where are you going? I said you *can* go – not that you *may* go.' Soon he got wiser and would say instead: 'All right, but then go and report yourself to Sister.' You could not draw back then without being proved a fraud. I was once caught by this, and duly crept into Sister's presence. She was very gentle and said that she knew I was 'not very strong'; I made sure never to ask Mr Scott if I could go round the corner and hear those dreadful words again.

At this time I first discovered I was short-sighted. It came on quickly, because I had no inkling of it the previous term, or even in the summer holidays. But now, peer as I might, I could no longer read what was written on the blackboard. My father was short-sighted, but not enough to wear glasses all the time. Knowing I would never be a tough, I thought that wearing glasses would advertise this fact. The only escape was to pretend to the world that my eyesight was normal. Instinct came to my aid and I discovered what must be known to all myopics, including those in primitive stages of civilisation – that I could overcome the problem if I made a tiny triangular hole between the tips of the thumb, index finger and middle finger of one hand and squinted through it, adjusting its size to sharpen the focus. By this ruse I could read the blackboard and thus delay by all of two years my transformation into one of that dreaded species, a spectacle-wearer. Finally I could keep up the pretence no longer and boldly announced to Jevvy one day in class that I could not see the board. Confessing lifted a burden, and when I returned to school the next term wearing glasses I found that it was not so bad as I had feared.

In the autumn term of 1939, we played the new war songs over and over on the school gramophone. As well as patriotic ones like 'Wings over the ocean', 'The army, the navy and the air force' and 'He was a handsome territorial', sung *alla marcia* in a soldierly baritone, there were Flanagan and Allen singing 'We're gonna hang out the washing on the Siegfried Line', 'Mr Franklin D. Roosevelt Jones' and the nostalgic reverie of a 1914-18 veteran telling his newly conscripted son of the pitfalls of life on the Western Front, 'If a grey-haired lady says "How's yer father?", that'll be Ma-de-me-zelle [of Armentières]'. We had a feeling of history coming alive around us, with the re-opening of the historic 'Western Front' and the B.E.F. once again going out there to see the Germans off. The soldier of the hour was Viscount Gort, its commander, who had won the V.C. 'last time'. My mother noted that with his cap titled to one side, and without the leather gaiters and gold braid of the Great War generals, he looked a new type of soldier, a man for the times. The defeat of Poland and its carve-up between Hitler and Stalin were happening too far away to make us anxious, but a foretaste of things to come was the sinking of the old battleship *Royal Oak* in Scapa Flow with hundreds of men on board shortly before Christmas. The first good news came with the war in Finland. Although it wasn't our war and the Germans were not involved, it was hugely satisfying to see the Russians getting a pasting from the brave Finns. There was one splendid picture in the papers of a couple of Finnish soldiers on skis pointing their rifles at an incredibly long row of Russians, all with their hands up. Their lowered ear-flaps somehow made them look even more of a rabble. The elderly peasant-like president of Finland, Kyosti Kallio, with his long drooping moustaches, cut an unimpressive figure, but the glamorous Marshal Mannerheim, in charge of operations, made up for him. It was hard for us to understand why we did not help the Finns, and it was a sad disappointment when they had to surrender in spite of their heroic resistance, and give up the Karelian Isthmus and Lake Ladoga of which we had heard so much in the recent news bulletins.

The Old Order Changes

In July, on turning sixty, my father retired from the staff of Guy's Hospital and accepted a lectureship in clinical medicine at Oxford. Then the war started, and New Lodge Clinic closed; most of the patients had been rich (they included some Indian princes and the great Nellie Melba[*]) and apparently its continuation in war-time could

---

[*] Melba's legend lived on in our family. My father had an agitated manner, and Melba

not be justified. Thus plans for us to leave Ascot and move to Oxford were already afoot in the late summer, and we drove over to look at some houses. A rather grand one with a large garden, near the river – all three of these attributes appealed to me – was ruled out as likely to be damp and unhealthy. During the next term, while I was away, they decided to rent a house at Headington just outside Oxford which, being on a hill, passed the health test. At the same time they found a tenant for Heath End – Lady Waddilove, known in the snob world for organising charity balls. My father sent me a letter (it was always he and not my mother who wrote to tell me of grave matters) trying to put the move in not too discouraging a light, though admitting that we would all be sorry to leave Heath End.

By the time I went back to Ascot for the Christmas holidays, almost everything was packed up. The walls were bare and we ate off kitchen china. There was not even a holiday governess. The old order had all put passed. I felt grim but stoical. There might even be some compensation if the house we were moving to proved to be nice, but when we got there on a grey, freezing cold afternoon, this proved to have been a forlorn hope – it was irredeemably without character. Just for that first night, like a stay of execution, we put up in the Randolph Hotel while the two maids we had brought with us were getting the house ready. My parents were in typical form at dinner that evening in the hotel dining-room. Although Pam was seventeen, they forbade her to order the sweet course she had chosen on the menu because they did not think it would be good for her (it was stewed pears). The atmosphere became tense and unhappy. I was always prevented from eating spinach or rhubarb for the same reason, which possibly explains why I enjoy them so much now.

I never liked our new house. Perhaps my parents thought we would only be there for a short time, but they never moved from it. Also, my father's normal astuteness in business matters deserted him over this house. They sold Heath End in 1940 at the bottom of the market – to the rich Lady Waddilove (she acted through an agent so that they did not know she was the buyer till after the deal was struck) – and should have bought the Oxford house at the same time. Instead it was left for my mother, by then a widow,

---

would lay her hand on his and say '*Calmez-vous!*' In other situations it was she who showed agitation: she once threatened to throw her steak at the cook's head if it was not done to her liking – grey on the outside and pink inside. My mother, characteristically, was disapproving when the diva proclaimed that a talent such as hers occurred only once in a life-time.

to buy it at the end of the war, when property values had risen again. Once I confessed to Rosemary that I secretly pined for Heath End, and she reasonably argued that we had never needed such a large house with so much space and so many servants, and in addition that Ascot had been as dull as ditch-water. But so was Headington, or at least the London Road where we lived – a fast main thoroughfare which later claimed the lives of Sandy, our incumbent corgi, his successor Tim (a third corgi, Gwily, the only one without a pedigree and therefore tougher, survived three collisions with cars), and a white poodle my mother bought when Gwily succumbed after a fourth and final encounter. Finally, the house had a blush-making name – 'Red Gables'.

The garden of the new house was its best feature, and was what, at a more propitious time of year, had appealed to my mother. It was of about an acre and was cared for by a surly man called Jacobs, who had contracted 'trench feet' in the Great War and never fully recovered, and, having worked for the previous owners, plainly resented our presence. A daily woman, Mrs Wooton, was immediately hired. Even at Ascot, with a larger staff, such a person was employed to do the rough housework; her name was Mrs Ewart, and my mother told me of her surprise at finding that it was actually spelt as Mrs Ewart pronounced it, and not 'Hewart'. Mrs Wooton had – in my mother's reliable estimation – been a beauty; she had perfect downy skin and regular features, besides having learned impeccable manners through being in service as a parlour maid. To crown it all, Mr Wooton was the head ticket inspector at Oxford station (G.W.R.) and wore a cap with gold braid on the peak and a stiff white collar.

That winter was famously cold, and the water that flooded Port Meadow every year was now frozen solid. This meant that we could resume skating, without the restricted space of a Swiss hotel rink.

Although my father was now officially part of the University, his activities were confined to the Radcliffe Infirmary and he took no part in Oxford academic or social life. However two surviving dons from his undergraduate days were invited to the house when I was there. One, from his old college, Magdalen, was Paul Benecke, whom I remember only through having been told beforehand that he was the grandson of Felix Mendelssohn-Bartholdy. The other had been my father's medical tutor: Emeritus Professor Walter Ramsden of Pembroke College, known as 'the Rammer'. He was a gentle old bachelor, and my father's explanation for his single state was that when, in the nineteenth century, college fellows were permitted to marry without resigning their fellowships, Pembroke was accidentally left out of the ordinance. Be that as it may, he was happy breeding silkworms, which he fed on the leaves of Pembroke's famous mulberry tree. He was also an Esperantist, and after my father died he sweetly befriended me, taking me on the river and later sending me a packet of Esperanto books at school. I heard that when he himself died, he lay in his room for a couple of days before being found. As an undergraduate I went to hear John Betjeman reading his poems, and he declaimed his piece 'I.M. Walter Ramsden' – I had not known of its existence, or that he knew the Rammer. Somehow I felt that the poem struck a false note.

In the early summer of 1940 my life was shaken up by two radical changes, one at home and the other at school. I received a crisis letter from my father to say that Rosemary was going to Canada with a group of fifty girls and two mistresses from her school, Roedean. The offer came at short notice, calling for an immediate decision, and as she wanted to go he and my mother agreed. Then my own school was evacuated to Devon. Of the two changes the second affected me more dramatically, while the first could only be felt as time passed. When I heard about it, Rosemary was due to sail one or two days later, and we could not meet again before the long parting. Perhaps this was just as well; because of some mysterious emotional anaesthesia, all three of us had deep inhibitions about expressing kindness or affection, real or formal, towards eachother, and saying good-bye face to face would have been agonising. As children the only ending to a letter that we knew was 'Love from', but if we had to write to each other we would follow 'Love' with the letters 'HH', meaning 'hem-hem', a verbalised clearing of the throat to signify that we didn't mean it.

Of the three of us Rosemary was the least inhibited. Passionate and instinctive, she had felt the need from the very beginning to fight her corner. My father had a special attachment to Pam, his long-awaited first child who also inherited his pulmonary weakness, and so Rosemary's earliest imperative was to elbow her way into the spotlight in their nursery jungle by undermining Pam's fragile defences – Pam being shy and retiring, this was easily done – and in the world at large through charm.[*] When I appeared, the even longer-awaited son and heir, a threatening 'second front' in the battle for centre-stage opened up. She resented Nanny's protective presence, and found the attention I received when I started playing the piano by ear at the age of four unbearable. One line of attack was to

---

[*] Our family visitors' book contained an eloquent testimony to her success. One of my father's patients was a retired brigadier-general, divorced and lonely, who had become a family friend and occasional house guest. When he signed the book, he invariably mentioned 'Pam and darling Romy'.

say that I was still a baby and would only cease to be one on my next birthday; when that birthday came, the end of babyhood would have shifted to the next year. Another, which struck my nascent male pride in its tenderest spot, was to call me 'Christine' and say that she wished I were a girl. One day, when Miss Reed had been looking after me for a short time, she made the true observation that 'Nanny wrapped him up in cotton wool'. Unfortunately Rosemary heard it, and that neat phrase, with its tripping rhythm, was turned into a little ditty, just as she had one for Pam, sung to the tune of 'Mary had a little lamb', which began 'Pam'la had a sister dear, her sister's name was Romy'. Any blows, kicks or scratches that passed between us came exclusively from me; Rosemary's weapons were words – and looks. She knew she could get a rise out of me by flashing a terrible forced smile; it was most effective when visitors were present and I could not react. But towards the end of our time at Heath End we began to play certain games together. The arrival of our first corgi, Sandy, united us – ever inventive, she evolved a whole series of linguistic distortions for talking to him, which we all to some degree fell into. With the brief appearance of Thomas, childish feuds finally ended.

So it was bad news that Rosemary was about to disappear from our lives. Pam, though never an enemy as Rosemary had once been, was not so close, and anyway was now grown up. Rosemary had a more definite personality and more vitality than either of us, and her removal made our whole family life duller, and me more lonely. As for her, she went with her Roedean contingent to a strict church school in Windsor, Nova Scotia (she later gave a wonderful rendering of the school song), and from there after a couple of years to a junior college in Illinois. When she came back in 1944, she was the possessor of a whole new world, and although she served in the W.R.N.S. till the end of the war and then studied and worked in theatrical costume design till the early 1950s, it always seemed only a matter of time before she would return to America. She went in the summer of 1952 and married Thomas a year later.

But I am running ahead. In May 1940, one morning during break-time, we stood outside the school building with the wireless turned up loud inside, listening to the news that the Germans had invaded France, Holland and Belgium. In June St Ronan's went through the same upheaval that we had done at Heath End a few months before. The school was going to move out of the supposed flight path of German bombers on their way to London, and go to South Devon. The parents of one of the boys, who lived there, had heard on the local grapevine that Lord Clinton was willing to let out his mansion Bicton House near the village of East Budleigh – he had another one to move to in the north of the county. One day in June we all made the journey together, boys and staff, by train and from Exeter onwards by motor coach.

As our convoy rounded the last turn in the long drive and we caught our first sight of Bicton House, we must all have been bemused – none of us lived at home in anything approaching the splendour we now saw rising before us. Bicton was not architecturally beautiful – the front block was indeterminate late Georgian, red brick, with a colonnade of white-painted wooden pillars – but it was very grand. It stood on an eminence looking across a flat gravel expanse and down a long gentle grassy slope to a lake, with big trees on either side, but some way off, so that in front of the house there was a broad space which became our general area for messing about. Only senior boys were allowed to pass beyond the boundary formed by the trees. Deer and sheep roamed in the park. The lake had a small wooded island, and beyond it was a renowned arboretum. To the left of the lake, looking down from the house, was a dark wood of evergreens, with a path through it leading to the extremely formal Italian garden,* with Paxton-style glasshouses, walks, flowerbeds and geometrical stretches of water. Across the bottom was a very high grassy bank of uniform height and gradient, topped with thick trees and pierced in the centre by a broad green avenue at right angles to it, similarly embanked, at the end of which a ploughed field rose to a point where an obelisk stood, completing the vista. Every Sunday morning we walked through this garden to and from the grey mid-Victorian Bicton church.

The appointments of the house were palatial. In the front hall at the foot of the grand staircase was the seated marble figure of Lord Rolle, owner of the house in the early nineteenth century. The hall was flanked by sumptuous rooms: on one side the library, which was soon filled to the ceiling with stored furniture, and which had a small study leading from it which became Vinter's hide-away; and on the other the dining-room, emptied for our use, leaving only a set of great dark maroon velvet curtains edged with gold brocade. On the first floor were three drawing-rooms filling the whole front block, all locked up; here the furniture remained, and there were great crystal chandeliers. I only ever saw these Aladdin's caves through the keyholes. On the top floor were the bedrooms which became our principal dormitories. Behind the main block was an older two-storeyed range around a courtyard containing all the offices, and

---

* Today this part is open to the public, while the house is an agricultural college.

at the front, where the main block and this range met, the corners were punctuated on each side by a beautiful oval room; one of these was now Dick's study. At one end of the corridor running across the back of the main block was the billiard room, which became our 'reading room' for general converse, billards on our small table, and the morning prayer session with a hymn and the evening one without. Jack bought a full-sized Broadwood grand piano with an ornate case at a saleroom in Exeter for £2, and on it Andrew Davidson and I alternately played the hymn in the morning, he by sight and I by ear.

Lord Clinton was a *grand seigneur* of the old school, born in 1863 and sporting mutton-chop whiskers. For a day or two after our arrival, the corridor already mentioned and the cavernous stone staircase at the opposite end of the front block from the billiard room, which we used to go up to our dormitories, were crowded with the family's portraits, but these regrettably were taken down. In one room of indeterminate use, from which we were not banished, there were, besides a Broadwood grand of 1820, some framed photographs of house parties in the 1920s, one including Edward Prince of Wales and another the Duke and Duchess of York. Lord Clinton's barony dated from 1299, and in the absence of a son his two daughters were co-heiresses. The genetic stock was badly flawed; in the 1980s there was a nine-days' wonder when the papers revealed that two female Bowes-Lyon cousins of Queen Elizabeth II had spent all their adult lives in a mental institution. They were grandchildren of Lord and Lady Clinton. That was not all: of their other daughter's offspring two had similar congenital mental disorders.

Thus we spent our schooldays in this aristocratic paradise and returned to our middle-class homes in the holidays.[*] Strangely some of us did not take to it at first, and repined for our hugga-mugga

[*] Up till this time I knew absolutely nothing about the aristocracy and landed gentry or their way of life – second-hand knowledge was to come in ample measure when I moved on to Eton. Ascot had contained a few plutocrats who, though rich enough to marry their daughters to peers (as Lady Weigall did), would have been quietly ridiculed for their vulgarity if they had set up house in the shires instead of outer suburbia where their ascendancy was unquestioned. When my mother saw Bicton, she remarked to my surprise that once in her life she had stayed in an equally large house – Lord Fortescue's seat in Devon, Castle Hill, to which she and my father were invited from Seale Hayne Military Hospital in the levelling circumstances of war. Normally such people never entered into their conversation, yet my father was remarkably knowledgeable about them. Once, when *Life* magazine published a feature on the twenty-six British dukes, with a photo of each, he examined it with me and pointed to a fair proportion who (or their fathers, wives or close affines) had been his patients. Shortly before his death, he took me out to lunch from Eton when on his way to wait on George VI, who wanted to hear of the progress of his cousin the Duchess of Beaufort.

at Worthing, which now became nostalgically known as 'Old St Ronan's'. For a few days the Prof, one other boy and I met in the breaks and solemnly planned to run away. But I knew that I was attracted to Bicton: it provided a counter-weight to our cheerless, frumpish house outside Oxford. Inhabited now by the St Ronan's extended family, Bicton became a welcoming place and seemed almost designed for our informal style. The end of breaks was signalled by a bugle call expertly blown by a new addition to our staff, Captain Gilbert Beal, in appearance and manner a stereotype of the Indian Army officer of old, but an accomplished writer and raconteur who had written under a pseudonym for Indian newspapers, and whose wife taught us drawing. He had been a boy at St Ronan's in the Great War, and told us of his excitement at hearing the news of 'Jutland', rather as we heard about the sinking of the *Bismarck*. Beal was still under forty, but his health had been broken in India and he died before the end of the war. We were fonder of him than of any of our other war-time replacements.

Once when I was walking in front of the house, I suddenly knew that I could no longer pronounce the 'w' sound without stammering. Because so many questions begin with 'what', 'why', 'which' and 'when', this was going to cause difficulties. It was not so bad if the 'w' came in the middle of a word or sentence, so I got into the way of taking a run at the interrogative words by using circumlocutions like 'Could you please tell me why...' Even that could not be guaranteed to work, though it usually did. This continued for years, and even today, if I am preparing a *bon mot*, the words become hard to utter as I get to the critical point. I never admitted this affliction to anyone, although it was the same kind of condition as my father had cured in the Great War. The worst incident was in a class at Eton when my turn came to read something. I was totally bereft of speech, and after some embarrassed titters the master tactfully moved on to the next boy.

In the summer of 1941, while Hitler's and Stalin's hordes were beginning their titanic struggle, and many schoolboys in the heart of Europe would have been starving or facing imminent violent death, I was having a bad time of a tamer sort. There was a boy, Stuart-Roche, with whom I always had a bond of natural sympathy based partly on our explicit interest in sex within the narrow confines of what we then knew or could imagine. He was sophisticated beyond his age and told adult jokes (for example, a French officer says to an English tart *'Je t'adore'*, and she replies 'Shut it yourself'[*]). Another

---

[*] I was told years later of a similar occurrence in real life by a man who, shortly after

bond was that, almost alone in our narrow age-group, neither of us belonged to the B.L.I. – short for 'Bicton Light Infantry'. This phenomenon sprang up in our first term at Bicton, and was started by two boys – one was the head prefect and the other (already mentioned) aged only ten and with prodigious leadership powers, Bill Shelley. After that term Shelley was left in sole command – of boys mostly older than himself. The B.L.I. appropriated one of the majestic trees on one side of the large green expanse in front of the house as its headquarters, erecting a strong palisade of fallen branches around it. It drilled under Shelley's command and fought set-piece skirmishes – it was something like a public school officer training corps in miniature. In place of rifles the 'soldiers' carried long, well-honed sticks. Its supreme moment of glory came one Sunday afternoon in the summer of 1941 when it was presented with its regimental 'colours' – a beautiful imitation of the real thing, embroidered by Mrs Vass. The parade took place in front of the house, and I stood in the colonnade, like a conscientious objector, as the ceremony unfolded. At one point the 'men on parade' intoned the national anthem, and Dick removed my hat for me – somehow it had not occurred to me to take this play-acting by my chums so seriously. I congratulate myself that I always detested the B.L.I. and the conformism it imposed. The thought of obeying Shelley's commands, if nothing else, was enough to keep me out of it.

In the volatile atmosphere of a prep school a close conspiratorial alliance, as had existed between Stuart-Roche and me since we had been virtual leaders of the 'vulgar' pranks of two years before, can turn to rivalry and enmity for no clear reason. I was more advanced academically than he, and although he had some musical ability, I had more. But this kind of thing did not count in our world. Suddenly, with support from Shelley, he started orchestrating a campaign of persecution against me, giving me a hurtful nickname which, even after all these years, I cannot bring myself to repeat. Soon most of the school, including my juniors, were using it. Stuart-Roche was small, and although I was anything but tough, I could have beaten him in a fight. But I did not seem capable of cold-bloodedly attacking him, or of losing my temper and lashing out, either of which might have brought the campaign to an end. He also used irregular tactics. I became aware that the Prof now made excuses not to join me on our story-telling walks, and asked him the reason. Reluctantly

---

his marriage, heard his wife say, apropos of nothing very obvious, 'I love Star Trek'. Unable to say with conviction 'So do I', he replied 'Oh really?' He later discovered that what she had said was 'I lust after you'. By then it was a little late to rekindle the fires of passion.

he admitted that Stuart-Roche had persuaded him to stop seeing me
– by offering him some sweets which he accepted, thus preventing
him from going back on his promise. Although this betrayal made
me despise the Prof and ended our friendship, mysteriously it was
not long before my relations with Stuart-Roche were almost back
to what they had been before, and we once again exchanged meaningful
smiles while I played the hymns and he, a member of the choir,
sang.

There was one boy among us – perhaps the traditional stranger
within the gates – who was pathologically odd. His name was Tombs
and he was a collateral member of a 'St Ronan's family' and the
only child of rich parents: in the grounds of his home he had his
own miniature railway which was large enough to carry him around.
He was known for his furious rages, but I never saw one: his usual
state was a somewhat distracted bonhomie – he never gave eye-contact
for more than a split second and one could not converse with him.
If highly amused he would jump up and down, working his jaws
and rubbing his hands together low down like a chimpanzee. He
had heard one funny rhyme and repeated it to everyone: 'Dearly
beloved brethren, is it not a sin to go behind a parson and prick
him with a pin?' (It was characteristic of the gentle-natured Mr Poole
that he was especially kind to Tombs – as he was to McMurtrie,
who was unfortunate for different reasons.)

At Bicton he came into his own and developed a craze for tractors.
Calling himself 'Tommy Tractor', he moved about the place shuffling
his feet and making a gentle tractor noise that we all came to know
and imitate. One day a representative from Massey-Fergusson, the
tractor manufacturers, arrived at the front door sitting atop a gleaming
new model. He had received a request for an inspection and try-out
from a Mr John Tombs of Bicton House.... Poor Tombs did not
last out his full time at the school, and after he left his cousin
told us in hushed tones that he would never be like other people
and would become odder as he got older.

Dick had been a classics master at Lancing, but he now only
taught English and related subjects to the senior forms. We always
looked forward avidly to his classes, and took in every word. He
introduced us to Tennyson; *In Memoriam*, on which he concentrated,
was very much his sort of poem, being about the pure love of
one man for another. And we read with him some of the more
colourful and dramatic episodes from the Old Testament – about Saul
and Jonathan, Nathan and his rebuke to David ('Thou art the man'),
Absalom, Gideon, Jephthah, Deborah and Barak, Samson and Delilah,
Ahab and Jezebel. He reached into wider cultural realms when he

took us through the styles of architecture, using Frederick Gibberd's *The Architecture of England* (Architectural Press, 1938) as a text. The first page of the book was on 'antecedents', including of course Greek temples, which gave Dick the chance to explain not only what triglyphs and entablatures were but also, memorably, how the Greeks introduced imperceptible curves to correct optical illusions. One of my comrades, Peter Collymore, took up architecture as a career and dates his interest in it from those lessons. For me they crystallised an unconscious fascination with buildings and topography. Once Dick told us to write an imaginary letter to Lord Clinton, asking him to concede some minor favour. Most of us began 'Dear Sir' or 'My Lord', and ended with some flowery phrase like 'Your obedient servant', and it came as a surprise and a bit of a disappointment to learn that the correct forms were 'Dear Lord Clinton' and 'Yours sincerely' – for us at least, since we were not servants or tradesmen but gentlemen. Dick was not a snob, only a realist.

The school dining hall was a low broad room on one side of the back range; in Lord Clinton's time it had been used by the servants and estate workers. There were five or six long tables at the end of which a member of staff sat at breakfast and lunch and a prefect at tea. Dick sat at the head of the centre table with his back to the sideboards and windows, and it was here at the end of lunch that he gave out the daily notices, including minor punishments. It was remarkable that all his requests to us included the word 'please' (I remembered this a few years later as an officer cadet in the army when told that no order was complete without the words *'You will'*). On a rare occasion it might be that a senior boy had won a scholarship to a public school and we were to be granted an extra half-holiday; or that the strawberries and cream we were eating for tea were the gift of Mr and Mrs So-and-so. Cheers would follow. The most alarming announcement was that a certain prefect, also the school's best scholar, was to be stripped of his privileges for allowing and taking part in unruly behaviour in the dormitory of which he had charge. If ever Dick or anyone else said that some property had been stolen, I would immediately feel guilty and expect suspicious glances to fall on me, although I never stole anything. For one term I sat next to the master at the head of my table, and this was old Vinter. He suffered from arthritis in his right hand, and to relieve it would stretch all the fingers and jerk it up simultaneously almost level with his shoulder, thus irresistibly suggesting to the childish mind the act of cocking a snook. Fond as we were of him, we kept a watchful eye open for these gestures and would smile furtively – they were made even more bizarre because he would always give a loud snort at the same moment as he raised his hand.

I had one experience in this room about which it is hard not to be sententious. Our traditional Sunday breakfast consisted of cornflakes instead of lumpy porridge, then sausages, accompanied by rolls instead of hunks of bread. It was permissible to ask for a second roll by putting up one's hand. I did this once, and the roll was brought over by one of 'Jack's men', on a large plate. Being unfamiliar with the refinements of good service, I found the plate comical and sniggered to my neighbour as the young manservant returned to his place by the sideboard. Jack was kindly, wise, humorous, of seemingly inexhaustible equability and a friend to us all, but this time, observing the little scene from afar, he descended like a wolf on a herd of sheep and snatched the roll away saying 'That'll teach you to laugh at my men when they're doing their duty.' Dick could not have mustered more authority at that moment.

It is now time to begin drawing the curtain on St Ronan's. In my last term there I let myself in for a new, if brief, bout of mockery by unguardedly repeating what a doctor had said after giving me an ear-test during the holidays: that I had 'remarkably good hearing' – something which for some reason had begun to be doubted. Of course I did not intend to boast, but that was how it was taken. Thus I learnt early the wisdom of the standard English response when asked after one's health – that one 'mustn't grumble' or 'could be worse'. I was also prepared for confirmation, with others, by Dick with occasional visits from the florid-faced, Jorrocks-like local parson Mr Gardiner. One of his jokes was that he had told another class that words beginning with the Greek-derived prefix 'eu-' or 'ev-' usually mean something good, like evangelist and eucharist, and immediately a boy put his hand up and asked 'What about evil, sir?' As in this story, Mr Gardiner was accident-prone: once when he was walking along the village street close to a high wall with a chestnut tree behind it, a boy on the other side threw up a brick to bring down conkers, and it fell on Mr Gardiner's head. Re-visiting Bicton church a few decades later, I found on the wall two brass plates close together – one commemorating the passage of St Ronan's and the other Mr Gardiner.

The confirmation sessions with Dick were held in his oval study late in the evening, with a fire burning and the lights low. Because we loved him, these sessions were prized – and perhaps it was because he knew this that he encouraged us to be confirmed early, under his aegis. If we had been prepared at our public schools – which I found at Eton to be much more usual – the impact would have been less. There were a very few boys in the school who showed signs of being more pious than the rest of us. One who showed the most obvious signs became a diocesan bishop. More typical was another whose college room at Oxford I shared one night because we talked till after the porter's lodge closed; he excused himself before getting into bed and knelt beside it for a minute or two in silence, saying afterwards that it was a habit he had acquired at St Ronan's and been unable to break. I was never like that, but all of us confirmands were imbued with a fleeting keenness, laced with a sense that it marked a stage in growing up. Serious interest in religion was something of which I had no inkling before my mid-twenties, having been innoculated against it by massive over-exposure at school. But never by a single breath did Dick use any tricks of evangelistic persuasion, or evince either low-church fundamentalism or high-church ecclesiasticism. He loved the Bible and the Anglican tradition, but somehow as a connoisseur – it was such terrific stuff, he might have said.

Each of us had a final one-to-one session with Dick a few days before leaving the school for ever, and this too was held in an atmosphere of comradely intimacy and wellbeing. The object was to introduce us to the subject of adult sex, shorn of schoolboy 'smut'. We were put on oath not to blab about it to our fellows in the few remaining days, but as it happened my father had talked to me at length about – or, more precisely, around – the subject two whole years before, and I had eagerly passed on his garbled version to my friends. It was a Sunday morning in winter when he and I set off for a long walk from our house to the top of Shotover hill, and he began discoursing on the human digestive system and particularly excretion. This, partly involving the same organ, must have seemed to him the logical way to lead on to 'reproduction', and how the vital fluid is 'passed' from the man to the woman – by using this clinical word he suggested the elimination of bodily wastes. I asked if it happened when one was awake or asleep. 'Oh, very much awake', he said, and added, 'It is a curious sensation.' It was also a way that a husband and wife expressed 'interest' in one another. He said not a word about passion, desire, erection and penetration, orgasms or anything that might suggest it was enjoyable as well as curious.

Dick at least built up a more real picture, and explained about erections. Of course I had had any number, but still did not understand their real purpose. About the female side he said little (my father had said nothing), and with good reason because it could not have been enlightening for thirteen-year-old middle-class boys in 1943.

He did speak vaguely of menstrual periods, and of how we should be considerate towards our maids at home, and take the hint if a girl of our class said she didn't feel like playing tennis. As for homosexuality he said that at public schools it was known for bigger boys to lure good-looking smaller boys ('and you are good-looking', he said, which I certainly did not believe) to out-of-the-way places and kiss them. There had even been a clergyman in Worthing who did it – I recalled the two ill-favoured old men who took our Sunday evening services, and wondered if Dick meant either of them. He moved on to 'shagging' but did not elaborate what it really meant, presumably so as not to encourage experimentation. He quoted as his authority for warning against it the head of music at a public school, who had said he could always tell which boys in his choir shagged because their reactions were slow. Could merely touching one's private parts have such an effect? When I joined the army I made the additional discovery that the working-class and public-school meanings of 'shag' were different.

Music became important in my last term at St Ronan's as Miss Wright, the visiting piano teacher, prepared me to face the renowned Eton Precentor, Dr Henry Ley (pronounced Lee). She taught me Beethoven's sonatina in G major, op. 49, no. 2, and I played it to him the following term adequately. A tall, austere elderly woman with snow-white hair and black eyebrows, she inspired a certain awe, but at our last parting she betrayed a touch of tenderness, shaking my hand and asking me to write to her. Anyone following the sweet-natured Mrs Scott, who left at the end of our first term in Devon, might have taken some time to win over our confidence, but poor Miss Wright, who seemed stern and charmless, quickly became 'Miss Wrong' and was subjected to a low-level hate campaign. What supposedly started it off was her remark, indiscreet if authentic, that our revered Mr Vinter, who played the piano by ear, did not play properly. From that it was a short step, in 1940, for a bunch of credulous small boys to believe that with her deep voice, flat chest and black eyebrows she was really a German parachutist in disguise. Dick acted swiftly, summoning all music-learners into his study where he made us sit on the floor and explain to him what we had against Miss Wright. The explanations were lame and she was accepted without question from that moment on.

(My Hertz grandfather had been a cellist, his brother Fred a violinist and their father Martin a conductor – all skilled amateurs while they plied the wool trade in Bradford. My grandfather and Uncle Fred were evidently good enough to play chamber music with Frederick Delius, a fellow Bradfordian destined for higher things. But what truly determined my musical development, or lack of it, was my father's near-total imperviousness to music and my mother's ability to play a few popular tunes of a generation earlier quite well from memory. Her influence was thus the dominant one, but it was not in her nature to apply strict musical discipline to me or even get someone else to apply it – from which alone my inherited facility might have turned into genuine musical ability. My father, for his part, would sometimes lean over the piano, cupping his ears, as I banged out 'Men of Harlech', 'The Road to Mandalay' or the waltzes from Lehar's 'Count of Luxembourg', learned from a gramophone record. He was a realist when he said that my gift would be valuable socially.)

I went back again to St Ronan's for the first time late in 1947, soon after leaving Eton, and sitting with Dick after supper, in company with two other 'old boys' of my generation, I shocked myself and almost certainly Dick and my other companions with the cynical way I spoke of Eton when asked a few harmless questions about life there and the character of certain housemasters. It just burst out. I should have guarded my tongue, but perhaps being questioned by the Prospero of such a benign yet effective school regime made the recollection of something so different hard to bear. That visit also revealed to me another side of Dick from the one I had previously known. Earlier in the day I was alone with him for a time in his study. He poured some sherry and we talked about books – he had just read Duff Cooper's *King David* – and about some of my contemporaries whom I had not seen or heard of since 1943. The almost juvenile jollity and jokiness, superimposed on seriousness, that marked his off-duty dealings with us as young boys was now completely switched off. He had ceased to be the schoolmaster but spoke with relaxed ease, as an equal. His tone was sophisticated. Here in private I got a faint glimpse of world-weariness, of his great energy ebbing; after all, he had a coronary in my time, and was now sixty. His old team – Vinter, Jevvy, Hood, Poole, Mrs Vass and Jack – was still intact, but it could not last much longer.

I have already mentioned my delighted surprise, when I arrived on this visit, to find Poole re-telling the legendary tale about his hair being parted by a bullet. I was equally surprised to find among the assembled company in the staff dining-room Michael Edwardes-Evans, who had been in my house at Eton. He was filling in some time as an usher, having got the job through Gabbitas and Thring and not by any personal connection. I was not able to see much of him on this visit, but the next time we met he told me that he had disliked St Ronan's. The irreverent throng round Dick and the custom of boys slapping masters on the shoulder and appearing to wrestle with them when the masters gently teased them – a ritualised and structured form of anarchy – could only baffle someone who had seen nothing like it before. To him it spelt indiscipline, chaos and moral danger. But perhaps an Anglican divine like Cosmo Gordon Lang or Geoffrey Fisher might have felt similarly shocked if he had been confronted by Jesus in action. I remonstrated with Michael that we all adored Dick as a kind of Jesus.

As part of the process of canonisation, Roman saints have to notch up three authenticated 'miracles'. It seems that Dick may have performed at least one. He told us during that 1947 visit that he had recently appeared in a dream to one of his old boys, who was serving as a platoon officer with the army in occupied Germany, and told him that when he saw a solitary horse and cart on a country road he would be in grave danger. Soon after that, the young man had been marching his platoon along a country road, and they were closing in on a horse-drawn cart moving slowly along directly in front of them. At first he did not remember the warning, but then he heard from far behind the scream of a powerful vehicle approaching at full throttle. Without thinking he shouted to his men to scatter off the road, and a few moments later an army lorry out of control crashed headlong into the cart.

My Mother Again

My mother had been exceptionally beautiful. It was what people who knew her as a young woman always remarked upon, and something of it still clung to her well into middle age; not only her looks but a consciousness of her power to attract. After my father died, she let fall to us that one of his friends had fallen desperately in love with her, and in one encounter had bowed his head over the mantel-piece and wept. All she would say was that he was someone whom we children had met. She did not censure this anonymous would-be lover, though her own conduct never departed from the highest propriety.

As a young wife she soon found herself in deep water. Her older husband's absorption in his work was as absolute at thirty-three as at sixty-three, and it was hard for her at times to communicate with him. Also, he suffered such terrible asthmatic attacks at night that she was afraid he would die there beside her. Once in the Great

War she had a breakdown and lost her memory. In addition, she had to remind him that if they did not do certain things occasionally they would never have children. Also in the war, he was giving her a driving lesson in an open touring car along a straight road through a wood near Henley-on-Thames, when suddenly a dog ran into the road. She swerved to avoid it, then swerved back to avoid the ditch and ended up in the ditch opposite. The car overturned and descended slowly into its final position – resting on her head. My father could not move it, and 'swore like a trooper' (her words) at a passing carter who was not sufficiently helpful. My mother became an excellent driver, but she always claimed that this accident affected her concentration.

Nanny, who was not a naive observer, said to me several times after their deaths that my parents' marriage had been 'made in heaven'. Certainly he loved her exclusively and unreservedly – to the end of his life his letters to her began and ended with extravagant endearments – and she is turn ministered to him. When he needed advice on any problem he turned to her, and she claimed that her common sense was superior to his because of her 'woman's instinct'. She also had a completely spontaneous sense of the ridiculous, and could collapse for a few seconds with helpless laughter – when this happened, her face would change and undergo a kind of dissolution. She could tease and make fun of my father so gently that he only felt pleasure. He could cope with a set-piece joke, but showed unexpected sensitivity when his pride was hurt; he once challenged me to a game of chess and when I won, got up without a word and stalked off.

My mother did not expect to score in passages of wit and skill, but she could use other less tangible gifts. Soon after she was widowed, a bachelor doctor came to dinner, a man probably some years younger than she was, intelligent and companionable. I could hardly believe what I saw: the course of the conversation was being confidently guided by her, and she was, quite unmistakably, flirting with our visitor. I felt proud of her. I only saw her behave like this once again, when she was in her sixties, ill and with her looks gone. I brought my Italian father-in-law, a widower in his late seventies who cared little about his appearance, to have tea with her. By this time all her social activities had ceased and she usually refused to meet either new people or those who had known her in happier times, but for him she made an exception. She dressed up and looked prettier than she had done for years. Again she talked with the assurance of a woman who knows she has the power to attract. He was enchanted and spoke of the visit several times afterwards.

At Ascot, with nannies and governesses minding her children, time hung heavy and the days passed in a slow, monotonous round. But she had a weekly break when my father went to London for his rounds at Guy's and to see his private patients in Harley Street. They would go to the theatre together and stay at one of their two favourite hotels, the Metropole in Northumberland Avenue and the Langham opposite the B.B.C. Typically, these were not like the Savoy or Claridges but solid 'family' hotels – several notches above the dowdy establishments in South Kensington which my mother later favoured as a widow. She did her shopping and had lunch, not at Harrods or Fortnum and Mason, but in or near Oxford Street at places like Debenham's, Marshall and Snellgrove – where the commissionaire, 'little Henry', was a particular friend of Hitchcock's – and D.H. Evans.

Gardening was her one creative talent, or compensation, and in Bravery she had the right partner. Together they laid out a formal rose garden, herbaceous borders, a pergola across the lawn, and patches of bulbs among the trees: her hand was also behind the creepers that covered most of the house. Another definite thing about her was her stout defence of the Empire, to which she saw herself as belonging in a special way through being a New Zealander. On her first visit to America in 1919, the famous Dr Mayo of the Mayo Clinic, a man of Irish origins (for her synonymous with unreliability and 'disloyalty' in contrast to the 'loyal' Ulstermen), asked her when New Zealand was going to break away from the Empire; she replied with spirit that it didn't want to, but failed to convince him. I was not in the habit of saying to my mother 'A penny for your thoughts', as she sometimes said to me, but it was clear the she spent a lot of time day-dreaming. Her absent-mindedness was an unspoken joke between my sisters and me. One summer afternoon when the two of us were sitting together in the garden, I had to speak to her three times before I could bring her down to earth. This happened often, but by the time of her long-drawn-out final illness, she was so alert that she would know if there was something special that I wanted to say to her before I had even begun to speak.

In the war, along with a number of other Oxford ladies, mostly much more formidable than she, my mother assisted in the setting up and running of the Greek famine relief gift shop on the corner of Broad Street and Cornmarket, the acorn from which Oxfam later grew. Even aged eleven or so, I felt that too many nice objects in our house for which there did not appear to be room were finding their way there – especially a Biedermeyer coffee set of exquisite delicacy recently bequeathed to my father by a childless aunt. One meeting of the local great and good brought her into the august company of the doyenne of Oxfordshire county society, the Duchess of Marlborough. The Duchess mentioned in passing that she had seen the Duke's cousin Winston Churchill the previous week, and when the goodbyes were being said, my mother in her artless way, which was charming or H.M. Bateman-like according to how one saw it, said to her spontaneously, 'Do give Winston my love the next time you see him.' Of course she hardly meant her words to be taken literally but, as she told us afterwards, the Duchess was visibly taken aback and stammered something to the effect that of course she would do so. To all but diehard politicians of left and right, Winston Churchill was the saviour of the country; he was my mother's hero and thus in a way her property, which was much more important than being the Marlboroughs' cousin. My mother, fortunately, was still a colonial at heart, and amused rather than upset by the Duchess's po-faced response. My school friend the Prof, after I had taken him out from school one visiting-day with my mother, remarked afterwards that she was 'not like a Lady'. The Duchess of Marlborough would have agreed.

At this time, as part of her staunch patriotism, she fell a willing prey to spy-fever. She was on a train with my sister Pam and noticed that one of their fellow-passengers looked out of the window with great interest as they passed a R.A.F. aerodrome. This act, combined with something about his appearance, made her suspicious and so, when they got home, although Pam remonstrated that any mildly curious person would have done the same, she insisted on phoning the police. Another time, a young man came to the house from the water board and asked to inspect any appliances in the garden. I was at home, and showed them to him. He was friendly and slightly pathetic. But he was also fair-haired and spoke with a foreign accent – so could easily have been a German. She could hardly wait till he had gone to get on the phone. Finally I fell victim myself. We stopped our car, as one always did, to pick up an airman who was thumbing a lift. As he sat beside me in the back seat, my heart missed a beat as I noticed that the 'eagle' shoulder flash on his uniform was incorrect: the eagle's head was supposed to look to the rear on *both* shoulders, whereas the one I was looking at faced towards the front. I knew this because Pam was by then in the W.A.A.F. Surely this airman, nice as he seemed, was a fraud if not actually a Nazi spy. I burst out with my discovery as soon as we had dropped him off, but we took a chance and did nothing about it. The Allies still won the war.

My mother could be as hard on compatriots who did not seem to act as if there was 'a war on' as she was on suspected spies.

In the classy Victoria Hotel at Sidmouth where she stayed on a visit to me at Bicton, she struck up a hotel friendship with the lady at the next table in the dining-room – Miss Foley – and thought it strange that such a pleasant and nice-looking woman had never married. But the friendship was short-lived. One evening at dinner Miss Foley complained tartly to the waiter that her toast was not well enough done, and the next day my mother told me that she could never feel the same again about someone who let her selfish concerns obtrude at such a time, while our young men were risking their lives to keep us alive. It was unpatriotic. And on the platform at Exeter station we both watched transfixed as a woman dressed like a *poule de luxe*, with a leopardskin coat (how did her clothing coupons stretch to it?), took an unopened packet of 'Petit Beurre' biscuits from her handbag and started feeding them to her pekinese. When this operation was completed, she wiped the dog's muzzle with her lacy hanky and threw the hanky on the track. The woman's behaviour struck us both as inconceivably unpatriotic.

'Floreat' in a Minor Key[*]

Eton makes good copy. In my time the book which best combined readability and verisimilitude, and with its superb photographs and sumptuous production made a nice gift for parents, was Bernard Fergusson's *Eton Portrait*. It was the unashamedly romantic view of someone who came from an 'Eton family' and did well at the school, as he did in the big world afterwards. However, when I came upon *A Question of Upbringing* by Anthony Powell I recognised the part about Eton as a classic portrait that perfectly conveyed the peculiar atmosphere and ethos of the place. Wilfrid Blunt's second volume of memoirs, *Slow on the Feather*,[**] is the ironic view of an outsider, ambivalent about the school but warmly honest about the people. For anyone who knew some of those people and Wilfrid himself, it is likely to be irresistible.

The Eton summer 'half' (= term) in 1943 started early, before

---

[*] The reference is to Eton's motto, *Floreat Etona*. (However desirable it may be in Eton's eyes that it should flourish, this seems a strange departure from the normal practice of having an uplifting motto like Oxford's *'Dominus Illuminatio Mea'*.)

[**] Published by Michael Russell, 1986.

the end of April. A day or two earlier, at a juvenile tennis party in North Oxford, the wife of a Dragon School master asked me if I had taken Remove, and I felt a touch of elation at being able to answer that I had (how short-lived it was). During that holiday-time, too, one of my New Zealand cousins, Valerie Riddiford, was married from our house and a St Ronan's contemporary who lived in Oxford came along to keep me company: he was staying on there another term, and I felt rather superior. My father, who was to have given the bride away, was ill and spending a day or two in the Acland nursing home, so I went down after the fun was over to tell him about it. There he was, sitting cross-legged in bed with a sea of papers spread out before him. He said he had read an article in *The Times* that day about the planned reforms to the diplomatic service after the war: I was good at French, so why didn't I think of going in for that as my career? Up till then I had always said, with scarcely a thought, that I wanted to be a doctor, but from now on, again without thinking about it, I said that I wanted to be a diplomat. Once before this, my father had raised the possibility of my not passing the medical exams – he knew that I had never shown much staying power – but this cold douche of realism only shook me momentarily.

On the great day, my mother came as far as Slough station, where I fell in with a slightly older boy and shared a taxi with him over to the school. He was friendly – his father, I later discovered, was a well-known musician, which perhaps made him atypical – and any growing nervousness partly abated. On arriving at 'G.W. Nickson's, Esq.' I went up to my room and waited for Nickson to appear. There was the standard furniture – a bureau (pronounced 'burry') of which 'lower boys' were only allowed the lower (desk) portion, an ottoman to hold sporting tackle, and the folding bed behind a curtain. This was my own room, my symbol of emancipation. I had not met Nickson before, so the wait was sharpened by curiosity.* Dick

---

* A couple of vacations earlier, my mother and I went over and visited the two houses which had been recommended. We met J.D. Upcott who was unshaven and dressed in his oldest clothes, and sat with one leg dangling over the arm of his chair. He held a cigarette in a shaking gloved hand. My mother was not impressed, but Upcott, who allegedly drank heavily to drown the pain of wounds received in the previous war, soon retired. Nickson had not been available but we met his 'dame' Penny Haughton. In any history of Eton one can read of how originally all the boys' boarding houses were run by dames, without housemasters, but these ladies – in my time they were always 'ladies', middle-aged and either unmarried or (rarely) widows – survived with their original function of housekeeping and sending us to the doctor if we were unwell. For reasons I could never fathom, our dame (we referred to her in the third person as 'M'Dame', just as we referred to Nickson as 'M'Tutor', and addressed her as 'Ma'am') was unpopular in the

Harris had warned us that relations with masters at our public schools were unlikely to be anything like what we knew at St Ronan's – and now here was Nickson, slight, neat, in his early forties, with thinning hair neatly brushed, and his face attractively creased all over as he smiled in greeting. Compared with the St Ronan's masters, he exuded urbanity. He would now take me, he said, on a 'Cook's tour' of the school. On our way we met a boy who had also come to Nickson's this half from St Ronan's, Richard T. We were utterly different, he a mathematician who also happened not to have a shred of artistic sensibility, and a voice, appearance and personality that jangled on me. In the previous term the knowledge of our shared destiny had briefly brought us together, but we now found that we had no thought, feeling or view in common and at moments could barely refrain from physically attacking each other. He took particular delight in slagging off doctors. What miserable luck to be banged up with him for the next five years. It gave me some satisfaction later when I pointed him out in the house photograph to my mother that she remarked how odd he looked.

The next morning Toby Gibson, a boy of my age who had been at Eton two halves longer than me, came across the passage and helped me do up the peculiar Eton bow-tie. His nonchalant friendliness was subtly different from anything to be seen at St Ronan's. As soon as we were all moving about our business, something of the anatomy of this strange world began to solidify. Our black tail-suits, relieved only by sparkling white collar and tie, were funereal, but the members of 'Pop', with their spongebag trousers, coloured waistcoats and carnations in their buttonholes, dazzled my innocent eyes.[*] (Wasn't

---

house, but I never bore her any ill will, nor she me. Once, memorably, we had a 'human biology' class with a master known as 'Botany Bill' Weatherall. He spoke with a Yorkshire accent and was uninhibited in tackling the subject. On wet dreams he said that they might be about some woman we knew – like our dame.

[*] To have been at Eton and not be for ever after sensitive to the minutest nuances of dress must be difficult, for there were many rules, explicit and implicit. Among the first, you wore a top-hat all day on Sunday, and on weekdays when going further down Eton High Street in the direction of Windsor than the parish church (about half-way) – this was a relaxation of the pre-war rule of wearing it all the time out of doors. With 'change' (sports clothes) or 'half-change' (sports jacket on top of regulation uniform) you wore a cap. Only members of Sixth Form could go bare-headed. In winter you could not wear an overcoat without the collar turned up – unless you were a member of 'Pop'. Among informal dress rules, it was unthinkable to do up the bottom button of one's waistcoat, to have a pen clipped into one's breast-pocket, or to keep loose change in a purse. To walk along with both hands in one's pockets looked 'idle', but with no hand in either pocket you risked looking slightly ingenuous. For an Etonian the never fully explained joke in *A Question of Upbringing* about Widmerpool's overcoat strikes an immediate chord.

such finery a bit strange in the middle of a war?) Some of the
Eton boarding houses were Victorian warrens, similar to the pre-war
St Ronan's, but Nickson's was a building of recent date (and dull
like everything else about it), and only the front portion, where Nickson
lived with his family, and a few senior boys had rooms under the
eaves, was eighteenth-century. Each of the three floors had a 'boys'
maid' or bed-maker, and throughout my time there the top floor
– I was usually on it – had the best in Mabel Hinckley, a solid,
ageless, slow-speaking woman with what, if I had been older, I
might have thought suspiciously dark skin. She had been in service,
and her manners, though in no way servile, were impeccably respectful;
we were always 'sir' or, where appropriate, 'm'lord'. The floor below
had a battle-axe called Mrs Green, and it was a rite of passage
when her boys were permitted to call her 'Greenie'. There was a
rough-hewn, gentle-mannered Welsh odd job man called Roberts who
cleaned our shoes every day.

I did not qualify to attend College Chapel till the next year,
but Lower Chapel seemed enormous. The young clergyman, also
a distinguished scholar, who took the services, G.C. ('Jesus') Stead,
was intensely pious – in prayer, his face uncovered and his hands
clasped, he was like a Baroque saint – but the general atmosphere
was relaxed and irreverent. On the other hand, the sheer loudness
of the organ and the singing – they were louder still in College Chapel
– could not but uplift us in some way.

For the last hour of every weekday morning, the 'lower boys'
– there were about a dozen of us – had to attend Nickson's 'pupil
room' and do a task, usually the completion of a Latin prose. He
sat on a dais facing us, and we all, on finishing the task and being
allowed to go, would get up and shout 'Goodmorning sir' as we
went out of the door. We sat strictly in the order in which our
names appeared in the Calendar – likewise in the house dining-room
and in chapel. The houses all had their own distinctive characteristics,
but I always had the feeling that several other houses were brighter
and friendlier than ours. St Ronan's might have been light years
away. Deep down (I could not have admitted it to anyone) I wished
I had the intellect to have passed the scholarship exam and got
into College.[*]

Richard T. and I were the only new boys in the house and had

---

[*] College housed the seventy foundation scholars, and was obviously, above all else, an
intellectually stimulating environment. Yet my father did not understand this; he said to
me that even if I could have won the scholarship, he would not have wanted me to take
it up because he could afford the full fees. In my time the immensely rich Jonathan
Guinness was a Colleger.

both taken Remove. Neither of us was a typical Etonian, but he swam in this strange sea with a certain confidence that I lacked. To my surprise I had done better in the classical entrance exam than he, and therefore got into a higher 'division' (form); I was also in the top French division with the *creme de la creme* of Remove, under René Ledésert, one of the interesting assortment of wartime masters (another was the patrician art dealer Geoffrey Agnew). Ledésert later won fame as a lexicographer, but seemed bored with us.

The school work bothered me straight away. At the end of every session, the division master would set us a task, and seemingly it was quite simple. It would consist of reading a few pages of a set book, learning a passage of Latin, Greek or French to translate ('construe') at sight, or mastering a mathematical problem. It was the essential feature of the Eton system that you did this work – not in 'prep', all together under a master's supervision, but alone in your room. This called for concentration and enough self-discipline not to spend the evening chatting with your mates, or simply reading a book of your own choice – which there was no external force to prevent you from doing. Then, on the next occasion that you went to the class, the master would open the proceedings with a simple test – largely of memory – written on scraps of paper. The next time we saw him, the pieces of paper would be handed back, and if the test had not been done almost perfectly, it would have a tear in the side – a 'rip'. The ripped test paper had to be shown to M'Tutor in 'pupil room' later that morning and initialled by him. If you got enough 'rips', the master concerned would decree that you were on a 'white ticket'. To collect it you had to go on the 'bill'; that is, you were summoned to the presence of the Lower Master, or the Head Master if you were in the upper school, by a sixth-form boy – a *praepostor* (an office similar to that of orderly officer in the army) – calling at your division room in the course of the morning and announcing this for all to hear. The Lower or Head Master would give a warning that if all your division masters did not sign it at the end of the week to say that your work was satisfactory, you would be 'flogged' (i.e. birched or 'swiped' in boys' parlance). Two white tickets in one half would usually result in a flogging automatically.

At St Ronan's I had done modestly well in all subjects and never lagged behind, so how did I get into a quagmire of rips and white tickets during my first two years at Eton and eventually get 'swiped'? It was not that I was incapable of doing the work, but somehow I could not gather my forces to do it, and so escape trouble. A contributory cause could have been that Eton was such a heady place – there was so much more to engage the attention than merely learning one's lessons. There were the all-important social shibboleths, and before long, too, Cupid got to work. It seemed a gratuitous privation that English and modern history, two subjects I found congenial, were not on the syllabus. I simply could not interest myself in ancient history, which we did as part of the classical syllabus. It was not till we had been in the school for a minimum of two years that we came back to the modern era – in my case the eighteenth century. In maths I had the feeling at first that the work was easier and less sophisticated than what we had done for some terms past with old Vinter. In my first half the 'beak' (master) I was 'up to' for maths was an affable, ageing fellow called Dick Young; he had been a housemaster but, mysteriously, for only one or two halves – something went wrong. He had also been a patient at New Lodge Clinic, and gleefully told me with the whole class listening that my father had not found out what was wrong with him. He had a way of sitting on the bench beside one to help with an equation, and wrapping his arm tightly round one's shoulders so that one shrank within the embrace (the Lower Master, A.E. Conybeare, was known for this too, but had a more genial personality). For this reason, and possibly also because like our boys' maid he had dark skin, his nickname was 'Dirty Dick'. Never at Eton did I encounter a master with Vinter's ability to make maths not only possible for me to understand but interesting, especially the theorems of Euclid and Pythagoras. And always these men were strangers – we would 'cap' them in the street (raising the right hand to where the brim of a hat would have been if we had been wearing one) and be capped by them in return, but our acquaintance with most of them was fleeting and impersonal.

Science was a compulsory subject, but my first teacher, 'Taxi' Hillard (son of the famed co-author of Hillard and Botting's classical textbooks) – heavy, aloof, unsmiling and probably bitter at never having been given a boys' house – made our hours with him a penance. One wartime replacement science master called Duchesne, elderly, pale, hairless and shrivelled, was catastrophically incapable of maintaining discipline. His junior classes regularly degenerated into uproar, with boys shrieking 'Cheese! Dutch cheese!' (a corruption of his name). I was never 'up to' him, which was just as well because I would surely have joined in the persecution. There was an upstairs room in the Science Schools that housed a small natural history museum. Among its exhibits was a kitten with one head but four eyes and two mouths, by which I was morbidly fascinated. There was also a framed photograph of a young Eton boy who had died at the school and in whose memory the museum was founded.

In my first half, and then to my despair in my second one too, my Latin master was a supercilious, apparently bored fellow called D.C. Wilkinson. In my last half by accident he narrowly saved me from a fearful embarrassment, but that was far in the future. In 1943 my sessions in his enormous class were like a treadmill. Any idea that classical literature was fine or beautiful – Jevvy had made the *Aeneid* and Xenophon's *Anabasis* come alive – might have been a bad joke. To emphasise the harshness and ugliness of it all, the 'old' pronunciation of Latin –already abandoned at St Ronan's before I went there – still lingered on, and even after the change was made around 1944, the unspeakable Charlie Rowlatt, with grim relish, refused to give it up. (When I became familiar with Italian, it struck me that not even the 'new' pronunciation had much in common with how Latin was presumably spoken in ancient Rome.)

In my first half, a ray of light was provided by Greek classes with Julian Harold Legge Lambart (known as 'Leggy'). He was a middle-aged bachelor with soft pink cheeks, gold-rimmed spectacles, and an unworldly, slightly fussy air, as if he would be easily shocked[*] – as he was, deeply, by bad work or philistinism. He was keenly musical, and a lover of art. Once I was in the street carrying a framed drawing by Samuel Prout which my father had given me to hang in my room, and Leggy, who was passing, asked me to show him the picture and spoke about it without a trace of condescension. Even Nickson would have found this difficult. He also told us in class that we should go to the National Gallery to see Titian's *Triumph of Bacchus*. He pleased me even more in a divinity class a year or two later by saying that I was the best reader. In my end of term report he wrote that I was a nicer boy than I had been that first half – I hate to think what I was like in those early days; at least, as time passed, I was getting used to Eton and vice versa. Other classics masters who brought some warmth to their task were Jack Peterson, with whom I did much better than usual, and my own Geoffrey Nickson – though my inability to cope with Homer clouded the half I spent in his division, and stung him to his one outburst of real (or skillfully feigned) anger at my shortcomings, in the privacy of my room on his regular nightly round of the

---

[*] A doubtless apocryphal tale was told about Leggy. One day he asked the boys in his pupil room if they knew any Latin tags. A hand went up and the first boy said *'Rara avis*, sir'. Asked by Leggy what it meant, the boy correctly replied 'A rare bird'. Another hand went up and the second boy volunteered *'Virgo intacta'*. Leggy paled, but bravely asked for a translation. The reply was 'A *rara avis*, sir'.

house (itself a wonderfully humane custom). He probably felt despair that anyone should waste the opportunity of enjoying Homer.*

I had my audition with Dr Ley, and was sent for piano lessons to Belle Dunhill, the much younger second wife of the eminent composer Thomas F. Dunhill, who had been a music master at Eton at the turn of the century and now, in old age, was filling-in and taking pupils again. Belle spoke with a soft Lincolnshire intonation and, though with greying hair, was pretty and lively (if there was any female member of staff I was going to have dreams about, it was her and not M'Dame). I didn't warm to the old man or, when I later heard some of it, his music, but her kindness and gentle charm had some influence on me, and under her guidance I learned to play some nice pieces – easier Chopin including the *Grande Valse Brilliante*, Debussy (prompting her innocent little joke – 'Who wrote "Kitten on the Keys"?' Answer: 'De Pussy') and Schubert (the A flat major Impromptu), and for a competition the slow movement of Beethoven's *'Pathetique'* sonata and the gavotte from one of J.S. Bach's French suites. But from time to time she complained, with ample justice, that I did not try hard enough – it was true that I hardly practised at all. Nickson would have liked one of his boys to perform in the great end-of-term School Concert, but he was not to reap that reward through me. However I did play a Chopin Nocturne at a small mid-term concert, and Nickson and a sprinkling of loyal friends sportingly turned up, one of the latter saying what a boring piece it was.

Meanwhile, back in the summer half of 1943, my social life was faltering. The bumping races between the house fours were held early in the half, and I had barely been at the school a couple of weeks when, for the only time in history, Nickson's four was the winner, with a double bump. The whole crew won their 'Lower Boats' colours. I was scarcely aware of what was going on, and on the evening of the great victory set out late for the river. Before I could get there, I came face to face with a joyous group of my house contemporaries, including Richard T., on their way back from cheering our victorious house four from the towpath and witnessing its moment of glory – *our* moment of glory. I was one with those 'gentlemen in England now a-bed' who would for ever 'think themselves accurs't they were not there'.

Nickson ensured that I made my number with Wilfrid Blunt, the

---

* I nearly added 'Which comes once in a lifetime', but such conventional thinking has been up-ended by my dear friend Richard Rhodes, then a *'kappa'* (non-Greeker), who decided to learn classical Greek in middle life – with such success that he has become a member of the exalted 'Cercle de la Lecture Grecque' in his adopted city of Geneva.

master in charge of drawing and painting, and joined the Musical Society – a large inexpert choir that rehearsed choral works at evening practices throughout the half and then performed them at the School Concert – or at the Christmas carol service in College Chapel. Ridiculously I put myself among the basses even before my voice broke – mortified at the very idea of singing treble. (Very much later, by singing in a parish church choir, I discovered that my true register is tenor or, at the lowest, baritone.)

'Messing' was a part of Eton culture. Breakfast, lunch and supper were eaten in the boys' dining-room, but at tea time we gathered in one of our rooms with our messmates – there would be two or at most three of us – and the boys' maid brought a pot of tea and other basic ingredients. In winter we could make toast by the roaring stove in the boys' entrance. At the end of each half the messing arrangements would be made for the following half; usually existing messes continued, but there would also be some re-shuffling. I started my first half, naturally enough, with Richard T. – also with an eccentric boy a year or so older who had been absent the previous half and had no messmate. This was Timothy Beaumont, whose father was an anti-Churchill Tory M.P. (at that time, in my world, to be anti-Churchill was tantamount to being pro-Hitler), and who was apt to stand on his chair and proclaim that the country was going to the dogs. Later he inherited a fortune, became a clergyman, owned *Time and Tide*, and was made a Liberal peer. But at the end of the summer of 1943 he had a breakdown and left the school permanently. Richard T. announced that the next half he would be messing with two other boys – I was genuinely amazed that these two wanted his company. But despite my relief that we would no longer be involved with eachother, it was humiliating to be thus left high and dry and so obviously friendless. This meant that in September I would mess with a new boy, who turned out to be Randle Cooke. He was remarkably scruffy, but this was of a piece with his underlying distinctiveness of character, and strong natural inclination for country pursuits like fishing and bird-watching. He came from an Eton family – and was musical and reflective though not intellectual. We messed together on and off, sometimes with a third companion, for the rest of my time at Eton. Once my mother turned up in my room unexpectedly and found Randle there instead of me, kitted out for beagling. She liked him, which from her was a tribute to his genuineness. After an Eton career almost more undistinguished than mine, he was commissioned in a cavalry regiment, and in the early 1950s a friend told me he had been killed in Korea. I never knew otherwise until in the early 1970s I noticed a reference on the court page of *The*

Times to the Duke of Edinburgh being accompanied by his equerry – Major Randle Cooke. The name was sufficiently unusual for me to write to him at his place of employment and ask if he was my old friend, and he replied that indeed he was (he had been a prisoner of the Chinese for two years). Since then we have been in constant if intermittent touch. He remains as he always was, real and distinctive.

My sister Rosemary came back from America in the spring of 1944, now nineteen, and I found it exciting getting to know her afresh and hearing about America – for example, that President Roosevelt was not a universally revered figure as we imagined, and that there were things called 'race riots'. She soon enlisted in the W.R.N.S., but before that my father gave a family lunch party for her at his favourite Trocadero restaurant, after which we went to see a Rattigan play, *While the Sun Shines*. This was still wartime London, and we had only just started venturing back there on occasional visits from Oxford, which had mysteriously escaped the bombing. Another such visit was for the funeral of my father's old colleague John Venables, who died aged fifty-five. My father and I made the journey to Golders Green – it was my first experience of the Underground (as we waited on the platform, he mentioned the name of an earl who had jumped in front of a tube train), and of visiting a crematorium.

In August 1944 my father also died. He was staying overnight in Edgbaston with one of his medical friends, Professor Lionel Hardy, and simply expired in an armchair, with the manuscript of his autobiography on his knee. He was alone in the room and Hardy found him later. It was extraordinary that his heart held out for so long under the punishment of his asthmatic attacks and injections of adrenalin. He also regularly imbibed hydrochloric acid mixed in freshly squeezed orange juice. It was a sunny afternoon when I heard L.J. Witts, the professor of clinical medicine at the University, unexpectedly being ushered into our house – and, straining to hear what he and my mother were talking about, I picked up the words 'Arthur died....' We had parted from him the day before in Stratford-on-Avon, and he drove on to Birmingham while we returned to Oxford by train. My mother said later that his farewell kiss was unusually tender.

For a few days the importance that comes with death lapped round us – though, because we never saw the body, there was also a feeling of unreality. The funeral was at the bleak local crematorium, at the far end of a housing estate on the outskirts of Headington. When the hearse arrived outside our house, the undertaker offered to bring the coffin inside and remove the lid so we could see him for the last time. I hoped that my mother would say yes, but without much conviction she declined. Perhaps she was afraid that it would set off a fresh release of emotion, but obscurely I felt – and who knows if she did not too – that we were missing the one thing that would have made the day real for us, more real than when we heard the news of his death, and certainly more real than the dreamlike ritual at the crematorium. After the ceremony was over, an usher asked my mother if she wanted a plaque put up in the colonnade outside, and when she said no, assured her that the ashes would be 'reverently scattered'. This was what, quoting Galsworthy (once his patient), he had asked for in a handwritten adjunct to his will – but in such a place?

Interlude: The Hertzes – Uncle Gerald

My Uncle Gerald stayed with us over the period of my father's funeral. His eldest children were old enough to have been my parents, but none the less it was understood that in the absence of my father I would now have a closer relationship with him. It meant little more than occasional mutual visiting: by him to me at school and by me to him and Aunt Margaret in the holidays. The death of his brilliant only son in North Africa in 1941 had created a void in his life, but he bore it stoically. Without in the least trying to do so, he and Aunt Margaret, with their large family which obviously 'worked', made me feel a sense of inadequacy about my own rather feeble family, and about myself. My father was a more remarkable figure than any of them, but he had gone – and I had hardly known him.

One thing Gerald and I had in common was an interest in our family antecedents – though in me, with little more to my name than bad school reports, this was considered rather unhealthy. Here I indulge it once again, to salute my paternal ancestors. After publishing his autobiography *Closed Chapters* (Manchester University Press, 1942), Gerald wrote two further chapters, which were typed out but not meant for publication, 'Family Origins' and 'Parents'. What he knew about earlier generations of the Hertz family, before the arrival of his grandfather Martin Hertz in England, was based on 'oral tradition' and a handful of surviving letters. On a visit to Hamburg in the late 1970s I acquired by chance a family tree containing some more precise detail. This revealed that we had been mistaken in always thinking of Hamburg as our original family home; it was in Hildesheim that Benjamin-Wolf Hertz (died 1788) was a jeweller and banker, the *Hoffaktor* (court contractor) to the prince-bishop and *Vorsteher* (superintendent) of the Jewish community. Benjamin-Wolf's father, the earliest ancestor shown in the family tree, was called Naphthali – our tribal name of which Hertz is a Germanisation, as mentioned elsewhere. His four sons continued in the jewellery business and as public-spirited Jews, but in different North German cities; only the youngest David Wolf (1757-1822) lived in Hamburg, and he became rich there. His son Wolf David (1790-1859) was a man of leisure and cultured tastes, and his wife, Rosa Haarbleicher, brought music into the family. Still named as a jeweller in the family tree, he was also interested in the Yorkshire woollens business. His younger brother Heinrich, who divided his commercial activities between Hamburg and Leeds, marked a characteristic departure replicated in England later: his son David Gustav was not in business but an advocate and a Hamburg senator, and David Gustav's son was our family's most glittering ornament, Heinrich Rudolf Hertz (1857-94), the physicist – the mega-Hertz, if a pun is permitted.

Wolff David's son Martin (1821-85) was sent by his father as a young man to Yorkshire to set up in the wool business, and thus founded M. Hertz & Co., which went on trading first in Bradford and after 1894 in Manchester into the 1950s. He also became a Freemason. His wife Josephine de Lemos belonged to a Portuguese-Jewish family settled in Altona (just across the Elbe from Hamburg but then in the Danish kingdom) who spoke Ladino at home. After she died in 1875 Martin retired and spent his last years on a farm he bought in Holstein. He was highly musical: a cherished boast in the family was that he conducted the first performance of Mendelssohn's *Elijah* to be given in Bradford. His eldest son William Martin (1846-1912), my grandfather, played the cello, the younger sons Uncle Fred and Uncle Martin played the violin, and the girls sang. Only William had sons, but none of the three (my father was the youngest) entered the business, which was managed in their generation by a first cousin through the female line, Charles Kukla. The three marked a departure too in that they were all unmusical, and since music in a family can only be nurtured through continuity, this killed off our musical tradition. The Hertzes abandoned the Jewish religion soon after 1820, and with baptism their given names changed to Christian ones: Moses (in my great-grandfather's case) to Martin, David to Ferdinand, Frumet to Fanny and so on. Religion, like music, was not part of the make-up of any of my father's generation.

W.M. Hertz's wife Fanny was the daughter of an immigrant from the Frankfurt ghetto, Julius Baruch Halle,[*] who grew rich in the City of London and left £204,000 when he died in 1904. Fanny was artistic and well-read, and being in love with William accepted the constraining life of a striving merchant in Bradford in the 1870s and '80s. In an extended portrait of the two of them in Uncle Gerald's unpublished memoir, one passage stands out: 'My mother inspired most of my early ideas. Unlike my father, whose understanding of young children was very limited, she had deep sympathy with their impressionable minds. My father was intensely interested in other people and their affairs. He spoke to every fellow traveller. It was, however, a curiosity only in the ideas and occupations of adults. He had none of the patience and imagination which attract the very young. My mother was a born romantic. She could not help illuminating the child's mind. With her own children she also sought to build character, and to make their early years happier than her own had been.'

I can instantly identity with William's curiosity about people and urge to speak to fellow travellers. But in the context the glowing picture of Fanny, doubtless true as far as it goes, is significant; surely there was willfulness in her treatment of Willy, the eldest boy (already mentioned) and the passionate partiality she felt for Gerald, the second son, right up to the end of her life.

The maternal love which Gerald received bore abundant fruit: he proved a model son, husband and father, and a devoted public man. Scholarships and prizes strewed his path. It is all recorded in his autobiography, together with his exemplary career as student, teacher, barrister, backbench Conservative M.P., Territorial officer and county court judge. As a child I regarded his wife, Aunt Margaret, with awe: she was the archetypal formidable female relative, imposing in appearance like a bourgeois version of Queen Mary, and given to pointed remarks and devastating judgements. But if any couple exemplified the honeysuckle and the bee it was Gerald and Margaret. He had a wonderfully efficient and discriminating mind; he could write or speak on demand with elegance and fluency; but in his own words (in a letter to my father) 'I have no creative or original mind *al all.*' While Margaret's handwriting expressed striving, his – allegedly copied from his mother at her request – was flowing, undisturbed, feminine. He was a commanding figure, energetic, conscientious, if lacking some of the niceties of behaviour that are supposed

---

[*] To the Frankfurt Jews Napoleon came as a liberator, and Julius's father, Simon Marcus Baruch, born in 1794, served as an infantryman on the French side. Simon's first cousin Ludwig Börne, born Baruch (1786-1837), rates a brief mention in *Encyclopaedia Britannica* as a journalist a⋅d satirist of the emancipation period.

to be the mark of an English gentleman;* but Margaret ruled the roost. My mother, a typical Protestant, thought it ironic that Gerald, a transparently good man, had not a shred of religious belief, while Margaret, whom she thought uncharitable and rather selfish, was a staunch churchwoman.

The nearest Gerald came to creativity was in bringing up their family of five daughters and one son, born between 1906 and 1919 and thus a generation older than me. He was assiduous in educating them from the earliest age, and had great story-telling abilities, informed by his historical scholarship and love of narrative verse in the Macaulay style. But above all, with his energetic inculcation of learning, Margaret's subtle wisdom, his abiding love for her and their combined belief in goodness, their children grew up stable and free from neurosis, able to love others and eachother. If this is what Fanny's partiality achieved, then it paid off.

Shortly before he died, I walked with Gerald, by then portly and slow-moving, from the Athenaeum to Charing Cross station, and as we stood briefly in the concourse before parting, he said that he had been handicapped in his career by not going to a public school (he didn't mention the German surname); otherwise, he thought, he would have had a better chance of becoming Attorney-General under Baldwin and a judge of the high court instead of the county courts. He had no pomposity and was always frank about himself, which I found endearing, but this shook me. Could it really be true? Reading and Birkenhead might have been more brilliant and more ambitious than he was, but they rose to the top of the totem pole from obscurer origins. Was this man, whose life seemed so harmonious, really disturbed in his depths by frustrated ambition and a sense of failure? Because he was an old-style imperialist and patriot, with a particular detestation for the Nazis, he could not have doubted that his dead son Quentin had been sacrificed in a worthy cause. But the irony that Quentin did go to a public school and to all appearances was English through and through, and now all these advantages had gone to waste, could not have been lost on him. Whatever his true feelings, the final chapter in his autobiography, which is devoted to Quentin's life, stands as a solid monument to the characters of both men.

---

* ·At an early age I was told by my mother, without malice, that Uncle Gerald had no sense of humour – and sniffed downwards. She also said that he was once considered for a fellowship at an Oxford college, but after being invited to dine at high table was turned down because of his poor table manners. This was told to me as a cautionary tale and I doubted its authenticity, but revised my opinion after he took me out to lunch from Eton and made a loud slurping sound as he imbibed his soup.

Life without Father

In September 1944 before the end of the school holiday, my mother and I were invited to stay in a splendid manor house on the southern slope of the Quantock hills near Minehead. It was the family home of one of my father's patients, a young woman (before the war, she had been to the Clintons' balls at Bicton, not many miles away). The family was large, and Betty was the only one of about eight children left at home. One day the aged father took me to the top of the hill behind the house – still on his land – and we looked out far over the Bristol Channel. In his early days he had farmed in Kenya, and at dinner he told a long story about a plague of ants, which he pronounced like 'aunts'. Betty, who must have heard the tale often, asked if there were any uncles too, and my mother succumbed to one of her waves of giggles. We also stayed with an elderly New Zealand cousin and visited other connections, and at each place I heard my mother tell, in almost identical words, the lengthy saga of my father's death and last days. Something close to irritation with her awoke within me for the first time, not so much at hearing the story yet again – which, though boring, was inevitable – but at her artless style of narration. She was fond too of telling how, when Rosemary returned from America earlier in the year, she phoned from Liverpool and said 'This is Rose-*mary* Hurst speaking', with the American-style emphasis on the second syllable. She had no compunction about doing so, with a toe-curling rendering of an American accent, even when Rosemary was present. Once, when my habitually bad school report arrived, she talked about it to our 'lady help' in front of me. A new era was beginning.

Among the mass of letters of sympathy that had arrived were two for me. One was from Dick Harris, who predicted that I would miss my father more as time passed,[*] and the other was from a science master at Eton, Dick Assheton, whom I was 'up to' the

---

[*] In fact I believe that my father and I would have had difficulty in understanding eachother as I got older, and that my godfather John Venables would have been much easier to talk to and was in that way a greater loss to me. But selfishly I realised that with my father around, our house would always have been an interesting place to be and to bring my friends, whereas without him the lapse into torpor was rapid and permanent.

previous half. On my first presenting myself in his division, he referred laconically but kindly to his having once been my father's patient; in my report he wrote at the beginning 'an idle boy', and at the end 'a nice boy'. The man had warmth. Nickson of course wrote to my mother, and after expressing his condolences in stereotypical form asked her to convey his sympathy to me also. I felt aggrieved that he did not think it worthwhile to write to me separately.

Life went on at school, and probably the subject of my father's death only came up with one or two of my intimates in the house, but the next spring it acted as a catalyst. I was in the same classical division as a boy in another house – friendly and likeable but a mere acquaintance. One day we were chatting during a break and he must have made some impersonal allusion to fathers, and I simply mentioned that mine had recently died. With genuine surprise and concern he said that he was sorry. Could this be Eton? In a moment, my feelings towards him were transformed. I had been fleetingly infatuated with three other boys whom I can think of, all contemporaries, since coming to Eton nearly two years before (one of them had been in Dick Assheton's science division, thus causing me to look forward particularly to attending it), but I was older now. This boy came, as I did, from a prosperous, unfashionable mercantile family, probably at least half-Jewish, was the youngest child, had an elderly father, and was rather hedonistic and easygoing. We both affected to like the 'good things of life' as exemplified not by art, music or poetry (he had little apparent interest in any of those things, then or later) but by smart hotels, cars and clothes. My greatest teen-age love had begun and was only to fade out towards the end of our time at Eton. It was never expressed in words, even less in deeds; 'consummation', beyond perhaps an embrace, never even came into my mind. But the friendship was close on both sides.

There was an undercurrent of pederasty in the school, just as Dick Harris had warned. But when stories, real or imaginary, were told of well-known senior boys fancying or actually 'crashing on' good-looking juniors – the notorious willing ones (there was one at Nickson's) were called 'tarts' – and when, as I got older, I heard appreciative comments being made about this or that fanciable 'lower boy' or 'choir oik' (i.e. one of the trebles in the College Chapel choir, who were recruited from the local townspeople), I could not even pretend to be interested. Passionate love for a contemporary was such a taboo subject that there was not even a name for it – 'crushes' only happened in girls' schools. Admitting to it would have risked being regarded as despicable, unmanly and subversive, whereas the other thing was natural and one could even boast of it.*

When I met the great *ami particulier* of my school time at Oxford after we had both done military service, one evening together was enough to show that we had practically nothing in common, or even to talk about. He had done well in the army, became a barrister after leaving Oxford, and today is a force in the City and, deservedly in the light of his record, one of the Great and Good. Much of his old charm has survived, but he is apt to deliver himself of weighty truisms.

Dick Assheton was a tall, rangy man with a shaggy moustache and a distant expression in his eyes. There was a hint of stoicism and suffering – the boys in his house alleged that his childless marriage was unhappy. There was a hint of the romantic too; the way he described seeing a total eclipse of the sun in Spain, and urged us to miss no opportunity of seeing one, was not purely scientific. Then one day I saw him in the street bowed and haggard and supporting himself on a stick. It was obvious he was extremely ill, and shortly afterwards we heard that he had died. A memorial service was held for him in College Chapel, early in the afternoon, and remembering his one but significant kindness to me, I went – I had not done such a thing before but it seemed so natural that I didn't hesitate. However, my deviant act somehow got back to the boys in my house, and at dinner the next day I was taken to task for showing off and sucking up to authority. Another dinner-time, apropos the impending retirement of the aged Provost of Eton, Lord Quickswood, I said that I enjoyed the short extempore orations which he gave every morning as he stood at the lectern in Chapel, wearing his green eyeshade, on the Lesson he was about to read. Coming from a Cecil, a man of learning and piety who had been one of the great House of Commons debaters of his day, these seemed to me gems, to be treasured. But the reaction in my house was astonishment that anyone could possibly enjoy the prosings of such an unspeakable old bore.

In 1945 the world witnessed more horrors than triumphs. That year also saw the nadir of my Eton career, the darkest hour before some sort of glimmering dawn. In the spring half, for the second time running, I was 'up to' Charlie Rowlatt for classics – it was in his division room that I had the casual conversation that sprouted into instant love. Rowlatt doubtless meant well by me, because he wrote in my report that he knew of no other boy who so neglected his education, and how it pained him to listen to my halting construing.

---

* We also affected enthusiasm for the sexier female stars of the silver screen. For our predecessors in the 1930s it was Jessie Matthews; for us it was Jane Russell, who starred with Gregory Peck in the steamy 'Duel in the Sun' (otherwise known as 'Lust in the Dust' or 'Spasm in the Chasm').

ABOVE *William and Fanny Hertz and their children: Willy (seated), Gerald (beside his mother), Arthur, the author's father – behind) and Josephine. Bradford, c. 1884.* BELOW *The Riddifords in their prime, with Edward (King) Riddiford seated centre. Cushla, the author's mother, is standing far left. Orongorongo (?), c. 1905.*

ABOVE *Cushla Hurst, with the dog Sandy, in the garden at Heath End, Ascot, c. 1938.* BELOW *Arthur Hurst, Ascot, c. 1938.*

ABOVE *The author and his sisters Pam (centre) and Rosemary.*
BELOW *With his Nanny, Gladys Cullen. Both pictures c. 1933.*

ABOVE *Charles Hitchcock with ALN 205.* BELOW *Joseph Bravery in the kitchen garden. Both at Heath End, Ascot, mid-1930s.*

ABOVE *William Martin-Hurst, the author's uncle, with part of his collection of Chinese art, Roehampton, mid-1930s.* BELOW *Gerald Hurst, the author's uncle, and his wife Margaret, 1940s.*

ABOVE *M. and Mme Brunet-Joli, world figure skating champions, fellow hotel guests at Villars, Switzerland, late 1930s.* BELOW *The author and his future brother-in-law, Thomas Naegele, just after the outbreak of war, 1939.*

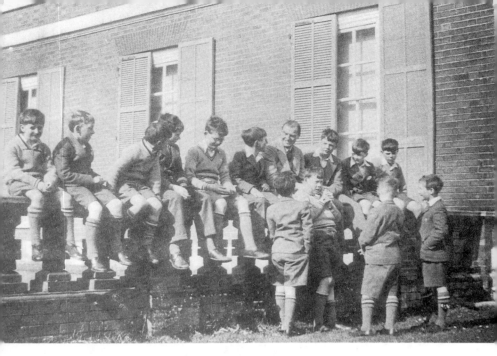

ABOVE *W.B. (Dick) Harris with a group of boys at Bicton House, where St Ronan's preparatory school spent most of the war years.* BELOW *The author and his father, Bicton House. Both 1941-2.*

G.W. Nickson's House group, Eton, July 1945. 'S.P. Bentley Earl', 'Toby Gibson', 'Ramrod-Rich' and the 'jolly Irish peer' all appear in this picture. Charles Booth-Jones, wearing white pants, sits near the right. Randle Cooke is at the far right, back row. Besides the author (centre row, 3rd from left), there are two future publishers: Ben Glazebrook (back row, 3rd from right) and Anthony Blond (seated, right).

He came from a prominent family, his father having been the judge responsible for the draconian Rowlatt Act in India. In the Great War he was badly wounded – it was said that he had a 'tin stomach' – and gassed, so that he talked, looked and moved strangely. Perhaps it was because of this that he had never married. My only evidence of his character was in his teaching methods – he turned classical literature into a field of dry bones.

Rowlatt had already put me on a white ticket once during that spring half, and when I failed again to construe properly, he put me on another one. This could only mean one thing, as we both knew. That day at noon I went before the Head Master, Claude Aurelius Elliott. He sat at a table, dressed in his satin cassock, with the *praepostor* (who became an even greater City luminary than my flame) standing behind him. Elliott had a big mask-like face with heavily hooded eyes and round gold-rimmed glasses,[*] and his wide thin lips seemed hardly to part when he spoke. He said to me: 'I shall have to flog you.' Accordingly I went over to Upper School – in the Wren block that separates School Yard from the road – and climbed the stairs to the great room where the School Messenger was waiting. As soon as Elliott and the future City luminary arrived, I quickly bared my bottom, knelt on the famous block – highly polished in contrast to the rough ancient floorboards – and the blows fell. My six strokes of the birch were not particularly painful, but I found later with a mirror that the twigs had left many livid marks. The School Messenger held me down and by the time I rose and dressed myself, the two of us were alone again. His round red peasant face looked far from unsympathetic, and I knew that part of his function was to administer rough comfort if it was necessary. I felt a dim sense of gratitude, but was too proud to show any sign of distress, and hurried away – to take part in a drill practice on the Parade Ground by the Drawing Schools. I was a recruit in the Training

[*] In my twenties, by pure chance, I was a fellow house-guest with his predecessor Cyril Alington, who told the company at lunch of the meeting of the Provost and Fellows at which Elliott's appointment was decided. The real contest was between Robert Birley, who succeeded Elliott but was then only thirty, and another strong but much older candidate, Elliott being an outsider on whom no one was very keen. The meeting could not make up its mind between the two favourites, and Alington, who was present only to advise and did not feel he could contribute any more, went out. But as he walked away he suddenly felt convinced that Birley was the only right choice, and hurried back, only to be told as he re-entered the room that the choice had fallen on Elliott. With greatness thus thrust upon him – before his elevation he was a tutor in medieval history at Cambridge – it cannot be said that Elliott was unimpressive in his role. Wilfrid Blunt portrays him as an alien being, altogether philistine; the *DNB* notice praises his administrative skill, also his 'manliness' (it acknowledges that he was the 'dark horse' candidate for the post, but without a hint of what Alington revealed).

Corps, being just fifteen, but not having yet 'passed out' we still
drilled without uniform. The sergeant-major in charge may have known
where I had been – or his breezy remark, when I reported to him,
that he hoped it had not hurt too much may have been an inspired
sally of spontaneous good humour. Anyway he meant it kindly. I
knew most of the squad well and as I took my place their faces
were blank and unseeing. But I noticed one boy, whom I had never
seen before, smirking unpleasantly. On inquiring later, I found that
he was a Colleger called (Douglas) Hurd. Nickson, on his rounds
that night, said that he admired my stoical acceptance of this and
my other less grave punishments for bad work; perhaps he felt rather
stoical about the whole business himself. If only his kindly words
had suddenly triggered –a 'great awaking', but my paralysis was to
last for some time longer.

When V.E. Day came in May 1945 there was a sense of unreality.
Eton had received a few small bombs before I went there, and the
scars were visible. We spent a couple of nights in the house air-raid
shelter during the flying-bomb scare, but none fell nearby. Oxford
was never bombed. My father had died, but he had not been on
any kind of war service because of his age and health. One cousin,
Uncle Gerald's son Quentin, and John Venables's son Hugh – both,
as I now know, exceptionally gifted and fine-natured young men
– had been killed, but I scarcely knew either of them. So what,
apart from various changes in home and school life, Rosemary going
to Canada and Pam joining the W.A.A.F., had the war meant to
me? Two young men who were still boys at Eton in my first half
had been killed in action – one an obscure fellow at Nickson's, the
other president of 'Pop'. There was an intercession in College Chapel
once a week during the war, which (unlike masters' memorial services)
it was considered OK and not 'wet' to attend. Claude Elliott, in
his strangulated voice which on these occasions seemed oddly appropriate, read out the names of Etonians whose deaths in action
had been announced in the past week, at the end of which he pronounced
the words 'Rest eternal grant to them, O Lord, and let light perpetual
shine upon them.'* Earlier in the war, when I first saw pictures
in the papers of Nazi atrocities – though mild compared with the
heaps of corpses at Belsen, they were ghastly enough – I had dreams

---

* By the time of the Falklands war in 1982 educated public opinion had completely
changed in its attitude to war. Every single death of a British serviceman was reported
and agonised over. Was the cause worth their sacrifice – or, come to that, any sacrifice?
And although some of the Argentine soldiers behaved badly, there was a distinct awareness
here that they were mothers' sons too, and their deaths deplorable. With the vast slaughter
of the two world wars, any similar reflection would have driven us all into the madhouse.

about them. But anyone growing up at that time was indeed fortunate to be living in the British Isles, where most of the horrors got no closer than the pages of the newspapers.

After the news of the German surrender, life at school went into a brief period of licensed anarchy. Some boys threw buckets of water at eachother and spun rolls of lavatory paper out of the windows. The future City luminary who attended my birching was the object of a sudden hue and cry – he was more unpopular than I knew. We assembled in School Yard to hear Churchill's victory broadcast. Then followed the general election and Churchill's defeat (the victorious Labour candidate for Eton and Slough was the playwright Benn Levy, a class traitor *and* a Jew). I knew how my mother would lament the fall of her hero – I did not understand then that it marked (so I believe) the high-point of my compatriots' political maturity – and she never spoke of Attlee and his ministers other than with ridicule. The worst were the class traitors like Stafford Cripps and John Strachey who, unlike the others, should have known better and had no excuse; however, she reserved special loathing for Aneurin Bevan, always putting the stress on the second syllable to distinguish him from the more acceptable Bevin.

My mother was concerned around this time that I showed no interest in serious reading. In this she was carrying on a campaign started by my father, who put into my hands the copies of Henty's adventure novels that he had read as a boy: why didn't I try these books which had once been his favourites? The bindings, with coloured pictures printed straight on to the cloth, would appeal to the bibliophile in me now, but then they just seemed fusty, and the immense length of the books and the tiny print were a fatal deterrent. Despite my pleas to her to desist, my mother wrote to Nickson asking for his advice, and he, in an agreeably relaxed way, wrote out a short reading list that included *The Good Companions*, *The Importance of Being Earnest* and *The Bridge of San Luis Rey*. I read the last of these and was fascinated by it, but the Priestley was simply too fat. Then at home I lighted on an even fatter volume which, if she had thought about it, my mother might have kept out of my way: the collected short stories of Somerset Maugham. These opened the floodgates and I devoured each in turn (as I did the Bulldog Drummond books when I was eight or nine). The world in which they were set was unmistakably adult and many of them were explicitly on sexual themes. One was 'Rain', the notorious story of the 'fallen' missionary. I also discovered *Rebecca* and read it almost at one sitting. The only other modern novel that ever sucked me into its entrails in the same way was another melodrama, albeit a more sophisticated one: L.P. Hartley's *The Go-Between.*

That summer, unexpectedly, I received an invitation to stay for three weeks with a much older cousin I scarcely knew, Barbara Wilks (daughter of Uncle Will), and her three small sons at a rented house in Freshwater, Isle of Wight. Her husband would come and go as his work permitted – shy and modest, he was a brilliant motor-car designer and later invented the Rover gas turbine engine. Barbara was big-boned, ruddy-faced, robust and sensual, and had married the slightly younger Maurice in her mid-thirties. She was a total contrast to my mother: above all, fussing about infection and over-exertion would have been unthinkable. What I had no inkling of at the time was that the invitation had been engineered to get me out of the way at home, where a family crisis was in progress.

Barbara and I were alone most evenings, and we had more adult talk than I was used to. She told me at length and with passion about the sins of her 'common' sister-in-law and the alleged sorrows of her brother – how she would keep the light on in the bedroom when he wanted to go to sleep, buy expensive clothes, and have her idle sister to stay for six months; and how, at the wedding, the bride's unspeakable father had strutted up to her and said 'A nice day for 'unting, Miss 'urst'. She afforded me my first glimpse of a woman's bare breasts when we were all changing into our bathing clothes on the beach. I had some more vigorous exercise when Maurice was down one weekend and we went sailing with his toothless and slightly batty elder brother Eason, who kept his boat in the roads at Newport. I was cackhanded and, despite Maurice's amiability, felt inadequate. Early on the Sunday morning, I rowed ashore in a dinghy (as a wet-bob at Eton I could at least handle a pair of oars) to buy some milk from a nearby farm. The moment the need was mentioned, I said I would go for it – I had to prove that I could do something, and was prepared to scour the whole island if I had to. When I rowed back – with a bottle of milk – Eason told me I had lost him a bet of two shillings to Maurice, since he had been sure I would not succeed in my mission.

I had been staying at Uncle Gerald's in Chislehurst for the night, *en route* to the Isle of Wight, when news of the Hiroshima atomic bomb came through. We were awestruck as we heard it on the wireless, but if we felt at all that the world had changed, it was merely that history had been given a prod and the war would be over sooner, which no one regretted. At Freshwater we did not even bother to go into town to see the 'fun' on V.J. Day. The night sky momentarily brightened with a few fireworks, but that was all.

At the end of my time there, Barbara let me stay an extra night to see *Rebecca*, with Olivier and Joan Fontaine, which was opening at the local cinema.

Soon after I returned home from the Isle of Wight, my mother said that the two of us were going on a driving holiday – the first time such a thing had been possible since the start of the war. She gave the appearance of being in high spirits. Our first stop was in the Cotswolds at Minchinhampton and our last was at Ross-on-Wye; at Symond's Yat we went out in a rowing boat along that exciting stretch of the river with steep and rocky wooded hills on either side. After Minchinhampton we stopped for an uneventful few days outside Cheltenham at a hotel called the Lilybrook, where an unexpected touch of tarnished glamour was provided by the proprietor, an aristocrat of the most blue-blooded lineage called Charles Fitzroy, only son and heir of the fourth Baron Southampton. He did not fraternise with his guests, and we only saw him at lunch when he came in clasping a large gin in a gloved hand, with a blowsy companion who appeared to be his wife (*Who's Who* states that he was divorced the previous year, in 1944, and did not remarry till 1951) and his son, who was a year or two older than me. Tall, languid, with smooth dark hair and boyish if ravaged good looks, every inch of him proclaimed his breeding. The son was scruffy and talked with a plebeian accent. Some pregnant facts in *Who's Who* about Charles Fitzroy's career helped to explain this scenario: early in life he held a commission in the Royal Horse Guards, was a vice-M.F.H., and married an archdeacon's daughter – but she died when their son was three years old. Back at Eton in the autumn, I found that he was the godfather of one of my intimates.

Of the large intake of new boys at Nickson's in my second half (Michaelmas 1943), most took Lower Fourth, and one, a hereditary City panjandrum now a man of great power and influence with a knighthood, took the third form, the lowest of all (he had as little charm as he had brains). None took Remove, as Richard T. and I did the previous half, but one took Upper Fourth – Stanley Peverel Bentley Earl, Charles Fitzroy's godson. The moment he entered our lives, it became clear that he was completely a law unto himself. While my Eton career teetered on the edge of disaster to the anguish of my parents and M'Tutor, Earl's was a smooth, stately progression of determined mediocrity. Tall, erect, a shade obese, his face so chubby that his eyes almost disappeared when he laughed (never aloud – that was too vulgar), with a fine pink and white complexion and curly auburn-coloured hair brilliantined and brushed back, he was precociously worldly and knowing. His father was a landowner in the far north of England, and he was an only son with several plain unmarried elder sisters. Like his father, whom I once had the joy of seeing on the Fourth of June, S.P.B. Earl was in appearance and in fact a great dandy and a great snob, though his snobbery had a consciously outrageous element in which self-mockery was mixed. The Earls of – Grange may have had a high opinion of themselves and a low opinion of all but the most ancient and respected county families, but their wealth was comparatively recent. My friend had one weakness which he did not try to hide: desperate aversion to his first name. Calling him 'Stan' to his face, which we sometimes found irresistible, was paid out as a matter of course by a not very powerful punch aimed at the offender's nose. The name was a constant threat to his dignity; Peverel was much better. 'Call me Earl', he enjoined sternly.

His Eton clothes were always perfectly brushed and pressed, his linen sparkling white, and his top hat glossy (Randle Cooke's, which he referred to as his 'lid', might have belonged to a knockabout comedian). When dressed in 'change' (ordinary clothes), again his turnout was flawless. A valued possession of mine is a blue spotted bow-tie that he gave me. He pleased himself in all things, within what was permitted, doing only enough school work and playing enough games to keep out of trouble. He was the only boy in the house, and perhaps in the school, who never had a mess-mate – by deliberate choice. Whom a boy messed with was a tacitly acknowledged sign of how he rated with his fellows, but Stan was above such shaming considerations. He showed his independence in having the *Daily Mirror* delivered, from his first day in the school to his last.

Stan was above all concerned with deportment – bearing appropriate to one's social status. One wore a hat, he said, to show that one knew when to take it off. His word for *'pas comme il faut'* was 'ponko'. One of the sisters had had a local suitor who was 'ponko', and for that reason alone Stan saw him off with a good boot to the posterior – or so he claimed. He viewed school achievements, indeed all achievements in the world of action or learning, with quizzical condescension. What determined a person's true merit was the way he dressed, walked, stood, spent his time, spoke (the right accent was assumed; the choice of words and expressions was what counted). He in turn was treated by most of the other boys in the house with amused tolerance, bordering on grudging respect; a group might descend on his room in the morning to consume the juicier morsels in his *Daily Mirror*, but once that was done, there was nothing more to say and he was left to his own devices. On the whole he and I got on well – he called me 'Hertz' – and he was prepared to tell me about his home and family. He had a quick brain; for him a joke had to be witty and preferably salacious. On a characteristic occasion, he and I and a group of other boys were lounging together by the house notice-board during a break, and among our number was one of Nickson's classical pupils from Herbert's, a neighbouring house. This boy was suddenly asked 'Who's stroking Herbert's Two?' In Eton lingo 'Herbert's Two' was that house's second boat in the bumping races; if one was the oarsman immediately facing the cox, one was 'stroking' the boat. Stan's face creased up with silent laughter, as he pretended that what he had heard was 'Who's stroking Herbert's tool?' The boy from Herbert's, who was serious and pious, said to me afterwards, 'I really believe Bentley Earl is *evil*.' Stan and I met for the last time in the half after I left, when he too was about to leave; we went to one of the Eton tea shops together and he insisted on doing the honours.

In an earlier, more comfortable age, Stan might have been able, like Oblomov, to lead the life of structured idleness to which he was so well suited. But the general odiousness of humanity would always have troubled him; he respected almost nobody, and found particularly risible his scapegrace godfather Charles Fitzroy – and his 'oik' son, to whom Stan had once administered the traditional Earl punishment of a kick to the rear for pissing in his barnyard. However, Charles's aged father Lord Southampton was a rare paragon, the one person alive whom Stan admitted that he ungrudgingly called 'sir'.

I heard nothing more of Stan after our last meeting in 1947 until I saw Randle Cooke again in the 1970s. Stan's father had been a cavalryman, and he in turn was commissioned in a smart cavalry regiment. But soon disaster struck, and he left his regiment under a cloud. He was well used to not being taken seriously but this was different. He took up a career as a con-man and spent many years intermittently in gaol. When I heard this, I wondered about getting in touch with him, but the family no longer rated an entry in *Burke's Landed Gentry* as in the past, and I could think of no way of tracing him.

There was another contemporary of mine at Nickson's who, like Stan, had an unusually clearcut personality for his years, and I mention him reluctantly because we were by no means friends. But it is like the Ancient Mariner's tale, that must be told, for he had an influence over me which, like a tattoo mark or some tell-tale dye, went deep and was irremoveable. This was Toby Gibson who, as already related, helped me to tie my tie on my first morning at Eton. That was the only uncomplicated episode in our long and

utterly sterile relationship. The last time but one that I saw Toby
(the last time of all was in a mirror in a crowded City pub – I
quickly turned away) was at Harrod's in the early 1960s. I was
with my then wife, Christine, and held our baby daughter in my
arms. We were passing from one department to another through a
narrow passage, and too late I observed Toby approaching from the
other side with his wife (I knew that he had recently married for
the second time, as I had). I kept my eyes averted, and we went
our ways. My heart was thumping and my mouth dry, and when
we got through Christine said that I looked as if I had seen a ghost.
I answered with a shaking voice that I and the man we had just
passed were at school together. 'Then why didn't you stop and say
something?' she asked.* Little did she know!

On arriving at Eton, I had not taken easily to the sudden change
to a stylised, self-conscious mode of behaviour after the all-embracing
easiness and foolery of St Ronan's. Of all my new companions none
personified this new mode more than Toby. He had been at Eton
somewhat longer than me, and his father and uncles (who were
a generation younger than my father and uncles as well as being
totally different from them) had all been there before him. But that
need not have signified much. What marked Toby out was his social
accomplishment, which he owed to both sides of his family. His
father belonged to a rich and vigorous clan, with its roots in the
shires and its financial base in the City, but was himself a bohemian
of far from typical political views. His mother was an eminent novelist.
They had recently divorced. Toby was not intellectually brilliant or
adventurous, but had enough brainpower and application to achieve
moderate academic success; and though not an athletic prodigy, he
was large and strongly built and won the highest colours in his
chosen sport. His Eton career meant much to him.

When my sister Rosemary saw his 'leaving photograph' in my
collection, she commented that he was good-looking – it had not occurred
to me. From a high, broad forehead with smooth brown hair, his
face tapered noticeably towards a narrow rounded chin. His eyes
were large and baleful, his mouth small and tight-lipped. The ensemble
was impressive, but I saw and felt it as menacing, a kind of death's

---

* Once, as a small child, I went for a walk with my father near Ascot. A very unkempt
old man passed us and my father said 'Good morning'. I asked my father why he had
done so and he unhesitatingly replied 'Because we went to school together'. Apart from
surprise that his old school companion looked so much older than he did, I believed
him. My father enjoyed sallies of this kind: he told a woman friend of the family, known
for her gullibility, that his club, the Athenaeum, had its own private tube station, and
she believed that.

head. But what transcended his very ordinary abilities was his taut, tense personality. He dominated our schoolboy conversations, being skilled at repartee and with a plentiful stock of pithy and mainly cynical epigrammatic phrases. At my first army unit, I borrowed one of his mother's books from the library – my first acquaintance with her writing – and it gave me a bleak satisfaction to find in it several of Toby's finest witticisms; the others doubtless originated from Noël Coward, Evelyn Waugh, Augustus John and other grandees of that world who were his parents' friends. But he had not an ounce of interest in music or the visual arts, or indeed in literature considered as anything other than what was OK at home. Perhaps part of the strong emotion he excited in me was due to my only half-acknowledged feeling that I had more in common with him generally than with almost any of my other contemporaries in the house but seemed totally unable to make contact. In our schizoid existence we often had exchanges of a civil but quasi-formal nature at lunch or supper. Occasionally he lent me books – like Waugh's early novels, and one by another well-known writer of Waugh's generation which bore a dedication to Toby and his sister, a fact on which neither of us commented; later I discovered that its author had been his mother's lover. We were sometimes in the same division, and because we were so close together in school seniority, we sat either next or opposite to eachother in the boys' dining-room throughout our time, and civil conversation was unavoidable. As history specialists in our last year we were both in a party that went to Shaftesbury Avenue to see *Richard II* with Alec Guinness, and had supper alone together in the dining-room when we got back, served by the nightwatch, a pale-faced 'distressed gentlewoman' to whom Toby showed conspicuous courtesy, thus exemplifying the admirable upper-class creed that, foul as you might be to others in the same broad social band who did not come up to the mark, you show the utmost consideration to underlings. But he was never in my company by choice, nor would I ever have sought his, for fear of a rebuff, except for some specific practical purpose that could be rapidly dealt with. If we passed eachother in the street – he wore metal clips on his heels which clicked in a sinister fashion as he walked – he would cut me dead whether or not anyone else was in sight. Twice he attacked me physically, once kicking me under the dining-room table when he had army boots on, to settle some small score, and the other time pushing me out of Stan's room when he and his circle were enjoying the *Daily Mirror*. To have responded in kind with any effect, so unequal were we in strength, would have been impossible.

There was a jolly Irish peer in the house, a little older than

Toby and me, and when I was about fifteen we became friends.
For a half or two we chatted endlessly, in the summer we went
on river excursious, and he even talked of inviting me to his home
in Ireland. Then one day, coming back from the river, after being
unusually taciturn, he suddenly strode ahead at a pace I could only
match by running, so I didn't try. Our friendship was over. I could
not ask the reason, but it naturally crossed my mind that Toby had
nobbled him for having such an unsuitable relationship.

In my last half Toby and I were both members of 'the Library',
a self-elected society of senior boys in each house with prefectorial
functions,* and this brought us together several times a day in our
common room – namely the house library, to which non-members
could only come before chapel in the morning to borrow books.
But despite this regular contact, I never deceived myself that it would
last for a moment outside the confines of the school. And so it
turned out. We met briefly in the army and on one of my visits
to Cambridge when he was an undergraduate there. Each time he
was nice as pie, and when we bumped into eachother at Eton one
Fourth of June (George III's birthday, the greatest day in the Eton
year) he introduced me to his fiancée. But when I was working
in the City a year or two later, I walked into Leadenhall Market
one day and my stomach churned as I sighted Toby bearing down
from directly ahead. We would have to pass within a few feet of
eachother, and clearly this was going to be the moment of truth.
I said 'Hello Toby', but with his best death's head look he marched
by. So that was it: the bad Eton days were back, or had never
gone away. After the lapse of another year or two, I was crossing
St James's Park and caught sight of him walking in the same direction
as me about fifty yards ahead, and at first was not sure if he had
noticed my presence or not. To my amazement I soon realised that
he was deliberately slowing his pace, allowing me to come abreast
with him before giving a sidelong glance and saying 'Hello Christopher'.
Anyone else would have stopped, turned right around at once and
given a normal greeting, but with the weight of past history this
grudging acknowledgement was almost better than the Prodigal Son
being embraced by his father. We walked together as far as far
as Queen Anne's Gate, where my office was, chatting warily the
while – how brittle his manner was, I thought. He civilly declined

---

* For most people a library is a place of refuge, refreshment and even beauty: what are
the massed and variegated spines of volumes along the shelves if not beautiful? Perhaps
only Eton could have endowed that word with an aura of menace – since it was always
in the library that boys were admonished or beaten by their seniors. Above all, it was
a place of exclusion.

my suggestion of a drink, saying he had to get back to the City.. This has mainly been an account of my own weakness and insecurity. If our small circle in the house was dominated by Toby's personality – and one did not speak or make a move in his presence, and sometimes out of it, without considering his reaction – it was hardly his fault. His influence was to instil a dull, cautious conformity, consistent with the stale values of contemporary Eton 'Oppidan' society (Oppidans are the great majority of boys who are not foundation scholars) and at odds with the human values I had imbibed at St Ronan's. In a dream I had in my twenties, I opened the front door of my house to find Toby on the doorstep. He said 'I want to be fucked', and I woke up. I am sure that this was not a sexual dream but merely wish-fulfilment – the destruction of my long-time oppressor. Even as I write, I do not believe that my vulnerability has completely ceased, but it is a long time since it was last put to the test.

And what of Toby's later career? Once when I asked him what he intended to 'do', he said 'be a farmer', and this, on inheriting his grandfather's estate (his father having been cut out for political deviancy), he has done. For some years before that he worked in the City – not, if what he told me when we met in St James's Park was the truth, with much enjoyment. At Eton he even said that he wanted to join a distaff uncle who had recently set up a publishing house (it soon folded). Perhaps I should be grateful that we never had to meet professionally.

I can think of two things I can be grateful for as the result of the Toby experience. One is that at the first hint of Toby-like behaviour in someone else today, I react strongly: *Nemo me impune lacessit.* The other, due to his precepts and example, is an acute sensitivity to boring conversation. Toby was ruthless in crushing obvious or sententious remarks. Compared to him, I had the severe handicap of having a father who did not know what conversation was, and a mother who had an awful lot of it and, due either to my father's deafness or his kind nature, had never been given a high standard to aspire to. Telling a friend once that rhubarb leaves are poisonous, she added: 'There was a clergyman who died after eating them.' Toby would have appreciated that.

Many of my contemporaries took Schools Certificate in the summer of 1945 and thereafter became 'specialists'. Because of my bad work record Nickson was not prepared to let me move on to this exalted status so soon; I had to carry on as a non-specialist for another year – a condition I did not mind, not least because the few 'Greekers' in the same boat as myself formed an agreeable group. Who are they? I can immediately name Martin Jacomb, Simon Wallis, Simon Sainsbury and Robin Jessel. Simon Wallis, a wit whose *bon mots* were made more piquant by his slight stammer, lived in Windsor and once invited me to tea at his parents' Georgian house near the Castle gates; he is the only one of them I have not seen or heard of since leaving the school.

But my *annus terribilis** was not yet over. In the autumn half of 1945 I fell foul of the senior boys at Nickson's – the 'Library'. I was thought to be getting above myself and insufficiently respectful of those in authority over me. Helplessly I sensed through various signs that nemesis was approaching, and one evening an absurd incident sealed my fate. I was returning to my room from the bathroom, and Ramrod-Rich, a member of the Library, an uptight Roman Catholic with whom I had hardly ever exchanged a word, was standing just outside looking at the house notice-board. In the good Eton fashion he said goodnight to me, and I said goodnight to him and then closed the door. He immediately opened it again with a stormy look and accused me of slamming it in his face. I muttered what was the truth, that the door had somehow slipped out of my grasp – I could not deny that it had slammed – and that I had intended no offence.

One or two evenings later after supper, I was summoned to the Library and told by the house captain, Charles Booth-Jones, that my recent conduct had been generally 'poor' and 'not good enough', I had been slacking at games, and to crown everything I had slammed my door in Ramrod-Rich's face. Charles was a contradictory character: a mighty oarsman and fencer, and an immaculate dandy (not even Stan could fault his deportment), he could none the less draw and sing with moderate competence. But his speaking voice, low and nasal with the vowels clipped and all expression squeezed out, was deeply unaesthetic. As he harangued me, the three other Library members – Peter Swinnerton-Dyer, Anthony Blond and Ramrod-Rich himself – sat in their armchairs reading, like Chinese monkeys. Charles asked me if I had anything to say, and apart from protesting that the accusations were misplaced, I had not. I was then ordered to wait outside, called back and given six strokes with a very hard cane. It did not draw blood like Claude Elliott's birch, but was much more painful. 'Now get out', he said at the end. I went out. It was a typical Eton occasion. Sadism was not encouraged, and

* No plagiarism here – this phrase was in my first draft before the Queen used a similar one.

although Charles Booth-Jones did not intend my chastisement to be painless, honour had been preserved on both sides. The incident was closed. A few years later he and I bumped into eachother at Lord's and exchanged not unfriendly greetings and inquiries about what we were respectively doing. He was a regular officer in the Household Cavalry, and finds a place in the autobiography of Auberon Waugh, whose squadron commander he was in Cyprus during the campaign against EOKA.

Eton perceptibly brightened for me when, in my last year or two, I got to know Jeremy Thorpe. As one of the group of returnees from America who started to appear around the end of 1943, he soon lit up the firmament. In the school concert at the end of his first half, he played a violin solo with characteristic bravura and won thunderous applause (did that addictive sound spur on his political ambitions?). I was able to place him right away because he had an older sister Camilla, whom he resembled and who had been to the same school at Ascot as my sisters and become known there for precocious and unschool-like behaviour – similar to Jeremy's at Eton. He and I truly fell in with eachother when we discovered a much closer connection. His father and my Uncle Gerald had been closely associated for a time in Manchester Conservative politics soon after the Great War, in which they served together in the 7th Manchester (Territorial) Regiment in the Middle East. I found that my uncle and his children, who were small at the time, had vivid memories of Jack Thorpe, for various reasons – he was remembered by all of them for his charm and by Gerald for his ill-disguised ambition and quest for a rich wife.[*]

Jeremy talked with relish about his strategy for scaling the political heights – through the apparently moribund Liberal Party, and through liberal use of his winning way with the middle-aged and old of both sexes; all this had been worked out by the time he was sixteen. So obvious was it, incidentally, that his ambitions were real and that he would carry them out that I consciously allowed certain fantasies I had previously toyed with of a political career myself

---

[*] Gerald's daughter Peggy, in her eighties, gave an example of his charm: at their family dinner table he had just referred to 'the most beautiful woman I have ever seen' and quickly added, looking round at the little girls, 'present company excepted'. Gerald laconically reported that when Jack Thorpe got into Parliament his family never saw him again. He had a few stories about the matrimonial quest, but it is history that Jack Thorpe eventually married the monocle-wearing Ursula, daughter of the would-be tycoon 'Empire Jack' Norton-Griffiths, who soon afterwards went bust and shot himself. Having once been a weekend guest at Ursula Thorpe's house and observed (on TV) how she bore up during her son's trial, I can only conclude that Jack Thorpe's final choice was triumphantly successful.

to wither and die, and for this – as well as for life-enhancement
– I am grateful to Jeremy. I am also grateful that through him I
came to know Simon Barrington-Ward, already a friend of his; the
three of us used to smoke cigars together in the farther recesses
of Luxmoore's Garden and exchange the latest gossip and risqué
stories. (One was on the unlikely subject of 'Routh's sponge'. C.R.N.
Routh, Simon's housemaster and a bachelor, was known to have
told his boys that if they felt the urge to masturbate, the application
of a cold sponge to the offending member worked wonders. Someone
had been into the housemaster's bathroom and noticed that his sponge
had a hole through the centre.)

Jeremy and I made a habit of visiting a certain dreary shop half-way
down the High Street called Wells, which sold furnishings and anaemic
water-colour views of Eton by a local lady; these were displayed
in the window. The door was always kept locked, but one rang
the bell and from the back would emerge a tall and extremely thin
woman of uncertain age, with no teeth and a look of infinite long-
suffering. This was Miss Wells, who ran the business with her married
niece, and it was out of fascination with her that we made these
pilgrimages. With unfeigned reluctance she would let us in and then
stand waiting, with pursed lips, while we affected a deep interest
in the water-colours. Once we asked the prices, and she told us
in her complaining voice that she didn't know but would have to
ask her niece, who was away that day resting because 'like the
rest of us she isn't very strong'. Whenever we met for some time
afterwards, we would unkindly repeat Miss Wells's comment about
her niece and 'the rest of us' in the same tone – Jeremy was already
a skilled mimic. I treasure the memory of his un-Etonian ebullience
and wit, agreeably mixed with a touch of rascality that I never thought
of as other than benign.

In my last 'trials' (end of term exams) before taking Schools
Cert., I was in the 'first class', having always previously hugged
the bottom of the second, and then in the great exam itself got
distinctions in Greek, Latin and French, and credits in all the other
subjects. Nickson was at last not unhappy with my performance,
and I moved on into my last year as a history specialist free at
last of the fear of imminent persecution. Nickson, though I slept
in his house, was no longer my tutor; that responsibility had passed
to G.B. Smith, a stimulating teacher who took pleasure in paradox
– in his youth, he said, he had been known as 'Gadarene B. Swine'.
He was a master at Osborne naval college early in the century,
and gave evidence in the Archer-Shee case; later he was headmaster
of Sedbergh, and only came to Eton out of retirement to fill the

sudden dearth of beaks in the war. He was very stout and completely bald – 'Egg' Smith was his nickname – and sang alto in the College Chapel choir on Sunday evenings. He founded a select madrigal club and, when I became his pupil, invited me to join, but the fear of being ridiculed by my philistine housemates was too great and I refused, to my lasting regret.

In the year or two after my father's death, a couple of his eminent medical friends visited our house in Oxford, bringing with them a rousing echo of the past. The first was Professor Lionel Hardy, in whose house my father died. He stayed the night and we had an evening of unaccustomed liveliness.* A musical man with a deft social manner, he promised to buy me a gramophone record on the way to Oxford station next morning. Fortunately, I did not let my unformed musical taste interfere with his choice, which was the *Magic Flute* overture, conducted by Toscanini; it has remained a favourite ever since. He mentioned to my mother that his wife was 'not quite a hundred per cent' and soon afterwards she died. Twice thereafter this delightful man wrote in the most courtly and tactful way inviting my mother to visit him in Birmingham, but she was not to be tempted. The other visitor was Dr John Hay from Liverpool; my father had been a good draughtsman with a knack for accurate portraiture, but Hay's pictures were more professional. I always had some talent for drawing, but had never tried to paint, and the good doctor questioned me, gave me various tips and sent me a book. The effect was miraculous.

My final year at Eton was about to begin, and as soon as I got back there I started using the Drawing Schools. Although I made a wobbly beginning, doing grotesque fantasies, the masters detected promise, set me to draw from life, and before long I was inviting

---

* To my embarrassment, my mother told Lionel Hardy that there was to be an agricultural camp in the coming summer holidays, arranged through Eton and for which boys were encouraged to volunteer. Neither Nickson nor anyone else there put any pressure on us to go, but I incautiously told my mother about it and she thought it was a wonderful idea and would do me good, as well as helping to win the war. I said that I did not want to go. She clearly hoped that Hardy could talk me round, but when I demurred he made it clear, whatever he may have thought to himself, that he would not try to influence me against my will. My relief and gratitude were compounded with sadness: I would really have liked to go, but feared the absence of personal privacy in a camp and the effect this would have on me – St Ronan's and Eton had fortunately never posed the problem in an acute form. If I had known Hardy better and been slightly older, I might have confided in him as a doctor and a father-figure, and he might have helped. When I was older I had no choice but to brave the situation in the army, and as if by magic the curse withdrew – only for as long as it was absolutely necessary for my survival. But in my mid-teens I had to keep these anxieties strictly to myself.

friends along to have their portraits painted. It came as a shock to me and to the two drawing masters that I had a hitherto undiscovered knack for catching a likeness, obviously inherited. This would emerge in the very first applications of paint, and might get overlaid and be hard to recapture. I could do the same with a pencil or charcoal, but paint was a more satisfying medium. This new state of being came to a head only in my last half, when I was never away from the Drawing Schools unless otherwise compulsorily occupied. I was mercifully no longer obliged to take daily exercise, and could now go boating if I wanted to with a friend, instead of compulsorily sculling to Boveney lock and back in an outrigger.

This seemed like art under halcyon conditions. I only needed to tell Engleheart, the sweet-natured handyman, that I wanted more paint, boards or brushes, and they were immediately to hand; the cost went on my school bill. The staffing of the Drawing Schools is amply treated in Wilfrid Blunt's *Slow on the Feather*. I had little to do with the titular head, Menzies-Jones ('Mones') the potter, except during one earlier term when I tried to do pottery. He was single-minded and inspired, but also mentally unbalanced and subject to dangerous rages, when the only wise course was to flee. Once I inadvertently mixed red and white clay – his particular phobia – and his voice went quiet and his face darkened. Blunt does full justice in his book to Engleheart but only alludes once indirectly to his closest colleague Gerald Leet, with whom he did not get on. Leet was an accomplished professional painter in his mid-thirties, and it was lucky for me that my own burst of activity coincided with his very short stint as assistant drawing master. He would watch my pictures proceeding and give tactful advice or add a brushstroke himself. He was also sophisticated and gossipy, and it was liberating for me as a schoolboy to converse with him. A year or two later he was living in a small grace-and-favour house inside Windsor Castle, having been commissioned by the then Queen to paint portraits of royal servants – a commission abruptly terminated when the King died in 1952 and his patroness became Queen Mother.

The antipathy between Blunt and Leet[*] could have had something to do with certain similarities in their natures, and with their extreme physical dissimilarity, Leet being small and sleek and Blunt huge and shaggy. But professional jealousy could have played a part too. Leet had one talent and brought it to perfection, whereas Blunt had several which he had worked up to a level which would be the despair of the untalented, yet without attaining ultimate mastery in

---

[*] When I asked Blunt to explain it at the end of his life, he replied, 'Oh just "Dr Fell", I suppose'.

any. He sang with a splendid baritone voice, studied singing in Munich and gave a recital at the Wigmore Hall before deciding not to become a professional singer. I was once included, through Nickson's kind intervention, in a party of musical and arty boys invited to a soiree at the boathouse home of the future mandarin John Maud at which Blunt sang *Lieder* and Mrs Maud (alias Jean Hamilton) accompanied him as well as playing piano solos. Blunt was no mean painter; a copy, perfect to my eyes, of El Greco's *Agony in the Garden*, done in the National Gallery when he was a student, hung in the Drawing Schools together with a handful of competent portraits and still-lifes. Both before leaving Eton and after, when he took up a creative sinecure as director of the Watts Museum near Guildford, he wrote perhaps twenty books on a pot-pourri of subjects – travel, orientalism, byways of history, and two delectable 'packaged' coffee-table biographies of Ludwig II of Bavaria (*The Dream King*) and Mendelssohn (*On Wings of Song*). Perhaps he came nearest to perfection as a botanical illustrator, and the book of his most likely to live is *The Art of Botanical Illustration*, with its King Penguin addendum *Tulipomania*. His interest in propagating Italic handwriting, to which several of my contemporaries became permanent converts, resulted in yet another book, *Sweet Roman Hand*. It was strange to read in his first volume of autobiography, *Married to a Single Life*, that at the very time when I entered Eton and first knew him, the hitherto greatest love of his life had just been killed in the war. This man, who was married, left a letter of wise advice to his two young sons, which was published in a newspaper – my mother made me read it as an example of right thinking.[*]

My ability to paint portraits made rapid strides – within strict limits where painterliness was concerned. My subjects were two friends at Nickson's, Bill Glazebrook and Ian Monins; Tom Stacey, who had the decency to buy the picture from me at the end of the Fourth of June exhibition in which it was hung; John Pierson Shirley Dixon, who took away his portrait, one of my best, without offering to pay for it; Peter Glazebrook, Bill's younger brother (my best effort, for which Leet said I could ask his family for a fee – I never did); Simon Barrington-Ward; Giles St Aubyn, an engaging new history master whom I was 'up to' (i.e. in his class); and 'M'Tutor', Geoffrey Nickson himself. An attempt at a self-portrait had uncertain results, and I used it selectively as a 'leaving photograph' – it was an Eton custom to send this little memento to one's friends, and it was a

---

[*] For the same reason she often quoted to me snippets from Harold Nicolson's weekly 'Marginal Comment' in the *Spectator*. If she had known what we know about Nicolson's private life, she would surely have cancelled her subscription.

sign of status to have a large number pinned to one's wall while still at the school (my only friend who left at the same time as myself who neglected to observe the custom was John Dixon).

The portrait of Nickson, which he offered to sit for with kind condescension, made him look grim – as he said, like a drunkard or a man facing ruin. He alluded to it several times, only half-humorously and even hinting that I was taking an unfair opportunity to get my own back at him. It was useless protesting that I had no malicious intent, or indeed any intent at all – it just came out that way. I hadn't the skill to touch it up and make him look less forbidding. He must have suffered having it on public view on the Fourth of June, aware that if he objected publicly he would make a fool of himself. I now feel sad about it.

Blunt told me that I was good enough to go to an art school, but I had no idea of what being a professional artist meant – and I felt no desire to go to an art school. When I did go to one briefly aged thirty, I realised how like a butterfly – bright and transient – that earlier facility was, and how much hard work would have been needed to turn it into a solid ability on which art could be founded. In the holidays after my last half I painted a girl, my first female subject, and found it difficult to catch her likeness; the harder I tried, and more elusive it became. Also, if I was to continue, I would have to find a good teacher and buy my own materials. Indolence, inertia and tight-fistedness took over. However, I did continue drawing portraits throughout my time in the army and at university. The Eton painting prize for 1947 went deservedly to Raef Payne, but I was given the drawing prize; I had not done much drawing, but it must have been a *proxime accessit*. It was mildly satisfying to go before Claude Elliott to receive the prize and be greeted with something resembling a smile rather than the look of a hangman.

In spite of the horrors recounted above, I am finally grateful not to have been sent to some other school where I might have fitted in better. For a start, Eton's music was incomparable, and there was so much of it. The College Chapel choir, though smaller than a cathedral choir, was trained up to no less high a standard, and we heard it every day. Henry Ley became precentor in 1926 and did not retire till the end of 1945, which gave me four halves of his dominance of College Chapel. He was short, very stout and somewhat dishevelled, and limped – he caught some of the blast from the bomb which fell on his house in Weston's Yard. Yet he played both the piano and the organ divinely. There was a daily choral service in the early afternoon for the town, which the boys did not attend

– one of the few people who did was the ancient and shrivelled Miss Goodford, whose father became Head Master in 1852. Robin Jessel, one of Henry's piano pupils, regularly turned the pages for him in the organ loft; once he took me with him, and occasionally after that I was asked to do the same office on my own.

Henry's feet were nimble on the pedals, despite his unwieldy body, and he had a mannerism of wrinkling his face and sticking his tongue out while simultaneously rubbing his hands rapidly together as he waited for his entry. He coached us at Musical Society practices for the choruses we would sing at the School Concert (the Shepherds' Chorus from Schubert's *Rosamunde* and 'Brightly Dawns Our Wedding Day' from *The Mikado* were the ones I found the most delicious) and at the two carol services held in College Chapel, one for the school and the other for the town; here the greatest thrill was singing 'For Unto Us a Child is Born'. He was fond of playing the sweetly melancholy shorter movements from Mendelssohn's organ sonatas as voluntaries. At long intervals, groups of perhaps a hundred boys would go in school time to the Music Schools for a music lecture from Henry. These were treated as social more than musical events by most of his hearers, but because of his enthusiasm, mannerisms and dazzling piano illustrations he was universally loved.

When Sydney Watson took Henry's place at the beginning of 1946, we did not have to wait long to find that we were in for a radical change. Hearing Sydney play the organ for the first time, it might have been a different instrument, and my immediate feeling was of grievous disappointment. Henry had put the maximum of light and shade into his playing, enjoying the fortissimi but giving soft expressive passages a silvery glow. Sydney's style was matter-of-fact to the point of woodenness; here was an academic musician, whose artistic sensibilities had to be well reined in. And the man himself was of a piece with his music – tall, gaunt and unattractive, he had a harsh stammer that made being in his presence an ordeal. When he addressed the whole school – unaccompanied weekly singing practices, which he conducted from the aisle, were instituted without delay – his unease seemed to melt away and he stammered less; and when he sang a passage in his surprisingly melodious tenor (Henry could do no more than croak in tune) the words flowed forth uninterrupted. At his first School Concert there were incredulous gasps as soon as the orchestra struck up under his baton; with Henry it never played together or in tune, and this agonising cacophony was considered the norm, but it was now a pleasure to hear. Now anyone caught strumming or, much worse, playing jazz in the Music Schools ('musical pornography', Sydney called it) was warned that if ever caught at it again he would be thrown out and not allowed to return.

How fortunate we were musically is exemplified for me by the strange institution of 'French singing' and the more select 'German singing' under Hugh Haworth, a senior teacher of those languages who had a tenor voice of stunning beauty trained, like Wilfrid's, in Germany. With the Precentor at the piano, he would train us in the course of an hour to give some sort of rendering of, for example, *'Au jardin de mon père les lauriers sont fleuris....'* or – a privilege indeed, especially after we had heard Haworth sing it through first himself – *'In einem Bächlein helle, da schoss in froher Eil die launische Forelle vorüber wie ein Pfeil....'*

There were other rare and wonderful experiences: going to the pupil room of George Lyttelton, one of the older beaks, when our own division master was ill, and listening to him read a tale by Saki with a full panoply of dramatic effects, and watching his then unknown son Humphrey giving masterly extemporisations on the clarinet at jam sessions in the almost deserted School Hall on Sunday afternoons; listening to Ernest Bevin, as Foreign Secretary, address the Political Society with majestic authority and wisdom (the father of the aforementioned John Dixon, Sir Pierson, was Bevin's Permanent Under-Secretary and, according to John, his wife was detailed to keep an eye on Dame Florence Bevin to make sure she did not eat peas off her knife); seeing Claude Beasley-Robinson, an ebullient maths master who later became a Cowley Father, driving his roaring yellow 'Prince Henry' Vauxhall of the early 1920s, at last returned to the road after being laid up throughout the war; hearing the mummy-like Canon Crawley of Windsor preach – he whistled with every sibilant (there are three in 'Jesus Christ' alone) and this was wondrously magnified by the microphone, reducing the whole school to helpless laughter; hearing Lord Quickswood on the very eve of his retirement as Provost preach his farewell sermon, in which he recalled his childhood (he was the youngest son of the 3rd Marquess of Salisbury), and read a lesson from *Ecclesiastes* – in both his voice faltered as emotion overcame him; seeing his successor, C.H.K. Marten, Princess Elizabeth's tutor, knighted by George VI on the Chapel steps; and making an immensely long expedition by bicycle with the school Archaeological Society to The Vyne, a most beautiful house in Hampshire.

This last happened on a whole-day holiday, and the weather was warm. There were perhaps not more than half a dozen boys and two beaks in the party. The Vyne was still owned by the Chute family, and Mr Chute, who had the air of an unworldly senior don rather than a grandee, showed us round. The equally dowdy Mrs

Chute dispensed tea. In the long gallery I took a sudden backward step to avoid colliding with someone, and collided instead with a wooden pedestal on which stood a china vase. Vase and pedestal started to topple over, but one of the masters, D.C. Wilkinson, in whose classical division I had suffered during my first two halves, caught it and averted a cataclysm. On our return journey we made a short visit to Ockwells at Bray, a small and exquisite medieval manor house. The aged owner, Sir Edward Barry, Bart., had commanded a regiment of the Household Cavalry in the 1890s. On the stairs I noticed a small print of a Tudor manor house called Hampton Gay in Oxfordshire, and asked Sir Edward why it was there; he replied that his brother had lived in it.*

There were so many beautiful parts of Eton – all the original college buildings, School Yard with its intricate paving, the cloister, the walk out from its small back exit past 'the Wall' and across Sheep's Bridge to the cricket fields, College Chapel with its mighty buttresses outside and dark wooden roof inside which harmonised with the whole better than the stone one that replaced it can ever do, Luxmoore's Garden, the river. And, among the sounds of the place, I had a fondness for the distant rattle – only audible at night as one lay in

---

* In the summer of 1943 I camped for a few days with a St Ronan's friend and his family in the grounds of Shipton Manor, a house of no great distinction but with a nice walled garden just off the Banbury road a few miles north of Oxford, owned then by a Dr Wells and now by the tycoon Richard Branson. It is a short and intriguing walk down a steep path from Shipton to, first, the Oxford canal, then the river Cherwell and finally the old L.M.S. railway line, all within a short distance of eachother, and it was natural for our little party to cross these arteries to explore the world beyond. There was no bridge over the railway, but merely gates in the wire fencing on either side; the trains came by at speed and there was a whiff of danger. The world beyond consisted of a large meadow with cattle in it, and some farmhouses on the far side. Isolated within the meadow and completely surrounded by it were two buildings. The smaller was the parish church of Hampton Gay, its tiny churchyard raised up a few feet and enclosed by a ha-ha. The large building, being deeply enveloped amidst tall trees, at first appeared as no more than a shape, but when you climbed over the iron railings, ignoring the 'Keep out' sign, it emerged as a stone house of considerable grandeur, with the outer walls standing, but roofless and gutted, with just a few black stains to show that it had been burned down. My romantic instincts latched on to this place. I used to fantasise about growing rich and rebuilding it, and made selected friends accompany me there from Oxford – it was an easy bicycle ride. There were all sorts of rumours about the last owner – that the conflagration had happened after a wild party and that he had torched it to get the insurance money and pay his debts. This was Sir Edward Barry's brother.

In a Wordsworthian scene I once came upon a very ancient man in the churchyard – he was contemplating the grave of his wife, and told me about her. The next time I went there, he was buried beside her. Also in that churchyard is the grave of a seventeen-year-old fireman, killed in one of the earliest major English train accidents in 1874, when an express left the line just north of the hamlet and plunged into the Cherwell where it turns and flows under the track.

bed, and faint or clear according to the direction of the wind – of the G.W.R. train crossing the long viaduct of brick arches between the outskirts of Slough and the Thames bridge close to where it terminated in the heart of Windsor opposite the Castle gates (conveniently for royal funerals). For the long time that it continued, I would strain my ears until it faded into silence, and think of escaping to London.

But I am becoming sentimental, which must mean that Eton is 'winning' the battle within me that still remains unresolved. This has nothing to do with the wounds I received there or the undoubted beauties of the place, physical and spiritual, which I imbibed without effort. In spite of all these things, Eton in my time was the ultimate citadel of a way of thinking and being totally alien to my own family's traditions.* To someone from an 'Eton family' this will be meaningless, or merely seem arrogant. My father was probably all but blind to the problem, but my mother was not, and used to chide me gently me if she thought I was being too 'Etonian'. All my life I have been schizoid about it, sometimes complacent but sometimes feeling corruption in my veins.

A Damascus Road

I faced a gap of a few months between leaving Eton in July 1947 and joining the army, which I could not do before my eighteenth birthday in December. I had left, strange to say, without any arrangements having been made for me to go to university. Nickson had encouraged me to leave when I did and go on a language course during the holidays on the continent, following the example of an older contemporary of mine in the house; but since it was the custom for university entrance formalities to be completed while a boy was still at Eton, it might seem that he did not think me 'university material', something I can hardly believe possible. He surely could not have

---

* My contemporary and friend Simon Barrington-Ward, when elected to 'Pop', took the perhaps unique step of asking for a day to think about it before finally accepting. Since he was already committed to his future priestly calling, this may have been motivated purely by fear of falling into the sin of pride. I prefer to think that, coming like me from a high-minded middle-class professional family, he was even more afraid of being 'taken over' by Pop's aristocratic ethos – against which every bone in his middle-class body would naturally have rebelled.

been paying me back for having been such an unsatisfactory pupil; whatever the truth, I just drifted along with typical fecklessness and let it happen.

At that time my mother used to house one or two undergraduates during term as 'P.G.s'; she did so without any false shame, probably because her motive, as far as I know, was not really economic. The first one was a mature man who had been in the war, a Scottish laird called David Hotham. On going down from the University he spent a few months working in the London docks, and before leaving Eton I decided that when I got back from my course (it was in Geneva, and devoid of incident except for getting to know an Eton contemporary, Tim Brinton, who was also there and going with him on our first brief visit to Italy) I would fill in the time before being called up by following David's example. He gave me the name of the Bermondsey man who would arrange my job and digs in a pub called 'The Grapes'. I met this man and a date was fixed. My sister Rosemary thoroughly approved, thinking that I was showing some signs of life at last, and my mother, with whom I no longer got on, annoyingly remarked that she was 'letting' me do it.

A few days before the planned start of this adventure, I was walking along Broad Street in Oxford when I spied on the opposite pavement David Edwin Bulwer Lutyens, who had been the most spectacular misfit of my generation at Eton. Sending him to Eton instead of a place like Dartington had been a cruel act of his grotesquely misallied parents – Robert Lutyens, only son of the great architect Sir Edwin, and an architect and painter himself (he had moved in the circle of Toby Gibson's parents), and his older Polish-Jewish wife Eva, niece of Chaim Weizmann, a science graduate and powerful personality. In adolescence David was strange-looking, short and feeble-bodied, with a disproportionately big head and lugubrious heavy-lidded eyes, thick lips of which the upper one curled upwards, and short wiry hair – 'like a bush', as someone remarked. His voice was a vibrant baritone, and he spoke like a classical actor, even the most mundane statement being intoned with perfect diction. But mundane was the one thing he could never be; he was deeply serious and intellectual, and although with a pawky sense of fun, he had nothing resembling a conventional sense of humour. He was virtually incapable of laughter, though he had a range of meaningful smiles from the pained to the pruriently suggestive. He was seldom ragged at Eton, and his nickname – 'Bill' Lutyens – indicated a degree of tolerance for someone so far removed from the norm; he spoke of Eton as 'civilised', which from him was high praise. He somehow survived being in Charlie Rowlatt's house and, having never shown any academic distinction before, won a history exhibition to Wadham College, Oxford.

Life for him now began, and his creative springs flowed. In the 1950s he flourished as a classical narrative poet out of his period, mining Graeco-Roman legend and Renaissance historical melodrama for his plots; he was staggeringly productive, and his verse plays were broadcast on the Third Programme. Secker and Warburg published a collection of shorter poems, with an accolade from Edith Sitwell. But exposed to a harsher world after Oxford – he had expensive tastes but no money to speak of – his mental balance gave way, and between periods in psychiatric hospitals there was a series of tragi-comic episodes in his income-earning and love life. At one time he was a reader in the theology department at Longman's; at another he worked under a museum director in London, whom he so despised that he told him to his face what a miserable creature he was, and had the satisfaction of seeing him popping heart pills; he had an ethereal girlfriend who only talked about hoopoes; and went through a marriage ceremony in America with a woman (I never met her) of whom his mother would only say that she had a hideously deformed nose and that they did to eachother things of which she felt unable to speak. Eva Lutyens provided David with a comfortable home – after her divorce she became an *haute couturière* and lived in 15 Palace Street, Westminster, a delectable house (now demolished) designed by Robert Lutyens – and pocket-money. David flirted with Roman Catholicism and with homosexuality, and once propounded to me the enticing theory that sin was salutary because it induced feelings of repentance, leading the sinner into the arms of Mother Church. He for ever oscillated between sybaritism and asceticism. We saw eachother often in the mid-1950s when I was working not far from Palace Street, and before his life started to go seriously wrong; once in the 1960s, after we had been out of touch for several years, he suddenly phoned when my wife and I were in bed, and I put him off; not least because I felt I could not cope with him any more. That was our last contact. Then in the early 1990s someone I had never previously heard of, called Candia Lutyens, was featured in the *Observer*'s weekend magazine and in the background of the photograph were a number of the objects I remembered from Eva Lutyens's house, including a marvellous pair of painted wooden caricature figures of George V and Queen Mary made by Eric Gill – and, according to Eva, actually seen and admired by Edward Prince of Wales on a visit to the house before she could think of hiding them. Candia was thirty years younger than David and the child of Robert Lutyens's old age. I wrote to her to ask about David, and she phoned to tell me that he had spent many years in mental institutions, which had become increasingly basic after Eva's money ran out, and finally – two years before this conversation – had fallen downstairs, after which, though still fully conscious, he never spoke again and died a few days later.

To return to the moment of seeing David in Oxford on that autumn day in 1947 – I crossed the street and he took me back the short distance to his room at Wadham. It was my first introduction to any private area of his life, and I was struck by the originality of his chairs, lent by his mother, which were exactly like upright deck-chairs but with upholstery of grey velvet instead of canvas. He said how much he was enjoying life – his obvious physical inadequacy had spared him military service – and asked me when I was coming up. The moment I told him what I was about to do, he launched into a passionate tirade, accusing me of Dostoyevskian self-abasement, and insisted that I find a tutor to enable me to get into the University. Thus I got in touch, through him, with Dorothy Erskine Muir, and settled down comfortably with her for a course of tutorials in history. She had been one of the many children of a late Victorian Bishop of Norwich, and been widowed young; she later published a book on Machiavelli and several who-dun-its. We found a source of gossip in the fact that her niece had been briefly engaged to my late cousin Quentin Hurst; she also told scurrilous stories about the royal family. My late conversion to serious study meant cancelling the intended move to Dockland and postponing my call-up. Not surprisingly I failed the Magdalen scholarship exam which I tried for first, but got a place at Lincoln College for the Michaelmas term of 1950. It was the college where Uncle Gerald (he lent me his study notes) and Quentin were undergraduates, and this connection cannot have been a hindrance.

David Lutyens did much more than merely fire me with a desire to enter the University. Of course I have sometimes thought it would have done no harm if I had gone and worked in the docks, answered my call-up at the appointed time, and after coming out of the army found a job or gone travelling. At least it would have made me independent sooner. But he made me instead, at a touch, a lifelong addict to reading. Pictures and music may be capable of giving me more acute pleasure, but the need for a book, or interesting reading matter of some sort, has never left me since then, wherever I am. Thus the form of reading known as editing – which requires total immersion in the text – is the catalyst that makes much of my professional work 'as enjoyable as a hobby'.

In the autumn of 1947, when I was trying to work every minute of the day at my books, Jo, a girlfriend of my sister's who wanted to go into the theatre, boarded in our house and earned her living as an assistant in one of the Oxford music shops while she involved herself in the undergraduate theatrical scene. One day I went down with David Lutyens into the basement record department where she worked, and two things happened: David instantly fell in love with Jo, and while I was sampling a record in one of the cubicles, I found that M., another girl in the department, was flirting with me – outrageously compared with anything I had ever known. David's high-flown romantic passion for Jo unfortunately soon became a bad joke in the shop, and meanwhile M. and I got to know eachother. She was short, slim and dark-eyed – the elder daughter of a German-Jewish professor of Greek who with his wife and three young children had come to Oxford just before the war. He soon skedaddled with another woman (dishonourably excluding all mention of his first family when he came to rate an entry in *Who's Who*), and M.'s mother, who was only in her early forties but prematurely stout and grey, was reduced to working as a char in an old people's home. Mrs Z., who was undoubtedly every bit as cultured as her learned husband, was proud and hypersensitive, and must have found this new pick-up of M.'s crude and self-satisfied. M., like the rest of her family, was intelligent, but she was resolutely unintellectual. At her house in the remoter reaches of North Oxford, the atmosphere was friendly and relatively relaxed except for Mrs Z.'s tendency to pick me up on any ill-considered remark, but the one time I brought her to my home, I realised painfully that her social manners were vulgar. I took her once to Eton for the day, and there we met Jeremy Thorpe and a girl on the staff of a prep school where he was filling in time as an usher before being called up. He later told me that his friend observed M. making eyes at him, of which I was unaware – so her flirting was mere knee-jerk stuff. Yet we did have some physical contact. We used to go to the cinema and in the dark our fingers intertwined and we nuzzled together. Once when we were supposed to be watching a film about Mayerling in which John Cabot Lodge played Rudolf, I got such an erection – my first 'public' one – that stars danced before my eyes and I felt dizzy. But when afterwards we were walking down Merton Street, deserted and dimly lit, with our arms around eachother, and I tried to kiss her lips, I got a quick brush-off; she had her pride, she said. She had been out with Ken Tynan, and I wonder what they did if they did not make love.

During this time, the strain of studying unremittingly for the first time in my life brought on an attack of eczema. Soon my whole body was covered with revolting sores, from which a golden ooze emerged and formed itself into little scabs, which itched so atrociously that I fell to rubbing them off. They would then re-form, and so it went on in a Promethean cycle. I spent a week in the Acland nursing home, and arranged on the mantelpiece in my room a long row of books. Having imagined that during this time of idleness I would read half of them, I actually read about half of *David Copperfield.* A course of baths in a purple solution of permanganate of potash relieved my conditions. While I was in the nursing home, a letter arrived from M. saying that she was about to leave for America, and I never saw her again.

With M.'s departure, I began after a short interval to see something of her precocious younger sister G., who was still only fifteen and at school, and went in for intense friendship rather than dalliance. On the evening before enlisting, I went out with her in a row-boat on the Isis (the Oxford stretch of the Thames) and bathed. I arrived home about eleven o'clock to find my mother waiting for me, weeping and wringing her hands. Maybe I had been selfish spending this precious last evening enjoying myself instead of with her, but that was not why she was upset: she already imagined G. pregnant with my child, a gunshot marriage, and herself baling us out.

Aux Armes, Citoyen!

I arrived at the Green Jackets* training battalion at Barton Stacey camp near Andover on 20 May, 1948, and in my intake of about sixty eighteen-year-olds was the only one who had been at a public school. On the first night I thought I might be in for a difficult time. The Rifle Brigade was a London regiment, and almost all my companions were from the traditional East End, with just a few from the less affluent suburbs. Speaking the same argot, they immediately behaved like friends and neighbours who had been together all their

---

* The Green Jackets consisted of two famous regiments, the King's Royal Rifle Corps (60th Rifles) and the Rifle Brigade (95th and last of the line). The training battalion at Barton Stacey in the summer of 1948 was run by the 60th; another battalion of the regiment returned to the camp from Palestine, which had just become Israel, while we were there. I had joined the Rifle Brigade – not that there was much difference between the two regiments except in their uniforms. The 1st Battalion of the Rifle Brigade was stationed in Germany.

lives. I was an object of curiosity, not at first very friendly. On that first night in the barrack-room nicknames were established (I was soon known as 'Ginge' because of my red hair) and boasts of sexual conquests and times spent in penal institutions were exchanged. The beds did not have sheets, and my companions all got in wearing underclothes; I naturally did the same, and left my pyjamas inside my bag. Soon after lights-out, I had an anxious moment when someone made a vaguely threatening obscene comment about me, but another voice told the first to pack it in, and gradually calm descended. The next day we all had to strip naked for a shower and the least inhibited of our 'mob', a Deptford Irishman soon to be discharged for failing the I.Q. test (he also used to throw his bayonet in the barrack-room for sport), commented approvingly on the size of my prick. Progress was being made.

We were encouraged on the first evening to go to the N.A.A.F.I. Most of my mob were enjoying eachother's company too much to leave the barrack-room, but I went and immediately fell in with some schoolmates – with whom *I* shared an argot (earlier in the day, within moments of arriving, I met John Dixon and we greeted eachother warmly, but to my regret he was on the point of leaving for Eaton Hall, the officer cadet school for National Servicemen). They introduced me to one of their company, who struck me as being not so much handsome as beautiful in the manner of a Dresden china shepherd: tall, fair and with a peach-bloom complexion. But his character belied this exquisite appearance: he was also acute, capable and sophisticated, though always enigmatic. His name was John Wilberforce: a Yorkshire landowner (his father having been killed in the war) and a Catholic, he had won a classical scholarship from Ampleforth to Christ Church, Oxford. We at once became friendly and so remained until we both left Oxford five years later. That evening, the regimental band was belting out light music from the current shows (one of them was 'Finian's Rainbow'), and in the N.A.A.F.I. with its low ceiling it was deafening but also exhilarating.

I got a particularly close hair cut in Oxford the day before joining to avoid notice, but like everyone else lost most of what remained in the regimental barber's shop. We also had to watch a film called *Joining Up* – its cheerful little theme-tune still runs through my head sometimes – and rather later, and not for the last time during my service, that wartime classic *The Way Ahead* in which a platoon of 'civilian soldiers' (officered by David Niven) is followed from the day of enlistment until it goes into action in North Africa.[*]

---

[*] When I met Raymond Huntley, one of the cast, on joining the Garrick Club thirty-five

On the very first day, still wearing civvies, we were marched before the commanding officer, Colonel Mitford-Slade, for a quick handshake, never to come face to face with him again. It was a humane ritual. Our immediate superiors were Corporal Seaton, a ginger-haired Grimsby fisherman whose bunk was in a small room at the end of our barrack-room; Sergeant Wood, who disliked Americans more than Germans; and Second-Lieutenant B., the platoon commander, who – compared to the brisk, down-to-earth N.C.O.s – seemed terribly wet, but cannot really have been since commissions in the Green Jackets could only be obtained by cadets of exceptional merit or with exceptional connections not unaccompanied by merit. Corporal Seaton, a fine N.C.O. and sweet man, only emphasised the class-ridden nature of the army by invariably addressing me, without sarcasm, as 'Mister Hurst'. Since sexual boasting was *de rigueur*, he informed us that in Trieste, where he had been stationed, you could have a shag on the beach with a local tart for half-a-crown.

I increasingly enjoyed the company of my mob, and they got used to me, but we were separated as soon as our six weeks of primary training were over; they went to the 1st Battalion of the Rifle Brigade in Germany and I to a squad of potential officers and N.C.O.s. It never occurred to me, any more than it evidently did to those who controlled our destinies, to wonder whether I was truly 'officer material', or to think that my service might be more enjoyable and profitable if I stayed in the ranks. It was certainly not a sense of duty that drove me on, through 'Wosby' (W.O.S.B. – War Office Selection Board) to Officer Cadet School, but rather an ignoble conformism and a feeling that it would be a disgrace for me, and a disappointment for my family, if I was not commissioned. Barton Stacey, in those first few weeks, built me up physically and psychologically, and barring accidents this wellbeing might have continued till my demob if I had stayed with the battalion – doubtless I would have been drafted into some specialist job, like being a clerk in the company or even battalion office, or intelligence, in keeping with my supposed ability. The main problem with this course would have been social; many of the officers were old Etonians, and even while I was at Barton Stacey two of my schoolmates, who had enlisted a few months ahead of me, arrived with pips on their shoulders. I viewed them with anxiety: if I bumped into one of them in a remote part of the camp with no one else nearby, would we stop for a chat and use first names, or would I stiffen,

years later and mentioned this film and his superb performance in it, a far-away look came into his eyes. He said that films of that calibre were not made any more, adding that Olivier's *Henry V* was being made at the same time in the next studio.

throw up a salute and rap out 'Goodmorning sir' without stopping? When I in turn joined my unsmart regiment in Cyprus as a second-lieutenant, one of the privates who worked in the battalion office was someone I remembered as having been at Eton briefly before being expelled. The nearest we came to a direct encounter was when he saluted me and said 'Goodmorning sir' in a disconcertingly Jeeves-like tone. On the same theme, I was returning to camp one Sunday evening from weekend leave, and asked at the booking office at Waterloo for a forces (reduced price) ticket to Andover. Maliciously the clerk gave me a first-class ticket to Salisbury (further on down the line) together with change for the vast sum of 13 shillings, almost half my weekly pay, and had turned to the next person before I could protest. Determined not to be completely outdone, I sought out a first-class compartment and sat down in the first empty seat I saw – between two senior subalterns in my regiment wearing civilian clothes (they were among those recently returned from Palestine), stalwart characters who had been members of Pop and great sporting heroes in my early days at Eton; they were inseparable then as they still seemed to be now. I wondered what they would do if they wanted to communicate with eachother – would they beg my pardon and speak across me? Strong and silent, they remained immersed in their reading matter and conducted themselves like total strangers throughout the journey.

My new, smaller mob was not as easygoing and warm as my first one, but there were compensations. For one thing, our officer was Stuart Symington of the soup family, a big, relaxed, humorous man who taught us what we needed to learn painlessly; the sort of officer we would have intinctively followed in battle. It was a hot summer and his attacks of hay fever were even worse than mine – once he threw himself into the long grass and rolled over as the sneezes convulsed him. We all felt bereft when he was granted leave of absence to play cricket for his county, Leicestershire.

Here we had one soldier who, as he lay stretched out on his bunk in rest periods during the day, delivered himself, with heart-wrenching emotion, of such current sentimental hit songs as 'Galway Bay', 'I love you as I've never loved before', and 'Dance, ballerina, dance'. The manic 'Hu-hu-hu-*ha-ha*!' of the 'Woody Woodpecker's song' was heard everywhere. The humour was a little less crude than in my first platoon, but still mostly sexual and scatological. Training in the use of the various infantry weapons, which had so many well-oiled parts that slid into one another, gave the N.C.O. instructors frequent opportunities to rehearse their repertoire of *doubles entendres*. A non-verbal one occurred in the indoor rifle range, where we were being trained to fire rapidly on the appearance of a signal – which consisted of a phallic-shaped piece of metal about two feet long with a pivot at one end and a rounded nob at the other, which hung down vertically. The signal to fire was when the N.C.O. pulled a string and the rounded end would lurch up to just above the horizontal. We also spent enjoyable days out map-reading in the Hampshire countryside.

A fellow-member of that platoon, John Brownjohn, was the son of a four-star general, then British commandant in Berlin, where he met numerous V.I.P.s, of whom he especially liked the Russian commander, Marshal Rokossovsky. He had also, as an only child, spent a year before the war in Germany with his mother, from which stemmed his later profession as a translator. He would doubtless have had a good start if he had wanted a military career, but although militarily competent he apparently never considered it. Yet his reaction to his father's calling was mild compared to that of an Eton contemporary, Michael McCreery, whose father was one of the leading British generals in World War II. Michael had a slightly ingenuous charm combined with remarkable good looks, and at first seemed destined for a conventional life of moderate privilege. While at Oxford he was a fellow guest at Badminton with the young Queen, and said afterwards that he would do anything for her. But a few years later his attitude had changed. Our places of employment – his the National Trust, mine the Architectural Press – were then both in Queen Anne's Gate, and we sometimes met for lunch. Once, as we crossed St James's Park, a bugle call wafted across from Wellington Barracks, and he said, as if stung, 'How I hate that sound!' He also felt distaste for the fact that one of the Queen's ceremonial horses was named McCreery after his father (who, if the *D.N.B.* is to be believed, was an admirable man). It became clear that something even more radical had changed when he told me of his clandestine involvement in a business scheme to turn a Georgian house in Chelsea into a shop by removing its bow-front while simultaneously his employer, the National Trust, was trying to prevent it. Not long afterwards he became a Maoist and left his old haunts to live with a working-class girlfriend and his new companions in Kentish Town. The last time we met, he opined that I would not be unsympathetic when the Revolution came. At the age of thirty he died of cancer. It was as if anger had eaten him up. Of the other two generals' sons I know, one is an ascetic Catholic priest (a convert) and the other a rabid pacifist.

Back in our select little squad in the summer of 1948, the time came for us to go off to our Wosbies. Mine was at Midhurst, and on the first evening two fellow-candidates and I dined at the best local hotel and afterwards wandered in the fading light into the ruins of the Elizabethan Cowdray House. An elderly female servant of the family fell in with us and said that it had been burnt in the year of the French Revolution – Constable sketched the august shell. She took us inside an adjoining wood and showed us a wide circle of yew trees, as old as the house itself and now of vast height but completely hidden by the surrounding trees of later growth.

Wosby (the first military establishment where I slept between sheets) seemed extraordinarily easy. The mild assault courses, on which one was expected to show leadership in a small group, and the general discussions were a push-over, but in a one-to-one interview I was floored by what seemed the simplest question of all: 'What do you think is an officer's job?' Surely it was...maintaining discipline, and leading one's men...in battle? The answer the fatherly middle-aged major wanted, and which did not occur to me, was 'seeing to the welfare of one's men'. Why didn't he note that this candidate had all the wrong ideas and was unfit to be commissioned? However, I passed, and so did Brownjohn; and the fact that the third candidate among us failed was some sort of restorative to my self-esteem. But in my last day or two before quitting Barton Stacey, some doubts assailed me. I was now sharing a hut with two regular soldiers on the permanent staff. Both worked in the cookhouse – one was quiet and passive, but the other, an overweight fellow called Hughes, was a stronger character. I came in once when they were both extended on their bunks, and as I sat down on my bunk it collapsed. Taking this jape in good part was easy enough, but as soon as I rose from the floor to put the bunk straight, the bulky Hughes advanced on me and tipped me off-balance with a gentle push. This was repeated, and I began to feel my composure slipping. Extreme passivity seemed to be called for, and none too soon Hughes desisted. Considering my unworthiness of the commission for which I was destined, perhaps he and his friend showed restraint.

We were not allowed weekend leave during the six weeks of primary training; it may have been assumed that some working-class recruits needed weaning from the all-enveloping maternal care they had just left – but after the quarantine was over I would go and wait outside the camp gates on Saturday mornings, wearing uniform, and thumb a lift from passing cars. Having seen little of England, I went once to Canterbury and another time to Bath. As I waited alone one evening for a lift that would start me on my intended journey to Oxford, the battalion second-in-command, Major Douglas-Pennant, called to me as he drove out through the gates, 'Want a lift to London, Hurst?' We had hardly ever come into contact and I was surprised he knew my name. I had seen him in action when a wooden building on the camp caught fire and there was a furious blaze that threatened to spread. This unmilitary-seeming figure, bachelorish and bespectacled, took charge and command shot out of him like Vulcan's darts. It was easy to see how he won his D.S.O. in the war. I declined the lift but immediately felt a pang of regret, thinking I should have accepted it for at least some of the way. This lack of formality and pomposity – a senior field officer unconcerned at sharing a ride with a rifleman – was a mark of the Green Jackets. In our earlier training the N.C.O.s had made it clear that we did not need to go in for 'bags of bull' like the Guards; we just knew we were bloody good without having to tell the world about it. We wore black buttons, not brass ones (this saved a lot of polishing), and marched in the light infantry style – with a rapid pace and our rifles held parallel to the ground instead of shouldered. Visible swank was, after all, against all our tradition: our dress, with its absence of scarlet, had been dictated by the need for camouflage in the American War of Independence – the redcoats were too easily picked off by the colonial irregulars.

Yet snobbery of the conventional kind was inevitable. On the Fourth of June I travelled to Eton for the day's celebrations in company with two of my contemporaries – Fergus, who was about to go to Sandhurst en route for a regular commission, and Stephen, recently commissioned into the regiment as a National Service officer. The two were friends and were discussing the officers at Barton Stacey, among whom the odd-one-out was a senior subaltern, P. He was guilty of the unforgiveable solecism of throwing his weight about excessively with the Other Ranks – not surprising since he wasn't a gent. It was the Thermopylae principle – that those with whom one could naturally form close relationships were also the safest companions in battle. And whereas there was a strong bond in a good regiment between the officers and O.R.s (Other Ranks), who never relaxed together, the officer who was an O.R. at heart with pips on his shoulder threw everything off-balance. Fergus was a large, handsome, charming creature, patrician to his finger-tips – capable of amusing frivolity, but at the same time solid and serious. One evening I was returning to camp by bus from Andover with Appleton, whom I scarcely knew and fell in with by chance at the Salvation Army canteen. He was an educated working-class man and a socialist, and happened to be in the same mob as Fergus, about whom he remarked venomously that with his background he would drift through life, a useless parasite, maybe being nice to people but otherwise achieving nothing. Obviously Fergus's niceness got under his skin; he could not reciprocate it without becoming a class traitor, so derision was the only alternative.

There were some poignantly unforgettable characters among the O.R.s in the battalion – like the fattest man, Busty Morgan; Rifleman Walters, a National Serviceman like myself who had lost an eye in an accident on the firing range, and was obviously bitter about it; and an elderly storeman, known as 'Boots', with snow-white hair and a rather rat-like look, and the only common soldier I ever saw when I myself was serving who wore the 1914-18 ribbons. He was a former sergeant-major who had been 'busted' for some misdemeanour. The army, which had demoted him, was also his refuge.

I was eventually granted ten days' leave, and had to give a contact address to my company office in case my transfer to Eaton Hall came through while I was away. Because I was going on a rapid trip to France, the address I gave was Thomas Cook in Paris. But my first stop was Nîmes, where I walked across the top of the Pont du Gard in the last rays of the evening sun, and next day I went on to Avignon. While wandering round the castle of Villeneuve across the Rhone from the papal palace and the Bridge, I met a friendly Pole from England, who said that I should visit Corsica if I had a few days to spare. So I thought, why not? I got on the next fast train to Marseille, took a flight to Bastia, and stayed that night in a one-star hotel of true old-fashioned squalor. The next day I moved on to Ajaccio and visited Napoleon's birthplace, a modest apartment where they displayed the Sedan chair in which Madame Mere was brought home from a social engagement when she felt the first labour pains that resulted in the birth of the future Emperor. Then down to Bonifacio, an unspoiled little medieval town on a rock with a distant view of Sardinia, and by train and boat quickly northward to be in Barton Stacey by the time my leave expired. My abiding memories of Corsica are of the wonderful beauty of the young women (many with a high colour and brown – not black – hair); the tiny fast-moving carts carrying one man and his load, and drawn by a single blindfolded donkey which the driver whacked incessantly with a thick whip, and the heaps of domestic garbage outside the front of each house, surmounted by any number of scavenging cats.

As soon as I got to Barton Stacey I learned that my summons to Eaton Hall had come a few days earlier, and that a telegram ordering my immediate return had been sent to Thomas Cook in Paris. From the moment of leaving the camp gates no thought of contacting Cooks had entered my head, and when I was told to report to the Company Commander, I expected to find myself in severe trouble for disobeying orders. But I need not have worried, because the Green Jackets spirit prevailed. Major Scott was a big expansive man, and in a benevolent mood. He seemed to think that the way I had spent my leave showed enterprise, and when I lied that I had contacted Cooks but the telegram was not there, he guffawed 'Never trust Cooks!' That was the end of the matter.

However, my mother had started a minor panic by phoning the regiment when she did not hear·from me during my leave. She spoke to the Adjutant, Captain Radcliffe, a Hampshire landowner who wore black gloves and drove a fine vintage Rolls-Royce, and when she apologised for troubling him, he replied that being troubled was what adjutants were for. A further dimension to my crime was added when, after my removal to Eaton Hall, I got a letter from Uncle Gerald saying that Aunt Margaret thought I should understand how irresponsible I had been in not telling my mother of my whereabouts. *There might have been questions in the House....*

A Taste of Hell

No change of environment and atmosphere could have been more total than that between Barton Stacey and Eaton Hall, the training establishment for aspirants to National Service commissions in the infantry. The Hall itself was a palatial mansion in the classic High Victorian Gothic style, complete with a clock tower, which the War Office rented from the Duke of Westminster. All the ducal contents had gone, except for a single painting which hung over the main staircase: Rubens's *Adoration of the Magi.** It was kind of the Duke to leave it for us to enjoy – not to mention the formal gardens and the park. Our recreation rooms and the officers' quarters were in the house, but we lived in barrack-rooms laid out in rows at a discreet distance.

My platoon was dominated by Guards cadets, several of whom

---

* Later it beat all auction records for its time, and it now hangs behind the altar in King's College Chapel, Cambridge. It is too sumptuous and sensuous to blend into a non-Catholic religious setting, and at the same time its peculiar radiance is largely lost in the cavernous vastness of King's. In its dark but intimate setting at Eaton Hall it looked perfectly at home, but it could not have stayed there after the army moved out, because the house was demolished.

I already knew. They formed a *corps d'élite*, partly because they had been more intensively trained, at Caterham barracks, than the rest of us – they arrived at Eaton Hall in large batches at intervals of about two months, and blind chance had thrown me into their company – but also because the great majority had been to school at Eton, Winchester and a few similar establishments, including the ace Catholic schools, Downside and Ampleforth. It was perhaps unfortunate that one man, Charlie G., came from Caterham with them, having been selected for officer training after serving for a year or more as a plain Guardsman – but he was not put through the kind of training before leaving Caterham that would lead him eventually to a commission in one of the Guards regiments. His plebeian accent and demeanour explained why.

I was quickly drawn to the company of some of the Catholics, a breed of whom I had previously known little. They struck me as different from Etonians of our age – was it that their education was underpinned by the spiritual as well as intellectual rigour of the Benedictines and Dominicans who were their pastors as well as masters, while religion for us was largely a formality? To us the ease with which they could expound Catholic doctrine could appear glib and a little arrogant, but at least, unlike us, they had all been obliged to think about those things. One of the cadets in our intake, who was a little older, had been a monk at Ampleforth and he was the only one of the group who prayed visibly each night in the barrack-room – he and the boys from the school knew eachother, but socially he stood apart, like Charlie G., and was not destined for the Guards. Of those who had been at the Catholic schools as pupils, one had an irresistible blend of humour, quiet intelligence and modesty, and quickly Cupid's dart struck me again after a long intermission. This person's attraction lay in the spiritual side of his nature being uppermost; largely concealed at that time, it later emerged fully when he entered the priesthood after briefly trying a mundane job in business. While still in his forties, he was one of the senior prelates in the English hierarchy.

Eaton Hall had some of the worst characteristics of a boys' boarding school – it was acknowledged to be an emotional hothouse, and competitiveness was rife. On how we were rated would depend whether we would get to be commissioned in the regiments of our choice; a bad rating could result in 'relegation' – having an extra month tacked on to the end of our training – and, at the worst, there was the supreme penalty of 'R.T.U.', or being returned to our unit of origin. Thus we strove to attract the favourable attention of either or both of our two platoon officers, Captain Aylmer of the King's Dragoon

Guards (a cavalry regiment) and Captain Colvile of the Oxfordshire and Buckinghamshire Light Infantry (the 'Ox and Bucks'). The similarity to my own earlier days at Eton was given an ironic twist by my unawareness of approaching doom.

The course lasted four months. To begin with, there were endless lectures, for each of which we were given duplicated texts to study – my interest in these, and ability to absorb them, were all but non-existent. There followed TEWTs (tactical exercises without troops), and the final test came with the week-long 'Battle Camp', based in a desolate, wind-blown old barracks on the edge of Dartmoor above Okehampton. Here we went through a succession of tactical exercises with live ammunition being fired just above. our heads, and a marathon endurance march in full kit, much of it at the double; at one point we waded through a bog with the black water shoulder-high, holding our packs and rifles aloft. Of course, drill was important. All the sergeant-majors and drill sergeants were from Guards regiments, and very impressive on the parade ground, with the peaks of their caps so steep that they had to hold their heads back in order to see, and with their unsurpassed capacity for swagger and exaggerated movements, and screamed words of command.

The event in the calendar that I dreaded most was the weekly company parade on the gravelled expanse between the front of the big house and the magnificent iron gates (it should have been the most enjoyable, because drill and parades – 'bags of bull' – appealed to me). It was essentially an inspection of our turnout. We stood to attention for a seeming eternity while the Adjutant, a runt-like little Guards captain, proceeded at a snail's pace along the ranks, closely attended by the dreaded R.S.M. Copp. This man, with jutting chest and gleaming pace-stick under his arm, seemed about twice the size of the Adjutant, and was equally ill-favoured but in a different way. Under the gleaming peak of his Coldstreamer's cap a bulbous nose protruded and bloodshot eyes peered. Beneath a pencil-line moustache his mouth curved downwards. His voice – the object of endless mimicry by the cadets – combined being loud and staccato with giving a painfully refined edge to his vowels. His choicest utterance was 'I've had enough of your San-Fairy-Ann [*ça ne me fait rien*] attitude!' – was this an echo of 1914-18 or of our earlier wars *against* the French? R.S.M. Copp once pronounced me the wettest-looking officer cadet he had ever seen and ordered the sergeant attending him to take my name ('Sir!' shrieked the sergeant). I knew I looked wet but there was not much I could do about it; even if I went on parade having doffed my glasses, which I usually did, it made no difference. Like all my fellows, I spent hours ironing my pants, applying blanco (a khaki-coloured powder) to my belt and anklets, polishing my brasses (here I could be thankful for Green Jackets black buttons but not for the white metal Rifle Brigade cap-badge [Fergus, already mentioned, had inherited one of solid silver]) and spit-and-polishing my boots with a cleaning rag wrapped over the handle of a toothbrush – but still I couldn't manage to look smart. What was it about me – something inherited from my Jewish ancestors before they emerged from the ghettos? Or had I simply not yet 'come together' as a person? The others did not seem to have this problem, except to a trivial extent, and most of them were fundamentally no more 'military' than I was. It should have become blindingly clear to me at this moment that in my journey towards commissioned rank I had hit the buffers. If Copp thought I looked wet, what about the soldiers – and N.C.O.s – who might find themselves under my command only a few months hence? I should have let my rifle drop, which would have been a signal for the R.S.M. to have me marched off in double quick time to the guardroom. It would not have been an ignoble exit and the Green Jackets would have received me back, if not with open arms, then at least with comradely regret at the failure of a misconceived enterprise.

As the result of having my name taken, I was on 'company orders' and confined to barracks for three days. This was no great privation since going into Chester by bus for a meal or a flick was the only recreation outside the camp. When in civilian clothes – we could not go to Chester in uniform – we were bound by the rules to wear trilby hats, and I proudly sported an ancient light brown one of my father's with an unfashionably wide band, which to my grief was blown away in a gust of wind one dark night during Battle Camp. It happened as I was leaving a little canteen on the camp compound run by a deceptively mild-mannered silver-haired man with a plastic white collar, who, as one prepared to leave, started to expound his rabid brand of Christian fundamentalism. I went there with an intellectually precocious fellow-cadet John Dow (also a skilled amateur book-binder, watch-mender and pianist), who fought the man at every turn and, as we left, chided me for not supporting him.

Battalion parades, held in a large field, were mild affairs by comparison with company ones, and took place only once a month when there was a passing-out, i.e. when a platoon finished its course and its members were about to receive their commissions and join their regiments. However there was a special one on the morning after the birth of Prince Charles, when the commandant, Colonel Gibbs, D.S.O., ordered us to remove our caps and give three cheers 'for His Majesty the King' – I wondered why it was not for the child's mother Princess Elizabeth. There were three companies and the senior platoon in each provided the 'under-officers', one senior and three junior, for the whole company – they wore distinguishing bands round the sleeves of their battledress. Of the three 'S.U.O.s' in the battalion (i.e. the entire Cadet School) one was awarded the coveted Belt of Honour for the best cadet (at Sandhurst, where cadets were trained for regular commissions and the course was much longer, the best cadet got a Sword of Honour).

It would be inaccurate to say that competition for the Belt was keen, because the vast majority of us knew we were not in the running for it outside our dreams. But there was undoubtedly an undercurrent of hero-worship, favouritism and sucking-up accompanying the distribution of these honours. In my platoon, when the time came, there were two obvious contenders for the position of S.U.O. One was an Etonian of my generation, Paul Graham-Watson, who had a spectacularly brilliant school career both as a scholar and as an athlete; a chilly Scot, totally lacking in artistic impulses and with an immense self-conceit quietly expressed, he emerged on top because of his exceptionally well coordinated abilities. The other contender, L.W., was not from a public school background (or if he was – and I don't remember – his had been a very *minor* public school) and it occurred to me even then, when he was awarded the palm, that this was 'positive discrimination' to redress the obvious class bias in the commissioned ranks. But his 'leadership quality' was real enough – it was essentially the accompaniment of a strong but modest and unassertive personality – and I found it fascinating to see it emerge because he and I had been at Wosby together a few months before, and apart from his obviously being a pleasant chap I had been struck by nothing else very special, which one could never have said after meeting Paul. However, Paul won the Belt of Honour on passing out[*] and was killed the next year on a patrol while serving with the Scots Guards in Malaya. A glittering career (perhaps in the mould of Oliver Franks) would have awaited him if he had lived.

[*] At the rehearsal for the passing-out parade, R.S.M. Copp permitted himself a shaft of sarcasm at the expense of this paragon: as Paul presented himself before the invisible general and went through the motions of receiving the Belt, apparently with overmuch reticence, Copp yelled 'Don't you *want* it, sir?' and a ripple of laughter passed through the ranks.

Interlude: Personalities

Life at Eaton Hall had its better moments, and for me these were without exception provided by the company of my fellows, many of whom were highly intelligent and interesting people. One whom I came to know for the first time, through John Wilberforce (mentioned earlier), was a fellow-member of his platoon called S. That he was too young to figure in the novels of Anthony Powell is a loss to mid-century English fiction. Born into a 'good' middle-class family, expensively schooled like so many of us, and with the kind of dark, Stewart Granger-like good looks that might not inspire total confidence in either sex, and a purring, affected voice, S. was unusually full of contradictions. A cadet in a famous Highland regiment and the son of a senior naval officer, he seemed none the less unable to avoid cock-ups. I happened once to be looking on while he was drilling his platoon on the parade ground in front of the great house, and when it came to marching his men off through one of the open gateways at either end of the screen of iron railings, he contrived to bring them face to face with the railings themselves, and they marked time until a N.C.O. gave the necessary commands to rescue them. I watched this little comedy with the comforting sense that there was at least one other incompetent cadet around besides myself.

S. was not popular in his platoon, which could have been partly because he was about to abandon his proud Highland regiment, having applied for, and been offered, a commission in the Guards – a move surely motivated by social ambition. This took him to Malaya, with a particularly baleful result, of the reverse sort to that which befell Paul Graham-Watson. He was leading his platoon in a hunt for communist guerrillas in a Malay village, and accidentally shot and killed a woman in the doorway of her hut. Presumably he couldn't control his nerves. This tragedy cast a blight over his later life ('There but for the grace of God....', I sometimes think). When I came back to Oxford after my demob early in 1950, he was already up at a fashionable college, and embroiled in a passionate and very public affair with an intelligent and beautiful girl undergraduate from a Southeast Asian country. S. was passionately in love, but here too he was prone to embarrassing accidents. One friend of both of us reported entering his room, knocking as he did so, to find the two in bed together

(S. should have 'sported his oak – i.e. closed the outer door – to bar intruders). And I myself, out punting on the Cherwell, came upon a scene of confusion: S. had got his punt at right-angles to the flow of this narrow river, thus blocking the passage of other boats from both directions. His *belle amie* was putting a brave face on this unromantic situation. The inevitable end to the affair came when, in obedience to the rules of her high-caste family, she returned home and entered an arranged marriage. S. had wanted to marry her and was heartbroken. (She died only a few years later, and a warmly appreciative obituary, anonymous as usual, appeared in *The Times*.)

Yet at Oxford too he was disliked; an American student described to me how, at a drinks party, he would let his glance roam round the room as he conversed with you, ever watchful for someone more important and interesting to buttonhole. Yet S. had an engaging warmth too. During a vacation from Oxford he and I met by chance in the Louvre – we were both alone and he said he had won a large sum at Longchamps the day before, so why didn't I let him buy me a good lunch? In the restaurant we traded confessions and much gossip, and the occasion was only momentarily marred when S., after tasting the wine, refused to accept it. We also spent the evening together – visiting the famous *cabaret féminin*, 'Le Monocle', where he made the unforgettable observation that he wished he could be a lesbian. Some of the younger girls, in their tuxedos, were very fetching.

By the time I got to Eaton Hall, John Dixon was near the end of his time as a cadet, having clearly done rather well: though not my idea of a leader of men, he had been made an under-officer. He was still amiable in manner, but a disturbing change had come over him. When I called him 'John', he informed me that his name was now 'Piers' – from Pierson, one of his middle names (inherited from his eminent father, the Foreign Office mandarin Sir Pierson Dixon, known to his friends as Bob) – and made it clear, on seeing me involuntarily smile, that this was not a matter for levity. Quite simply, the made-up 'Piers' sounded more distinguished than his plain unpretentious given name. And, though still wearing the Rifle Brigade cap-badge, he was going to be commissioned in the Grenadiers, the senior Foot Guards regiment and the one with the greatest social *cachet*. That was bad enough, but it had been arranged that he would be a general's aide-de-camp and, as such, immediately leapfrog to the rank of captain. I couldn't help expressing indignation at this blatant piece of fixing – a reaction he certainly put down to envy.

Near the End at Eaton Hall

As time passed and the training course went into top gear, the gulf between the social and military sides of my life widened. I was like an untrained mountaineer stranded on a narrow ledge with a vertical drop below and an overhanging ascent above. Nemesis came after Battle Camp. All of us were interviewed in turn by the two platoon instructors, Captains Aylmer and Colvile, to be given our grading. I had expected my interview to be sticky but not a disaster. But they said bluntly that my performance was in every way below standard, and that they were going to recommend that I be 'returned to my unit' – in other words, to the Rifle Brigade. My heart should have leapt for joy, but to be 'R.T.U.'d' was the ultimate degradation at Eaton Hall. I thought of the shame, and asked the captains if I could be 'relegated' instead. This less drastic alternative meant being transferred to the platoon immediately behind, extending one's stay by a month and enduring Battle Camp a second time: it had been cold, wet and miserable in November, and would be worse in December. Aylmer and Colvile said they didn't see much point in my being relegated, but the final decision would rest with the company commander – a sweet-natured Scot, Major Sim – whom I was to see next. I faced this second interview with a shred of hope and was not disappointed. I pleaded my cause, and he relented: my fate was to be relegation. I appeared the next morning for the one and only time before the commandant, into whose presence I was marched by none other than R.S.M. Copp himself. It was a formality: a few words of rebuke and stern encouragement, and it was over. I was saved, but for what? If I had received the sentence of 'R.T.U.', the R.S.M. might have said a few kind words to me after I was dismissed – for such men were usually kind under the hard exterior. But what could Copp, whose lowly origins and rudimentary education had prevented him from reaching commissioned rank, have thought on contemplating the army's future with me as an officer, technically of senior rank to him, holding the very lives of other men in my hands? Why could I not see all this: that I would be happier, and the army and the country freed from a liability, if I returned to the dear old Green Jackets, settling for an existence at my proper level?

I was relegated to a platoon with just one other Etonian in it – fortunately a nice one, Jack Stewart-Clark. We shared a room and often listened to his records, in particular one of Fats Waller singing 'My very good friend the milkman' and 'Shortnin' bread'. Our 'S.U.O.' had a rather unhealthy relationship of mutual admiration with the platoon officer, and we were not a socially exalted mob like my previous one – on marches and in the back of trucks going out to exercises we sang songs like 'The Good Ship Venus', 'Roll me Over' and 'The Ball at Kirriemuir' rather than 'A Partridge in a Pear Tree' and 'I'll give you one-oh, green grow the rushes-oh'. Charlie G., the former Guardsman, was there too – he had been relegated with me. Perhaps – who knows? – the lot of us were more representative as a mob than my last one of the young manhood of the nation, even if we were hardly natural leaders. Somehow I managed to pass out, on my nineteenth birthday, with a commission in the Loyal Regiment (North Lancashire), the 47th of Foot. My face was saved; in their ignorance my mother would be proud of me and Uncle Gerald not ashamed. Later in life, when I told people I had been an officer, it would be assumed that I had some stuffing in me. A year or two before the time of writing, I was visiting Nanny in Lincoln and she produced a studio photo of me wearing my second-lieutenant's uniform. The very sight of it appalled me: R.S.M. Copp had been exactly right when he said I looked wet. It was the last print in existence, and Nanny obligingly let me tear it into small pieces.

Although the interview with Aylmer and Colvile had been painful, strangely the decency and comradeliness that could be part of service life conspired to restore some balm to my soul after they had ceased to be responsible for my fate. One day, as cadet orderly sergeant, I found that the orderly officer was Aylmer. After we saluted, he greeted me warmly, and asked how I was getting on in my new platoon. Another time, I bumped into Colvile on the touchline watching a football match and we talked a little. He remarked that he had been invited to his old prep school for a celebration during the coming weekend, but had declined. I asked if the school was St Ronan's and the celebration that of Vinter's half-century as a master. It was, and I was going to be there. The next year our paths crossed in Cyprus. He affected not to have met me before – more, I suspect, out of tact than amnesia.

To the Island of Venus

In our last days before being commissioned, we were called together to be told which regiments we had been assigned to, and where they were currently stationed. The Loyals, I learned, were in East Africa. One of our group, on hearing that he was going to Trieste with another Lancashire regiment, bewailed his fate, and I immediately offered to swap postings with him, because of all the routine destinations Trieste was the one I had been praying to be sent to. Our platoon officer told me it would be good for me to go to East Africa (never mind the East Africans).

We were also told the precise wording to use when we wrote to our future Commanding Officers announcing our arrival. The letter was to begin with the single word 'Sir' and end 'I have the honour to be, / Sir, / Your obedient servant'. This done, I turned up in January at the Lancastrian Brigade Training Centre outside Carlisle, having travelled up first-class, the prerogative of all commissioned ranks. The new second-lieutenant would become a platoon commander, with a platoon sergeant, two corporals and about thirty private soldiers 'under' him. The men here were all new recruits doing their primary training, as I had been doing only eight months earlier. The change was vertiginous: these northern counterparts to my old Cockney mob were, and would for ever be, 'Smith' and 'Brown' instead of 'Bill' and 'Bob', and would address me as 'Sir', standing to attention. I was to share a batman with two others of my ilk; he was an old soldier and did as he liked. (When I joined my battalion, I could choose my own, and he would be a National Serviceman glad of a job which, except in battle when he would become the platoon commander's runner, was dead cushy.)

I had no experience of a Green Jackets officers' mess, but it would have to be less stuffy and status-conscious than the Lancastrian one. Few of these officers were 'gentlemen' – the county gentry, wherever they hailed from, normally preferred to be with their own kind in the Guards or cavalry, or in the Green Jackets and a small number of more select light infantry or county regiments, or Highland ones (the Black Watch, especially) if they were Scots. My Barton Stacey friend John Wilberforce, for example, went into the King's Own Yorkshire Light Infantry, a battalion of which his father commanded

130

till his death in action. The older officers in this mess tended to leave the likes of us severely alone, but two who belonged to my new regiment, the Loyals, were friendly. With one I went to a concert by the East Lancashires' regimental band, which gave an inspired performance of the *William Tell* overture. This was followed by a small unaccompanied choir of soldiers singing 'Abide with me' to an unfamiliar but movingly sentimental melody. The other Loyals officer was John Arrigo, a short, plump man with jet-black hair and moustache and a certain animal force about him. Being Maltese, though from a wealthy flour-milling family, he did not have the clout to get into a classy regiment – or the nerve to insist that his surname be pronounced correctly, with the accent on the second and not the first syllable. He had been stationed in Cyprus – where, to my delight, I soon discovered that I was to go. Our 1st Battalion was about to move there from Mogadishu. John told me that in Famagusta I must make a point of looking up his good friend Elvira Carlucci.

With my new platoon I was soon involved in a storm in a teacup. The sergeant was, by army standards, old and nearing the end of his service. He was also a bit of a card, with that permanently hoarse voice that seems peculiar to North Country comedians, and fancied himself as warm-hearted; he would do anything for his lads. In practice this translated itself into a determination that at the passing-out parade which marked the end of their training they would outshine the other platoons of recruits. He was a man obsessed, and would take his lads out on the parade ground and drill them in normal drill hours and out of them, even to the point of keeping them away from other items in their programme, notably 'education' and 'padre's hour'. I thought this unreasonable and said so – they drilled well and it was hard to see how they could be made much better; indeed they might get sick of it – but it was no use arguing with Sergeant C. Our two corporals were disaffected with him and poured poison into my ready ear. For there was another irregularity: Sergeant C. had a favourite in the platoon, whom I saw him shamelessly hold up to the others as an example, and whom he even moved into a small single room at the end of the barrack-room normally reserved for N.C.O.s. This young man was undersized, quiet, unmilitary and a goody-goody. The next time I heard that Sergeant C. intended to take the men off other activities to practise their drill, I intervened and said that the set programme must be adhered to. Sergeant C. cut up rough and we had it out in the company office. My point of view was allowed to prevail, and the Company Commander decently mollified Sergeant C.'s wrath by saying I was new and perhaps over-enthusiastic. The sergeant's favourite lost his privileges, but this was not mentioned before the Company Commander.

Twice I had to fill in educational hours myself. Once I talked about V.D. and got so carried away that, as we were going out afterwards I jokingly apologised to one of the men, who replied that I had gone red in the face. The other time, I delivered a conflated version of Dick Harris's lectures on architectural styles, and I can still see the mystified look on the men's faces.

My platoon passed out with credit, Sergeant C. was vindicated, and I felt proud. The inspection was taken by the Deputy Lieutenant of the county, a baronet called Graham. When it came to his turn to address a few words of approval and uplift to the parade, he unexpectedly launched into a passionate sermon about a soldier's duty to observe discipline. His unctuous voice rose and quavered as he repeated that word, and he told with relish the terrible story of the *Birkenhead*, a troopship which foundered off Southern Africa in the 1890s. The point of it was that the soldiers were mustered on deck and held their formation as the vessel went down, drowning in hundreds. This might have been something with which to point a moral and adorn a tale at the time when it happened or even during the Battle of the Somme, but was it how we wanted to present the idea of discipline to my raw eighteen-year-old Lancastrian conscripts in 1949? They probably never gave the Deputy Lieutenant's pep-talk another thought, but it filled me with indignation.

Nothing could have pleased me more than the prospect of going to Cyprus. Militarily it was a 'cushy billet', as the last of the thousands of immigrants to Israel who had been holed up there had recently been allowed to leave, and there had not been a serious outbreak of Greek nationalist agitation since 1931. There was no sign of any now. At the Eton Film Society I had seen a government documentary called *Cyprus is an Island*; the place looked a paradise, and with the few scraps of knowledge I had about Crusader kingdoms and surviving Gothic cathedrals and castles, my cup overflowed.

One other newly-commissioned (regular) Loyal officer, a keen and unpretentious man called Ken, travelled out on the same troopship, and we were met on landing at Famagusta by the officer in charge of our battalion's advance party – the rest were due to arrive from Mogadishu soon after us. But before we landed we had our first significant encounter. This was on a landing craft that came out to fetch us from the ship, which remained anchored offshore because of the shallowness of the harbour. Standing among the police and porters aboard this conveyance was a short man wearing an ancient three-piece drill suit and a hat of which the brim was pulled down all round; one could only see his hook nose, little moustache and gap-toothed smile. This was Theophilus Mogabgab, M.B.E., Serving Brother of the Order of St John, Deputy Director of Antiquities for Famagusta District. John Arrigo had mentioned him but given me little idea of what to expect. He regularly came out on the landing-craft to be the first to meet any newly-arrived officer. I said I knew of him and that was enough; he invited me to call at his home, Caraolos Plantation, near my camp, for tea. Ken was invited too, but I could see he did not want to befriend such an odd specimen.

The sight from our camp of the massive Venetian bastions of Famagusta and the twin towers of its one-time cathedral about a mile away was a lure I could not resist, and as we had nothing else to do, I persuaded Ken on our first afternoon in camp to come along with me to explore. The road to it led across waste ground, barren except where it passed right between two small houses, surrounded by trees and a rather dusty garden like an oasis; this was Mr Mogabgab's compound. We wore civilian clothes – only military police could go into the Old City wearing uniform. Much of the area within the walls was also waste ground, but there were still an extraordinary number of medieval buildings (many more were said to have been cannibalised to provide building stone for the Suez Canal in the time of Turkish rule). Goats, chickens and evil-looking mongrel dogs abounded. It was a Turkish quarter – the Greeks lived in the modern town of Varosha nearby. But at once we caught sight of a black woman, who I was later told was one of a handful of descendants of slaves who lived in the island – another, a cheerful man called Ramadan Ali, was the latrine cleaner in our camp. Before the cathedral – now a mosque, the interior richly carpeted and with the whiteness of the walls only relieved by the *mihrab* – was a small piazza, with cafés where old men smoked hubble-bubbles and played tric-trac. Here we sat and had coffee and strips of rubbery feta cheese and olives. We were seeing 'the East' for the first time.

That weekend I took a shared taxi to Nicosia, about 40 miles away. Wilfrid Blunt had given me an introduction to a painter called Diamantis, one of his fellow-students at the Royal College of Art in the early 1920s, at whose wedding in London he had been best man. I found my way to his small house in Achilles Street, and the door was opened by a man with a beautiful, almost ethereal face, ringed with thick, wavy white hair. He was obviously pleased that Blunt had sent a friend to meet him, and ushered me inside. Antoinette, his wife, was sharp in both wits and features, down-to-earth and somewhat lacking in charm; she worked in the court of the

Chief Justice (a Briton). He was an art teacher at the Pan-Cyprian Gymnasium, the island's principal Greek secondary school, and he showed me some work by his pupils – a collection of coloured patterns on squared paper struck me particularly. Then he let me see his own work, which had had to proceed slowly under the pressure of his job at the Gymnasium, where he obviously gave of himself unstintingly – mostly they were gentle Impressionist-inspired Cypriot landscapes and still-lifes. In a back room I was astounded to see, dominating one wall, a fine copy of El Greco's *Agony in the Garden*, exactly like the one by Wilfrid Blunt which hung in the Eton Drawing Schools (mentioned on page 103). I said that presumably he and Wilfrid had made their copies together, but Diamantis looked puzzled. Then, over a distance of nearly thirty years, a tiny incident came back to him: as he sat in the National Gallery working on his copy, he felt a touch on his shoulder. There was Wilfrid, who smiled at him quizzically and immediately went away. From that moment he had never thought of it again.

I continued at longish intervals throughout my stay in Cyprus to see Diamantis and Antoinette (his first name, Adamantios, was never heard, and even his wife referred to him simply as 'Diamantis'), and from the first visit I saw that this was a relationship I had to treat in a special way. Over time, I took a few of my brother-officers to visit Mogabgab, but I could not have done this with Diamantis. He and Antoinette were fervent nationalists and as such believed in *Énosis*, a union of Cyprus with Greece – no one then even thought of independence. I would not find a single Greek Cypriot, they said, who favoured a continuation of the *status quo* – except, maybe, a few people like the lawyer Sir Panayiotis Kakoyannis (to whom I had an introduction from Uncle Gerald) who worked for the occupying power and accepted its rewards. I have wondered whether it was through self-delusion or a certain cynicism that people like Diamantis and his wife held so firmly to their aspiration, knowing, as they must have done, that it could never be realised with the consent of the Turkish minority. Yet the common response of the British to *Enósis* (as they invariably pronounced it) – that it was baseless because 'Cyprus never belonged to Greece' – was based on ignorance, as I realised even before meeting Diamantis, since the Greece they referred to had only existed since 1830; of course Cyprus had never belonged to the modern Greek state, but it had been a Greek colony in classical times and then part of the Byzantine empire and church for centuries before it belonged to any outside power, and was overwhelmingly a Greek *ethnos*. The Turks only arrived after 1571. When I mentioned at the Diamantis house, with obvious eagerness, that

I had seen some of the island's Crusader Gothic monuments, Antoinette immediately said that they had nothing to do with Cyprus, and Diamantis more gently named a number of Byzantine churches in the Troodos foothills that I should visit, notably Panaghia tou Arakou and Stavros tou Dhiosmati – as well as the better known Kiti and Asinou. They told me late in my stay that as a matter of principle they never received members of the British colonial establishment at their house, but they had made an exception for me because I was a friend of Blunt. At least we remained in touch later.

Diamantis and his wife were a formidable pair with their contrasted but complementary characters. He came from a Cyprus village, where his father was a furniture-maker, and by winning a scholarship was able to study at a famous English art school. Antoinette was from the Corfiote upper bourgeoisie, and through the accident of her father being the first Greek officer to be killed in the Balkan war of 1912, she and her sister were educated, mainly in France and England, at the expense of the Greek royal family. One evening in Nicosia I passed Diamantis sitting in the street in company with a dark unshaven man, to whom he did not introduce me. Each was dandling a small child on his lap; this, he said, was the way they brought up children, to mix with the wide world. He told me the next time we met that the dark man was an artist called Kanthos, whose anti-British feelings were less controlled than his own.

When the regiment arrived from Mogadishu, there was a quick flurry as it organised itself. I was assigned to a platoon, with Sergeant Priestner in charge of it. He was a man of energy and wit and I could safely leave everything in his hands. Our only task out of the ordinary was to patrol the recently vacated refugee/immigrant camp, which was alongside our own, at night, with pickaxe handles as weapons to ward off looters, not that there was anything of value to loot. One Sunday I hired a motorbike, and Priestner and I went off on it into the hills – this was so that he could teach me how to ride it, which he quickly did. As we sat over our mid-day snack in a wayside cafe, he revealed details of his complicated sex life – with close-cropped red hair, prominent teeth, a squint and magnifying spectacles he was an improbable Lothario. He was soon posted home, to my great regret, but I grew fond of his successor, the mild and humorous Sergeant Fitzgerald – one of the many Irishmen in all the Lancashire regiments. Like Priestner, our Company Sergeant Major was also an impressive soldier, brisk and immaculately turned out. It amazed me to hear that he was only thirty-one – his face was ruddy and weather-beaten and his voice permanently husky. But one day C.S.M. Banks failed to appear in the Company office because he was under close arrest. The previous evening he had got drunk and gone into a certain corporal's room and made a very unmistakable sexual proposition to him. I knew that his nickname was 'Bugger Banks' but assumed this was due to the alliteration, combined with a C.S.M.'s normal reputation for strict discipline. He looked anything but a 'poof' and, besides, had the name 'Gladys' and a pierced heart tattooed on his arm. He was 'busted' down to the rank of corporal and that was the last we saw of him.

I shared a room with another second-lieutenant, a regular who had gone through Sandhurst (with Charles Booth-Jones, who gave me such a beating at Eton). This was Ian Mackie. On first acquaintance I found him intriguing. His father was a Hebridean who made good in Glasgow, and abandoned an unpronounceable Gaelic surname. Ian – tall, bony and with close-cropped, ginger hair – went to a small English public school and became a Catholic convert. His Gaelic background gave him a romantic interest in his own race and race in general, and soon he was talking excitedly about (northern) racial purity. When I told him that I had Jewish ancestors he was genuinely shocked. I took him with me on my first visit to Mr Mogabgab, and again when I followed up John Arrigo's introduction and called to pay my respects on the Carlucci family. I understood from Antoinette Diamantis that in his younger days Mr Carlucci had been a handsome blade. He was now a rather sour-faced, paunchy man of about fifty but still with an air about him. His Turkish wife, once a beauty, wore a plain black dress and hovered in the background while we were in the house. Ian Mackie, anxious to show off the little Italian he had learned in Somalia, said *'Come sta, signore'*, to which Mr Carlucci replied politely that he was not Italian. His great-grandfather, a Neapolitan physician, had entered the service of the Turkish pasha here in the last century. But of course, like Mr Mogabgab who was Lebanese, he was an eternal outsider in Cyprus, being neither Greek nor Turkish. The quixotic act of marrying a Turkish woman had distanced him from the Greek majority. Of their two daughters the elder had married an English N.C.O. who then settled in the island and opened a sports shop in Varosha. The younger, Elvira, was still unmarried. We did not meet her on this occasion, but a date for an evening outing was fixed; I was told she would join me for a party in a restaurant with her sister as chaperone, a practice still *de rigueur* among respectable Cypriot families – one could only be with a girl alone in the 'reception room' of her family home. In the event the brother-in-law came too (Elvira must have realised from her parents' description of us that the evening had no romantic possibilities) and I, similarly persuaded, brought along a fellow-subaltern (not Ian this time).

Elvira, though not exactly beautiful, had striking looks of a pronounced Turkish character – unlike her sister, who was fair. She made it plain from the start that she was bored with me and my companion, and remarked that she had expected me, as a friend of John Arrigo, to be older. Her sister made up for Elvira's taciturnity and talked for much of the time about her only baby, who had died, and her wish to have another. Her English husband, David, was very pleasant. I would never have met Elvira again had I not, several months later, been passing the sports shop and decided on a whim to go inside. There was nobody in the shop, but a moment later David appeared from upstairs wearing his best suit with a flower in the buttonhole and holding a glass. 'You won't guess', he said, 'you've come just at the right time. Elvira got married this morning and we are drinking to their future happiness.' Only the nearest relations were there, and Elvira, flushed with happiness beside her prosperous-looking Greek bridegroom, looked ravishing in a knee-length white dress. Mr Carlucci, the old Romeo, was displaying his considerable charm. Coming in so unexpectedly on this rite of passage and being handed a glass of champagne, I felt that the earlier failure to connect had been redeemed.

Just as my non-Aryan origins upset my room-mate Mackie, some of his ways upset me. The camp was a natural habitat for a quantity of 'curs of low degree' which scurried about in small packs, looking perpetually hungry. Mackie adopted one which seemed less woebegone than most and, by some genetic quirk, seemed a near-perfect version of an Alsatian, the one telltale sign of impurity being that while one of his ears stood up in the usual way, the other flopped down. Torquhil, as he now became, moved in to share our quarters, and was immediately subjected to a ferocious training regime. Utter obedience was demanded, failing which he would be beaten. Mackie was fond of going out in boats, and told me with relish that he regularly keel-hauled Torquhil with a long rope. One night, because of some tiny breach of Mackie's regime, Torquhil had his collar tied to his master's bedstead so that he could not lie down. At this I accused Mackie of cruelty, and said he was making life intolerable for me as well as Torquhil. But he did not relent and dared me to go and complain to the Adjutant. Circumstances soon parted us, to my great relief.

Mackie was the assistant battalion M.T.O. (motor transport officer), and one day I had to make a journey in a 15-cwt. truck with one of the M.T. unit's drivers, Benson. Because of my fixation with architecture, I looked constantly at the buildings we passed, and Benson goodnaturedly commented on it. He was ill-educated but bright and high-spirited, and talked volubly about his large happy family of eight or ten siblings to whom he would soon return. Being both National Servicemen, we had more in common with eachother than either of us would generally have had with regulars of our own ranks. But perhaps the most memorable thing about Benson was that he had a glowing physical beauty such as one rarely sees – another Billy Budd. I made the great mistake of referring to Benson's good looks when I told Mackie afterwards of my agreeable encounter with him. Mackie gave me the dirtiest of looks, as if to say 'We don't want degenerates like you here', whereas Benson had inspired no feelings of that kind in me whatever. Some fifteen years later I caught sight of Mackie in Holborn tube station, wearing a light-coloured mackintosh and a black Homburg hat – by then totally out of fashion. I kept my head down and hurried on.

In the summer of 1949 my company went on detachment to a camp outside Nicosia. The area was empty and wild, and one had a direct view of the barren southern flank of the Kyrenia mountain range. Just outside the camp perimeter was a military correctional establishment, quite separate from us with its own warrant officer in charge and a fanatical staff sergeant who, when he saluted, lifted his foot to what must have been an unprecedented height before banging it down and yelling 'Sir!'. However it had a part-time officer in command, with responsibility for handing out punishments for disciplinary infractions, and this happened to be our company num-ber-two: Captain Allen Patrick. I have introduced Allen in this connection because some months later, after he was drafted home to the U.K., the humane warrant officer in charge said to me one day with feeling that he believed Captain Patrick to be mad. Allen clearly revelled in these duties. He was aged twenty-nine, and wore six campaign ribbons from the recent war. One would not have noticed him in a crowd; he was slight in build, totally undistinguished in appearance, and his face showed no animation except when an unpleasant joke – usually his own – twisted his features into something distantly resem-bling a smile. He possessed a pure-bred Alsatian which he boasted he had trained to kill wogs; but he had brought it not long before from East Africa, and it was, mercifully, still in quarantine. In one of his nasty moods he said that he would set it on me, and I replied that if he did I would feel free to kill it. He said he would then feel free to kill me.

Our company commander lived in married quarters, and so Allen, a regular second-lieutenant called Maurice, and I shared a primitive

mess consisting of a small main room, a kitchen and a shower compartment. We slept in tents. I met Maurice again twenty years later
when our regiment was amalgamated, and as we talked a sudden
reminiscence lit up his face in a broad smile. He asked if I remembered
Allen Patrick. I said that I did, very well, and Maurice admitted
that he had mistakenly thought him a great guy in those weeks
when we were all together. The admiration was mutual, because
it tickled Allen to have an acolyte who even aped his mannerisms.
Allen's biggest line was sexual boasting, which became more fantastic
the more he drank. He claimed to have had four hundred women
in one year during the war in Malta. But although that was certainly
a lie, Maurice and I knew, through having spent evenings with him
on the town, that he regularly enjoyed the services of one of the
foremost cabaret 'hostesses' in Nicosia. Maurice confessed that although
he and his *de facto* fiancee back in England had often reached,
and passed, the point of maximum mutual stimulation together, they
always stopped short of penetration. I couldn't even boast that much
– or that little. Allen was unable to identify with anything like this,
where the restraint was due to love, because he openly despised
the female sex. Ignorant as I was, I understood the signs: once he
told us of a raid he had led as a military police officer in Germany
just after the war – on a brothel. There they found a chamber-pot
in the room, *'full of women's pee'* – the disgust in his mocking
voice said it all.

Towards the end of my time in Cyprus, after Allen went home,
Maurice and I became quite friendly, something that would have
been impossible with Allen. Our mutual antipathy ran deep, but on
my side there was fear too: he was a 'loose cannon'. I felt it once
when the two of us were alone and he challenged me to a game
of chess. Why didn't I let him win? But I won, and although obviously
put out – he was slightly drunk – he disguised it by telling me several
times that I was a better player than I thought (I knew this to
be untrue) and should take the game up seriously. Another time,
we were both in the battalion officers' mess at Famagusta late one
evening, and he, evidently calculating that he would get a favourable
response from the two or three others present, said brightly 'Let's
throw Hurst into the sea'. The shore was not more than fifty yards
away and was all sharp rock – and it was dark. I said 'Let's throw
Allen into the sea' and the moment passed. He was my senior officer
and I had to be careful. One of Allen's habits was speaking offensively
to Other Ranks, who could not reply in kind without a breach of
military discipline.

It was a long summer, largely of pleasant inactivity. I became the detachment M.T.O. when my company was stationed in Nicosia, away from the battalion, and spent much of each morning reading in my office. I was never going to understand the workings of the internal combustion engine, so when I bought a 1931 Morris Minor from Sigmund Pollitzer (to be introduced shortly) it was the little M.T. unit that looked it over – and gave it a bill of ill-health, remarking that I had been 'jipped'.* As for my reading, there was a library in town, run for the British community, where I came upon the Scott Moncrieff translation of Proust (the lady librarian called him 'Prowst'). They only had the first volume, *Swann's Way*, but that was enough (at my request my mother sent me the whole set for Christmas, but regretted it later when she somehow discovered that Proust is not 'nice'). Reading it gave me a new experience: I kept finding thoughts and feelings articulated which I instantly recognised but had never seen or heard expressed in words before. The army education office had a tiny record library, and from there I borrowed almost the only complete long work by any composer that it contained, Mozart's violin concerto in D (K. 216), and the last record of the Brahms St Antoni variations – the rest was missing. I played these in my tent one hot afternoon on a borrowed gramophone. It was months since I had heard any music, and the final Brahms variation gave me a mighty thrill. But as I listened to the Mozart, especially the slow movement, the extraordinarily beautiful landscape of the north coast of Cyprus rose up before me. This was not a happy thought that I searched for; it just happened. The phrase 'classical landscape' suddenly took on meaning.

My circle of acquaintance grew. Prompted by Diamantis, I called on a late middle-aged couple in Kyrenia – a retired colonel and his wife who lived an idyllic, sleepy life as amateur painters. With them lived a man of fifty, from a distinguished intellectual family, who needed looking after – Geoffrey de Selincourt. Tall, with a fine hawk-like head, he too painted, and wrote poetry as well, but his talents remained at an unformed stage. After I was with them for an hour or two, they said 'Why don't we take him to meet Pollitzer?' They remarked that this man had an extraordinary voice.

When I later told Diamantis that their introduction had led me on indirectly to Pollitzer, Antoinette remarked that there was something 'Café Royal' about him – at the time I did not grasp the allusion to Oscar Wilde. The colonel had said he was a draughtsman. Whatever I may have expected from this label, the door of the small isolated

---

* Presumably being 'jipped' was what one expected from 'Jippoes' (i.e. Egyptians) or by extension anyone hailing from east of Gibraltar.

one-storeyed Turkish house to which we drove on the eastern edge of Kyrenia opened to reveal a heavily tanned, slim man wearing dark glasses, with a lot of fuzzy light brown hair around a bald patch, and a warm smile. He asked us inside – his voice was indeed a high tenor with an expressive lilt – and we went round the well-planted courtyard and sat on an east-facing verandah from which the whole sweep of the forested northern slope of the Kyrenia mountains could be seen stretching away until it faded into invisibility. This was the scene which Mozart's concerto had conjured up.

Sigmund Pollitzer, who was then thirty-six, belonged to a Jewish family which made its fortune through the transport and exhibition business, Beck and Pollitzer; the elder brother Edward managed it while Sigmund lived on a comfortable income. In England a few years earlier he had produced pen drawings of cornstooks and gnarled tree-trunks; now he drew Cypriot *objets trouvés* – sunflowers (he had many growing in his courtyard), gourds, goat skulls and male figure studies – and produced ceramics. The technical mastery and artistic completeness of the drawings, clearly the result of intense concentration, seemed to me prodigious. He lived a frugal, disciplined life, rising early and working in the morning only. I never saw him at work, or other than taking his ease and in a good humour.

As he was seeing the colonel, his wife and me off the premises at the end of our visit, Pollitzer said to me quietly 'Come again'. He had been so welcoming to my companions that one could never have suspected that, as he later admitted, he regarded them as bores and incompetents. However much his parting invitation might have been a similar courtesy, I decided to call again – he was not on the phone – and, when I did so, felt for the first time that there was someone in the island in whose company I could completely relax. He was not an intellectual but, by my standards at the time, he had read and travelled widely, and having been a sergeant in the Intelligence Corps during the war knew something of the army. It was also clear that I was one of the few compatible people around by his standards.

Once he dropped a remark in passing that made it obvious that he was in the habit of consorting with prostitutes – he talked of having had a 'bit of nonsense' in the Old City of Famagusta. I innocently imagined that he meant female ones, but later it came out that he was talking of boys. He had had one particular love, a Greek Cypriot called Dino, who after a brief carefree period had shown signs of a nasty character and caused all sorts of grief, finally ending up in prison. These revelations did not change our relationship because it was quite clear that he had no designs on me; he liked younger males, and I had no illusion that I was attractive to either sex. But there was another revelation. This was my first conversation ever about homosexuality with an adult homosexual, and I acknowledged to him my own ambivalence. I had always, with the large compartment of myself that was conditioned by my upbringing, assumed that I would sooner or later be heterosexual. The females who had appealed to me hitherto were either young girls who did not share my sort of background – and I had only got close enough to one such girl to feel sexually excited – or older women who did share it. My adolescent wet dreams had not been of women, as the rudimentary sex education of the time told us was normal, and instinct told me that their obstinately homosexual character was telling me the truth about myself. Yet whereas most teenage boys, either cheerfully or anxiously, masturbate, and at boarding schools the activity is sometimes engaged in with others, none of this happened to me. My school love affairs were always undeclared, and indeed my mind hardly made any connection between spiritual and physical love, *agape* and *eros.*

Sigmund Pollitzer died in the early 1980s, so there is no harm in saying here something he never told me himself: that during the war he and a small group of homosexuals – one of whom, Brian X., a notorious *homme fatal*, was the great love of his life – were betrayed to the police, tried and gaoled, not for corrupting the youth or any offence but engaging in homosexual acts in private. This left him with a distaste for living in England. A few years later, when EOKA's dirty war began, he moved to Positano where he lived for the rest of his life.

Also during that summer I was recommended for musical reasons to make the acquaintance of Richard W., a young Englishman recently arrived in Cyprus who was staying at a small hotel in Nicosia. He was said to be an accomplished pianist and a man of parts. The first time I called at the hotel he was out, but in the hall a short rotund man nearly walked into me and apologised in a fruity English voice. I realised he was drunk. He reappeared a moment later and asked me to join him in the bar. He said at once that he was going to ground because Mountbatten was due to arrive in the island the next day, with much to-do, and he wanted at all costs to avoid meeting him: they had been naval cadets in the same year at Dartmouth. He introduced himself as Commander Cobley – generally known as Uncle Tom. Unabashed, he told me that he had been dismissed from the navy for insubordination; drink had combined fatally with his sardonic intelligence, and he had told his admiral what he thought of him. He said he was once married and had children, but I later heard that this was untrue. Going on 'blinds' and drying out, it soon transpired, was the pattern of his life, but in the sober intervals he was good company. He was not frank about his sexual proclivities, because after leaving the island I heard from Pollitzer that he had made Cyprus too hot to hold him. First he had gone into a Greek Orthodox church on Easter Day and sat with his legs crossed, which was taboo; when asked to uncross them he refused and was thrown out. Then he committed an act of 'gross indecency' with a boy in full view of everybody on the beach at Kyrenia and was put in prison.

Uncle Tom was only one of a small colony of expatriate English pederasts. A member of it with whom I had lunch one Sunday in Kyrenia was 'Ozzy' Darell, an aristocrat (he later became a seventh baronet) in his forties, with the innate poise of his breed and in addition a fund of amusing conversation. As the painting colonel remarked sadly, what a disappointment Ozzy must have been to his father, an ancient brigadier-general. Tall and no doubt good-looking in his day, he was now pale and shaky and never without dark glasses. Without self-pity he bemoaned the emptiness of his existence – which, unlike poor Uncle Tom, he at least had the means to sustain in some style.

To return to Richard W., he was about thirty and remarkably ugly – his features were small and pinched. But I at once realised that here was another congenial spirit. On his gramophone, at our first meeting in his hotel room, he put on Yehudi and Hepzibah Menuhin playing Mozart's dazzling A major violin sonata (K. 526), which I had never heard before. He had bought a share in a dry-cleaning business in the heart of Nicosia, and was about to rent a house – most of his books and other possessions were still in store. The incongruity of a man of his kind engaging in such an occupation struck me with force when I called at the establishment once in passing and found him being berated by a dissatisfied woman customer. When she flounced out, he smiled and shrugged his shoulders, and then proceeded to tell me of his previous night's adventure. It was apparent by this time that the reason for his strange existence was the easy availability in Cyprus of young boys, for whom his craving appeared insatiable. He spoke with nostalgic regret of the boys in the Sorrento peninsula who, he said, were genuinely affectionate, unlike the mercenary Cypriots.

Along with all this, his artistic sensibility and critical intelligence were acute – not creative, perhaps, but I heard him in a violin and piano duo at the British Council, when he expertly played the piano part in the Ravel sonata. He introduced me also to the works of Graham Greene, Kafka and, of special importance to him, Thomas

Mann whose *Magic Mountain* he thought the greatest novel ever written. He disliked Proust, whom he likened to someone pulling the wings off a butterfly. He once visited Pollitzer at my suggestion, but the meeting was not a success, as I should have foreseen. Pollitzer, to whom beauty was everything, found Richard repellent – and was affronted when he kept bringing the conversation round to his erotic adventures, apparently presuming that with their shared pederasty Pollitzer would find them interesting. When I was about to Leave Cyprus, Richard W. sent me a farewell letter, referring to my 'rainbow future'; from someone most of whose rainbows had long since dimmed and who might have been excused for feeling sorry for himself, this was kind and generous. But whereas Pollitzer and I corresponded on and off till his death, I got no answer when I wrote to Richard after my return home.

Mr Mogabgab, though not married, showed no sign of being of the same tendency as these other friends of mine; if he had been, it would have behoved him to keep it well hidden, since he aspired to enjoy the favour of the colonial Establishment, and his position was too humble to afford him any freedom for eccentricities. I procured an invitation for him and his sister Mathilde, who kept house for him, to a drinks party at our officers' mess in Caraolos camp, and this made him very happy.

His residence consisted of two houses, one containing a drawing room, a dining room and servants' offices, the other his library and the bedrooms. The cart-track from Caraolos to Famagusta passed between the two. Heavily furnished in Victorian style, the house also contained a collection of rare wooden top-lidded chests from Greek churches. Most were in the dining-room, which had no windows and where I only entered once, when they invited me to a farewell dinner just before I left the island.

Mr Mogabgab had been presented to Princess Mary when she visited Cyprus sometime between the wars, and the glow of this meeting still lingered. One day, walking to Famagusta, and passing the north-west bastion of the Old City, I espied him atop its massive bulk in the company of two young men. He signalled to me to go up there for what, judging from his dark suit and trim panama hat, I assumed to be a special reason. When I got there, panting after a long and hurried circumambulation, he presented 'Lieutenant Hurst' to the two. They were the sons of a daughter of King Victor Emmanuel III of Italy who married a German prince and, with him, became a Nazi; both parents died in a bombing raid and now the boys, their German title of Hesse italianised to 'Assio', lived with the exiled king in Cairo. I was clearly not required to stay around but, being susceptible to the charms of blue blood, I was touched by my friend's gesture in sharing his pleasure with me.

Beneath the surface of Mr Mogabgab's courtly manners and general good humour lay some historic unappeased resentments. He was, as already mentioned, an Assistant Director of Antiquities under the colonial government, and his writ ran no further than Famagusta district. The Director, based at the Cyprus Museum in Nicosia, was A.H.S. ('Peter') Megaw, a classical archaeologist trained at the British School in Athens. It was obviously sensible that the Director of Antiquities should be a Hellenist of high credentials[*] rather than a self-taught medievalist like Mogabgab, but nonetheless Mogabgab, who was over sixty while Megaw was barely forty, felt that he had been done out of what should rightfully have been his. This straightforward disappointment had spread out into deep suspicion of all Megaw's motives. British officialdom, in its bone-headed application of the rule book, had sometimes reduced him to despair: once a newly discovered cache of Venetian weaponry – muskets with precious intaglio and so on – was taken out to sea and dropped overboard by order of the police commissioner. But he reserved his most virulent denunciations for a choice specimen: Rupert Gunnis, the secretary at Government House when the scholarly Sir Ronald Storrs was Governor of Cyprus. Storrs was a proconsul in the Curzon mould, instigating the island's splendid definitive set of postage stamps, and filling Government House with local archaeological treasures – it was not his fault that they were destroyed, along with his private collection amassed elsewhere, when the building was burnt down in the uprising of 1931, during his governorship. But Gunnis, at the end of his tour, apparently took home to England much loot to which he was not entitled and which should have entered public collections on the island. I had no means of knowing whether this was true or not, but meeting him once, a middle-aged bachelor in the company of a group of handsome undergraduates at Oxford, I understood how he would have made Mogabgab's hackles rise; he had probably been insufferably patronising to someone he could only have seen as an obscure crackpot. Another object of my friend's dislike was Polybios

---

[*] The most eminent Cypriot archaeologist was Dikaios, who had no official appointment but was engaged on the long-term excavation of a Mycenaean site a mile or two inland from Salamis, north of Famagusta. An English friend introduced me to him on the site, but another time I went alone. The place was deserted and unguarded and I saw sticking out of the side of a hole in the ground a characteristic Mycenaean pottery figure of a bull, complete and unblemished. I was terribly tempted to a steal it. If I had done, I would probably be returning it to the Cyprus Museum about now. More out of fear than virtue, I desisted. It would be nice to think that it was a fake and had been put there by Dikaios deliberately.

Georghiou, a painter who moved into a house inside the Old City of Famagusta which had an authentic Venetian façade, and built modern rooms behind it, including one that he had decorated entirely with Byzantine-type murals, like the ones in the small village churches of the Troodos foothills. This, in Mogabgab's view, was bad enough, but he was also an Enosist, of the radical-chic rather than active variety: the Byzantine paintings had more political than religious significance – this particularly incensed the ultra pro-Establishment Mogabgab. In contrast to Diamantis, Georghiou admired Pollitzer; in further contrast he was a bohemian figure who cohabited with a comfortable Viennese lady. I once called on him, using Pollitzer's name as a *laissez-passer*, and he was welcoming.

Megaw was conventionally friendly but dry and reserved; he and Mogabgab were men of totally different types. To Megaw I owe one great boon, an introduction to his erstwhile director (in Athens) and travelling companion, R.M. Dawkins (1871-1955), emeritus professor of Byzantine and Modern Greek at Oxford. But to Mogabgab I owe much more; my connection with him, warm if not close, provided me with a haven of congenial company for a whole year of my life. At our final parting he gave me his (incomplete) set of Molmenti's *History of Venice*.

Perhaps the strangest people I met in the island were a late middle-aged trio, Dr and Mrs Campion and Mrs Campion's bachelor brother Dr Shelley. All three radiated a special kind of wellbeing: they were members of a fundamentalist Christian sect. The Campions had lived for years in the Middle East – they had a faithful, long-serving Egyptian manservant – and now lived in considerable comfort in the island, with houses in both the Troodos and the northern mountains and another in Famagusta. They were a fine pair, and apart from the absence of alcohol and their remark, *en passant* as they brought out a pack of 'Happy Families' after supper, that ordinary cards were playthings of the Devil, there was nothing unusual about an evening in their company. On my first visit they took me in to see Mrs Campion's father, an incredibly ancient man, transparent and feeble, who lay in a large bed. In the distant past he had been a bank manager in Jerusalem. On another visit soon afterwards I heard that the old man had died, while they stood round his bed 'singing him to glory'. Dr Shelley, an eye specialist, lived alone in a primitive house, part of which was his surgery while another part was a canteen for servicemen. Round the walls were Biblical texts and coloured pictures of the Apocalypse. In his own spartan quarters he took a small object off a shelf and handed it to me. It was the tooth of an extinct mammal, found in a cave near the top of a 3,000-foot mountain in the Kyrenia range. He pointed out that it was embedded in sand, which salt had cemented hard, so proving that the mountain was once under the sea, and that the Biblical story of the flood was true. He also produced a photograph of a well-known prehistoric carving from central Europe, of a woman with grotesquely huge breasts. While some might have seen it as an innocent fertility symbol, to Dr Shelley it meant only one thing: that the people who could make such a thing were destined to disappear off the face of the earth because of their degeneracy. It was said that the whole family camped out for several nights on a hilltop in Palestine sometime in the 1930s, expecting to be the first witnesses of the Second Coming.

Dr Campion showed what kind of man he was by insisting, although we were little more than acquaintances, on coming to the quayside in Famagusta to see me off when my troopship left.

Late in 1949, when most of the National Servicemen who had been in my platoon when I arrived had gone home on demob, a large new batch arrived.* I interviewed them in turn and perhaps they were surprised when I asked them the number and sex of their siblings, whether both their parents were still alive, and what were their ambitions when they returned to civilian life. At last, instead of being a greenhorn, I was becoming an old hand. I always liked

---

* This was true of the National Service officers too. A new one was William J., whose father was the Chief Justice in the colony (it was in his court that Antoinette Diamantis was the clerk, though when I mentioned to him that I knew her, it was as if I had said I knew the doorman). William and I shared a room and one Sunday he offered to take me, with his parents, to lunch with a true exotic: Major-General Sir Courtenay Manifold. He lived at Kyrenia, worlds apart from the artists and queers, in a mansion from the Turkish period, enclosed in a very private garden. The house had to be large to accommodate his astonishing collection of treasures. In 1900 he had been with the British part of the expedition that put down the Boxer Bebellion, and it was generally assumed that the numerous large and precious Chinese objects he had in his house, the foremost being a bell from the Temple of Heaven, studded with gems and said to be of solid gold (I lifted it and it was heavy), had been carted out as loot. I also remember an impressive but unaesthetic screen made of tortoise-shell.

His first wife had been a sugar heiress from one of the Caribbean islands, called Josephine, who came to identify herself with the first wife of Napoleon. The house contained an equally extraordinary collection of relics of Napoleon, including a gilded throne on which he was said to have received the homage of the Italian princes in Milan. When the first Lady Manifold died, it fell to Lady J. to sort out her personal effects – and these included seven or eight hundred pairs of shoes and the same number of pairs of gloves. The dead woman's gravestone in Kyrenia's Anglican cemetery bore the single word 'Josephine'. The old man, now well on in his eighties, married his nurse, a quiet dignified lady; when I remarked to William J.'s parents afterwards that he made me think of a Chinese mandarin, they agreed – so perhaps he, like Josephine, had suffered a shift of identity.

the Lancashire soldier, but now I felt a new possessive fatherly instinct towards my little mob. Only once during my time in Cyprus were we ever on alert: in early 1950, when the Greek Orthodox Church organised a referendum on the future of the island, of which the result – since only the Greeks voted – was of course overwhelmingly in favour of Énosis. There were a few scuffles, but an unexpected result was the low turnout; the reason for this was that for the first time in many years there was snow on the ground, and the younger people found voting less fun than throwing snowballs. The army, fortunately, was not involved.

From our detachment camp outside Nicosia I took my platoon on an overnight exercise camping out high in the northern mountains – just below Buffavento castle. On the way down we stopped at the monastery of Ayios Chrysostomos, and trooped into the courtyard where I asked the monks if we could inspect the church and have some of their wine. Here we stayed for a short time before marching on to meet our transport. This must have been the only close sight of any of the island's monuments that these men ever had.*

Soon afterwards a battalion of the Oxfordshire and Buckinghamshire Light Infantry, an élite regiment with an affinity to the Green Jackets, arrived, thus doubling infantry strength in the island – a first sign of things to come. They moved into our detachment camp, which we shared with them briefly before moving off to Famagusta to rejoin our parent unit. This meant that we shared the 'Ox and Bucks' officers' mess, which was a revelation to me of how such an institution can be a friendly place without any sacrifice of 'good order and military discipline': subalterns and majors were all on first-name terms with eachother, and the C.O. was addressed not as 'Sir' but as 'Colonel' – all this in the privacy of the mess only. Our mess, by contrast, seemed obsessed with rank and bullshit; subalterns called the majors 'Sir', and when the C.O. came in, a sycophantic coterie gathered round him in a half-circle and laughed uproariously at his attempts at humour. Of our periodic 'mess nights' the best thing I can say is that the regimental band, under its gentlemanly bandmaster Mr Palmer, played well in an adjoining room; it was the year of *Bless the Bride* with its touching song 'This is my lovely day'.**

Of the older Loyals officers the one I remember most fondly

---

* Buffavento is described in Nagel's Guide as 'almost accessible'; I presume this means 'almost inaccessible', which it is. None the less, I spent the night within its walls, while the platoon ensconced itself some way below.

** One of the happier dividends of joining the Garrick Club was meeting Vivian Ellis (1904-96), the composer of this and the equally delightful 'Spread a little happiness'. As one would expect, the music matches the man.

is John Jeffery, the Captain Quartermaster, who had been commissioned in mid-career from Regimental Sergeant Major, a well-worn promotion route even today. He helped me after I handed over a large load of the regiment's cookhouse equipment to a warrant-officer in charge of a catering course being held in our detachment camp, but without obtaining a signature – the warrant-officer was twice my age and I trusted him – and at the end of the course found that some of the implements were missing. Technically I should have had a lot to pay, but John found a pan here and a ladle there to make up the losses, until in the end I only had to pay out a pound or two. I met him and all the rest (except, thank God, for Allen Patrick) once again at Dover Castle in 1970 when the Loyals amalgamated – no one could have been more surprised than I to find myself the only National Service officer present and as such an object of friendly curiosity. John was by then long retired and in charge of the Regimental Association at Preston. And 'Mr Rolfe', another of nature's gentlemen who had been our R.S.M. in 1949, had risen by the same route as John to become Major Rolfe. He was a short man of impeccable bearing who never shouted or resorted to vulgarity – a more polished version of Hitchcock. Once our Adjutant, who thought that I did not salute properly, ordered me to report to Mr Rolfe for a lesson. I did so twice, but with consummate tact he made the excuse each time that he was too busy.

Talking of 'gentlemen', with and without quotation-marks, I have to mention St John (pronounced 'Singeon') McConnell, a captain in his early thirties who had served with an Indian regiment in the war. He was a Roman Catholic with distant aristocratic connections, and had a rather fée wife called Myrtle, and no children. In spite of commanding a company and being liked by his men, he teetered on the edge of being a figure of ridicule among the other officers. Short and slight, but with a large head, prominent teeth and a straggly moustache, he spoke volubly in a lisping upper-class accent, and involuntarily snorted when he giggled, which was often. Because he had been in India, he organised the mess dinners at which curry was to be eaten, and a great fuss he made of it. He got drunk on a low intake, and in the singing, recitations and horseplay that followed dinner on mess nights, had to be watched in case he hurt himself; once he climbed on to a table, and I caught his tiny body as he fell off it. The distaste of our vigorous C.O., Colonel Robin Boyle, for him was well known, and Ian Mackie, a fellow Catholic, was incensed when St John commented one Sunday on his absence from mass. I was once detailed to sit on a court of inquiry into an alleged petty crime by one of our soldiers. It was presided over

by St John, and he did what was required with a perfect combination
of firmness and good manners, restraining me at one point when
I pursued a point over-zealously. The buffoon was forgotten, and
his true officer-quality shone out. I saw it again on another occasion.
Every afternoon, the few men in the battalion who were currently
being treated for V.D. had to parade in full kit in an inconspicuous
part of the camp and be inspected by the orderly officer. The first
time this task fell to me, I was on my way to do the inspection
with the orderly sergeant when we met St John, who advised me
to dismiss the parade as soon as we arrived; he rightly regarded
this regulation as an affront to decency. In the 1950s I bumped
into him in the West End of London, immaculately turned out, full
of bonhomie as ever, but underneath rather sad. He had left the
army and was working in insurance, Myrtle had left him, and he
lived with his aged mother and aunt in Ealing. It did not seem
a joyful prospect.

In the last minutes before leaving Caraolos camp for the docks
to board my ship home, I was called in for a farewell meeting
with Colonel Boyle. Apart from one very formal visit to his house
for mid-day drinks on a Sunday, we had seldom exchanged words
other than in a highly ritualised way. I had recently beaten all the
other officers in the battalion in a cross-country run (and all but
two of the regiment besides), and been rewarded by him saying
in the mess 'Well done Hurst, have a drink'. That was all, and
now I hoped that with our formal relationship about to end, we
would talk, even for a few moments, as man to man. At this moment
of parting I was feeling sad. But the Colonel spent the entire interview
haranguing me on how important it was for National Service officers
to continue serving in the Territorials. He got entirely carried away
– for him it was not me there at all. And of course my conscience
pricked me because I did not intend to become a Territorial. So
that was that.

The voyage home – with the beautiful island, the friends I had
made there and would mostly never see again, and my regiment
all receding behind me – was dispiriting. We didn't sail directly to
England but stopped for a few days in the army transit camp at
Port Said. My stay coincided with King Farouk's thirtieth birthday,
when flags were flown in the camp. On Sunday I narrowly missed
the only bus that would have got me to Cairo and back in one
day, so had to wait nearly forty years to see it, and spent a tedious
day by the Canal. There was a certain grandeur about the area round
the de Lesseps statue, augmented by the famed Simon Arzt emporium
with its own excellent brand of cigarettes and a book department

as good as any in the West. Back in England. I was glad not to have to spend more than one night in the camp at Aldershot from which I was discharged. Watching a Robert Donat film on my last evening in the army about northern working-class life and hearing those familiar accents again, I felt sharp withdrawal pangs.

Even then, it was not quite all over, because on the night before my departure from Cyprus I called my platoon together and offered to visit the family of any man who wished me to. Four accepted, and I duly made the visits. Two of the families were in Liverpool. The first one I called on, in a slum, consisted of the man's careworn mother and much younger sister, who was half-blind and of whom her mother kept saying 'They say this one favours [looks like] our Bill.' Bill, whom I remembered as an awkward lad with a bedwetting problem, would be 'thrilled to bits' to hear of my visit. The other Liverpool family lived in relative prosperity out in the suburbs. My batman's family in the mill town of Bolton, motherless and with numerous siblings, was poor but self-respecting and happy. 'Sid's a good lad', the father said several times of his absent son. All I could do was reassure them that their lads were OK; possibly they realised that I was doing this to reassure myself as well as them.

Muted Homecoming

Naturally I looked forward to seeing my mother again, but our reunion was a mixture of disappointment and farce. At the actual moment when the taxi brought me to the house, the only person at home was Mrs Seward, the female half of my mother's resident married couple, and we greeted eachother warmly. Her first act was to show me a copy of my father's autobiography, *A Twentieth Century Physician*, which had just been published, five years after his death. My father left it incomplete; the early part is an excellent, racy account of his contemporaries and seniors at Oxford and Guy's Hospital, with delightful personal observations, but his pioneering psychiatric work in the Great War and his work at New Lodge Clinic and with the 'Medical Pilgrims' in the 1920s and '30s, when he was at the summit of his activity and influence, was little more than sketched. The most amusing chapter, a devastating portrait of Sir Arbuthnot Lane, Bt., the fashionable surgeon whose belief in colostomy as a panacea led to many of his patients losing their colons unnecessarily, was excised at the urging of Uncle Gerald, who felt that it would give people 'the wrong idea about Arthur'. My father, though ever supportive towards his juniors, was notoriously caustic about contemporaries with whom he disagreed. So the chapter would have given the right idea about him. Clearly Edward Arnold, as the publisher of some of his earlier books, took on this not very appealing project out of loyalty and *pietas*, but my mother repaid them ill. She sat on the proofs for several years, so virtually killing the book; I cannot think why, after giving her a final warning, the firm did not assume the proofs to be passed by default and go ahead – it is a shame that in her short paragraph of acknowledgement she did not thank Mr Clare, the partner at Edward Arnold, for his forbearance. The text was printed on good paper, but the illustrations are poorly reproduced, the captions to two pages of rather good pencil portrait sketches and clay models by my father of his medical colleagues do not say that they are by him, and finally the captions of a boring page-full of medals are muddled up. This was my first experience of opening a book and feeling my spirits sink rather than rise at the look and feel of it. Mrs Seward of course thought it was marvellous.

Now my mother returned, with my sister Rosemary and Elizabeth, a friend of hers staying in the house. The two were wardrobe mistresses for the O.U.D.S. production of *Othello* showing that week. My mother was no sooner indoors and we had exchanged a perfunctory embrace than she launched into an anguished complaint against Elizabeth, whom I had never met till this moment. This was because she had been briefly mentioned in the gossip-column of the latest *Isis* (the undergraduate magazine) that could have suggested to a suspicious mind that she had been involved in some kind of flirtation at a party. My mother asserted that she was responsible to Elizabeth's parents for her safety while under our roof – which Elizabeth, who had just had her twenty-first birthday, politely denied. The situation seemed drearily familiar.

After a quick round of calls on friends who were already at the University, I went up north to discharge my promise to the four soldiers in my platoon. As a base for these forays I stayed with my father's cousin Charles Kukla,* then aged nearly eighty and still

---

* His mother was one of the three sisters of my grandfather Hertz, all of whom married in Germany. The older Kukla, a Czech born in Brno but living in Hamburg, was a musician – his son remembered Brahms coming to the house – and in middle age, after his children were grown up, left home one morning as usual to go to the Conservatorium. However he did not return and none of them ever saw him again. He turned up in South America where he became a concert pianist, as well as starting a new family. Years

managing our family business, M. Hurst & Co., in his comfortable old-fashioned house in Didsbury outside Manchester. This gave me a rare taste of luxury and good living of a kind scrupulously eschewed by my more puritanically inclined closer relations, who even carped at the fact that Charles apparently spent none of his considerable income on good works. Indeed he was an unashamed *Lebenskünstler*: in his house only the best wines and cigars were produced, and his Portuguese wife Emmy cooked exquisite meals. She was getting deaf and was anyway far from able to match his mental powers, and he would show his irritation at her slowness in grasping points in conversation. She for her part plaintively remarked that chronic sinus trouble made it impossible for her to taste the food she prepared. He took me on my only visit to the business in its antique premises in Chepstow Street South, where I was introduced to old chaps who had known my grandfather 'Mr William' and great-uncle 'Mr Fred', and shown over the warehouse, full of bales of gaudy cloth about to be exported to Africa. We also went to a cinema club to see Marcel Pagnol's *Marius*. As we got out of the car, he pointed to the number plate and said 'You see – "KNF": one of my friends says it stands for "Kukla no fool".' I drew a pencil portrait of him, which was the best I ever did, and in the euphoria afterwards said to him, on an impulse: 'Cousin Charles, would you give me a job?' His reply came back like a flash: 'Out of the question.' I said it would only be for a few months till I went to Oxford, but he repeated his refusal and there was an end to it. Even if he did not think that my presence would clog up the works, it was more than thirty years since there had been a Hurst in the business, and Charles's own son Ernest was in line for the succession; the wrong signals might be given. While I was there, Ernest took me to lunch at his club, and asked me if I would object if, when his father died, he changed his name to Hurst. I seem to remember saying that if I had a distinctive name like Kukla I would want to keep it, but of course I could not possibly object to his adopting our name. However, by the time Charles died in the mid-1960s, the business had already been defunct for ten years, and there was no name-change.

---

later one of his daughters – Mimi Weinstein, who had second sight – heard a piece of music in the ether which her father had often played – and later discovered that at that moment he had died while on the concert platform. Mimi moved with her husband before 1914 to Portugal, and her descendants still live there. As an old lady she was visiting Germany with her grandson and suddenly said that she must return home to Lisbon because she was going to die the following week. Her grandson said that she was in as good health as ever and suffering a delusion, but she returned none the less, and did die the following week.

Interlude: The Dales

The problem of how to fill the coming months was unexpectedly solved by a chance meeting one evening soon after my return at a North Oxford dance. I had been going to these little functions for the offspring of dons and local professionals since my mid-teens, dressed in my father's antediluvian dinner jacket. This one, held in a private hotel, was an amalgam of separate parties, each under the tutelage of a middle-aged lady or couple. When things were already in full swing, a man and a girl entered who immediately drew the eye, the man especially because he, alone in the room, wore full evening dress. He looked much older the rest of us, who were green youths. He was actually thirty, over six foot tall, nearly bald and wearing the pebble glasses of the very myopic; he had a large mask-like face over which a look of faint amusement hovered. His smile, when it appeared, was warm and frank, and his hearty, clear laugh had the same quality. He spoke loud and with a plummy accent. He certainly was not conventionally good-looking, but he was not unattractive either, as I could see from the behaviour of his companion.

It turned out that he was an architect called Simon Dale. I could immediately place him – as the son of Lawrence Dale, also an architect and the author of *Towards a Plan for Oxford City* (Faber, 1944), in which a road across Christ Church Meadow was mooted as a way of relieving the traffic congestion in 'the High' that was slowly ruining its magnificent buildings. My mother gave me a copy of the book. Simon and I soon got talking, and I said I was thinking of studying architecture (although this was true, the idea had shallow roots). He at once generously offered to ask his father if he would agree to my working in his office – unpaid, but also not paying a fee – doing odd jobs like holding a tape-measure out on sites and even making a few simple drawings Simon explained that he and his father were in partnership, sharing the office and its facilities but working independently, each with his own clients and jobs. Lawrence Dale was the official architect to the diocese of Oxford, and two local parish churches had recently been built to his designs – robust-looking and rooted in the arts and crafts tradition. Most of his diocesan work consisted of small additions and alterations to existing churches;

my first task was designing a collection plate. His work for private clients was all small beer.

I presented myself a day or two later at Lawrence Dale's office on the attic floor of Lloyd's Bank Chambers at Carfax. The scene there would have made a good subject for a painting by Sickert. With its sloping ceiling and irregular shape it had a cramped air. Drawing-boards filled the window bays, and at one end was the desk where Lawrence always sat, mostly ruminating and giving instructions to Bernard, his assistant. With frayed brown linoleum on the floor, it had no hint of smartness or modernity. Everywhere the neo-Georgian style was in evidence. Much of the space on the inside wall was taken up by two large and finely executed colour-washed measured drawings – external and internal elevations – of Lawrence's masterpiece: his design for the Masonic headquarters in Great Queen Street, for which a competition was held in the 1920s. Lawrence won the second prize of £500, but by failing to win the competition forfeited the chance to leave a substantial artistic legacy, or to move out of his allotted sphere as a minor provincial architect. Anyone comparing the building which actually materialised, and stands for all (too plainly) to see in Great Queen Street, with Lawrence's design would have to wonder how he failed to win the first prize. Possibly the winning design's echoes of ancient Egypt appealed to the Masons more than Lawrence's Lutyensian classicism – good-mannered but rising grandly to the occasion – but, according to Simon, his father always believed that the competition result was arrived at by graft. He was thus an acutely disappointed man. Also on the wall were a photograph of a quite large, textbook neo-Georgian house he built for a wealthy client between the wars, and a head-and-shoulders oil portrait by Peter Greenham of his elder daughter Angela, painted just before she joined a closed order of nuns. Lawrence was a skilled watercolourist, and also on that wall were some examples of landscapes by him in this medium. Simon had no such talent.

In both personality and appearance father and son were utterly different. Lawrence, in his late sixties, was short and florid-faced with jutting features reminiscent of Mr Punch and a ring of wavy white hair around a shiny pink patch. He invariably wore an old tweed suit and a bow-tie, and was seldom without a pipe clamped between his teeth; he had a way of droning as he lit or puffed on it. He had a wonderful laugh – almost silent, his face turning puce and breaking into a thousand wrinkles, and punctuated by groans and gurgles. His laughter tended to be directed, with half-charitable mockery, at the follies of mankind. Had he been more successful, he might have given his strain of bohemianism fuller rein and been another Munnings or Albert Richardson. But he also stood for old-fashioned virtues like hard work and responsibility.

The office staff consisted of a young trainee surveyor, Bernard, and a part-time secretary, Mary Heptonstall, whom Lawrence addressed as 'Mrs H'. Bernard, who spoke with the Oxfordshire burr, was Lawrence's right-hand man and called him 'sir'. 'Mr Simon', he told me, was building up a practice with the county families, which was why he spent so much time out and about, while 'the old man' concentrated on his diocesan and local private work. The total income of Lawrence's practice was about £2,000 a year. Simon's aim of reaching beyond the enclosed society of Oxford burghers and clerics was understandable as a means of escaping from his father's shadow, but it was also in character in a different way. While Lawrence spoke accentless English, muffled and distorted only by his ill-fitting dentures and his pipe, Simon had the kind of upper-class drawl and clipped vowels I had become used to hearing and almost capable of copying at Eton. Yet he had not been at Eton or in the Guards, but at a 'minor public school', St Bees, and in the Royal Engineers (allegedly passing the compulsory eye-test by slipping into the examination room beforehand and memorising the rows of letters on the test sheet). He also affected cavalry twill pants and well-cut tweed hacking jackets. When he came sauntering into the office, probably adopting an exaggerated dandyism and languid air for the occasion, there was a hint of electricity in the air.

I got on well with both of them, and made occasional forays outside with one or the other. Lawrence was invited by his old friend Vincent Harris, architect of the massive neo-classical stone-clad Ministry of Defence building between Whilehall and the Embankment (then half-finished and just the kind of job Lawrence himself might have masterminded if he had been luckier) to visit the site, and took me with him. There we saw the grand office soon to be occupied by the Secretary of State, with a huge black marble fireplace; and, somewhere deep below ground, a red-brick vaulted chamber of Tudor date, saved from destruction at the express bidding of Queen Mary. Another time I accompanied Simon to Cambridge and back on some forgotten errand in his old Lagonda tourer. Obviously it was more fun being with him, but I felt uncomfortably conscious of his sexual frustration. He scoffed that Bernard, as soon as he passed his surveyor's exams, would marry and tie himself down to the same kind of life he was living now as an only child living in dingy respectability outside Oxford with his widowed mother. Mary, the part-time secretary, whose husband was a North Country undergraduate of mature age and notorious infidelity, told me when we were alone in the office

that Simon had once laid a hot hand on her shoulder. She declined
the implied proposition. She liked him, was amused by Bernard,
and disliked the old man, whom she thought malevolent.

Once, in his capacity as my master, Lawrence sent me out to
make a measured drawing of the Jacobean gateway in the blank
wall at the back of Christ Church, facing Oriel Square (in the great
wave of Oxford restorations, this little landmark has escaped attention
and is now badly eroded). I climbed a ladder and did my measuring
oblivious of all around me. At one point I looked down and saw
a man I had known slightly at Eton passing by. It was the old
syndrome of whether to show recognition or not; he looked at me
but we did not acknowledge eachother.

Towards the end of the summer I left the Dales and went on
a long trip to southern Italy and Sicily. After a year or two, Simon
Dale moved to London and joined the fashionable but distinctly unmodern
practice of (the Hon.) Claud Phillimore, which specialised in country
houses, as an assistant architect. He now shared a flat in Finsbury
with his sister Alison, and we met from time to time for a drink.
He was much given – like his father, but with a sardonic edge –
to an epigrammatic form of utterance. One of his observations which
had a prophetic twist was that Catholics were more interested in
being Catholic than in being Christian.

I also kept up with Lawrence after leaving the University. By
this time Bernard had qualified and moved on, and the old man,
now a widower, had given up his office at Carfax and lived in
a flat in North Oxford where he continued to do odd bits of work.
I tried to persuade my mother to commission him to build a house
on the land at the end of her garden, which was more than big
enough and had become overgrown and impenetrable. Drawings were
made, and planning permission was obtained, but nothing materialised.
Early in 1955 I was looking for a job, and while on a visit to
Oxford went to see him – not to ask for help but to pass the time.
He offered to house me, my wife Suzanne and my son, then not
quite a year old, and to pay me £500 a year if I would be his
assistant. He was convinced I had the necessary understanding of
architecture, even without any training (he had never attended an
architecture school himself but been apprenticed), and that I could
revive his practice. When I expressed doubts he suggested that I
take up architectural journalism instead. This sounded like a good
idea, and he agreed to write to his friend John Betjeman on my
behalf. Betjeman wrote to Hubert de Cronin Hastings, co-proprietor
and co-editor of the *Architectural Review*, and I was duly hired.
Lawrence wrote, in reply to my letter of thanks, that he deplored

the modernistic style of the *AR*, but that I could change it once I had become established to something more conservative.

On my last.visit to him, in 1959, I asked after Simon. 'Simon has married into the landed gentry,' Lawrence pronounced, 'name of Wilberforce.' The interesting reflection that Simon seemed well on the way to realising his social ambitions, with which his professional ones were so closely bound up, was quite overlaid by astonishment that his wife Susan, whom I had never met, was the sister of my old friend John Wilberforce, now a rising diplomat. When Lawrence died a year later, I wrote to Simon telling him of my fondness for the old man, and he invited me to visit him and Susan at their flat in the Old Brompton Road. I duly went, and it was clear that Simon's life had gone through a revolutionary change for the better. The flat was light and full of pleasant things, and the bachelorish frowstiness that had surrounded him before was gone. Susan was young, fresh and attractive in the centaur-like way of some well-bred young Englishwomen, and Simon was relaxed and happy; their baby Alexander lay in a carry-cot on the floor. They were unmistakably in love. A framed photograph of brother John stood on a shelf, mitigating the impression, which they tactfully conveyed, that the marriage had caused a rift in her family. On the wall was an impressive reminder of Susan's inheritance: a finished full-length drawing of William Pitt the Younger by Gainsborough.

They showed me photographs of a decayed seventeenth-century brick-built mansion in Herefordshire which they were thinking of buying for a song – ostensibly to save it from demolition. They had plans to do it up and then live there, while Simon established a local practice which of course would be mainly concerned with restoring similar houses. If they had merely been thinking of restoring this house while remaining based and practising in London, it would have seemed like an exciting venture. But when they spoke with bright-eyed enthusiasm and complete seriousness of abandoning everything for this not very inspiring decayed heap of bricks and mortar, I felt alarmed. Maybe Susan had enough money for the venture, but such places were capable of swallowing up fortunes – and for what? Would they take on a life-style commensurate with the house? Simon, infatuated with Susan and with her grand background, and never a great realist, was seeing his Shangri-la come into view.

Susan, aristocratically born and bred in a large country house, subjected to a strict Roman Catholic upbringing and squired by blue-blooded young men, evidently found release in Simon Dale's more easygoing style. He was intelligent, and finding at long last an attractive and much younger woman to love him and even reject her whole past for his sake, the tenderness and kindness which undoubtedly lay concealed under his affectations would have flowed forth after being dammed up for so long. His former rather silly social pretensions might have subsided with the upper-class girl he had dreamed about now actually present in the flesh, but the snag was that he could never fit in comfortably with the sort of people among whom she had always lived – the incompatibility being personified in her brother John, with whom Simon probably shared not a single interest or mental attitude. The marriage had to work. If only they had settled for what they had and stayed put! But the house in Herefordshire beckoned and became their *folie à deux*, the curse implanted so soon after their rapturous union.

After this one meeting I never saw Susan again, and only met Simon after a lapse of about twenty years. I was surprised to see some years later that Heath House, Leintwardine – owner Simon Dale, Esq. – was listed in the supplement to the handbook *Houses and Castles open to the Public*, among the places not regularly open but which can be visited by appointment. For me it was a matter of waiting for a time when I would be in or near that remote part of the country. I also once looked up the Wilberforce entry in *Burke's Landed Gentry*, and found that Susan and Simon had had four sons and a daughter in quick succession; the first names of the second and third sons were Ilgerus and Xenophon. Eventually, in 1978, my wife Rachel and I were in the Border region and I phoned from a call-box. Simon answered with his unmistable drawl. I asked if he and Susan would mind if we called; he replied that they had been divorced for some time and added for good measure that he was now nearly blind. But we would be welcome, and so we went. We parked in an unkempt area at the back of the house, facing the Jacobean portion which I recognised from the photograph they showed me years before. Simon was waiting for us, peering out from one of the windows on the other, classical side. He was as jovial as I ever remembered him, and led us into the kitchen and made tea. He then took me on a tour of the house. It was basically a rectangular building of the Wren period, but with a Jacobean central staircase. Upstairs were rooms which still contained children's furniture and toys, but were now abandoned, *Marie Celeste* fashion. Only one room was completely furnished. He could not have shown the house to anyone who spotted it in the *Handbook* without a lot of explaining.

What had happened, he told us with his usual lapidary understatement and no apparent bitterness, was that his eyesight had 'packed up' a few years before, forcing him to give up his work and thus his only source of income. Most of Susan's money was by then spent, with the house only half restored, and in a panic she decamped, taking all the children with her. They stayed briefly with John Wilberforce in Yorkshire before moving to a cottage not far from Heath House. The screw was given a further turn when she changed the family name of herself and the children from Dale to Wilberforce, and returned to the Catholic faith from which she lapsed on her marriage. With my age-old link to Simon and his father, I found the change of name painful, and have sought in vain for an explanation of why, as adults, none of the children wanted to change back to their true family surname. Simon told us that Susan now desperately wanted him out of the house so that she could sell it, but he was already destitute and if he left he would be on the streets. I could only sympathise with him. He told us further that he had made some interesting archaeological discoveries about the site on which the house was built, and this was another reason why he did not want to leave. He had written copiously about it – somehow the ancient Armenians were involved – and showed me a pile of typescript. Here was a curious echo of his father, who left a great hoard of unpublished and unpublishable mystical writings.

Rachel and I felt oppressed by what we heard and saw, and talked several times about Simon's predicament. Soon after our visit I had a typed letter from him saying that he wanted to patent a design for a small house in the neo-Georgian style, to sell to developers: with my appreciation of good architecture, would I be interested in joining him in this project? With Mrs Thatcher's revolution soon to break, it might have been a good idea, but I answered that all my energy was now devoted to publishing. Gradually the immediacy of it all faded. Then one day in 1989 I read in the paper that a certain Baroness de Stempel had been arrested and charged with the murder of her divorced husband. The item attracted my attention because there was a photograph of Michael de Stempel whom I once met in the company of John Wilberforce when we were all undergraduates at Oxford. So had he been murdered? As I idly read the story, it became clear that the Baroness was the erstwhile Susan Dale, née Wilberforce, and the murdered man was Simon Dale. I had missed the news of his death more than a year before in the autumn of 1987.

Susan was tried for the crime, put up a spirited defence, and was acquitted, but she was found guilty at a second trial of defrauding her aged aunt Lady Illingworth of a great deal of property, and sent to prison along with de Stempel and two of her children. After the acquittal I wrote to John Wilberforce, trying to convey some fellow-feeling over the horrors he and his family had suffered. We had met once since Oxford – some time after my one visit to Simon in Herefordshire – and, cordial as the occasion was, I carefully did not say that I knew Simon. But I now told him of my long friendship with Simon and his father, and fondness for them, and of how happy Simon and Susan were the one time I saw them together. John replied that, just as I only met Susan once, he only met Simon once – also in the Old Brompton Road flat. This was an imperfect analogy; whereas the first of these two facts was natural, the second was not. In 1978 Simon, without a hint of malice, made it clear that he and John had never had more than a frigid business relationship, with letters beginning 'Dear Dale' and 'Dear Wilberforce'. If John feared from the start for a bad outcome to the marriage, he was proved right, and the financial and emotional burden on him over the years must have been appalling.

John passed my letter to (Ilgerus) Sebastian, the one of the five children who returned to live with Simon soon after the mass exodus and was closest to him, and an unexpected consequence of this was that when a memorial service was held for Simon in the church at Hopton Castle, a mile or so from Heath House, in the summer of 1990, the vicar phoned me beforehand and asked if I would read the second lesson from St John's Gospel. Sebastian gave an affectionate address. Alison Dale, Simon's sister, was there and so too were some posh cousins of Susan's. It was somewhat horrifying that the guests were entertained after the service in Heath House, and we all had to enter through the kitchen door which had admitted the murderer, and over the very spot where Simon was battered to death. At the time of writing nobody has been able to identify the killer.*

To Where the Lemons Grow

I set off on my summer trip to Italy in August 1950 with a rucksack and very little money, hitching a lift to London from the Headington roundabout. The man driving the car must have asked me what I

---

* Two books were published on the case in 1991: *The Trials of the Baroness* by Terry Kirby (Mandarin) and *Blood Money* by Kate Wharton (Headline). I was interviewed by Terry Kirby.

was going to do in life, because we talked for a while about architecture: and I must have praised high-rise apartment blocks – all the ground they save for recreational space, and the Corbusian idea of 'unity' – because he stolidly but kindly remarked that an Englishman's home, i.e. small house, is his castle. (I now live in a small suburban house.)

Once across the Channel, I travelled by train in the cheapest class, spending all night in the corridor, and watching enviously as an Italian family, all seated in the nearest compartment, tucked into their salami rolls, grapes and red wine out of a cheap suitcase open on their laps. The man spoke with extreme volubility, and the truly wonderful thing was how, with the meal finished, the torrent of speech dried up almost within seconds and he fell asleep. In the early morning, as we passed through a deep, dark Alpine valley, a French girl student could not stop exclaiming to her friends *'Formidable!'*, but I looked in her face vainly for any sign of enjoyment. I stopped for the night in Pisa and saw on a news-stand that our Princess Anne had been born. I didn't stop in Rome because this was to be a trip to the south, but spent one or two days in Naples, visiting Pompeii and Herculaneum. On the local bus I caught in my glasses the reflection of something moving behind me, and turned round to see a solitary unshaven man in the back seat conversing silently with himself and emphasising his points with wide-sweeping gestures. In Pompeii itself I fell into the company of a short, chubby, ugly and friendly American college lecturer who soon revealed that he was homosexual and regularly had intercourse with his former lovers who had married; for good measure he said that the film star Tyrone Power was of the fraternity.

I took the train south, got out in the middle of the hot afternoon at Paestum, and walked to the temples. As I wandered about the site, a neatly dressed young man with an intelligent face, coming towards me, raised his straw hat and asked if I spoke English, but it soon transpired that he could not do so very well and we dropped into French. This was a twenty-three-year-old German called Harald Vocke. He too planned to catch the next train south, so with an hour or two to spare we went and had a swim in the warm sea from the deserted beach. Whereas I was at the start of my journey, he had already been in Italy for several weeks and stopped to learn Italian in Florence which he already spoke with some facility. He planned to spend less time in Sicily than I did, but we decided to travel together for as long as it suited us. Both of us had come to Italy with the intention of calling on an eminent writer of our own nationality. I carried a letter of introduction from Professor Dawkins in Oxford to Norman Douglas, and would present it in Capri on my way home. Harald had already met Hermann Hesse, arriving at his villa in southern Switzerland unannounced.

We reached Messina early the next morning and took the train along the north coast to Cefalù. In Cyprus I had borrowed from Mr Mogabgab Otto Demus's *Byzantine Mosaic Decoration* (Kegan Paul, 1947), and with this inspiration visited all the great sites, among which Cefalù and Palermo ranked high. My need to see every mosaic and closely examine the Romanesque capitals in the cloister of Monreale cathedral amused Harald, who said that I was like Don Quixote to his Sancho Panza, and had more enthusiasm for my hobby than he had for his *métier*, papyrology, which he was studying as a postgraduate at the Sorbonne. Despite his fresh and youthful appearance he had been conscripted into the Wehrmacht shortly before the end of the war, and spent some time as a prisoner in Russia.

We travelled together as far as Segesta, where the unfinished but – as far as it went – complete Doric temple stands on a rocky outcrop with a cliff behind it. As we looked at it from a distance, with it standing directly between us and the blazing sun, all shadows on the temple became invisible and it seemed to disappear as if merged into the cliff – it was built of the same stone. Before Harald left to catch a train to Agrigento, we picked and ate some half-ripe plums in an orchard. Later that day I was attacked by a sharp stomach pain, and by the time I reached Trapani on the far west coast, where I had intended to stay for one night at the most, was bent double. The next day I could not move from my cheap hotel room, desperately hoping that I would not have to visit a doctor. Fortunately I recovered quickly.

The bandit Giuliano had been killed by police at Castelvetrano, also in the west of Sicily, only a few weeks before, and Harald had detected among the uneducated Sicilians we met an equivocal attitude towards him: Giuliano was not such a bad man – he had only ever killed policemen, which showed that he was on the side of the common people. More unexpected was the belief, which cropped up in several conversations, that Hitler was still alive.

I met Harald twice again in our student days – first in Paris, where he lived in a waterless garret in the early 17th-century Place Dauphine on the Île de la Cité, and then on my first visit to Germany when I stayed at his parents' apartment in Frankfurt. His father was an eminent central banker and a *Geheimrat* of the empire, and the family's ethos, profoundly anti-Hitlerian, was that of the Berlin professional grande bourgeoisie, the same cultured and humane stratum that produced Dietrich Bonhoeffer and other 20 July (1944) plotters. Soon after this visit I heard from Harald that, while in Egypt working on his papyri, he started to study Arabic – '*eine passionerend interessante Sprache*', he called it – and this determined his later career. After some years in the Federal German diplomatic service, he became Middle East correspondent of the *Frankfurter Allgemeine Zeitung*. In the mid-1970s I was walking along one of the aisles at the Frankfurt Book Fair and saw coming towards me a portly man with a shock of grey hair, under which were the unmistakable quizzical features of Harald Vocke. I had not seen him for over twenty years – by now his English was fluent. We immediately agreed to lunch together the next day, and have met from time to time ever since.

Having fully recovered from my indigestion, I climbed the mountain of Erice behind Trapani and from that high point the view stretched far away to the west. From shore level an island could be seen a few miles out – this was part of the Egadi group – but from higher up it was possible to discern, much further off and directly behind the first island, another which seemed to consist mainly of mountainous cliffs. I immediately decided to go there, come what might, and hurried back into the town. It was Sunday morning, and a boat was leaving within the next hour – there were daily trips to the nearer island, but the boat only visited the far one, Marettimo, twice a week, including today.

On the boat everyone seemed to know everyone else, and I got talking with a middle-aged schoolmaster from Ferrara who spoke French. He had been born in Marettimo and was now returning to visit his aged mother. He told me that his father, as a boy, had acted as guide and servant to Samuel Butler, who went there while writing his strange book *The Authoress of the Odyssey* (1897), which argued that Nausicaa, not Homer, had written the epic and that Marettimo was Ithaca. The schoolmaster was in no doubt that I was the first Englishman to visit Marettimo since Butler – a few American soldiers passed through at the end of the war, but they didn't count.

The place was wild and barren. There was a single community which lived on the side facing the mainland – precipitous as this side of the island was, the far side was almost a sheer drop to the sea from a height of around 1,000 metres. There was a small irregular-shaped piazza, filled with drying nets. There was no resident priest; but one was supposed to come over from Trapani with the Sunday boat and return after saying mass, but he did not come this Sunday. A big friendly-looking policeman, who despite his size reminded me of the diminutive American comic Lou Costello, met the boat and gave us all a look-over: Marettimo was one of the last fragments of Italian territory before North Africa and a favourite jumping-off point for fugitives from justice. The schoolmaster told the policeman that I was harmless. He also escorted me to the *albergo*, where the tariff was 150 lire a night – a little over one shilling and sixpence – which suited my budget. It was a friendly place, run by a young couple with a baby called Giuseppe whom the mother continually petted and called by every possible diminutive – Pipo, Pupo, Peppino, Peppuccio. There was an emaciated old granny who spat on the floor behind the counter.

Upstairs the bedrooms were in a row without a passage, each one leading into the next; I was put in the last, and in the penultimate one was a skipper whose continuous snores were unbelievably loud. Here and there was an electric socket and a wire cut off an inch or two from the wall: there had once been electricity on the island, but supplying it proved unprofitable for the power company, and so it was withdrawn.

On the afternoon of my arrival I went down to the harbour to swim from the jetty, and my arms were raised for a dive when a hand touched my shoulder. There, accompanied by the nice policeman I had seen before, was another – a rat-faced fellow, unmistakably the senior of the two. He was unshaven and had the collar of his tunic unbuttoned and his cap pushed back – and his breath smelt of booze. With no attempt at courtesy he said the one word '*interrogazione*'. That, at least, I understood. He was the *maresciallo,* the local chief of police – his rank equivalent to sergeant-major.

When I had dressed we went to my room where the *maresciallo* asked to inspect my rucksack. Now my heart sank, because I remembered that among the few possessions I brought over from Trapani was a rusty Arab dagger obtained in Egypt by Uncle Gerald in the Great War. I carried it as a kind of mascot, but could not even attempt to explain this across the insurmountable language barrier. As he took the dagger out of the bag and held it up, triumph lit up the *maresciallo*'s face. A routine piece of officiousness had turned into a genuine police matter. He pocketed my passport and said that I would hear from him when he wanted to see me again. This interview took place the next day in his office, and he told me that I could not leave until instructions were received from the mainland. It was clear that the mid-week boat to Trapani would go without me, and with the prospect of spending a whole week there, Marettimo lost some of its charm. Also my inability to counter the *maresciallo*'s hectoring in any way made me begin to feel rather sorry for myself, as well as cursing my stupidity.

When the schoolmaster heard about my plight he shrugged his

shoulders. It was unfortunate, but I should make allowances for the *maresciallo*, who had spent most of the war as a prisoner of the British in East Africa; also, his wife had gone off with another man. I could be sure that the matter would soon be solved. My days were passed swimming in the clear, warm water or hiking up and down the mountain or along the coast, and each evening I went to the same old woman for a generous bowl of *pastina in brodo* and chunks of rough bread (it was all I could get to eat during the entire day). *'Buono'*, she would say, putting one finger to her cheek and turning it – a Sicilian gesture of approval. Setting forth from her house afterwards in the dark, one saw blobs of light out at sea – the local fishing boats carried powerful lamps in the stern which shone down into the depths.

On Saturday evening I spent some time with the schoolmaster, sitting in the roadway outside his house. By previous arrangement the *maresciallo*, now well shaven, came and handed me a long typewritten document. If I would sign it he would return my passport. The schoolmaster translated the essential parts: it was an elaborate statement of my lack of criminal intention, and a promise to abide by the laws of Italy henceforward. The final sentence stated that my treatment by the Italian police had been exemplary. I made a flowery signature. The *maresciallo*, with many cringing gestures to my host and a handshake for me, withdrew.

The next day, on my way to the jetty to catch the boat, I passed two uniformed figures coming the other way. One was the *maresciallo* who, though now smartly turned out, looked strangely diminished beside the other, his chief from Trapani. I was told that the chief had not been pleased to hear about our little drama. The priest once again did not turn up. I found 'Lou Costello' on the dockside, and as I was about to board the boat, he held out his hand and said *'Buon viaggio'*. As I grasped it, struggling in vain to think of an appropriate Italian word in the second I had to respond, I let out the same words *'Buon viaggio'* instead of *'Grazie – arrivederci'*, and he turned about in despair and sauntered off.

This last sorry incident in my Marettimo adventure came back to me about thirty-five years later at a tourist hotel in Morocco. There, in the breakfast room, set apart from the main buffet, was a little stove on which a solemn, noble-looking Berber fried eggs on demand for those who wanted them. One day I used his services and as we trooped out at the end of breakfast gave him a perfunctory farewell smile. In return he said *'Bon appetit'*.

Much has been written about Norman Douglas, and there is no need here for a *tour de force* on the famous old rascal. As has often been remarked, he had a noble head, still unbowed in 1950 by his eighty-two years, and thick yellowy-white hair parted in the centre. At Eton my history tutor G.B. Smith advised us to read *South Wind*, but a much stronger recommendation came from that discerning guide Richard W. in Cyprus (it was he who told me about Paestum); he regarded Douglas's scholarly travel books, in particular *Old Calabria*, as in a class of their own. Richard claimed to have won the old man's friendship, and he possessed copies of many of his works, each with an affectionate personal inscription on the flyleaf. When I mentioned Richard to one of the gang at the villa where Douglas lived, I got the unmistakable impression that he pushed his way in and appeared a shameless crawler; also that grand queers dislike being confronted with a queer of a different sort, socially a nobody, with only their queerness as a bond – those who were beddable could be common, but that was not the same thing. With Douglas, that prince of pederasts, Richard presumably made a strong suit of his pederasty, especially as he found the boys of the Neapolitan region so much to his liking. The old man had a hard core of decency, not to say nobility, and was far above any petty snobbery. In the 1890s he was a diplomat, well connected and well married, with two sons, but for decades now he had been an impoverished exile, often in trouble with the police. Now he was fortunate enough to be passing his last days as the guest of Kenneth Macpherson who, thanks to a long-defunct marriage, lived off a slice of the Ellerman shipping fortune. It was entirely credible that after all his own vicissitudes Douglas felt genuine compassion for poor Richard, a much younger exile, and valued him at his true worth.

On the evening when I was bidden to the villa, having handed in Dawkins's letter in the morning, the company sitting on the terrace consisted of the expansive Macpherson, Islay Lyons his agreeable young male companion, David Jeffries who was on his way to Athens to tutor Crown Prince Constantine (he was a vigorous man, and it was he who spoke with bile about Richard), a rich Australian Mick Sandford and his young man (a German), and the daughter of a renowned former mayor of Capri, obviously much in favour with them all. Baron Schack, elderly, courtly and completely bald, presented himself late in the evening; he had 'lived abroad' ever since the great homosexual scandal in the upper reaches of official society in Wilhelmine Germany.

Douglas said little, and made only occasional interjections which, though sardonic in tone, were never small-minded or bitchy – the prevailing tone of those around him. Even when he made a meaningful grunt, everyone laughed. Scruffy and lacking in social poise, I felt pretty much out of it. When someone inquired about my travels, I mentioned that in Trapani I had seen a beauty contest, with the winner declared 'Miss Nestlé'. Douglas at once inquired if she was the girl with the biggest breasts – a fine point I had overlooked.

When the time came to leave, Douglas invited me to meet the party again in the piazza the next evening for drinks, and said that in the mean time I should visit a cave containing a Roman shrine, in a remote part of the island off the tourist track. Macpherson's boyfriend showed kindness in asking about my immediate travel plans, and suggested that I visit Venice ˙on the way home. I thought this a good idea. I broke the journey north at Ravenna and from Venice took a *vaporetto* to Torcello, thus making further additions to my Byzantine mosaic repertoire. I stayed for an extraordinarily low price in a small palazzo on the Giudecca, Casa Frollo, where Dawkins later told me he had stayed around 1910 when he knew 'Baron Corvo'. The gentle, cultivated proprietress, last of the Frollos, wore clothes that were literally torn.

A Not Quite Fresh Freshman

Going up to Oxford as an undergraduate should be a moment of elation, and if one has only been to this majestic city for the entrance exam and just left school, it can hardly be anything else. But I knew Oxford in all its dreariest aspects, starting with my own parental home, and in the three years since leaving school had got out of the habit of deferring to tutors and college hierarchs. I was not academically promising. Having got in by passing exams in history, I decided during the summer to switch to English – probably a good choice, because the main syllabus at Eton contained no English whatever. The classics masters there prescribed English 'saying lessons' – poems to memorise – but these were more a recurring penance than an introduction to the beauties, let alone the joys, of literature. The books I had to read as 'holiday tasks' (a chilling phrase) at different times were *Kim* and *Julius Caesar*, and our Shakespeare play for Schools Certificate was *The Tempest*, for which there was no preliminary class work. The experience of reading Shakespeare can be enhanced, or at least not diminished, if the edition is pleasant to handle and the type attractive; these school texts were puny and unappealing. *Julius Caesar* only came alive for me when I saw Gielgud playing

Cassius in the film, and *The Tempest* likewise in a Stratford production I saw as an undergraduate.

I had my rooms not inside the College (Lincoln has both a medieval and a Jacobean quadrangle) but in a characterless annexe on the opposite side of Turl Street; my room looked out on to the roof of the covered market, a place infested with rats. My 'scout' (bed-maker) was an unsavoury little woman, ever with a fag between her lips at the end of which hung a great length of ash before it fell off on to the carpet; the fag-ends she was apt to drop between the window sashes. Her blonde daughter sometimes accompanied her – not to help, I suspected the first time I saw her, but to case the joint. Before the end of my first term Mrs K. was sacked for stealing, and the daughter had the nerve to come round begging for a donation because her mother had 'had a bit of bad luck'. Indeed I don't remember any of the College's domestic staff with whom I had any dealings, from the steward (who also had a fag-end perpetually attached to his lower lip) to the porters, who did not seem in some way menacing and corrupt. It was quite a change from Eton.

The Rector of the College was Keith Murray (1903-93), much lauded by Uncle Gerald, a loyal senior member, as a coming man – young (for a head of house) and forward-looking. The son of a Scottish judge, he was an agricultural economist with a powerful bent for administration, who became College bursar in his thirties, and then Rector as well as bursar when barely forty. On the surface, there was nothing donnish about him. He wore a tweed jacket, flannels and pullover like an undergraduate, and had a round, fresh-complexioned face over which played a remote half-smile, and a full head of wavy brown hair. He spoke softly with a hint of a Scots intonation. He could not have been Chairman of the University Grants Committee (where he moved after Lincoln) and held numerous other public posts, temporary and permanent, if he had not had an effective mind, albeit a narrow one, and able to dedicate himself to the task in hand. He was one of the great apparatchiks of his day. Yet he was surely deficient as a head of house because he never played the part of a father to his flock. Being a bachelor need not have stopped him from showing some desire to get to know us individually by, say, asking small groups of us to eat, drink or merely sip Nescafe with him in his Lodgings. What made this apparent personal aloofness worse was that he had a few favourites among the undergraduates, one of whom, a great athletic star, had a room in the Lodgings. There were rumours that he was a practising homosexual, though very much a 'closet' one, and I have recently heard evidence of this from what I believe to be an unimpeachable source.

A few years later, visiting Oxford to seek material for a feature I was writing for the *Architectural Review*, I called on his successor Walter Oakeshott who, sadly for me, took office as Rector of Lincoln the term after I went down. This former headmaster of Winchester, whom I already revered as the discoverer of a manuscript of Malory's *Morte d'Arthur* in the College Library there, was warm, scholarly, sincere, exactly the right person to encourage and when necessary console undergraduates – yet Murray, the technocrat, the fresh-faced master of deception, will be remembered in the College annals as the great man of his time. When Oakeshott wrote to me after our meeting, he began the letter 'Dear Hurst' as to an equal; Murray always used the formal 'Mister'.

The first time I spoke with Murray, except to say 'goodmorning' in the quad, was at the beginning of my third year; it was about my tutorial arrangements. I sought the meeting because I was dissatisfied with the idle habits of my tutor W.W. Robson, a College Fellow who, like Murray, enjoyed a great reputation among people who never had close dealings with him. His pupils often had to put up with him either postponing tutorials or cutting them altogether. To us it was a joke that he had a reputation as a lady's man, for we had seldom seen anyone so unprepossessing; he looked unwashed and as if he had just been in bed wearing all his clothes. His tutorials were opinionated monologues – modest *tours de force*, because he had a gift for quoting long passages by heart and these were from good rather than merely 'interesting' poems, but when you dipped into the writings of F.R. Leavis you saw, sometimes word for word (his good memory again), where it all came from. With sublime hubris he took every opportunity to traduce the great polymath and most attractive of lecturers, C.S. Lewis, beside whom he was a midget. The last straw came when he said he could not tutor me on Coleridge because he was not sufficiently well versed in the subject. So I told Murray I didn't feel I was getting adequate tuition and asked to be transferred permanently to another tutor, Dennis Burden, an impoverished freelance from the north who did some stringing for Robson. Murray made no comment but with diabolical wisdom said I should go and say to Robson's face what I had said to him. This was hard, but emboldened by this oblique encouragement I went directly and did it. Robson seemed mildly shocked, which almost made me feel sorry for him, but I got my transfer.

Then, one Sunday morning during the next vacation (the last before my finals), I opened the review page in the *Observer* and there, staring me in the face, was a review by Robson of a new book by a fellow member of the Oxford English department, Humphrey

House – on Coleridge. This was another last straw. I wrote Robson a short letter pointing out that he was prepared to do for money what he was not prepared to do because it was his duty. A few days later Murray summoned me to an interview. I went, and as usual he spoke quietly and with no sign of emotion or animation. He said the consensus among the College Fellows was that I should be sent down, despite my family's connection with the College, but he disagreed with them, feeling I should be given a chance to make amends. This meant writing another letter to Robson withdrawing the earlier one; if I did that, all would be forgiven. At first I protested that what I had written was true, but he patiently pointed out that the Fellows were not obliged to take pupils – to my continuing astonishment, because Robson was clearly not averse to taking them, and the College received our tutorial fees. When I showed this momentary sign of anger, he said he had not realised I had this in me, and had recently written a favourable report on me to the University Appointments Board (on what this was based I cannot imagine because he knew nothing of me personally, good or bad). If I refused to withdraw my letter, he said, I still would not be sent down; I could take my finals, but would not be allowed to enter the College or enjoy, then or later, any of the privileges of membership. Fortunately I saw that we were both engaged in a *pas de deux*, and having said I would go away and think about it, immediately wrote the letter of recantation. If I ever regret not having gone through with my protest and suffered for it, I console myself by reflecting that Murray must have known that my climb-down was a lie.*

I took a third-class degree, although I had read a lot and imagined myself to be working hard (my weekly essays, written when the subject was fresh, were better than my exam papers). Such was my lack of enthusiasm when it was all over that I had to flog myself to make the effort to attend the degree ceremony the following term. Years later my beloved Lincoln and army friend John Brownjohn told me how much he had enjoyed going to a College Gaudy, and this made me think I was missing something. So I paid the requisite sum to receive my M.A., without which one cannot attend Gaudies, and then waited ten years. At last an invitation came, and I stared

---

* Robson, late in life, got his come-uppance. While enjoying the relative eminence of a chair of English at Edinburgh University, he evidently felt homesick for Oxford, and applied for the vacant fellowship in English at one of its richest colleges where he could have lived off the fat of the land. It was between him and another man, and he was passed over. Dining in that college while writing this book, I was shrewdly placed by my host at dessert next to the 'better man' and told him I once had Robson as my tutor. We had a liberating roar of laughter. Nothing more needed to be said on the subject.

at it on and off for a several days before finally declining. One deterrent was the thought that Murray might be there.

I continued in my first year to see friends and acquaintances from earlier epochs, which meant that my social connections were almost exclusively outside my College. One of these friends was Tom Stacey, who to my sorrow left at the end of our second term, joined *Lilliput* and got married. I am sorry I did not escape at the same time, but Tom knew what he wanted to do and I did not, so it was easier to stay put. Jeremy Thorpe was on the threshold of realising his first major ambition, to be president of the Oxford Union. He was amusing as ever, and affected a three-piece suit of Edwardian cut and a brown bowler hat. We were once chatting in the Broad, when we saw a car do a U-turn, and as he commented acidly on women drivers, I realised that the culprit was my mother. When she saw us and stopped, he continued with the bold badinage at which he was so adept and told her a risqué joke, with clear allusions to *'soixante-neuf'*. I would never have dared, but she laughed immoderately. John Wilberforce was ensconced in a vast room in Canterbury Quad in Christ Church, ever friendly and ever sphinx-like. He drafted me into a small select club, the Chatham, which used to meet in the smarter colleges, drink mulled wine and hear a speaker – it could be an eminent don like G.N. Clark, Robert Blake or David Cecil or an ancient politician like John Simon or L.S. Amery. We acted like young fogeys.

Through an accidental meeting in the street I took up again with Ian E. He had been one of the nicer boys at St Ronan's, some two years older than me, and at that time a cheerful extravert. At the beginning of one term we heard that during the previous holidays Ian had gone into the family's private wood with a gun, and seeing what he thought was a small animal moving in the undergrowth levelled up and fired. He found that he had killed his younger sister and only sibling.

For once we suppressed any tendency to gossip or speculate. To all appearance Ian was no different from usual, and Dick Harris, doubtless to fill his mind with other concerns, quickly promoted him to head prefect. I had not thought about him for a long time when we bumped into eachother in Oxford. His open smile was the same, but his hair was tinged with grey, and an air of solitude hung about him. He said that we hadn't met sooner because he had had a nervous breakdown and been away from Oxford for some months – this was out of character with the Ian I had once known. Now, after all his contemporaries had gone down, he was back and hoping to take his finals soon. We had dinner together, and he asked me if I knew.... I said I remembered hearing something about it. This was the sole cause of his troubles. Quite recently his mother had revealed that she believed he shot his sister intentionally, and now he could not be absolutely sure his mother was wrong. (Yet, from what I had learned of his character over the years, the idea was utterly outlandish.) A little later I heard that Ian had another breakdown and left the University for good.

My sexual self, hitherto inactive, had long been divided into separate compartments. There was my long history of crushes on other boys at Eton, which recrudesced in the army, once for a fellow-officer cadet and later for a soldier in my platoon, but they were never accompanied by physical desire, and I now tend to think they were a not very abnormal, if slightly over-prolonged, phase of growing up. I only once felt physical desire for a girl, M. – on an occasion already described – but nothing happened. In Cyprus a friendly tart called Dora, who came to our detachment camp with us late one evening with one of her girl-friends, encouraged me to take her to my tent, but my nerve failed: one reason was that Allen Patrick was around and I feared an ambush, of which he would have been capable – another, more basic reason was that she got hold of me through my trousers in the taxi and I immediately came off.

After returning from the army, I saw something of M.'s bright but serious and unflirtatious younger sister, G.; also of a girl at the Ruskin art school. Both were from intellectual German-Jewish families, and both had the same first name – my sister Rosemary would not have been human if she had not teased me about this. G. and I even lay in a field near Marston Ferry one hot summer evening exchanging kisses as hard as we could go, but genuine desire never kindled, and early in my first term she shrugged off my advances, and so ended our non-affair. I already knew that the other G. had only ever been happy in the arms of a French girl the previous summer. In the background all this time was the lingering after-effect of my encounters with Sigmund Pollitzer and Richard W. in Cyprus – since meeting them, the idea that I was queer had grown on me, although this never quite drove out a deeply ingrained belief that one day I would marry and have children. It was not cynical calculation that made me entertain these two very different thoughts in tandem – but merely inability to put my thoughts together, combined with profound ignorance of the female sex.

Some sort of experimentation was urgently needed, but I was now in Oxford, not in Nicosia where someone like Dora would have obliged for the asking. The homosexual route seemed equally difficult: I had no idea of how and where to begin. Then it happened. Just before the start of my second term and within days of my twenty-first birthday, I was in the Oxford public library consulting the card-index when a laughing Siamese with spectacles boldly engaged me in conversation. I gladly accepted his invitation to go to his bedsitter for tea – he was swatting to take the University entrance exam – and then we went to the cinema. While we were there, I became certain with a pounding heart that something momentous was about to happen, and it did a few days later. With anyone else I might have panicked, overcome with guilt, and bolted – and because of his easygoing good humour and decency, I could also have bolted from T. if I had wanted without embarrassment. But he did not function in the British way. Everything that followed seemed easy and natural.

The reason why it 'worked' was that as a young oriental, smooth-skinned and graceful, he was physically attractive in a way that the objects of my ancient crushes had not been, as well as being amusing company. I became very fond of T. (though certainly not 'in love'), but in craven fashion I kept him away from my social circle – not out of protective jealousy but, ignobly, because I thought they would not find him interesting, as indeed they would not: he was resolutely frivolous and unintellectual. He grasped this intuitively and was baffled by what he saw as my split personality, referring to the part of me that didn't 'belong' to him as 'Mister Christopher Hurst'. At the end of the summer term we had to go our separate ways, and although we occasionally met again, he never returned to Oxford because he failed the entrance exam.

In the way that these things happen, another lover soon appeared on the scene. This was A., a Ph.D. student in a highly specialised corner of art history (he already had a Ph.D. from another British university, but was now attached to my College where the world's leading authority on his subject was a Fellow). He came from a southern European country. We first met in the College boat-house after a rowing practice, and for the walk back into the town I sought out his company. On some pretext I brought the sculptor Ernst Barlach into the conversation and, being an intellectual snob, A. was impressed.

He was in his late twenties and had lived in his country while it was occupied by the Nazis. Before the war his father was one of the richest merchants in their city, and he himself was sophisticated and highly cultivated, with fine manners and an engaging sense of humour. But he took culture seriously in a way I was not used to, and we would read poetry and Ibsen plays out aloud. His favourite one was *When we Dead Awaken*: what he cared about was not dramatic effect or subtlety, which this final play of the master certainly lacks, but that it embodied 'the quest for the Absolute', an idea that possessed him. The drama was in the mind, and he found the idea of the great sculptor and his former mistress, meeting again after many years in a mountain resort and walking off together up the mountain into a blizzard to die, supremely exciting. I was temporarily infected with A.'s enthusiasm and started to think about art in all its forms in terms of 'the Absolute', but he wanted to apply it to human relationships as well, with a fiery and demanding romanticism. When we saw *The Three Sisters* together in a London theatre, he gave a genuine sob as the curtain came down at the end. But he did laugh when, as he often did, he quoted Leopardi's line *'Il naufragar m'è dolce in questo mare'* – shipwreck in this sea is sweet.

There was nothing unmanly, in manner or in character, about A. He despised campness and the tendency of queers in places like Oxford to congregate and form cabals – he would have nothing to do with them. Morally he disapproved of pederasty, and aesthetically he could not bear the idea of two queers cosily cohabiting. So, being exclusively drawn to young men, he had to be content with short-lived amours, in the course of which he gave and demanded fidelity. While in England he also had an affair with a French girl, whom he first penetrated in a secluded corner of a public garden. 'At least it showed me I could do it,' he said. He liked her and she was in love with him, but the dependence, domesticity and com- promises of marriage were not for him, leaving aside his aesthetic preferences. (The pleasure-loving T. had also made love with girls – his grandmother kept a hotel and he sometimes slept with the maids.) A. spoke of his first love in his own country, with an older man who later married, and of a recent one with a German student as of something natural – though in the later affair the romanticism took a morbid turn (A. did not see it that way) with talk of *Liebestod*.

A., as well as being likeable, was a more interesting person than anyone I had ever known well before, but our attitudes were so different – his intense and exclusive, and mine casual and amused (he was openly contemptuous of most of my friends whom he met) – that a break was bound to come. It came, at his behest, because he felt I was robbing him of his freedom – an excellent reason, but ironic because I had been struggling, not quite consciously, to prevent him from dominating me; the force of his character made him a natural dominator. After avoiding eachother for a few months, we met again occasionally, without ever discussing or even alluding to what had passed. A few years later he became a full professor and head of department at a university in another English-speaking country.

He has joined the small band of path-breaking scholars in his field, and his published works have entered the canon. Today he is emeritus but he remains in charge of a museum attached to his own department and a research school in his native country, which he helped to found. He has received a grand *Festschrift* and the highest decoration in the country of his adoption. When I met him again in 1994 after twenty-eight years out of touch, there was a feeling that our friendship is indestructible.

How quickly it was all over – T had left town, and a few months later I had parted from A. I settled into a mood of pessimism – it seemed impossible that either the brief rapture with T. or the stimulating time with A. could ever be repeated with anyone else – and drifted into the society of Oxford queers, but this solved nothing. I partly envied those who had crossed the Rubicon and seemed at ease with themselves, but I knew, and most of those who knew me also knew, that I hung back. Deliverance came, stumblingly, when I became the lover of an older woman – probably the only way the transition could have come about. I now felt, with perhaps exaggerated conviction, that the other thing was not for me and that I had to avoid it like the plague. It seemed to be a choice between dissolution and integrity. At first, after meeting Suzanne, I felt the zeal and intolerance of the new convert, perhaps a natural defence against doubt or any temptation to backslide.

Summer in Holland – A Second Student Winter

My first long summer vacation, in 1951, was an enjoyable time. Wandering one day round the Ashmolean museum in Oxford, I came upon a notice advertising a three-week course in the history of Dutch art in The Hague. I enrolled and duly turned up. I shared digs with a picture restorer from Bristol in the house of an eminent architectural historian, Professor Ter Kuile, whose forte was Jacob van Kampen, contemporary and counterpart of Inigo Jones. I met the family at breakfast only, and they were amiable in a dry way.

We were an odd assortment of people at the Art-Historical Institute. From Belgium a girl student came for one week only, to be replaced by another. The third and last one, Andree, went with me on the final Sunday by train to Middleburg on the island of Walcheren. Here for the only time I saw women in traditional costume wearing heavy gold ornaments, but the town had one rather sinister feature. Walking down a long empty street of old houses, we had an odd feeling of being watched, and suddenly discovered the reason: the first-floor windows had little *espion* mirrors attached at right-angles to the outside wall, so that the housewife inside could watch the world go by, and by extension spy on her neighbours, while remaining unseen herself. As we went along, we saw impassive faces reflected in several of these mirrors. Andree was a lively *jolie laide*, and when I think of her I regret that I was not keen on women at the time. We walked several miles through empty countryside to the village of Veere with its vast church, converted by Napoleon into a military hospital and never restored. We were young and on holiday, and she may have wondered why I didn't take advantage of such a good opportunity.

There were two women curators from the Louvre, the sour middle-aged Mme Dreyfus and the sweet, flaxen-haired, wise Sylvie Beguin. Aged little more than thirty, Sylvie was already a widow, with a small child whom she had left in Paris, her husband having died of T.B. Fortunately her English was worse than my French, so we conversed in her language; we usually went for a drink together after the day's activities were over. Italy was the country she loved, whose art she studied, and where she spent much time with her husband; for her, coming to Holland was an exotic experience. She made piquant observations about our colleagues on the course – Mr Williams, my fellow lodger, a small man with a large moustache which she said propped up his entire personality, or Mme Dreyfus, about whom she had a store of *'méchant'* anecdotes. I contrived to sit with her on our coach journeys to outlying monuments and collections, and once she was entranced when I swiftly averted my eyes as we passed a little girl having her knickers pulled down by her mother at the roadside; she had *'une belle petite arrière'*, Sylvie teased. One evening several of us were in a café and an Austrian male student regaled us on the piano with light operetta music, heavily rendered. When at length he retired, I sat down and just played *'Bist du bei mir'*, by ear but convincingly – helped by the desire to impress Sylvie. It was a cheap trick but it worked; after all the other stuff, she said, the Bach had been *'ravissant'*. Despite our endless, quite intimate conversations, our only mode of address was *'Madame'* and *'Monsieur'*.

I sent Sylvie my photographs of her, and received a charming letter of thanks for the additions to her 'iconography', but never saw her again except, in 1994, in a TV programme about a disputed Leonardo da Vinci attribution. She was now an authority on Italian Renaissance painting, Junoesque in appearance, and if her name had not been flashed on the screen I would never have recognised her. However, I forged a lasting bond with a remarkable visitor from London, Count Alexis Bobrinskoy. Descended from Catherine the Great and her lover Orlov, he was born (in 1893) to great wealth, and inherited a love of art from his father, a famous collector of oriental bronzes. His early life was carefree – his favourite pastime was stalking game in the Caucasus – and he married young, fathering five children. After the Revolution he moved to Paris, where his wife died; and now he lived with his second wife in Earls Court. He was portly, dressed with complete lack of style, and was determinedly jovial, indulging in little exhibitionistic turns like swallowing slices of raw herring whole in what was supposed to be the Dutch manner. The Ter Kuiles' daughter, who worked at the Institute, thought his bonhomie skin-deep, and Sylvie characterised him as *'malin'*. A photograph I took of him standing in front of some Rococo stucco-work in a palace we visited made him look melancholy, but when he saw it he only commented on the appropriateness of the setting.

When we met again, it was at his flat in Penywern Road, which was full of modest works of art bought cheap in salerooms, the least ordinary being the Russian icons; he had not brought any of them from Russia. There were photographs and a coloured chalk drawing by Alexandre Benois of the family's palace in St Petersburg. The one tangible relic of this former glory was an elaborate brass wall-candelabrum, one of a large set which had adorned the ballroom. A dealer from Paris, visiting in 1914, asked to borrow one example to have it copied, and was not able to return it before the war started. Alexis reclaimed it after the war and here it was. Whenever we met he gave droll imitations of the solemn Dutch art historians we had met, and teased me gently about my eponymous *béguin* (I had not known that this word means a love affair).

Alexis never talked about his large family, and I suspected he was not able to provide for them in exile while they were growing up; all I learned was that one son was an Orthodox priest in Paris. Giving a few Russian lessons, and various shadowy comings and goings in the world of art dealing, seemed his only sustenance. But only a year or two after this, a more prosperous chapter in his life opened. One day I got a card from him telling me to tune in to B.B.C. radio at a certain time. He had written some true, if embellished, stories about his own and his family's life in Russia, and now he broadcast a series of them. His natural showmanship came into play, and with his strong Russian accent and plenty of histrionic modulation the effect was engaging. The best story was one called 'The Constantine Rouble' about an extremely rare gold coin which his father produced at a dinner party and encouraged the guests to hand round from one to the next to admire; but while circulating it disappeared, nobody knew how. The social embarrassments that followed were well described. Next he appeared on TV panel games and, strangest of all, took to modelling: his face appeared on advertisement hoardings, always registering exaggerated happiness, surprise or horror. He was also now officially an adviser to Christie's on Russian art. When he died, I wrote an obituary sketch for *The Times*, which was printed. At his funeral in the Emperor's Gate Orthodox church, his face, waxen and unrecognisable, lay open to view and at one point in the long ceremony the congregation filed past the coffin to plant a kiss on the strip of paper, printed with a phrase from the Gospels, which lay across his forehead.

To return to Holland, this was the chance of a lifetime to visit genuinely private art collections. There was the cabinet of drawings in the Lugt house overlooking the Vijver in the centre of The Hague; the Six mansion in Amsterdam containing Rembrandt's incomparable portrait of Jan Six pulling on a glove; and the van Beuningen collection, the most astonishing private treasure-house I have ever seen. The house was not out of the ordinary, but to find oneself suddenly facing Breughel's 'Tower of Babel' in the crowded living room was a strange experience. Mr van Beuningen was a short elderly man with a red face and plebeian appearance; perhaps it was appropriate, as his family made its fortune out of coal, that he looked like an old miner. He was very friendly. In his study a superannuated calendar hung above his desk, which showed Hans van Meegeren's best known Vermeer forgery, the 'Christ at Emmaus'. Van Meegeren had died in disgrace, and his forgeries were locked away in the vaults of the Boymans Museum (now Boymans-Van Beuningen) in Rotterdam, which acquired them with Van Beuningen's money. Following my thoughts, the old man said to me that he did not regret having supported the forger, and still admired his productions.

The two art historians of whom we saw most at the Institute were Mr de Vries, the rather flashy director of the Mauritshuis, and Horst Gerson, a shy, humorous German Jew – the more intelligent of the two and the better scholar. To him I owe a lasting love of Jacob van Ruysdael. In later years he upset the Rembrandt establishment by de-authenticating certain pictures previously accepted as from the hand of the master. In spite of the heavy emphasis on the 17th-century golden age, we did not overlook Van Gogh, and looking at the 'mad' paintings of his last days, at the Kroller-Muller museum, it was impossible not to think of my lover A.'s 'quest of the Absolute'.

Going back to my digs each night along the leafy suburban avenues, it was impossible not to notice that all Dutch families left their living-room windows uncurtained. Inside, as if in a picture by a classical *genre* painter, there was a scene of domestic tranquillity: father with book or newspaper, mother doing needlework, the children peaceably and usefully occupied. On my last day I dared to ask Professor Ter Kuile why the Dutch didn't draw their curtains as we did in England. The answer came pat, without a smile: 'We have nothing to hide.'

From The Hague I went via Aachen to Cologne for my first sight of Germany. Half way across the makeshift bridge over the Rhine in the centre of the great destroyed city I asked an elderly man the way to the Wallraff-Richartz Museum. I was able to address him in a semblance of his own language but he gently corrected me by saying I should preface questions to strangers with the words *'Entschuldigen Sie eine Frage'*, and then insisted on standing me a cup of coffee, on condition that I at some time helped a young German. He joked about pompous German names, and pretended not to know if it was Wallraff-Richartz or Richartz-Wallraff. German politeness had already impressed me on the rickety tram between the Dutch border and Aachen: the conductor punctiliously said *'Danke schön'* to each passenger on receiving the fare and *'Bitte schön'* on handing back the ticket. Were these the people who had so recently terrorised Europe?

In Frankfurt I stayed with Harald Vocke in his family's comfortable apartment, and from there took a bus to Kassel, where I was met by the benign avuncular figure of my father's first cousin Dr Ferdinand Rohr, a paediatrician – 'Onkel Freddy'. I heard of this family from Uncle Gerald, who had corresponded with them over Uncle Fred's will (of which more later): they were excluded from receiving the share in the estate to which they would normally have been entitled because they were, legally, still 'enemy aliens'. Gerald did not want me to contact them, anticipating that they might expect some tangible favour in return for entertaining me, but I went ahead, and had an enjoyable time with them. Onkel Freddy lost a brother in the First World War and nephews in the Second, and some of the clan were now in the East. His own two sons both served in Hitler's army and were taken prisoner; because the older, Klaus, was held in France, compelled to work for a farmer till 1947, we talked in French which alone made communication with the rest of the family possible. Klaus, being 25% of Jewish blood, could only attain non-commissioned rank, and that after intercessions at a high level. We had a carefree few days, and on Sunday afternoon wandered in the

Wilhelmshöhe park with its spectacular cascades and fountains. The centre of Kassel city was still a flattened ruin.

Overflowing with *Gemütlichkeit*, Onkel Freddy sent postcards to my mother, and to our family's Methusaleh, Uncle Martin, whom he remembered from the distant past, signed by Tante Hildegund and all the family. Little could he have imagined that by addressing my mother as *'Liebe Cousine'* and writing a message of greeting in German he caused her dreadful anxiety; she had not recovered from war fever, and seriously thought that this postcard would be eagerly scrutinised at our local post office and set tongues wagging in the neighbourhood about her German family connections. Uncle Gerald's unwelcome realism about my trip proved well-founded. Klaus soon wrote to me that Jutta, the youngest in the family, who was still at school, wanted to come over to learn English: could I help? I asked around all my relations who could possibly put her up – my mother was clearly out of the reckoning – and had the odious task of replying that I could not help. It was hardly surprising that I never heard from Onkel Freddy's family again.

After this, I went straight to the small Warwickshire town of Kenilworth to take over the editorial chair of the *Kenilworth Weekly News*, an eight-page tabloid newspaper with a circulation of 2,000. This assignment came about through my chance meeting with Vivienne, a woman of independent means who did the job as a hobby, at an Oxford party the previous term; when she told me she needed a replacement during her five-week holiday in Sicily, I volunteered and got the job without more ado.

The second-generation owner of the paper was a small printer-stationer called Jim, youngish, married to an attractive wife, and of limited imagination, who found his inheritance a burden rather than an opportunity. The compositor, Charlie, was a self-educated cycling-mad socialist, rather older than Jim. Charlie and I were quickly in cahoots. The paper's front page offered me an immediate challenge: the columns went right up to the top, and such a thing as a banner headline had never been seen. Accounts of weddings, with the halftone block of the group standing at the church door provided by the photographer, were staple front-page fare; flower shows were big news. Gradually, with Charlie's cooperation, I undertook my hubristic task of altering the layout of the paper.

I was expected to report the highlights from the magistrate's court, and this was disturbing. I felt deeply for an innocent cyclist who was spotted by a constable riding straight out of a side road into a main road in the depth of the country, ignoring the 'stop' sign although no vehicle was in sight; he was fined. And the pathetic-looking vicar of a local parish was charged with drink-driving after visiting pubs in his locality to raise money – an admirable way of doing so. His defence was that only a little drink went to his head because he was hungry, being exceedingly poor. His flock had offered to pay his fine if one were levied, and one duly was. The magistrate in this case was the one most feared for harsh sentencing, Mrs More O'Ferrall of the advertising contractors.

I met a few local luminaries, but my only personal brush with fame came when I interviewed George Formby, who was staying with his wife Beryl at the hotel right across the road from the *News* 'office' while doing a show in nearby Coventry. Ten years earlier I could not have missed a new George Formby film, but meeting him was a disappointment. He hardly had a word to say.

What gave these short five weeks a special buzz was the chance that a general election campaign was in full swing, and Kenilworth was in Anthony Eden's constituency. I went to one of his meetings, and discovered how pedestrian and uninspiring as a speaker this immensely prestigious figure could be. Even an election was not enough to raise the temperature at the *News*, but then the incumbent Labour candidate was suddenly dropped by his party at the last moment because of a sex scandal. A new candidate had to be drafted in just three weeks before polling day. Charlie and I resolved to do our bit. He came up with a large block of a flattering portrait of the candidate to put on the front page, and we went to town with an *Evening Standard*-style banner headline. I meanwhile interviewed the candidate on the phone – he hadn't time to see me – and cobbled together a story.

The best part of this little episode was when Eden's agent came into the office on the morning of publication to register a discreet complaint. He said that while of course our independence was respected, he had still always counted on Vivienne as an ally. I merely said that Eden couldn't lose, so what was wrong with giving the Labour man a bit of a fillip? Yes, he said, but did we really need to give him the whole front page *and* a photograph? With a menacing smile he withdrew. From then on Jim, who was dyspeptic and self-pitying at the best of times, turned bitter. He accused Charlie of letting the Labour people nobble him, possibly even with a bribe, and as for me, I couldn't be expected to understand what hot water I had got him into.

The Basil Spence design for the new Coventry cathedral had just been approved, and I wrote an editorial praising it for the next issue. When this was already set up in type, Jim joyfully pulled it out and penned an illiterate pro-Tory tirade himself to replace it. The time had anyway come for me to depart.

Before leaving Oxford at the end of the summer term, already knowing that I would have to live out of College in my second year, I omitted to visit the Delegacy of Lodgings, which kept details of all vacant rooms in houses vetted as respectable by the University authorities. The result was that when I called there on my return from Kenilworth, there were very few left. But I had somehow settled into a state of mind in which things like that didn't matter to me. So I moved into the first room offered, in the North Oxford house of Mrs Walton, a divorced middle-aged woman of obvious breeding. She made it clear when I arrived that taking in a lodger was a painful necessity for her, and did the next best thing to having no lodger: she pretended not to have one. She never tidied the room, into which, small though it was, she had put all her largest pieces of furniture that she could not use elsewhere – I had to get into the bed from the foot. Nor did she employ a cleaner. Because she cooked the breakfast and left it on the table before calling me, it was already cold by the time I got to it. When A. saw the place, he remarked that it was like Raskolnikov's garret in *Crime and Punishment*. One night I came back late and, thinking Mrs Walton was asleep, crept into the kitchen and helped myself to a bowlful of Rice Krispies. Suddenly she appeared in her dressing gown and, quivering with rage, demanded how I dared to steal her food. We both apologised the next morning. A few nights later I went to a ball, and she could not do enough to help me get my evening rig looking respectable.

The dance in question was at the Randolph Hotel, and was held to raise funds for the Oxford branch of the United Nations Association. The branch secretary was a friend of mine, Erich Alport, a Hamburg Jew (in the same sense – secular, cultivated, comfortable – as my great-grandfather) who came to live in England with his mother before the rise of Hitler. Due to old Mrs Alport's connection with the family that made Nivea Creme (a source of amusement to the many people who despised Erich and knew about his habits), they were wealthy and by timing their departure from Germany so astutely were able to keep their fortune and bring with them a fine set of chattels.

When I knew them, Erich was nearing fifty and the old lady was about eighty. Her English was heavily accented, Erich's virtually accentless though too precise to be quite real. She had an earthy vigour and toughness and considerable charm and humour, notwithstanding her hunched and shrivelled body, and an ugly, partly paralysed face under an engaging mop of grey curls. Erich had smooth black hair, sallow skin and expressive grey eyes. His colouring and the shape of his head reminded me of my father, but otherwise they could not have been more different. Poor Erich led a vapid existence. He had studied at Heidelberg and acquired a doctorate, then come to Oxford for more study, and except for serving loyally in the British army during the war (in the Pioneer Corps), had never done a job. He structured the vacuity of his life to give all his comings and goings, for pleasure or business, an air of importance.

This extended to sex. As a young man he had one or two great love affairs, which he said he destroyed through jealousy, but by the time I knew him he resorted to travelling to places where there was an established network of local boys available to well-off homosexuals from northern countries at a price. To anyone knowing only the prim, smiling figure in North Oxford these activities would have been incredible. I first met him at one of the tea parties that Mary Stanley Smith, of whom more later, gave every Sunday during term at her house in Ship Street, and he immediately befriended me. There was never more than the most discreet hint that he might have amorous designs, but he did see me as a kindred spirit, maybe even an *alter ego*; this worried me as time went on. During the winter of 1951-2 my mother was in New Zealand and had let our house, and because Mrs Walton's house was only a few minutes' walk from Erich's, he invited me fairly often and I went willingly.

The Alports were art collectors of no mean order; those who dismissed their pieces as good merchandise were probably envious. The old lady had a Chagall portrait of a clown dating from 1914, and in Erich's study there was a calm and low-toned Van Gogh painting of some buildings, now in the Ashmolean, which I found beautiful. I also remember a watercolour sketch by Cezanne and a charming bronze by Henry Moore of a woman holding a baby, in a rocking chair which rocked. While I knew him he bought a small seascape by Bonnard of which naturally he was proud – he solemnly called it 'important', which I thought both deadening and exaggerated. Even his well-stocked modern library had its embarrassing aspects: he once started to pull out volume after volume signed by their authors, often with a dedication to him – but because he was so colourless, it was hard not to think that he had brazenly put the books before the authors and given them no choice. However, there was a contemporary writer, Stephen Spender, whom he had once undoubtedly known intimately, entertained at his family home in Hamburg and tried in vain to seduce. The character called Dr

Jessel in Spender's recently published *World within World* was, he said, himself – something about which I would have wanted to keep quiet if it had been me.

On the night of the U.N.A. dance he gave me a treat. As my partner he invited an intelligent, well-bred and gentle-natured girl undergraduate, the daughter of one of his patrician Hamburg Jewish acquaintances but brought up in England. We met for supper first at the Alports', and Mrs Alport clucked over her like an old hen: how rarely she must have had a girl in the house to make a fuss of! Erich never made jokes himself, but he was apt to quote the supposedly humorous remarks of eminent people he had known, and did so on this occasion, with a quip his professor at Heidelberg, Ernst Curtius, had made about a pair of spectacles; it was painfully unfunny, but the girl laughed charmingly.

In the summer of 1952 Erich went on a long trip through the Middle East of a kind which has long been impossible. Earlier in the year he asked me to go with him, offering to pay all but a fraction of the expenses. He reeled off the names of people in many cities to whom he had introductions; there was also an implied agenda of sexual adventures. At first I agreed, but the feeling that I would be entering some sort of trap grew – not least after he told his mother in my presence that I was going with him and it seemed that the shrewd old woman looked at me with something between incomprehension and pity. I eventually excused myself on the (true) grounds that my mother had come back from New Zealand suffering from a mysterious illness and I was the last of her children left in England. In any case, by the summer I was already seeing Suzanne. It still took me several more years before I understood that I am *au fond* heterosexual, with a spontaneous liking for women – their bodies and minds. It might have been better if I had known that from the beginning, but it did not happen that way, so there is little point in repining. Clearly, though, my gut antipathy to queer-cliquishness and effeminacy had genuine roots. A friend of both Erich and myself reported him as saying of me later, 'I don't think he was ever really happy with us.'

At the end of the term, despite my rapprochement with Mrs Walton, I moved to a large house in Norham Gardens, nearer to the city. Because of my mother's absence, coupled with my own unadventurousness, I had to find somewhere to stay through the Christmas vacation – Oxford digs usually let rooms for the term only. The new place seemed just right for the purpose. It had something of the atmosphere of a cultured German-Jewish home, and the landlady Mrs Frankenthal was willing to let me share their meals in the evenings and at weekends if I wanted to – this also was unheard-of in normal student digs, and the price for each meal, 2 shillings, was incredibly low. We said '[*Gesegnete*] *Mahlzeit*' and shook hands at the end of dinner. Mrs Frankenthal and her husband were both about sixty; she was a big woman, with a warm, straightforward personality and natural dignity. He was short, dark and shabby, with a lurking sense of comedy. They lived apart in the same house. She had been a paediatrician but no longer practised; he was a Freudian psychiatrist, and received one or two patients in the house, who paid him a pittance. She was a Berliner, he a Viennese with a Slav forename. Music was his passion, and we sat together, with scores on our knees, listening to *Tristan* and *Die Meistersinger* on the radio. Their son, who was my contemporary and studying medicine at the university, was often at home.

Another lodger moved in after me, a lonely middle-aged bachelor who worked at the Food Office in town – Mr Worth. Mrs Frankenthal obviously thought him compatible with the rest of the household but it quickly became clear that she had been mistaken. In meal-time conversations he was continuously out of his depth, and his occasional attempts at breezy conviviality fell flat. One day at breakfast the talk turned to President Auriol of France, who was in England on a state visit. Mr Worth now saw his opportunity to make an interesting contribution at last, and said helpfully, 'I once knew an Oriel man' (Oriel is an Oxford college). There were a few groans round the table, then we fell silent. Seldom, outside a fairy tale, can an innocent gaffe have led to such dire punishment for its perpetrator: Mrs Frankenthal told us that evening that she had asked Mr Worth to leave.

As Easter approached, I took a vacant room in one of the old houses in Longwall Street, looking over the Magdalen deer park in front and with the tops of the trees in New College garden just visible over the medieval city wall at the back. The landlady, Mrs Shrimpton, was the wife of a New College porter, and spoke with the local accent; she had no pretensions to being either a lady like Mrs Walton or cultured like Mrs Frankenthal. It helped that I recognised her homely features from when she had worked in a shoe-shop in Broad Street during the war. I stayed at her house for the rest of my time in the University, and we became friends.

Mrs Frankenthal may have had a noble nature, but it was warped by the sordid business of running a boarding house. She could easily have installed a pay-phone, but preferred to have a home-made money-box beside the house phone, which was just outside her room, and which we were on our honour to feed each time we made a call. She once accused me politely, on aural evidence alone, of not putting in enough money. I thought I had done so meticulously. And to have a bath one had to borrow the key to the hot water cistern from her, and she added sixpence to the week's rent. The greatest tragedy came when I broke a little electric lamp in my room, its base consisting of the hollow leaden figure of an owl. It had already once been broken, and the two halves crudely soldered together; I had broken the solder. Unfortunately it had sentimental associations for Mrs F. and she asked me to get it repaired – but when the time of my departure came I had forgotten about it. On my last day in the house, I took several tins of food, which my mother had sent me from New Zealand but I had no means of using, and offered them to Mrs F. For some reason I was feeling generous. She replied that I was very kind, but she would prefer to have the lamp repaired. Braving this insult, I persisted, saying that I could not take the tins away with me. At last she relented, saying that she would send them to her old servant in Germany; she also agreed to repair the lamp and let me know the cost. A year later she sent me a postcard asking for five shillings.

Interlude: Lovely Lovely Ludwig Van

This title is anachronistic, since it comes from *The Clockwork Orange*, but how lovely we did find Beethoven. We would go to eachother's rooms and sit round the record-player listening with intense concentration to any one of the quartets from Opus 95 onwards, silent except to mutter something like how amazing it was that every phrase, as it followed the preceding one, was so obviously just right. Someone lent me a book by a man called Sullivan, just called *Beethoven* (he was not a musician but a common-or-garden Beethoven freak like us); he claimed that the fugue at the beginning of the Opus 131 quartet was the greatest piece of music ever written. I felt that perhaps he was right, but I couldn't help actually liking some of the less ethereal music better. As well as the quartets there were the piano trios – the two in Op. 70 and the Archduke (again some claimed that the slow set of variations in it was the greatest etc.) – and the Op. 20 septet with its elegiac slow movement. I thought I knew the symphonies (for my friend A. they were too rumbustious), but an impecunious friend in my College owned just a single record and one day he played it to me: it was the Eroica symphony. I

had heard the eight-note opening phrase of the first movement hummed
by Dick Harris at St Ronan's, but through some oversight had never
actually heard the whole work or even part of it, and nothing could
have prepared me for the excitement of listening to it for the first
time.

We had a chance to hear some great performers in Oxford while
I was there: Kathleen Ferrier, Dietrich Fischer-Dieskau, Rudolf Serkin.
I was not moved by Solomon's playing, but Serkin's was something
different. It was at an annual commemorative recital given in Balliol
College Hall, and the presiding geniuses were two well-known lady
dons, the Miss Denekes. The occasion began with a little speech
by one of them, and she then sat down at the piano with Serkin
to play a duet – composed by her. It limped along, and at the end,
rather ungallantly Serkin galloped ahead and left her a bar or two
behind. When the ordeal was over he charmingly took her hand
as they bowed to the audience. He was small, bespectacled, the
sort of figure that must almost have typified for the Nazis the indestructible Jew – ugly and awkward – and I had not seen or heard
of him before. Then he sat down and played Beethoven's Opus
109 sonata, and I knew I was in the presence of an interpreter
of the supreme composer who was himself supreme. The Hall is
not a large space, and the power of the playing filled every corner.
I often heard him later and was never disappointed.

When I met Suzanne soon afterwards, I took along – on one of
my first visits to her place, knowing she had a player – a record
of the Opus 110 piano sonata, played by Artur Schnabel, which
I had out of the record library. It was a fairly callow thing to do.
She had a greater love for J.S. Bach, but conceded that Opus 110
was good music for lovers, and said that if we ever had a row
we should stop and say 'hundred-and-ten'. What a nice, practical
idea that was!

But it is many years now since I have listened to Beethoven's
late quartets, or even the Rassoumovskys and the trios – partly for
the corny reason that they are associated with a particular time of
my life that seems remote and uninviting; partly too because the
experience of hearing them is too intense to be enjoyable; and partly
because they became so engraved in my brain that every phrase
is familiar and I simply have no need to hear them again. Now
a more lyrical sort of sublimity – that of the ever-young Schubert
– appeals to me more. Mozart at times produces transports of incomparable pleasure. And the 'just-so' solemnity of Mendelssohn,
the sunny optimism of Schumann for whom the world always seems
to be young, and the agonies of Chopin, together with much else

on the lower slopes of Parnassus, have a comfortable and not too demanding charm that never fails.

Yet Beethoven only needs to raise his voice to have the last word. The final part of the fourth movement of the Ninth Symphony moves bad men like the Nazi leaders (there is a documentary film that shows them at a performance in an opera house and almost jumping out of their seats with excitement) and the anti-hero of *The Clockwork Orange*, and good men like us. Ludwig surely has an unequalled power over the human mind and emotions.

Back on the Mainland

Suzanne and I first met at one of Mary Stanley Smith's Sunday afternoon tea parties in Ship Street. With her was a small boy, and I assumed, because of her unassuming but extremely polite manner and slight foreign accent, that she was his governess. We did not get into conversation till another Sunday, when she invited me to a party at her place in North Oxford. She then revealed that she was Italian and had recently divorced her husband, an English coffee planter in Mysore State, South India; the boy was her son. In spite of being only five years old, he was a boarder at a prep school on the south coast where his father had been before him.

At her party she signalled that I should not hurry away, and when all the other guests had gone, we settled down to a scratch supper. Around the room were some oil paintings she had done, mostly in India; the most striking one was of a female servant, seen from the back. The colours were bright and the drawing was strong – Van Gogh had provided some of the inspiration.

She was a beautiful woman in the Botticelli style, with firm but delicate classical features, light brown hair and blue eyes. At this time she was still re-shaping her life, using the same broad brushstrokes with which she painted. She had met her husband before the war when they were in their teens and both alone in England; his parents were in India and she had come over from Italy to complete her schooling. They were staying briefly in the same house and there were stolen kisses in the potting-shed which he never forgot. During the war he wooed her from afar, and she agreed to marry him after an unrequited passion for an Irish doctor, sailing to India on a troopship while the war was still on. On the voyage she got swept up in a

typical shipboard flirtation with a Guards officer, and was so sorry
to part from him on their arrival in Bombay that tears were in her
eyes when she and her husband met on the quayside. He realised they
were not tears of joy on seeing him, and so things started badly.

Life on the coffee estate was never her style. Her mother-in-law
was the practical domestic type, with a husband in his eighties, who
ran the place and jealously watched over the welfare of her darling
only child, who she thought was not being properly looked after
by his wife. There were two middle-aged male cousins on nearby
estates – Humphrey Trevelyan mentions them in his memoirs – whom
Suzanne liked better than the immediate family. She also found a
Russian doctor at nearby Ooty who acted as a father confessor. A
son was born – some of the most ravishing photographs of her are
with him as a baby – but the marriage did not prosper. One of the
estate servants, a woman whom she befriended, fell sick and died,
and Suzanne's husband, who already viewed this relationship dis-
approvingly, could not understand or cope with her distress. Then
her nascent interest in painting aroused his jealousy. After about
four years she wanted to spend some time in Italy, where she had
not been since before the war, and her husband agreed to let her
go. So with her son she made the journey and settled for some
time in Turin, where she had two half-sisters, and took art lessons
at the Accademia under the famous master Felice Casorati.

Her family background was complicated. Her father, Giancarlo
Antinori, was a somewhat impoverished member of an old family
from Perugia with the title of *marchese* – an uncle of his, Orazio
Antinori, was a celebrated explorer. The *palazzo* that now houses
the university for foreigners was said to have been theirs in the
distant past; certainly it was formerly called Palazzo Antinori. Giancarlo
owned a small apartment in a house in the heart of the city; his
family house was at Riccione on the Adriatic. He had an English
mother and spoke her language without an accent except that of
a Victorian gentleman. He qualified as an engineer at the Crystal
Palace and spent a few active years in distant parts of the British
empire, working on the Victoria Falls bridge. But around the age
of thirty he contracted a mysterious disease which permanently reduced
his energy, and he never worked again; his English qualifications
were apparently of no use in Italy. He had enough money to marry
– his wife was a very plain Scots lady. She unfortunately fell ill
with cancer after little more than ten years, and a governess was
hired, also from Scotland, to look after their three little girls. Before
Giancarlo's wife died, the governess had to leave in a hurry and,
rejected by her strict family, gave birth in London to a daughter

by Giancarlo. The girl was given the forenames Ida Antinori, but was known by her mother's surname. For the first five years she remained in an orphanage while her mother earned a living and visited her on Sundays – there is a photograph taken of her there, sitting on a swing and looking wistful but very pretty. She had both a romantic, self-dramatising streak and a robust sense of humour, and used to say without self-pity that this picture reminded her of how she longed for love in those days – a longing she always felt and which was never fully satisfied.

Giancarlo had an unmarried sister, religious and devoted to good works, who insisted that her brother, by now a widower, should do the decent thing and marry Ida's mother, which he duly did though without enthusiasm. Suzanne (Ida adopted this name in her teens) remembered being at the wedding party and wondering why everyone looked so glum while she was cheerful and danced round the room. A son, Davide, was born, Giancarlo's fifth and youngest child. Suzanne's mother, like her predecessor, died early; by Suzanne's account, she grew thin and faded away, and was constantly miserable.

Of the three older sisters the youngest emigrated, and the remaining two married brothers: Erica, the stalwart eldest one, married the neurotic younger brother some time after the romantic and artistic Peggy married the rock-solid elder one. These two women, both intelligent and well educated, largely brought Suzanne up, and the debt she owed them, later shared by her two sons and by me, was unrepayable. But she and they were very different – they practical and tending to be bossy towards their much younger half-sister, she vague and instinctive – and in her teens she rebelled and insisted on going to England.

Now, at the end of the 1940s, Suzanne was back in Italy after a very long absence. Davide was doing his military service. After a few months her husband joined them, and she later recalled one happy day when the three of them – she, her husband and Davide – were briefly together in Naples. Soon after her return to India, she received the news that Davide had shot himself. He evidently felt hopeless about his future, and a close friend of his had done the same a short time before. When I knew Giancarlo he was – under a thin veneer of courtly manners, good humour and intelligent discourse – a man eaten up by a sense of failure. He had not had a career; both his marriages had ended unhappily, especially for his wives; though a puritan by instinct, he had committed a very public sexual misdemeanour; and, worst of all, his only son had committed suicide, for which he blamed himself. He was apt to quote his family's motto *'Duris non frangar'* (I shall not be broken by adversities); certainly he appeared to live up to it.

Suzanne's long stay in Italy and a visit from a liberated woman friend from England deepened her dissatisfaction with life on the coffee estate with a man who had so little in common with her. The estrangement grew until she finally decided to go – significantly she chose England and not Italy as her destination. Her husband was taken aback when it came to this point, but he quickly restored his self-esteem by marrying again, and in a letter he told Suzanne, to her great amusement, what a good manager his new wife was and how excellently she made jam.

I admired the way she continually met her fate head-on, leaving her family before the war when it became oppressive, taking a long break from her married existence when she needed one and at the same time starting to paint, and then walking away from it when there seemed no hope. Now she was about to make another decisive move. She had observed my movements while I boarded with Mrs Frankenthal, and by the evening when I went to her party I had by some mysterious process entered her consciousness as someone who would play a part in this new, still unfolding stage of her life. At first I did not realise what was happening. On parting from her that night I invited her, in normal Oxford fashion, to have coffee with me the next morning. She agreed to come, but the appointed time passed and I thought that, again in normal Oxford fashion, this was the sort of minor stand-up that might happen after any party where a certain amount had been drunk. I picked up my books and was just coming out of my digs to go to the library when, right there in front of me, she collided on her bicycle with another cyclist as she was about to dismount. No damage was done, and there was laughter all round. I got her to leave her bike in the Shrimptons' back yard, and we went off to a coffee house. There, as if it was utterly natural, she said that I could come with her to the house in the Italian Alps that her sisters were renting for the summer, and where she and her son had been invited. Because the next academic year was my last, I had to spend a lot of time reading, but this prospect seemed very inviting, and of course I could take some books with me. What was implied by this invitation soon became plain – in a thoroughly disarming way. I yielded willingly.

Mary Stanley Smith, at one of whose tea-parties I met Suzanne, was one of the characters of Oxford. At this time she was in her late forties, with beautiful straight flaxen hair tinged with white, a radiant smile in which lurked a mischievous glint, and a deliberately, almost provocatively affected voice. She rented a small, primitive house in the heart of Oxford: 12 Ship Street, with one room only on each of its three floors. There was no bath and no telephone, and Mary did not own a car.

Each Sunday she dispensed mugs of tea and pieces of plain cake to – as my friend A. remarked after his only visit – young men in need of a mother-figure. Girls were in a minority, and those few tended not to be very exciting. A few older friends of Mary's appeared, and some quite eminent writers turned up from time to time like Joyce Cary, Rosamond Lehmann, John Heath-Stubbs and the folklorist Christina Hole.

Mary was the Oxfordshire Country Librarian, and as an unmarried woman in such a job might have been expected to live in moderate comfort, but she was prevented from doing so by family complications. Some time after getting to know her, I called at 12 Ship Street one evening, hoping to find out what she was like when not doing her thing among the tea guests. Of course she was alert and shrewd behind the persiflage, and knew exactly what was going on around her. When, the following year, I told her that Suzanne and I had started something together, she instantly replied that of course it could not be permanent. I was unnerved, especially as she read the situation more accurately than she knew. Suzanne had already talked about marriage almost casually. So why didn't I say to her, just as casually, that I was not thinking of it yet? One reason was the novel one that the idea was no longer automatically barred. Another was that I did not know how a man is supposed to feel when the time has come to think about it. How would I find out? Would I ever meet the 'right girl' and, if I did, would she conceivably be interested in me? And what would she – and her family – think of my recent adventures? So why should the right girl not be Suzanne? After all, I owed to her my liberation from the life of an amateur queer; I was grateful and, in addition, we were having fun. I could love her even if I was not swept away by an overwhelming passion.

Feeling not a little pleased with myself, I plunged ahead and made plans for our holiday. On the day we were to leave – by train and boat – I met Suzanne and her five-year-old son in the portico of the National Gallery. It was my first meeting with Christopher since getting to know his mother. Yes, his name was – and is – Christopher, but to avoid the difficulty of the two males in her life having the same name, she at once started calling him by his second name, Anthony. And Anthony he remained during all the time that we were together. I should not have allowed this to happen; it would have been easy to devise a not too unflattering nickname for myself so that Christopher Anthony could keep his true given name.

On the journey we had a disaster. It was around midnight and the train was approaching Modane, the last station on the French side of the Italian frontier. I put my hand inside my jacket to take out my passport and it was not there. It was not in any other pocket, or in Suzanne's bag, or in any of my pieces of luggage, or behind the seat, or on the floor of the compartment. It was gone completely. My sister Rosemary later suggested that Christopher Anthony might have thrown it out of the train window. In short, Suzanne and Christopher Anthony travelled on while I stayed behind at Modane, where the station staff advised me to wait till the border police clocked on in the morning. I was confident that matters would be sorted out, but I was wrong; I would have to go to the nearest British consulate, which was in Lyon. I went there, to be told that the only hope was to go on to the consulate-general in Marseille. I spent a not very happy night in a hotel there, and visited the office in the morning. A sympathetic compatriot gave me a travel document that enabled me to return to England, but not go anywhere else. I could only get a new passport at the Passport Office in London.

If it ever crossed my mind to change my plans and spend the rest of the vacation in England, I must have rejected it instantly. Like Don Quixote, I called to my aid the medieval knightly ethos that permeated the works of Chaucer and Spenser that I had been reading so enthusiastically in the English syllabus. According to that way of thinking such a setback would only be taken as an excuse for retreat by the faint-hearted. It was a test of my mettle: I had to go through with my original worthy intention.

And so I arrived in Turin a week later, to be welcomed warmly by Suzanne's half-sisters and their husbands, who lived in two houses on a single countryfied hillside site close to the city. The sisters spoke perfect English with a Scots accent, and language problems only obtruded with the husbands. We soon moved up to Gressoney in the Alps, where a house had been rented, There was no room in it for Suzanne and me, so one was found in a peasant house nearby; it was directly above the byre and smelt overpoweringly of cow-dung.

Of the two half-sisters Peggy, the younger, had three young sons, while Erica, the older, already over forty, had a son barely one year old. They each had a family maid who came with them on holiday: Erica's, called Redenta (short for Italia Redenta, 'Italy Redeemed', a slogan of the Risorgimento), was unhappily married and had switched all her love and possessiveness to her employers. She bossed everyone, and was seldom without Erica's little boy, then known as Chicco, in her arms, cooing and repeating his name in endless variants. She was shocked to find at bath-time that Suzanne's son was circumcised, and remarked '*Non è bello come Chicco*'. A year or two later, Erica finally could not stand Redenta's dominant behaviour any longer and gave her the sack.

I went off on one climbing expedition with Gino and Paolo, Suzanne's brothers-in-law; we intended to reach the top of Monte Rosa, but heavy snow at about 10,000 feet forced us back. One sunny afternoon I was sitting idly with Erica outside her rented house when a man whom the family knew slightly walked up. As he approached, he said '*Permesso*' (Excuse me) in a grave, humble voice, and went on inside where he sat down and ate a plate of pasta. He was about fifty, tall and big-boned but emaciated, with a fine head, a sunburned deeply-lined face, sunken mouth and eyes, and steel-grey curly hair. His clothes were of a piece with his neglected appearance. Erica told me his story and why he looked as he did.

His name was Giuseppe, and he was the only child of a successful engineer, still vigorous aged well over eighty. At some time in the distant past, the father took it into his head that his son was too vague, poetic and idealistic to be any good to him as a partner in his profession. He publicly pronounced his son mad and would talk of getting him certified and shut away in an asylum. In the end Giuseppe went off to Somaliland and stayed there, working in some menial capacity, until his mother, who was always too terrified to defend her son, died and left him a property that she owned independently. It contained enough farmland to give him an adequate income, and he returned to Italy to take possession of it. But his father's persecutions began again, old though he was, and he made mischief with the *contadini* on Giuseppe's property, telling them that it did not belong to Giuseppe but to him. At one point Giuseppe was going to marry, but he began to suspect that his financée was a fortune-hunter and broke the engagement off. And here he was.

In a flash it came to me that the story of Giuseppe and his father was different only in detail and in degree from that of the two Dales, Lawrence and Simon. I remembered a light-hearted bet Mary Heptonstall, Lawrence's secretary, had made with me – that whichever of us first wrote a novel about the old man would be treated to a slap-up dinner by the other. With this elemental tragedy for a plot, I was sure that I could win the bet. Bernard, the trainee in Lawrence's office, could play an Iago-like role, cunningly stirring the old man against his son after the latter's return from exile in the hope of taking his place and eventually getting his hands on the estate which the son had inherited from his mother. Bernard would also bribe the farmer who managed it to make life impossible for him, and drive him over the brink. Having done that, he would bump off the farmer and marry his attractive but frustrated wife, who had a passing fancy for the noble Giuseppe character. I got to work in the train going home immediately after it left Turin. At first it seemed to go well; the opening episode consisted of a quarrel between the farmer and his wife, whom I modelled on Suzanne and her planter husband, but the difficulty of turning this melodramatic plot into a credible novel soon became insuperable – for me, with my lack of experience and human insight. I spent a lot of time at the beginning of my last student year writing a first draft, but it would not come alive outside my own brain, and in the next few years I wrote it to death.

Throughout the next year I visited Suzanne at her new digs in Chelsea – again following some unspoken instinct, she moved from Oxford to London at the end of the term in which we met – and the plan that I would marry her as soon as I had taken my exams became fixed. Various attempts were made to dissuade me – and her. The following spring, I stayed for a night with Uncle Gerald and Aunt Margaret in Chislehurst, as I did every vacation. Suzanne had already been invited there without me, and was duly pronounced by Margaret to be a lady, which for her, while not in itself the highest praise, was still an indispensable seal of approval. A typical scene was played out in the moments before I left for the station. Gerald said how satisfactory it was that I would now be settled, but Margaret cut in with two questions. If I married, wouldn't I miss my freedom to travel, which she knew I enjoyed? That was easy: I now wanted to write. She then asked if I loved Suzanne, and at this point Gerald literally snorted and charged out of the room. 'Gerald only sees things in black and white', said my aunt. She did not press me for an answer.

The fact that I could not afford to get married never seemed to come up in any of the conversations I had with various people on whether or not it was the right thing to do, and it never troubled me. I was soon to have a job but it was low-paid and, once its unsuitability for me and mine for it became apparent, without prospects. My personal capital, inherited from my father, was also pitifully small and had been losing value ever since he died because it was all invested in government stocks – which I could not touch because, small as it was, it was in trust and could only be released with the consent of his trustees, who were my mother and the manager of the Trustee Department at Williams Deacons Bank in the City. (When I got them, a little later, to release enough of it for me to buy a decrepit seaside cottage as our true 'married home', at double its true market value, I felt rich. Suzanne had nothing except her alimony and that would cease as soon as the knot between us was made legal. My mother came to the rescue and paid me an allowance from which, even with slightly improved finances in the following years, I was never able to slip free.

I was at home one afternoon during the spring vacation of 1953, probably doing some last-minute swatting for schools the following term, when the phone rang. It was my old Siamese lover, T., who was in Oxford. We had not met for more than a year – he was now at a university in the Mildlands – and we had made no effort to see each other in that time. But I was glad at the thought of a meeting (by then I had met A. again without a word or the twitch of a muscle to hint at what had passed between us), and with perhaps surprising naivety took the bus into town expecting no more than an enjoyable drink or two in the bar at the Eastgate Hotel, where we had agreed to meet.

T. worked by different rules from A., and while we were there I soon got an idea of what was in his mind. We went out of the hotel and walked along Merton Street, which is always nearly deserted. As we passed the open garage of one of the houses, he pulled me inside, we embraced, and he said 'I want to spend the night with you.' I was incapable of resistance, and as if in a dream we made our way to the King's Arms, where he checked in. As soon as we were inside his room, we fell to in the impatient and almost perfunctory way which had been our habit as beginners two years before. When it was over, I looked sadly at T. for the last time, said good-bye, and fled. I felt very bad at abandoning him, but so overcome by remorse and self-disgust that I was simply carried along, just as I had been by attraction a few moments before.

It didn't dawn on me till many years afterwards what had happened. If I had stayed at the King's Arms long enough for revulsion to subside and gone through with the original plan, probably some instinct of decency would have compelled me to break off my understanding with Suzanne. I had never intended to lead a bisexual life, and never had the remotest intention of doing so with her, but if I could now spend a whole night with T., then I would have proved to myself that I could do no better – that was if I did not take the easy way and settle for a homosexual life. And that could never be, because everything I knew or could imagine about it repelled me. On the other hand, the kind of family life in which I had been brought up and had been drawn into with Suzanne's relations in Italy, and which was inseparable from heterosexuality, seemed preferable to an inexpressible degree. So on that day there was a parting of the ways that proved final. T., always gentle and stoical, would probably not have resented the catalytic role he played.

Suzanne's landlord in Chelsea, a wily Suffolk man, had a small cottage for sale at Felixstowe Ferry, by the mouth of the river Deben. Would she – would I – like to buy it? As I discovered too late, it was riddled with dry rot as the result of the great East Coast storms that spring and had to be re-timbered throughout. Suzanne realised that having access to a place like this – which, of course, I could not afford to run – was going to be necessary for her new life to be tolerable. We spent six weeks there after the actual ceremony at Chelsea Town Hall, and I came under the spell of the estuary and the coast north of Bawdsey. She often stayed there for long stretches while I started my wage-slavery in London.

Suzanne was already pregnant when I returned to London to start work, and Andrew was born in St George's Hospital in May 1954. He was healthy, Christopher Anthony was delighted and not jealous, and Suzanne was a good mother. Although Andrew suffered when we parted in 1958, and expressed his feelings about it to me outspokenly at the time, he has an emotional solidity which he owes to her love and basic soundness. He also inherits her (and my mother's) sense of the ridiculous. Her Italian family were always a rock, for her and (to this day) for him. We had him christened in a village church in Suffolk, without attendants: it was too far for the godparents to come. As the young vicar recited the baptism service from the Prayer Book, I could not hold back the tears. Andrew seemed so small to be host to the 'Old Man' or be a 'soldier of Christ'.

Suzanne again went to an art school after we parted (what triggered the parting is explained later), and then moved to Cambridge, where she suffered her first serious mental disturbance and had to enter hospital. After that, attacks became more frequent. She moved next to Cornwall, and in the late 1970s we heard that she had swum out to sea from near her house in St Just and been winched out alive by a helicopter. In October 1978 she did the same again and was drowned.

Hi-ho, Hi-ho

The question of how to earn a living only intruded slowly on the even tenour of my last year at Oxford. It was customary to visit the University Appointments Board at the beginning of that year and collect a sheaf of job descriptions corresponding to one's ambitions or tastes. I went rather late and was told that many of the desirable openings (that meant traineeships with mighty concerns like Shell and ICI) had already gone. At the interview I said more or less straight out that I needed something not very demanding to keep the wolf from the door while I wrote my immortal prose. It was an extraordinarily foolish prescription for life in the real world, but the interviewer (whom I remember despising for the job he did) took the point: he realised that he would have me off his books in record time. The City, he said, was the one place where the Old Boy network still operated – why didn't I try that? With that sentence he determined the course of my life for the next year. I went straight off and wrote to Frederic Seebohm, a son-in-law of Uncle Gerald, then regional director of Barclays Bank in the Midlands, who gave me the names of two of his friends, the chairman of a 'discount house', otherwise known as a bill-broker, of which he was a non-executive director representing Barclays (they were both Quakers), and a partner in a small merchant bank. (He also said he thought I was unwise to think of getting married so soon.) He added that if I took up his introductions, I should attend for my interviews wearing a dark suit and a white shirt. I sent off applications to both these people, and both wrote back that they were willing to see me.

I went to Cornhill one Saturday morning to see Mr O'Leary, a director of Wilkinson Brothers Discount Co. Ltd., who received me in the directors' dining room. He was a heavily-built, florid-faced man in his late forties, rather like John Bull, and was the moving spirit of the firm. A waiter brought in two large glasses of sherry. The upshot was that the firm hired me as a clerk, and I started work there on the first of October.

Wilkinson's has long since become part of a financial conglomerate, but it was then small, with three executive directors including the chairman Ronnie Wilkinson, and three assistant directors. The Wilkinson family once owned a 'farmers' bank' in Oxford, which Barclays bought out in the 1860s. In the outer office three sub-managers sat just outside the green baize door from the directors' room, awaiting and relaying their instructions. The youngest and keenest of these was Mr Coward, tall and forward-leaning, with brilliantined black hair and huge hornrimmed glasses. His particular friend in the office, Mr Flower, whom he persuaded, when Flower married and left home, to go and live near him in Cheam, guided me round during my first week. Both had done National Service in the army and been commissioned. While Coward was highly imbued with *esprit de corps*, Flower was already cynical. Coward would pass the time enthusiastically imparting precise information about his garden or house-decorating and, when he heard that my wife was pregnant, the fact that his wife carried a lot of water during her pregnancy. Flower talked about his rugby games and the follies of women, including his young wife.

Further into the outer office were the stock department and the bill department, and finally the chief clerk, Mr Stenhouse, and his deputy, Mr Cady, men in their late fifties, and a small pool of two or three general stooges of whom I was one. The total sub-managerial and clerical staff, excluding two female secretaries, four messengers and the waiter, can barely have numbered a dozen. On arriving in the morning, all the outer office staff took turns to go out for coffee in groups of two or three, and while this was happening the directors (Mr O'Leary would first be served a double brandy), wearing top hats with their city suits, went out to do the rounds and ascertain their customers' wishes. On their return dealing began, and the messengers and stooges – and, when the supply dried up, clerks with fixed occupations – were detailed by the sub-managers to carry bills of exchange or Treasury bills to and from banks round the City (the interesting and even romantic names of some of these establishments, and the atmosphere of the narrow lanes, some containing Wren churches, which one used for short cuts – helped me to endure this tedious occupation). The commonest value was £5,000. The stooges filled in record books with the particulars of all transactions. One big ledger was used by Mr Stenhouse to strike a balance at the close of each day's business, and as soon as be did so we were free to go; it could be as early as 4 o'clock. If there was an error, we had to stay until it had been tracked down.

On paper colossal wealth appeared to flow in and out of the house every day. With the money it held on short loan – it could be for only a day or two – the firm dealt in gilt-edged stocks, and the broker would turn up every morning at sherry time, also wearing a top hat. How the discount market works is described in a book published by Chapman and Hall in 1952, called *The Bill on London*. Superficially it was not very complex, and at the time I thought I understood its principles.

Leaving aside the work, the environment was different from anything I had experienced before. Joining the army and being the only public-schoolboy in an intake of sixty with whom I spent every minute of every day had been a culture shock of sorts, but one that I could cope with easily. At Wilkinsons the shock was greater. While the army had been socially liberating, this was constricting. Several of my colleagues were in their twenties, but we all called eachother 'Mister'. They were destined to pass their entire working lives together, so it was important that nothing should disturb the little rituals of bonhomie and equability. We saw the ill-effects of mutual dislike going beyond proper bounds in the two elders, Mr Stenhouse and Mr Cady, who were united only in their hatred of Mr Plater, a man slightly younger than them and from similar beginnings, who had been promoted to the sub-managers' office. Both of them were veterans of the Great War and both, too, had been born and brought up in Finsbury, on the western fringes of the City, and recruited into the firm soon after the war from a working men's club there by the present chairman's father, who was one of its patrons. Each one married, moved out to an Essex suburb, and begot one son. Mr Stenhouse was a solid, straightforward character who did his work like clockwork, for ever puffing at his pipe; his regularity extended to going upstairs to the lavatory with his newspaper each morning immediately after hanging up his hat and coat. His talk was economical and, like much else at Wilkinsons, had a ritualised quality. A matter of more than passing significance in his life was his recent acquisition of an expensive gas heater, which was delivered to him with a small bit of the enamel chipped off. His battle with the suppliers to obtain a replacement became a heroic saga of the little man fighting for his rights, and we were given daily instalments for weeks on end. Mr Cady was not solid: he talked and laughed a lot, and was devious. With obvious reference to Mr Stenhouse, he sometimes said that some people mistook kindness for weakness. But under his stolid exterior Mr Stenhouse was kind too; and he regarded Mr Cady with silent contempt. Mr Cady had been the favourite of Ronnie Wilkinson's predecessor as chairman, a Mr Parsons, who let him and his wife occupy his private box at the Albert Hall for the Prom concerts as often as they liked, and his colleagues suspected that he informed on them. But he had no such advantages now. Cady had one noxious habit. He had been gassed in the war, and this left him with a persistent cough, but he made matters worse by seldom being without a cigarette stuck between his lips, so that when he coughed there was a shower of ash.

This was truly a job for life. After being with the company a certain time, and particularly on getting married, you could buy a house with a 100% mortgage at 2% interest. There were generous non-contributory pension and insurance schemes, and even the surveyor's fee for your house purchase was taken care of. Once you had accepted all this largesse, with no private financial resources, how could you extricate yourself? I realised early on that this was serfdom, however benignly it was dressed up. I had been there a month or two when Mr Coward took me aside and, looking eagerly though his horn rims, explained to me the company pension scheme. As soon as he let fall the words 'When you are sixty....', a bell rang in my brain. Of course I knew that I would be leaving Wilkinsons a long time before I was sixty, but now my original reason for coming here began to seem inadequate. The very thought of a lifelong attachment to this life – on the wrong side of the green baize door, as seemed to be the pre-destined lot of most of my confederates – struck me with dread, and I felt danger to myself in being so close to it.

Some of the other clerks were delightful people. Of my near contemporaries one, Mr Harrison, was about to get married when I joined and under Wilkinsons' auspices had just bought a house in Hornchurch. This quiet man had done his National Service as a private in British Honduras, and looked back on this brief interlude nostalgically as a magical adventure of a kind that could never be repeated. When he disappeared for the fortnight of his wedding and honeymoon, the place hummed with well controlled prurience, which briefly broke out when he returned. One colleague who differed from the rest in being, at around twenty-two, a mature personality and a confirmed bachelor was 'Bunny' W. An allergy prevented him from doing National Service, and although more than bright enough, he missed university and headed straight from school into the City. He, alone in the outer office, read *The Times;* well brushed and dapper, he was convivial, quick on the draw, sure of himself. Yet there was a weakness somewhere. Though slight of figure, he was known for downing a vast quantity of liquor when out on the town. I met him in the street a year or two later and over a quick pint he told me he had left Wilkinsons and gone to a foreign bank in the City, but was now looking round again.

One of whom I have poignant memories is Chris Cuthbert. His father was general manager at the head office of a clearing bank, which put him in a higher social stratum than the others. Instead of living in a place like Upminster, Hornchurch or Cheam, he went home each evening to Dorking, an important distinction. But even in such a gentle, uncompetitive place as Wilkinsons you needed a modicum of toughness, and this Cuthbert lacked. He was relatively tall, but seemed like a big version of a little boy with curly hair, a chubby face and large eyes with curling lashes. He had a suburban accent like the rest, but without a Cockney edge to it like Mr Flower and some others. Crude parental pressure brought him to Wilkinsons. When he was demobbed after National Service, he was sufficiently emboldened by that short taste of freedom from home influence to strike out by joining Novello, the music publisher. He was keenly musical, with a penchant for twentieth-century English composers – Vaughan-Williams lived near his home and his one serious ambition was to meet the great man. But his father thought that his oddball only son needed security, which meant the City. Chris had a girlfriend with whom he went to concerts, and later married her; she too worked in the City and one lunchtime I caught sight of them together in Leadenhall Market and was surprised by how attractive she was: dark and slender, and obviously ·in love. Cuthbert was a bit of a card; he could give a passable imitation of a French horn, and when Bunny W. said one day that there should be a phone upstairs in the lavatory so that they could remain in contact with Mr Stenhouse, he made the sound of a raspberry. He was also sly. He let fall that it had been noticed when I was served sherry at my interview; none of them had been given such privileged treatment. Also none of them, except Chris, would have mentioned it. I called in at Wilkinsons more than twenty years later hoping to do a small bit of business with them. Most of the old gang were still around, but in a much expanded organisation they had been promoted at least to assistant directorships – except for Chris. I cheerily said 'Hello Mr Cuthbert' but he was unforthcoming. I learned later that his marriage came apart and he died before reaching retirement.

Although we in the outer office were definitely beyond the green baize door, the non-clerical staff, except for the two lady secretaries, were in a yet humbler category. Joe Myers, the rascally chief messenger, was a well-known character around the City pubs. His marriage was childless and loveless, and he joyfully escaped every weekend to enjoy his favourite sport, angling. He loved to show his special penny which had 'heads' on both sides and, as an occasional treat, a photograph of himself, taken in West Africa during the war, holding an African woman's bare breasts. The butler Mr Farmer, was a character of even rarer vintage than Joe; but for his striped trousers and black jacket and waistcoat, he would have been ideally cast as a comic porter in a Shakespeare play, with his jug-ears and a vacant, slightly worried expression reminiscent of Stan Laurel. He served the directors' lunch, which was brought in from a caterer, and then joined the second shift in the dining room of a pub on the other side of Leadenhall Market where, every day, the outer office staff and the messengers received lunch, which was free up to a value of five shillings, plus a sixpenny tip for the waitress. This truck payment was said to be due to the directors' concern that all employees should have at least one square meal a day (don't tell the wife). The three sub-managers and the secretaries were fed together at a more fancy establishment to the value of seven-and-sixpence.

The pub dining room was ministered to by Florrie, a boot-faced, ageless woman dressed entirely in black like all of her vanished breed of pub waitresses, and as respectable as my colleagues. Despite her lugubrious expression, she tolerated the gentle banter with which we regaled her day by day. Then one¹ day Florrie asked us how we would like our fish 'done' (grilled or in batter). I was sitting next to Mr Farmer. He was a man of few words and up till then had been in his habitual trance. Suddenly his face brightened and he said 'Have you ever been done, Florrie?' Mr Stenhouse said 'Don't mind him', and the gaffe passed with no more than confusion on Florrie's part and embarrassment on ours. The strange thing was that, despite his apparent dim-wittedness, Mr Farmer had remarkable abilities. As a headwaiter he was much in demand to organise the waiting at banquets and big functions all over London, including Buckingham Palace, and it was said that the Duke of Edinburgh greeted him like an old friend. This was no myth: one of the junior messengers had been asked by him to make up his numbers, and said that on his big nights Mr Farmer was a changed man: he managed his team of waiters and kept them on their toes like a general commanding an army. His other talent was the horses: he made more money racing than he ever did with his free-lance waiting and at Wilkinsons, and had been seen driving his wife around in a large black Daimler.

I had been at Wilkinsons for a few months when I came in one morning to find in the office a man I knew from Oxford, Richard Judge. Although we had been no more than acquaintances before, I greeted him now, involuntarily, as if we were the closest friends – perhaps this and our automatic use of first names showed lack of feeling because, like my glass of sherry, it so obviously set us apart from our fellows. It was all I could do not to say 'What the hell are you doing here?' He was a classical scholar and a competent musician, but very much a man of the world – more so than most of Wilkinsons' directors – and he knew perfectly well what he was doing. Having worked for a time in a small merchant bank, he was riveted by the world of finance, and convinced that the discount market offered him the best chance of enjoying himself – going about the City with access, in the daily quest for business, to many influential financiers – and of making some money. At the same time it was not too demanding to curtail his many extramural activities. Within a week or two of my leaving Wilkinsons, we met by accident on the steps outside Urbino cathedral. He was on his honeymoon, about which there would certainly be no ribaldry when he returned to the office. I was alone but on my way to Riccione to meet Suzanne's father, Giancarlo Antinori, for the first time; Richard and his bride were driving in the same direction and offered to take me there. When we arrived at Giancarlo's house, they accepted my offer to introduce them to the old man, and as we confronted him on the doorstep, he immediately misidentified us: Richard was a few years older than me, and being prematurely bald looked older still (Suzanne was always sensitive about how much younger than her I not only was – eight years – but also looked). We then had the pain of sitting in his house for what seemed an endless time as he prepared cups of tepid tea. In spite of this inauspicious start, Giancarlo and I did establish a rapport.

At the first of my two interviews with Ronnie Wilkinson, my starting salary of £360 was raised to £500, and he said that I was just the kind of chap they wanted. In the late summer of 1954 I was unexpectedly summoned to see the chairman again and he informed me in a thoroughly pleasant way that Mr Stenhouse did not think I showed the interest or application necessary for a career with the firm. I did not argue. I could have three months to look around, and they would help me to find another job. He thought publishing might be in my line, and suggested that I had a talk with Ralph Snagge, one of the junior directors, who was known to have many contacts. Snagge said he knew one of the newer, brighter publishers, Derek Verschoyle, whom he promised to telephone. Accordingly I went the very next day to 14 Carlisle Street, Soho, to the interviewed, and Verschoyle offered me a job which I accepted. So I was out of Wilkinsons within a week of being fired – a salve to my battered pride.

That tight little society was behind me. I was glad to be gone but wistful all the same at saying goodbye. When I took leave of Mr Flower, the cynic, he said 'I envy you'. That was a difficult moment, especially as I felt I had let them down, barely working my passage but noting their peculiarities like a voyeur. The work I had to do was repetitive and lacked mental stimulus beyond anything I could have imagined. One day Bunny W. said to me 'Mr Hurst, I think you would even be happy in prison.' I took it as a compliment, but my psyche was rebelling. To make the mechanical work endurable I used to form mental patterns, but one night I stayed half-awake imagining for what seemed hours that I was entering details of transactions in one of the big ledgers in the outer office at Wilkinsons; I knew that something more needed to be done but could not think what it was. Then one evening I went to a recital of Beethoven quartets in the large hall at the Victoria and Albert Museum that contains the Raphael cartoons. My seat was near the back. The recital started with the famous Cavatina, which was not on the programme but was played in memory of Kathleen Ferrier who had just died. Very soon, as the programme went on, three of the four players began to take the shape of members of the staff at Wilkinsons, including Mr Stenhouse; the fourth player simply did not look like any of them. I knew it was an illusion, but it was very real and lasted right through the evening.

Interlude: The Wills of Uncle Fred and Uncle Martin

I was invited about this time by Uncle Gerald and Aunt Margaret to spend the night with them at Chislehurst. Their son-in-law Kenneth Elphinstone, a pious and handsome barrister, appeared after dinner, Margaret made herself scarce, and the two lawyers began to explain to me that there had been a small terminological slip in the drafting of the will of my great-uncle Frederick M. Hurst (1858-1918), which they had only recently noticed and which had ramifications affecting me. If the ramifications had been pleasant ones, they would surely not have gone to this trouble to tell me about them.

My great-grandfather Martin Hertz had three sons: my grandfather William Hertz, Uncle Fred and Uncle Martin. There were several daughters, all of whom married Germans and lived in Germany. Uncle Fred was the joint managing director of M. Hertz & Co. (the firm changed its name along with the family in 1916). He established a branch in Manchester in 1883, and this became more important than the Bradford branch which William closed in 1894, following Fred to Manchester. 'This development' (to quote Gerald in *Closed Chapters*, p.9) 'was due to the steady decline in the continental market for Bradford stuffs and the contemporaneous expansion of the far larger markets of Asia and Africa for Lancastrian cotton textiles.'

Fred died a much wealthier man just after the war than William was at his death in 1912. He had no children, and willed that his estate be shared out among the numerous progeny of his siblings. However, his widow had a life interest in it, and the family had to wait a long time for their turn; she outlived my father, dying at the end of 1944. Aunt Em was far richer in her own right than any of us because her father, a Tyneside shipbuilder called Redhead, left £700,000 early in the century, which was shared between her and just one brother. She regarded the Hursts as out to get their hands on her fortune, and throughout her long widowhood refused to see any of them. Gerald was Uncle Fred's executor, and when Aunt Em finally died, he remarked that the charities to which she bequeathed her money were quite respectable ones – not the cats' home as he had feared. Under Uncle Fred's will there were life interests for my father and Charles Kukla, Uncle Fred's nephew and successor as manager of M. Hurst & Co.; these, despite the error in drafting that affected them, were safe, and extended to their widows, but the interests of their offspring (there were four of us: my sisters, myself and Charles's son Ernest) could only be obtained for us, and then in a depleted form, through a lengthy process of persuading the numerous other legatees to renounce their residuary interest in our portions. I did not understand then, and still do not, why the fatal words 'to his widow if any', which followed the names of Arthur Hertz and Charles Kukla in the will, had this effect, but so it proved. Gerald and Kenneth asked me if I accepted this interpretation, which they assured me was legally correct. They also said that the firm of solicitors in Manchester which drafted the will had agreed to sort out the confusion resulting from their error as best they could, for nominal fees. So my hand had been forced, but it did not enter my head to take issue with Gerald and Kenneth mainly because I naively disdained to feel upset about it. My mother, like Charles Kukla would continue to enjoy her life interest as long as she lived, and Gerald asked me particularly not to tell her since it would only worry her to no purpose. I agreed to this too. Ernest Kukla, was so angry that he ceased all communication with our side of the family.

The obstacles to our ever seeing more than a fraction of this bequest were overwhelming. Those who had to make disclaimers were, to start with, all the living descendants of Martin Hertz, Uncle Fred's father, who had died in 1885 – that is, all except those living in Germany. My first cousins were easy enough, even the fairly numerous Australian progeny of my father's sister Aunt Jo, but Uncle Martin had a hard-up only daughter, and as expected she refused. Then there was the 'Custodian of Enemy Property', who still, ten years after the war, had responsibility for the descendants of the German aunts; half-Jewish though they were, Hitler's action in going to war with us had disqualified them from any automatic right to inherit property in the U.K. And finally, as residuary legatees, there were Aunt Em's admirable charities, and with them it could only be a question of striking a poor bargain. It was a lawyer's field day. My mother died in 1961 and Charles Kukla some years later in his nineties. At the end of the 1960s I finally received from the Manchester solicitors a cheque for approximately one-third of my proper share. My sister Rosemary in New York spent some of her share on a large ice-chest which she christened 'Fred'.

As time passed I felt less equably about what had happened. No wonder Gerald and Kenneth asked me not to talk to my mother, because she had a strong sense of justice and would have asked why Uncle Fred's intentions could not be carried out since it was quite obvious what they were. In the 1970s Kenneth said to me that if he had discovered the slip later (for it was he who had pointed it out to Gerald), rather than when he was younger and keener, he would have been strongly inclined to let sleeping dogs lie and hope for the best. This generous admission went a long way to turn away wrath.

I had a soft spot for Uncle Martin, the youngest by far of my great-grandfather Martin Hertz's children, born in 1864 and brought up in Germany, whither the older Martin returned in his last years, and cannot let the opportunity pass of recording something about him. His *curriculum vitae* is a virtual blank, but there were plenty of anecdotes, starting with his baptism, when the pastor said that he presumed the baby was being named after Martin Luther, and his father indignantly replied 'No, after me!' He did not have the brain-power or mature character of his older brothers and never succeeded in making a career for himself. An agency of the business was set up in London to give him something useful to do, but it did not work. Thereafter he was a remittance man for the rest of a long life, and the burden of writing annual cheques for Uncle Martin passed down the generations of the family.

He saw service in Malta as an intelligence officer (a source of hilarity in the family) in the Great War, though well into middle age, and thus came to be known as Major Hurst. He was also at one time Portuguese vice-consul in Manchester.

For him poverty had to be worn with style: he, his wife Aunt Jeannette and their daughter Kathleen always lived in the 'West One' postal district of London, even if it meant being under the rafters in a cold-water apartment. This, like everything else about Uncle Martin, profoundly irritated Uncle Gerald who, as general overseer of the remittances, believed he should cut his suit according to his cloth; Uncle Martin even had the temerity to reproach Gerald for letting the side down when, with a family of six children, he set up house in Ladbroke Grove, which was 'West Eleven'. Like his older siblings he was musical, and in Bradford played second fiddle to Uncle Fred, with Grandfather William Hertz on the cello and Frederick Delius on the viola.

Aunt Jeannette, remembered by Onkel Freddy in Germany as '*sehr hässlich*' (very ugly), slit her wrists in a Brighton boarding house when a doctor diagnosed as cancerous a small growth which the post-mortem proved to be benign. Uncle Martin's most famous remark was made to Gerald who, after spending a day in Brighton helping him with the formalities after Aunt Jeannette's death, was about to catch the train back to London. Uncle Martin slipped away to buy an evening paper, and hurried back elated. 'Look at this, Gerald!' he exclaimed, pointing to a small news item. 'It's about poor Nettie – the headline reads "Mayfair woman commits suicide"!'

Remembering him only from an outing to Ranelagh Gardens before the war, with his strange-looking daughter 'Cousin Kathleen' (her face bizarrely made-up, and wearing a black dress that came down to the ground), I was anxious, as a teenager, to meet this unique relic of our continental past. He spent the war in 'rooms' in Torquay, and there we caught up with him at the beginning of 1945. We were staying at the Imperial Hotel, and Uncle Martin came there to tea, a tiny old man dressed with Edwardian formality, looking distinctly Jewish (did he not once deplore the over-abundance of 'dirty Jews' at a holiday resort?) and with an unmistakable German accent. We brought him up to date with family news. He invited me to walk back with him to his digs, where he had a single room with only a modicum of possessions, including some child-like paintings he had done himself. He told me warm-hearted tales about various inconsequential encounters over the years, but was not disposed to talk about the distant past. After the war, living I know not where, he spent his days in the Junior United Services Club, a long-vanished late nineteenth-century Baroque extravaganza on the east side of Lower Regent Street. One day, as an undergraduate, I called there and inquired if Major Hurst was in. The porter led me into a cavernous saloon, and there the little figure, his skin now seemingly half-mummified, received me with traces of his old jauntiness (a quality rare in our sedate family). He produced a box of unlabelled Turkish cigarettes and offered me one, adding 'I have them specially made, y'know'. Early in 1952 I received a black-edged card announcing his death – incongruously in Birkenhead, where his daughter lived with the ex-ship's steward she married after an adventurous career as a 'journalist' on the continent after the outbreak of war, about which Uncle Gerald would only say that 'truth is stranger that fiction'.

Uncle Martin too made a will, and bequeathed £50 to my Australian cousin Mary, his god-daughter, but the cupboard was bare and it could not be paid. Charles Kukla remarked to me once that Uncle Martin was unjustly maligned by some members of the family.

One of the Brighter Publishers

I have to be thankful that the transition from being a clerk at Wilkinson Brothers Discount Company was so quick and painless. It was a blind date with Derck Verschoyle, but I saw nothing wrong in that.

Verschoyle was a man famed for his charm. As I entered his room he rose in a cloud of cigarette smoke and, holding out his hand, asked 'Are you like me, a writer *manqué*?' It was not a question I was yet prepared to answer with either a 'yes' or a 'no', but it showed that we were on the same wavelength. He also asked me within minutes if I wanted to invest money in the firm, and miraculously my wiser instinct prevailed and I said 'no'. Although I could tell him almost nothing about myself, he offered me a job at £500 a year, with the remarkable bonus of four weeks' annual holiday. I was not to be fitted into any department but given a general grounding. He wanted me to start at once, which of course suited me very well, but my only time off that year had been the week immediately after Andrew's birth, and I asked if I could join him at the end of a fortnight. He agreed reluctantly, saying that my prospects would be better if I could get down to work at once.

When I did start, it was clear that Verschoyle's words about prospects had not been idle. He said the firm was facing difficulties, and wanted me to tell him at the end of the week how I thought they might be put right. This was heady stuff for a total novice, and I briefly visualised myself as the saviour of the firm. He must have needed to convince himself that hiring me had not been – as it clearly was – yet another of those impulsive mistakes that had brought the firm to its present pass.

My first task, besides taking manuscripts home to read in the evenings, was typing invoices in the general office downstairs under the eye of Mr Braybrooke, a man in his late sixties who had been in publishing all his working life since early in the century, and had known some of its famous figures such as Otto Kyllmann of Constable and Wren Howard of Jonathan Cape. Short, stout and suffering from chronic dyspepsia due to worry, he talked for much of the time in his high-pitched voice about these worries. He had been production manager at Cape – 'making beautiful books', he said, was the only work he really cared about (and Cape's books at that time were beautiful) – until invited by Verschoyle in 1950, when he was starting up his business, to join him as general manager at a salary of £1,000. At the time the offer seemed flattering and lucrative, but he was now the dogsbody of the trade department, and a short time before my arrival Verschoyle cut him down to £500 a year. He was powerless to resist, since he was far too old to find another job. His all-absorbing concern now was to pay off the mortgage on his house in Ruislip before it was too late. I, meanwhile, was being paid the confiscated half of Braybrooke's rightful salary. Considering this, he was amazingly kind to me.

At the end of 1954 Verschoyle probably had about forty titles in print, not many of them classifiable as solid backlist. Production was at most a dozen titles a year – and the flow was now tacitly halted because his printers refused to do any more work for the firm until their bills were paid. Yet in the autumn of 1954 this house of cards still had many mansions. The only one of the five floors at 14 Carlisle Street not in use for the business was the attic where, after Verschoyle's departure, it was found that he had left just one article behind – a full-dress officer's uniform of the Royal Air Force, in which he served during the war. In the basement was the book store and packing area, with two full-time packers; there was a delivery van inscribed with the company's name and a part-time driver. In our department, besides Braybrooke and myself, there was a tea-and-telephone girl and an occasional helper with odd clerical jobs like stuffing envelopes, an actor called Harry Hancock. The production department had a highly-qualified manager: first it was the renowned book designer Francis Minns, whom Verschoyle lured away from André Deutsch when he was flush, but who returned to Deutsch soon after my arrival to be replaced by Keith Vaughan.[*] In addition there was a bright production assistant called Jackie on whom, as a lady, Verschoyle had felt free to use his wiles to obtain a financial injection into his business. She gave him £500, which she never saw again, so in effect she worked there for something like a year without payment. I was told that she lost her heart as well as her money to her employer. Produced by such skilled hands, the firm's publications looked pretty good. Cash was no object: I saw a finished pen and wash drawing by John Minton, done for the jacket of a novel but never used. It cost £100.

Then there was a resident 'reader' – first John Wyndham, soon

---

[*] Keith ended his career in the 1980s as head of the publishing course at Oxford Polytechnic.

to be an established critic, and after his departure John Rosenberg, a young writer and actor from New York who had recently married Elizabeth King, a reader at Longmans (who were about to publish John's first novel *The Desperate Art*). Mr Barham, the book-keeper, was a man of contrasts: elderly, toothless, with an Old Bill moustache and with fallen arches, he was irrespressibly amorous, and all the attractive girls in the office accepted an invitation from him at one time or another to go to the cinema, and lived in dread of being asked again. He was, he told me, a life-long revolutionary socialist. A rare bird in this aviary was Rudy Rothschild-Davidson, a darkly handsome but rootless antiquarian bookseller; his signet ring bore the five arrows of the Rothschilds, but he showed no other signs of affluence. He was entrusted with a programme of publishing massive bibliographies; two came out in his 2-3 years' tenure. He was the firm's highest-paid employee, at £2,500 a year, and he had a tall, tanned blonde assistant called Lesley whom he desperately lusted after, but who spent all her spare time sailing with her boyfriend. 'D.V.' himself (those initials were inevitably the subject of quips about our chances of being paid our next month's salaries) sat in a fine office with Regency furniture, and he had a personal secretary, Pam, who like Braybrooke, joined the firm at the very beginning. Heavily made up, dressed in daring colours, with streamlined blue-rimmed glasses, she was efficient, loyal, kind-hearted and, not surprisingly, a cynic. Finally, there was the salaried London salesman, a Scot called Chalmers.

Of the four directors one spent odd hours in the office working on publicity and press relations. This was John Walter Jr, then in his forties, a director of *The Times*. The suffix 'Junior' was no vulgar Americanism but full of snob-value. Until his father, who was still alive, sold out to Northcliffe, a John Walter was chief proprietor of the paper from its foundation. Everything about John Walter Jr (who died in 1980) proclaimed the decline of his family's greatness. His manner was fussy and ineffective. However, his name was an adornment on the firm's stylish two-coloured letterhead, which also bore the typically snobbish colophon of a heraldic boar's head. The financial backing came from the two non-executive directors, the immensely rich Graham Eyres-Monsell and Ian Whigham. Speculation among the staff about these two was rife. All we knew for certain about Whigham was that he was a cousin of the Duchess of Argyll, who as Margaret Whigham had been the most renowned débutante of all time, and was now involved in a well publicised divorce suit with the Duke.

Derek Verschoyle, a sprig of the Anglo-Irish gentry, was the only

non-Etonian director and in strength of personality he far outshone
the others. He had moved in London literary circles before the war
and after it was a diplomat for a few years; according to rumour,
Burgess and Maclean were his friends. It was 'common knowledge'
that he had had five wives, although *Who's Who* only showed two
– his first, Anne Scott-James, and the current one, who used to come
in and discuss manuscripts with John Rosenberg. He was tall, fair
and very bald, with a narrow bony face, and smoked incessantly.
His pale blue eyes glittered under heavy lids, and I was not alone
in being almost mesmerised by him; it seemed a pleasure to do
his bidding. When I went to him with my half-baked ideas for reforming
the business, based on a week's experience downstairs with Mr
Braybrooke, Chalmers the rep was in the room and poured scorn
on them. Any possible usefulness I may have had in D.V.'s eyes
probably vanished at that moment, and he was anyway so preoccupied
from then on that we scarcely ever came face to face again.

If Verschoyle seemed to bear up under his mounting tribulations,
the effect on John Walter was the reverse. He was born too late
to enjoy the power of his name; he had never found a niche in
life and the D.V. venture for a time seemed a belated means of
giving himself one. He was said to have invested £10,000, which
for him, unlike the two main backers, was not a trifling sum. Now
his dreams and his money were slipping away. His private life was
also in ruins; Rudy alleged that his wife's lover actually lived in
their house. He was drinking steadily and in a terrible state, yet
he must have been a genuine bibliophile because he had separately
set Rudy up in an antiquarian book business at 1 Monmouth Street,
from which he could not have hoped to garner either riches or glory.
That did not collapse with Verschoyle, but it did perforce about
two years later when Rudy, on holiday in France, stepped out of
his car to buy some cigarettes and was knocked over and killed.

Early in 1955, as the wolves were gathering, a new general manager
called Johnston was hired at a salary of £750. He was also a sleeping
director of Sidgwick and Jackson, and only a short time before had
been sailing the ocean wave as an officer on passenger liners. Although
we were never on first-name terms, we often had beer and sandwiches
together, when he would tell me about his Lothario-like exploits
at sea and maudlin reunions with his wife. He also told me that
John Walter asked him at their first meeting if he wanted to be
addressed by his maritime rank of 'Commander' or as 'Mister', and
when Johnston replied 'Mister', said that he thought 'Commander'
would be better for discipline in the office. One day D.V. took
the 'Commander' and me round the corner to Rupert Hart-Davis's

office in Soho Square to see, as he disarmingly said, how a real publishing house was run. A director called Townsend – tall, debonair, relaxed, the epitome of an English gentleman publisher – showed us round. The firm was in the euphoric aftermath of Heinrich Harrer's bestseller *Seven Years in Tibet* and the place throbbed with energy and confidence.

Even in the closing days there were moments when the gloom lightened. Late one afternoon an excited D.V. burst into the production department, where I was proofreading, and asked Keith Vaughan to cost the Duchess of Windsor's ghostwritten memoirs, which he had been offered. Perhaps this might convince our backers that the corner could at last be turned. The calculation was done and that was the last we ever heard about it.

By his works shall a man be known, so on that reckoning how did D.V. score? The manuscript D.V. gave me to read on my first day in his employment I warmly recommended, which made me suspect myself (D.V. probably shared the suspicion) of naive enthusiasm. This was a modest but gripping biography by Hope Costley-White of Mary Cole, a butcher's daughter of Gloucester who in the late 18th century was duped into a fraudulent marriage with the aged Earl of Berkeley of Berkeley Castle, and restored the ailing fortunes of his estate, only to find after the birth of five sons that they were all illegitimate. When Harrap published it later I felt vindicated. Of Verschoyle's actual publications the most charming were two illustrated children's stories by Ludwig Bemelmans about a naughty girl in a convent school called Madeline; then there were novels by Christopher Sykes, James Hanley and Manes Sperber; Patrick Leigh-Fermor's over-blown novelette *The Violins of Saint Jacques*; a lengthy work of political analysis by Raymond Aron (doubtless expensively translated); and a book by Randolph Churchill called *Fifteen Famous English Country Homes*. His bestseller was a biography of Nehru by M.R. Masani of which a large number were sold to Rupa in India. D.V.'s very first list announced a book by James Laver called *Memorable Balls*, which had still not appeared when the firm folded and was quietly dropped. Our most published author was Roy Fuller, with two novels and one book of poems. Years later Fuller told me that he sent one of his mss. in on spec. After weeks of silence he phoned, to be told that the book was already with the printer, though there had been no agreement. Fortunately he thought it was nice to have such a publisher.

The end came in the early spring of 1955. André Deutsch took over the stock, D.V.'s few promising futures, its many debts and its premises. Verschoyle left one day without saying goodbye to anyone, not even to Pam who had served him so faithfully ever since the day he started in Park Place, St James's (an expensive address for an unknown publisher, but it was across the street from Brooks's Club, to which all the directors belonged). Normally hardboiled, Pam was in tears. D.V. immediately resumed his publishing career with his friend Michael Joseph, but he later moved into other fields and died in the 1970s.

Deutsch did not take over D.V.'s loss; that was bought for tax purposes by Enid Blyton, who was no Noddy when it came to business. A few months later every literary agent in London was sending Deutsch juvenile mss. – word had got around that he had fallen into the Blyton net too. Deutsch had to scotch this rumour because he did not want to be a juvenile publisher, but on the other hand he was determined to keep Bemelmans, whom D.V. tried unsuccessfully to take with him to Michael Joseph. The Carlisle Street premises were the main attraction to Deutsch and there was no question, under the circumstances, of money changing hands for the lease. However, just to make the transaction 'feel right' his lawyer Stanley Rubinstein proposed a nominal price of 10 shillings, and handed D.V.'s lawyer a 10s. note from his pocket. Deutsch had a sleepless night, and next day repaid Rubinstein the 10s. – 'just in case you think you own the lease'. He eventually sold the lease to Secker and Warburg for £10,000.

Playing at one-upmanship to the last, D.V. turned to Deutsch during a pause in the negotiations and asked him what the weather was like in Bangkok – he was about to go there on an important mission (we had been told that this was why the R.A.F. uniform was hanging in the attic). In the event the mission went without him.

Professionalism had arrived in Carlisle Street – there was also a different approach to staff relations. No place could be found for poor Braybrooke and he had to go, but hearing that I was married and had a child, Deutsch offered me a job as assistant to his book-keeper Mrs Howell. After considering it overnight I turned the offer down, but sat with Mrs Howell long enough to learn that on the day Derek Verschoyle Ltd started business in 1950, it paid Dylan Thomas £100. The reason for the payment was not recorded, but I suspect it was protection money to the gods, as well as an early example of the firm's *folie de grandeur*.

The Passion for Architecture

After being introduced to the Architectural Press (hereafter A.P.) by John Betjeman on the recommendation of Lawrence Dale, as mentioned earlier, I was called to an interview at 9-13 Queen Anne's Gate some two months after leaving Carlisle Street. The entrance foyer was cunningly designed in the ascetic but spirited style of the Festival of Britain, with stark black and white and much use of mirrors and visual tricks. Immediately below it, in total contrast, was 'The Bride of Denmark', the famous basement bar furnished with relics salvaged from bombed or dismantled Victorian pubs. Here I met Ian McCallum, the 'executive editor' of the monthly *Architectural Review*, and Ian Nairn. McCallum was in his mid-thirties, always dressed like a model and without a hair on his head out of place. He was almost excessively good-looking (a perceptive secretary nicknamed him 'Fishface'), and his low, dulcet voice matched the easy flashing smile, uneasily accompanied as it often was by a smell of toothpaste. Ian Nairn was McCallum's opposite. Physically large, ungainly and dressed anyhow, he was intense and spoke in a high-pitched, strangulated voice with just a trace of a north-of-the-Trent accent. He seemed warm and was unaffected. We chatted, and among other things McCallum asked me what I thought of the Methodist Central Hall, just round the corner. Since then I have developed a strong taste for late Victorian and Edwardian public buildings but have never much liked that one; however, I knew I was supposed to say that I did like it and obliged. I was also asked to produce a piece of my own writing; all I had to offer was an article on Sigmund Pollitzer which *Studio* published, and paid me £3 for, in 1953. In short I was hired as an assistant to the production editor – Ian Nairn.

The reason why he needed one became clear after I joined in early May 1955. In my first week a special number of the *Review* was published, called 'Outrage'. On the cover was a drawing by Gordon Cullen, the A.P.'s brilliant resident artist and architectural visualiser, showing a view along a main road at the entrance to any large town in England, from Carlisle to Southampton, with spec-built 'ribbon development' semis and gibbet-like concrete lampstandards stretching away into infinity. The issue set out to expose the abysmally unimaginative and frequently hideous work of local authority architects' and planners' departments. The research and most of the photography were done by Nairn himself. He had enthused H. de C. Hastings, co-proprietor of the A.P. and paramount chief among the *Review*'s five editors, with the idea for the issue and been hired on the strength of it; in that sense the production job was a blind, although he in fact did the donkey work to layouts by Ian McCallum and J.M. Richards, another more senior editor. Now, with me sharing it, he could devote time to related projects, and cope with the after-effects of 'Outrage'.

These came in a deluge. As soon as the special issue appeared, most national papers carried sympathetic features on it. However, one borough architect, picking up one of Ian Nairn's phrases, 'Things in Fields' (structures housing electricity generators – Nairn also had fun with concrete bus shelters), pathetically asked if he and his kind were 'things in town halls'. Duncan Sandys, the Minister of Housing, took up the theme (doubtless with some opportunism because the worst 'outrages' emanated from Labour-controlled councils), and the result was the founding of the Civic Trust, which still exists. Nigel Nicolson, a prominent Conservative backbench M.P., took an interest (H. de C. had once been closely associated with Nicolson's publishing partner George Weidenfeld, which may explain this). Within weeks the Duke of Edinburgh used in a speech the keyword of the new campaign, 'Subtopia', which Ian coined himself and has long been in standard dictionaries. He was on the verge of being enrolled in the select band of the mid-1950s Angry Young Men.

Ian Nairn combined admirable and very disagreeable characteristics, and the latter gave me the final push in deciding to leave the A.P. just over two years later. I had to mention these to Hastings at our farewell interview, and he replied judiciously that although I showed talent as a writer, Ian had genius, which was why he hired him and would hold on to him, difficult as he was known to be. When Ian first came to the office, Hastings said, he entered by sidling round the door, so shy and gauche was he. What was Ian's genius? He was the only child of a minor civil servant, born and brought up in the Surrey outer suburbs although the family were originally from the north: his great-grandfather was stationmaster somewhere near the Scottish border, and this seemed to be the lodestone in his search for identity. He studied mathematics at Birmingham University and there met his first wife Joan, a librarian – homely, kind and polite. When I knew him they lived in a one-room flat and seemed enviably close, but only a few years later he left her, saying she was not sufficiently interested in sex. Also she quietly wanted children and he noisily did not. From the university he went into the R.A.F. and was commissioned. It was jokingly said at the A.P. that Ian flew his Meteor over the countryside looking down longingly at Soane mansions, but the truth was more bizarre. One day, riding a bicycle, he had a bad spill and was knocked unconscious. When he came to, his burning interest in architecture, till then latent and recognised, was fully in place.

This did not take the form of wanting to be an architect or a town-planner; far from it. He would be a critic and interpreter – a tireless collector of facts and impressions from his unending travels, at first around Britain and later on the continent and in North America. For me, coming to the A.P. was a first taste of doing work that really fired me, even down to the humdrum detail of interpreting page layouts by McCallum or Richards. In Ian Nairn, of all the people at the A.P., I sensed a similar sort of interest in architecture to my own – from the gut and not merely from the intellect. Ian was proudly indifferent to creature comforts, and dressed as unaesthetically as possible in baggy flannels and jacket and an open-necked Air Force shirt. He claimed to have worn a suit only once, when he married Joan – she was under twenty-one at the time, and her parents only consented to the marriage on condition that it took place in church, hence the suit. He spoke of this as if it still rankled. For a time we shared a top-floor office, and in winter, with its small gas-fire, it took some time to get warm. One cold day I was in there first and both turned on the fire and shut the window. When Ian came in, he made a dart for the fire and turned it off, and opened the window, spluttering in his high whine that if I didn't like it I could wear my overcoat. Once I read a description he had written of the domed ante-chapel at Clare College, Cambridge, in which he said that the architect's genius made him nearly sink involuntarily to his knees – an effect of the spatial dynamics, be it understood, not of reverence for the architect or for the Lord. I was incautious enough to ask him rhetorically if that was really how it made him feel. He snarled back that he would not have written it if he had not meant it, which was unanswerable, but when I look at his once trendy book *Nairn's London* today, I find it often over-written and sentimental. Yet through it speaks the authentic Ian: quirky, restless, truculently anglophile, investing the working class and especially its mean streets, pubs, snack bars and transport caffs with a romantic, even heroic aura. He respected the aristocracy because of their beautiful houses. What he couldn't abide was the middle class, with its compromises and pretences that he lumped together as the 'little life'.

We agreed more often than not, but we were unambiguously united in our dislike for McCallum, our immediate boss, whom Ian Nairn compared to Professor Welsh in *Lucky Jim*. His male subordinates had a way of getting up and leaving, unable to bear his smooth-tongued yet stinging way of addressing us. McCallum's secretary Maureen, with honey-coloured hair and an enchanting figure, was the prettiest girl in the whole office, and several of the young men, including Ian Nairn and myself, lusted after her; so it was galling when it appeared that she only really liked McCallum, who was invariably polite and considerate to the opposite sex. One day, walking into McCallum's room on a routine errand, I had the nasty shock of finding with him Colin F., a homosexual young man I had known at Oxford, for whom I felt unmixed contempt: his speciality was vamping much older men, preferably those with money and position (they included Professor Dawkins and John Sparrow, Warden of All Souls), and combined with this went an unappealing ingenuousness. He was now employed by a top wine firm in the West End, and looked every inch the smooth showroom attendant. 'I believe you know eachother', said McCallum. I have seldom exchanged a more unpleasant handshake. My secret was out, but so was McCallum's; I had suspected his orientation before but not been certain.

I had another job in the house besides production of the *Review*, as secretary to the weekly meetings of the five editors: H. de C. Hastings, McCallum, Jim Richards, Nikolaus Pevsner and Hugh Casson. Pevsner was a temporary member of the A.P. staff during the war while technically an 'enemy alien', and this created a strong bond of mutual respect and loyalty between him and H. de C. He was also close to another, more powerful publisher, Allen Lane, who was the patron of his large-scale projects. He had already edited Penguin's magnificent architectural histories, and was how working on his most colossal project, *The Buildings of England*. For the volume on Surrey Pevsner recruited Ian Nairn as co-author – for Ian, Surrey's many country houses by Lutyens and his contemporaries made it a Mecca – but mostly the series was Pevsner's own unaided work. To be so prodigiously productive needed special qualities, and he did indeed function with a machine-like ease and precision, without obvious hang-ups and with a blameless, contented domestic life – in the potted biography on his books his marriage and three children always came first. He had an engaging dry manner, and as far as I know his only enemy was John Betjeman, to whom he must have appeared like a Japanese trawler to a fisherman in an open boat. His gift for writing English went far beyond simple mastery of the language to an intuitive inventiveness – he could juggle with the idiom like an academic Conrad. He and Ian Nairn, nearly thirty years apart in age, died in 1982 within a few days of eachother so that, in

architectural periodicals at least, their obituaries appeared together,
Inevitably the much-honoured architectural historian rated more column-
inches in the national press than the maverick critic. Ian Nairn surely
deserved an entry in the *D.N.B.*, but did not get one.

Hugh Casson, who was as friendly and uncondescending as Pevsner,
made his name and got his knighthood early as one of the masters
of ceremonies of the Festival of Britain. By the mid-'50s he was
already an inside figure and on friendly terms with the royal family.
Once when I asked Ian Nairn, without satirical intent, if he could
name any buildings Casson had designed – I could not – he gave a
hollow laugh and said 'Exactly'.

Jim Richards had trained and worked for a short time as an architect,
but soon turned to journalism and from the early 1930s, with a
break in the war, he worked on one or other or both of the Press's
two periodicals, the monthly *Review* and the money-making weekly
Architects' Journal. His *An Introduction to Modern Architecture* (1940)
is lucid, workmanlike and a touch didactic. He could not avoid seeming
rather severe and pompous, addressing Ian Nairn, Bill Slack (layout
man on the magazines for forty years), myself and other juniors
by our surnames *tout court*. He was a member of the Royal Fine
Art Commission and architectural correspondent of *The Times*, and
got his C.B.E. and joined the Athenaeum while I was at the A.P.;
he was working his way slowly up the ladder which Casson somehow
managed to by-pass altogether. His pomposity was more than skin-deep,
because he gave his recreation in *Who's Who* as 'work'. But under
the outward exterior was an attractive man, decent and warm-blooded.
I was delighted to note how, during one editorial meeting, he let
his eyes lingeringly follow the shapely Maureen as she passed round
the room serving the coffee. When McCallum was away, Jim did
the layout and some of the writing of the *Review*, and the male
staff sighed with relief.

The only thing about Jim which bothered me was his excessive
deference to Hastings who, I thought, very gently made a fool of
him. Of the five editors Hastings alone had no professional connection
with architecture. He studied art briefly at the Slade School, then
became editor of both journals in his mid-twenties. His achievements
in this role need no elaboration here; Richards's autobiography *Memoirs
of an Unjust Fella* (1980) describes these as well as portraying the
man. 'Townscape', a favourite theme of the *Review*, was his invention,
and Gordon Cullen's drawings brought it to life. He espoused modernism
early, imposing his personality on the stuffy periodicals he inherited,
and became, through the transformed organs, a shaper of opinion
and taste. The 'Functional Tradition', a cult of the robust, unadorned

building forms of early industrialism, was another theme he embraced, helped by Eric de Maré's photographs.

Not only was the modern *Review* his creation, but so was the interior of the three mid-Georgian houses the firm rented form Christ's Hospital. Apart from the confection of mirrors and black and white décor in the entrance, the rest was camped-up Georgian, the walls painted viridian green or terra-cotta red, with the cornices and woodwork white. Vernacular objects such as topographical prints, Staffordshire china plates and old handbills adorned the walls. Most sumptuous was the boardroom and Hastings's own sanctum adjoining it on the first floor – a true *piano nobile* with many surprises. In one way Hastings resembled Evelyn Waugh: both were sons of solidly middle-class technical publishers, both had genius, and both resorted to elaborate and expensive affectations to shield a fragile ego from scrutiny by the vulgar. They were alike too in aping aristocratic dress, behaviour and general appurtenances. We, as the staff of his pet child the *Review,* had easier access to him than most of our other colleagues, but the mystique of the omnipotent recluse, invisible within his hall of mirrors, who rewarded the just and unjust strictly according to their deserts, was sedulously maintained.

I had to write up the minutes of the weekly editorial meetings and see that decisions were carried out. This minimum of chores was more than outweighed by the enjoyment of being in at the planning of our future issues, the consideration of architects' recent jobs for publication, and post-mortems on the issues as they appeared, and of course hearing gossip and watching these five very different men together. The design of the Shell building on the South Bank let loose a torrent of condemnation, which became muted after an incautious anonymous comment by Jim in the *Journal*'s 'Astragal' gossip column on how the architects secured the commission for it resulted in a libel writ.

Although the layout of every feature was designed by either Jim or Ian McCallum, I had some discretion over both layout and content when it came to filling up the rest of the paper. An inspired space-filler was our literary editor Peter (Reyner) Banham. His knowledge of the modern movement was encyclopaedic, and he would knock off elegant and engaging little pieces to order, in the rather blasé style that was our hallmark. Here I had my first introduction to typography. In the *Review* there was a preference for robust Victorian faces: Scotch for the main texts, a large size of Clarendon for the introductions to features (usually written by Peter) and Doric italic for the captions to jobs. For certain headings a rare shadow italic of the 'Egyptian' family was used; this could only be obtained from a nearly blind typographer Charles Hasler, who produced the settings to order. Several such faces were widely used on buildings for a decade or so after the Festival of Britain. The *Review* regularly published articles about lettering, mostly by Nicolete Gray. When McCallum asked me, not just once, to set something in 'Scotch Roman Italic', I realised that he had not a clue about typography.

In and Out of Queen Anne's Gate

I had only been with the A.P. a few weeks when we moved to Greenwich. After Andrew's birth the previous spring, Suzanne did not want to go back to our furnished flat in Chelsea, and while the two of them remained in our cottage at Felixstowe Ferry, it was left to me to find a new flat. Taking the line of least resistance, I got one from my Verschoyle colleague Rudy. He had three floors of a house in Warwick Road, Earls Court, and this was the empty first floor. Then as now, Warwick Road carried heavy traffic up from the Embankment to the trunk roads leading to the west; and directly outside our windows was a zebra crossing with beacons that flashed all night. Suzanne did not object to it, but for me it quickly became a place out of hell, utterly soulless, and I longed to get away from it. Doris Lessing lived above us on the top floor. Her young son Peter and Christopher Anthony played together, but Suzanne and she did not click. I would sometimes be invited upstairs to have wine or coffee with her visitors when I was alone, and was fascinated by her panther-like movements. Suzanne could not bear the sound of her typewriter going on till late at night, and once asked me to go up and ask her to stop. Motivated by cowardice and high principles in about equal measure, I refused and we had an alarming row.

Suzanne was away in Italy when, walking through Shepherd's Market, I came on a handwritten card in a newsagent's window advertising a freehold Georgian house in Greenwich. The owner, it turned out, was Martin Boyd, an Australian novelist; he had bought the house a few years before for a niece and nephew visiting England, but they had left and the house was empty. It was one of a trio facing south over Greenwich Park – the pediment of the central one contained an oval medallion saying 'PARK PLACE 1791'. I beat Boyd down fractionally from his asking price and agreed to buy the house for £3,000. It had nice proportions, though most of the original fireplaces and window shutters had gone; it had space; and above all it was not in Earls Court. Greenwich had appealed to me for some time, and it never occurred to me that Suzanne could be anything but delighted with it and its location. Unfortunately I was wrong. Park Vista (the road's new subtopian title) was about a quarter of a mile to leeward of the imposing but grimy Greenwich power station, which deposited a coating of soot on cills below open windows on the north side. Also it was a vertical type of house, with four floors including the basement, each with two rooms. The dirt and the need to go constantly up and down became a settled bugbear. For her, with her yearning for the warm south, the ugliness and noise of the Greenwich High Road about a hundred yards to our rear, with its small, unattractive shops, grim-faced people and endless lorries thundering through, was as hellish as Earls Court had been for me. Matters were not improved by the 'Plume of Feathers' pub three doors away. This was a traditional pub whose blotchy-faced landlord, a former chief petty officer, told me when we met late one night as he was taking his dog for a walk after closing time, that he was a tolerant man who would put up with almost anything, 'but I won't serve niggers.' One night I heard a baby persistently crying and at last went out to inspect, and tracked the sound down to the back of a car in the road where it lay screaming while the parents were inside. This was normal. Another time I saw two small children at the entrance trying to call their parents, only to be chased away by their mother with a mouthful of abuse. On Friday and Saturday nights at closing time revellers regularly vomited in the road just below our windows.

Croom's Hill, on the west side of Greenwich Park, has a wonderful collection of 17th- and 18th-century houses, and before we even went to Earls Court I answered an advertisement in the 'Personal' column of *The Times* for a furnished flat on the top floor of one of them. The house belonged to Noël and Bernard Adeney, and although it turned out that they did not want to let it to a family with children, we got on famously at first meeting and became friends as soon as we arrived in Greenwich to live. They were both painters (he was born in 1878, she in 1890), he the less productive and fluent of the two; he was tall and handsome, and though charming, also remote. Noël was a tiny *jolie laide,* intense and eager to establish a completely frank and intimate relationship almost from first meeting. She was Bernard's second wife – his first, Therese Lessore, went on to marry Sickert. As a young woman she moved on the fringes of 'Bloomsbury', but the 'defining' relationship of her later life was with Denton Welch, a neighbour in Kent where they lived before coming to Greenwich at the end of the war. As an art student in the 1930s he broke his back in a cycling accident, and thereafter had a slow and agonising decline till his death in 1948. Noël gave him love and support and tried to fight off the unpleasant ex-sailor who looked after him. She was no writer, but she followed the example of Denton Welch himself, who wrote three autobiographical novels, and produced her own effort in that genre, *No Coward Soul*, about their friendship (to disguise Welch's homosexuality, the ogreish protector was depicted as female). It was accepted by Chatto and Windus, and was going though the works soon after we came to Greenwich. She was thrilled to be taken for a routine author's lunch by Cecil Day-Lewis, the partner at Chatto's editing the book, but was less charmed by his suggestions for revision, which she considered insensitive; it had been difficult enough for her to write it in the first place. It came out to a muted reception. Not long afterwards Day-Lewis came to live in Greenwich, and Noel expected a lovely friendship to blossom between them, but when she went to call she got a swift brush-off. The hurt festered. A cross she had to bear over a longer time-span was Bernard's conversion to Roman Catholicism after a near-mortal illness. She flirted with his monsignor, but as an atheist convinced of Bernard's error, she would give him no peace and argued with him until he became desperate.

Another compatible but quite different set of neighbours were the Grays who lived in a Georgian house in Maze Hill, on the other side of the Park: Nicolete (already mentioned); Basil, Keeper of the Oriental Department at the British Museum; and their five children of my generation but slightly younger – for a time the Russian-speaking Camilla and I sought out eachother's company on our daily train rides from Maze Hill station to Charing Cross. They were a spiky, precious family who failed to make their splendid house comfortable inside; the picture in the place of honour was by Mondriaan. Basil was a charming, sophisticated man who knew many eminent people; when Macmillan became prime minister, he remarked that they had once been fellow house-guests – at Viceregal Lodge in Delhi. He had shared digs with John Betjeman at Oxford.

I began going to church shortly before arriving in Greenwich. The typically inconsequential occasion was reading in the A.P.'s idiosyncratic pocket guide to London that Charles Smyth, the rector of St Margaret's, Westminister, preached 'good intellectual sermons'. I went, and found myself entranced – by more than the rector's sermons, good as these were. The Anglicanism that had washed around me in my schooldays had never touched me before but it did now. St Alfege's, the Hawksmoor parish church of Greenwich, practised a high but mainline Anglicanism that suited me in a way that Evangelicanism and 'bells and smells' Anglo-Catholicism could never have done. Blissfully unconscious, I sought diversion from my difficulties at home in the seemingly innocuous pursuit of milk and water religion and 'good works'. I joined in various activities at the church, even briefly taking a Sunday School class, and became a prison visitor at Brixton. I went there at first on one evening a week, but sometimes twice as closer relationships with prisoners developed. Suzanne didn't know how to cope with all this, being well aware that these seemingly admirable activities won me approval and that I got a kick out of them, but that the underlying motivation was dubious.

Then, in spite of having a highly congenial job, I began to feel an urge for a more 'committed' way of life. I even inquired at my father's hospital, Guy's, about the possibility of entering the Medical School. The Dean, who remembered me in kneepants, was accommodating and said I could be admitted (probably shrewdly calculating that by so doing he was making it less likely that I would go ahead with the idea), but I put my head in the noose when I told the crusty veteran Guy's physician Sir John Conybeare, whom I got to know socially after coming to London, about this chimera. He, not conceding an inch, said that scientific curiosity rather than a sentimental urge to benefit humanity should be the motive for taking up medicine – an exaggeration containing much truth. We had this conversation over tea in the Athenaeum and within hours he phoned me to say that if I wanted a chat with his old comrade-in-arms from the Great War and father of one of my Oxford friends, the stockbroker Graham Greenwell, he would see me. So I called on him in the early evening at his flat above Prunier's restaurant in St James's, and he plied me with gin as he expounded his wisdom. His line was: 'You're doing well at your present job – why change?' I went away drunk but momentarily purged of illusions.

The two Nestors had worked the necessary cure, but for the time being it was only a local cure and the generalised malaise remained. Another symptom soon appeared when I began to have fantasies of myself as a priest. This could never be translated into a concrete plan, because my status as the husband of a divorced woman automatically precluded me from Anglican orders. I was detached enough to realise how outrageous the idea was, and confessed it as a sin to Father M., whom I used to visit at the Cowley Fathers' house in Westminister. This sweet man, who was decorated for gallantry in the Great War, is still remembered long after his death for his seeing eye. As soon as the words had passed my lips he sat bolt upright and, galvanised with passion, exclaimed, 'This is the work of the Adversary – and how!'

My practice of religion was precariously balanced. It depended on 'everything in the garden' being 'lovely'. It also depended, at another level, on being seriously pursued. (It didn't depend on belief in the articles of faith in the Creeds, which I never possessed.[*]) Father M. once enunciated a great truth about religious practice in Sunday School parlance: 'Prayer knocks sin on the head, and sin knocks prayer on the head.' But prayer of the kind that he meant needs more strength of will and staying power than I have ever possessed in internal matters. It was therefore a question of chance how long I would continue to be free from sin or serious temptation.

A 'one evening stand' that resulted from my offering a lift back to London to a woman I met at Mary Stanley Smith's one Sunday after a week-end with my mother caused no serious problem; it was obviously not going to continue and could be wiped off the slate according to good Catholic practice. It was rather different when I fell in love with a young student at Oxford whom I already knew in another context. Being invited to her room for tea after a chance meeting in the street and watching her sitting on the floor as we talked worked upon me; I knew, and she knew, that we were never going to bed together, but she encouraged the friendship, and we met clandestinely and enjoyably until she and her acknowledged lover, whom I did not meet till their wedding day, were actually married. This infatuation shook my complacent religiosity out of place. I still went to church but my heart was not in it. I once said to Father M. that I was thinking about divorce, and he literally threw up his hands. It could not be thought about.

My involvement with the church has been like sitting on a see-saw with the world, the flesh and (Father M. would insist) the Devil at the other end. When (as will be related shortly) I met Christine, who like me had been a church member and whom ironically I met via the church, the church and I parted company until, in desperation when my marriage to her entered an impasse, I went running back. I married Rachel in 1974, and partly because we both had young children but for other less tangible reasons, we became members of our local Anglo-Catholic church – bells, smells and all. She dropped out first, about ten years later, and then I did, again because of a passing infatuation. Since then I have felt that the see-saw has

---

[*] Except for one: the trial and crucifixion, for which there is independent evidence. For me this happens to be the most important, because willingness to undergo crucifixion in the sense of denial of self seems the one unavoidable requirement placed upon anyone who would be a true follower of Jesus.

achieved equilibrium (Father M. would doubtless say that the Devil, grown fat on my former good resolutions, is sitting with his feet on the ground laughing, while I am stuck helpless high in the air). I have concluded that the infinite subtleties of the physical, animal and vegetable world, not to mention the intellectual, spiritual and artistic worlds, can not be considered other than as a 'creation', though how they were created must for ever elude us. As for Jesus of Nazareth, he was the mightiest spiritual genius among the Jewish prophets, also powerful in prayer because of his virtuous and ascetic life, who enunciated a system of conduct which he illustrated in seductive, exhilarating sermons and parables, humane but uncompromising, which we can all profitably endeavour to follow. Thus I confess flatly to being a Nazarite rather than a 'Christian' in the strict sense of a believer in Jesus as 'Christ'. A great man of the spirit like William Temple hesitated before being ordained as a priest because he had 'difficulties' over the resurrection and the virgin birth; I, as a lesser man of the spirit, have at times ignored or forgotten those difficulties, but now prefer to remind myself of them.

According to my theory, the early fathers of the church realised that no rational and educated person could believe these things, so they had a very rational idea: to decree that they must be believed, on pain of eternal hellfire and more immediate penalties in the here and now. It worked. Then came the Enlightenment and, above all, the scientific and therefore rational 19th century. 'Faith' was under threat, so what did the Pope do? He decreed a series of irrational dogmas: papal infallibity, the immaculate conception of Mary and the assumption of Mary. It is a wonderful way of controlling people.

My name means 'bearer of Christ'. Of all the 'sons of God' Jesus was the closest to his 'father', but I cannot believe that he is the 'only-begotten' son of God, in the technical sense of the trinitarian doctrine. He is our 'brother', and as such I 'bear' him gladly. How can anyone express such opinions who surveys the great buildings, paintings, music and literature inspired by devotion to this very Jesus – but as the Christ and only-begotten son of God? I am fortunate in having been left as an infant on the steps of the Anglican church where, perhaps more than in any other church, people have been allowed to find their own salvation. I will always be roused to devotion by reading the offices and collects in the 1662 Prayer Book and by the words and music of our great hymns, and I hope that eventually the order for the Burial of the Dead will be read over my body.

Not many years ago I was invited to give a Sunday morning sermon at a 'broad' Anglican church in Blackheath. My subject was the ever-growing squeamishness in the mainline C. of E. about saying anything nasty on the terribly politically-incorrect concept of sin – as evidenced in the various liturgies that have replaced the Prayer Book. If Jesus's main *raison d'être* was not saving sinners, what was it? Does a sin-blind church have any excuse to exist except as a social club?

H. de C. Hastings was both jealous taskmaster and enlightened patron. He made Ian Nairn's career by giving him a free rein with 'Outrage', and had employed Ian McCallum at intervals ever since he went to prison at the outbreak of war in 1939 on registering as a conscientious objector – something Ian Nairn and I, having been in the forces, smugly took as an additional reason for despising him. Hastings, by giving Pevsner a job early in the war, saved him from virtual destitution, and in return this great scholar went on contributing articles to the *Review* long after peace brought him prestige and demanding employment elsewhere. I was given two feature articles to write. One, on electricity pylons in the landscape (I ended up liking them), was signed by Hugh Casson. The other, of rather more moment, appeared as the work of 'the Editors': it was on traffic congestion in the heart of Oxford and the plan, then under serious consideration by the city fathers, to cut a relief road through Church Church Meadow – or possibly further away from the city beyond the Isis (Thames) to the east, although that alternative was always seen as too cumbrous and inconvenient. At that time the old working-class faubourg of St Ebbe's, south-west of Carfax, still stood homogeneous and intact and undisguisedly slummy. The area would have carried the continuation of any southern relief road; as it is, the whole of St Ebbe's has been swept away and is the site of a truncated relief road and large car park. Christ Church Meadow remains undissected, and presumably will remain so. But at that time, while the controversy was at its height, I was ordered by H. de C. to go for some days to Oxford and write a report on it. This involved interviewing heads of colleges and other luminaries such as the City Architect and Thomas Sharp, whose book *Oxford Replanned* the A.P. published and who revealed alarming signs of paranoia when we dined together. If it had not been for this assignment, I would never have had lengthy conversations with such figures as Maurice Bowra, A.L. Goodhart and John Sparrow, or the delightful new Rector of my College, Walter Oakeshott; nor would I have discovered that in the colleges north of the High the idea of a road through the Meadow was regarded almost with equanimity, which was far from being the case on the south side, where it would almost have been within sight and earshot.

In 1957 the Royal Institute of British Architects held its annual conference in Oxford. It had done so the year before in Norwich, and Ian Nairn wrote a special number of the *Architect's Journal* as a conference guide – topographical and architectural. This year, to my surprise, they asked me to do the same for Oxford. With one of the firm's Rolleiflexes I went and took a series of shots of unfolding vistas – e.g. as one walks along Catte Street from the Broad towards Radcliffe Square, New College Lane and New College itself, Merton Street, Christ Church, Queen's, Worcester and even my own modest Lincoln – all offer choice trails in which one vista opens as another closes, the fascination increased by its being first perceived through a narrow alleyway or low arch. I even began to wonder if one of these vistas had inspired the rabbit-hole in *Alice in Wonderland*. I had a wonderful time, and when the issue came out Ian Nairn approved and he could not lie. The architects probably considered it poor value since it said nothing about restaurants or places of entertainment – but it did have an appendix about Oxford ghosts, supplied by Mary Stanley Smith.

During the winter of 1956-7, while I was still at the A.P., a holiday in the Alps with Suzanne's family gave us a chance to go south to Rome for a few days without the children. I had never been there before, and we stayed in a guest house kept by German nuns close to the Vatican. Ian Nairn was never short of suggestions about what to see if I was going away even for a weekend, and both he and Peter Banham extolled Borromini; Peter had said that Sant' Ivo was not to be missed, but because it was only open to the public during Sunday mass, I had to stand through it – frequently lifting my eyes to heaven because the óval dome is its most remarkable feature. Basil Gray, on the other hand, particularly praised the area of the city round the Pantheon; and I fell under the spell of the Pantheon itself, which remains for me one of the world's most magnetic buildings. The force of Michelangelo's Moses, as one comes upon it in a modest parish church, only hit me on my next visit, with Rachel on our honeymoon seventeen years later; this time I got my only genuine *frisson* from seeing Velazquez's portrait of Pope Innocent X illuminated at the end of a long dark corridor in the Doria-Pamphili palace.

From Rome Suzanne returned north to the Alps, while I set off on a journey to the east side of Italy starting at San Giovanni Rotondo in the wild Gargano peninsula, and going on to Riccione to visit my father-in-law. San Giovanni, as well as being near the birthplace of Al Capone, was the home of Padre Pio, the stigmatist Franciscan priest, and in my current phase of piety I wanted to see him in action. He said mass publicly only at 5 a.m., long before dawn – it was freezing day and night – and I attended on both days of my stay. A few determined local women formed a knot round the church door, and as soon as the sacristan unlocked it, rushed in and occupied their accustomed places by the communion rail of the side chapel where the Padre celebrated. On the hour, followed by his altar-boy, he materialised out of the darkness, a ruggedly handsome figure, and the women avidly fingered his vestment as he passed. The stain, supposedly of blood oozing from the ever-open wounds on the palms of his hands, was clearly visible on his mittens. I had talked with a man in the small pilgrims' hotel, and he told me about the many marvels connected with Padre Pio: especially bilocations and conversions of even the hardest cases – the Padre was reputed to know as soon as such a person, or anyone in spiritual turmoil, appeared in the back of the church where he was at any time. This man suggested that, as I could not receive the sacrament from him, I should ask the Padre for his blessing in the sacristy after his mass; he spoke no foreign language and the recommended experience of a short confession would have been impossible. On the second morning I did indeed go into the sacristy when the Padre was de-robing. There was quite a crowd, so I was not conspicuous, but even so I could not advance towards him; I felt an outsider, separated from the living saint by tradition and my own inadequacies, and hurried out, feeling empty and angry with myself.

During my one full day at San Giovanni, I got to know the place a little. On one side there was the 'Padre Pio industry', with the large hospital donated by American devotees, and *bondieuserie* shops where every badge, locket and piece of ceramic that did not bear a picture of Jesus or Mary showed the strong features of the Padre rather than the gentle, ascetic Pius XII. Not surprisingly this cult was frowned on in Rome. On the other side there was a chronically impoverished southern village where a crowd of men of all ages, many wearing thick cloaks against the cold, stood about idly for most of the day in the piazza talking, smoking and spitting. To pass the time I walked out towards the highest point in the locality – 1,000 metres or so – and two young men joined me. It was bitterly cold but the air and light were beautiful. One told me that he had been as a migrant worker to Germany a year or two back, and got a local girl pregnant. She gave birth to a living child, a son, but died herself. He was still distracted with grief. I suggested that he talked to Padre Pio, but he was not yet ready for such a remedy.

My accommodation at the simple hotel in San Giovanni and the early rising were spartan, but nothing compared to life in my father-in-law's house at Riccione. He was in his late seventies and lived alone. The house was pleasant in summer but, being unheated, was utterly miserable in January. He tried to light the stove with pine needles, but of course they went out immediately. I hoped that on retiring for the night I might get warm, but my bed turned out to be so damp that I could only get into it wearing my overcoat. Added to that, in the attic above my room, a window had lost its catch and constantly banged as it blew to and fro in the gale off the Adriatic; this I was at least able to fix by climbing up a ladder with some string. Cooking was painfully slow and totally disorganised; once he took me on a walk in the rain lasting at least a quarter of an hour to buy a few ounces of butter. But he valued his independence so much that there was little I could do to help.

The A.P. was an agreeable place. The editorial staffs of the two periodicals, the advertising staff, the two photographers, the book department, Connie (Miss Constable) the photographic librarian, the artists, the drawing office – all used to come together for coffee every morning in the 'Bride of Denmark', summoned by a handbell. Only the few people in the building who were stuffy and status-conscious (Jim Richards was one such) didn't join us. The 'Bride' was also used for our wild Christmas parties, when ordinarily staid people behaved in surprising ways, the most fiercely amorous being a man of transparent virtue. I could have enjoyed working with these people for a long time, but the pleasure was going out of it through constant exposure to Ian Nairn's moods and the highly-strung McCallum's muffled tantrums. There was also a violently unstable man in the advertising department; at first I found him interesting because he was writing a novel, but he then started to take a fancy to me. Having wondered for a time whether to send letters of application to some of the well-known book publishers, I had my attention caught by an advertisement for the job of assistant to the publicity manager of a 'leading' motor-car manufacturer. I suspected it might be Rolls-Royce, and sent in an application for the hell of it. My guess proved correct and I was offered the job. I accepted it and gave notice. McCallum fumed quietly. The change to Rolls-Royce was nonsensical, and I may have left the A.P. too soon. Both Nairn and McCallum left soon after I did, and for the rest of his life McCallum was director of the American museum at Bath, and made a great success of it. So that problem would have been out of the way. I told H. de C. at our final meeting that I would have liked to learn something about the business side of the firm, but he dismissed the idea; again, if I had been patient, I might have been allowed to take an interest in the book department, which then and long afterwards was in the doldrums. Its excellent production man, Tom Colverson, moved to the lusher pastures of Oxford University Press while I was there and was not replaced, and apart from two part-timers there was only the manager, Raymond Philp, who had severe war injuries and was in a bad way. As successor to Raymond, I might possibly have done a buy-out when the whole firm started to come apart. As it was, it expanded in its last days under Godfrey Golzen before being sold off to become part of Butterworth. The Hastings and Regan younger generation proved unable to manage the firm and sold up, and then Robert Maxwell bought it – which caused its pensioners problems after Maxwell's death. I went to the retirement party in the 'Bride' for my last remaining A.P. contemporary, Bill Slack, in 1991, shortly before Maxwell moved the magazines to new premises. The 'Bride' was abandoned, amid talk that some enthusiasts, led by Dan Cruikshank, might turn it into an architectural club. I wanted to be a founder member, but it never happened. It is now officially 'listed' and may somehow be saved.

Nothing Extenuate....[*]

Here it is necessary to go forward to a point about half way through my time at Rolls-Royce, to record the ending of my cohabitation with Suzanne. The parting was undramatic; not so my re-coupling.

Our house at Greenwich had been a cause of low-level running disagreement for almost our whole three years there, but in 1958 we seemed to strike a historic compromise. Up till a time not long before our arrival there, the house had no bathroom at all, but then a primitive and inconvenient one was tacked on to the back of the ground floor. The quality of life was bound to improve if one were installed upstairs. The idea of actually doing this was mine and there was an unspoken accord between Suzanne and me that with this improvement she would no longer agitate to move away. I got in a good modern architect who lived nearby, and the job was nicely done. As it turned out, I only lay in that bath once.

In the late summer of 1958 we drove out to Riccione and had

...nothing extenuate nor set down aught in malice: ....' (*Othello*, Act V, Sc. ii).

a nice holiday, mainly on the beach. Christopher Anthony and Andrew had the company of their Italian cousins. It might have seemed that providence was watching over us because after we crossed the Alps on the way out, the clutch pedal of our Morris Minor gave way under my foot – just as I was turning into a parking space in the centre of Milan; I was able to push it those last few feet. One day Giancarlo, my father-in-law, and I made a long expedition from Riccione to Urbino, Sansepolcro and a small rural chapel to see paintings by Piero della Francesca.

At the end of my allotted time I went home alone, and as I drove away from the house along the tree-shaded road, saw in my car mirror Suzanne leading Andrew by the hand back indoors after they had waved goodbye. I registered that this was a fateful moment, and years later by a chance remark Andrew revealed that he remembered it too, in the same way. I took the route over the Brenner pass, stopping in Innsbruck and Munich and seeing various magnificent Baroque and Rococo monuments recommended by Ian Nairn and the *Pieta* by Botticelli in Munich recommended years before by Sigmund Pollitzer. In Brussels I visited the famous Expo. Suzanne was not going to return till after the building work was finished; naturally she did not fancy being there with builders in the house and the plumbing cut off. Andrew had been going to kindergarten, but he was still only four and not yet obliged to go to school.

In the congregation at St Alfege, Greenwich, was one late middle-aged widow, who had appeared there after I did, Mrs S. She was a friendly, shy, dignified woman and we never spoke until one Sunday after mattins we were crossing the bottom of Greenwich Park in the same direction. I had no idea where she lived, and was astonished when she said that she was the mother of a woman who lived in my road; both this woman and her husband, a painter, whom I knew slightly, seemed the very opposite to church types, as indeed they were. All of them came from South Africa.

In the course of this conversation Mrs S. told me that she had a younger daughter Christine who, having studied the piano in the music department at the University of Cape Town, had now won a scholarship to study at the Guildhall School in London. In fact it was this daughter's departure for England, leaving her on her own in South Africa, that made Mrs S. decided to come over herself and take a teaching job in London. She added that Christine could not find a suitable piano locally for practising and was making do with a beat-up old upright in the house of the newsagent. I told Mrs S. that I had in my house a splendid inherited Blüthner grand, which I used very little and never to anything like its potential.

As this was when we were about to go on our Italian holiday and leave the house empty, I said that Christine was welcome to use the piano as often as she pleased. Of course Mrs S. and especially Christine herself, whom I had only set eyes on once, gardening at the front of her sister's house, were delighted with this offer.

I had already bitten the serpent's apple, because I did not tell Suzanne till I was back in London and she was safely in Italy about the arrangement over the piano – she reacted sharply, but I assured her it was harmless. It would be untrue to say that as I drove back from Italy I did not look forward to making the acquaintance of this talented girl. She continued using the piano after I returned, during my working hours. Eventually, one Saturday morning, we met and at my urging she played the pieces she was currently working on – a march by Schumann and J.S. Bach's Prelude and Fugue no. 3 (of the 'Forty-eight') in C sharp minor. I had never heard anything like this at such close quarters before, and was overwhelmed by the force and polish of her playing.

One evening I was invited to have dinner with her, Mrs S. and the son of the family who was about to emigrate to America – not with the sister and brother-in-law, who lived in a different part of the house. Christine cooked, and it was a pleasant and undemanding occasion. I went round on another evening, and this time the only person at dinner besides Christine was her sister's mother-in-law, who also lived in the house and with whom Christine got on especially well. Afterwards I proposed a walk and in a deserted alley I kissed her. So an affair began, which was Christine's first. She was twenty-two and I felt, at the age of only twenty-eight myself, that – but for inconvenient reality – the situation was quite normal. I had fallen in love – such was my excitement that for several days I could hardly eat.

We had been seeing eachother for barely a fortnight – going out and having a fine time – when the whole dream edifice fell to pieces. Christine was frank about herself; she told me that at the music academy in Cape Town she had been desperately in love with one of the professors (he happened to be queer) and had got so wrought up that she blacked out and had a bad fall; the implication was that she was liable to behave oddly. This experience was long past, but now she started pulling away, saying we had better stop, that it was all her fault and she had no right to carry on with a married man. I thought I had convinced her that my marriage did not work, but then a lot of philandering males say that. Christine had a very clear mind, and it was particularly clear when she was disturbed. And I only realised by stages – rapid ones, inevitably – how disturbed she was. In no time she had gone into hospital with a severe mental breakdown. She recovered over the next few months, but the effect of this first attack never left her, and she had recurrences at various times when we were together throughout the 1960s and decreasingly later. Mrs S. came round to my house early one morning and handed me a bag containing the few small presents I had given Christine. I did not see Christine again for nearly a year, but I had already written to Suzanne that I wanted to leave her.

There were deep ironies in this situation. The one I found most appalling was that Christine gave up her place at the Guildhall and ceased playing the piano altogether. Her sister said to me that she would never have made a first-class performer, and at best might have become a music teacher, but I found no consolation in this. Only when Christine decided twelve years later that she wanted me out of her life – I had had an affair and been found out – did she start playing again (I remember the Beethoven and Schubert she learned at that stage as poignantly as I do the Bach and Schumann she was playing when we first met). Of course if she had been someone with the maturity of her sister, our affair, if it had ever started at all, might have run its course, and we could have resumed our separate lives. It is unlikely that I would have gone back to Suzanne, but a new marriage that brought little satisfaction and a great deal of acute misery at various times might not have happened. (Since we had three children, it is impossible to say it *should* not have happened.) If she had not met me, Christine might have had a happier life.

When Mrs S. returned the gifts, she said to me 'Why don't you act like a man and never see Christine again?' I saw the vicar not long after that – obviously I had to leave the church – and he said much the same thing, adding that at present I was blind. My mother, pragmatic as ever, wrote to me that as Christine suffered from mental instability, it was obvious that our relationship could not go on. But my interpretation was the opposite to that of Mrs S.; 'manly' conduct in this case surely did not consist of abandoning Christine since I alone was the cause of her trouble. It did not occur to me that perhaps the knowledge of my *not* being around would have helped her recovery more than the knowledge that I was around. But having been cut off in mid-flight, the feelings Christine had (unwittingly) awakened in me were intensified and, as the vicar said, I was indeed blind to aspects of the affair that did not accord with my own devices and desires.

My mother, again showing a shrewd instinct, wrote to Suzanne off her own bat before my affair started, saying that she did not think it was a good idea for us to be parted for so long – by that time Suzanne had been away for about two months. But Suzanne did not plan to come back till after Christmas, when she hoped I would go out there – another two months ahead. In fact I got a few days' leave from Rolls-Royce in January and flew out, knowing that I had to talk with Suzanne face to face. She welcomed me and clearly hoped that I could be made to change my mind. Andrew was already becoming bilingual, and for the next few years he spoke English with an Italian accent; I took him to the archaeological museum in Turin and as we looked at the Roman sculptures he remarked that some of them were not wearing '*vestiti*'. Saying good-bye at Turin station to Gino, the *de facto* head of Suzanne's excellent family, gave me a severe pang. During the few hours I spent in Milan before catching the plane home, I went to see Leonardo da Vinci's *Last Supper*.

At the beginning of 1960, when snow was on the ground, I finally had to provide evidence for Suzanne to divorce me under the old rules. Of the three standard grounds, cruelty was not in question, and Christine, whom by then I had been seeing again for several weeks, did not want us to wait the whole time it would take to provide evidence of desertion. That only left adultery. Of course we all knew that adultery had taken place, but a gentleman was not supposed to implicate his girlfriend in the sordid charade of committing it before witnesses.* My solicitor gave me the name of a private detective agency which could find a discreet companion to go with me to one of the hotels specially favoured for this purpose. It would all be strictly business. But when I told Christine of this plan, she would not hear of me spending a weekend with another woman and volunteered to go with me. So, in spite of the snow, we had an enjoyable weekend at Skindle's Hotel at Maidenhead, where the staff were trained to understand the significance of an apparently married pair handing out generous tips on arrival, and sitting up very visibly in bed when the early morning tea was brought to them, and not dozing with the bedclothes pulled up.

It may sound as if by this time Christine reciprocated my feeling for her. We did indeed quickly become lovers after our reunion at the end of 1959, and in the first half of 1960 we were looking forward eagerly to the future. It was the best time we ever spent together, but I managed to spoil it, and things were never the same once we got married the following year.

---

* A.P. Herbert wrote the classic account of old-style divorce and its pitfalls in *Holy Deadlock* (1934), which I read on the advice of my solicitor.

Glorious Machines

It might have seemed by this time that my career as a rolling stone was running out of control. There could be no logic in swerving sideways out of publishing, and what would I learn from working in a motor-car company, even one as full of legend and mystique as Rolls-Royce? I was unlikely to be among such a generally congenial lot of people there as at the AP, but on the other hand my new boss, Rollo Waterhouse, was a refreshing contrast to Ian McCallum. They were the same age, but in the war Rollo had been a Spitfire pilot, and he was happily married (to the widow of a wartime comrade) with a brood of small children. He was a decent and also a sensitive man. His boss was the sales director Jack Scott, a one-time engineering apprentice at Talbots who, in Rollo's words, lived on his nerves. The ultimate chief, based in the motor-car division's factory at Crewe, was Dr F. Llewellyn Smith ('Doc Smith'). We were housed in the division's sales office at 14 Conduit Street, Mayfair. Only one representative of the aero engine division had a desk there – the Anglo-American millionaire and former gentleman racing driver Whitney Straight, who emanated a greater air of power and dynamism than any of the others.

Rollo took his duties like a wartime assignment, in a relaxed, jovial style which he must have acquired as an antidote to the strain of chasing the Hun over southern England in the summer of 1940. He was aware that not all the owners of our cars were as nice as the cars themselves, but he knew what his job was and did it. There was one thing about the cars that he reiterated with patient regularity: their safety. When I joined, Rollo, Jack Scott and 'Doc' were just back from a great joint promotional campaign at the famed Neiman-Marcus department store in Dallas, Texas. To help sell the new cars, the famous Silver Ghost built by Henry Royce in 1905 had been shipped out, along with a new Silver Cloud, and a photograph was taken of Doc atop the 'Ghost' wearing a ten-gallon hat and grinning broadly. Rollo handed me the company's house journal containing his own professionally upbeat article on the Texas jaunt, to give me some background on our activities. I immediately noticed, as he had not, the phrase 'pubic relations exercise' (*sic*) in the first sentence and pointed it out thinking that it would at least evoke

237

a smile. But he furrowed his brows. Solemnity about our product and everything to do with it was the rule.

The allure of the Rolls-Royce is strong, and for me there was a touch of nostalgia because my father had owned one throughout my childhood. My mother remarked without irony that Hitchcock would have been proud of me, but I doubted it; for him I would have been on the wrong side of the counter. The Company's heroic past still had living echoes in the late 1950s. Royce, to save his health, was persuaded long before his death to take up residence in the south of France, and Everndon, one of a crack team of engineers who worked with him there, still had a little office at the Crewe works although he was semi-retired – the sole remaining link with the great man at that level. The manager of the Conduit Street showroom, a man with a distinguished appearance but rough manners, had been taken to visit Royce as a boy and remembered his penetrating cold blue eyes – evidently he was more feared than loved. And I was once called down to the showroom to talk with an octogenarian baronet called Chance who had owned a 10 h.p. Royce during the short period when they were made. A 'vanity' book on the car called *The Magic of a Name* by Harold Nockolds was handed out at every opportunity, and I had to read it as part of my indoctrination. It was a poor piece of work, permeated by the company's peculiar semi-apologetic style of boasting.

To complete my initiation I was sent to the Crewe factory for a few days and stayed at the apprentices' hostel. (One evening I went to a wrestling bout in the town at which the women spectators did most of the rooting.) I hoped the visit might improve my understanding of the internal combustion engine – I told Rollo at my interview that it was pretty weak. But I was now doubly dumbfounded by the mysteries of the automatic gearbox, which was fitted to all the cars except for a select handful destined for connoisseurs. I was assigned to one of the mechanics (Royce always used that term to describe himself), each of whom was responsible for a single car – first the chassis only and then the whole car with the body added – as it progressed through the works, performing numerous tests and adjustments himself, and doing nothing else until the car was passed as fit to leave the factory. This had a beauty about it. I saw one engine on a test-bed being run to destruction – the sacrificial lamb – and visited the workshop where the leather and the walnut veneer for the interior trim were worked. The Silver Cloud and its companion the 'S' type Bentley were the company's staple product, and of course it was our job, ever discreetly of course, to laud their virtues. But they were strictly a standard product – the identical body shells were manufactured at the Pressed Steel works in Cowley and shipped to Crewe for assembly. The company's own man, Mr Blatchley, had designed the standard saloon (my friend Simon Dale derided it as 'like a fat cigar'), but no one denied it was a far cry from the Rolls-Royce and Bentley of old. Purists could not accept that the post-1931 Bentley deserved the name at all, nor would they admit that there had ever been a nobler car than the Phantom II (50 h.p.) Continental model of the mid-1920s, which Royce insisted should have *two* spare wheels attached to the boot at the rear for perfect balance. That was true style.

Before the Silver Cloud and 'S' type, which sold for around £5,500, every car had its coachwork hand-built by craftsmen at one of the old specialist coachbuilders: Hooper, the most staid, which had existed since the 18th century; H.J. Mulliner, Park Ward, James Young, or Freestone and Webb. The Silver Wraith, a pre-war car still exclusively coachbuilt to order, was only phased out while I was there; the Phantom IV, with its larger chassis, was built for heads of state only – General Franco and the Shah were among current owners. The coachbuilders hand-beat the panels over wooden templates. Mulliner alone built the glamorous high-performance Bentley Continentals (the two-door with the long sloping back was the only one of the firm's cars which could still be made with manual gear-change). Park Ward had been bought by Rolls-Royce ('nationalised', as a nostalgic old hand at Conduit Street put it); and James Young of Bromley belonged to Jack Barclay, the hugely successful retailer (exclusively of the firm's cars). In a last gasp before ceasing production, Freestone and Webb showed a model at Earls Court in 1957 with high tail-fins, deplored by Conduit Street as more suitable for a Studebaker.

My job mostly consisted of producing publicity literature, and I had some small part in the conception of press advertisements. (I once watched Rollo patiently listening while a Swede tried to sell him the idea of getting some V.I.P. to start a speech to an important gathering with the words 'Ladies and Bentleymen'.) For the catalogues and brochures I inherited a designer, Pat Kemmish, and a small litho printer called Colorprint near the North Circular Road, founded and run by a Leipzig Jew, Walter Herz. This wheedling salesman had persuaded Rollo of the superior virtues of litho as against letterpress, and of his firm's ability to get the delicate tints of the cars' paintwork exactly right, but I always thought he got them a shade wrong. (After a time Herz began to woo me as a potential partner and successor but I was not tempted.) Herz's catalogues, elegantly designed by Pat Kemmish, struck a traditional note, but I accidentally picked up a pocket-sized brochure for Mercedes cars, using simplified coloured profiles of various models and no photographs, which I thought more modern and suitable, and persuaded Rollo to copy it. Pat redesigned it, competitive quotes were obtained, and this time Herz lost out to a letterpress firm in Sussex. For a time we referred to it in the office as 'the Mercedes book' until Rollo checked himself and said we had to stop using that expression.

When the Phantom V came on the market, replacing the Silver Wraith and the kings-and-dictators-only Phantom IV at one blow, a more regal and discreet promotion piece was required than Herz was thought capable of. I happened to meet, outside Hamleys in Regent Street, an Oxford acquaintance who was now a director of his family's high-quality printing house, the Curwen Press. This was Timothy Simon. His father Oliver Simon, author of the invaluable *Introduction to Typography,* had dominated the firm (and Timothy) but died in the mid-1950s comparatively young, leaving Timothy with greatly increased freedom though not in charge. I got Rollo to agree that we might ask Curwen Press for a design and an estimate. He had already asked W.S. Cowell to do the same, and the very gentlemanly director of Cowell's, a friend of Rollo, showed pained surprise when he came into the office all smiles, expecting to take away the order, to find that it was going to Curwen.

Timothy, like me, was half German-Jewish by descent on his father's side, and at Oxford this, besides a shared interest in art and his considerable personal charm, gave me the feeling that we were friends. But a tiny incident revealed a peculiarity about him that I was to see later in higher relief. In Paris during one vacation I met him in the street with two other fellow students whom I knew slightly; both later made their careers as museum experts, one (then a pupil of E.H. Gombrich[*]) on painting and the other on porcelain. We instantly decided to go together to the Louvre to see a loan exhibition from the Kaiser-Friedrich Museum in Berlin. This passed

---

[*] He was Slade Professor of Fine Art at Oxford in 1950-3, i.e. throughout my time as an undergraduate. His immediate predecessor was Sir Kenneth Clark, whose lectures packed the theatre at the Taylorian Institute: his fluent, slightly affected style is well known. Having heard him lecture at the end of 1947, I was sad that my army service prevented me from hearing more. As a freshman in 1950 I went to Gombrich's inaugural, and as this ungainly, moon-faced man, then barely forty, took the rostrum and began speaking in his heavy German accent, I felt a sinking of the heart and wished we still had Clark. The subject of his first term's lectures was Ghiberti's Baptistery doors in Florence, and he explored every minutia with relentless thoroughness. This was real art history. Soon, with his unyielding integrity, vast scholarship and occasional shafts of dry humour, he won us over, and Clark began to seem like an accomplished showman. In the last term of his Slade professorship Gombrich lectured with complete authority on Picasso, and his victory over our minds and hearts was complete.

off agreeably, and we met again in a restaurant that evening. It was soon apparent that the two embryo experts wanted to have some fun at my expense, my dilettantism being so obvious. After tripping me up on a few points of expertise, one of them raised his glass and said 'Let's drink a toast – art stinks! I don't suppose you'll subscribe to that, Christopher.' Timothy was not taking part but obviously enjoyed the sport, and I would not have spoken to him again after that evening had we not met so unexpectedly in 1959 and then done some business.

He invited me to Plaistow to see his factory, where he had set up a studio for artists to make lithographs with real stones, and soon afterwards to a party at his flat to meet his American fiancee. One Sunday evening during that year – by then I was living alone – I felt an instantaneous and overwhelming attraction to a girl on a tube train, and seeing the label on her suitcase, which said that she was a nurse at Guy's Hospital, wrote to her and asked if she would meet me. Months passed and, not being an Alain-Fournier, I had all but forgotten our fleeting encounter when a letter arrived, saying that she accepted my invitation. We met in Piccadilly underground station, and went off to see a play at the Royal Court and then dine at a restaurant. She was the daughter of a miner in Aberdare and her mother had died of T.B. I did not mention my marital status (by the time we were about to part I did not dare to mention it), and in spite of signs that were not discouraging – we had a nice evening – I threw away my victory at long odds over chance and did not contact her again. As Timothy and I sat having lunch in the Curwen Press canteen I told him this story. The poor man said that it was hard for him to hear about such a delectable adventure now that he was embarking on matrimony.

Among the choicer denizens of Conduit Street were the uniformed drivers. There were four of them, and their white-haired doyen, Mr Garner, was a rock-like stalwart of the old school like Hitchcock. They often had royal assignments and in my time, when the Queen Mother visited Nigeria, a Phantom IV and Garner were shipped out there together to ensure that, whatever else might go awry, the driving – at the royal snail's pace which is so demanding – would be faultless. Once he told me that he drove Edward VIII as Prince of Wales on a tour of the Midlands. They got to a fork in the road, and were about to take the pre-arranged route through a string of villages where the people had prepared a welcome, when the prince said that he was fed up and wanted to get quickly to his final destination, the grand house of one of his friends, which meant taking the other route. After a quick but furious altercation with his secretary, the prince's will prevailed as a matter of course and the people were disappointed.

More important for the company's business was a small team of young men who drove round the country in Silver Clouds visiting owners and dealers, and trying to drum up new custom. One of them was Raymond Salisbury-Jones, son of the *vigneron* of Hambledon* who was also Marshal of the Diplomatic Corps and, as such, had an official residence in St James's Palace. Raymond gave parties there, and with typical flamboyance and generosity would invite some of the humblest staff at Conduit Street. Because of his social connections the firm reckoned him to be useful on the country house circuit. A brilliant sight-reader, he played piano duets with the chief engineer at Crewe, Harry Grylls, and when he met Princess Margaret at parties used to be commanded by her to sit down and play her favourite hymns – this was during her holy phase after the Townsend affair. The team was joined in my time by a keen young man who, just after joining, piped up at a sales meeting chaired by Jack Scott, the sales director, with words that stuck in my memory: 'It seems to me, J.S., that what we have to do is get people to adopt the Rolls-Royce way of thinking.' It was meaningless, but struck the right note. His name was David Plastow, and he went on to head Rolls-Royce, and later Vickers after it bought Rolls-Royce out.

One of Rollo's achievements was commissioning David Ogilvy, the great British advertising phenomenon in New York, to work out a campaign for the United States, where the Rolls-Royce image needed refurbishing. The budget would be smaller than Ogilvy normally accepted, but the 'magic of the name' made up for it. A tip-top photographer took a very ordinary picture of a Silver Cloud parked outside a village grocery store in New England, and under it was a slab of matter-of-fact prose, eulogising the car's performance. However, the heading 'The loudest noise in the Rolls-Royce is the electric clock' became one of the most quoted advertising slogans ever coined.

---

* I was once invited by Raymond to spend a weekend at Hambledon, and witnessed a scene of suppressed drama. His father Sir Guy Salisbury-Jones happened to be entertaining to lunch on the Saturday two mighty men of the wine trade, Mr Sichel and the octogenarian Mr Langenbach, in order that they should taste his wine, which was still at a semi-experimental stage. All eyes were on the old man especially, since much would depend on his judgement. As the meal progressed, almost to the end, he refused to talk shop and kept relentlessly to generalities. At last with a great effort Sir Guy asked Mr Langenbach what he thought of the wine. 'Like a Moselle', he said, and added one or two words of polite appreciation, then the conversation moved on again. It was distinctly oracular, but the old man would not be drawn further.

There was some heart-searching at Conduit Street over its obvious inaccuracy – the electric clock made no noise at all.

Rollo and I both knew, almost from the first day, that ours was a misalliance, and the week before Christmas 1959 he told me – kindly, just as Ronnie Wilkinson had done five years before – that I could have three months to look for other job. And again I left within a week. For the past term I had been going to evening classes at the Byam Shaw art school on Campden Hill, and spent most evenings and weekends during that year in the streets of Covent Garden where I was living, in the City, and occasionally in the country drawing and painting. The Byam Shaw school was suggested by Peter Greenham, to whom I showed the work I had accumulated. When the axe fell at Rolls-Royce I enrolled as a full-time student at the Byam Shaw and left Conduit Street for ever on my thirtieth birthday. Rollo had evidently dabbled at painting in his time and said 'I envy you' as we were about to part, thus echoing Mr Flower when I left Wilkinsons.

Less than a month later I got a letter from Rollo's secretary, Kathleen Stewart, saying that he had been killed driving home to Guildford late at night from some promotional event in London. A newspaper report she enclosed said that he had been in a company car and driven at high speed straight into a tree – according to the police, the alcohol level in his blood was 'not significant'. There was talk of a heart attack. Rollo could not have been less loyal to Rolls-Royce than he was to the country when he was flying Spitfires during the war. He survived the 'real' ordeal only to die selling luxury motor-cars whose safety on the road he had never ceased to extol.

Anxious Interlude with Paintbrushes

About the time when the stifling summer of 1959 was ending, I saw an advertisement in the *Evening Standard* for an unfurnished flat in Notting Hill. It was on the ground floor of a Victorian house near Holland Park Avenue (27 Portland Road). The rent was £100 a year, and there was a 'premium', also of £100. It seemed impossible, but it was true. This house and no. 29 next door had belonged since 1919 to a high-minded lady, Miss Binckes, now past eighty, who never lived there but let out the rooms cheaply to people she deemed needy or otherwise deserving. She came up from her house in Dulwich to vet me, the deal with the outgoing tenant was completed, and I moved in.

The tenants were a mixed bunch. In one of the two small rooms on the top floor lived Miss Ogilvy, an old friend and contemporary of Miss Binckes, who from the early years of the century was companion and housekeeper to her bachelor brother, the vicar of a parish near Lancaster; on his death in 1937 she accepted her friend's offer of a room in one of the houses. The room was spartan; on the faded blue-green walls were just two small pictures – one of Jesus and the other of King George V. She ate almost nothing – the smell of boiled cabbage was ever present – and was skeletally thin. She went every day to All Saints, Margaret Street (temple of Anglo-Catholicism), where she cleaned the church and mothered the boys of the choir school, but the real passion of her life was watching cricket at Lord's (never at the Oval, which was too rowdy). Next to her on the same floor lived Mr Robinson, 'a nice little man though not a gentleman'; he was just old enough to have served in the Great War (letters arrived addressed to him as 'Trench Brother'), and worked as a rep in the rag trade north of Oxford Street. He had long been separated from his wife, who would not divorce him 'for religious reasons' – thoroughly un-Christian, Miss Ogilvy opined – and had a settled relationship with an extremely respectable woman; they spent all their free time in a caravan on the south coast. The remaining tenants in my house were a childless middle-aged couple who both worked at the head office of Schweppes, he as a commissionaire and she as a secretary; both were overweight, fishy-eyed and obsessed with their poor health.

My relationship with them was soon to change, because I heard after a few weeks that Miss Binckes wanted to sell the two houses. I immediately wrote to her and asked how much she wanted for them. The answer was £3,000. I would have paid that sum whatever their condition, but a survey revealed that the joist in the back wall of no. 29 next door was consumed with dry rot – 'it came out in spoonfuls', the surveyor said – and when Miss Binckes learned of this she insisted on taking £100 off the price. I had not hitherto met the tenants in no. 29. Like those in no. 27 they were all far from young. On the top floor was Miss Bicz (prounced 'bitch'), a Polish Jewess, whose emotional quarrels with her sister Mrs Rappoport were the despair of Miss Ogilvy, who lived on the other side of the party wall. On the first floor lived the ingratiating Miss Smith, who had worked in a bank and therefore considered herself superior to the two other ladies in the house: Miss Acock, a retired parlour-maid, and Miss Waterman, who had owned a tea-shop. However much it cost to repair and re-decorate the houses, I could not help making a profit, and thus when the moment of destiny came at Rolls-Royce, I did not feel too irresponsible in not taking another job at once. The Byam Shaw school was barely a ten-minute walk away.

I realised soon after joining this small and serious school and mixing with the full-time students rather than the evening ones that I had made yet another mistake. Whatever might have happened if I had built on the promise I clearly showed at seventeen and become an art student then, the moment had passed. I could only, at best, be a Sunday painter and dabble at portraiture, and for that a year or two of evening classes might have sufficed. But by plunging in and inviting comparison with some exceptionally gifted young students I laid a trap for myself and disappointment was bound to follow.

Some of the visiting professors were awesomely good. The star was Peter Greenham, a big shambling man of fifty – he was soon to marry one of the students. And there were Bernard Dunstan, James Mahoney and Patrick Phillips. Seeing these professionals draw a few lines or paint a few strokes was acutely pleasurable. The full-time professors were Peter Garrard, a much younger disciple of Greenham's, and R.W., the only one who told me I was good enough to go on – he was also the least gifted of the bunch and I was not swayed by his opinion. By the time the school closed for the summer vacation, work on the houses was finished and they looked a lot brighter. Meanwhile I received a windfall when six of the rooms became vacant: Miss Smith died and 'Trench Brother' Robinson moved permanently to the seaside. His set gave me the whole basement in no. 27, which I linked to the ground floor with an internal staircase, and a spare room on the top floor next to Miss Ogilvy. I bought Miss Smith's furniture and let her rooms. Suddenly I had a decent home and a bit of income.

My second marriage to Christine was in prospect and I went to the Labour Exchange to find a job which I could start at once, while I angled at more leisure for something permanent: it was now clear to me that my future had to be in publishing. The Labour Exchange sent me to the J. Lyons factory at Cadby Hall in West Kensington. They were already making Christmas puddings four months in advance, and these had to be wrapped. I was hired for the night shift wrapping puddings. This was done in a manner barely worthy of the name of automation: there were two rows of simple hand-operated machines, before which we sat, with a conveyor belt passing slowly between them, along which the puddings progressed. You grabbed a new one as you finished wrapping the last. This went on interminably, and it was like the work I did at Wilkinson Brothers Discount Company in that it left the mind free.

Among my fellow workers were Geoffrey, who had been a cavalry officer and was here to clear his debts; Ali, a Pakistani, married with three children, who also did a full-time job during the day; and Paddy, a nice-looking and apparently well-knit young Irishman. There was a scrawny little Glaswegian who appointed himself as charge-hand, and once Geoffrey, unable to bear his loud-mouthed rudeness and arrogance any longer, nearly had a stand-up fight with him, but they were pulled apart. The outcome was less fortunate when Paddy came in on Friday night, as he regularly did, fighting drunk. At first nothing happened; he sat at his machine, muttering and swearing to himself. The tension made us quiet. He was not wrapping his puddings properly, and sensing rather than hearing criticism – of course we were were not going to tolerate one of our number doing less than his share of the work – he lashed out. Ali was the target, but on the first occasion everything quickly calmed down and in another hour or so Paddy was his usual cheerful self. The next Friday he suddenly turned round and from his position at the front of one of the two rows threw a ·pudding straight at the head of Ali, accompanying it with explicit insults about his colour. Ali jumped to his feet but the foreman was close at hand, and this time Paddy was thrown out, never to return.

We had an hour's break at midnight, and sat, often snoozing, in the canteen. During the second half of the shift it was easy to get drowsy, and I tried not to wonder how I could bear it. Sometimes the supply of puddings ceased before the end of the shift, and if we were lucky we might be dismissed. Or we might be sent to the contract catering department to fill bridge rolls with substances like fish paste or egg mayonnaise for some grand reception. One Friday night, soon after we were given our weekly pay packets, I found that mine was missing. It never occurred to me that it might have been stolen, and I immediately reported the loss to the foreman, who was sympathetic and ordered a search. It could not be found – sorry, bad luck. I went home reflecting that although the actual sum I had lost was not large, it represented a whole week of this unspeakable toil. But what could I do? I duly clocked on the next night, and long after the start of the shift, when the conveyor belt had been sending Christmas puddings down the line for an hour or two, I suddenly saw coming towards me, on the conveyor, something that looked like a pay packet. It turned out to be mine. I never knew who played the trick or how, but I was as overjoyed as if

I had won the pools, and spent much of it the next day taking Christine to the Trocadero.

After two months it seemed like time to change to a day job, and I went back to the Labour Exchange. This time they sent me to Barker's department store in Kensington High Street, where an assistant was wanted in the weeks leading up to Christmas on the tobacco counter. The tobacconist Mr Emm was a considerate and fatherly boss and together we selected our stock for the counter from the storeroom each morning. I was also sent down to provide an extra pair of hands in the wine cellar. From the foreman Mr Pope, I learned never to say '*vin rosé*', with an accent, but 'vin rose' pronounced as if it were English. I also learned that it was OK to play games with wine labels, like putting vintage ones on bottles which were really non-vintage; we knew because we bottled the more 'plonkish' wine ourselves. Of the rest of the mob, there were two Irishmen, a tall portly one with the *gravitas* of a butler, broken only when from time to time he broke into ditties sung with an exaggerated brogue, and his mercurial friend and foil Maurice, a short, broken-nosed ex-boxer. Maurice was gentle and amiable; he had seen better days but he bore the world no ill-will. Our youngest colleague was filling in time before joining the customs service for which he had already been accepted, and not surprisingly he felt pleased with himself. Once, thinking it would be taken in good part, he called Maurice punch-drunk and in a moment Maurice had him pinned in a corner whimpering for mercy.

With Mr Emm at the counter, much as I enjoyed selling things (a foretaste of the future), I was intermittently haunted by the archetypal fear of a bourgeois in this position, of being recognised by someone I knew, like an Eton contemporary. At the age of thirty it was less easy to laugh off than if I had been twenty, and it would be an insult to Mr Emm if I explained to my acquaintance that I was going through a bad patch. It never happened. When I was asked to take some cases of wine on a trolley to a restaurant on the other side of the High Street, the owner tipped me three shillings and I was surprised by how pleasant it was to feel the money being pressed into my palm.

In the early weeks of 1961 I wrote letters of application to publishers and waited for replies. Timothy Simon gave me useful leads – as a high-class printer he knew most of the publishers who mattered – but in the end chance played a greater part. I got to see the charming Norman Askew, sales manager at Cape, but no job was on offer. And I went at least twice to the Oxford University Press office at Amen House in the City, and had a long interview with David

Neal, head of 'Overseas Editorial'. I was even summoned before Eric Parnwell, the Deputy Publisher and pioneer in earlier days of Overseas Editorial. He was an impressive man of small stature who had once been an office boy but now sat at a vast mahogany desk. His manner was fatherly but smug, and he told me 'We have ways of finding out about people' – presumably he meant writing to one's College for a report, which in my case was not likely to be favourable. Later in my protracted negotiations with the Press I was told that there could be an opening in the Bombay office: to have worked there under the famous 'Hawk' – Mr Hawkins, the last expatriate general manager – would have been a great experience, but going abroad at this juncture in my life was out of the question.

An advertisement in the *New Statesman* caught my eye: it was for the job of advertising manager at Barrie and Rockliff. This was a firm I had barely heard of, and it didn't sound exciting. But I applied and at my first interview – with John Bunting, who was joined half way through by the managing director Leopold Ullstein – I was offered the job. I still hung back, reluctant to let go of the chance of entering O.U.P. after laying seige to it for so long, and to settle for such an obscure firm. It would be a better prospect than Derek Verschoyle, but I could imagine the blank looks I would get when I told people where I worked. Timothy Simon knew the firm, but simply remarked that he found the name cacophonous. Christine providentially made up my mind for me and I accepted the job at a salary of £900.

Not long after joining I knew that this was my sort of life. The consummation of starting my own firm was still over the horizon, but I was at the start of a journey towards it.

Slow To Its Close Ebbs Out Life's Little Day

After my father died in August 1944, my mother's life lost its centre; she no longer had an automatic source of love and support. She was not left badly off – my father invested his sizeable professional earnings wisely – but clearly there would be strains as she tried to live within her income, yet without sacrificing the comforts she could not do without. She did not succeed but, apart from an occasional sale of shares, never had to make any serious change in her general style of life. I stayed at Eton for three more years after 1944, and although we talked about moving (to London, to be nearer the bright lights) she could never screw herself up to sell 'Red Gables' – seeming so puny when we arrived from Ascot but a white elephant long before her death in 1961.

Blows of different kinds fell on her. There was a grave and unexpected one just a year after my father's death, right within the heart of our immediate family.* I knew nothing about it at the time and, as has been related, was packed off to stay with cousins in the Isle of Wight. During my last year at school I started to see my mother with an unfriendly critical eye. It happened in a flash, only a day or two after I had told her that no one could have a more intelligent or adorable mother than I had. I was much too self-willed and self-righteous not to let her feel this sudden new chill, never thinking for more than a moment how much it hurt her and how hopeless she felt. In 1947, while I was enjoying my last half at Eton, she fell ill with pleurisy and took a long time to recover. She later reproached me, with justice, for being too absorbed in my own concerns to care about her.

In the autumn of 1951 she left the house and went to her native New Zealand for the winter. She had not been there since the Great War when still in her early twenties and ravishingly beautiful. Pam, my elder sister, had already emigrated to Canada *en route* for the United States in 1949, but Rosemary and I speculated about what my mother's momentous journey might bring. Would she possibly decide to stay in New Zealand? Or might she meet a nice widower on the ship and marry again? Neither of these things happened, and in fact it was a fixed idea of hers that she must be back in time for the English spring. But two inauspicious things happened on the way out. First she fell in her cabin when the ship lurched, so that when she went ashore in Sydney, where my father's only sister, Aunt Jo, met her, she had to be taken around in a wheelchair. Then, as the ship was about to depart for the last leg of the outward journey, she missed the general embarkation and was taken out in a launch and winched on board. Next day a local paper drew attention to this undignified proceeding with the headline 'Titled lady hauled aboard liner'.

Rosemary and I met her in London when she got back in the early spring, and she seemed subdued. The visit had not been quite the happy experience she had hoped for. The residents of an old people's home in Headington, whom she used to visit and who loved her, gave her a little leather-bound travel diary before the trip, and

---

* The explanation of this comes at the appropriate moment later in the book.

she wrote it up assiduously until her arrival in New Zealand. There followed a long gap until, already on her voyage home, she wrote just one page about her impressions. The main drift was that the New Zealanders were good, kind people but that the women, including her sisters, spent all their time keeping their houses spick and span, and preparing food. They had not learned, like their British cousins, simple labour-saving tricks like opening tins. Always susceptible to looks, good and bad, she commented that the women were better looking than the men. She wrote all this as an outsider looking in. She was no longer a New Zealander.

Only a few months after returning, my mother started to show some alarming symptoms. She could no longer completely control her gait, her handwriting or her speech, which became slurred. Her G.P. advised her to see a renowned neurologist, Macdonald Critchley, at the National Hospital for Nervous Diseases in Queen Square, and she spent the week of the Coronation under observation there. A diagnosis emerged: she was suffering from deterioration of the cerebellum. But if she felt anxiety before, she did doubly now, not only because of her physical condition. Critchley was never one of my father's associates, and she came away from the consultation with the shocked realisation that, eight years after his death, the big men of the medical profession were no longer as deferential to the name of Hurst as they had once been. For the first time since her marriage forty years before, she felt that she was being treated as just another patient and a rather difficult and demanding one at that. She had the humiliation of breaking down in tears while talking to Critchley, which she was apt to do now whenever she alluded to a much worse fear: that there might be a suspicion among the doctors that her disease was not 'real' – that she was covering up a secret addiction to drink or drugs. Avoiding any contact with alcohol now obsessed her.

She was alone – her husband dead, both daughters now living permanently in America, and her selfish son at university. She had no intimate or childhood friends. And, as if this was not enough, she became convinced that my father's unmarried niece Daphne Martin-Hurst, now in her late forties, was a viper in her bosom. Daphne, as a hospital almoner, was a big cheese in the Oxford medical world, and the principal local neurologist, Ritchie Russell, was her chief. My mother now remembered a minor tiff they had in happier times some twenty years before, and an unpleasant smirk Daphne tried to conceal when they were talking about the harrowing episode in my mother's life soon after she was widowed. These and other signs convinced her that Daphne wished her ill, and that through Dr Russell a false account of her character had preceded her to the consultation with Macdonald Critchley in London. Earlier the same year my Australian Aunt Jo (for many years a widow) visited England and stayed with Daphne; the two were close. My aunt had been the companion of her widowed father (Grandfather Hertz) in the last years of his life, and she planned, when the old man died, to keep house for my father, her favourite brother, who was already in his thirties and still unmarried. She herself was past thirty, bookish and plain. This scheme aborted when my father married the beautiful young New Zealander. Aunt Jo, buoyed up by a bequest of £20,000 from her father, went off on a world trip, met her future husband and bought a farm in Australia, where she remained. My mother thought that this sister-in-law bore a grudge against her (as I found out, she had no fondness for Gerald and Margaret either). This could be ignored while my father was alive and Aunt Jo was safely on the other side of the world, but now, with her nearby and in cahoots with her suspected enemy Daphne, she imagined the worst and, as both women were cleverer than she, felt horribly exposed.

Life now closed in on my mother. She had long had a married couple living in, the husband working at Cowley and the wife cooking and minding the house, but now in addition a personal 'companion' became necessary. A succession came and went, none quite satisfactory, until at last she had a wonderful stroke of luck. After the death of Lady Mary Murray, Kathleen Haynes, who was nurse-companion to her and, up till his death, the great humanist Gilbert Murray as well, came into my mother's life. Kathleen was not a 'lady' as her people were tenant farmers in west Oxfordshire, but she was a person of superior qualities, overflowing with love and concern for her charges; after an unhappy romance she had to look for a vocation and found it looking after the old. She was rigidly principled and self-disciplined, and in the house would never allow herself any indulgences or even self-expression other than through her work. She was alert and energetic to the point of being jumpy. Her years in Boar's Hill with the Murrays, with their numerous progeny to whom she was devoted and who apparently were equally fond of her, accustomed her to varied and stimulating company, which she certainly didn't get with my mother. It was not a fault, but it could become faintly irritating, that she never tired of telling us in fulsome terms of the Murrays and their doings and of the consideration they had shown her. It had been, and would doubtless remain, the high point of her life.

Superficially my mother's existence went on smoothly enough. She saw almost nobody, but read the *Daily Telegraph* from cover to cover, watching the movements of her shares with special attention, and became a telly addict, so that there was not only a set at the end of her chaise-longue in the drawing-room, but a second one in her bedroom. Near the end of her life, she often breathed noisily as she slept, and one would come down at night and from her room hear both sounds simultaneously – laughs and snatches of pop music from the TV, which was still on after she had fallen asleep, and my mother's groans which all of us who heard them found a dreadful intimation of approaching mortality. For years since our last corgi succumbed to the traffic outside in the London Road, she had a little black poodle, Sambo, and as time passed she became increasingly attached to him, and he would sit by her feet during the day and sleep in her bedroom at night. If he was out of her sight for a moment she would assume that he was on the road and cry out with alarm. She never worried so much about her small grandchildren, much as she loved them.

I should have wished for my mother a quick end but when she once actually told me she wanted to die, I felt a painful shock. Kathleen did more, day by day, to lighten the burden of her existence than anyone else could have done, but my mother did not seem quite as grateful to her as she might have been; she remarked rather cattily that Kathleen needed to be constantly praised. No doubt my mother struggled to say nice things occasionally, but effusiveness was alien to her nature, and she remained firmly undemonstrative except towards her own family. Kathleen's solitariness was deepened because they did not communicate except over routine things.

A domestic crisis blew up in the last months because of friction between Kathleen and the female half of the married couple, Mrs D., a Catholic woman from Wigan with a strong personality and considerable intelligence who outshone her small, timid husband. She was as blunt and outspoken as Kathleen was refined and reticent, and having been with my mother for some ten years resented Kathleen's superior airs and my mother's reliance on her. One weekend Kathleen poured out to me a catalogue of petty annoyances and pinpricks she had suffered at the hands of Mrs D. I liked Mrs D., and wrote her what I thought was a tactful letter, expressing gratitude for her years of excellent service but pleading with her to tolerate Kathleen, even if she found her irritating, for the short remaining period of my mother's life. So much for my good intentions. Mrs D. stormed into my mother's room brandishing my letter and announced that she, her husband and her son were moving out immediately. So for the last few weeks a charming grey-haired couple kept house – they also adopted Sambo a little later when he found himself without a home. Mr P., I remember, was particularly pleasant, and it was strange when we found out, after they had left, that he had a police record for petty fraud.

Anticipating that my mother was about to die (the extraction of a tooth speeded up her decline), I took a week's leave from Barrie and Rockliff, and she died on the Thursday night, 22 September 1961. She had willed that her eyes should be taken for medical use, and we immediately telephoned to arrange for this to be done. A young doctor came with a metal container, and went into her room to extract her eyes. Kathleen went with him, something I was far too squeamish to do under any circumstances, but least of all when the eyes were those light brown ones with small pupils I knew particularly well.

The funeral was in the Anglo-Catholic parish church at Old Headington, where her coffin lay all through the night before with a candle burning at the head and foot. We did not follow the hearse to the crematorium after the service but saw it off at the church gate. The other people hung back around the porch as Christine and I, alone, watched it drive away. As we stood there she told me that she did not want to entertain a lot of guests – I had already invited everyone back to the house for tea. I said that Kathleen would take care of everything, and we had a slight altercation. Word of this later came to Kathleen's ears.

That night, from our bedroom, we heard her weeping loudly and passionately in her bedroom next door. It was a terrible sound, from a woman normally so controlled, and we thought that she was finally letting go after all the stresses of the past days and weeks. That probably had more to do with it than she cared to admit, but she told me next day with her habitual air of innocence that she wept to think that Christine and I had been having a disagreement at such a moment.

For the next few days, even after returning to London, I felt my mother's presence near me. I became convinced, as I have been ever since, that she was a good person who consistently did right and avoided wrong by choice if not always by inclination. I had the sensation, both happy and disturbing, that she was watching over me – her son who was not a good person either by nature or to any great extent by choice. The feeling of her presence soon faded, but I still sometimes dream that I am back in her house, which contains many more beautiful things than it ever did in real life, but they are decayed and in disorder. I am faced with the hopeless task of rescuing them from dissolution. My mother is alive – old and ill – in another part of the house, but then I remember she is dead and wake up.

Book II

The Road to King Street
and the View therefrom

'He ran a business which any ordinary businessman would have abandoned; but his heart was in it ....' (from the obituary of John Sebastian Morley, harp maker, died 11 July 1988, *The Independent,* London)

'Up jumped the swagman and jumped into the billabong – "You'll never catch me alive", said he.' (from the last verse of *Waltzing Matilda*)

Ullstein's Way

Barrie and Rockliff's office was in a tall and gaunt late Victorian block in a gated alley off the Strand beside the Law Courts: 2 Clement's Inn. The lift was worked by pulling a rope, and it seemed in keeping with the place when a window-cleaner fell off a ledge high up its cliff-like frontage on to the flagstones below.

Our workforce was compact. Besides Leopold Ullstein and John Bunting, the two executive directors, there were Bobby, Leopold's wife, who officially did the book-keeping and wrote the salary cheques, but was also involved in politicking and some editorial decisions; Geoffrey Robinson, the editor; Richard Wadleigh, the production manager, and his busty Jewish assistant Brenda; a couple of secretaries; and the London rep, Jack Caspall. Some months after I arrived, Peter Willmore, who had been with Harrap for more than ten years, also joined in the new post of sales manager, on which I briefly set my sights. The chairman was Tony Samuel – the Honourable A.G. Samuel, a younger brother of Lord Bearstead of the banking family (M. Samuel & Co., later Hill Samuel) and grandson of Marcus Samuel, the founder of Shell. He was therefore enormously rich. The other non-executive director was Humphrey Hare, a convivial middle-aged bachelor who translated the works of Maurice Druon from French and worked only at night. Both were Old Etonians.

The history of the firm is both complicated and relatively short. At different times various imprints flowed into it and partly changed its character, and finally the whole lot disappeared into a larger entity which in turn disappeared into a yet larger one. I came along when it was just short of half way through its combined independent career of rather less than thirty years. The story begins with James Barrie, a peripheral figure in the literary life of post-war London who seems to have been a buccaneer, rather in the style of Derek Verschoyle. He founded his own imprint after being an agent with Curtis Brown, and one of his authors for a time was L.P. Hartley – sadly for him, the best-selling masterpiece, *The Go-Between*, was the one that got away. Barrie went bust twice, and each time the firm was re-created. The second time, his partner was Leopold Ullstein, and after various twists and turns his residual interest was bought out by Leopold's acquaintance Tony Samuel. Tony was not interested in banking, had once tried farming in Rhodesia, and now thought that publishing might be fun. When it came to the point, Barrie was unwilling to go, but after making a nuisance of himself and trying to set Leopold and Tony against eachother, he was pushed out. That left Leopold and Bobby running the firm, with Jack Caspall still selling its books to the trade as he had done for some years before. Never anything but loyal to his new employers, Jack nevertheless always had a special regard for James Barrie. All this happened around 1954.

Leopold was unlike any of the other Jewish refugees from Germany and central Europe who made a mark in London publishing. Probably this was at least partly because in the terms of our profession he was an aristocrat; he started at the very top, and the sort of ambition that would have driven a man from a less exalted background did not touch him. His father was the eldest of five brothers who were the joint owners of the great German firm of Ullstein. Born in 1905, he was more than old enough to have become a partner before the rise of Hitler, but 'formidable' disagreements between the brothers delayed his coming into his inheritance, and instead he joined the firm of Rowohlt. Just as a solution finally appeared which would have let him into the family firm, the Nazis came to power and he had to leave.

John Bunting, only child of the writer Daniel George (Bunting), briefly had an imprint of his own, the Turnstile Press (under the umbrella of the *New Statesman*, whose offices were at Great Turnstile), at the end of the war: he decided to give this up voluntarily, and moved successively to Heinemann (as advertising manager) and Baillière, the medical publishers. He became interested in the Barrie venture, clicked with Leopold, and was hired. The two were utterly different. Bunting (born in 1919) was intelligent, sophisticated, kind and humorous, and knowledgeable about the trade and alert to the ways of the market place, but in a peculiar way was physically unco-ordinated: he had an awkward speech impediment, and was unkempt, with dirty finger-nails and cigarette ash all over his clothes. Ullstein was a man of baffling character, unimpressive-looking but well-dressed, even-tempered, without neuroses and often disarmingly friendly, but also loftily paternalistic in accordance the management style in which he had been brought up.

I saw John Bunting several times in the early 1990s when he was living in retirement in the Charterhouse, and never disguised my gratitude to him for opening the door in 1961 that led me on to the Pall Mall Press and my own independence. We could talk as fellow-workers in the vineyard, and discussed the Barrie experience at length. The fact that both he and Leopold died in 1995, and Bobby in 1996, frees me (morally) to reproduce here part of a letter he wrote me in March 1992, the main purpose of which was to correct an impression he thought he had given in conversation that he did not rate Leopold's abilities very highly. Of course I also knew Leopold and his contradictory qualities, and needed no such reassurance. It is as lifelike a portrait as could be hoped for.

Of course he had [talent]. He had firstly immense energy and enthusiasm which he could infect, and could command loyalty even when he infuriated. He also had an uncanny sense of predicting 'figures' which he seemed to work out in his head, often confounding others who had predicted it all 'scientifically'. On a number of occasions he was proved right about matters on which any reasonable person would assume he must be wrong, on the basis of available evidence. [...] I can say I have never met or even heard of anybody with a character so complex and so apparently contradictory. He could be so absurdly overmodest and at times arrogant, he could be patient and understanding and at other times unbelievably insensitive and ill-mannered. I remember Richard Wadleigh remarking very aptly 'The trouble with Leopold is that he is totally without any social antennae'. When I joined him I did my best to politely educate him in book trade 'basics', urging him for example to read the *Bookseller* carefully each week (he had not previously been aware it existed, I think) but he never did except to see if there was any reference to Barrie. He would never go to any meetings such as P.A. Book Centre when we were heavily involved or attend any kind of Trade semi-social functions. He rarely set foot in a bookshop or took the trouble to inquire which booksellers were worth talking to either for public relations or to seek opinions.

He would get enthusiasms for books – that he should usually do so when they were ones he had personally picked or somehow been responsible for was natural – and would then convince himself that they could become relative best-sellers and demand large print runs and much advertising, when it was patently obvious that, interesting though they might be in some quarters, they would never possibly command more than minority appeal. Had the price been higher, advertising less and had not most of them been translations requiring hours of editorial discussion because of his often correct objections to relatively minor errors of the translator, they would have been books that did not disgrace the list and might even have made a small profit. But he would never understand that very few book readers other than those with a very specialised interest would read for example a biography of a person of whom neither they nor any of their friends had ever heard, unless of course it had some very marked literary style or was in some way scandalous, sensational or very comic.

Considering he came to England with little more than remembered English from his school days, he quickly acquired a remarkable fluency, not only spoken but written. His long letters which he always made me vet very seldom required to be corrected or revised as far as the English was concerned. They had to be revised and sometimes totally re-written because of inordinate length and because the important points he was endeavouring to make would be totally lost in a mass of verbiage, jokes, asides etc. He would have a sentence of 8 lines and few paragraphs.

He had a good sense of visual things, but even here he could not understand why what he saw as a very good drawing made an unsuitable jacket, though this was obvious to everyone else.

. . . . . .

This letter is simply written because I feel I may have given the impression [talking face to face] that I always considered L. a complete idiot. This was far from so. But I do think he was unsuitable to run a business once it had got beyond 'hobby trading'.

He and Bobby took very little salary all the time.

. . . . . .

This letter is getting like one of Leopold's that I complain I had to cut down and redraft.

Around 1957 they were looking for a new list, and homed in on the 'Rockliff Publishing Corporation', which was for sale. This firm published books on the theatre, music and the more mystical end of the religious spectrum. It also had a textbook series on the hotel and catering trade. The founder Mr Rockliff retired, but his manager and editor Geoffrey Robinson, a high-minded autodidact who had little in common with his new colleagues, joined the team. Barrie and Rockliff was thus formed, and the firm had backlist, but it only achieved commercial viability when it acquired Herbert Jenkins, the publishers of P.G. Wodehouse, soon after I left. This was an especially shrewd deal because, having absorbed the Jenkins operation, it was able to sell off that firm's old premises in Duke of York Street, St James's, and by so doing recover its entire outlay on the acquisition.

I faced a moment of truth within a day or two of joining the firm. An advertisement had to be designed: it was very small, but as I looked at the space to be filled, panic came over me. In spite of being immersed in typography at the *Architectural Review* and even at Rolls-Royce, I always worked to layouts designed by others and never did one myself. Yet this was precisely what I had been hired to do. Confidence came quickly, and I was spared having to admit to being a fraud.

Right at the start I asked for manuscripts to read and proofs to correct, and Geoffrey Robinson kept me supplied. Also, to my delight, the production manager Richard Wadleigh asked me to design a jacket: the subject was church architecture, the design suggested itself naturally, and Richard was pleased. But the most seminal of my extra-curricular experiences was going out with a bag to sell books to the trade – repping. Jack Caspall would come into the office at lunchtime and talk about the calls he had made during the morning. His father had been the butler at the British embassy in Brussels, and his speech and manner always had a well-modulated, respectful tone – in a different era he might have followed his father's profession. It was amusing to see how Leopold addressed him as 'Caspall' as if he had been the butler, and Jack obligingly called him 'sir' in return. Humphrey Hare at least called him 'Mr Caspall', but in his own way was equally patronising, which Jack, who thought him no end of a lad, lapped up. But the essential thing was that he was highly regarded in the trade, as I was often to hear and as Peter Giddy of Hatchards stressed in his obituary of Jack in the *Bookseller* about twenty years later. I got the impression from talking with Jack that repping in central London was a somewhat ritualised affair. It was important, he said, to accept your place in the queue calmly if there were several reps already waiting to see the buyer. From this it appeared that a single important call could take up a rep's whole working day (calls were hardly ever made in the afternoon), most of which would be spent gossiping with colleagues.

At an early stage I asked Jack if, with the agreement of Leopold and John (this was readily given), he would take me with him on some of his calls. He had a better idea: that I should go by myself to accounts which he could not visit easily – outside central London but not so far out as to fall within the territory of the Southern England rep, a freelance. The nearest calls were in Notting Hill (Mandarin Books and Mary Glasgow), Euston Road (the Friends' Bookshop), Caledonian Road (Houseman's Peace Bookshop) and Hampstead (High Hill). My favourite regular call was at Mandarin; the orders from the discerning Irish owner Mr Sanderson were modest but gratifying. I had an unpleasant experience on one of my visits to that part of town when, waiting with my bag in W.H. Smith at Notting Hill Gate to see the buyer, I came face to face with the most beautiful and spirited (also quite talented) girl student at the Byam Shaw school, where I had been the previous year. As we never knew eachother well, we exchanged banalities; I could not appear to make apologies for my present occupation, but I felt a jerk – all the more so because for almost the only time in my life I was sporting a ridiculous tweed hat.

Ian Norrie's High Hill Bookshop was my major call in North London, and with him I had my first taste of 'returns', of which he must have been something of a pioneer. Before ordering anything new he would go round the shelves and hunt down unsold Barrie books, which I had to agree to take back. Another memorably expert and rebarbative customer whom I visited in Islington was Arthur Mendelson, then selling left-wing books on his own account and later to become manager of Collets in Charing Cross Road. When I made my way to the W.H. Smith branch at Heathrow airport, I amazed myself and everyone else by taking an order for fifty copies of a new novel by the softporn Norwegian novelist Agnar Mykle. I never had the chance to repeat that triumph because Jack immediately decided to go there in future himself.

Writing blurbs was one of my tasks, and in despair one day I took a German novel to John Bunting and said I was stumped, although I had even gone to the length of reading it. Did he have any ideas? Innocently he asked me to describe the book. I started doing so. Then he asked me what I thought of it and I told him. At the end he said 'Write what you have just said'. I did and it worked first time. He also told me not to exaggerate or use such standbys as 'penetrating' and 'controversial' without good reason. I still strive to write or edit blurbs on the Bunting principle.

As advertising manager I had to deal with my opposite numbers on various organs – such as the lordly John Latham of the *Sunday Times*; the handsome Jerome Foster of the *Times Lit. Supp.* whose marriage, I was told, caused grief among his unattached female colleagues; and the amiable, gossipy Michael Roberts of the *New Statesman*. Through Michael I got an invitation to his paper's great half-century reception at the Connaught Rooms in 1962 – David Low, Kingsley Martin and Harold Wilson (not yet prime minister) were a few of the eminent guests; a less eminent one was my Oxford tutor, W.W. Robson. I suddenly ran into one of my fellow-students in the Oxford English school, Catherine Dove (whom Robson had at one time pursued), and asked her gaily what she was doing there. With a brilliant smile she said she was the wife of the editor, John Freeman, and thus my hostess. At this party I met for the first time John Hitchin, then near the beginning of his career at Penguin, who took pains to impress on me that his firm was the best publisher in the country. I had not seen it in that way before, but on most counts he was right. Among the advertising reps who came visiting at Clement's Inn the greatest 'card' was the man from the *Liverpool Daily Post*, whose stories were so funny that when he suddenly stopped and said 'Well, Mr Hurst, I can't keep you all day – what about a small insertion on our book page?', it would have needed a heart of stone to refuse him.

None of the novels Barrie & Rockliff published while I was there entered the canon, or came anywhere near it. I have mentioned Agnar Mykle, and one of his was described as 'the greatest novel I have ever read' by a reviewer in the *Aberdeen Press and Journal*. Unfortunately the reaction elsewhere was lukewarm, and the provenance of this quote meant that if we had used it in press ads it would have caused mirth rather than a rush to the bookshops. We published several books by an Australian, Gerald Glaskin, who wrote extraordinarily well – but there was something that prevented them catching on, probably a combination of the Australian setting and our unglamorous imprint. We suffered agonies when Glaskin offered us a novella about a dim-witted pair of teenage lovers – it was explicit and told with a cloying sentimentality that suggested real-life experience insufficiently digested. We all found it repellent, and it was rejected. Too many of the rest were translations that had excited Leopold or Geoffrey Robinson, and in which an inordinate amount of time and money was sunk; Jack's best efforts cannot have sold many copies of any of them. An exception to this gloomy picture of largely wasted effort may have been J.L. Carr's first novel, *A Day in Summer*; I was given the manuscript to read and recommended it, and then, once it had been accepted, edited it. Jim's subsequent output and reputation would seem to vindicate the choice. He inscribed the copy he gave me 'To my secret sharer', and we remained friends. Barrie did not keep him, because he could not help hopping from one firm to another, and published his last two novels himself.

Barrie and Rockliff had its own warehouse on the North Circular Road. The manager, Mr Hunter, was another German Jew, though belonging to a different world from Leopold's *haute juiverie*. From overheard talk between Leopold and John Bunting, one had the impression that he was 'our son of a bitch', the subject of endless complaint and even suspicion but none the less indispensable. Small, paunchy, bespectacled and perspiring, he was a total contrast to his faithful assistant Miss S., a local lady – like him, middle-aged though well preserved and still shapely. Without her, it was generally agreed, the whole outfit would collapse into chaos. There was a mixture of astonishment, amusement and genuine pleasure in Clement's Inn when we heard that this incongruous pair had got married.

John MacCallum Scott and Fred Praeger

Another publishing house for which Barrie and Rockliff provided warehousing was the Pall Mall Press. This was later extended and became a complete service: sales through Jack Caspall and the commission reps, production by Richard Wadleigh and advertising by me. This firm was the creation of John Hutchinson MacCallum Scott, born in 1911, the only child of a Scottish Liberal M.P. and barrister. An intelligent, sensitive man, he lost both his parents in an air crash while still at school, and on leaving Oxford went to the Bar, adopting his father's first name, MacCallum, as an additional surname to boost his career. He immediately married Nora, another only child, and they departed on a two-years-long world trip. Both were comfortably off, and without the spur of necessity he never practised as a barrister. Instead he wrote two books about his travels which were commercially published. He had an 'interesting' war, in uniform but non-combatant, ending it in Scandinavia – an abiding love for him though it never figured in his publishing. With the war over, as well as standing for Parliament a couple of times, he helped to found the Liberal International, becoming its first secretary-general and editing a periodical called *World Liberalism* and various propaganda pamphlets. The publishing side of the operation slowly grew, with John taking increasing editorial and financial responsibility, so that by 1957, when he gave up the secretaryship in favour of Derick Mirfin, a list of short books as well as pamphlets was in existence – in transit between the phasing out of the L.I. propaganda programme and the inception of an independent publishing house directed by John. This evolution coincided with removal of the L.I. office to the garret of 123 Pall Mall (a few steps from his club, the Reform), where John wove his plans for full-fledged publishing.

John had big soulful eyes, a short upper lip that revealed his teeth in a perpetual worried smile, and flabby jowls; he looked slightly like the actor Alastair Sim, even down to a mild Scots accent. He was well read and an acute observer of the political scene, but tone-deaf and without any aesthetic sense. Thirty years after their early marriage, the childless John and Nora were like oil and water; she was fiery, blunt-spoken and frustrated, and his response to her barbs was to smile feebly and say nothing. One night I stayed in their comfortable old farmhouse in Dunmow, and after dinner she insisted on playing records of Beethoven quartets, until I nearly went mad; John simply retired to bed in despair. (Dear friend as Leopold Ullstein became, I never got to know him and Bobby socially. He once invited me and Christine to cross London from Notting Hill to Hampstead on a Saturday night to have coffee after a dinner at which they were entertaining one of the firm's authors. By the lights of Leopold's old-fashioned paternalism this was quite in order, but I found it insulting and declined. Twenty years later I made a point of inviting him as my first lunch guest after joining the Garrick. We bumped into André Deutsch in the entrance and I re-introduced them – they barely knew eachother. During lunch Leopold suddenly chuckled and said that while he was at Barrie's a Sri Lankan woman offered him a manuscript that he found mildly interesting but did not feel moved to find a place for. He advised the author to send it to André Deutsch and to tell him that he, Leopold, was extremely interested in it. André took it. Whatever the precise truth of the story, I have found it convenient ever since to think of this standard publishing experience as the 'André Deutsch syndrome'.)

Typical long-standing Pall Mall authors were luminaries of the international Liberal movement like Massimo Salvadori, Wilhelm Röpke and Salvador de Madariaga ('Madders'), not a constellation to brighten the publishing sky in London. But John brought in some more interesting younger authors: S.E. (Sammy) Finer, professor of government at Keele and later at Manchester, who made an instant impact with his *Anonymous Empire*, on the political lobby in Britain; Colin Legum, Commonwealth correspondent of the *Observer*, left-wing South African exile and evangelist of 'Uhuru', had produced his classic *Pan-Africanism*, linking contemporary events in Africa with their Black transatlantic intellectual origins; and Hugh Tinker, professor of South Asian history at London University and another one-time Liberal candidate, complex individual and graceful writer, whose *India and Pakistan* was the first in a projected Pall Mall series on modern polities that never came to pass. The Pall Mall books of this type attracted the attention of Frederick A. Praeger, publisher, of 111 Fourth Avenue, New York, who co-published them. The old-style Pall Mall books became non-moving backlist, but even the new ones looked dreadfully unexciting, with amateurish jackets.

Meeting John, and discovering the kind of publisher he was, opened a window in my mind. I knew that with all his good qualities – kindness, generosity, political astuteness and inability to hurt anyone – he was amateurish in his approach to business. But his publishing *idea* at once slotted into concerns of mine that went back even before the start of the war in 1939, when my main interest was stamp collecting. Having 'old' parents who talked sagely in my presence about Hitler, Mussolini and Neville Chamberlain brought international affairs into my ken early, and when the war started there was no rest from news bulletins on the wireless, sometimes announcing cataclysms like the invasion of Russia and the attack on Pearl Harbor. Artistic interests, as distinct from innate endowments, came later, but the attraction of grand politics never slackened. Now here was someone who had created a publishing enterprise out of it. It was different from publishing big books of contemporary history or biographies of, and autobiographies by, big political figures. Barrie and Rockliff were potentially publishers of that sort, and Leopold Ullstein considered his most important book to have been a history by Alexander Werth of the struggle between Russia and Germany in 1941-5. But the firm had not the economic power or, above all, the flair and the energy (both of which George Weidenfeld had in an extreme form) to bring it off. John knew he was a foot-soldier, a humble tiller of the soil in the world of political publishing. Fred Praeger was much more than that.

When I carried a bag round the shops, I was all too well aware that a book on India and Pakistan, in hard covers with a dull, tract-like jacket, was not going to enthuse any buyers, who would look hard and long and then with luck order a single copy 'see-safe'. An early exception among London booksellers, which endeared the Pall Mall list to the ever-optimistic Jack Caspall, was the Economists' Bookshop, then run with an iron hand by the domineering Gerti Kvergic, assisted by young Gerald Bartlett, to whom Jack introduced me. Somewhere within me a sense of mission was developing.

Before I knew John, he had already left 123 Pall Mall and turned an attic room at the house in Dunmow into an office, where a locally recruited secretary typed his letters (he could not type himself) and helped him produce a mailing list. Fired by an unfortunate macho desire to be more like a 'real' publisher, he published some novels and a non-political book of memoirs (by Lionel Leslie, a first cousin of Winston Churchill on his mother's side). They were the no-hopers of the agents' lists, the jackets were as frightful as ever, and they made no impact. Jack did his best but was too polite to express his misgivings other than in a roundabout fashion. At this time too, John agreed to vanity-publish the memoirs of his old Liberal crony and a director of Pall Mall, Sir Andrew MacFadyean, who also happened to be S.E. Finer's father-in-law. Of course it only sold a handful of copies. This was just when John's subjection to Praeger was beginning, and his specious arguments to try and persuade Fred to co-publish MacFadyean in the States, and indeed his publishing it at all, proved a powerful irritant. It was not in John's nature to grasp the need to preserve his identity as a serious publisher, which was compromised by every book he published that was not squarely of the Pall Mall type.

It was because the Pall Mall list contained authors of the calibre of Finer, Legum and Tinker that Praeger conceived the idea of a closer alliance with this odd little British firm, which he saw – with the enchantment lent by distance – as a sales outlet for his much bigger list and as an editorial stalking-horse. This happened in the nick of time. John's service contract with Barrie and Rockliff was costing him much more than he was gaining from it in increased sales, and he would certainly have had to give up if Praeger had not intervened. Taking 80 per cent of the equity, Praeger ordered an expanded set-up. The Pall Mall name would be retained, and John would be managing director. In addition there would be an editor, a promotion manager and a production manager, plus a personal assistant for John. The local girl who assisted him in Dunmow would also be retained.

The editor was Derick Mirfin, a man of my age who had been president of the Cambridge Union and carried off a 'starred' first in his history finals. Like John he was a zealous Liberal, convivial and a wit. He had turned aside from the broader path to worldly success which must have been open to someone of his attainments by following John as secretary of the Liberal International. He was also Liberal candidate for Stratford-on-Avon, where John Profumo was the sitting M.P., and in the late summer of 1963, just as we were starting up the new Pall Mall office in London, he suddenly found himself pitched into an unusually newsworthy by-election when the 'Profumo scandal' left the seat vacant. A little later John proved the reliability of his political intuition by predicting, early in the Macmillan resignation crisis, that Home would be the next prime minister.

John targeted me to do the promotion and I accepted. My responsibility was not described as 'sales' because that continued to be handled by Barrie, but there was no one in charge of export sales and I quickly took that on myself. The European continent was covered by an agency in Zurich, Boxerbooks, which was typical in having more clients than it could cope with and favouring the ones that published art books, which sell best in that market. It only served Pall Mall well in the Nordic countries and Benelux, which were covered by Boxer's Danish stringer Björn Hansen. The world outside Europe was a blank for us. We started off in a small office in Great Ormond Street and then moved to a larger one in Charlotte Street.

From the first moment there was no doubt who was running Pall Mall. Fred Praeger himself directed his attention to the activities of John and Derick, while my province was overseen by his partner George Aldor, another Viennese Jew. He was some years older than Fred and only came to the book business around the age of fifty after dealing in nylon stockings, but he had an instinctive grasp – something John could never hope to emulate. Distinguished in looks and with a certain charm, he none the less had a foxy air, unlike the apparently relaxed and extrovert Fred. George spoke with a strong German accent and only his business phraseology betrayed the years he had spent in America. Fred had a more American style; whereas George looked good in a well-cut suit, Fred's preferred attire was sporty, and a lumberjack shirt was his virtual trademark. Short and stocky, he constantly toned up his fibres with vigorous exercise, ski'd and played tennis, and travelled with a rowing machine. He was a big spender. In short he had charisma.

My first major assignment on behalf of the reconstituted Pall Mall was a tour of the principal general and university bookshops up and down the country. The specific purpose of the trip was to set up a system of involving the shops in recommendations of Praeger paperbacks for university courses. It was something most of the book-sellers I met found to their liking; that the scheme never took off is another matter.

I met several heavyweights for the first time, like Ernest Hochland in Manchester, Paul Austick in Leeds, Robert Clow in Glasgow and Jan Janiurek in York. J.S.D. Thornton of 11 Broad Street, Oxford, whom I first saw on his return from war service as a comparatively young man, received me courteously in his little eyrie high up in that wonderful shop, with his rolltop desk and portraits of all his predecessors. Ross Higgins, manager of the fashionable Wylie's bookshop in Sauchiehall Street, Glasgow, received reps sitting at a table, not a desk, in the middle of the shop, and as soon as I sat down he asked me straight away why our distribution was not more efficient. The strain of being polite for so many days was telling on me, and I snapped back. He looked at me in way that I remembered uneasily over the next few days, but I pressed on under his beady gaze and concluded my business. A courteous letter from him awaited me on my return to London, agreeing to cooperate in the Praeger paperback scheme.

I went for the first time to Maxwell's path-breaking new store at the Plain in Oxford. In keeping with its owner's publishing interests, it stocked mainly science books; and it had an open plan with a café in the basement. This marked a departure from the establishments traditionally patronised by town and gown in Oxford. Hans Zell, though not the manager, seemed effectively in charge. This young Swiss had an intense energy and a high-pitched voice that reminded me of Ian Nairn. He had already served his apprenticeship with Almqvist and Wiksell in Stockholm, assisting Davids Thomsen there to set up a new documentation-promotion scheme for new 'scientific' books (in the continental sense of all academic disciplines), which was to be operated by just one major academic bookstore in each country, and by Maxwell's in Britain; and he later went on to manage in succession Max Holmes's Africana publishing programme in New York and two university bookshops in West Africa: Fourah Bay and Ife. Since then he has made for himself an unchallenged position as bibliographer and recorder of the African publishing scene, and after Sisyphean labours started up in Oxford a distribution point for serious books from all over Africa, for the Euro-American market and for Africa itself (to overcome the huge barriers to trade *between* many African countries). I have written about him at this length because he is one of the international book trade's most unusual and admirable figures.

At Blackwell's I met the manager of the oriental department, Mr G., soon to leave under a cloud and be replaced by the two young Ring brothers: the robust-looking Bob, who died a few years later from food poisoning picked up in Yugoslavia, and Dick who ran the department alone for many years longer and with whom I had dealings over all that time. The oriental specialist at Heffer's in Cambridge was R.A. Gooch, a man with a gentlemanly and authoritative air. He seemed too large a personality to fit in the cramped atmosphere of Petty Cury, and no doubt the notoriously low salaries paid there hastened his departure to found a new business, Ad Orientem Ltd, in a large terraced house at St Leonards on Sea. Many of his customers followed him, and in the late 1960s, aided only by a secretary, he was producing a fine thrice-yearly catalogue and turning over a quarter of a million pounds a year. Another well-remembered meeting was with Barry Hudson, one of two brothers and one sister who still owned and managed Birmingham's foremost bookselling business. By the same route as my erstwhile Nanny became a partner (and the brains) in her family's funeral carriage business because of her brothers' absence at the war, Pat Hudson became the head of Hudson's. (Women have never been so dominant in bookselling as when she, Una Dillon, Christina Foyle, Gerti Kvergic and Hilary Pattison ruled in their domains – strange that none of them became office-holders in the Booksellers Association.) Barry looked at the backlist in the Pall Mall catalogue and remarked that the dates of publication were not given, thus depriving users of essential information; this was something I would certainly never be told a second time.

Pall Mall were still using Barrie and Rockliff's force of commission reps, and John Bunting's remark that they were more often ill, or their cars were off the road, than they were out selling books has echoed down the years. On my trip I received particular help from the Midland rep, who lived in Cambridge. It was a treat for me to go around with him, because he was excellent at his job and *persona grata* everywhere. This was because of his hyperactive and obsessive character, and his being a 'card' always quipping away in his North Midlands accent. As a matter of course he invited me to stay in his house, and on arriving in town I had to meet him after Benediction at an Anglo-Catholic church where he was a server; in this as in everything else he knew no half-measures, and his wife let on that she looked back wistfully to the time before he took up religion. His name for her was the first syllable of the word 'treasure', which cannot be spelt with English orthography. Not for the first time in this sort of relationship I was discouraged from getting on to first-name terms, but soon found that everyone, including his wife, called him by the first syllable of his surname. This kept people from getting too close. I kept in touch with Jack Caspall at this time by meeting him occasionally for pub lunches. He was just as friendly and obliging as ever.

There were three categories of books I had to deal with at Pall Mall. First, there were our own Pall Mall originals: it was assumed, especially since Pall Mall's editorial policy was now (in theory) under Praeger's control, that these would be co-published by Praeger in the United States as a matter of course (Canada still, quaintly, counted as part of the British publisher's market). Then there were Praeger originals which it was decided – by Fred and George, not by us – would be co-published in Britain with the Pall Mall imprint. It was clear that the best ones would never come to us, and before long it also became clear that some of those which did come to us as co-editions would have been better supplied in small quantities under the next category, distinguished by the rude-sounding acronym FAPUK (Frederick A. Praeger – U.K.), of those Praeger originals which were not considered suitable for co-publication, but which we would distribute and promote. Of these last the most hopeful were of course the Praeger paperbacks for which Praeger held world rights – these included U.S.-policy-oriented volumes edited by academics called Henry A. Kissinger and Zbigniew Brzezinski.

Derick Mirfin was the focus of Fred Praeger's aspiration that

Pall Mall would become his editorial outpost in London. He knew by instinct that he could expect little or nothing from John MacCallum Scott, who was neither a hands-on editor nor a source of inspiration for the kinds of book Fred wanted. The authors he was after were star political and diplomatic journalists and a sprinkling of academics strong in 'area studies'. Memorable books of the Pall Mall type which gestated in our Charlotte Street office during my time there were Robert Stephens's *A Place of Arms* (about Cyprus), Peter Nichols's *Politics of the Vatican*, S.E. Finer's *The Man on Horseback* (on the military in politics), Colin and Margaret Legum's *South Africa: Crisis for the West*, Hugh Tinker's *History of South Asia, The Modern Culture of Latin America* by Jean Franco, Alexandre Bennigsen's *Islam in the Soviet Union* and (mentioned reluctantly) Emmanuel Hevi's *An African Student in China*. The last of these recommended itself to Fred because of his close links with U.S. national policy at the time; one side of him was a typical American enemy of European imperialism who rode the Uhuru bandwaggon with the best, but the other was a committed Cold Warrior. All Derick's efforts were needed to wrestle Hevi's book into shape, but because it exposed the racism of the Chinese despite their official 'internationalism', it was good Cold War material and received C.I.A. support. Our involvement came about because the author was Ghanaian – and because it was not a front runner that would appeal to a bigger British publisher. Books on the Soviet Union, the Vietnam conflict and U.S. national security formed the staple of Praeger's contemporary affairs list, and a classic he published in this area was *The Communist Party of the Soviet Union* by Leonard Schapiro – who took offence at the vulgarism of a Praeger blurb-writer describing him, a full professor, as 'teaching' at the London School of Economics. Schapiro was one of a panel of advisers, also including Finer and Legum, whom John MacCallum Scott retained on Praeger's behalf.

On one of Fred's visits I was included in a lavish private dinner at the Reform Club which all of them attended. Fred, as already mentioned, was an open-handed man, but it was the quintessentially clubbable John who was in his element on such an occasion, although he was only surrogate host. Fred, dressed out of character in a dark suit and in an alien setting, looked awkward and spoke little. When cigars were passed round I incautiously took one, but it quickly interacted with the rich food I had eaten and I had to make a dash for the lavatory. I returned, feeling shaky, to find that the party had settled down to the serious talk of the evening, and was just in time to hear Finer starting to enunciate a publishing idea of classic beauty and simplicity. It was that Pall Mall should commission a series of extended essays by different authors called 'Key Concepts in Political Science'. Finer had already inspired the initiation of re-issues, in new translations, of neglected classic political texts: the only two to appear were *What is the Third Estate?* by the Abbé Sieyes and *The Sociological Works of Vilfredo Pareto*, which Derick translated from Italian and Finer edited. The 'Key Concepts' idea germinated, and in the early 1970s several titles appeared, originated in hard covers by Pall Mall and from 1971 issued in paperback by Macmillan.*

My own relations with Fred Praeger were at first formal and distant. He was not personally interested in my department, and unlike George Aldor, who said what he felt spontaneously, his personality tended towards reserve and careful calculation of the effect of his words, which were always uttered with deliberation. If George didn't agree with you, he would say so at once, sometimes in crude language spiced with New York slang. For Fred disagreement would have the quality of *odium theologicum*, turning, if unresolved by sweet reasoning, to deep and permanent grudges. John MacCallum Scott had a peculiar ability to get up Fred's nose: on the one hand he showed a pathetic and undignified anxiety to please him, while on the other he persisted, sometimes deviously, in actions that could only anger him and thus weaken his own position. For example, he insisted that it was necessary for the firm to keep an office in Dunmow, but we all knew it was not necessary and just a way for John to keep some of the action under his exclusive control. And he made a typical mistake in the course of commissioning a book called *The Craft of Diplomacy* from a well-read but bland and complacent retired ambassador, Sir Douglas Busk. In his idle moments Busk had penned a short, elegant but unsaleable manuscript called *The Curse of Tongues* and put it away where it belonged, in a bottom drawer. When John appeared, unsure, gullible and armed with fresh capital, Busk succeeded in making the publication of *The Curse of Tongues* part of the deal, so that it appeared before the diplomacy book. Fred was furious at the bungling way his London operation had been entrapped by this vain old *poseur*; the dismal commercial outlook for *Tongues* was almost secondary. (I too had a minor row with John over these books, when he told me that the author had asked that his name should appear without the 'Sir' on the cover and title page. I protested that the name 'Douglas

---

* Some titles in the series were: Martin Albrow, *Bureaucracy* (1970); Brian Chapman, *Police State* (1970); Peter Calvert, *Revolution* (1970); John Plamenatz, *Ideology* (1970); Ioan Davies, *Social Mobility and Social Change* (1970); Joseph Frankel, *National Interest* (1970); P.H. Partridge, *Consent and Consensus* (1971); A.H. Birch, *Representation* (1971); Henry Tudor, *Political Myth* (1972); C.J. Friedrich, *Tradition and Authority* (1972).

Busk' meant nothing to any except a select few, but that the magic handle might just make one or two potential buyers stop and take a second look. But of course John had already agreed without thinking of the consequences. (My conviction that Busk's request sprang from arrogance and not modesty is reinforced by the fact that none of the handful of knighted ex-colonial governors whose memoirs my firm has published made such a request and probably, being genuinely modest men, never even thought of it.) There was also a life of Friedrich Engels by a nice female amateur scholar which somehow found its way on to the firm's list of futures. It needed to be virtually rewritten by Derick, thus occupying large chunks of his valuable time, and its copublication was refused by New York. The battle lines for a future set-to were being drawn up.

George Aldor thought that I achieved good results when travelling, and so in August 1964 I was sent off on a three-month tour of the English-speaking markets of Africa. Pall Mall was in the process of inaugurating two series to be co-published with Praeger: a Library of African Affairs and a Library of World Affairs with no geographical limitation, though its first volume, *The Somali Dispute* by John Drysdale, and its third, *Algeria: the Revolution that Failed* by Arslan Humbaraci, happened also to be about Africa. At this time Drysdale's book was just out and the first two volumes of the Africa series were in preparation. Legum was considered to have unrivalled contacts with the emerging African leaders – as a banned South African left-winger he had the right credentials – and was also looked up to as a guru not only by the firm but by a number of British journalists of about my age who were then seeking their fortunes in the newly independent countries. He played his part with due solemnity. It was from this circle that Legum confidently expected to find authors to cover various African countries, but although several were signed up, few delivered the goods. Of those who did the most significant was Richard Hall, whose book on Zambia in the series was the first of several distinguished books he has written on Central African history. The first book to appear in the African series was a massive tome on Ethiopia by Richard Greenfield, who with his slight physique, boyish appearance and conspiratorial air suggested a latter-day Lawrence of Arabia. It offended the old Ethiopian regime, but not quite enough to provoke a lawsuit. Outside either series was the Legums' *South Africa: Crisis for the West*. It was this book especially that I was expected to sell on my travels – though obviously not in South Africa itself, where the authors were 'banned persons'.

Before leaving for Africa I phoned Tony Pocock the general sales manager at Oxford University Press, and asked if he would be willing to give me a briefing. He agreed without hesitation, though he could not have been more than dimly aware of Pall Mall's existence, and at Amen House in the City I sat for more than an hour at his feet and those of an old hand, Freddie London, whom he called in. They told me who was who and where in the African book trade as I scribbled notes. This willing sacrifice of their time was typical of O.U.P.'s public-spiritedness; like the British Council and even the Foreign Office, they had a mission to the world.

At about this time Pocock wrote a paper which the Publishers Association circulated, urging British overseas sales staff, and heads of houses going on their travels, to investigate local conditions in the territories they visited more thoroughly than they had been wont to do in the past. Eager handshakes and the mouthing of platitudes were no longer enough.

Africa, 1964

Till the previous year, when I went with Christine and our daughter Jo to her brother's wedding in New York, I had been no further beyond mainland Europe than Cyprus and Port Said. Remembering Pocock's injunction, I panicked slightly as the VC-10 was flying into Khartoum, my first stop, as I realised that I did not know the name of the Sudanese head of state. A British expatriate on the bus into the city put me wise (as it happened, General Abboud was displaced in a coup before I left Africa).

In Khartoum I immediately felt at home. The grand avenue along the Nile lined with gnarled old trees and the imposing red government offices built after Kitchener's conquest had a solid, reassuring air, and likewise the Grand Hotel, where I stayed. Sitting in the vast dining-room as the numerous waiters in white jellabas and head-cloths sped around and the ceiling fans spun gave me a most satisfying sense of luxury. (In spite of eating only English-style food, I immediately developed diarrhoea.) I was directed to certain members of the Sudanese élite by a friend, Peter Kilner, whom I had grown up with in Headington, Oxford, and who joined the Ottoman Bank on leaving the University, but moved sideways in Khartoum and worked for several years there as a journalist. He said I should introduce myself to these people by saying that he and I came from the same village. One person whose name came up in every conversation I had in Khartoum was

Jamal Mohamed Ahmed, the Sudanese ambassador in Addis Ababa, my next stop. 'You must meet Jamal,' they all said. It was not part of my brief to look for new books, but I wanted not to miss the chance of meeting potential authors as I went along.

Of the local booksellers the one that obviously thrived was the Khartoum Bookshop, owned by the Greek Flanginis family. The staple of their business, as in so many places of the same sort, was the agency for *Time* and *Newsweek*. They also sold hundreds of the Dell paperback edition of Alan Moorehead's *The White Nile* and *The Blue Nile*. I stayed in contact with P.N. Flanginis, then a young man, for long afterwards. He was someone who would not take 'no' for an answer: when I published a book on Nubia on my own account and sold 1,000 copies to the Khartoum University Press, Flanginis visited me in London and asked over and over again if I would sell copies to him as well, ignoring my repeated protestations that it was impossible. Greeks and Armenians made up most of the book trade in Khartoum; a Sudanese enterprise was starting up under British tutelage but it showed little sign of life.

One evening I was taken to a night-spot, and there was a pretty but smallpox-ravaged young 'hostess', heavily made up, behind the bar who had an Ethiopian mother and a long-vanished Italian father. As she calmly told me these facts, a fat middle-aged Sudanese standing next to me muttered something I did not catch but she did, and immediately she spat in his face and shouted 'You can insult me, but His Imperial Majesty – never!'

Addis Ababa was a squalid city compared to Khartoum, and although it had its imperial residences, built in a late-nineteenth-century South Kensington Italianate style, one could look over a parapet alongside a modern made-up street and see below a miserable jumble of shanties with people living like animals. One important-looking concrete-paved avenue broke off suddenly in the middle of town. Haile Sellassie is reputed to have commented on returning to his liberated capital and seeing so many fine civil engineering works left half finished by the departing Italians, 'It looks as if I have come back too soon.'

I phoned Jamal Mohamed Ahmed late on the afternoon of my arrival, and he asked me to come round to his house right away. As soon as I got there he ushered me into his ambassadorial limousine and we went off to a welcoming reception for the newly arrived secretary-general of the Organisation of African Unity, the Guinean Diallo Telli. The venue was small compared to the O.A.U.'s imposing new headquarters, but African ambassadors and Ethiopian notables filled it to capacity. Apart from a German, seemingly as unimportant as myself, I was the only white person there. I did not realise till much later that, with the O.A.U. only a year old and Diallo Telli the first secretary-general, I had assisted at a historic occasion. (After his term of office, Diallo Telli was murdered by his own countrymen.)

Earlier that year Jamal Mohamed Ahmed had gone to his native region, Nubia, and spent some time among his own people while they were being evacuated in preparation for its flooding by the rising waters of the Aswan High Dam. I encouraged him to write about this experience – he had already had a book published in England, and it seemed a real possibility. At first he agreed to do so, and this chimera kept us in touch through his subsequent ambassadorial career at the U.N. and in London, but he never wrote anything.

Another man I was urged to see in Addis Ababa was Stephen Wright, a former British Council representative who had stayed on after retiring and was now old and in poor health. He asked me to lunch and while we ate, his servant silently came and went. He told me how, as a child living in Battersea, South London, he went to his local public library for the first time. Not knowing what to look for, he opened the subject-catalogue at the beginning, and his eye naturally fell on 'Abyssinia'. There were two books about that mysterious country and he took both of them out and read them from cover to cover. He was already middle-aged when his chance came to go to Ethiopia for the first time: it had just been freed from the Italians, and someone was needed to run a British Council office there. He got the job on the strength of his great knowledge of the country, all gleaned from books. Then, when the time came for him to retire, he gave up his house, bade farewell to his servant, and left for 'home'. But after only a month, alone in London as an ageing bachelor, he came to the verge of a nervous collapse, and escaped back to Addis Ababa to live out the rest of his life. His servant was waiting, and told him that he knew it would be only a matter of time before they were reunited.

I also met there one of my firm's future authors, Hans Lockot, a Latvian-born German and a wanderer until he took up the post of head of the research division in the National Library in Addis Ababa. From his twenty-year tenure he developed a deep respect for the Emperor, and eventually wrote a portrait of him in defence against the best-selling denigratory one by Ryszard Kapuzinski. When Lockot re-surfaced in my life in the late 1980s through an introduction from Richard Pankhurst, I dimly remembered a colourless man sitting in a bare office. The connection with Latvia made me sure it was the same person.

In Addis Ababa, as in Khartoum, the retailing of books in English seemed to be largely in the hands of Greeks and Armenians; there

was one bookshop run by American Mennonite missionaries which
showed some interest in my wares. But this was as nothing compared
with Nairobi, my next stop, where the book market seemed buoyant.
My first call, on D.L. Patel Press, produced an order for six dozen
copies of *The Somali Dispute*. At S.J. Moore, an old British-owned
business, I obtained a small handful of single-copy orders. *South
Africa: Crisis for the West* was my *pièce de résistance*, but it did
not sell. I quickly found that, whatever might be said at the U.N.
and the O.A.U., South Africa's problems were of very minor concern
in other African countries north of the Limpopo.

Mr Upadhyay of D.L. Patel Press, who gave me my splendid
order, invited me to join him and his family for an outing on the
coming Sunday, but I had already agreed to go rock-climbing with
Charles Richards, the Oxford University Press manager, and some
of his friends. When we got to the climb which was our main objective,
I went up it quickly and with ease – to his surprise and, even more,
my own. I had never attacked a vertical rock face before and never
did again. One of the party, a deeply bronzed, melancholy Englishman,
looked out from the top of our outcrop at some farming land which
had been British-owned but was now in the hands of Africans, and
commented laconically about its dilapidated state. Charles whispered
that this man had been unlucky with his own farm, and his wife
had gone home without him. Charles himself was cultured, clubbable,
a keen Anglican and a typical O.U.P. man of his generation – like
John MacCallum Scott too in his transparent decency and idealism
and apparent lack of commercialism. One of his daughters was there
on a visit from England – auburn-haired and with beautiful fair skin,
she was in full bloom as well as being intelligent and lively, and
because we got on well I felt pangs of desire and regret. I asked
Charles if he would take on Pall Mall as one of his sales agencies;
the answer, some time later, was 'no'.

Colin Legum was in town and introduced me to a circle of young
British journalists and academics, and I went to a stimulating supper
party at the house of one of them. All the whites present, including
the girls, had African partners and they appeared to be riding high
aboard the Uhuru bandwaggon. Late in the evening Peter Kenyatta,
the President's pale-skinned son by his one-time English wife, arrived
alone, and though warmly welcomed seemed ill-at-ease. A young
Englishman not of this group, whom Legum had singled out to write
a book for us on Kenya, was John Nottingham, an out-and-out idealist
who lectured at the university and ran the East African Publishing
House, an enterprise founded by André Deutsch in an act of enlightened

self-interest, but only controlled by him for a short time before he was obliged to sell it for a pittance.

I convinced myself that it would be a wasted opportunity if I did not look for editorial openings as well as sales. Thus in Kampala, where I did not manage to sell anything, I spent most of my short time there on the campus of Makerere University. Ali Mazrui was the reigning guru whom everyone passing through had to meet – in conformity to what seemed a fashionable pattern among more sophisticated African academics, he had an English wife though she seemed to me relatively unsophisticated. I did not succeed in persuading him to write one of his many books for us. The pioneering African cultural periodical *Transition* was then at its peak and the editor Rajat Neogy, a highly westernised Ugandan Indian, who lived and operated in Kampala, was by far the most interesting person I met there. His young Swedish wife had just had her first baby, and in the restaurant the two of them cooed over it ecstatically: when I met him again a few years late by chance and asked after her, he said they had parted. Mazrui's marriage to his Englishwoman didn't survive either.

In Dar es Salaam, a much more exotic city, there was plenty to imprint itself on the memory: the houses in the Indian quarter with big enclosed balconies projecting over the walkways, on which poverty-stricken Africans lay inert; a dancing procession along the main avenue overlooking the harbour; a German cemetery on the seashore just outside the town – the black marble headstones incised with gold-painted Gothic letters – under tall palm trees; and suddenly arriving on a nocturnal walk at a Catholic religious house in what I thought was no man's land, and being led by the doorman to an open garden-house where a German bishop sat, presumably meditating before my arrival. All this was in darkness – there was no moon or light of any other description. I must have talked with the bishop for at least half an hour without ever seeing him, but I had the sensation that he was physically large.

On the flight down to Malawi I sat next to a young African accountant, John, who lived in Highfield, one of the two main 'townships' outside Salisbury, Rhodesia – the plane's final destination. He gave me his phone number. In Blantyre I arrived at a modest colonial-style hotel and, when addressing the white woman behind the desk, was innocent enough to refer to an African as 'that gentleman' in the way one would do at home. She repeated the word with deep sarcasm and I realised that we were now in the magnetic field of Southern Africa. At Zomba I was the guest of a British hydrologist, John Pike, who had been commissioned to write the Pall Mall volume

Private Sid Haywood, the Loyal Regiment (N. Lancs), the author's batman. Famagusta, Cyprus, 1950. Drawing by the author.

T. Lawrence Dale, architect, Oxford, 1959. Rapid sketch by the author.

ABOVE *Suzanne, the author's first wife, Felixstowe, 1953.* BELOW
*The author's children, Greenwich, 1969. Left to right: Andrew,
Josephine, Martin, Daniel.*

ABOVE Cashla Hurst, the author's mother. BELOW Kathleen Haynes, her companion. Both drawn by the author at Oxford, 1960.

ABOVE *Leopold Ullstein.* BELOW *John Bunting.*

ABOVE *John MacCallum Scott and (left) his wife Nora, mid-1950s. Photo courtesy of Liberal International.* BELOW *Derick Mirfin. Photo taken in the Pall Mall Press office, mid-1960s, by Stella Heiden.*

ABOVE *Frederick A. Praeger.* BELOW *Marguerite Gwendolen Ogilvy and the author's son Daniel, Notting Hill, 1965. When Miss Ogilvy, then aged 84, saw this picture, she said it should be entitled* 'Nunc Dimittis'.

ABOVE *The author with Eduardo de Laiglesia, Madrid, 1993.* BELOW
Michael Dwyer, 1997.

ABOVE *Gustav Nachtigal and Humphrey Fisher.* BELOW *The ceremonial lamp lit by President J.R. Jayewardene before the launch of* A History of Sri Lanka *by K.M. de Silva, Colombo, 1981. From left, K.M. de Silva, the author, Mr Parthasarathy (Oxford University Press, Madras), the President.*

on the country, and eventually delivered. We drove through the town early the next morning, and passing President Banda's office had to halt because the Kamuzu himself, preceded by uniformed security men like *Tontons Macoutes*, arrived at that moment. Emerging from the limousine and walking up the steps in his dark three-piece suit and black Homburg hat he was as spooky as Baron Samedi. This turned out to be a historic Day of the Long Knives, when Banda dismissed several of his ministers, supposedly to pre-empt a coup. I saw just enough of Malawi to realise that it is a green and very beautiful place, but over-populated. The only bookshop I was able to do business with was a modest Asian enterprise.

My brief stay in Lusaka was mainly memorable for meeting Richard Hall. He was the editor of the weekly *African Mail*, and superficially appeared fairly typical of a seasoned British journalist who knew all the tricks of his profession. But before the demise of the Central African Federation the previous year, attempts had been made on his life because of his paper's opposition to it and support for Kaunda. Everything he has done since leaving Zambia, not least being the last journalist to leave Biafra before its collapse in 1970, has marked him out as a man of principle, with an unwavering dedication to Africa. His talented wife Barbara, from whom he later parted, was the *Mail*'s agony aunt – a collection of her columns was later published by Deutsch with the title *Tell me, Josephine* – and the creator of its crossword. A dinner party in their house included a Namibian who had trekked overland to escape from his country, and a small assortment of local white businessmen and expatriate adventurers. The only guest who didn't appear to me distinctly odd was the Namibian.

Salisbury was a boom city with an outcrop of high-rise modern buildings downtown. The Sunday of my stay was Pioneers Day, when a great gathering of loyal whites, including the Governor, performed a ceremony round a memorial in the city centre to the first settlers who arrived in 1890. None of the original pioneers was alive, but the widow of one was there. The general demeanour and style of dress of white Rhodesians reminded me of my New Zealand relations, also the offspring of colonists who had subdued an indigenous population. When I met one of those cousins for the first time in New Zealand a couple of years later, almost his opening gambit was to declare his admiration for Ian Smith.

There was one bookseller in town who clearly outshone all the others – Victor Tarica of the Book Centre. When I first called he was absent – it was Jewish new year – but the wait for his return was well rewarded. He was a man of fine manners and engaging personality, well described by the Italian word *signorile*, and when

I met his widow, still a bookseller, in Cape Town in 1991, she greeted me as an old friend and insisted that she remembered me, which I did not believe but took as proof that in this quality she and Victor were as one. In the Pall Mall list of new titles I had a large bibliographical work with the high price of five guineas. Victor ordered ten copies, remarking truly that no one else in the country would have taken half that quantity. After U.D.I. he moved south, buying Joe Zion's Pilgrim Bookshop in Cape Town.

I phoned John, my flight companion from Dar es Salaam, on arrival, and asked if I could visit him at Highfield, but he said I would not be welcome there. Instead he agreed to come for lunch to the Jameson Hotel where I was staying, the only European-style place which admitted Africans to the dining room, and to go from there to the Agricultural Show. It was Saturday and the busiest day. Naively I had not realised what I would be letting myself in for by going to this citadel of settlerdom with a stroppy African. The first salvo of abuse came from a passing car as we walked down the road to the showground. The next time was when we went into a bar and as I was about to order, the barman said to me, without discourtesy, 'I can't serve him here.' And finally, as we stood watching a stunt car driver making spectacular leaps through the air over an ever-lengthening row of other near-wrecks, a cowboy-like character sidled up and said I should watch out or my companion would pick my pockets. Increasingly anxious to avoid an incident – and to save my skin – I persuaded John to leave with me. He had planned to join in a demo the next morning at the Pioneers ceremony, though in the event, unlike some previous years, nothing happened.

I was asked to dinner by a journalist, Eileen Haddon, another friend of Legum's. A fellow-guest was a young German businessman from Johannesburg, who had observed me with John at the Jameson Hotel – after living in South Africa, he said, one could not fail to notice such things. Judith Todd, the politically radical and still very young (and beautiful) daughter of the former Southern Rhodesian prime minister Garfield Todd, was also there. Late in the evening Eileen told Judith to phone her parents, and said to me 'Why don't you go and see Garfield?' It was arranged almost before I knew what was happening.

That visit to the Todd ranch was my farthest foray into the African bush. Driving a hired car from Bulawayo along a strip road in the dusk required concentration, and the thought of what would happen if it broke down nagged at me. It was astonishing when I arrived to find the ranch house as well appointed as a stockbroker's villa in the English Home Counties; the chintzy style of furnishing and

the dark uniform and white frills worn by the African maid carried
me back to pre-1939 Ascot. Todd was a New Zealander who first
went to Rhodesia as a missionary. He said grace before dinner and
we all drank Coke. But he showed his sporting instinct afterwards,
when we went out in his Land Rover. Suddenly a buck's eyes were
caught in the headlights and he leaped out and shot it. As he threw
the carcass on to the car roof, blood was spattered over my shirt.
'Don't worry', he said, 'put it in cold water overnight and it'll be
gone in the morning' – and it was. The next day he took me to
a headland near the house and looking down to the river below
we saw a hippopotamus slowly coming out of the water for a lie-down
on the bank. Todd had been apprehensive about my coming because
on the faint phone line he had only caught the word 'press' and
assumed I was a journalist; when he heard I was a book publisher
he was relieved. He was not contemplating an autobiography, but
would I be interested in a collection of his speeches? This was
clearly hopeless and I demurred.

I already knew that he was setting off somewhere early the next
day and when the morning came he told me where he was going
– far up-country to Gonakudzingwa detention camp near the Mozambique
border to visit Joshua Nkomo. Did I want to go with him? Such
a swift change in my plans, with the car due back in Bulawayo
and my flight to Johannesburg booked for that afternoon, seemed
impossible and I said no, but as soon as I had left, gracefully waved
off by Todd and his wife, an enormous regret hit me, and for long
afterwards I cursed myself whenever I thought about it. What would
a missed flight have mattered compared with making such a journey?
I got to know Nkomo later in London, but this would have been
different, and I would here learned much from two days spent in
Todd's company.

The rest of the day was miserable for different reasons. On my
immigration card I wrote 'publisher' as my occupation, which of
course was to invite suspicion in South Africa. At Jan Smuts airport
the customs officer asked me if I had any books, and when I replied
'One or two' he opened my suitcase and, as my knees began to
wobble, put his hand down to the bottom and unerringly took out
the one book I didn't want him to see: the Legums' *South Africa:
Crisis for the West*, which was automatically banned since both authors
were officially banned persons. The man also took the totally respectable
Penguin History of Africa by Fage and Oliver, which I had for
reading matter. He said the books would be examined and returned
to me if found unobjectionable. That was all, and I staggered out
into the concourse, to be immediately accosted by a flashy Jewish

man who said he was some sort of middle manager from the Central News Agency (C.N.A.), the South African counterpart of W.H. Smith. I never discovered how he knew I was on the plane, or knew about me at all.

Clearly never doubting that I would welcome his ministrations, he said that a hotel room had been booked for me in the city and we would drive there. I bitterly reflected that if I had gone to Gonakud-zingwa with Garfield Todd I would not now be having this disagreeable ordeal. As soon as I had got rid of him and was in my room, I phoned Vanguard, a renowned liberal bookshop and under-the-counter dealer in banned literature – another of Colin Legum's recommendations. The owners, Fanny Kleneman and Joe Moed, were about to close for the day, and I pleaded with them to come round on their way home for a drink with me. Colin's name was persuasion enough, and they quickly made me feel better; they knew the ways of the South African immigration authorities and the C.N.A. all too well. It was only sad that I no longer had Colin's book, which I had all along planned to leave with them, not least in the hope that they might surreptitiously sell a few.

While the grid-plan centre of Johannesburg was reminiscent of an American city, Pretoria's Church Square, with its ornate late nineteenth-century public buildings and mighty statue of Kruger in his frock coat and hat, was reminiscent of provincial France although it encapsulates as nowhere else the homely pomp of the old Transvaal Republic. Yet Pretoria exemplified another architectural phenomenon – the vigour of new Afrikaner public building, much of which used the modern idiom daringly and successfully. I met Jan van Schaik, the bookseller and publisher, and Albert Geyser, a liberal Dutch Reformed theologian who had recently undergone a trial for heresy. A bookseller who took an interest in my books was the owner of Veritas, which had premises off the street on the first floor of an office block. She was a blonde German of about fifty and made no effort to conceal her admiration for Adolf Hitler – which, she said, explained the name she had given to her business.

In Cape Town I was due to meet Christine, my South African-born wife, who was coming out by sea with Jo, aged three, and Dan, not yet six months old. But that was still some days off, and on the way south I spent an unproductive day in Bloemfontein, from where I was going to make a side journey into Lesotho. That city had a *verkrampte* atmosphere. The professor of political science in the university seemed embarrassed by my presence and repeatedly asked if I was 'comfortable' in South Africa; a bookseller whom I met asked with mounting anger in his voice why, if I published books that were 'against South Africa', I had bothered to come to see him.

Getting to Maseru, some ninety miles away, took all night. The train ended its run at a little place near the border called Marseilles, and there I had to accommodate myself in the station waiting room, which had nothing but shiny wooden benches. There was a full moon, and the only sounds were those of nature, I hardly slept a wink. In the early morning I found that I was not alone. In a separate compound nearby a sizeable number of Africans had been sleeping – soundly, it would seem – and now they were stirring. The place came alive, and soon a huge, closed articulated truck also stirred into life; it was to take us to the border. The Africans were herded into the back and the door was fastened. I was placed in the front cabin between the driver and his mate, both rural Afrikaners who spoke little English. We had only gone a mile or two when there was loud rattling in the back, the truck came to a halt and the driver's mate went round and opened the door. The men only wanted to get out for a pee, having doubtless saved it up to annoy the drivers, and we then continued. The driver pressed his thermos of sweet tea on me and when I sipped a token amount he would not be satisfied until I took more. At the border they both shook hands with me. The stamp in my passport read 'Basutoland Mounted Police, Caledon Bridge'.

My first call in Maseru was on the British information officer, Mr Tristram, in his very modest office with a Union Jack flying over it. The country was still nominally under British tutelage, but the true locus of power soon became clear. The Roman Catholic church owned the radio network, and the young priest who ran it told me he had warned Tristram to cease broadcasting British government propaganda or else be denied access to the network. I went by bus out to Roma, seat of the university – at the bus park people waited to take their departure to every corner of the mountainous kingdom, mostly wearing boldly patterned blankets. Two large stone buildings faced me on arrival at Roma: the Catholic seminaries, both run by French Canadian priests. At the senior one I was admitted as a guest for the night, and had a long conversation with the urbane and scholarly Father Superior in his study. He was apprehensive of the hotting-up of the battle between the political factions, one of them financed by the Chinese – as we talked, a loud-speaker van passed nearby. He was convinced that the people were unprepared for the political manipulation that would follow independence – when their renowned high standard of education, given to them by the churches, would count for nothing.

The professor of English at the university was driving to Bloemfontein the next day and offered to take me along. The two of us and a third Englishman set off with a picnic lunch on board, but a short way out of town we stopped when a solitary African walking along the road thumbed a lift. He was nearly starving and when our picnic was put before him, he ate a large part of it. He gave us his card and we found that he was an 'archbishop' of one of the country's myriad independent Christian churches. He left us on the outskirts of Bloemfontein to walk on alone, thinking it wiser not to be seen in our company.

In Cape Town, where I climbed Table Mountain on the afternoon of my arrival, I visited C. Struik's wonderful Africana bookshop – as well as antiquarian stock, it carried all good current material it could get hold of, and I picked up a nice order from Mr H. Waterberg, the manager. Both Mr Struik and he were 'Hollanders', as the Dutch were called in South Africa. Struik cornered the market for South African historical reprints, which included G.M. Theal's multi-volume *Records of South Eastern Africa*, and published some less striking original scholarly works. It was a fine enterprise, parallel to the Frank Cass operation in London, and was reputed, like Vanguard in Johannesburg, to sell banned books on the side, but after the old man's death in the 1970s his sons, who had been bred up in prosperity and lacked their father's calibre, concentrated on publishing touristic coffee-table picture books, and the bookselling was abandoned (their place as the scholarly bookseller *par excellence* in Cape Town has been taken by Clarke's in Long Street). Another interesting bookshop, long defunct, was Foyle's; unlike the parent business in Charing Cross Road it was a quiet place, and the manager, another Hollander called Pama, who worked upstairs in his office all day on the heraldry of Afrikaner families, on which he was the acknowledged authority, obviously liked it that way. At the university I met two of my firm's future authors, Jack Simons and David Welch.

My family holiday was spread between Cape Town, a small town in the rural Western Cape where Christine knew the vicar, and Durban where she had an old school friend with whom we stayed. One evening O.U.P.'s veteran South African supremo, Freddie Cannon, entertained us with his wife to dinner at the smart Kelvingrove Club. He, like Eric Parnwell who had once interviewed me for a job at Amen House, was one of those Oxford stalwarts who had risen from the lower deck, missing out the academic entrée. He was something of a Napoleon, aping the discontinued metropolitan custom of putting the publisher's personal name above the Press's imprint on the title page of the branch's publications. He was cataleptic and on this occasion briefly nodded off several times at the table and then continued talking as if nothing had happened. By contrast I also met Leon Rousseau, partner in the newly-founded Afrikaans literary publishing house Human and Rousseau, which later published the novels of André Brink. Rousseau was warm, outgoing and camp, quite unlike any of the Afrikaners I had met hitherto, with their warm but stiff manners always accompanied by uneasy defensiveness. Proud of his culture, he could yet talk about it with detachment and total lack of solemnity. Publishing of this kind and on this scale attracted me strongly. (Needless to say the firm lost its independence, and Mr Human later became a powerful figure in schoolbook publishing.)

There was a wonderful example of Afrikaner collective hysteria while I was in South Africa. The world president of the Rotarian movement came on a visit from America and, when he was interviewed at Jan Smuts airport on arrival, made a mildly critical remark about apartheid to reporters, doubtless not for the edification of the South Africans but to avoid censure from his constituency worldwide. Immediately politicians, businessmen and the nationalist press strove to outdo eachother in denouncing the man and his organisation. The controversy occupied the headlines for about a fortnight till the visitor's departure, when he made what I read as a very ambiguous retraction of his earlier statement. This was seized on as proof that South African values had triumphed, and incidentally that Rotary was not such a bad mob after all.

I broke the journey to Durban at Port Elizabeth, from where I hired a car to Grahamstown, home of Rhodes University, and thence to Alice. After a fruitless call on Fogarty's bookshop in Port Elizabeth, I went to the famous 'snake park', in reality a small zoo with reptiles only. The most evil-looking of a sinister lot was a large speckled lizard which spat venom into the eyes of its enemies. The sun was at its zenith as I promenaded alone among the enclosures, the heavy silence broken only by the mutterings of the custodian's parrot. At Grahamstown I saw, among others, Guy Butler, eminent poet and professor of English, in his office. A call on such an interesting man should have been a treat, but it turned out to be a mistake because I dried up: probably through the combination of having to adjust my patter to someone who was not a social scientist and sheer mental fatigue. I simply could not think of anything to say. We laughed it off and I withdrew.

The Ultima Thule of this excursion was Alice, home of Fort Hare University College. Fort Hare had recently been emasculated by the Afrikaner Nationalists; from being a Mecca for bright African students from all over the country and even beyond, it had been turned by decree into a tribal college for Xosa only – the wave of liberal outrage had spent itself by this time, since there was obviously nothing to be done. The professor of 'missiology' under the new dispensation was G.C. Oosthuizen, whom Monica Wilson, the eminent professor of anthropology in Cape Town, had recommended that I meet. As soon as I contacted him he invited me to stay the night in his house, and the first thing I noticed about him was his courtesy to Africans. A Dutch Reformed dominie who had served as a chaplain with the South African forces during the war, he made the indigenous 'independent' churches his specialisation. He had a completed manuscript on their practices, called 'Post-Christianity in Africa', which I thought would be an interesting departure for Pall Mall. He in turn took me to visit Alexander Kerr, who had been the first principal of Fort Hare, from 1915 to 1948, and still lived there in retirement. He did not have a ms. but I suggested he should write his memoirs.

He had been a young Scots Presbyterian minister when he was sent out here, and the whole place was infused with religion, but the pursuit of academic excellence was purely secular. Fort Hare had been a heroic enterprise, and Kerr had a story to tell. I failed to interest Fred Praeger in either Kerr or Oosthuizen, and published both myself in 1968, my first year of independence. When I was there, the Federal Theological Seminary – federating four denominations, including Anglicanism as represented by the Mirfield Fathers – was being built, right alongside Fort Hare, to the profound annoyance of the Afrikaner Nationalist academic establishment, who saw it (rightly) as a deliberate provocation, dangling non-apartheid practices under their noses, and with a strong Anglo-Saxon flavour. The seminary of course trained African candidates, and there was no segregation in worship. It finally migrated to Natal and still flourishes there.

I had met the South African scholar and patriot Zachariah K. Matthews, Fort Hare's first graduate, in London shortly before leaving for this trip; he advised me to see the new African leaders, which I lacked the chutzpah to do. The meeting was in the Pall Mall office because he had offered us an autobiographical ms. – the first part heavily re-written by an American well-wisher, the rest in a very raw state. It was far from covering his life adequately, and he seemed uninterested in completing it. Pall Mall rejected it, and although I looked at it again later on behalf of C. Hurst & Co., I concluded it was unpublishable, but that Z.K. would make an excellent subject for a biography by someone else.

In Pietermaritzburg I had two contradictory experiences. One was at the long-established bookselling and publishing business, Shooter and Shuter, where the managing director (of British descent) told me that he employed as an editor for Zulu-medium schoolbooks a distinguished Zulu professor of literature, C.L.M. Nyembezi, who had been sacked from his university post for political reasons. This was typical of the reaction of decent people in South Africa to the race laws, but the professor's desk had to be accommodated in the warehouse, among other Africans, and not in the office among whites, so as not to provoke an outright clash with the authorities. On the same day I went to the Voortrekker museum, which I found moving beyond all expectations.

During my last day in South Africa I had a few hours in Johannesburg after flying up early from Durban, and called at the South African Institute of International Affairs. A female senior staff member received me in a dignified panelled office, and as it became clear to her that she could talk freely, she described some of the absurdities of recent government legislation and then suddenly started laughing and couldn't stop. As she mopped her eyes and apologised, it was plain that she was near to despair. Many of the people I met seemed to be living life at a more intense and dramatic level than I was used to, and I felt on leaving that my time in South Africa had been the most exciting I had ever spent anywhere.

From Johannesburg I flew by Panam to Lagos, arriving late at night and staying in a hotel which, though far from luxurious, was expensive. The two girls at the front desk seemed to spend all their time plaiting each other's hair, and the Lebanese owner flitted about listlessly. Going out into the street the next morning and seeing Africans carefree, noisy, seemingly beholden to no one but eachother, I felt – perhaps naively and presumptuously – a sense of liberation myself after the restrictions of South Africa. The best bookshop in Nigeria from Pall Mall's point of view was the one on the campus at Ibadan University, but unfortunately the English manager was on the verge of a breakdown, which made doing business with him impossible. He could only talk about the fecklessness of his African staff – I got a dose of it as soon as I was introduced to him beside the faculty swimming pool, and then again in his office.

In the east I saw the unfinished bridge over the mighty Niger, and the famous book market at Onitsha, where at one end of the main street stood a statue of Nnamdi Azikiwe, then Federal President and the East's most famous son. In Enugu I had my only experience of staying in an African hotel, the Atlantic, where guests wrote their ethnic group in the register under 'nationality'. In the evening, as one sat in the lounge, a very young prostitute made the rounds of the seated guests, all of whom were male, offering her services. I never travelled in a 'mammy wagon', one of those ancient, over-loaded buses, elaborately painted in gay colours, the decoration always including a religious or otherwise uplifting slogan. Outside a prison a party of prisoners worked contentedly while three of their number stood close together beating out syncopated rhythm for them with sticks that had some sort of xylophonic properties.

Ghana, which I visited next, was still ruled by Kwame Nkrumah. There were many new prestige buildings in Accra, and many interesting expatriates in the country, attracted by the Osagyefo's reputation, who did not come from the traditional colonial echelons or countries. I was told not to miss the Kwame Nkrumah Ideological Institute at Winneba, near the sea west of Accra, and duly stopped off there on my way to Cape Coast. A nice Dr Twomasi showed me round – the library had a limited range of titles but multiple copies of each – and as he enumerated the subjects of instruction, I expressed surprise that 'art' was included. This, he explained (and I laughed briefly before noting his serious expression), was how students were taught political cartooning. At Cape Coast itself, one of my Australian cousins was part of an international team teaching at a secondary school, and I stayed in his house. Around noon the next day I walked alone to the castle of Elmina by the sea. No one else was there except for a guard, and at first, as I wandered round, I could think only of the topographical interest of this well-preserved relic of a vanished maritime empire. Then as I looked down from the battlements into the enclosed courtyard – more like an open dungeon – it suddenly came upon me that in this very place countless captives had been herded before being shipped off to the New World.

At Kumasi my first call was on the aristocratic bookseller Kwaku Mensah, cousin of the Asantehene, who was most welcoming – a tape of church music played in the background – and invited me to lunch with him the next day at the fashionable Hotel de Kingsway. The lunch did not take place because I fell ill overnight with flu, including a severe gastric upset. However I was better by the next day, and in the evening rode with Mensah in his Mercedes back to Accra. I sat beside the driver, and in front of me was a deck for playing 45 r.p.m. records, with which I was bidden to make free. Most were of African dance music, but one had the choir of St Clement's Danes church in London singing 'Jerusalem', and as I heard that rich and peculiarly English sound, homesickness welled up. I had been away for long enough.

My remaining visits were to Monrovia and Freetown, where the transatlantic influence made for a certain picturesqueness. There were any number of two-storeyed colonial-style villas with deep verandahs, though in Monrovia most of them were blackened with grime and seemed on the point of collapse – in contrast to Tubman's gleaming new white and gold presidential palace standing on a promontory by the sea. Also, the beach at the bottom of Randall Street, the town's main artery, was strewn with the wrecks of American limousines. It was not a cheerful place, and the people I met had a downtrodden air, yet the peculiar Liberian handshake, combined with a flick of the finger and thumb, suggested an unwillingness to accept fate. It was noticeable that women held a number of important positions in the academic and public arenas than was usual in Africa.* Just as I could not reason myself out of feeling attracted by the Afrikaner myth, the black settler republic's mythology also cast a spell, with its homespun Great Seal showing a sailing ship, a palm tree, a peace dove and a plough, and the motto 'The Love of Liberty Brought Us Here' – although amid the all-pervading squalor there could not be much liberty. A hard-headed young Lebanese, Wadih Captan, was the only bookseller of note. We spent an evening together, but I did not get an order from him; American pocketbooks and those standbys *Time* and *Newsweek* were his staple fare.

Having stayed at a Lebanese establishment in Monrovia, I went to Freetown's seedy City Hotel, 'immortalised', as everyone knows, in Graham Greene's *The Heart of the Matter*. The impossibility of stepping beyond the hotel's front steps without being accosted continually by touts, combined with the extreme humidity, made me glad I was about to leave for home. On my last morning I waited with the local Longman representative for a brief interview with Siaka Stevens, then mayor of Freetown and a future President of the country. It was the only time I felt I was following Z.K. Matthews's advice.

Low-Intensity Power Struggles

It was generally thought that my trip had been successful, and the moment of welcome as I came into the office was pleasant. Certainly the name of Pall Mall was now known in new places, and some respectable orders had been obtained. As for setting up agencies, I achieved little; arrangements came into being in East and West

---

* They included the country's consul-general in London, and I was warned by Cook's when preparing for my journey that if the requisite letter of application for a visa began 'Dear Madam' and not 'Dear Sir', it would be automatically rejected (yes, it was that way round).

Africa but were obstinately unproductive. An agency with O.U.P. was the snark I was hunting in all those markets, but our books – among which were an increasing number reflecting American concerns – were unlikely to generate enough sales to earn them a worthwhile commission; also they had elements of similarity and thus of competitiveness with their own output. O.U.P. people are mostly delightful, but they know their own value. Thus the end I most sought eluded us. I did not realise then that the *publisher* visiting a distant market for the first time can come away with a much more impressive order than an agent, who calls regularly with a whole portfolio of publishers' lists, could get even if he tried hard. There was also the flavour of our type of publishing; it was almost impossible anywhere to persuade the buyer in a bookshop that any customer browsing round the shelves would decide to buy a bulky hardback on a subject like Algerian politics. There were prospects of library business, but our list was 'special' even in that context.

At this time Fred Praeger was initiating a series, which has continued to this day and spawned many imitators, called 'Praeger Special Studies': they were in a relatively large (royal 8vo) format, well bound but unjacketed, and the text was set, usually by the author, on a superior typewriter. The print-runs were low and the prices high. The trade discount was a flat 20%, and it was in vain that I pleaded with George Aldor that it might be increased for orders placed by booksellers on spec; they were not bookshop items at all, and my attempts to sell the first of the series, *Israel in Africa*, in Africa were unsuccessful. However, they sold well otherwise and made money, and were probably Fred's most influential innovation.

As a consequence of the trip, I was to have an assistant to look after advertising and publicity while my attention turned more to sales and (unbidden) to editorial matters. Anne Wade, a Yorkshire girl from Ilkley who had graduated in history from Durham University, got the job and stayed at Pall Mall longer I than did; we are still friends. I was then directly involved in the hiring of someone else soon after Anne's arrival. Derick advertised for an assistant editor and received a large batch of applications. One was from a recently retired Royal Air Force intelligence officer, Michael ffolliott-Foster (the name caused amusement in the office when we first heard it), who had served in the Arabian emirates and knew Arabic, but because he was forty-four Derick thought he was too old for the job. By chance I saw his letter and Derick's reply, forestalled its dispatch, and got clearance to write asking him if, failing the editorial job which I said was already filled, he would be interested in joining as home sales manager and London representative, thus replacing the sales force of Barrie and Jenkins which now seemed increasingly anomalous. From that job he might move on eventually to the one he had originally wanted, and would be a better editor for having first been a salesman. He accepted my reasoning and stayed with the firm for several years – eventually going to New Zealand and joining A.H. and A.W. Reed, the country's archetypal indigenous schoolbook and general publisher.

In the spring of 1965 John MacCallum Scott went off with his wife on a five-week Caribbean cruise, and like the mouse when the cat is away, I told New York, almost the moment he had walked out through the door, that I thought it was essential for me to go on a trip to see if our continental agencies were working well. Accordingly I went to Holland, visiting several cities there, and then to Hamburg, Stockholm, Copenhagen and Zurich visiting book dealers and meeting our agents. The main agent was John Boxer in Zurich, who had been a classmate of Fred Praeger's in Vienna (from where, as a Jew, he too had to flee) – he told a nice story of how Fred found out which textbooks were to be used in the class and then obtained them in bulk to sell to his fellow pupils. Boxer was friendly, effervescent and most un-Swiss, and he accumulated many agencies. His faithful lady assistant was, by contrast, very Swiss and incidentally unmarried and no longer young. He told me that she had worked for him for several years before she shyly invited him to lunch one Sunday at her family home. When he did so he found that she lived in unimaginable opulence in a large villa by the lake. Boxer's Danish sub-agent for the Nordic countries, Holland and Belgium, Björn Hansen, was the main strength of the agency as far as we were concerned. This big, cheerful, witty man, formerly a bookseller with Arnold Busck, was loved by all the British publishers who used his services. Few people have ever made me laugh as he did – the only one of his quips I remember was when he and his wife Jandje were taking me round the Louisiana modern art gallery near their home, and I paused momentaily in front of a huge canvas of a grotesque female nude. He immediately said, 'Come on, Christopher, surely you haven't been away from home that long?' I had once used his first name in correspondence and it was not reciprocated – but earlier that evening in their house, as we went into the living room after dinner, Björn and Jandje stood together and said, with smiles, that their names were Björn and Jandje and they hoped I would use them in future.

Returning to Holland for the first time since my student visit in 1951, I saw attractions that had not been apparent earlier. This time I was staying not as a humble paying guest in an academic household but in a comfortable hotel, the Corona, in the centre of The Hague. Each table in the downstairs restaurent had a Turkey carpet spread under the tablecloth, there were newspapers to read, and the silver-haired, dark-suited waiters were as respectable-looking as their customers. Smugness was perhaps a national characteristic, but there was also an unabashed appreciation of the good things of life – especially good food, drink and cigars. It seemed that the well-upholstered world of the seventeenth-century Dutch *genre* painters lived on.

The emporium of the eminent bookseller Martinus Nijhoff was particularly redolent of this atmosphere. The main room was laid out like a scholar's library with big free-standing bookcases, the floor was richly carpeted, and there were leather-covered armchairs in which Mr Strijker the manager could talk and smoke with his visitors. Being in that magnificent street, Lange Voorhout, with the Hôtel des Indes (in my parents' opinion the best in the world) at one end, and close to all the major government offices, embassies and bank headquarters, he was in the rare position of actually wanting to place good orders for Pall Mall books. Several Dutch firms combined bookselling and publishing under one roof, and Nijhoff was one of them, but its own publications seemed like dissertatious that nobody else would accept. The only firm that gave both functions equal weight was E.J. Brill of Leiden, founded in the 1680s, though its greatest achievements in oriental publishing were in the past: it was now reputed to seek large subsidies for most of its publications. On the other hand the bookselling business, under its manager Mr van Dijk, was entrepreneurial and depended on frequent and comprehensive catalogues. Like Nijhoff, and like that other oriental giant Otto Harrassowitz of Wiesbaden, it cast its net worldwide. In Amsterdam there were two oriental booksellers of smaller scope: C.J. van der Peet, specialist in Southeast Asia (especially Indonesia) with a strong antiquarian and art side, and Gé Nabrink, with premises in the red light district near the railway station; I got orders from the ancient, cigar-smoking Mr Nabrink but was later told that he was uncreditworthy and few publishers would deal with him.

An intriguing publishing business, located with its own printing works under the same roof right in the commercial centre of The Hague, was Mouton, a world specialist in linguistics and anthropology. For years its international link was Kees van der Wilk, who showed me round on this occasion. Then in Leiden there was the international law publisher with a sideline in art history, A.W. Sijthoff, headed by the urbane and amusing John Landwehr. I often met both him and van der Wilk, and because almost all of their publishing was in English, I tried to explore means of collaboration, especially with Praeger in the U.S. Other Dutch publishers of this sort that I knew about were Van Gorcum of Assen (who offered us a sociological work on Zimbabwe), W. Junk (because its speciality was natural science, our paths did not cross), D. Reidel of Dordrecht (quite recently started by a printer, and specialising in science) and Van Hoeve in the Hague, a moribund firm which had published in its time many distinguished works of Indonesian history. The English-language books of these houses were almost all distinguished by their solidity and handsome appearance, and their being published here, as an integral part of this non-English-speaking country's long humanistic tradition, combined with the fact that these publishers were independent of the great Dutch scientific houses Elsevier and North-Holland, endowed the whole enterprise in my eyes with an aura of fascination, almost of romance. Today, without going into detail, the scene has changed utterly. Brill is still there, but the rump of its bookselling business has disappeared into a German firm. Mouton belongs to De Gruyter of Berlin. Nijhoff's wonderful shop moved soon after I saw it into an adjoining space – the owners' pride and joy – with as much atmosphere as an airport concourse. It, like Sijthoff, has been absorbed into one of the Dutch conglomerates. Van der Peet and Nabrink have disappeared.

While in The Hague I went out one evening to see the film of John Fowles's *The Collector*, and it scared me so much that I lay awake all night.

The other side of Dutch *Gemütlichkeit* showed itself when I was foolish enough to visit the leading academic bookseller at Groningen in the north, Scholtens en Zoon. The rather elderly and very complacent manager looked at my list and started asking me silly questions about it in the middle of the shop, for the amusement of his staff, who dutifully sniggered. I quickly escaped.

It was from this town that I took the train to Hamburg, and even as I sat in the compartment with three men all puffing cigars I was still thinking about the charm and the wellbeing of so much that I had seen during the past week. Not far into the journey the three men got out and I was alone. As the train sped on and I looked out of the window at a more variegated landscape, a quite unexpected feeling of relief and liberation came over me. This was because the train had now entered Germany. Holland, the entrancing dolls' house, lay behind. This pleasure was tinged with historical guilt-feelings, but these were assuaged by the knowledge that I was heading for the city from which my father's paternal grandparents set out for Yorkshire in the 1840s. When I got there it was no disappointment. It was the weekend, the spring weather was fine, and with no local connections I could only sightsee, and went for a ride on one of the boats that tour the harbour. On board I fell into the company of a Pakistani man of about my age, and thus (both) emboldened we decided to head off for the St Pauli district and visit a strip club, something I had never done before (and have not done again). What was most striking was its appearance of respectability; sitting at one table were two elderly couples with expensive, sober clothes and white hair. The compere was well-dressed and debonair, and I wished I had been able to understand one of his jokes which included the words 'Elizabeth and Philip' and even made the old people smile. The girls came on one by one to do their turns, and it was above all a study in contrasts – certainly unintended. The Catholic ones from southern Europe looked chaste, and clearly their thoughts were resolutely elsewhere; they did nothing but remove their clothes slowly to the music bow and withdraw. The really obscene turn was done by a neurotic-looking blonde girl who was obviously German. The only girl who took off every last stitch was black, a special thrill for the strait-laced burghers.

On the Monday I went out of town to visit the large wholesale warehouse of Hans Heinrich Petersen, whom Fred Praeger, while in the American occupation forces, had helped to set up in business just after the war as a channel for English-language books to enter the country. I met Petersen – he seemed an autocrat whose powers were failing – but in charge was Egon Schormann, slightly foppish with his bow-tie and longish hair, but a man I shall always remember fondly. Once again it was not possible to fix up a stocking arrangement, but he gave me some useful names and addresses, and after my own firm was in existence we would never meet without his giving me a small order. When he prematurely died, Tony Pocock wrote a glowing obituary in the *Bookseller*. I also called on the newly founded Buch- und Zeitschriften Union, managed by a svelte and quietly dynamic young man called Rosenthal, which did not have a bookshop but used advance information from publishers to make offers to their customers; they would offer individual titles (obviously the more highly priced the better), in the manner of numerous German specialist and academic booksellers, unlike our own academic booksellers who depended on catalogues. I always found this an appealing way of doing business.

Also in the spring of 1965 I went for the first time to Ireland, north and south. My original intention was to explore the market for our books, slender though I knew it to be, and before boarding the ferry at Holyhead I made a routine phone call to the office. Fred Praeger was in town and came on the line. Why didn't I try to find a good author for a book on Ireland? My trip had given him the idea. I was pleased to be given an editorial mission at last, and began to look forward eagerly to what lay ahead.

My first call in Dublin that I remember was on Liam Miller, man of letters and founder of the uncompromisingly high-quality all-Irish literary publishing house, the Dolmen Press – a bookseller must have referred me to him on hearing of my quest. The firm's publications had the distinction of being distributed in all countries outside Ireland by O.U.P. – but Liam was not enough of a businessman to keep it going as an independent enterprise for more than a few years. He suggested that Con Howard, an information official in the Foreign Ministry, might be able to help me, but as a Pall Mall reflex I also sought out Basil Chubb, the professor of politics at Trinity College (T.C.D.) – fortunately, as it turned out, he was already committed and we were saved from commissioning a work of political science. Con Howard took me for a luxurious lunch at the Royal Hibernian Hotel, and for the book recommended a lecturer at University College (U.C.D.), the Catholic university, well known as a character and for his contacts. I met this man in a bar, and he apologised on two counts – one, that he could not write the sort of book he thought I was looking for and, two, that he was not free for dinner. As remedies he suggested that for the book I try Tim Pat Coogan, a young journalist, and for dinner he passed me over to his two companions, middle-aged dark-suited senior business executives who took me on to another pub. At the beginning of the meal, searching for something original to say, I fell headlong into a deep trap – by remarking on the large number of interesting pubs I had noticed in central Dublin. What I meant to imply was that they were like English pubs had been decades earlier, with Victorian furnishings, cut-glass mirrors, brass, mahogany and open fires, but my aesthetic musings went for nothing. They chose to believe that I was insulting the city of Dublin and placing it on the same level as any godforsaken small place in County Sligo. A lot of bars indeed! Their sarcastic comments went on for so long that I nearly got up and left, but in the end we managed to last out the evening. I had quickly learned something about Irish networking and Irish sensitivities.

At the weekend I hired a car and drove across to Achill Island on the west coast, by way of Connemara. Needless to say, it was very beautiful. As I left the city a well-dressed, 'lady-like' young woman of about thirty standing by the roadside thumbed a lift – she was on her way home. Well educated and unprovincial as she was, she had never left Ireland. I felt I was learning something else. It was only at the beginning of the following week that I met Tim Pat, and he agreed to write the book that made his name: *Ireland since the Rising*. It was followed a year or two later by its sequel, *The I.R.A.* We meet whenever I am in Dublin, and perhaps 'discovering' him was the best service I ever did for Pall Mall.

Derick Mirfin was much closer to John MacCallum Scott than I was, by reason of their long-standing collaboration, but in the eyes of George Aldor and possibly even of Fred Praeger my recent travels had made me appear a modest asset to the London end of their business. I witnessed some of the tussles between them and John over such things as his Dunmow office and felt embarrassed at John's understated but unmistakable way of conveying that he understood the British market and the British way of thinking and doing things in a way they could never hope to do. I felt most of my sympathy swing over to Fred and George. It was ironical that on the eve of the final bust-up George sent John a memo telling him that within a few days it would be Fred's fiftieth birthday; and John, never at a loss for well-turned phrases, composed a long cable using an extended cricketing metaphor to congratulate him.

Fred and George were not pleasant enemies, and as the battle warmed up I felt for John; but I felt for them still more. They were professional publishers, impatient to see some results from their investment, and became ever more infuriated as John seemed only to respond to their direct tactics with a combination of blarney and one-upmanship. It was soon a straight fight. John had to find enough cash to buy out their 80 per cent stake or else sell them his 20 per cent and resign. He did his utmost to drum it up and sought the advice of his fellow Reform Club member Sir Stanley Unwin, among others. For the sake of good publishing I wanted Praeger to win and made my position plain to both sides, aware that this would hurt John, to whom I owed a lot.

My honourable course would have been to leave and look for another job, but with frankly ignoble motives I held on. As we approached the crunch, Fred sent a memo requesting John and myself to fly immediately to New York. John replied that they must surely have made a mistake in naming me rather than Derick, who was discreetly keeping his head down, but John and I duly went. On one of the days we were there, Fred had a hired car with a driver to take him to the funeral of one of his authors, an army general, at West Point, and made John go along with him. Throughout the day they battled together inside the car, breaking off briefly to stand by the graveside. John could not cope with the strain and from not having smoked at all since I knew him, was soon smoking most of the time and developed a persistent hacking cough.

Praeger was then at its peak, although it apparently never made money. The chief editors were Arnold Dolin, Morton Puner and Lou Barron, a specialist in books on Africa; Stella Heiden, whom I had last met in 1955 when she was André Deutsch's secretary, had an editorial role; and Matthew Held, who in the distant future was to be Fred's successor at Westview Press, was production manager. The place was full of optimism. Here surely lay Pall Mall's future. Fred and George seemed ideal partners; at times, such was their euphoria, they engaged in cross-talk like a pair of stand-up comics, but over the Praeger enterprise and what, in their eyes, it stood for they were in deadly earnest.

The agony was soon over, and John said farewell to us and left. I felt a shit, especially as things did not settle down. Derick and I were now the directors of the firm *in situ*, but neither of us had a genuine managerial function, this being exercised from New York. We tended to watch eachother warily at times, Derick with the more reason because I could not suppress my interest in editorial matters. At the same time I became aware of an anomaly in our position at Pall Mall *vis-à-vis* New York. Praeger assured us that they would not force books on us which were unsuitable for our market, but this continually happened; and for good reasons there were some of our books which they refused. But there was also a conflict in principle between us over the 'open markets' of continental Europe and Japan. In spite of such receptive markets as Germany, Holland and Scandinavia being on our doorstep, we found Praeger unwilling to let us sell their books which we co-published or distributed into those markets through our agents, preferring to keep them as the preserve of their worldwide agents Feffer and Simons, owned by Doubleday, who received a massive U.S. government subsidy to underwrite credit in uncreditworthy Third World countries. This may have been better for them, but it was restricting for us, and meant that we were prevented from giving our agents on the continent and elsewhere what would been a valuable additional incentive.

Pall Mall's production manager – Richard Barber, who had come in as John MacCallum Scott's protégé (he was the son of his local physician) – left at about the same time as John himself. I was put in charge of production, having been sagely counselled by Fred to choose an appropriate model for each book and copy it; we had a freelance jacket designer. Then, one day as I came out of our Charlotte Street office into the street at lunchtime, I bumped into

Timothy Simon – my earlier dealings with him have already been narrated. We got on together with the ease of old friends, with numerous acquaintances and other reference points in common. We had not seen each other for a year or two, and I was cheered by the encounter. He said he was out of a job – did I know where he could find one? This was astonishing because it had been to him that I turned after my painting interlude in 1960 for exactly the same advice because of his good connections with most of the mainline publishers (his wife, in addition, was Hamish Hamilton's niece). We had only talked for a little while when he suggested that he might do some production work for Pall Mall – he had hardly been aware of the firm up till that moment – and I promised to put the idea to Fred and George. The answer was not encouraging, but the next time one of them visited London a meeting was arranged and it was fixed that Tim would work part-time overseeing production – and design jackets and publicity material (he had recently given the *New Statesman* a typographical facelift).

Tim had left the Curwen Press after a family row. The firm owed its pre-eminence to his father Oliver Simon (incidentally an oppressive figure where Tim was concerned), but Oliver died in the 1950s when Tim was relatively new in the firm, leaving his brother Richard in control. Richard had a son with whom Tim did not get on. So, from having been virtual crown prince, he now saw himself excluded from the succession. One day Tim was driving his car past the Natural History Museum in South Kensington and stopped at traffic lights. In the next car he spied an old acquaintance, Basil Harley, and called out a greeting. Basil Harley told him that he was looking for a job. On an impulse – was it generous or machiavellian? – Tim took out his card and was just in time to throw it into Harley's car before the lights changed. The result was that Harley joined the firm – but Tim found, contrary to expectation, that he had not acquired an ally in his family feud. In due course Richard Simon's son left the Curwen Press and Harley became managing director. Finding this situation intolerable, Tim left.

Tim had absorbed the art of book design through his pores, and soon Pall Mall's productions were unrecognisably improved. A house style was established and a new Pall Mall logo invented; some of the books were printed at the Curwen Press. Tim started to take an interest in the way the office was organised and proposed some new systems. I was not averse and neither was Derick (who at first, for a mixture of reasons, viewed Tim's arrival without enthusiasm). Both of us were wedded to our own specialised functions and prepared to leave administration to others. But now two sensational developments burst upon us.

Fred and George suddenly arrived in London in an atmosphere of excitement for reasons we were not told about, and Tim was called to confer with them at their hotel – without Derick and myself. What was up? We soon found out. On intelligence supplied by Tim, and derived from one of the many contacts with publishers he had built up as a book printer, the firm of Praeger had bid for and acquired the Phaidon Press. To me Phaidon had always represented the acme of scholarly distinction in art book publishing – with an author like Ernst Gombrich it could not be otherwise – and clearly Fred and George thought the same way. Acquiring it would give them a new enhanced image in the whole international publishing scene, and because one good turn deserved another, Tim was appointed managing director of Pall Mall. He quickly ensconced himself in John MacCallum Scott's old office, and brought in a new assistant of his own, Juliana Powney. It was in that office that he said to me one day with his habitual nonchalance, 'You've heard about this managing director thing, have you?' Up till that moment I hadn't. This was the man whom, for the sake of our old but not particularly close friendship, I had invited in off the street just a few months earlier. He had done to me what Basil Harley did to him, but more quickly.

Only a few weeks later, in the summer of 1966, Derick came into my office looking as if he had seen a ghost. The London office of Encyclopaedia Britannica had just phoned him to say that that organisation was now the sole owner of Praeger, and thus of ourselves at Pall Mall. We had not heard a word from New York. Fred and George, we were told, would be staying on, and it was Fred's outstanding personality, reputation etc. which had attracted Britannica. The Praeger company would be a fine jewel in their crown. This was all stated in a press release. The consideration was $2.5 million. Tim Simon was bullish; we would be able to do more and worry less. He also saw a chance of realising his cherished plan to publish some books on music (he was not musical himself but had a friend, John Warrack, who was a musician and whom he had earmarked as the editor of a series). I was unable to digest the news; it meant nothing to me, and when Derick and I were bidden to join the former Senator William Benton, owner and president of Britannica, for dinner in London, I made excuses while Derick went.

The situation at Pall Mall during the year after John's departure could not have gone on for long. It was essentially a 'holding operation' because there was never any question of either Derick or, even less, myself becoming manager – we simply accepted direction from New

York. The appointment of a managing director might well have seemed to the two of us a welcome and wise change – if we had been consulted and allowed to express our opinion on the candidates being considered. What I could not tolerate was the way it had been done and the choice of the individual. Tim Simon was someone I could happily have worked with as an equal, but not as my boss.

George Aldor had been pressing me for some time to go on another big trip – this time to Asia and Australasia. To prevent myself brooding about the new situation, I told George I was prepared to go at any time, so it was fixed that after a couple of days with him and Fred at Frankfurt in October, I would fly on to Beirut and thence to Nicosia, Tel Aviv, Tehran, Pakistan, India, Singapore, Kuala Lumpur, Bangkok, Hong Kong, Tokyo, Australia and New Zealand. From there I would cross the Pacific and call at the Praeger office for debriefing on the way home. To go off on the trip knowing that I would not stay with Pall Mall for long after my return required a steadying of my nerves. To extend the physical metaphor, I also had to harden my heart, as I did over the battle between Fred Praeger and John MacCallum Scott. I knew it would be more honourable to leave straight away, but I had no immediate alternative plans and no intention while travelling on behalf of Pall Mall other than to work for its benefit – although I would inevitably acquire experience that could be put to good use later. I reasoned with myself that I had been 'constructively dismissed', and that this journey would balance the account.

My marriage to Christine suffered as the result of my new-found enthusiasm for business. Her life looking after three tiny children was tough, and although I thought of myself as a loving parent I did not do much to ease her burdens. Then, with Praeger opening up my career by sending me on long overseas trips, I was twice away from home for three months at a stretch. The first time, when I went to Africa, she joined me; it was her first and only return visit to her homeland, and all went well. Our last child Martin was conceived just after we got back.

Before I left on my round-the-world trip in 1966 we went on a family holiday in England and I had a distinct sensation that our marriage was maturing and we were getting to understand and care for eachother more. Something told me that if I could only stay at home instead of going away, we might just manage to consolidate things permanently. (I now think that this was an illusion – which is not to say that it wouldn't have been worth acting upon it.) There was no question this time of her joining me for any part of the trip. But I went none the less, and her mother, who taught at a girls' secondary school near our home, moved in.

Martin was born on 5 October 1965. It was a breech birth, and although we had planned for it to take place at home, as with Dan the previous spring, we had to rush to Hammersmith Hospital, where Martin was delivered in one of the examination cubicles in the outpatients department. My first sight of him was in a doctor's arms being taken to an oxygen tent. It was the only time in my life that I prayed spontaneously. The Frankfurt fair was due to start a few days later and it had been arranged that I was to go there – for the first time – under the wing of Fred Praeger and George Aldor. These were the euphoric early days of the 'new' Pall Mall, without MacCallum Scott and before the sell-out to Britannica or the sudden promotion of Tim Simon. It was self-evidently a great opportunity. I went, but to Christine – and even to me – it felt like desertion.

Journey in Borrowed Time

My trip in 1966 had its moments. Beirut had a well developed book trade. Marco Hazan, the dynamic Jewish proprietor of the Librairie du Liban, gave me a nice order, but I found a close rapport with Berj Jamkojian, the young Armenian manager of Khayat's bookstore. Here was a superb business built up over decades by old Mr Khayat, who had lived frugally and virtuously. Now his two sons were in charge, and wasting his substance; a visitor immediately got the new flavour on entering Paul Khayat's vulgar office with its thick-pile carpet and jumbo-sized desk. Although he talked airily about publishing reprints, I was told that his greatest interest was his real estate in Florida. After Berj and I had lunched together, he drove me out of town to meet the Armenian bishop in his house because I had said I would be glad to publish a book about the Armenians. Nothing came of this, but I was honoured by the introduction. Later he settled in Vienna and became a representative selling books throughout the Middle East.

When I arrived in Nicosia it inevitably felt like a homecoming. I was met at the airport, unexpectedly, by Mr Michaelides of 'M.A.M.' – whom Antoinette Diamantis characterised, when I met her later, as 'one of our EOKA heroes', which presumably meant that he had shot a number of British soldiers. Casually meeting this agreeable fellow, such a thought would never have entered my mind. Diamantis and Antoinette entertained me to dinner on my first night in the island, and took me out next day in his ancient car to the Troodos foothills where we visited a village church with medieval wall-paintings. After leaving their house that first evening, I walked to where another old friend had lived – Vartan Malian, alias 'Jimmy', the Loyal Regiment's camp contractor and, unknown to his military clients, a man of various talents. Approaching the house in Victoria Street, I was challenged from an upstairs balcony in a very polite voice with a Scandinavian accent. It was exactly on the border between the Greek and Turkish parts of the town, and the Malian family were long gone. I was allowed into the well-remembered Turkish quarter and, wandering in the bright moonlight close to the Great Mosque, once a cathedral, fell in with a Turkish constable, who also, in the most oblique and courteous way possible, wanted to find out what I was doing there. Soon we were deep in conversation.

The next day I was back in the same part of the city to visit Kemal Rüstem. This gentlemanly character set up as a bookseller in his teens, and at the time of writing, after many vicissitudes, is still flourishing in his late seventies.[*] On this occasion he described, more in sorrow than in anger, how he was at the mercy of the postal authorities on the Greek side who deliberately held up his deliveries. On an impulse I said that my firm might consider a book on the Cyprus problem seen from the under-appreciated Turkish view-point. He immediately sent a messenger to fetch Mr Osman Örek, a nattily-dressed lawyer who had been a senior government minister in the short-lived bi-ethnic government after independence – he claimed to be the only Turk who had ever attended a Commonwealth conference. He was willing to write a book on the lines I was thinking of, and we agreed to resume detailed discussion later.

Tehran gave me a first taste of a style of driving different from anything known in the West. In West Africa I had been impressed by the panache of drivers but never thought them dangerous. In the streets of Tehran, with a fully laden bus bearing down from straight ahead on the car in which one was travelling, one could only cower in abject fear. In India one did not meet such apparent recklessness but merely the hegemony of the larger vehicle over the smaller – whether of truck over car, car over scooter, or scooter over bicycle and handcart. In Tehran, as in Israel, the larger booksellers would not open an account for Pall Mall books when they could obtain Praeger books through the ubiquitous Feffer and Simons on

[*] I published a 'profile' of him in the *Bookseller* on 2 June 1989.

easy terms. Mesrob Grigorian, another sophisticated cosmopolitan bookseller, told me that as an Armenian and a perpetual outsider he was, as an article of faith, loyal to the government in power.

In India (about which I was briefed in advance by Roy North of Longman) I made the acquaintance of several bookmen who were to remain friends and sometimes collaborators in the years to come: in Bombay Ramdas Bhatkal of Popular Prakashan and Mr Shanbhag, whose Strand Bookstore was for long up till very recent times unique in India for the variety of its hardcover imported stock – he placed a large order for Pall Mall books and, twenty years later, for mine; in Delhi Mohan Chawla and in Calcutta Gulab Primlani. Mohan, still in his twenties, was about to transform a business started by his father in Kanpur, the Universal Book Stall, into UBS Publishers Distributors, a leading wholesaler of imported books and of Indian books both within India and abroad.

Mohan had an economics degree and took a deeply serious approach to his work. He had married a fellow graduate who was both clever and beautiful, and they lived over the shop in Ansari Road, Daryaganj, the Paternoster Row of Old Delhi. When I went there to dinner, it bothered me, with my Western liberal sensibilities, that Mohan's sister, while helping to prepare and serve the meal, was not really treated as one of the party. Her sister-in-law clearly outshone her intellectually, in looks and in social graces. I did not think much about this nice, homely girl again – not even when, a year or two later, a young Indian man called at my office by appointment to say that he was on his way to Delhi and would be seeing Mohan Chawla there: did I have anything that he could carry to Mohan for me? I hadn't, so we merely chatted, and he mentioned as if by the way that he was going home to get married – and had not yet met his bride. Then, after another year or two, Mohan was in London and invited me to go out to Harrow, where he was staying, to spend an evening. On my arrival at the house, the door was opened by none other than Mohan's sister, who looked radiantly happy and beautiful and was carrying a very young baby. Her husband was of course the man who had called at my office.

In Delhi too, Mohan gave a small tea party in Connaught Circus to introduce me to booksellers – and took me to Agra and Fatehpur Sikri (his car expired just as we were approaching the station – we left it where it stood and ran to catch the train). Altogether it was hospitality of a high order, and at one point it was slightly more than that. Pall Mall had just published a book about Nehru by an old boxwallah called Tyson, and Mohan, who was co-publishing it, took me along to Indira Gandhi's prime ministerial morning durbar at her residence to present her with a copy. We approached her in the throng – there was no visible 'security' – and, as well as making the presentation, each of us asked her to sign a copy. She did so with an indecipherable scrawl, and finding such a trophy merely embarrassing, I presented it to an Indian academic I later met in New Zealand. I had thought Indira a beautiful woman.

From Calcutta I made a side trip to meet a serving Indian Army general, D.K. Palit, with whom I had corresponded; he wrote to Pall Mall asking for books to review in a military journal and I replied. It seemed worthwhile to find out in advance if I could meet this intellectual soldier on my journey, and as it turned out he would be staying in Darjeeling, at his old school St Paul's, when I was in Calcutta. So I flew to Siliguri in the plain just short of the foothills, and from there took a bus up the mountain road alongside a classic narrow-gauge steam railway, stopping for refreshment at an equally classic Victorian station on the way up. I had booked myself in at a hotel, but was extracted by Palit's A.D.C. and taken straight to the headmaster's house in the school compound. I was then taken to attend a regimental function under canvas in a nearby army camp and there introduced to 'Monty' Palit, short and lithe and remarkably dashing in his dress uniform. A Gurkha pipe band was playing Scottish music outside the marquee. Thus began a friendship which has lasted till the present, involving co-publishing, a few years of non-communication due to an ill-advised business deal, my acting as the originating publisher of one of his many books (a critique of the Indian government's conduct of the 1962 Himalayan war with China, in which he commanded a division), and numerous social meetings in London and in India. At the time of this writing, aged seventy-seven, he still plays first-class polo.

Next morning at about six, I became aware of a brilliant golden light filling my bedroom window, and immediately grabbed my glasses. There in the dawn rays, was Kanchenjunga which, even seen from 8,000 feet up, appeared immeasurably high. A few moments later cloud covered it and I never saw it again. Palit and the A.D.C. drove off in a jeep after breakfast to Sikkim; he said he would have taken me along, but for it being forbidden territory for unauthorised persons.

My acquaintance with Malaysia is confined to a couple of days in Kuala Lumpur, and it left a disagreeable impression. It all boiled down to Malay chauvinism, public notices of all kinds being in that language only. I witnessed a wonderful example of it as I was about to depart. President Lyndon Johnson was due to arrive in the country shortly after the scheduled departure time of my flight to Bangkok – and the impending visit had Kuala Lumpur in a jumpy state during the whole time I was there. Squads of mobile riot police were going through their motions at various strategic points in the town, their scarlet paddy-wagons freshly painted for the occasion. It was no surprise when the Bangkok flight was postponed till after the President's arrival, but irritating because I was due to be met at Bangkok airport. However, there was the unlooked-for bonus of a grandstand view of L.B.J.'s arrival – all the passengers for Bangkok assembled at the waving base and watched the two planes (the first containing the press corps and security men) fly in. The President, who as a very tall man cut an imposing figure, was met on the tarmac by the current King, dressed in exotic native costume, and speeches were exchanged. The King's was in Malay, although there was no reason to doubt that he had been at Sandhurst, Oxbridge or the Inns of Court and could speak flawless English. When he had finished, an interpreter gave a flat rendering of the speech and the President replied, raising a muted laugh when he came out with rehearsed quip that one thing Malaysia and the United States had in common was that both were federations formerly ruled by the British. He then spoke up for the Vietnam war effort. After we had got away, we were about half an hour into our flight, over thickly wooded hills, when the plane banked steeply and did a 180-degree turn. Out hearts were edging up into our mouths by the time the captain announced that one of the engines was overheating and we were returning – not to Kuala Lumpur but to Singapore, the only airport in the region where the necessary repairs could be done. My hardbitten Canadian neighbour told me how a plane in which he had been a passenger had dropped to earth from 1,000 feet and he had survived. We landed in Singapore at an alarmingly high speed, and several fire engines were waiting beside the runway. Donald Moore's representative in Bangkok, Raymond Li, had been waiting for me at the airport there all day when I at last arrived.

I remembered that my National Service contemporaries stationed in Malaya spent exotic leaves in Bangkok. At my hotel several G.I.s from Vietnam were hard at it, and the pity of their situation, if nothing else, would have dampened any desire to relive my youth. I met a Thai Buddhist intellectual, Sulak Sivaraksa, who had recently set up his own Social Sciences Publishing House, from which I was soon to buy books when I set up my own business.

Then, as now, my company's representative in Japan was Sumio Saito, a man of panache and independent spirit. He was from a wine-growing family but had decided to join Donald Moore's book distribution business, then burgeoning throughout South-East Asia, when it opened a branch in Japan. Donald was a charming and wily fellow who had been a naval officer in those parts during the war, and he liked books. But he was constantly in financial trouble because his customers – particularly government departments – took excessive credit which of course meant that his client publishers back home were paid late too. Every year or two, a meeting of restive creditors was held in London, where the combined persuasion of Paull Harrap, their unofficial convenor, and Donald himself always succeeded in putting off the day of reckoning.

To return to Sumio, he had made D.M.J. (Donald Moore Japan) efficient and successful, and when Donald eventually sold out he became its owner. But most of my memories of Japan have little to do with business. I will only mention the weekend I spent in Kyoto with Makoto Kobayashi, Sumio's young publicity manager – still today with the firm. The Katsure imperial villa (I realised at once how often it has been imitated in the West) and the Ryoan-ji abstract garden with its raked sand and rocks are places I have often re-visited in memory because, although they leave behind an overflowing satisfaction, they also stir up a craving for more.

I had a minor misadventure on arriving in Brisbane from Hong Kong. In advance of Britain, Australia had gone over to decimal currency, and when I used it for the first time to pay the taximan who drove me into town from the airport, I handed him a 10-dollar note momentarily believing that this was equivalent to 10 shillings. Since it was clear to him that I expected no change despite having paid ten times the actual fare, he looked at me first inquiringly and then gratefully, and only as he slowly drove off did it dawn on me what I had done. The Australians to whom I told this sad tale, more out of amusement than self-pity, were touchingly distressed that any Australian was capable of such turpitude.

I met a number of publishers whose books I thought could interest Pall Mall – in each case I was wrong. In Brisbane, the American immigrant Frank Thompson was at the start of his long career as manager of the Queensland University Press, and Brian Clouston ran Jacaranda Press, an educational house he had founded with close links to New Guinea, but by then owned, along with Lloyd O'Neil's Lansdowne Press, by F.W. Cheshire of Melbourne. The Melbourne University Press, under its British director Peter Ryan, had just published a bestseller on Indonesia by an Australian academic – a rare exception to the tendency of Australian publishing to be largely Australia-centred. In Canberra the Australian National University Press, contrary to what might have been expected, was little more than a campus publisher, but it soon blossomed under an Amercian director, William ('Chip')

Wood, publishing series on the Aboriginals and Pacific history, and I took a few as co-publications. An exciting publisher in the 'serious trade' sector was Brian Stonier, with his newly founded independent non-fiction paperback imprint that was attracting attention. Altogether I found the scene vigorous and invigorating. In Sydney I had lunch with James Bennett, an Englishman who emigrated in 1930 to escape the Depression and was currently making a great success of offering British books to Australasian libraries at British prices. His object was to supplant Blackwell, who did that as a matter of course, but loud cries of pain were heard from the entrenched local retail trade, who were accustomed to marking-up the prices of British books heavily and getting away with it. Bennett was about to open an office in London, operating clandestinely under a different name, to buy books embargoed for direct sale to Australia because of closed market agreements. Andrew Fabinyi, the Hungarian immigrant who headed F.W. Cheshire, had visited Pall Mall in London and I wanted while in Melbourne to promote two-way traffic, but again Australian topics monopolised his list and these barely sold at all in Britain or America. Pall Mall was actually represented in Australia at this time by Thomas Nelson, with results that did not justify the effort expended by them or us.

If Nicosia was a homecoming of sorts, arriving in New Zealand was an almost mystical reunion with the spirits of my ancestors. On the morning when I was due to take the four-hour flight across the Tasman Sea, I was at the Monash University Bookshop in Melbourne and broke off my talk with the manager when I looked at the clock and noticed that time was getting rather short. At the airport I had to run across the tarmac to the plane just before it closed its doors for take-off.

That evening, form my hotel in the dour southern city of Christchurch, I phoned my aunt Alys Arkwright at her home in the North Island and we fixed our rendez-vous for a few days later. Christchurch was the unlikely home of the cultural enterprises of Charles Brasch, a rich bachelor who is unflatteringly portrayed in Janet Frame's *Autobiography* – Caxton Press had published the literary periodical *Landfall* in the early years after the Second World War, books of poetry, and fancies such as *The Ballad of Sir Patrick Spens* and *The Demon Lover* each exquisitely yet unpretentiously produced as an individual booklet. New Zealand was too small and generally philistine for such an enterprise to outlast the enthusiasm of its founders, and by the time of my visit Caxton's great days were long past. All the more reason for thinking there was scope for a new literary publisher with outside links, and for a few days I tortured my conscience by entertaining the fantasy that I might set myself up in that role. I knew it would pass as soon as I left the country.

I plunged into family visiting first in Nelson, a small and isolated but friendly. town (notably un-philistine: they had once invited the Amadeus Quartet to play there) at the north of the South Island where a cousin, last seen at our home in Ascot before the war, and her husband, a carnation farmer, lived in happy penury; her twin sister was married to a member of a commercial dynasty in Edinburgh and much better off. Their younger brother Earle, posthumous son of my mother's brother (also Earle), was the only male Riddiford among my first cousins, and indeed the only one not of the rich senior line, and he devoted his life to making up for it. Earle was the prime mover of the New Zealand Himalayan expeditions of the early 1950s, and went with Edmund Hillary on the first one in 1952/3. He practised as a lawyer, but a turning point came in his life when a magnificent estate called Orongorongo (the final 'o' is silent) on a strip of wild coast south of Wellington came up for sale. This was one of the properties of our great-grandfather Daniel Riddford the First; much of it was unyielding mountainside and it was therefore not very productive, but because of its romantic associations and its situation it was somehow seen by the whole family as the most precious jewel in the diadem of historic Riddiford sheep-runs. From Great-uncle Edward ('King'), Daniel I's eldest son and the inheritor of all his best properties, it passed to his son Eric, who lived and entertained there in style, but it was sold in the 1950s. For Earle its re-acquisition was a major step forward in his pursuit of the holy grail, but only a person with large means could afford to run it, and these Earle would never possess.

In Wellington I stayed in the basement of Earle's vernacular clap-boarded house as the guest of his mother, Aunt Helen, whom my mother thought the most interesting member of the family; certainly her long widowhood had bred an independent spirit. Earle and his family lived in the upper part. He was quick-witted and amusing, and no lover of Britain, especially over its treatment of Ian Smith and his U.D.I. His legal practice, which he shared with our rich second cousin Daniel Riddiford IV, a Conservative M.P., supposedly helped to finance the running of Orongorongo.

At the weekend we decamped there, in company with a nubile young cousin, Beverly, who worked for the publisher A.H. & A.W. Reed, and her mother acting as chaperone. The house lay in the wildest of natural settings between the mountains and the sea, but protected from the elements by a wood and a garden enclosed by hedges permanently bent by the wind. It was a long wooden bungalow, with suites opening on to a common verandah. At one end was a ballroom, with a small sun-room overhead, which Eric Riddiford added in the 1930s in the seaside hotel style of the period. Across the choppy grey sea, snowy mountain tops in the South Island were descernible. Earle, with his own hands, was fencing his 2,000 acres for sheep – he had a half-Maori factor and hired labour for shearing – and on the morning after our arrival he took me up the mountain to drive some heavy stakes into the hostile ground, a task at which I proved useless. Two of the rich Riddifords came over to visit – Daniel, the M.P., and his sister Philippa Williams, whose husband Tim was chairman of the conservative newspaper, *The Dominion*. Their father was 'Cousin Dan', King Riddford's last surviving son, and the only one who produced male heirs. Their attitude to Earle was somewhere between amused condescension and awe at his restless dynamism: was he not perhaps the true spiritual heir of King, while they had gone a bit soft? They might privately have thought him a parvenu, dispensing hospitality that he couldn't afford at *their* family's old stronghold, but his brashness was redeemed by the grace of his wife Rosemary, who certainly was to the manner born.

Orongorongo – the place and the set-up – made me think of *The Great Gatsby*, but it reminded Beverly's mother of Manderley in *Rebecca* – an evocation which was apt in one way, because after Earle's death in 1989 (by then it had been sold) the house went up in flames. In 1994 I saw the bare foundations – and the still immaculate garden laid out by Rosemary and now cared for by the people who bought the outbuildings as weekend homes. Just as nobody knows for sure whether Mrs Danvers torched Manderley, there are uncertainties about how exactly Orongorongo met its end. There were hints of an insurance scam.

I took a bus from Wellington to Marton visit to Alys Arkwright, and, as we had planned, she was waiting at the bus stop to meet me – a still good-looking and vigorous old lady now well on in her seventies. A few years before, she had moved to a small house from Overton, the Arkwright family homestead, now occupied and farmed by her middle son John (father of Beverly, whom I met at Orongorongo). Overton was a large late Victorian country house with half-timbering, surrounded by an English garden with conifers and rhododendrons; except for the grazing land outside the perimeter, it was very similar to the house where I passed my childhood at Ascot. One evening we had a slap-up family dinner there, in the middle of which my aunt went into the corridor outside and ran up and down to help her breathing. I was allowed to choose what we did and whom we saw: Ros, Alys's beautiful auburn-haired daughter whom I had last met at Ascot nearly thirty years before, and who lived on a farm nearby, was top of the list, and I also wanted to meet 'Cousin Dan'.

Alys's Wykehamist English husband Henry had inherited Overton from an uncle of his. Although she did not have the leisure or the money to visit the old country more than a couple of times in the last forty years, it remained 'home', and no rite of passage was endowed with more significance than an invitation to a weekend at Government House. She and Henry had been guests of Sir James Fergusson back in the 1920s – the A.D.C., Lord Claud Hamilton, fell in love with her – and when his son Bernard Fergusson was appointed Governor-General in the early 1960s, she was invited. Dearly as she wanted to go, she became ill at the critical time; was invited again, fell ill again, and eventually with great heaviness of heart realised that it was too late. In spite of being obviously frail she had far more vitality, even at this stage in her life, than her younger sister, my mother, and as we went about together, visiting, tidying up the house, endlessly conversing, I felt it was all unreal; here we were, like a mother and son still talking when she was in bed, or up and half dressed, and yet we had only ever met before for one weekend nearly twenty years earlier.

Cousin Dan still lived in his large estate house, Longwood, at Featherston. He had served in the Great War with the Grenadier Guards, which meant that he had friends in high places in England who regarded him as one of their own.* Now he was over eighty, a lonely widower, hard of hearing and nearly blind. Our tea-party was a desultory affair and I only remember him saying acidly 'I hear that in England now you've got a lot of niggers.' The old-fashioned atmosphere was strangely accentuated by the presence on the table of a huge fruit-cake, home-baked by his housekeeper and almost as tall as it was broad. But of the rich Riddifords it must be said that they helped the poor ones – notably the family of Earle (senior) after his early death – when times were hard.

For the last stage of my time with Alys we drove north, circling Mount Egmont and visiting the hot springs and Maori tribal showcase at Rotorua. We stayed overnight at the farm of Alys's youngest

---

* One of them was Captain Harry Crookshank, long-serving Conservative M.P. and a bachelor. Cousin Dan and his wife were staying once at our house for Ascot Week, and Crookshank was invited too. He had an unusually large head, a fact even commented on in his *D.N.B.* entry, and when the men were gathering up their top-hats before leaving for the Royal Enclosure, someone mistakenly picked up the gallant Captain's, and each hat that he tried on was too small. He had no sense of humour and was almost weeping with vexation. The drollery of the situation was remembered years later by my mother.

son Richard, deep in King Country and surrounded by 'native bush'; any expansion of his diminutive lot was ruled out because each of the neighbouring lots had more Maori names on the title deeds than could possibly be traced.

When I parted form Alys, knowing it was for the last time. I took the bus to Auckland and, in one day there before flying out, met an interesting small publisher, Janet Paul. She and her husband had run first-class bookshops (Paul's Book Arcade) here and in Hamilton, and as a late venture started their own publishing imprint, Blackwood and Janet Paul; Blackwood died soon afterwards. The house produced high-quality Zelandiana, much of it on the Maoris; and on this visit I spotted such a book in production which, in a co-edition split with Humanities Press in New York, became almost the first title to bear my independent imprint. Paul's did not retain its independence, but the name survives today in Longman Paul.

Interlude: Farewells

My debriefing in New York was a formality. Fred and George knew I was going to leave, and said no hard words about my doing so immediately after undertaking this big trip for the firm. A day or two after arriving back in London I had a last lunch with Timothy Simon. Again there were no hard words, and we talked as people who would not lose all contact. In the event he did not last long as managing director of Pall Mall; an appointee of George Aldor's, Roy Arnold, was brought in as joint managing director of both Phaidon and Pall Mall, which had been relocated to Phaidon's office in South Kensington. Seeing his advance within the firm blocked, he quickly started to look outside. (Afterwards Tim said to me: 'If you think it was hard being under me, you have no idea what it was like under Roy Arnold.')

He was eager to start up a publishing house on his own, and suggested to Colin Haycraft, an intellectually brilliant and pugnacious Oxford contemporary of ours then working with Weidenfeld, that they might do it together. The two were no more than social acquaintances. Colin was against Tim's scheme but happened to meet Mervyn Horder, who wanted to sell the firm he owned, Gerald Duckworth. Colin had no cash, but Tim was able to put up half the price, which enabled Colin to borrow the other half. So they acquired Duckworth and moved into its long-time premises in Henrietta Street where they inherited a languishing firm with a staff of fourteen people and a turnover of under £100,000 a year. Tim had ambitions – 'One day', he said to Colin, pointing to Moss Bros as they passed that emporium at the end of their street, 'we shall be like that.'

However, his life expectancy was poor. He had already had open-heart surgery and in the summer of 1970, against medical advice, he went on a buying trip to New York. There he fell ill with pneumonia and died. Colin was left an option on ·Tim's shares, which he was able to take up by increased borrowing, thus keeping control till near the end of the 1980s, and earning a rare reputation as an idiosyncratic general publisher running on low overheads. Tim's death almost certainly saved the business from going bust, since it would have been beyond Colin's power to restrain his big ideas. The Tim Simon story took on the dimensions of tragedy when his widow, Sue, died a few years later of cancer, leaving their three young sons orphans.

Fred Praeger's moment of triumph on selling out to Encyclopaedia Britannica soon turned to ashes. Senator Benton is known to have admired him and to have been willing to give him his head, but Fred found taking his orders in any form intolerable; it was strange that he had not anticipated this. A moment of truth came when the firm's senior staff were invited to the Senator's permanent suite at the Waldorf Astoria for indoctrination. They were served champagne and guided round by flunkeys who told them the prices of all the works of art on show. The reverence of Benton's own staff was at odds with the still independent spirit of the Praegerites. The culminating affront came when Benton delivered a homily in which he did not once mention Fred's name.

The whole experience wounded Fred so badly that he hastened back to his native Austria for solace. There he acquired the respected German imprint of Fritz Molden and one or two minor ones, employing Stella Heiden as his literary scout back in the United States. George Aldor took his place as chief executive of Praeger in New York. Fred regarded this as *lèse-majesté*, although it was hardly surprising, and it led to a permanent rupture between them; yet under George the firm became more successful than it ever was under him, and had a Book of the Month choice with *Charmed Circle* by James Mellow (1974). Since the 'circle' was that of Gertrude Stein, it marked a certain shift in emphasis.

Fred was to return to America for a renaissance with Westview Press in Boulder, Colorado, but that was still a few years ahead. Meanwhile his venture into German publishing was a failure because, although he had dealt with German art book publishers from the vantage point of New York, he knew nothing of trade publishing in Europe form within. At this time I ran into him at Frankfurt. He seemed strangely diminished and for once was not on his high horse with me. He observed wistfully, but as ever pithily: 'I am a big-time publisher on a mini-scale.' His misery was compounded by the collapse of his marriage to Heloise, who went back with him to Europe and then saw all they had gained materially from the sale to Britannica disappear. Later George Aldor returned permanently to Europe, and operated from Paris as a scout for Rizzoli.

Of my mentors I rank none higher than Fred Praeger.

Early Days of Independence

The idea of publishing independently first came to me while John MacCallum Scott was still running Pall Mall. I had just come back from Africa, and been unsuccessful in getting Fred Praeger to take the slightest interest in publishing the memoirs (still unwritten) of Alexander Kerr of Fort Hare. I was unwilling to let the idea drop completely; Fred may have been right that it was intrinsically a project of slight importance and not commercially viable, but I still thought it worth doing. So I asked John if it would be possible for me to publish the occasional book of 'my own' while staying under the Pall Mall roof – paying the costs and receiving the income, less a commission for Pall Mall's various services in producing, selling and distributing it. He was not averse to the idea and invited me to talk with him about it over lunch at the Reform Club. There he did a sum on the back of an envelope, showing that it would be very difficult for me to avoid losing money, certainly on such a project as Kerr's memoirs; he told me, as a warning, that his publishing only started to lose money seriously when he became a client of Barrie and Rockliff for every function of the publishing process except editing. The way we left it was that I would tell him if I wanted to go ahead with this or any other independent project, but once I had aired it, the urge to turn it into reality weakened.

Before the idea of leaving Pall Mall began to look realisable, I sought out the acquaintance of two independent publishers whose operations interested me, and for a time saw them quite often. They were Frank Cass, who was my age, and Clive Bingley, a few years younger. There was nothing particular I wanted to discuss with them;

I was merely trying, not quite consciously, to get the feel of being independent. Frank was way ahead of the field in Britain when the great 'reprint wave' started to roll in the 1960s – for him it was a natural progression from his first independent enterprise as an antiquarian bookseller, when he had quickly learned which out-of-print books in certain fields – such as colonial history and anthropology – were rare and in demand. Clive, due to the accident that his employer André Deutsch acquired the Grafton list of books on library science and gave it to him to look after, started up on his own as a library science publisher. The books were neatly produced with a distinctive livery, and Clive enjoyed a captive market. He started by doing everything himself, including packing and dispatching, and then took on the distribution of another fledgling independent, Arms and Armour Press, whose owner Lionel Leventhal and he soon started SPEX, a book exhibition that grew into the London Book Fair. Clive went into orbit as a cunning entrepreneur, leaving the admirable Clive Bingley Publishers far behind him, but he started in the classic way, and it was this which attracted me in the mid-1960s.

My relations with Frank Cass have remained close. His firm, which has steadily consolidated itself in Britain and in North America, is now best known for its scholarly journals – over fifty of them – but it also publishes new books in fields not far removed from mine, and in Judaica. Frank's son, having already established himself in management and finance, has recently joined him in the business – a phenomenon more often seen today in India than in Britain.

It was certainly as well that I had at least revolved many relevant thoughts in my head before the push came, because I would not have been able to work out a plan in a void. Everything, in a sense, was already in place. I knew that (as was my habit) I did not need to stir myself much. Publishing could just begin; there were a few manuscripts I was keen to do for which I could obtain contracts quickly. I would soon see how much skill I had learned, how much I had been born with and what it all added up to. I knew that co-publication deals were the key to healthy cash flow. If I was lucky, Praeger might take one or two of my books at the start, and allies such as the Praeger editors would guide me in the direction of other partners whom I did not yet know of.

C. Hurst & Co. began its life in January 1967 when I had a letter-head printed, with the address of my then home, 21 Gloucester Circus, Greenwich. Under the name were the words 'Bookseller and Wholesale Importer' – nowhere did it say 'Publisher'. The name itself was meant to echo that of the family's textile business founded by my great-grandfather in Bradford, M. Hertz (later Hurst) & Co. I based my colophon on the curious 'time-ball' on top of Flamsteed's observatory in Greenwich Park; the first version was drawn for me, but I later re-drew it myself more to my liking. Because I don't, finally, see much need for a colophon, I ceased using it in the early 1980s.

I did not delay in starting to publish, but my two recent journeys had awoken a fascination with English-language scholarly publishing outside Britain and North America. In the previous few years I had become aware of the extent of such publishing in the 'humanities' and the 'social sciences', and it also made me aware of the practice, among certain booksellers, of offering individual titles to their customers on slips of paper. I thought that I could make a small niche for myself selling expensive scholarly books published outside the English-speaking world – specifically in Japan, the Netherlands and the Nordic countries – by means of these individual offers to, at first, British libraries and then overseas ones. To this end I started collecting catalogues and sending out offers. The single title that did best for me was one published by Mouton in The Hague on the sociology of the military; I sold about fifty copies and Mouton were pleasantly surprised, though their discount remained niggardly. E.J. Brill had a lovely book on the rare white rhinoceros of Sumatra, but that did not sell as well. If the customer was not in central London I would ask the publisher to drop-ship. It was all delightfully simple. My most lucrative single sale was of a set of microfilms published in Japan which I sold to America for $600. I soon found that two other booksellers were also interested in this field. One was Christopher Foyle, who at that time was at W. and G. Foyle in Charing Cross Road being groomed as the successor to his aunt Christina; he was thinking of compiling a catalogue of English-language books published in non-English-speaking countries, but that went no further, and he did not stay at Foyle's for long. The other was Hans Zell, a man of much greater determination, who had been trained in precisely this field at Almqvist and Wiksell in Stockholm, but turned instead to Africana. I might have carried it much further than I did with little competition.

But my round-the-world trip in 1966 stimulated me to evolve a more ambitious plan. I had, as I thought, discovered a whole world of scholarly publishing in subjects other than the 'hard' sciences in India, Pakistan, Thailand, Singapore, Japan, Australia and New Zealand which had very little contact with the markets of Europe and America. South Africa, 'discovered' two years earlier, was another source. The then flourishing Asia Publishing House of Bombay, alone of Indian publishers, had branches in Britain and the U.S. and so had no need for my services, but there were several others worthy of attention. In Pakistan there was an Islamic publisher, Sh. Muhammad Ashraf, and the well-known bookstore in Lahore, Ferozsons Ltd, had published the autobiography of one of the prominent political figures of the independence period, Sir Firoz Khan Noon; I thought there must be a market in Britain for such a book, but when I saw the exceptionally bad quality of the printing I reluctantly let it go. In Bangkok the attraction was Sulak Sivaraksa's Social Science Association Press with its books on Buddhism, none of which had been sold in the West. In Japan there had been an English-language publishing firm, the Hokuseido Press, for many years. Its staple fare was Japanese literature (notably a four-volume collection of *Haiku*) but it also, intriguingly, had works on Yeats and even George Eliot. All these books were finely produced. At the time I approached Hokuseido it was about to publish two books of textual criticism by an English Jesuit, Peter Milward, at Sophia University, on Hopkins's *Wreck of the Deutschland* and Eliot's *Four Quartets*. I immediately offered to co-publish them, and took a small edition of each which sold out. In Australia the main quarry was the Australian National University Press in Canberra, which was about to enter a phase of productivity and excellence under its American director 'Chip' Wood, which alas did not last more that a few years. F.W. Cheshire in Melbourne had one book that I decided to co-publish – on the kangaroo. In New Zealand I went for the Maori books in Blackwood and Janet Paul's list.

It would not have been impossible to offer all these books around in the same way as I did the European ones, but I had the benighted idea of importing a small quantity of each and trying to sell them to booksellers. The Asian prices, at least, were so low that I could easily mark them up. When Gerald Bartlett, at the Economists' Bookshop, learned what I was doing on receiving my first, all too extensive list of offers, he warned me against it. He was quite right. I should have approached the idea as a publisher – as I did with certain titles in Australasia – singling out the most promising titles only. As it was, I placed sizeable orders with a few Indian publishers, buying firm – those titles whose publishers did not know how to supply exports direct I ordered through U.B.S. in Delhi, and Mohan Chawla obtained the best possible discounts for me. Mohan made his first visit to London at this time, and stayed briefly in our house. Wiser than I was, he advised caution in what I was doing. When he told me of his plan to found a publishing house, later Vikas, I advised him not to do it but to stick to his last.

Some of the Indian books did indeed prove immoveable, and

ended up in a skip a few years later, (a Polish neighbour came round and told me how fascinating he found them, and that he had helped himself to a great many), but some, such as the noble multi-volume *Linguistic Survey of India* and the 50-volume *Sacred Books of the East*, which Oxford surrendered to that tenacious Jain family firm Motilal Banarsidass, not to mention the *Cambridge History of India*, republished by S. Chand and with a permanently missing volume, sold easily. The Indian publisher whose books, with a few notable exceptions, I found hardest to sell was also the one who made incomparably the greatest impression on me when I was in India in 1966. This was K.L Mukhopadhyay of Calcutta, who had founded, and ran personally, his own scholarly publishing house. It was in a crumbling eighteenth-century town house, and he sat, a stout late middle-aged man wearing a *dhoti*, surrounded by his wares. We had two lengthy sessions, and he gave me the essential inspiration to start my own imprint. I never met him again, but we corresponded and at one point he wrote that, although we did not seem to succeed in doing much business, he valued our contact. From the time of my meeting with him, India has continued to be one of the few magnetic poles in my publishing life. Relatively modern history – not that standby of old-style Indian publishers, Indology – was Mukhopadhyay's speciality, and as well as somewhat arcane monographs he had published seminal works by the renowned Bengali historian, R.C. Majumdar, on the 1857 'Mutiny' and the Freedom Movement (in three volumes) – an enviable achievement for a personal publishing enterprise, and due to his reputation alone.

At this time I took another action which, like my wholesaling, I have sometimes looked back on with anguish. On leaving Greenwich in the late 1950s I kept my house there and when we came back again to Greenwich at the time of Martin's birth in 1965 I kept my two houses in Portland Road, Notting Hill. All were unmortgaged and producing rents. Collecting the rents in the Notting Hill houses, where the tenants were used to paying cash, was inconvenient from a distance – the Park Vista house was no trouble. No doubt there would be repairs in all three to attend to, and as the tenants left there would be the nuisance of finding new ones. Of course it could all have been handled by an agent, but even so I could imagine myself being distracted by the sordid preoccupations of a landlord from my new business. So I decided to sell them all. There would be a sizeable profit over what I had paid for them, but the stock market was buoyant and I thought I was making a shrewd move. Of course, had I kept them I would have had vastly more collateral, especially after the property market soared, for raising capital for the business.

When I put the Portland Road houses on the market I received a heart-rending appeal from Miss Ogilvy, my oldest tenant now aged eighty-five. We had got on well, and while I was there she had someone in the house for the first time during her long tenancy whom she perceived to be of her class, and therefore with whom she could communicate at more than a formal level. She also doted on my second son Daniel, who as a cheery ash-blond toddler completely stole her heart, and the letters which, for a short time, she sent me in almost every post mentioned 'Daniel, whom I love'. She even told me that she had included me in her will – and would not cancel it. A year or two later her solicitor sent me the bequest of £25, which I received with a very bad conscience. The retired parlour-maid, Gertrude Acock, with whom I had also chewed the fat on many occasions, was more philosophical. For a time she had been convinced that her room was infested with mice, which she said crawled over her in bed, bit away large chunks of the plaster skirting (she showed me where they had been broken off and I noticed that they had all long ago been painted over) and created a stench – she often repeated this word. We called the Council rodent exterminator, but nothing could dislodge her obsession and she accused me of not believing her. Then eventually she began to forget about 'the little gentlemen in grey waistcoats', and dropped dead one day when she tried to move a large chest of drawers unaided.

I soon realised that I could not continue for long working at home, and rented a single room, costing £5 a week, on the front of the second floor of 13 James Street, Covent Garden, a run-down building largely occupied by small fruit merchants and long since demolished. I had lived in Broad Court, alongside Bow Street magistrates' court, throughout the hot summer of 1959 and acquired a lasting fondness for the area. The market was still in full vigour, although by the time we office workers arrived, most activity had ceased and the porters played cards on fruit boxes in the open-fronted ground floor areas. Porters no longer carried the legendary stacks of round fruit baskets on their heads but one could still witness breathtaking displays of skill, as when, in James Street, two porters descending the steep gradient, each with a barrow piled high with produce behind him that he was holding back, converged at a very acute angle and, without either one slowing his pace, missed colliding with each other by inches. No girl could walk past the stalls and not be whistled at. Under the portico of St Paul's church in the Piazza was a grimy caravan from which a weatherbeaten, wheezy old man sold tea and stale cakes. In 1959, when I was working at Rolls-Royce, I often walked from Broad Court to Mayfair along King Street, where a pleasing large 18th-century house (No. 37) had a 'for sale' notice on it. I eventually phoned the agent to find that the freehold was going for £17,000. It was just before I made my much smaller investment in Notting Hill, but having rented an office in the adjoining house, No. 38, since 1980, I still suffer twinges of regret that I did not have that sum available at the time.

One of the advantages of being in Covent Garden was that I could cultivate relations with that remarkable breed, the oriental book-sellers of Great Russell Street: Arthur Probsthain at No. 41, Kegan Paul at No. 43, and Luzac at No. 46. Plainly they were my best hope of shifting a substantial quantity of my imports. (Apart from them, Dick Ring, in the oriental department at Blackwell's, was as helpful as he was able to be, and the Economists' Bookshop, despite Gerald Bartlett's warning, surprised itself and me by landing one astonishing library order for single copies of about fifty titles from my list.)

I first heard of Probsthain from Theophilus Mogabgab in Cyprus who, on his slender income, kept an account there and regularly paid sums into it but never enough for all his desiderata to be supplied at one time. Until only a few years before the time of writing, the shop had a dingy air; tattered parcels, obviously from the east, lay unopened in piles on the brown linoleum floor, and even the mint books on the shelves and in the window never looked entirely fresh. The owner Walter Sheringham was of German birth and trained as an engineer, but early in his career was brought to London to be taken into partnership by his uncle, the original Mr Probsthain, who founded the business in 1902 and died in 1939. Walter had a courteous and rather distracted manner, and seemed more like the librarian of a learned society than a trader. But he traded successfully, as is proved by the fact that of all the generically similar establishments in the street, his alone has survived. He made a careful choice from my offerings, including a full set of the *Sacred Books of the East* (50 volumes), but would buy them for no more that the price he could have paid to his Indian agent.

Bob Sawers, the manager of Kegan Paul at No. 43, wanted no Indian books but took the Japanese ones I had imported from Hokuseido Press. Alone of the three, the firm was interested in Oceania and 'native' America – the former came in useful when I started co-publishing books on the Pacific peoples with the Australian National University Press and Paul's of Auckland. Sawers soon departed to start his own business dealing in Japanese prints, leaving in charge the elderly and experienced but timid H. Coles, whose late brother had been the dominant figure in the business for years. He did not stay for long, and from having been the most comprehensive and modern of the three stores, this long-renowned business went into a decline and, after the sale of its parent company, Routledge, in the 1980s finally disappeared altogether.

But the most helpful and friendly of all was H. Reynolds of Luzac, whom I had not previously met. Once we got to know eachother, this wizened Cockney with a tortoise-like face traversed by wrinkles would receive me in his large top-lit back office, run his eye down my list and pick off a nice mixed order of 30-50 books, and then sit back and reminisce. He had joined the firm in 1919 as assistant to Mr Knight-Smith, its proprietor since the 1890s, whose grandson John now owned the business together with the freehold of the building. Reynolds was a director, but with no capital had never been able to carve out for himself the commanding position which his experience and character, and the training he had received from his revered mentor, merited. He and John Knight-Smith, whom he only ever referred to as 'my colleague', were no longer on speaking terms. John sat in the front of the shop and handled new books, while Reynolds dealt with the secondhand. He had also been a publisher of orientalia, and was still the exclusive distributor of the publications of the Pali Text Society, the School of Oriental and African Studies (S.O.A.S.), and some other similar learned institutions; in this and much else he was the true heir of John's grandfather. However, his great days in bookselling were long past: while the British Raj in India lasted and for a few years afterwards, he had bought the collections of former India hands, but what had once been a steady stream was now a trickle. Reynolds loved his business but it had turned sour. He was now well beyond the usual retiring age, but could not detach himself – for one thing he would die of idleness in retirement, for another he was rightly afraid of what would become of the business without his restraining hand. One day I went into Kegan Paul next door and found Reynolds there. I had once been in Probsthain's when he appeared and bought a book for one of his customers, but this was clearly not one of those occasions. He was now working alongside his old friend H. Coles as a fellow-employee. In answer to my questioning look he explained that his 'colleague' had turned the upper part of No. 46 into a flat for himself and his mistress, and this was the last straw. Within a short time he was dead, and Luzac folded not many years later.

A diversion arose from my trading in Indian books in 1969, when Ramdas Bhatkal of Popular Prakashan in Bombay talked me into taking a very small edition (about 125 copies), with my imprint, of a multi-author volume on the Indian economy edited by A.V. Bhuleshkar, a lecturer at a college in the English Midlands. The reason why Ramdas wanted a deal for this book, however puny, was that Mountbatten had written a short foreword (his actual letter was reproduced facsimile in the book). No doubt he had long ago forgotten about it, but I was determined to get a little fun out of this, and wrote reminding him of his generous act, and asking if we – the editor and I – could personally present him with a copy. He wrote back a civil letter (mentioning by the way that he had not written sooner because of a visit to Paris – I thought it charming that he felt moved to impart this gratuitous information to a complete stranger, but wondered if he had felt unable not to drop this hint that he had been staying with the Windsors), and we duly made our call at his house in Kinnerton Street, with Mrs Bhuleshkar and the (still today) ubiquitous photographer Madan Arora in tow.

Mountbatten, of course, was very affable, but one should never forget that such people are different from the rest of us. When Arora had posed our little group and stood back to take the shots, the great man started saying repeatedly 'Barbaroo, barbaroo' and I wondered what this curious, rude-sounding word meant (was I a barbaroo?) – it only clicked later that he was saying 'Rhubarb, rhubarb' and encouraging us to do the same. He then sat down to take a quick look at the book, which he said he would add to his India collection, and put on a pair of spectacles. One would never have recognised him with them on, and Arora could not resist another shot. Mountbatten immediately said, pleasantly enough but firmly, 'You mustn't publish that!' I told him that we were currently having one of our books printed in India, and he said this was good and we should do more of it. We now do so with some regularity.

Publishing Begins

I was not thinking very ·hard when I started simultaneously to trade as a publisher, a retail bookseller and a wholesaler. Even if I had engaged an assistant, as I did, it would have been too much – for me. Running an organisation was not then, nor did it ever become, even remotely what I wanted to do or thought myself capable of. Mine was going to be a personal business; I would do what I knew how to do and enjoyed doing, and follow the various hares I had released as far as they would lead me.

Publishing, curiously, did not intrigue me so much at first as my two other, novel activities, which immediately put me in touch with suppliers in an exotic range of places, and with customers who found what I was doing interesting. This was not the same at all as working for months on a single book, dealing with one author and one co-publisher, and a printer – which could be lonely and at times dreary work. But I had to stabilise things, and it was the publishing that naturally came to the fore. I went on duplicating the odd offer of an individual title from Mouton, Munksgaard or J.C.B. Mohr of Tübingen longer than I worked on the wholesale stock, but both just faded out.

My first publishing contract was very deliberately for a book which I knew would have no successor, but which I thought, as well as selling reasonably well, would be like a penny in the fountain. This was to be a history of Greenwich by David Leggatt, the Borough Librarian. No such book had been written in recent times, but there seemed an obvious market (Leggatt assured me that on the strength of his name alone every public library in the country would order it). Besides, the author knew the subject, and was a likeable fellow. He produced a convincing synopsis and promised to have the job done within a year. We were in business. But mysteriously he proved unable to deliver; my phone calls produced evasive answers, and once he was so incoherent that I wondered it he was having a quiet nervous breakdown. The plan finally had to be jettisoned. Not long afterwards Nigel Hamilton, who had already started the Greenwich Bookshop with his wife Hannelore, and later became the biographer of the Mann brothers, his godfather Field-Marshal Montgomery and that super-godfather Joseph Kennedy and his progeny, brought out a book called *Royal Greenwich* in collaboration with his mother and under the imprint of the bookshop. I could only grind my teeth: accessible and not very original, it sold well and filled a need. Commissioning Leggatt was my one deliberate professional act of *pietas*; I thought it meet and right for a publisher to publish a book about his home town – and, having no territorial roots, I was more attached to Greenwich than to anywhere else. I did not know at the time that many American university presses, alongside their academic specialisms, have a strong line in regional history.

In 1968 I brought out my first five books, and it would show a lack of *pietas* if I did not dwell on their genesis. The very first came ready-made and I did not have to go out and look for it. It was called *African Women: Their Legal Status in South Africa*,

CATALOGUS VAN
VIJFTIG BOEKEN EN BOEKJES
ZONDER TOESTEMMING
UITGEGEVEN IN DE
JAREN
1942—1945
DOOR
A.A.BALKEMA
TE
AMSTERDAM

JUNI 1945

ABOVE *Title-page of the catalogue of A.A. Balkema's war-time publications, Amsterdam, with the publisher's autograph.* OVERLEAF *two subsequent pages of the same. The typography is likely to have been by J. van Krimpen, who is acknowledged as the typographer of several of the books listed.*

1. H. J. SCHEEPMAKER, In memoriam Anton Marinus Pleyte. 19,5 × 13,5. 8 pp. 30 exx. Oktober-November 1943. Niet in den handel.

2. Zehn kleine Meckerlein, een satyrisch gedicht op het 3de Rijk. 15 × 13. 18 pp. 40 exx. December 1943. Niet in den handel.

3. VAN DEN VOS REYNAERDE. Een door Dr W. Gs Hellinga naar het Comburgsche handschrift uitgegeven diplomatische tekstuitgaaf. Typografie J. van Krimpen. 19 × 11. 138 pp. 200 exx. op Van Gelder. Februari 1944. f 12.50.

4. H. J. SCHEEPMAKER, Het Gedenken. Gedichten. 19,5 × 11. 36 pp. 100 exx. op Pannekoek. April 1944. f 3.—

5. A. ROLAND HOLST, Helena's Inkeer. Een fragment. 29 × 20. 14 pp. 50 exx. 2de druk voor vrienden van den schrijver en uitgever. April 1944. Niet in den handel.

6. JACOB GEEL, Gesprek op den Drachenfels. Typografie Reinold Kuipers. 21 × 13,5. 52 pp. 50 exx. op Hollandsch Antique de luxe; 100 exx. op Hollandsch, abusievelijk niet in den colophon vermeld. Mei 1944. f 5.—

7. F. DE LA ROCHEFOUCAULD, Maximes. 13 × 10,5. 94 pp. 200 exx. op Pannekoek. Juni 1944. f 5.—

8. W. B. YEATS, Selected Poems, gekozen door A.

Roland Holst. Typografie S. H. de Roos. 20 × 12,5. 60 pp. 200 exx. op Haesbeek Imperium. Juli 1944. f 7,50.

9. STENDHAL, Souvenirs d'Égotisme, 15 × 9,5. 192 pp. 300 exx. Augustus 1944. f 5.—.

10. OMAR KHAYYAM: Rubaiyat. Typografie J. van Krimpen. 19 × 11. 30 pp. 12 exx. op Barcham Green. Naar den eersten druk van de vertaling van Fitz Gerald, September 1944. Uitverkocht. In herdruk, zie pag. 14.

11. BERTUS AAFJES, Kleine Katechismus der Poëzie. 19,5 × 13. 16 pp. 100 exx. op Ossekop Van Gelder. September 1944. f 3.50.

12. EMILY DICKINSON, Selected Poems. Gekozen door S. Vestdijk. 16,5 × 11. 70 pp. 200 exx. op Ingres Van Gelder. September 1944. f 5.—.

13. HERAKLEITOS, Fragmenten. Grieksche tekst met Nederlandsche vertaling door Drs E. Hoek. Typografie J. van Krimpen. 20 × 13. 24 pp. 100 exx. op Van Gelder. September 1944. f 7.50.

14. THOMAS GRAY, An elegy wrote in a country church yard. 20 × 15. 12 pp. 100 exx. op Van Gelder. September 1944. f 3.50.

15. DANTE GABRIEL ROSSETTI, Selected Poems. Gekozen door H. J. Scheepmaker. 16,5 × 11. 64 pp. 200 exx. op Haesbeek Imperium en Prelu. Oktober 1944. f 7.50.

16. DEN CIX PSALM. 11,5 × 20. 8 pp. op Van Gelder. Oktober 1944. Niet in den handel.

17. ALEXANDER POESJKIN, Enkele Gedichten. Gekozen en vertaald door Aleida G. Schot. 16 × 12,5.

and was by H.J. (Jack) Simons, an authority on African government and law at the University of Cape Town, whom I had met there in 1964. Shortly after that, as a member of the South African Communist Party in the 1930s, he was banned and went into exile in Zambia, which meant that this book, which had been set up in type by the local publisher A.A, Balkema,[*] could not be published in South Africa. Balkema had once called on me at Pall Mall, and we discussed his acting as our agent. He now asked if I wanted to take on this book, and I jumped at it. He had prudently got the setting done in Holland, and all that remained for me to do was pay the printer's bill and a royalty to the author. Within a short time Northwestern University Press, then as now with an Africanist orientation, agreed to import 1,000 copies in a co-edition which more than covered my whole outlay. About ten years later my copies sold out, and I asked Northwestern if they could re-supply me. They answered that a few weeks earlier they could have done so, but in the mean time a freak snow storm had caused the roof of their warehouse to fall in, and all the remaining copies had been spoiled – except for eight, which I could have.

Almost at the same time as *African Women*, I brought out a book which its author, a serving Royal Air Force officer Eric Macro, had discussed interminably with Pall Mall, but which finally neither side had the heart to go on with. It was an amateur scholar's very painstaking study with the self-explanatory title *Yemen and the Western World*. He had been persuaded to cut and cut again till he thought it barely viable, but I simply took on the remains, Praeger bought 750, and it has sold steadily – Probsthain has always been an especially good customer.

Then my meeting in Addis Ababa in 1964 with the Sudanese intellectual and diplomat Jamal Mohamed Ahmed bore unexpected fruit. I heard in 1967 that he was now ambassador in London, and contacted him in the hope that he would soon write – for me – about his native Nubia. Within a day or two of our meeting and having a pleasant but unproductive chat, he called me to say that a Sudanese

---

[*] Originally a Dutch publisher and typographer, who earned undying respect by producing in Amsterdam during the German occupation a clandestine series of books, not openly subversive but intended to inspire his fellow-countrymen in their current travail. Because of the shortage of paper and power, they were in extremely short runs, and some consisted of one signature only – among them were selections of poetry in English by Emily Brontë, Emily Dickinson, Yeats and D.G. Rossetti; also Gray's *Elegy* and the 109th Psalm. He handset them and made the printing press run by linking it to the driving wheel of his bicycle, which he then pedalled. These books, of which he kept none himself, later became precious collectors' items. He gave me a copy of the catalogue of this production that he published after the war, and I asked him to autograph it.

friend of his was in town with a completed manuscript called *The Southern Sudan: Background to Conflict.* This was Mohamed Omer Beshir, an academic also involved in public life. M.O.B. was a ubiquitous figure, a prolific writer and voluble talker. He had been secretary to the 'Round Table Conference' on the South in 1965, which gave his writing added authority. The idea of publishing an ecumenical book on this subject, as this seemed to be, by a Northerner appealed to me and I took it. Praeger bought 750 of this one too. My edition did not take long to sell out, but it already seemed too late for a reprint; events had moved on. In the aftermath of the Addis Ababa conference in the early 1970s, M.O.B. gave me a new manuscript on the Southern question, which I also published, though he produced a number more that I did not. When he died in the early 1990s I heard that he had left an autobiography in English, but this has so far remained an unsubstantiated rumour. My other two 1968 books both resulted from my visit to Fort Hare in South Africa in 1964: the memoirs of Alexander Kerr, the College's first principal, which he evidently wrote at my inspiration, and G.C. Oosthuizen's book on the independent churches of South Africa. Both books contained photographs, which I had the pleasure of laying out, using what facility I had learned at the *Architectural Review.* Of Kerr's book *Fort Hare, 1915-1948* I sold 500 to Shuter and Shooter in Pieter-maritzburg and 250 to Simon Silverman at Humanities Press – because it was my first deal with him, he graciously paid half the purchase money up front.[*] Of Oosthuizen's *Post-Christianity in Africa* T. Wever in Stellenbosch took 500 and Wm. B. Eerdmans, the Evangelical publisher in Grand Rapids, Michigan, the staggering quantity of 3,000. *Post-Christianity* was the toughest editing job of my five 1968 titles. The author – an Afrikaner, and one writing on a religious subject

---

[*] Simon was scrupulously reliable and high-principled – accompanied by a certain amount of emotional hand-wringing. Up till this time the backbone of his business had been imports from two British publishers, and because of their copious offerings of works on his favourite subjects – philosophy, spirituality and sociology – he would have clung to them with hoops of steel: Allen & Unwin and Routledge & Kegan Paul. He limited his commitment by starting with a low order, 250 or so, and re-ordering when necessary. These eminent firms were happy with such an arrangement, and he tried to convince me that it would also serve me better to stick with him and sell my titles on this basis rather than going for initial orders of 750, 1,000 and above, which might well be the final ones – an unpersuasive argument for someone in need of quick cash recovery above all else, but of course uttered, as Simon uttered everything, in utter good faith. Then, at about the same time, A. & U. and R.K.P. both set up American sales offices. It did neither of them much good, but the tide was moving that way and they had to go with it. Simon was left high and dry, and although his business continued, much of the real joy and satisfaction went out of it for him. It is an achievement that, some years after his death, Humanities Press preserves much of the character Simon gave to it.

– had an idiom that was distinctly foreign and needed adaptation for a generally Anglo-Saxon readership; his only previous book, a thesis, had been published by Brill unamended. I knew at once that I enjoyed working on manuscripts like this one and Mohamed Omer Beshir's. I was in my element like a fish swimming in the sea. Whatever else I did as a publisher, this was the essential creative task, to which the design of the book – internal and external – became automatically ancillary. I had only done fragmentary bits of editorial work before, not enough to make this discovery. Every aspect of trading also appealed to me, perhaps a legacy from my long line of Jewish merchant ancestors. I knew publishing was 'me' already at Barrie and Rockliff, but this was the first time the spirit and the body had coalesced.

Not knowing which printer to go to with my first two edited texts, the ones on Yemen and Sudan, I phoned Frank Cass for advice. His production manager recommended Billing's of Guildford as being good and not too expensive. So by chance I began a relationship with Billing's that lasted till about 1980. The books were set in hot-metal Monotype, so one had to be careful about corrections.*

A love for typography, which had gestated since my time at the Architectural Press, also now came to birth. I had Beshir's book set in Plantin, with Perpetua bold for the jacket, and Macro's in Imprint. Neither were faces I used again. But for Oosthuizen I used Times, which ever since has seemed the ideal face for something straightforward and workmanlike, and which of all the classic typefaces has been most convincingly imitated in the new era of computer setting. Kerr was set in Bembo, again with Perpetua on the jacket. Much as I like Caslon in its proper place, it harks back to the 18th century, and in modern books has an antiquarian flavour, so I have never felt able to use it except once for the new introduction to a reprint, where the original had been set in it – by O.U.P. in the 1920s. Bembo has always been my choice where a sense of refinement has been needed, and I have also reserved it for books on East Asia, Eastern Europe and the former U.S.S.R. Baskerville has done service for many books on Africa. I never found hot metal

---

* 'Author's corrections', or ones not due to a fault of the compositor, were charged to the customer, and we were supposed to correct them in black ink and 'printer's errors' in red. I found it difficult to bother seriously about this because the printer could see quite clearly which were which without any differentiation by the customer. But I never could fathom the way printers worked out their charges for author's corrections anyway, and suspected that certain 'old Spanish customs' came into play. Sometimes when I knew I had wilfully done more of them than I should and fully expected a high charge, it came out surprisingly low, to my great relief. But, equally often, it came out higher than expected when the corrections had been painstakingly kept to the minimum.

setting so attractive as when it started to disappear: so inadequate were the alternatives then on offer that its phasing-out seemed traumatic, and I hoped that, just as the 'real ale' movement saved traditional draught beer for the discerning drinker within a hair's breadth of its extinction, Monotype metal setting with its barely definable qualities of 'colour', and letterpress printing with its equally elusive 'crispness', might also be rescued. It has not happened, although there are still houses that can offer it for limited use at high prices. At odd times after it disappeared in Britain, I had books set and printed in the old way in Hong Kong by the Libra Press and in Calcutta by Eastend Printers, but both those firms finally closed down in the early 1990s, and with the improvements in computer setting and a dulling of old memories I have had to admit that the comp with his stick, and his skills learned through long apprenticeships – not to mention that other vanished figure, the printer's 'reader', who examined proofs before they went to the publisher and marked queries that had attracted his attention – should be allowed to rest in peace.

To complete the account of my first crop, I must mention my second attempt to commission a book – which failed, like David Leggatt's would-be history of Greenwich, but which at least produced a replacement, and some amusement on the way. Ever since meeting Osman Orek, Turkish Cypriot lawyer and politician, in Kemal Rüstem's bookshop in Nicosia in 1966, I had wanted to activate the plan we discussed then for him to write a Turkish account of the Cyprus problem, which I thought deserved an airing. Early in my independent life I renewed the invitation, and he wrote that if I could send a good English secretary out to him, he would pay all expenses and dictate the book to her on the spot. This was the time that I was publishing David Steel's book *No Entry*, and I asked David's secretary Juliet Carpenter if she would like to spend her holiday that year taking up Orek's assignment. She was only too pleased at the prospect. Juliet arrived in Nicosia and reported for duty. Mr Orek apologised that he was busy that day and asked her to come back the next day. She did, and although he made an attempt to get started, he could not concentrate, and gave up after a few sentences. On the third day, he told her that it was hopeless and she should spend the rest of her time in a hotel by the sea at Famagusta. Thus the book never got written, but in Orek's first letter to me he asked if I could obtain for him a long out-of-print book which would be useful for his research: Sir Harry Luke's *Cyprus under the Turks, 1571-1878*, published by the Clarendon Press in 1921. No bookseller I knew had a copy, so I phoned Sir Harry, then aged eighty-four, and he at once suggested that I reprint the book, using his own copy.

When I called at his Kensington flat to collect it, he remarked that I was younger than he expected – which was exactly what I felt on first meeting Frank Cass (why are scholarly publishers expected to be old?). He was atypical of British proconsuls (he had been a governor in the Pacific and before that, more suitably, held senior posts in Malta and Cyprus); but I recalled R.M. Dawkins saying that his family name was originally (pronounced) Lukash. The books he had written about Malta and Cyprus lacked depth, in my opinion, or much light and shade. This early academic exercise was at least totally original. About the man himself there was an exotic air suggesting that his career might have had shadowy aspects of which the world knew nothing. His devout Anglicanism was bizarre, his devotion to the Order of St John less so.

I obtained the reprint rights to the book from O.U.P., and Sir Harry wrote a new introduction, which reflects his hellenophobia, though he does not refer to Archbishop Makarios in it as 'that evil man', as he did in conversation. (It was enjoyable getting it set in Monotype Caslon, which exactly matched the setting of the original edition.) The 1,000 hardback copies I printed, with a large *Tughra* (symbol of Ottoman sovereignty) on the front of the jacket and the British consular arms on the back, took twenty years to sell out; I then made a paperback reprint, of which Rüstem bought several hundred.

My only other straight reprint, apart from an Antarctic series published in the late 1970s, resulted from a visit to Tony Hopkins, economic historian of Africa, at Birmingham University. 'Have you heard of Sundström?' he asked; 'Sundström is the great man – you should reprint *The Exchange Economy of Pre-Colonial Tropical Africa.*' Lars Sundstrom was an anthropologist at the University of Uppsala. Hopkins showed me a copy of this master-work, which was beautifully but eccentrically produced (as part of one of those numerous Latin-titled monograph series which are so integral a feature of academic life in Scandinavia) in a format of exaggerated size, with huge margins. The format reflected the eccentricity of the work – which in turn, as I later discovered, reflected the man. It was a triumph of compilation, the sort of work that would now be done with a computer. Hopkins's recommendation was enough at that stage to make me take it on, and in the spring of 1973 I met Sundstrom himself. We spent a day together, first going to a country inn for lunch, then visiting a magnificent Renaissance castle, Skokloster, and finishing with dinner back in Uppsala.

He was a little older than me, and a striking figure, tall with a fine head. But, handsome as he was, his thick greying hair and his clothes were untidy as opposed to merely informal, and his face had a ravaged look. He was of course pleased – though he would have been untrue to himself if he had not expressed this ironically – that his work was going to receive greater exposure; it might help him too when the head of his department, Professor Lagerkrantz, retired in another year or two. As soon became apparent, this attractive and exceptionally intelligent and cultured man held the professor in sovereign contempt and regarded his own succession to the chair as not only overwhelmingly deserved, but also certain. Over his desire for the chair he could not be ironical; it was the motive spring of his being. Yet, being so intelligent, he must have known that he was an oddball. Though an 'Africanist', he had only been to Africa once – to Liberia for a week's holiday. His marriage had been damned in an unforgettable way. His wife was a Dutch woman with Indonesian blood, and their wedding ceremony took place in Southend-on-Sea, Essex, of all unlikely places, to get over the Swedish nationality laws. Then, after having two sons, his wife contracted tuberculosis, and he nursed her with total, self-denying devotion through years of agonising illness. At last she recovered and was declared fit – and immediately deserted Sundstrom and the two sons. He told me now that he had just ended an affair with a girl because he was afraid of hurting her. Like certain passages in Ingmar Bergman's films, this real-life biography was almost too much to bear. A few years later I learned that he did not get the professorship and never had any chance of getting it. His book is still in print but sells very slowly. In 1991 I sent Sundstrom a small cheque for five years' royalties, and the letter was returned with a message that he had died. (I knew the doyen of Uppsala Africanists, Bengt Sundkler. Unctuously friendly but impersonal, the great professor would address one as 'My dear friend'. He and I worked together on one book, while he was completing his super-*magnum opus*, an all-inclusive history of Christianity. I learned of him first while editing G.C. Oosthuizen's *Post-Christianity in Africa*, where there are many references to his path-breaking work *Bantu Prophets* (1948). Oosthuizen had worked with Sundkler when that book was being researched, and told me in the 1990s that it was still remembered how miserably he paid his African assistants. He and Sundström piquantly personified academic success and failure.)

Sundström, in 1973, told me to contact Axel-Ivar Berglund, a man of about forty who had just finished a thesis called 'Zulu Thought Patterns and Symbolism', which he said was one of the best pieces of work of its kind one was ever likely to find. Berglund, himself a missionary and the son of a missionary in Zululand, had learned the Zulu language as a child, and this dense, long book was drawn direct from oral sources. I co-published it with *Studia Ethnographica Upsaliensia*, and would have sold 750 to St Martin's Press if the editors had been willing to supply those copies in hard covers. But it was too difficult for them, and I had to make do without a co-edition. But fifteen years later, after selling out, we acquired the exclusive rights and sold nearly 2,000 copies to the Indiana University Press and more to David Philip in Cape Town. The only way we could sell the edition to Indiana at the low price John Gallman insisted upon was to go to a printer in Hong Kong, since when I have been regularly sending work to that same printer. But that is another story, that gets us too far away from Lars Sundström.

A Publishing Genealogy

Publishers can only be judged by the books they publish. My company edged its way forward slowly and at first in the dark; some glimmers and flashes began to appear in the early 1970s, and by the '80s it was daylight. The struggle for solvency has never ceased, but the outline, the 'profile', of the list had become clear. It is impossible not to give some account here of the books the firm published in its earlier life, and because the over-riding categorisation continues to be geographical, the only way of doing this is by tracing a geographical genealogy. In the absence of authors' agents, one book leads on to another, sometimes by direct descent, at other times indirectly. There is no attempt to describe C. Hurst & Co.'s current publishing.

Soon after moving into 13 James Street, Covent Garden, I took on a young Dane, Sven Nathan, who had advertised in the *Bookseller*. Having learned his trade with Arnold Busck in Copenhagen, he was settling in England to marry. Though Jewish-looking (he and his fiancée had met in a kibbutz), he was thoroughly Scandinavian in character with a pawky sense of humour and a tendency to smugness. We got on well. He was to garner information for mail-order selling, but because I decided to scale the work down to a manageable handful of titles, his job did not last long and I hired a secretary instead. But while he was with me he drew my attention to a title in Busck's catalogue: the *History of Greenland*, vol. 1: *Earliest Times to 1720* by Finn Gad (born in 1911). Gad had been his history master at high school. Sven's instinct proved correct: I was interested, and the book was translated with help from Danish government sources. The volume was royal 8vo, set in Baskerville with plates on art paper, and had a handsome appearance. I sold 1,000 copies to the McGill-Queen's University Press, then run by Robin Strachan, a Briton who had begun his career in the Sudan Political Service; this seemed something like a triumph. I went to Copenhagen in the cold early spring of 1969, and was invited to dinner at Gad's house. It was a formal, not to say stiff gathering, but in spite of finding Gad something of a martinet in our correspondence, insisting that the English edition replicate the Danish exactly, I took a liking to him. He had a personal warmth, unlike the translator, the English master at Gad's school (also at the dinner-party), who wrote pleasant letters but was a cold fish. My cherished Danish sales rep, Bjorn Hansen, told me how old Greenland hands, who knew the place before the war and the arrival of the Americans, became misty-eyed when they talked about it, and I saw this happen when Gad described how, as a young trainer of Greenlandic student-teachers in the 1930s, he and another Dane waited in the fjord at Godthab for the ship to arrive from home bearing their brides-to-be, and the whole hillside was covered with white-clad Greenlanders out to watch the scene.

Our good relations became strained after the publication of the second volume, which soon followed and took the story forward only another sixty years, covering the notable missionary enterprise of the Moravian Brethren headed by Hans Egede. I found this interesting enough but not thrilling like Vol. 1, which dealt with the material culture of the Eskimos and the episode of the medieval Norse settlement and its unexplained disappearance. Vol. 2, covering a conspicuously shorter period than its predecessor, was half as long again. This time, at my insistence, the Danes paid for the whole translation, but McGill-Queen's would only take 500. Exasperated, in the process of editing, by Gad's inability to leave out even the most trivial minutiae, I desperately made a few discreet cuts – perhaps the equivalent of one page out of a total of 500, and of course his eagle eye spotted them. He was reproachful – obliquely, without being able actually to spell out my unspeakable crime in words.

Greenland's early history was played on such a limited stage that it might be possible to include every recorded item, and this, it seemed, was Gad's mission. Alas he was a pedestrian chronicler rather than a historian, though in Vol. 1 he had achieved a certain majestic sweep. A few years later I was sent the English script of Vol. 3, at least as bulky as Vol. 2 and this time carrying the story only twenty-eight years further on to 1808. I had given a fairly clear understanding that I would publish it, but when I realised that Gad was writing more and more about less and less, I had a deep confabulation with Don Sutherland, by then the director of McGill-Queen's, as the result of which I pleaded that the market would no longer stand it and begged to be released. Ole Busck nobly took the line of accommodation and published Vol. 3 himself, but Gad was not satisfied and wanted *'force majeure'* used against me for 'private reasons' (was it because I had accepted his hospitality?). Gad died leaving the project beached around 1830, and it has not so far been carried any further.

Also during my visit to Copenhagen in 1969, I agreed to buy 250 copies of a beautiful small book in English recently published by Haase, *The Flora of Greenland*; I advertised it in the *British National Bibliography* and sold out within two years. And Knut Vinderskov, the manager of Busck's bookstore, advised me that two famous books by Henrik Rink, published in English in the 19th century, one on Eskimo customs and the other on the Greenland economy, had become very rare and could be reprinted with profit. I obtained new forewords from Helge Larsen, the doyen of Danish Eskimologists, and went ahead, selling McGill-Queen's 500 of each and Busck themselves 250, but apart from these satisfactory deals which covered my initial outlay, they sold very few copies. For a time I must have been indisputably the leading commercial publisher of hardcore Grœnlandica in the English-speaking world, and may be still, for the two volumes of Gad are still in print. At the time of writing I am trying to persuade a Danish Greenlandist, based in Aarhus, to produce a modern treatment, but this requires me to be as patient as an Eskimo fishing for seals through a hole in the ice.

From Sven Nathan's tip there descended a whole family of Nordica. It started with a visit to Bonniers in Stockholm, where an editor, Daniel Hjorth, showed me a book on the Lapps by a Swedish professor who was also a Lapp, Israel Ruong. It looked just the thing for me, so I acquired the rights, and a young Fenno-specialist in London who also understood Swedish, Michael Branch, agreed to translate it for me. We agreed a rather high fee by the standards of the time, and I am amazed at my optimism. As it happened, he never quite finished it – then as now he had a lot of projects on hand – and did not claim his fee. In consequence I could not proceed with the book. Some years later I received a letter from a Colonel Lort-Phillips saying that he had produced a translation of Ruong's book for his amusement, and offering it to me free. The colonel

332   *The Road to King Street and the View therefrom*

had failed to do his curb drill twice over; not only was his a duplicate translation, but the book had been superseded and there was no longer a need for it.

In the mean time Michael Branch introduced me to a junior librarian in London University, John Screen,* who was looking for a publisher for a biography of the Finnish national hero, Mannerheim, from his birth as a member of the Swedish-Finnish landed aristocracy to the end, caused by the Revolution in 1917, of his career in the Russian imperial army in which he rose to the rank of lieutenant-general. It was a fascinating story, elegantly written, and I published it in 1970 in an edition of 1,500 copies, though without being able to find an American partner. Aping the continental practice, and to cut down the investment, I produced it in paper covers only. Of course we and the author would have made more out of it if it had been hardbound; the price in the 1990s, when it sold out, would have been around £30 instead of £15, and we would probably have sold no fewer copies because of a not inconsiderable Mannerheim cult outside Finland. I discovered the extent of this in 1986 when we published a translation of the one-volume version of the monumental 8-volume biography of Mannerheim (enough to satisfy any cultist but not available in English) by his relation Stig Jägerskiold; John Screen played an indispensable part in producing this book. This time we sold a large quantity to the University of Minnesota Press – luckily because not long afterwards, with the retirement of its then director Jack Ervin, it ceased to publish Nordica, and remaindered a large number of copies (nearly 2,000, all of which I bought). Of Screen's book we sold the Finnish rights to Werner Söderström (WSOY), who sold out their edition long before we did ours. But then a strange thing happened. In 1993 we re-issued the book with a new preface and additions to the bibliography, which I had the satisfaction of getting set in hot-metal Monotype Bembo (supplied by Mould Type of Preston), exactly matching the original; this time the Finnish Foreign Ministry placed a sizeable order, as it did for the Jägerskiöld. In 1993 I was in Helsinki and as a matter of routine visited WSOY. When I mentioned to my interlocutor, Simo Maenpaa, that his firm had published the first version of Screen's biography, he knew nothing of it, but immediately decided that it would fit well into a new series he was doing and bought the rights for the second time, even paying an advance. Not surprisingly, Screen was quite pleased. He has never fulfilled his original intention of writing

---

* At the time of writing Michael Branch is the director and John Screen the librarian of the School of Slavonic and East European Studies at London University.

the 'second half' of his biography of the great hero, but I felt that the wheel had turned full circle in another way when he was awarded a decoration by the Finnish state and asked me, as his publisher, along to the intimate investiture and *vin d'honneur* at the embassy. He has helped me innumerable times when I have needed information or advice.

These books had a varied progeny. First there have been a succession of books on Finland, starting with a translation of one on the British and French involvement in the Winter War by an academic, diplomat and *littérateur*, Jukka Nevakivi. This was co-published by McGill-Queen's, and several years later, when the author was in my office, I asked him why the Finnish Foreign Ministry was not interested in the book. He immediately phoned Henrik Antell, the cultural attaché at the London embassy, who ordered 100 copies on the spot. By this time I had commissioned for the first time a general book on Finland by David Kirby, a young historian at London University. Whatever he writes has breadth and elegance. This time the Foreign Ministry dug deeper into its pocket, and I sold a sizeable edition to the University of Minnesota Press. At the time of writing we are about to publish, after this long interval, second books by both Nevakivi and Kirby. With my partiality for autobiography I will only mention, among the firm's other Finnish projects, two work in that genre, one by the English geographer W.R. Mead – an idiosyncratic account of fifty years' professional involvement with Finland, which consistently avoids using the first-person-singular – and the other by the former President, Mauno Koivisto.

A related line of descent has consisted of books on other Nordic countries. This started with one on the Faroes, which came as the direct result of Gad and had a slight but not fatal similarity to it, by a lecturer at Trent Polytechnic in Nottingham, John West. In a very English way he had been obsessed by the islands all his life, and in its time it was unique. He later appeared on the TV show 'Mastermind' – his special subject can be surmised. A few years later my wife Rachel and I were introduced in London to an Icelandic theatre director, Benedikt Arnason, who had recently married an old friend of hers, and he mentioned that a close friend of his – one of the country's most prominent men of letters, Sigurdur A. Magnusson – had written a ms. on Iceland in English but then put it in a bottom drawer when publication plans miscarried. Like West's book this was a general study but it had much more oomph. Having resurrected it, I suggested many cuts – mainly of the names and achievements of minor modern artists – but treasured such items as the road-builders in recent times who wanted to level a hillock that stood in their way, but were forced by the local community to divert the road round it because it was home to the fairies; and the two labourers laying drains and having a heated argument, which was found to be about who did what in one of the Sagas. We called the book *Northern Sphinx.*

Although I did a small deal with a bookdealer in Torsvik for the Faroe book, the tempting idea of a visit there never materialised. However, Rachel and I did go to Reykjavik in 1977 to help launch *Northern Sphinx.* A sort of press reception was held to which about half a dozen people turned up; coffee was served, alcohol being forbidden under Iceland's draconian drink laws. I only just met the deadline, and several cartons of books were airfreighted over through the good offices of Sigurdur's wife Svanhildur who worked at Icelandair; we went to the godown ourselves to pick them up. But one evil effect of the hurry was that for the only time in my career I lapsed on the publisher's over-riding duty to ensure that the proofs were properly read. There were a lot of typos, and Sigurdur suffered anguish – which I shared passively; with remarkable stoicism and chivalry he did not direct any blame at me.

While I was in Reykjavik the aforementioned Benedikt Arnason took me for a walk round the harbour. We went to the end of a long concrete mole, where a small vessel was moored and covered by a tarpaulin. This was the legendary fishery protection ship *Tyr,* which had wrought havoc with the nets of the Hull fishing fleet only a few years earlier during the Cod Wars. Not long afterwards a senior Icelandic diplomat offered me a book on those events (sad for the Brits but a triumph for the Icelanders) and I published it. This man personified in a fairly extreme form a kind of Icelander (and indeed Scandinavian) whom I did not encounter at all on my visit in 1977: dour, humourless, conservative, and with an upside-down view of the world, in extreme contrast to the free and easy, fun-loving but equally serious type represented by my friends. He snorted with contempt when I told him I knew Sigurdur. After *Northern Sphinx* sold out I was able partly to redeem myself by correcting all the literals with paste and scissors and ceding reprint rights to Snaebjorn Jonsson's 'English Bookshop'; I received 200 copies in lieu of an offset fee. I wished I could have published Sigurdur's next book, an autobiographical account of his harsh, impoverished childhood, which broke all records in Iceland by selling 14,000 copies.

We published a book on Svalbard (Spitsbergen) in the late 1970s after I had read a letter about it in *The Times* from a Norwegian politician; when I wrote to him he referred me to Willy Ostreng, the author of a recently published book, which in characteristic fashion he translated himself. He is now director of the Fridtjof Nansen Institute, a research centre which occupies Nansen's strange *Jugendstil* mansion outside Oslo, and from his desk looks out over a sloping lawn to the explorer's grave under a large tree. Because Greenland led me to look to the Far North as a possible generic area of publishing, I called at the Norwegian Polar Institute on one visit to Oslo, with little hope of results since its work was mainly in geology and glaciology. But the director, Tore Gjelsvik, had just published an account of his exploits in the resistance during the Nazi occupation, and soon we had made arrangements for a translation, which J.W. Cappelen, the publisher, financed. A little later I took a biography of Haakon VII – spotted at Frankfurt – from Gyldendal Norsk Forlag. At least it was translated, and 200 copies were bought with public money (books about royal persons are not my line, but I made an exception for this unusually admirable example of his breed). I sent a copy to King Olav, who wrote a short personal letter in reply; the translator, Kingston Derry, thought the King had turned down our proposal to present it to him in person because he was fed to the teeth with books about his father. My U.S. co-publisher in this case ignored requests for payment for over a year and only paid up after Lou Barron prodded him on my behalf. He sold out and re-ordered, and the cycle was repeated.

The Nordic tree branched out further when my eldest son Andrew, then beginning his career as a journalist in Brussels, was told by a young British staff member at the European Commission, John Fitzmaurice, that he was working on a study of politics in Denmark, his mother's native country, and referred him to me. I published it, and although it did not do particularly well, I soon commissioned John to write on similar lines about Belgium; the resulting work had gone into its third completely revised edition by the time of writing. It has resulted in a close editorial relationship with John; also to an informal series of political portraits of other European countries. By the end of the '80s, the last major lacuna on our Nordic map remaining to be filled was Sweden, so I reacted favourably when Chris Mosey, an English journalist who had worked there for ten years and recently left in a state of some disillusionment, offered me a book he had written around the assassination of Olof Palme, delving into the history of Swedish social democracy and Palme's family background, career and peculiar character. The portrait Mosey presents of Palme is closely observed and convincing; I would describe it as very human rather than deliberately unflattering, but clearly some of his friends objected to it. At first the book was accepted by Weidenfeld and Nicolson, who paid the author a decent advance and announced it in their catalogue. But then mysteriously they dropped it; the reason alleged by Mosey was that Weidenfeld himself came under pressure from Lord Rothschild, whose daughter had been a close friend of Palme. This tale awakened in me that dangerous psychological condition already described, the André Deutsch syndrome, which – added to my purely gut feeling of distaste for Palme – resulted in our publishing the book. It did not do well; by the time it came out, the world was forgetting about Palme, and even the Swedes were not much interested any more.

A Nordic spin-off was *A History of European Ideas* by three Danish scholars – a schoolmaster, a physicist and a theologian – which I took on at the urging of Ragnhild Hatton, a Norwegian with a powerful personality, then a professor of history at the London School of Economics, who offered to edit it for next to nothing. The translation, by another academic, was also inexpensive. Every Dane under the age of fifty has studied the book in senior school and it has been through countless editions, but with my paltry promotional equipment it failed miserably to achieve its potential in English, although I sold the American rights to Addison-Wesley – which gave me an early taste of the harsh trading conditions imposed by large American corporations. I was then having a couple of books printed in Czechoslovakia, and my contact in the printing house was a sad-faced but attractive woman in her forties who had lived in England during the war. I shall never forget the 'old-fashioned' look on her face as she told me it had been decided that they could not produce this book for me because it reflected a social-democratic and not a socialist viewpoint.

In those early days as my firm was becoming known for its Nordic interests, Dreyers Forlag of Oslo offered me an illustrated book on the Viking ships. I took 250 copies and quickly sold them. Dreyers was a printing company till the Second World War, when Bartold Butenschön, son of one of Norway's richest bankers who lost much of his fortune at the time of the Wall Street crash in 1929, and a man of great breath of vision, bought it and added publishing to its activities. It was Bartold's son Hans with whom I negotiated this deal, and although we have not done business since, we have become friends and sometimes stay in eachother's houses. Here I get the better side of the bargain because he and his family live in an enchanting house on the edge of their considerable acreage of forest and farmland which, unlike their town mansion (now the seat of the Nobel Peace Prize committee), did not go under the hammer as the result of the crash. Originally a farmhouse, it was converted into a dacha and filled with fine objects early in the twentieth century. The whole has a faintly Gallic flavour and exerts a potent charm redolent of the setting for a Chekhov play. In his extended family Hans plays the part of paterfamilias with a light touch, which he also brings to his strongly idealistic attitude to life.

Two branches that have been important for the list grew from the Nordic trunk. Early in the 1970s I saw on the Kohlhammer stand at Frankfurt a book I could not resist: a history of the three Baltic republics during their twenty-odd years of independence between the world wars, by George von Rauch (1904-91), a Baltic baron who had become a professor at Kiel University and written a respected history of Russia, published in translation by Praeger. This more modest work, an obvious labour of love, had escaped the notice of anglophone publishers and I snapped it up and got it professionally translated for £400. I never met von Rauch, a gentleman of the old school, but we had a cordial correspondence on editorial matters, each of us writing in his own language. I am susceptible to kind words about me in authors' prefaces, and when he thanked the publishers 'for the great understanding they have brought to the subject of the work' I felt especially touched. (I naturally did not tell him how much my interest owed to devouring Stanley Gibbons's stamp catalogue when I was a child.) I pondered deeply on hearing that his two sons belonged to the Baader-Meinhof gang and one was killed in a shoot-out with police. The University of California Press took a good-sized edition (Grant Barnes was the editor concerned) and ten years later we collaborated on a reprint, although in the mean time I had written the book off as a failure in the home market and offloaded hundreds of copies free to the still surviving legations in London of the three legitimate pre-1940 Baltic governments. The book later revived and, realising it had achieved a permanent place in the canon, we reprinted it in paperback in 1994.

Soon after its first appearance in English I asked von Rauch if he could write on the post-1940 period. He declined but put me in contact with three young Baltic American scholars of a generation younger than himself. Since the three scholars represented all the three Baltic nationalities, it was assumed at first that the book would be vertically divided, but it soon appeared better to approach the subject horizontally, each writer homing in on certain themes; this became unavoidable when the Latvian dropped out. The book, by Romuald Misiunas and Rein Taagepera, came out in 1983, and was completely revised in 1993 to include the end of Soviet rule. California were our partners for both editions. Taagepera is now back in Estonia at Tartu University, and Misiunas is a Lithuanian ambassador. It was while the von Rauch book was being prepared that I sought the advice of David Kirby, already mentioned, which led to a long and fruitful association with him. Taagepera has now completed a unique work on which he has laboured for many years: about the Finno-Ugric peoples within Russia – esoteric, no doubt, but an ornament to any list of the C. Hurst type.

Michael Branch, who had translated the book on the Lapps that I never published and pointed me in the direction of John Screen and our first Finnish book, took a further hand in the development of the list when I asked him – as director of the School of Soviet and East European Studies – who might write a book for us on contemporary Greek politics. We struck lucky with his first suggestion, the historian Richard Clogg, who wrote a dense book of greater solidity and stature than I had expected. During its gestation period Richard invited me to the launch, in King's College London, of another book of his, and as we stood around with drinks I noticed a tall, dark man enter whose fastidious manners and Mephistophelean looks made me think of a Proust aristocrat. This was Stevan Pavlowitch, son and grandson of Yugoslav diplomats under the monarchy, and for many years dividing his time between British and French universities. We soon got talking, and not long afterwards we published his elegant and profound essay *Yugoslavia: The Improbable Survivor*, which despite its title continues to be read. He had promised another short book, simply called *Tito*, to Robert Maxwell's firm Macdonald, but after the Maxwell *dégringolade* it was offloaded and we gladly picked it up. We have published a continuing stream of Balkan books in the 1990s, and the presence of Pavlowitch's books on our list, and his availability as an ever-willing adviser, has been a boon.

Finn Gad and Greenland led my thoughts into the snowy wastes of the Poles, and one day I called on Harry King, the librarian at the Scott Polar Research Institute in Cambridge. He immediately pointed to an empty quarter in the reprint market: the Antarctic, which had attracted many more scientific expeditions than the Arctic in the golden age from the end of the 19th century to the Great War. Each of these had resulted in at least one book – generally set in large type and therefore running to hundreds of pages, with many pictures and sometimes a few folding maps and plans, and with the scientific material in appendixes following a relatively light-hearted narrative of derring-do. Except for the main works on the Scott and Shackleton expeditions, these books had been out of print for decades and were rarities. We started in 1974 with *Antarctic Adventure* by Sir Raymond Priestley, who as a young geologist had been with Scott's 'Northern Party' and thus did not take part in the dash to the Pole. The book was published by T. Fisher Unwin in 1914, and of the 2,000 copies printed 1,000, still unbound, were destroyed in a Zeppelin raid. I got the rights from Fisher Unwin's successor, Benn (later absorbed into A. & C. Black), Vivian Fuchs wrote a new foreword, and Priestley himself, who died as the book was going to press having written to me the day before to say he hoped to live long enough to see it in print, provided the texts of songs written by the Northern Party, including a parody of 'I heard you calling me'. Because Priestley had been Vice-Chancellor of Melbourne University, the university press there bought 500 copies; McClelland and Stewart of Toronto co-published it in North America. Next came Roald Amundsen's *The South Pole*, published by John Murray in 1912 and never reprinted, despite its historic and scientific importance, and there followed the accounts by Jean Charcot, Otto Nordenskiöld and C.E. Borchgrevink (all translated, like Amundsen, immediately after appearing in their original languages) of the expeditions they led; *The Voyage of the 'Scotia'* by its three leaders, and the account of the *Belgica* expedition by Frederick Cook, the ship's American doctor Each had a new foreword. The *Belgica* captain, Baron de Gerlache, did not publish his own account till 1941 when Belgium was under German occupation (I imagine he thought it might inspire his countrymen at that time), and his two sons gave me a precious copy of it; they were as glad to see Cook's story in print again as, for a different reason, was Cook's grand-daughter who devoted her life to trying to rehabilitate his reputation, which was ruined after he supposedly made a false claim about his role in the Peary expedition to the North Pole. Of all these books, Amundsen's has sold easily the best.

Original copies of all these seven works sold to enthusiasts for much more than the price of my reprints, so the market was at first receptive. But there came a point when Harry King could only suggest books that he admitted were not in the first league; Mawson's *The Home of the Blizzard* was an exception, but although the original 2-volume edition published by Heinemann in 1915 was rare and reprintable, the market was flooded by a shortened version first published by Hodder and Stoughton in 1930. So we left it at seven. This flurry of activity had two offspring. One was *The History of Modern Whaling* by Tonnessen and Johnsen (I could not persuade Tonnessen to change '*The*' to '*A*'), a book of some 800 pages but, even so, reduced from a 4-volume Norwegian original. Like Tore Gjelsvik, mentioned earlier, Tönnessen had published a book about his experience in the Norwegian resistance – in a small edition – and I resisted his urging to publish a translation. California co-published the *History*, and I was saved from losing money by a large order from the Secretariat of Whaling in Sandefjord; like the Antarctic books, it occasionally brings buffs trekking to our door to buy a copy. We had more fun from a book called *Antarctic Law and Politics*. I had long wanted to find or commission such a book, and Harry King put me on to the one man in the world he reckoned competent to do it: Professor A. at a university in Australia. The completed ms. arrived on my desk on the precise date specificed in the contract, something that has happened to me on only one other occasion, when I commissioned Professor A. to write a second volume: again the ms. arrived from Australia by post on the very day promised eighteen months before, and I began to wonder if Professor A. was in league with the Devil. (Unfortunately this time publication did not result.) The first volume came out just after the Falklands invasion, and at a huge meeting hastily convened in the Royal Geographical Society, the chairman Lord Shackleton held it up to show the audience.

The 'China line' began far more randomly than the one just described. At a Christmas party in Greenwich in 1969 I met a British diplomat, Theo Peters, who had been at the embassy in Peking during the Cultural Revolution. Staying as his house guest, he told me, was Douwe Fokkema, a professor of comparative literature at the University of Utrecht who, because of his knowledge of Chinese, had been on secondment to Peking as Dutch *chargé d'affaires* at the same period. He had published a book about this experience and translated it into English. I went to meet Fokkema the next day. The book needed only light editing, and I sold editions of it in North America and Australia. It inaugurated a slowly maturing China list, but it was also important for me as the means of getting to know Fokkema himself, a sophisticated, quizzical man whose company I always enjoy. While *Report from Peking* was in the press late in 1970 I dined at his home and met his wife and teenage son and daughter; they joked that he was an exception among sinologists in not having a Chinese wife. At this time my marriage to Christine was in its death throes, and I felt envious of their happy ménage.

The two immediate successors to this book were both literary – with China we have never stuck solely to politics and recent history. One of them was that rare thing, a doctoral dissertation that is short and beautifully written, and refutes the time-honoured health warning against handling 'untreated theses'. The author, David Pollard, was then at S.O.A.S. but long ago took up permanent residence in Hong Kong; and at the time of writing it looks as if before long he will have a new and much more exciting work for the firm to publish. Douwe Fokkema took to letting me know of interesting new books on China that were appearing in German or Russian. He recommended

Jürgen Domes, then professor of political science at the University of Berlin and head of the Contemporary China Study Centre there, and we met in Berlin, where this great lover of the good things of life treated me to the first of several splendid meals on German soil. But that visit will always be memorable as my first introduction to the greatest of divided cities. Everything about the Berlin Wall, its creation and its history, was mean and horrible, yet it had – for me, at any rate – a unique fascination. Standing near it, you felt as if you were near a destructive natural phenomenon like a volcano or an immensely powerful waterfall. When one was travelling on the Western-run *U-Bahn*, the train rattled through some darkened stations without stopping – they were in a part of the eastern zone that jutted into the western one. (The roar could be heard on the eastern side as you passed the barred station entrances.) Checkpoint Charlie gave a *frisson* too as you passed into a world so far removed from the glitzy Kurfürstendamm. The uniformed female guard with her peroxide hair inevitably made me think of Nazi concentration camps. Yet Eastern 'peace' propaganda had potency. In the controllers' hut at Checkpoint Charlie was displayed a quotation from Brecht about the three Punic wars. It was to the effect that the first had been bad; the second worse; and after the third not one stone in Carthage was left standing on another. The greatest paradox of the Wall could not be appreciated till it had gone: that, despite its ugliness in every sense and the lives it claimed, it harboured and preserved a way of life for the mass of people that was not unequivocally worse than what has replaced it.

Having started his career as a specialist in German politics, Domes switched to China and quickly learned Chinese. He then made his name internationally with a monumental history of the Kuomintang, published in German by De Gruyter but never in English, although it had been completely translated. At one point I was interested in publishing it, but the unique copies of two chapters were missing and never found (a terrible warning to publishers and authors). Domes just could not be bothered to get them re-translated. However, I published in turn two books of his analysing recent Chinese politics, Praeger co-publishing the first and the University of California Press the second, and somewhat later his biography of the disgraced Marshal Peng Te-huai, which he wrote in English and Stanford took in the United States. Domes is a man of prodigious intellectual power, able to combine a copious output with invariably high quality. Although we had eaten and drunk together several times, the formalities were preserved for more than twenty years until, meeting him in Newcastle-upon-Tyne where he had been invited over to attend a seminar, I waited till we had glasses of whisky in our hands before dinner, and then suggested that in future we should call eachother by our Christian names. He responded with delight, and we rose and shook hands.

The first of Domes's books that I published was dedicated to 'Dr Ladislao La Dany...as a modest expression of gratitude for the comprehensive analytical work with which he, more than anyone else, has promoted the international study of Chinese politics in the last twenty years' (this was in the early 1970s). Who was this exotically named person? Better known as Laszlo Ladany (properly Ladanyi), he was a Hungarian Jesuit priest (1914-90), who studied the violin at the Budapest conservatoire and law at the University – as he told me, 'The people coming through nowadays tend to be more narrowly focused'. He went to China in 1940 and thence in 1949 to Hong Kong, where he lived for the rest of his life. For nearly thirty years he wrote single-handed an analytical digest of the output of Chinese radio stations, especially the provincial ones; his room in the Jesuit house Ricci Hall contained high-powered receivers, manned at various times round the clock by relays of listeners. I began to woo him soon after learning from Domes that all his output had gone into his fortnightly publication *China News Analysis*, and the great summation in book form was yet to come. We met just once, at Ricci Hall in 1979. Like any extremely clever bachelor don, he seemed to derive a simple pleasure from the complex intellectual game he played. I could not imagine him saying mass or hearing a confession. Another Hungarian staying in the house, Father S., who struck me in the same way only more so, explained that some of the Society's priests were called to the 'scholarly apostolate'; that, and not pastoral work, was their gift to God and man. Father S., on a whim, phoned up the printer of *China News Analysis* – yet another Hungarian, Francis Braun – whose firm Libra Press still used hot-metal type and letterpress printing only. Braun was getting old but remained very active, and I had five books produced by him over the next few years. At this time I was still not reconciled to the abandonment of letterpress, and here was a chance of holding on to it for some of my output.

One day in the mid-1980s Ladany's long-awaited ms. arrived. Entitled *The Communist Party of China and Marxism: A Self-Portrait*, it was very long and he suggested publishing it in two volumes; I unhesitatingly rejected this suggestion and it came out as a single volume of 600 pages, although with its racy style it is far from heavy. Ladany had already signed a separate contract with the vastly rich Hoover Institution at Stanford (as I later discovered, he excused them from paying royalties on the first 2,000 copies, an act of charity he did not extend to me). I thought briefly that this would make the whole proposition rather unattractive for me, but I was able to persuade Hoover to let me produce the book and sell them 1,000 copies at a pleasantly high price, which of course did not include royalty. The book came out in 1988 and not long afterwards Ladany offered me another much shorter ms., an afterthought to the bigger work, about China's ancient legal tradition and Mao's contempt for it. I could not see it selling and turned it down. A week after Ladany died at the end of 1990, the *New York Review of Books* gave its first five pages to a review of his big book, then more than two years old, by Simon Leys (the alias of Pierre Ryckmans, the Belgian-Australian sinologist). Shamefacedly I thought again about publishing the second work. I had rejected when Ladany was alive. The Jesuits in Hong Kong sent me two short mss. he had left, partly overlapping in subject matter. Domes, with his wife and collaborator Marie-Luise Näth, edited them for publication and wrote an introduction. An American deal was struck with the University of Hawaii Press, and we have even had to reprint our own edition.

An occasional contributor to *China News Analysis* was the British Vietnamologist P.J. (Paddy) Honey, and in 1979 Ladany advised me to get a book from him. Vietnam, on which Praeger had published so much in the 1960s, was now a nearly dead subject that, in my opinion, needed reviving. I contacted him in London – he was a senior member of the teaching staff at S.O.A.S. – and found him a representative of a dying breed: a gentleman orientalist without a Ph.D., who had lighted upon his speciality through the vicissitudes of war. As a young naval officer in the Far East when the Japanese surrendered, he heard that volunteers were being sought to learn Vietnamese for liaison and intelligence work in that country, which in the immediate aftermath of the surrender was under British control. 'As a classicist', he told me, 'I thought I could cope with it.' He was due to retire shortly, after which he would work on the book. We signed a contract, and meanwhile he put me on to an unusual former Ph.D. student of his, a serving colonel in the U.S. Air Force, Peter Dunn, who had written an account of the little-known British occupation of Vietnam in 1945. He had revisionist axes to grind, and the follies of F.D. Roosevelt and Mountbatten, and the villainies of the French, were dwelt on; the undoubted heroes were the British force and its commander, General Gracey. Dunn was born British, but his father was killed in the war and his mother was re-married to an American. I had an enjoyable moment, staying at a guest-house in Washington run by Quaker pacifists, when Dunn came to call for me, wearing his spendid uniform with a lot of gleaming insignia and several rows of medal ribbons, accompanied by a brother officer similarly attired.

His book was called *The First Vietnam War*. Soon after Paddy Honey's retirement his wife suddenly fell ill and died and he did not have the heart to write his book. Our only other Vietnam book – the autobiography of a prominent North Vietnamese self-exile, Bui Tin – appeared in 1995.

I published other China books on Domes's say-so, in particular a life of Chairman Hua Kuo-feng, Mao's immediate successor, written in Chinese by a Hong Kong journalist Ting Wang and translated solely at my expense. It was a competent rather than an inspiring work, but its topicality won the day and I sold a record number of co-editions: in North America, Australia, Singapore and Pakistan. Then Hua was ousted from power just as the book was rolling off the press, and interest in this virtual nonentity vanished overnight. I was like the ring-master at a circus when the seal refuses to balance the ball on its nose. It was not my fault that Hua fell but it was embarrassing that I had made a profit from the book while my four partners were certain to make thumping losses.

The Fokkema connection itself blossomed when he and his collaborator Elrud Ibsch, a professor at the Free University of Amsterdam, completed, in the late 1970s, a book called *Theories of Literature in the Twentieth Century: Structuralism, Marxism, Aesthetics of Reception, Semiotics*. Hard though this densely textured work was for a mere literary punter like myself to follow, I recognised its expository value. Now, nearly twenty years later, it has been through three reprintings, the latest with a long new introduction although the central text has remained unchanged except for my manual correction of the few literals, and been translated into four European languages and twice into Chinese, once legally by the Chinese University Press in Hong Kong and some years later illegally in the People's Republic. Then, to my delight, a far more accessible book came along called *Modernist Conjectures: A Mainstream in European Literature, 1910-1940* which, notwithstanding its serious analytical purpose, provides a highly pleasurable introduction to some of the most fascinating modern writers. Several of these were ones I read in my youth when I seemed to have infinite time, like Thomas Mann, Proust, Gide and Italo Svevo. Others, like Musil, have only a cult following, while two Dutch writers, Menno ter Braak and Charles Edgar du Perron, are still known almost exclusively to those who can read Dutch; they turned the key on Modernism with tragic aptness by both committing suicide on the day, in May 1940, that the Dutch army surrendered to the Nazis. This work introduced me belatedly to what has become one of my favourite books, James Joyce's *Dubliners*, and to the suggestive ideas of Modernism itself. During the run-up to publication of the first of these books, Fokkema, whose harmonious domestic life I had so envied just a few years before, wrote me a letter saying that he was now divorced from his wife and would soon marry his academic collaborator Elrud.

I turned to Fokkema at around this time for help in finding an author to write on a subject which had mildly obsessed me since well before the start of the firm. In the spring of 1962 the Dutch were forced by a powerful mixture of pressures to hand over their last colonial possession in the East – West New Guinea – to Indonesia. The expansionist Indonesians were able to exploit the false logic that because they had been the natural inheritors of the huge archipelago of the East Indies after its liberation from the Japanese, they had an equally valid claim to the only other Dutch colony in the region, although its Papuan inhabitants were totally different from the Indonesians. Powerful Dutch business interests represented by the Bilderberg group were impatient to re-establish their old and profitable links with Indonesia, but Indonesia refused to oblige them while its spurious claim to New Guinea remained outstanding. In the view of the Bilderberg group the Dutch government's reluctance to give up this remaining vestige of empire was sentimental and unrealistic; in the government's view it reflected a sacred responsibility for the backward Papuans, towards whom the Indonesians would feel no comparable scruples but more probably a racist superiority. When Indonesia threatened war, the U.S. administration of J.F. Kennedy in turn exerted pressure, which the Dutch were unable to resist. And so the territory was handed over. I was upset by this ignoble transaction and now, some fifteen years after the die had been cast, I could publish a book about it. It was a gesture of sorts.

Fokkema put me in touch with Dr L., once a district officer in New Guinea and now an anthropology lecturer at a Dutch university. He was amazed that a British publisher was interested in the subject and, memorably, flew over to London on a day trip to meet me. He had continued to visit Indonesia and Papua over the years, and was happy to accept my commission. I learned from him that, true to what one would expect, the Indonesians had sent thousands of landless peasants into New Guinea to colonise the country, and the Papuans had been 'driven back into the bush'; and, further, that a referendum of the Papuan population in 1969, on which the U.N. had insisted in 1962, had been blatantly rigged, without any international protest being made.

I visited Dr L. at his home as an overnight guest on three successive years while driving back from the Frankfurt book fair. The first time we finalised the synopsis and signed the contract, the second time we finalised the ms., and the third time we launched the book. Dr L. was a short, cherubic middle-aged man whom one could easily have mistaken for an old-style village *cure*; indeed he was a devout Catholic (there were several Baroque crucifixes scattered round the house) and, as he engagingly admitted, he had even allowed himself to be mistaken for a priest on some of his more distant travels. He was married to a woman ten years older than himself, a former missionary whom he met in New Guinea. They had no children, but he often mentioned two young nieces to whom he was specially devoted. Dr and Mrs L. were charming company, though I felt vicarious guilt when at the end of dinner he would immediately leave the table, throw himself into an armchair and light up a cigar. He appeared not to notice as his wife and I spent the next few minutes attending to the dishes.

On my third visit the book had just been released in the Netherlands – my close friend Lucas Bunge, an independent medical publisher, agreed to hold stock for me and supply local booksellers – and Dr L. had a briefcase bulging with the news clippings (we never had a single review in Britain). That night we watched him in a recorded TV interview, and he said that the government was re-considering its aid to Indonesia on the strength of the book. The next day we drove in two cars to The Hague for a news conference and Dr L., who was leading the way, stopped his car a few blocks short of our destination to pick up a young girl – one of his nieces. A few minutes later we were all together in the ante-room of the meeting hall, and after introducing me to his niece, Dr L. took her out for some reason, leaving Mrs L. and me alone together. Suddenly, in a low voice full of passion, this normally matter-of-fact woman hissed: 'You can see – anyone can see – she's his daughter!' She added that her husband had fathered two daughters, after their marriage, by a married woman; but there was no time for her to say any more before the others came back.

So meeting Theo Peters at a party in Greenwich had been productive, leading me to Fokkema and much besides.

Two lines of descent started simultaneously with my first crop of books in 1968. A succession of proposals came in the wake of Mohamed Omer Beshir's book *The Southern Sudan: Background to Conflict*. First there were two anthropological monographs – Tatal Asad's on the Kababish, which sold the prodigious number of 1,500 to Praeger alone, and one on the Berti by Ladislav Holy. I came to know of Holy as the result of discovering, when visiting Prague for the first time in 1970, a collection of essays edited by him, published by the Oriental Institute and left to moulder in its storeroom.

I bought the entire lot of 200 or more and quickly sold them. Holy, who was working in Zambia, then approached me. Through Asad I published a *Festschrift* of anthropological essays for E.E. Evans-Pritchard edited by Ian Cunnison, Asad's professor at Hull, and Wendy James. All these three books comfortably sold out their modest runs.

Then came something rather different. A young Sudanist, Peter Woodward, asked me if I would be interested in publishing a ms. he had been editing, namely the memoirs of the last Briton to hold real power in the Sudan: Sir James Robertson, Civil Secretary (and thus head of the small, elite Sudan Political Service) from 1945 till 1953, when he handed over to a Sudanese successor two years before independence. He followed this plum job with another, as Governor-General of Nigeria in the run-up to independence there. He was a Scot of massive physical bulk and presence to match, known to his former colleagues as 'John Willie'. His ms. had been given the uninspiring title *Transition in Africa*, but it was a well-wrought tale, modest and unpompous, and interspersed with telling anecdotes, some genuinely funny. I could not resist it, and went to town with the design, using the royal 8vo format and putting on the cover an impressive shot of the author standing in the archway of the Khartoum Secretariat between two Sudanese sentries. The most authentic echo in the book of 'all our pomp of yesterday' was in the foreword by Margery Perham, friend and biographer of Lord Lugard. It is a splendid short essay on the problems of decolonisation, replete with nostalgia, and in her paragraph of tribute to Robertson's wife she does more than sing the praises of one woman: '. . . . I know well from my travels over many years how much, as a lesser queen beside the gubernatorial representative of the British crown, the wife could help to make or mar her husband's work in the highly sensitive setting of a British dependency. All who have known Lady Robertson in her public life will endorse my opinion that. . . she has been the ideal partner.'

Soon after this, a Nubian ms. beyond my earlier dreams suddenly came to me via Ian Cunnison – a record of the whole process of evacuating Nubia before it was flooded by the rising Nile waters above the Aswan Dam, by Hassan Dafalla, the Sudanese government officer hand-picked for the delicate task of supervising it. His tasks ranged from breaking the news to the people to placing a cash value on every date palm that would be lost, not to mention arranging archaeological expeditions to survey ancient remains soon to be inundated. Margery Perham would surely have concurred that his British training showed not only in his efficiency but in his humanity and acute observation of the people's psychological reactions. His health was broken by the experience and my only meeting with him was in a Harley Street clinic, where this most attractive individual was all too visibly fading away. He died aged fifty just before the book came out. I had not been able to persuade him to cut or even shorten the long introductory chapters which were no more than a re-hashed history and topographical description of Nubia; the best part occupied barely half the length. When the book was already printed but not yet shipped to the Sudan (I had sold 1,000 copies to the Khartoum University Press), I had a call from the Sudanese embassy in St James's asking me to go there to meet the author's elder brother, a professor of law. I was told it was a matter connected with Hassan's will. But all that the professor, who had none of Hassan's charm, wanted was to ask me to remove a photograph of General Abboud, the former Sudanese dictator, which appeared quite justifiably because, as head of state, he had come to Nubia to console the people in their tribulation. Its presence in the book, I was told, might be 'misunderstood'. I told the professor it was too late, and anyway Abboud had fallen from power long before I received the ms., so Hassan could easily have removed the picture himself, but had not done so. I heard no more about it.

I did one rather strange book consisting of writings on the Sudan in the mid-nineteenth century by the Verona Fathers ('Comboniani'), translated by Father Elia Toniolo and edited by the Catholic Sudan historian Richard Hill. It was printed cheaply by a press in Slough, also run by Italian priests, and we had the unexpected mishap of the first run having to be scrapped due to a major printer's error. I surprised myself by refusing in rather strong language when the priest in charge of the press asked me on the phone to pay the cost of reprinting.

Our last Sudan book till recently was Sir Gawain Bell's memoir, *Shadows on the Sand* – anyone knowing this former 'Sudan Political' and wartime member of the Arab Legion would realise how characteristic it was to choose a title from Flecker's *Hassan*. I had met Gawain Bell by chance in Cyprus during my army service in 1949 and not forgotten either his charm, which made him seem a different species from the senior officers in my regiment (he was the same age as our C.O.), or his unusual name. So when Anthony Kirk-Greene put us in touch it was rather like a reunion with an old friend. He was easy to work with and agreed, albeit sadly, to shorten the rather lengthy opening section about his early life; none the less, I felt it was important to keep more of it than would be usual in the memoirs of man of action, because they so nicely conveyed Gawain's old-time high-mindedness and romanticism; among his particular heroes were an uncle and namesake, a Winchester master killed in the Great War, and John Buchan, who had told tales round the fire to a group of boys at his prep school. He was a punctilious diarist and letter-writer and relied heavily on these sources to build up the account of his service life; thus, although the interest never palls and there are many nice touches, there is a slight feel of artificial contrivance. Because of his popularity with his erstwhile peers, a mailing of Sudan Political Service pensioners produced a great harvest of full-price sales.

There was a slightly unhappy aftermath. Early on, Gawain had talked about a second volume dealing with his career after the Sudan – notably as the last Governor of Northern Nigeria (then, as before, under Robertson). Once I casually asked him about it, and he surprised me extremely by saying that he had yielded to the urging of his friend Wilfrid Thesiger to give it to his agent. I told him right out that this would not work and that the agent had only agreed to take it on as a favour to Thesiger; also, that by doing this he had released me from the obligation I had felt up till then to publish it, even if (as proved to be the case) it was less interesting than *Shadows*. The gallant knight could not understand my attitude, and when the inevitable happened and he finally offered the ms. to me, he was offended by my rejection of it after a cursory look. 'Yours ever' changed to 'Yours sincerely', but a man like Gawain could not bear a grudge for long, and amiability returned. In the end the book was respectably published by Lester Crook.

Soon afterwards Kirk-Greene steered my way another old hand from the colonies who had written some rather good memoirs, Sir Rex Niven. He was ten years older than Gawain, fought in the Great War, and then spent all his service of forty years in the 'Holy North' of Nigeria – at the end under Bell as Governor. The two were not friends – Gawain viewed him with a kind of fear. Niven gave the impression, with his quick brain and sharp tongue, that he might have been a difficult man to work with, but that he would have been meticulously impartial and a friend to the Africans; I remembered the type from my army days. The ms. was loosely structured and needed a lot of work to reduce it to a reasonable length and shape, but this was more than balanced by his irrepressible interest in human nature and the vividness of his descriptions. The book got reviews in two national newspapers, and the reason was his penchant for risqué stories. Here, not out of prudery but to shield the book from ridicule, I had to edit heavily; it was amazing that Sir Rex was always passing a colleague's house in the dark just as the colleague's wife was undressing and clearly visible through the blinds stripped naked. I left in just one incident that I thought would give the authentic Niven flavour. An officer's wife on the station sought an interview with him, and as she stood before his desk and he was talking, she slowly lifted her skirt until it was above her head – she had nothing on underneath – and then let it drop back again into place, the conversation continuing meanwhile as if nothing had happened. He was known in the service as Sexy Rexy.

But, although I liked all these memoirs, my two favourites were from a relatively humble level on the colonial totem pole. One was *Forgotten Mandate* by E.K. Lumley (the title alludes to the status of Tanganyika after it ceased to be a German colony). Lumley, born in 1900, was Irish, with a strong brogue, and as senior scholar at Trinity College Dublin applied for a post in the British colonial service. From the early 1920s he served in remote districts of Tanganyika, never rising above the rank of district officer; a tendency to speak his mind inhibited his progress in the service. The book gives an impression of the god-like power vested in such men, who administered justice and organised basic infrastructural works in their districts to improve the people's lives; he describes the back-breaking labour, in which he shared, of building roads with little or no mechanical aid. For me the overwhelming impression (never deliberately created by the author) was the sheer hardness of his life, without let-up; the dedication it required from its votaries was like that of a serving brother in a monastery. '*Dare quam accipere*' might have been the motto of the rank and file of the Colonial Service (as well as of Guy's Hospital); good men as Robertson, Bell and Niven were, their books have a slightly different focus. Lumley retired from Africa due to ill-health, and with a broken marriage, in the 1940s, and had obscure jobs till his retirement. The book came to me through meeting, at a friend's party in Greenwich, the journalist Douglas Brown, who at the time was editing the ms. on Lumley's behalf. The other book of this ilk to which I warmed especially was *Private Secretary/Gold Coast (Female)* by Erica Powell, Kwame Nkrumah's devoted secretary throughout his years of power – before him she served the last British governor. Erica had retired wounded from an aborted plan for it to be published by a prominent firm, and I can say that I rescued as well as completely re-edited it. Ungallantly a S.O.A.S. historian, Richard Rathbone, panned it in a review, but he missed the point. Erica deliberately confined herself within the bounds set by her profession, but she emerges as warm, a shade ingenuous, a great sport and unshakably loyal, as well as a shrewd observer of humanity.

There was a quick accretion of books on South Africa, and among these was the best work of literature I have ever published. It came via the journalist Colin Legum, who had been associated with Pall Mall Press, and was the autobiography of a Sotho South African, Naboth Mokgatle, who was born in a tribal village 100 miles north-west of Pretoria and migrated to that city to escape the tyranny of his father and the tribe, but of course found there a far harder tyranny. At first he worked as a grocer's roundsman, pedalling to white people's houses and scoring numerous amatory successes with the maids, but gradually he turned to active trade unionism and finally to Communism. He managed, to his great surprise, to get a visa to visit a conference in Romania, but knew that the authorities were ensuring that he exiled himself. As he passed the final barrier to go to the waiting plane, an Afrikaner policeman who knew him said 'Good luck, Mokgatle'. He settled in London and worked till he retired as a warehouseman at the Peter Jones store in Sloane Square – the sort of job he might have had in South Africa. He and his Sierra Leonean wife (who, he once told me in her hearing, was not his intellectual equal but had been loyal to him) lived in a dingy Council flat in Lambeth. Reading the ms. was like going inside a painting by Grandma Moses; it was startlingly vivid. Because Mokgatle had never met famous people or taken part in great events, he could recount his life straight, without disturbance from the magnetic fields that those elements set up. I am not sufficiently detached to compare it to better-known writings, but I was prepared to back my judgement. The University of California Press (U.C.P.) made it the first, 'keynote' volume in a series of Southern African Studies, which still exists, and ordered 3,000 copies.

We gave a launch party at the Royal Commonwealth Society, and Naboth asked if he could bring a few of his colleagues from Peter Jones. I assumed he meant at most half a dozen, which at first he probably did, but he was too good-hearted to leave anyone out, and the room filled up with a large crowd of people, who sat demurely in little knots talking quietly. They reduced to a small minority the journalists and stalwarts of the South African exile community I had invited along to do Naboth honour. I wondered if his colleagues had realised before what a remarkable man they had in their midst. The book was given the derivative title *The Autobiography of an Unknown South African*, and the *Morning Star* review complained a little speciously that Naboth was not unknown. A year or so later a letter came from an educated person in Durban, with a deliberately illegible signature, telling us that the book was on the open shelves in the public library there and much appreciated – it was officially banned. Strangely, neither U.C.P. nor we ourselves sold the book in any notable quantity, but it was reprinted in South Africa by Ad Donker after the end of the old regime. Naboth wrote incessantly – novels and a volume of African 'great lives' – but nothing more after the autobiography was publishable. He was a man with just one real book inside him.

We supplied U.C.P. with three of the first four books in their Southern Africa series. Besides Mokgatle, there were Peter Walshe's *The Rise of the African Nationalist Movement in South Africa*, about the A.N.C. from its foundation till 1952, and a personal account of Chief Leabua Jonathan's coup in Lesotho in 1970 by B.M. Khaketla, one of his political opponents, simply called *Lesotho 1970*. Publishing Walshe was straightforward, and various bonuses followed. It has become a source book and, like Mokgatle, was reprinted in South Africa after long being banned. After several years Walshe produced another book, on the opposition Christian Institute in South Africa, and this opened up a new American connection with Orbis, the Maryknoll community's publishing house which, like Walshe himself, represented liberal, liberationist Catholicism. Through Walshe we published in 1973 a collection called *Black Theology: the South African Voice* – a re-titled, re-edited and augmented version of a book rushed out in Johannesburg in 1972 by the University Christian Movement and immediately banned. John Knox Press were our co-publishers in America, and we launched our edition at the Africa Centre – a speaker was Desmond Tutu, then working in London and unknown to the wider world. Steve Biko had written one of the essays in the book, and after his infamous death it was reprinted in *The Times*. Wanting Biko's family to receive the fee, I sent the money to Canon L. John Collins, founder and director of the International Defence and Aid Fund, thinking that he if anyone would know how this could be done. He replied that the money would be used for defending Africans on trial in South Africa, in other words to serve the purposes of I.D.A.F. – which had not been my intention.

I came upon the Khaketla book when, after visiting an oculist in Marylebone, I called unannounced on my confrere Rex Collings in the next street. Khaketla's ms. was positioned prominently on his desk, and I must have expressed some curiosity about it because with a· lordly wave of the hand he implied that it was not worthy of notice. I asked, after giving it a glance, if I could take it away – and so I came to publish it. Rex hardly missed another *Watership Down* (his famous bestseller that had been rejected by fourteen publishers), but it was a good bit of 'lived' contemporary African history told by an educated and honourable man. U.C.P took 1,000 copies, and although South Africa, where Chief Jonathan was seen as a reliable ally, was not a market, I sold quantities in Lesotho itself, where censorship was less efficient, to the long-established missionary book depots of Morija and Mazenod. It seemed a mild coincidence that at this very time my old Nanny, Gladys Cullen, was raising money through her Soroptimist branch for the school in Lesotho where Khaketla's wife was headmistress.

The last main line of descent with which I shall burden the reader started with a phone call one day in 1968 from Julian Rea at Longmans. I had not heard of him before, but as a publisher with African responsibilities he had somehow heard that there was a new worker in this field who presumably wanted to build up a list. In the early 1950s his ancient and distinguished firm published fiction – even something as rich and strange as John Rosenberg's *The Desperate Art* (above, p. 212) – and had a theology department where David Lutyens (above, p. 110) was briefly employed while working up to a mental collapse. It was now shedding all its 'general' publishing (which meant everything not designed for use in courses), and was in the difficult position of having to turn away manuscripts and projects it might have been interested in only a short time before. I went from my squalid office in James Street to the dignified Longman headquarters in Grosvenor Street, Mayfair, to see Julian and we repaired to a nearby pub.

The books he passed or referred to me in quick succession were a study of the Organisation of African Unity (O.A.U.) by Zdenek Cervenka, already in existence as a scruffy short-run publication of the Czech Academy of Sciences and thought to deserve re-issuing in the West; a ms. on Biafra by two young Ibo graduates, Arthur Nwankwo and Sam Ifejika (its critical stance towards the Nigerian Federal government obviously made it impossible for Longmans to publish it with their big presence in Lagos); the already translated second volume of the Marxist historian Jean Suret-Canale's three-volume history of French colonisation in Africa, covering 1900-45 – already translated at Longmans' expense; Humphrey Fisher's short study *Slavery and Muslim Society in Africa*, based on the great travelogue by the Prussian physician Gustav Nachtigal, *Sahara und Sudan*, published in 1879-89 and then still unpublished in English; and, slightly later than the others, *Aden under British Rule, 1839-1967* by R.J. Gavin.

Of this splendid harvest there is least to say about the Aden book, which was an officially commissioned history, admirably organised and disciplined; it has produced no offspring for the list – only, twenty years into its life, a small reprint. Bob Gavin, a lecturer at Zaria,

Northern Nigeria, when the book was published, became in a later incarnation Principal of Magee College, Londonderry, and I made use of our connection on one visit to Northern Ireland in the 1980s to explore that claustrophobic walled city, and spent a day with him driving around County Donegal over the border.

Zdenek Cervenka was still in Czechoslovakia when our negotiations began – the 'Prague Spring' was not yet over. He was among many bright people from Communist Europe who had found jobs in Nkrumah's Ghana, where he was in the Osagyefo's personal secretariat. The events of August 1968 brought him through London on his way to Uppsala, where he was offered a job and has stayed ever since. All was settled between us painlessly. A sufferer from logorrhoea, he gave forth words, written and spoken, in an ever-rolling stream, his English being fluent. While I edited his published text, he made additions to bring the O.A.U. story up to date; I asked for a piece on the Nigerian war, and he sent me 100 pages describing its genesis and progress in exhaustive detail – when I said that it should have been ten pages long at the most, he cheerfully scrapped it and gave me ten pages instead. The book sold well: Praeger took 2,000[*] and Nelson a paperback edition of the same number for West Africa, and I sold out my own edition. An early consequence was that I received a letter ordering a copy of the book from one of the great men of Africa: Nnamdi Azikiwe, who succeeded Sir James Robertson as Governor-General of Nigeria in 1960 and became President when the country became a republic soon afterwards. When the Eastern region, of which he was Premier from 1947 to 1960, called itself the independent state of Biafra, he at first joined the secessionists

---

[*] They only decided to do so as an afterthought, having at first rejected it. By the time they changed their minds, I had already wooed a small New York importer and made a verbal agreement to sell him 500 copies. He, quite naturally, reproached me bitterly for gazumping, but earning the author four times more royalty (let alone earning four times more revenue for my struggling firm) seemed to me an ethical imperative higher than any obligation to stand by an earlier 'gentleman's agreement' that had not been formalised. That the latter was likely to be the attitude of the traditional British gentleman-publisher I had learned from an actual case. When still working for Praeger I called on Marion Kister, who with her husband – they were refugees from Hitler's Europe – founded and ran a small trade publishing house in New York. She told me that the number she usually imported of a book she liked was 500, and added that recently an eminent British publisher had agreed to sell her that quantity of one of his books, and stuck to the bargain even when another publisher later made him a much more attractive offer for it. There were still a few gentlemen around in British publishing, she said. In a flash of inspiration I asked if she was referring to Faber, and she admitted that she was, and to Peter du Sautoy in particular. (Would a true gentleman, I now wonder, have told her about the bigger offer?) I have continued to believe that this particular kind of 'gentlemanly' conduct, however admirable from the point of view of maintaining good relations between publishers (and these are necessary for the benefit of authors), is ultimately indefensible.

but later jumped ship while on a mission to London and lay low there until the Federal army's victory ended the war early in 1970. When I sent him his copy of Cervenka, I asked if he was thinking of writing anything himself. He immediately replied that he wanted to write a history of the war and would be happy to talk with me about it. So I went to see him in his flat on the North Circular Road, the first of many meetings with that extraordinarily attractive man. It was obvious that he could not begin working seriously on the book until the war was over, and that therefore this was a long-term project, but I was eager to sign him up, and even felt encouraged when he told me that he was writing some bits already. The advance was £1,000, with half payable on signature. At our first meeting, when it seemed that we had concluded our business, he suddenly said 'I have another manuscript that I can let you have', and there it was lying on a shelf; clearly it had been in existence for some time. This was his autobiography, from birth to becoming Premier of the Eastern region in 1947: *My Odyssey*. Although it was long and unwieldy in its structure, it deserved publication in full; not only did it provide documentation of an important career, but he also had a journalist's instinct for a good story. The description of his years in the United States (1925-33) studying and then teaching at Black universities, and above all of his return home to a hero's welcome – in his years away, he had come to be seen clearly as a future national leader – is a classic tale of self-improvement and of an awakening sensibility. Julian Rea told me it had been promised to Longman, but I had used no persuasion on Zik, and ungratefully I let my pleasure at this acquisition overcome scruple. Again I sold the book to Praeger in America and Nelson in West Africa – this time they took 5,000 copies. The book has been reprinted in Nigeria by a firm run by a European without authorisation from us.

But to return to the war history, Zik moved after the fall of Biafra into a flat in Belgravia, and worked steadily on. When I visited him, I uneasily noticed neat piles of typed foolscap sheets mounting ever higher. Our conversations would end with his bringing out a bottle of Bristol Cream and regaling me with table talk on some of his former opposite numbers in other West African states. If only he could have written as he talked. . . . I admired the meticulous organisation that went into assembling 'Military Revolution in Nigeria', but it emerged leaden and lifeless, a collage of communiqués and official documents quoted *in extenso* with almost no commentary, and nothing at all relating to Zik himself. It was politically understandable that he wanted to skate round his personal role, but how would the public react if such a vital element were missing? Far more serious was the matter of length. The contract had specified 130,000 words, but here we had 2,000 pages of about 500 words each – a million words. One could forget any thought of rescuing the project with vigorous editing. Zik had stayed on in London only to finish the ms. and was already back home when I went to pick it up. So we were never able to discuss the problem of what might be done face to face. There was talk for a time of his arranging a co-publication in Nigeria, perhaps financed by himself, but it came to nothing. Interest in America was nil. So I availed myself of my right under the contract to turn the work down. A pained letter came back, in which he said that he was about to reach man's allotted span of three score years and ten (he was to live another twenty-one years) and had learned to regard the evils of this world with equanimity; he stoically accepted that I must have been nobbled by his enemies. His lawyer wrote demanding that I pay the balance (50%) of the stipulated advance. I replied that I was not demanding repayment of the first 50%, as I was entitled to do, and that was how it was left. I deposited the ms. with Donald Simpson, librarian at the Royal Commonwealth Society.

The book by Nwankwo and Ifejika, for which I obtained a signed contract when they still lived in the shrinking Biafran redoubt, was written in cool, unemotional language, and made its case almost by understatement. I tacked on to the end a piece of reportage by Nwankwo alone on Biafra at war, which he had wanted published separately. I drew the cover artwork, showing the Biafran emblem of a flaming rising sun, myself. At first I could not sell an American edition, and did not bother much because a Biafran lobbying organisation in Washington ordered 1,000 copies; besides, time was short and I anticipated a sufficient sale in the home market. However, Praeger, having at first turned it down, decided to take it at the thirteenth hour so that I had to rush a reprint through specially for them. Their 2,000 copies were delivered to the docks more or less on the day Biafra surrendered, and George Aldor (by then in sole charge) cabled me to halt the shipment. Of course I did not do so. It was fortunate that the Biafran lobbying organisation had paid half of the agreed purchase money up front, because by the time the balance was due it had ceased to exist.

Arthur and Sam ('the boys', as Zik called them) came to London while Biafra was still fighting, to try and further its cause. These serious young men (Arthur the more extrovert of the two), seemingly ennobled by their people's suffering which they had shared, made a strong impression in London. They looked to me to open doors for them, and I made a start by introducing them to Richard Hall, journalist and one-time Pall Mall author, and David Steel, M.P., who had recently accepted a commission from me to write a book about the Commonwealth Immigrants Act of 1968. Dick Hall took advantage of my call to introduce me to a seasoned Ibo trade unionist, Wogu Ananaba, who had written a history of the Nigerian trade union movement, was looking for a publisher, and happened to be in Dick's office at the time I phoned. It was vigorously written, like Khaketla's Lesotho ms., and the author gave me two vivid 'primitive' ink drawings of the miners' strike in 1949, when several strikers were shot by police, to use as illustrations. The book, co-published in America by Max Holmes's Africana Publishing House (then run by Hans Zell) and in Nigeria by Ethiope (then run by the French scholar Abiola Irele), came to be regarded as a minor classic, and sold out. Ananaba was an official of the I.C.F.T.U. (International Commission of Free Trade Unions), based in Brussels, which during the Cold War was ranged against the W.F.T.U. (World Federation of Trade Unions), based in Bucharest. We got on well and when he died in his fifties, an element of farce supervened because it was impossible to establish for several years who were his legal heirs and thus entitled to his royalties: his wife or his children by a previous marriage, both of whom claimed them.

When 'the boys' returned to Nigeria, they were encouraged by some Ibo notables to start a publishing house in Enugu as a step towards re-establishing self-esteem in the defeated East. The result was the eponymous Nwamife. One of their backers was a brilliant academic constitutional lawyer, B.O. (Ben) Nwabueze, who spent several years after the war away from Nigeria at the University of Zambia. He had written, with his habitual lucidity and erudition, a work called *Constitutionalism in the Emergent States*. I saw the ms. and was interested in it but he had apparently signed a contract with a branch of a large and famous American publishing house, of which he sent me a copy. I was able to tell him that in fact his contract was with a small new independent firm set up by former editor of that famous publishing house, whose signature on it had confused him. He felt that he had been deliberately led up the garden path, and my reward for alerting him was to publish the ms., its two sequels in a trilogy, and two subsequent works. Nwamife imported editions of all these books except the final one, *A Constitutional History of Nigeria*, which was bought by Longman. I nearly lost my shirt on an order for large quantities of four of Ben's books that I printed specially and shipped to Nwamife just as Nigeria's oil-related exchange crisis was erupting in the early 1980s. By my standards the sums involved were large, and it was surely only through

Ben's influence* that they were eventually paid. The firm of Nwamife did not benefit from Arthur Nwankwo's burgeoning entrepreneurial skill for long. He quit and set up Fourth Dimension Publishing House, which has done well while Nwamife languished. Also, he and Sam Ifejika had been united in adversity, but their differences of character soon caused them to part. The quiet, sensitive Sam emigrated to Canada, took a doctorate on the role of the press in the Biafran war, and became a race relations officer in the Ontario state government. It was nice being greeted one year at Frankfurt by a stout and prosperous-looking Arthur, and told that he would always remember that he had got his first taste of publicity from me.

Jean Suret-Canale's big history of the French colonial empire in Africa had been contracted by Longman and the translation completed – by an Englishwoman living in Prague. The rights, obtained from Editions Sociales in Paris, were assigned to me, and all I had to do was pay the second half of the very modest translation fee. Praeger's former Africa editor, Lou Barron, who with two colleagues Gilman Park and Stella Heiden had taken over control of Universe Books in New York, imported 1,500 copies, and I later sold several hundred unbound sheets to Heinemann for sale in Africa. Neither of them did well with it, but for once I sold my own copies reasonably well and had to stock up by repurchasing copies from Universe. About 1980 Christopher Fyfe, the Edinburgh-based historian of West Africa, showed me a book of Suret-Canale's historical essays and suggested I should publish a translation. Suret, an excellent scholar, was an orthodox Marxist and as a Briton I complacently enjoyed this analysis being applied to French colonialism. I therefore felt inclined to do it but knew that the firm could not afford to finance a translation; then I suddenly had the idea of translating it myself. When Rachel, my wife, heard of this plan she rightly said that I could not run my business and chase wild geese at the same time. I instantly conceived the idea of a long summer trip in Sri Lanka (it was 1981) in which business could be commingled; while she spent the mornings on the beach, I, who love the heat but easily get sunburned, would work indoors on the translation. I found the chapters about anti-colonial currents in metropolitan France under the Third Republic especially fascinating. By this formula I translated the book, although I did not finish editing it and obtaining the author's comments for several more years. The American edition was published

---

* On returning to Nigeria from Zambia he accepted, in quick succession, two chairs of law before quitting academic life and becoming a banker. In the Babangida administration he was for a time Minister of Education.

by Kassahun Checole's Africa World Press in the first of a succession of deals. Other matters concerning that trip to Sri Lanka are related later.

Czechoslovakia – Nachtigal

In 1970 I left Frankfurt during the book fair week-end by train for Nuremberg, and from there, having looked at what is left of the old city and stood on the podium from which Hitler addressed the party rallies (there was no one in sight), went on to Prague. I almost get a fainting feeling when I experience the endless beauties of that city and reflect that if Britain and France had gone to war with Hitler over the Sudetenland in 1938, as so many right-thinking people thought we should, it would have been flattened. (This involuntary reaction is doubtless one that should be suppressed for the sake of historical perspective.)

My connections with Zdenek Cervenka, Till Gottheiner (the Suret-Canale translator) and the Sudanists at Hull University gave this visit a special justification, but I also realised at this time that I could not consider myself a citizen of the world if I did not very soon visit Communist Europe. I spent the first night in Prague at a spiritless 'botel' on the river but the next morning I called, without a previous appointment, at the Oriental and African department at Charles University and the scene brightened. I was received by the head of the department, the Sudanist Karel Petracek, who knew some of the same people as I did back home and made me realise at once that I had stepped into a transnational community. He was the only person I have ever met who suffered from acromegaly, the disorder of the pituitary gland that makes the facial features and hands grotesquely enlarged, but with this he was also gentle and courteous, which made him seem like the kind giant in a fairy tale. He called in younger colleagues – a rising Arabist, Lubos Kropacek, and Ladislav Venys, who had published a book on Mau Mau in an obscure departmental series. Kropacek was, stated crudely, serious and shy, while Venys was a lively extravert but serious too. Both were in their early thirties. Venys immediately told me that his wife was away and I could therefore stay in his apartment, which I did – not only this time but again a year later when his wife was at home. I was the only anglophone publisher any of them could remember visiting their department, and they all offered me their work in progress:

with Petracek and Venys it was edited collections, and Kropacek was planning a history of the Sultanate of Darfur. They were completely unaware of the restrictions placed by Dilia, the state agency for authors' rights, on contracts between Czechoslovak authors and foreign publishers. Without exception they were Dubcekites and regarded the current Husak regime with contempt tinged with fatalism, though in the case of Venys one felt it was something more; he and his wife had been at the end of a two-year study tour in the United States in August 1968 and their hosts implored them to stay, but he felt it necessary to return home. The older Petracek did not discuss politics but the others had no inhibitions and I wondered at their boldness as we sat in public eating-places. Two other members of their circle, the young Soviet-trained* anthropologist Peter Skalnik, whom I later got to know even better, and Vladimir Klima, a specialist in contemporary African literature at the Oriental Institute (housed in a lovely Baroque ex-convent in the old town), were the same. They expected their department to be purged soon, but until it was they were going to take things in a relaxed fashion. Their devil-may-care behaviour in public came back to me forcibly some years later when I was sitting in the Russian Nikolai restaurant in free Helsinki with a Finnish friend. I asked him quietly if he had not though it rather *infra dig* when President Kekkonen went to Moscow along with all the satellite leaders to greet Brezhnev on his seventieth birthday. He leaned forward and looked over his shoulder before whispering 'Yes, some of us thought so too.'

Ladislav Venys took me to visit his uncle Bohumil Janda (born 1900), whose creation, Sphinx, had dominated the publishing scene in Czechoslovakia between the wars, acquiring the rights to many of Europe's leading writers and forming a strong link, unsurprisngly, with the most distinguished and international in outlook of the British publishers at that time, Stanley Unwin. Unwin had acted as his banker

---

* Peter told me a 'Soviet' joke, which I have never heard anywhere else and venture to share with the reader. Two friends met in the street, and one, noticing that the other looked depressed, asked him what was the matter. The second man replied that he had just been expelled from the local Party committee. 'For heaven's sake, why?' asked the first man. The second explained. 'Well, it's been coming for a long time. The first thing happened just after Stalin died. The Party secretary told us proudly how much money had been spent on Stalin's funeral, and I said: "They could have buried the whole Central Committee for that." Then there was the time when Brezhnev replaced Khrushchev as General Secretary. We had a photograph of each of them on the wall in the Party office, and our secretary just said to me "Get rid of that idiot", and I asked: "Which idiot?" And just last week I met our secretary in the street, just as I'm meeting you now, and he asked me: "Why didn't you come to the last Party meeting?" I said to him: "If I had known it was going to be the last Party meeting, I would have come with my whole family." '

in bad times, and bought 1,000 copies of his glorious final production, a history of Slovakia illustrated with multi-coloured woodcuts, in 1948; after that, the Communists closed down Sphinx and sent him to work in the forests as a wood-cutter for four years, only allowing him back as a humble proof reader in the Publishing House of the Academy of Sciences before he retired. When I remarked that the inter-war period must have been like Arcadia compared to the three periods of foreign domination he had known, he said I was mistaken: the Habsburg days were far better. Once, a small figure wearing a beret, he turned up at my stand in Frankfurt and asked if I would go with him to the famous Bertelsmann party that evening to which he had been personally invited by Reinhard Mohn. I agreed – foolishly because Mohn, who looked sour enough as he received Janda, only needed to look at me to see I was in the wrong place. As we shook hands I felt that unmistakable little shove which says 'Beat it'. I stayed long enough to savour the spectacle of him standing at one end of the room flanked by his henchmen – almost uniformly grey and overweight while he looked lean and mean.

Nothing could hide the beauty of Prague, but it all had the run-down air of Western Europe just after the war. However, it felt different: hopelessness and cynicism reigned – Ladislav Venys, alone of my friends, seemed relatively immune to it. A depressing phenomenon was that none of the younger married people I talked with had more than one child; maternity leave was brief and the strain of raising a larger family was too much. For a visitor Budapest, where I also went, was less gloomy; it could hardly be otherwise when gypsy bands played in many restaurants. The Publishing House of the Academy of Sciences interested me in a plan to translate for the first time the 19th-century travelogue of Laszlo Magyar, who went native in central Africa and married the daughter of a local king – what little of it had escaped accidental burning. But nothing came of it, and later Judith Listowel published a book partly based on his writings. (Lubos Kropacek had a similar plan for the journal of a Czech traveller, Antonin Stecker, but he soon had to leave the university and.to this day it remains unrealised – I reminded him of it in 1991.) But I did co-publish one book with the Hungarians on Latin American economic development by Bela Kadar, then on the staff of a research institute but, after the fall of Communism, Minister of Economic Development in the Hungarian government. On each of my three visits to Budapest in the Communist period he took me to a first-class privately-owned restaurant. I did co-publish one other book as the result of this journey: a work on a Chinese writer by Anna Doleszalova that was just being published by the

Slovak Academy of Sciences in Bratislava, where I met her. It was highly specialised and therefore I only imported 500, to be shared equally with Paragon, an oriental specialist in New York, but the abysmal quality of the production made it something I hardly dared to offer for sale. The composition had been done on an office typewriter, and the paper was yellowish in some sections and dead white in others. Yet they had bound this monstrosity in hard covers.

I left Prague after my third visit, in 1972, feeling that the lights that had still shone with fitful brightness in 1970, in the afterglow of 1968, had gone out and that I would not be back for some time. The new director of the Oriental Institute, a creepy fellow-travelling academic, referred shamelessly to the policy that Moscow required him to follow. I took the train to Stuttgart – the journey lasted all day and my sole companion in the compartment was a girl, beautiful in her youth and extreme nubility, and with a mane of chestnut-coloured hair. She spoke only Greek and Czech – Greek because her parents had been in the mass exodus of Communists from Greece to Eastern bloc countries at the end of the civil war in 1949. She knew no more than a few words of English and German, and I had only a small vocabulary of ancient Greek, yet somehow we managed to converse. She was going to Stuttgart to be married to a Greek boy she had grown up with, and he worked in a garage. She would not be working, and I implied by mime – and she agreed – that she would soon be cooking his meals and ironing his clothes. When, exhausted by our conversation, she fell asleep, I admired her sadly, desperately wanting to touch her marvellous hair, and thought of her impending fate. I wished her good luck and made myself scarce before the train pulled into the station at Stuttgart – thinking it would not be a good idea if her swain saw her, at this moment, exchanging smiles with a strange male – but I could not resist peeping out to witness the encounter. There they were on the platform, two young Greeks – a good-looking one, all smiles, stood out in front, while an ill-favoured one hung back. It was the ill-favoured one who turned out to be her fiance.

When I published two books, by Czechs, that came my way in the early 1980s on the two tragic turning-points in Czechoslovakia's more recent history, I felt, aside from the obvious commercial expectations, that in a small way it was a repayment to my Czech friends for their great warmth to me ten years before, when everything around them must have seemed unrelievedly grim. The first one, which I imported from a tiny publisher in New York, Richard Karz, who had had it translated at great expense, was on the Prague spring and its consequences: *Night Frost in Prague*, by Zdenek Mlynar, one of Dubcek's ministers who had moved to Munich. The second, which I spotted by chance at Frankfurt in some dry-as-dust German historical series, was for me equally important although it was not so dramatic a story or so well written. It was piquantly called *The Short March*, and was about the three years between 1945 and 1948 when the Communists planned and finally executed their take-over. It is a beastly story. The author, Karel Kaplan, had been a C.P. official, and his account was based on documentation that he managed to abduct when he moved to the West. Very nobly my eldest American nephew Jolyon Naegele, who from about the age of ten studied every aspect of Czechoslovakia, collected its stamps (and those of no other country) and eventually learned the language at London University, translated the book for me, the *quid pro quo* being a negligible share of the royalty. He was working at the time in Vienna as Voice of America correspondent for Eastern Europe, and did the work anonymously, not wanting – for their sake or his – to endanger the excellent sources for his professional work inside Czechoslovakia. He almost made a silk purse out of a sow's ear. *Night Frost* sold well, and was made into a TV feature. I was invited to a private viewing, and at the end leaped to my feet, faced Mlynar who was sitting next to me, and clapped. Nobody else applauded, and I realised too late that this was not the thing to do in those blasé circles. *The Short March* alas did not sell.

My crop of introductions from Julian Rea ended with Humphrey Fisher – after that, I occasionally asked Julian if he had anything more for me, but the news that Longman were no longer doing 'general' books had quickly reached potential authors, and that was it. For what I had received I was duly thankful, and have always thought of Julian as a benefactor of the firm – almost founder's kin. Humphrey came to see me in James Street, and both of us remember this first meeting. He, seeing me sitting at a large table covered with disorderly piles of paper (as my office desk is today)*, thought this a typical publishing environment – a reaction perhaps typical of Humphrey's open, uncomplicated, sanguine view of life. He is very tall, certainly not handsome, but with a look of benevolence, boyish good humour, and above all *gravitas*. He speaks in measured tones with a half-American accent, the result of being at an American school when his father was an official in Washington during the war, and later a student at Harvard. I was not surprised to learn that he is a Quaker.

* Perhaps a characteristic of men of action: the disorder of Lord Kitchener's desk is described in Lord Edward Cecil's *Leisure of an Egyptian Official.*

Humphrey was then a lecturer (later promoted to Reader) in African history at S.O.A.S., specialising in the Islamic civilisation of West and Saharan Africa. From this he developed a natural interest in Gustav Nachtigal and his great, hitherto untranslated work *Sahara und Sudan*, already alluded to. With the help of his father, a retired economist, and his German wife, he was moving ahead with preparing an English edition, including full scholarly apparatus of introduction, notes, index etc. The original has three volumes, but for the English he planned four; and when I first met him he was at work on the fourth – the first, second and third to follow. But as an earnest of the work in progress, which would inevitably take a long time, he had produced a short manuscript called *Slavery and Muslim Society in Africa*, drawing heavily on the great avatar. This had been diverted from Longman to me, and I was only too glad to take it.

Doubleday already knew about the work. In the Africa euphoria of the 1960s, it had started an African series, managed by Chivuzo (Chi) Ude, one of the more fortunate members of the Biafran intellectual diaspora. Dealing with very large firms, a small publisher is often struck by meanness, not to say pettiness, over the conditions offered on co-publications. Doubleday were prepared to take this book but offered me a derisory offset fee, Chi making this worse by adding the typical big-company bullshit that this was in my interest – I didn't see how. Astonishingly Doubleday never offset the book at all but re-set it – whether to conform to their stylistic preferences or to give work to their company printing house I did not discover.

When Humphrey handed over the modest-sized typescript, he asked: 'Would you be interested in Nachtigal?' I answered that I would be, and so the four volumes were published, each of 500 royal 8vo pages or more, with the original line illustrations, folding maps, and, in the first volume (1972) and the last (1989), a portrait of Nachtigal. I feel various emotions when thinking about the Nachtigal enterprise. It was an ambitious project for a small publisher, and I stuck with it to the end. Therefore I can pat myself on the back. My co-publishers were not so steadfast. The University of California Press took 800 copies of the 1972 volume (Vol. IV) but when I offered them Vol. I in 1975, the editor I had dealt with before, an Englishman called Geoffrey Ashton, turned it down, saying they had only sold 500 of Vol. IV, which was not enough. I asked if they would take an edition of 500 instead, which seemed to me a reasonable proposal, but he was adamant, and my thoughts when I later heard that Geoffrey Ashton had done away with himself by walking into the sea were tinged with speculation that the ghost of Nachtigal might have had something to do with it. Barnes and

Noble eventually took 500 of Vol. I, but they declined Vol. II, of which I had to content myself with a sale of 100 copies to Holmes and Meier. Humanities Press, by then run by Simon Silverman's successor Keith Ashfield, took 250 copies of Vol. III. I still believe that U.C.P. proved themselves unworthy of their responsibilities to scholarship by taking one volume and then backing out. The book went through similar vicissitudes over printing, for which I alone was responsible. All was plain sailing with the 1972 and 1975 volumes, which were set in Monotype Baskerville, but by 1980 I had to opt for the dire alternative of using Linotype setting, which was all I could obtain at a price that was not prohibiive. But by the time Vol. III came along I was in touch with Libra Press in Hong Kong, who matched it perfectly with the first two volumes. But I made one lapse with the 1972 volume; when I showed it to Mr Coles at Kegan Paul, he took off the jacket and pointed out that I had not blocked the volume number on the spine. It reproaches me to this day, as does the fact that what should be a perfectly matching set does not completely match. Humphrey Fisher is the only one of my firm's authors whose mss. did not need to be copy-edited or his proofs double-checked. No publisher should ever seek to place these heavy responsibilities on an author alone, but in this unique instance there was no risk. Humphrey invited me and two distinguished historians of Africa, Roland Oliver and Antony Atmore, to a celebration dinner for *Slavery and Muslim Society* at his parents' house in Oxfordshire, and there was another dinner, this time in London but again with his parents present, for Vol. IV of Nachtigal. The way he made it all a family affair was delightful.

I should finally record that, while I published Vol. IV in 1972 without a penny of subsidy, we received for the subsequent ones increasingly generous amounts from German funds – and two smaller donations from British ones. Humphrey himself fixed all this up. He once arranged a meeting at S.O.A.S. of Africanists to discuss with me what other great works not in English, comparable to Nachtigal, might also be translated and edited.* Nothing came of this but it was a tantalising idea – more suitable for one of the larger and richer American university presses.

Volume IV of Nachtigal carried on its title-page the name of R.S. (Sean) O'Fahey, who had given Humphrey editorial assistance,

---

* A serious contender to be the most tempting of these must be Carlo Conti Rossini's *Storia d'Etiopia*, of which the '*prima parte*' was published in 1928. On a visit to Naples in 1984, I was told by the Ethiopianist Alessandro Triulzi that the '*seconda parte*' was completed, but remains unpublished due to some disagreement among Conti Rossini's heirs. This too is not without its tempting aspects.

and a few years later, by then a professor at the University of Bergen, he offered me a history of Dar Fur in the Western Sudan. It was at first hard for me, having courted the author of another book in the making on the Dar Fur sultanate, Lubos Kropacek, to accept another and thereby effectively jettison Kropacek; but with the passing of the years I had to realise that nothing was likely to come from that source, and O'Fahey's book came out in 1979. In 1990 we published his next book, on a Moroccan holy-man of the early 19th century and in 1992, as a direct result of his introducing to us Gabriel Warburg, professor at the University of Haifa, the latter's study of modern Sudanese historiography, *Historical Discord in the Nile Valley*. This branch of the tree is likely to bear further fruit.

I caught up with Kropacek in Prague in 1991, when I was there for Jolyon Naegele's wedding. He was finally back at the University, after being fired in 1974 for his ideological lukewarmness. During this long interval in his academic career, he had not been long without work. Czechoslovakia was a leading supplier of arms to the 'socialist' Arab regimes – Libya, Syria and Iraq – and an Arabic interpreter was needed for the top-level meetings. Kropacek was the obvious choice. I said over dinner with him that a best-seller could be written by someone with such experiences as his to relate, but in a touching echo of his fellow-countryman, the soldier Schweik, he said that 'those people' (Husak and company) had treated him well, and he could not do the dirty on them now they had fallen on evil days.

Bridge of Sighs

Not having employed anyone who could, even remotely, be described as a secretary since the mid-1980s (of course I have sometimes felt the need for one), it amazes me to think that, at the time when I parted company with Sven Nathan early in 1968, it seemed essential to engage one. Parkinson's Law was at work. Part of the job, admittedly, was to carry on with the non-stockholding retailing of expensive academic tomes in English published on the continent, but I even felt it behoved me to get my letters typed, although I had learned to type quickly, albeit in a rather hit-and-miss fashion, at about the age of ten when my sister Pam was taking a secretarial course and bought a typewriter to practise on.

If I had spent every day alone in that flyblown little room in

James Street, I might, in fits and starts, have worked more productively, but attacks of gloom might also have been worse. Anyway, I advertised in the *Bookseller* for someone intelligent, and the first answer came from Margaret Flack, then working for John Bush at Gollancz almost in the next street, whose eye had been caught by that word. She had been brought up, and had her married home, in Bromley, and her father was a potato merchant in the City who had refused to let her go to university. Her experience and secretarial skills were far beyond my deserts, and although working cooped up in that miserable place with one other person and no escape cannot have been very pleasant after Gollancz, she gave me continuous support and never succumbed to moods; on the contrary, her bright, upbeat personality always made me feel good. My first books had just appeared when she arrived and it was an exhilarating time. But soon after joining me she discovered she was pregnant, and left the next spring. In her place came Margaret Stephenson, a doctor's daughter from Sunderland, who had just left Oxford Polytechnic after doing two of the three years of the publishing course there. She copy-edited mss. and read proofs, and designed one jacket – for Ananaba's book on Nigerian trade unions. She had a gamin face and razor-cut blond hair, and wore a mini-skirt and, in cold weather, a maxi overcoat that nearly touched the ground. I liked her but knew she would not be able to stand the solitude and monotony for long. Her departure coincided with a major move.

During 1969 a particularly awful domestic happening – Christine took an overdose – made me so down-hearted that for a time I could see no point in carrying on the business. I talked with Frank Cass, thinking that with our different but somewhat complementary characteristics we might have gone into some sort of partnership. He would have been the boss, but our differences would probably have become uppermost, and I would soon have felt frustrated. Just at this time I met a man at a party in Highgate – I knew who he was as soon as we were introduced, because not only was he the son of an eminent banker but his sister had been a friend of mine at Oxford. When I told him what I was contemplating he at once pleaded passionately with me not to give up; and as I left to go home and looked back into the room where all the guests were talking, his eyes met mine from the other side and he vigorously shook his head. I have never met him again, but if I ever do there will be much to thank him for.

A prospect of fresh fields opened up when I found out that a little mews building was for sale in a yard off Royal Hill, Greenwich, not a quarter of a mile from where I lived. It belonged to a small family furnishing business in the Greenwich High Road, Newing's, and had been used till then as a workshop and a garage. I bought it for £4,000 and had the garage turned into a warehouse and the two-storeyed part into an office. I was going to be my own distributor.

Still a sole trader, I had no serious need of an accountant, but even before casting loose from Pall Mall I thought I should talk with one about the realities of independence, and managed to get in touch with Ray Noonan, who had done the audit at Barrie and Rockliffe while serving as an articled clerk at Chalmers Wade (the firm is now known as Kidsons Impey). I knew nothing of him except that during those days when he had been around the office he had struck me as rather nicer than some young auditors I had met, who I felt despised their clients. (On the other hand, Chalmers Wade once sent a man to Pall Mall, who was pleasant enough but spent the entire day sitting back in his chair staring out of the window – he was taken off the job soon afterwards with a nervous breakdown. Yet another auditor, with a thick Glaswegian accent, was introduced to Fred Praeger, who asked him brightly 'Are you Hungarian?') Ray was friendly and, an additional commendation, could be heard humming snatches of operatic arias as he went about his work.

He did one or two sets of figures for me, and one day in James Street (despite the limited space, I emulated the civilised custom of old-fashioned Dutch booksellers in having a couple of upholstered armchairs in which to talk business, whatever else might be lacking) I told him of my impending move to Greenwich. A day or so later he came back and offered to join me as a partner. He had been working for some years with an American manufacturer of ten-pin bowling alleys, and felt the need for something slightly more edifying. To this end he was after the job of chief accountant in Routledge & Kegan Paul, which was soon offered to him, but preferred the idea of having direct responsibility for building up a new business. He was willing to take a sizeable cut in salary in exchange for a 20 per cent share in my business. I accepted his offer, succumbing to my old vice of taking what seemed the easy option without thinking much about the possible consequences.

We started in Greenwich at the beginning of 1970 and at the same time became a limited company. Ray, who had not previously been able to type, invoiced the orders and then went downstairs to pack them. He also read some proofs, and prepared trial balances. The audit, naturally with skilled book-keeping, was a formality, and was done by Chalmers Impey; the partner in charge was Andrew Nairn. But it was not long before Ray found this activity too restricted, and suggested that we took in a distribution client recommended by Nairn, namely Maurice Temple Smith – a new independent of remarkable maturity, who mysteriously gave it all up voluntarily after a few years. I agreed. The distribution side of the business, which steadily increased (soon Rex Collings and Aidan Ellis joined too), was now Ray's sole concern – not that I find the subject of book distribution sterile or boring, as some editors do, but my interest only extended to our own books; *being* a distributor did not interest me at all. However, I was prepared to leave everything in that department under Ray's care.

Very quickly, C. Hurst & Co. became a firm of whose turnover only a minority was due to publishing. The distribution side could either subsidise my publishing if it went well, or wipe it out if it flopped. We had not been doing it for long when Ray proposed that the two activities be separated, and I did not demur. The new firm was to be called Noonan Hurst. Ray was to retain his 20% share in C. Hurst & Co. and have 51% of the new company; to finance his share, though married with two young children, he took out a second mortgage on his house in Coulsdon. We rented a floor of an old bonded gin warehouse by Deptford Bridge, Seager Buildings, and –again doing the opposite of what I should have done – I sold the building in Royal Hill, which had remained my personal property. The Noonan Hurst office was set up above a shop in Trafalgar Road, East Greenwich, a grim and noisy thoroughfare, and I meanwhile worked in one of the glazed cubicles in the gin warehouse, with the stacks of books all around me, and the packing bench and the three staff – Eddie, Terry and Gladys – within sight. I quite enjoyed this unconventionally 'bookish' setting.

During part of our three-year stay in Royal Hill, Alison Hodge worked with me as an editorial assistant; she applied after graduating from the Centre for West African Studies at Birmingham University. We worked well together, and after some further publishing experience and travels in Africa, she set up as an independent publisher and bookseller in her home town, Penzance. But Seager Buildings was not a place where I could take an assistant. No normal person could have done a sedentary job there; the ambience was prison-like, there was no central heating, and the sanitation was spartan. I would sometimes have meetings in the expansive atmosphere of the Charing Cross Hotel, because it seemed out of the question to receive visitors in Deptford, but one did come: Don Sutherland, director of McGill-Queen's University Press. We built up a relationship that was singularly fruitful for me, as he imported editions of a large variety of my titles over the next few years.

Why did I abandon my nice little nest in Royal Hill? Ray and

I discussed over lunch in London whether personally I wanted to go along with the idea of setting up Noonan Hurst; he said that, as far as he was concerned, I was free to refuse, and if I did he would return to 'the profession'. I claim no virtue in having thought that, however haphazardly our business relationship had started, it was a reality and we had to go on; whatever he might say to allay my scruples on his account, he would be placed in a bad position if we decided to call everything off (though not as bad as the one he got into later because we had gone ahead). After that, I let things happen as they would. I merely continued, day after day, with my publishing. The last of the Indian stock, as already mentioned, had been loaded into a skip outside my house

But in the middle of 1974, after I had been at Seager Buildings for more than a year, a new spirit of resistance stirred inside me. With Ray in East Greenwich I now seldom saw him, and we had no practical involvement with eachother's businesses; the cross-shareholdings seemed to have lost whatever point they once had. I told him one day that I wanted his 20% share in my firm back, and that he could have my 49% share in his with suitable financial adjustments. He agreed, of course, but his first reaction was emotional; he said he had never been given the sack before. But I saw it more like a divorce without any marital offence. Either way, I had suddenly become convinced that C. Hurst & Co. would not survive unless it reverted to my sole ownership free of the entanglement with Noonan Hurst. Therefore a break had to be made.

Still, the separation took time. When Noonan Hurst was first established, C. Hurst & Co. formally became its client, with a three-year contract, of which there were nearly two years still to run. With what I acknowledge was some irrationality, I felt that this relationship should be speedily ended now that Ray and I were no longer partners. But he had his company's wellbeing to think of, and not unreasonably held me to the letter of the contract. So we remained tied to eachother till the end of 1976. There was also – and this made me anxious whenever I thought about it – a clause in Noonan Hurst's lease on Seager Buildings that placed the ultimate responsibility for the tenancy on C. Hurst & Co. because, unlike Noonan Hurst, it had been trading for some time before the lease was taken out. This condition would have had appalling consequences for me if N.H. had ceased trading before the lease expired, and it only lapsed when the lease was renewed around 1980. While Ray and I were both working in Royal Hill, we became quite friendly – we had quite a range of tastes and interests in common – so it was painful when hard feelings supervened.

In the early 1980s, for reasons I do not know and have never wanted to know for fear of suffering psychological vertigo, Noonan Hurst was forced to cease business, with considerable debts to its clients, of whom Rex Collings was one, although Maurice Temple Smith and others had got out earlier. I have never been able to avoid a feeling of contingent moral responsibility, because without me Ray could never have embarked on this venture. But, looking at my own narrow escape, I could only think that for once I took the right decision. If I had stayed with N.H. I would have been finished – and a publisher who, as a distributor, is responsible for causing losses to a fellow publisher could hardly be in a more invidious position, as my old friend Tom Stacey was a few years later.

The urge to abandon everything which gripped me in the late 1960s did not disappear completely till after I had written to two British firms I admired, Blackwell and A.N. Other, offering my imprint and my own services for sale. With Blackwell I did have two serious conversations, one in Oxford and the other in Greenwich, before they said 'no'; A.N. Other only replied after a silence of several weeks, in the form of a two-line letter from the managing director, in which not a glimmer of human sympathy was expressed. This odious behaviour gave me fresh courage. But there was a more serious flirtation – with a newly-formed Dutch publishing conglomerate, V.N.U. Its ambitious managing director, Mari Pijnenborg, wanted to launch a grand series of 'basic' books in English more or less in the areas that concerned me – contemporary civilisations, geographically based. He had sought the advice of my treasured author Douwe Fokkema on the Chinese side to the project, and Douwe had advised him to contact me. We had an upbeat first meeting in Brown's Hotel, when he asked me to formulate some ideas. I took his approach more seriously than perhaps he intended, and drew up a detailed proposal. I was then invited over to attend a directors' meeting at V.N.U.'s headquarters in Haarlem, when we sat round a table having a very vague and directionless conversation for the whole afternoon. I felt that my ideas were clearer than theirs, although at least one genuine publisher, Aad Nuis of Het Spectrum, was present. We gradually began to talk about incorporating my firm as a unit within V.N.U. But meanwhile I would make some investigations, visiting academics who might act as series advisers, and going to New York and Boston to talk with publishers who might collaborate, at the end of which I would come back with a super-proposal. The final act in this drama, after my trip to America, was that Rachel (we were just married) and I were invited to the launching in Amsterdam of V.N.U.'s new encyclopaedia in which Mitchell Beazley, pioneers before Dorling Kindersley in the business of bringing virtual reality to the printed

page, were involved; information books with cunning colour illustrations
had become the flavour of the decade. We were opulently housed
in the Amstel Hotel, and attended various functions. James Mitchell,
who looked deceptively like a studious young clergyman, was there
and, because I had seen him pick up his wife and turn her upside
down at a party in London, and then try unsuccessfully to do the
same to another woman, I warned Rachel to beware. He did indeed
try it. Before leaving for London, the two of us had a last session
with Pijnenborg and the manager of one of the group's newspapers,
a delightful man called Frank Sweens, with whom I was told I
would be working if our project came to anything.

Pijnenborg always talked in abstractions – I wondered if he had
ever actually *published* a book, as I understand that expression, in
his life – and it was becoming clear that he would never get down
to brass tacks, so it was almost a relief when his letter came saying
that they would not proceed with the plan. Only Ray Noonan, who
thought it had represented the opportunity of a lifetime, was disappointed.
For V.N.U. it had been a small dummy run, and for me a mildly
entertaining diversion. One useful door in particular opened during
my researches. I decided to look for the first time into European
studies, and this took me to Loughborough University, where there
was a new centre. Here I met Tony Burkitt, who wrote a book
for me on West German political parties and elections, and John
Frears, who did the same thing for France; both convinced me that
a need existed for these volumes, and they sold quite well. The
format did not promise sparkling works of literature, but John's book
did sparkle – he proved to be a naturally gifted writer. The two,
in time-honoured fashion, became friends and allies, and when I
wanted to publish a similar book on the complex polity of Belgium,
John recommended John Fitzmaurice (mentioned earlier). His literary
ability seemed to be part and parcel of his unusual career: if Frears'
Biscuits, in its modest way a household name, had not been absorbed
into a conglomerate, he would probably have continued as he began,
as a biscuit manufacturer, instead of switching to further education
and Labour – later Social Democratic – politics.

When I finally left my family home in Greenwich in May 1971,
it was to move into a rather grand Italianate villa in Blackheath,
built in 1859.* I had not wanted to leave, but as has been adumbrated

---

* The owner was an interesting man: Michael Cary, eldest son of the novelist Joyce
Cary and a civil service mandarin who defied all stereotypes of that genus: darkly handsome,
relaxed and friendly without a trace of pomposity or condescension, and with a noticeable
liking for hard liquor. Even by the standards of old-fashioned Permanent Secretaries, he
had a remarkable intellect. For one thing he never took work home, but much more

earlier, all the wrong omens had been present at the start of my relationship with Christine. We were at least as one in thinking that almost everything that had gone wrong was my fault. For a long time after the balloon went up (she found a letter that revealed I was having an affair), I could not imagine that one day I would have to walk out of the house and leave our marriage, blighted as it was, and our three children behind. Was there no way of saving it? I thought of, and tried, everything but generally succeeded only in making matters worse. One thing I tried was enrolling with the Marriage Guidance Council. It was perhaps a pity that the counsellor was not a hard-bitten man fifteen or twenty years my senior, but an attractive, provocative woman a few years younger than me, who had qualified as a barrister, then spent some years as an air stewardess. She could fairly represent Christine's feelings and I tried to be honest about myself. Of course I hoped that Christine would go too, and that it might lead to a reconciliation (which for a time became more desirable the further the likelihood of it receded), but she played her cards skillfully, knowing that she had a trump card in her hand and that if she once threw it away, it might never be recovered. She made clear from the start that she would go to the Council only once – alone.

The counsellor and I, as people speaking the same language, became friends, and this led to an embarrassing situation. After I had been seeing her for some time, she said that she wished to write a book about her counsellor-client relationship with me, and the theoretical light it might shed on the practice of counselling, but of course only if I agreed. I disagreed at first quite vigorously, but she suggested that I owed it to her out of the mutual love and trust which were an essential part of the counselling relationship; by resisting I was being my old unregenerate self which I must surely wish to leave behind. I felt uncertain about her motive (why choose me?), but in the end consented. It turned out to be the wisest thing I could have done because she quickly lost interest in the idea.

One day our subject of discussion was a letter which I had written to *The Times* and she had seen. A British airliner had crashed from 2,000 feet straight after take-off in a field not far from the motorway

remarkable were his two hobbies. One was electronics – he could put together anything from a hi-fi installation to a bellows for the fire – but the other, which seemed to dominate his life, was making inlaid harpsichord cases of masterly workmanship around innards supplied by Thomas Goff. The front part of the large basement was his workshop, the back part a nursery school run by his wife. He already had a weak heart at this time, but this did not deter him from renting a removal van when they left and helping to load it himself. Clearly a driven man, he died while still in his fifties.

near Heathrow. Everyone on board was killed. Many passing drivers stopped their cars on the road-side just to stare at the scene, and as the result the emergency services had difficulty getting through. The newspaper reports next day, broadsheet as well as tabloid, went far beyond deploring this straightforward fact, and sermonised self-righteously about the ghoulishness of the British public and how disgraceful it was. I rallied to the support of the 'ghouls', saying that it might be once in a lifetime that anyone witnessed a disaster of this magnitude actually taking place, and it was natural if one succumbed to an overwhelming urge just to absorb it, think about all the lives that had been extinguished before one's eyes, reflect on one's own tenuous hold on life, and so on. In other words it was an encounter, however brief, with what we are pleased to call God. (I was once, in the late 1950s, similarly 'ghoulish' hurrying out of my house in Greenwich one foggy night after hearing on the radio about the Lewisham train crash; I drove to St John's and simply walked up on to the track among all the firemen and rescue workers, and saw under the arc-lights many of the 100-odd dead commuters trapped in the wreckage by the fallen bridge or laid out on the ground. I had never seen even one dead person before. Admittedly I had some vague notion of helping when I went out, but this was clearly unnecessary, and I felt no guilt at being a spectator.) The counsellor had clearly not thought me the kind of person who would propound this sort of ideology publicly. I am proud to say that the letter was reproduced in *Private Eye*'s 'Pseuds' Corner', that early pillory for the politically incorrect.

In the end, sheer exhaustion of spirit made me embark on that infallible restorative, house-hunting. One day I saw an advertisement in the *Evening Standard* for a small, cheap house in our locality. Why not move there? The agent told me that it was right between two railway lines where they bifurcated outside Lewisham station, but he had a house in Blackheath that was just on the market and not yet advertised. It was well outside my price range, but I thought all the same that the price was below its market value, and bought it after mortgaging myself to the limit, to convert and sell off the top two floors and live in the lower two. I felt a barbarian, because the house was much nicer in single occupation than carved up, and when I sold the end of the large garden to a rich neighbour to build a house, I had to watch the little orchard of fruit trees being bulldozed to make way for it. The year or so that it took to create and sell the flats coincided with the first steep rise in house prices, and when I left the house five years later, I had about the same sum in hand as all I had spent on it.

At the end of 1972 I went to Scotland, with my youngest son Martin, to spend Hogmanay with a cousin, and thus missed a party given by a near neighbour in Blackheath at which she wanted to introduce me to a young divorced woman who had just moved into the very next house to mine, and with whom she thought I might get on. This was Rachel, though at that stage I did not know her name. She had lived in Blackheath for a long time, and recently parted from her husband, an accomplished City solicitor who sailed every week-end and played the clarinet. Her daughter and son, who lived with her, were of the same ages as my two youngest children, and I called on her soon after getting back from the north to propose that we might meet one week-end soon and introduce our children to eachother. She was surprised to learn that my name was Christopher; she had thought it was Geoffrey, but had been told by a fortune-teller that she would soon form an important relationship with someone called Christopher (obviously the 'Geoffrey' next door could not be that person).

I could write another book about Rachel and the extraordinary things she has achieved – and about the effect she has had on my life – but will only say a little in this book directly about her. Both her parents were in the theatre and followers of the arts and crafts movement, and she herself went to a drama school, the Rose Bruford, at the age of sixteen. But first back trouble, which interrupted her studies for two years, and then early marriage meant that she never made a career in the theatre, although in her teens she acted in professional productions with her parents. Also, from latent beginnings she developed a form of muscular dystrophy which forced her to start using a wheelchair in 1975, rather more than a year after we were married. This at first sank her into despair, but gradually it opened up a public career as an activist in the local, national and international disability rights movement, where her vibrancy, intelligence, satirical wit, generosity of spirit combined with pugnacity, energy, organising ability and theatrical training all came into play. Even before becoming disabled, she never worked in my business, but has always supported me when I have needed it, and without the courage she gave me, I might not have made the saving break from Noonan Hurst when I did. And after I had made the break but was still working in the desolate solitude of Seager Buildings more than a year later, she urged me to move away.

Back to Covent Garden

For more than ten years I used no printer other than Billings of Guildford. As already related, I went to them first by chance, but they served me well and a friendly relationship grew up. I never had more than a formal acquaintance with the managing director, Robert Bradley, a former naval officer who had no background in printing; he was the appointee of the majority shareholder, the tycoon Sir Alfred Owens. But, as is the way, I knew the production staff at the factory through frequent phone calls, and after moving to Greenwich tended to drop in quite often at Billings's London office at 1-2 Henrietta Street, Covent Garden, above Lloyds Bank and Boulestin's restaurant, to leave or pick up parcels.

Sometime in the mid-1970s Sir Alfred Owens sold his shares, and Bradley left. The first buyers offered me the astonishing credit term of six months – it had previously been three – but within a short time they sold out to Blackwell's of Oxford, who installed David Hale as managing director. David, younger son of the publisher Robert Hale, had been a printer all his working life, and he now arrived, at a time of revolutionary change in the industry, to carry out revolutionary reforms. A time of enhanced collaboration with Billings began.

The opening phase was painful because David had to cut deeply into my new credit term; but he allowed me to float to earth slowly, as if with a capacious parachute, rather than fall with a bump. The two rooms in the Covent Garden offices which had been used for the firm's sales reps* to browse in on their short visits to base

---

* One of these was Peter, a keen man of about thirty, whom I got to know a little through lunching with him perhaps a couple of times. He once told me that he was an identical twin but had never known his brother, since both of them had been adopted at birth by different families. In the early 1990s, when I had been out of touch with Peter for at least ten years, I was in a clothes shop near Piccadilly Circus and suddenly heard his voice – it was unmistakable. I looked round but there was no sign of him; then I saw that the voice was coming from the assistant standing behind the counter – who, like Peter, was fairly tall and had a rather small head and a beak-like nose. There could be no doubt whatever that this was Peter's twin, although superficially they did not look particularly alike. My strong urge to speak to him could not prevail against my even stronger inhibitions. When I got back to my office, I said to Michael Dwyer (below, pp. 404-5) that if Peter should phone us that afternoon, it would be an exceptionally high-grade coincidence. While I was on the phone later, Michael took another call and told me

were vacated, and David offered them to me at a low rent. I did not need to think for long before accepting such an attractive proposal. So at the end of 1975 I turned my back on the gin warehouse. I have a fondness for Deptford despite its squalor – a characteristic especially in evidence where we were, directly across the street from one of London's biggest doss-houses. All day, like crows, the men sat or wandered about the Broadway, some holding bottles of drink; one little white-haired man, wearing a school cap and blazer, was never without a cheerful smile, and another – tall, distinguished-looking and with a Central European appearance, walked slowly up and down with a look of intense inward preoccupation; I imagined him to be a violinist playing great concertos in his imagination. For lunch I would sometimes meet Rachel in one of the nearby pubs, but she longed for me to get away from the place, which she thought was eating into my soul.

David Hale, determined and energetic, set up web-offset machinery in another printing works newly acquired by Blackwell at Worcester, which could print and bind in one operation – at low prices because of the labour saved, and of course at a hugely increased speed. He called it 'Bookplan', and for a time it was the market leader. This was a complete departure from the traditional flat-bed, sheet-fed printing. Because the new machines were fed from a long roll, the paper could no longer be cut in a way that ensured that the fore-edge of the resulting book would appear straight; it was now wavy. I did not like this, but we were all having to accept the disappearance of old refinements in book production. The savings in cost and time were persuasive.

Billings were comparatively late in closing down their hot-metal machines, and before the end were offering me setting from them a low prices because they were no longer being fully used. But David was soon experimenting with new computer-assisted setting, and allowed me to put two of my books through as guinea-pigs for the process, at specially low prices. These both came from Chatham

---

afterwards that it had been Billings, asking if we had any business for them. It had not been Peter, but it was a near miss, as if the god of coincidences was trying hard to bring a convincing one about. Later I did dare to say to the man in the shop that he reminded me of a friend of mine whose name I mentioned, but he looked blankly at me and denied any knowledge of what I was talking about. I did not say that I knew he was Peter's twin brother. At the London Book Fair in 1996 I found out by accident that Peter was now in a senior position with a multinational company, and went to his stand where we greeted eachother as old friends. I reminded him that he had long ago told me about his twin, and he said that till that day they had never met or been in touch with eachother. I gave him the name of the shop where I had seen him, although he had ceased working there some time before this.

House – the Royal Institute of International Affairs – and this fruitful connection compels another diversion.

I had just become a personal member of Chatham House, which helped, but it came about because Richard Brain, an editor at O.U.P. whom I knew from Oxford days, tipped me off that the Press was divesting itself of its long-standing role as the Institute's exclusive publisher, and if I stepped in smartly I might pick up a few good books. Chatham House then sponsored research in depth, not necessarily related to urgent policy issues, by various distinguished scholars – a practice that has since given way to 'less on more'. It also had its own house editors, highly qualified if eccentric people tied into a civil service career pattern, and not greatly constrained by considerations of time and money. At Richard's suggestion I phoned the director of studies, Ian Smart, and sure enough there were two splendid books which, because of O.U.P.'s defection, were looking for a publisher. I snapped them up on sight. They had confusingly similar titles – *The Turkish Experiment* (by Feroz Ahmad) and *The Yugoslav Experiment in Democracy* (by Dennison Rusinow). Both were heavyweight, and it was not difficult to arrange profitable American deals – with Fred Praeger's Westview Press for the first and the University of California Press for the second. The Chatham House editors, Rena Fenteman and Hermia Oliver, both nearing retirement, gave me and the authors a hard ride, but the result was an editorial standard I could be proud of. I made the jackets as well as the inside of the two uniform, and Chatham House expressed satisfaction. (Feroz Ahmad remains a friend and ally, and his book resulted directly in two other books on Turkey coming to us: one on Pan-Turkism by Jacob Landau of the Hebrew University, Jerusalem, and a collection of essays on Atatürk produced by Unesco for the centenary of the great man's birth in 1982. Both have been reprinted.)

The next Chatham House book I secured was undoubtedly of 'star quality', and Richard Brain later admitted that O.U.P. had been foolish to let it go. This was Ian Brownlie's *African Boundaries: a Diplomatic and Legal Encyclopaedia*, a work which, when published, made nearly 1,400 royal 8vo pages, and must be the chief monument to the fanatical industry of this extraordinary international lawyer. I had no hesitation in accepting it, despite its enormous size, and David Hale provided help throughout with the personal enthusiasm, interest and commitment of which only he among British printers I have known seemed capable. An editor, specially hired by Chatham House for job, relieved me of the burden of copy-editing and proof-reading; all I had to do was ensure that the book was appropriately splendid in appearance when finished, and was co-published in North

America. At first I obtained an agreement in principle to take 1,000 copies from the legal publisher, Oceana of Dobbs Ferry, with whom I had never previously done business – the firm's agent in England was a professor of law at the London School of Economics, which seemed to me strange. But I soon grew profoundly irritated at being passed around from the desk of one bland bureaucrat at Oceana to another, and when I was told (by their legal counsel of all people) the maximum sum they were prepared to pay although I told them truthfully that it was less than my cost, and at the same time exactly how the books were to be packed, I cancelled the negotiations. Chatham House were upset because I did not yet have another co-publisher, but the University of California Press soon agreed to take 500 at a much more reasonable price. Chatham House were still upset but there was nothing I could do to appease them. It was a good deal. The book still sells steadily after fifteen years, and it was for long the firm's best money-spinner.

By the time I took on a fourth Chatham House book, Tom Nossiter's *Communism in Kerala,* the Institute's old editors had retired (editing Tom's book was Rena Fenteman's swan-song) and been replaced by someone who would have overall responsibility for publishing matters. To ensure publication in India, and to cut down the cost of producing this quite lengthy book, I had it typeset and printed under the care of O.U.P.'s Delhi office, which would also be the local publisher. Finding an American co-publisher for a book like this would not be easy and might be impossible. However, I had not reckoned on the terribly long time the typesetting would take. Chatham House got agitated and put continuous pressure on me, which I tried, not very successfully, to pass on to India. It happened that I only fixed up the American deal when the typesetting was well advanced – and the preceding time had been anxious because I knew, and so did Chatham House because I had told them so, that I would lose heavily on the book if I failed to get a transatlantic deal. I was in San Francisco for a conference in June 1981, and remember the moment when the U.C.P. editor Bill McClung agreed, as we faced eachother in his office at Berkeley, to import 750 copies at a low price. It was as if a heavenly light had shone down upon him. I felt he was acting on impulse, and perhaps neither of us really believed he would sell that number, but I hastened to clinch the deal. While imparting the glad tidings a little later to the new publications supremo at Chatham House, I let fall a remark which I expected her, as someone who had worked for some years in an American publishing house, to understand instinctively: that the delays in the typesetting had turned out not to be so disastrous because they had allowed the American deal to be concluded in good time before we could have gone to press. About half a minute after the end of our conversation she rang back and delivered a scorching rebuke, saying that she wanted me to know how disgraceful she found my attitude. That marked the end of my publishing relations with Chatham House, except with their royalty department.

But as a member I occasionally went to lunch-time meetings there, and two of these resulted in my commissioning a book from the speaker. At the first, Admiral of the Fleet Sir Peter Hill-Norton spoke about NATO. He had just retired after a glittering career; in the preceding few years he had been successively First Sea Lord, Chief of the U.K. Defence Staff, and Chairman of the NATO Defence Committee – respectively the top job for a British naval officer, a British officer of any arm, and a NATO officer. The reason why I attended the Chatham House meeting was because I had seen him on the television news a few days earlier and been struck by the intensity of his replies to the interviewer. It was the same at the meeting (in the flesh he was a small man, though he had seemed massive on the screen). Again this Hamlet-like intensity emanated from him; all too clearly he felt that had been torn untimely from his seat at NATO, where he all but said there was still a job for him to do, and one which he knew how to do better than anyone else. He was sixty-three. He still lived NATO's problems, and there was obviously an extended essay there waiting to be written. I wrote to him and he asked me to meet him at the Royal Yacht Club in Knightsbridge. This gave me a foretaste of what was to come. We sat in the outer hall of the club, and he did not ask if I wanted even a cup of tea. He also did not smile once, but merely interrogated me about how our relationship would work. But my proposition had fired his imagination and we parted having agreed on a contract. He wrote the book quickly, and I published it quickly. I was determined not to be fazed by his graceless manners, of which I was to learn more later by hearsay from a friend who had served under him in the Navy, and by direct experience, and invited him and his wife to lunch with me and Rachel at Rule's; as a pair they were charming – they had married when he was twenty-one and she eighteen. He and I entered choppy waters when I read his first draft and sent my routine list of queries. How could I possibly not understand every word? The last thing he had expected was that his production would be subjected to questioning and stylistic tinkering like a school essay, and he phoned me to say that perhaps we had better call the whole exercise off. I asked if I could visit him at his house and go over the script; he agreed, and this lightened the atmosphere.

Again his wife came to the rescue, and he unbent a little as we drank whisky and soda before lunch. But a few days later I had to send him a short final list of still unresolved points, and once again he came on the phone and said he was really rather cross. This time I was getting quite cross myself and said that I had worked my balls off making his bloody manuscript publishable, and all he could do was complain. This explosion got us at last into calm seas. The book – entitled *No Soft Options* – would have had more impact if it had come from a large publisher, but it just happened that a small one had thought of it: a recurring dilemma.

The other Chatham House speaker I commissioned was Indar Jit Rikhye, in his time (he was born in 1920) the youngest general in the Indian Army, who was seconded to serve the United Nations first with UNEF I after the Suez war, and later in the key capacity of Military Adviser to the Secretary-General – first Dag Hammarskjöld and, after his death, U Thant – in the Congo. He agreed to write a book called *The Theory and Practice of Peacekeeping* (1987), and from this there descended a succession of books on U.N. peacekeeping operations, mostly by former participants, including Rikhye's own on the Congo. These have necessarily been heavily subsidised by guaranteed purchases, but I have liked publishing on this subject, which I dissociate utterly from 'militaria'.

Just before leaving Seager Buildings I advertised for a secretary to help me organise a small London office, and V. came to me from a large publishing house. She was a 'lady', with influential relations, aged twenty-eight and attractive without being pretty. The day she reported for work, she wore a pair of tinted spectacles with octagonal panes. At her interview she had not worn them, and they made a striking difference to her appearance; if anything, they made her look ill. I thought that perhaps she was wearing them that day because of migraine or a headache, but no, she wore them all day every day. Which of us was more sexist – she in figuring that as a lecherous male I would be put off by her unattractive glasses if she wore them at the interview, or I in feeling that this side of me had been exploited? She had a low opinion of men, having recently ended a cohabitation in the Far East, and as she showed one day when a printer's representative called touting for business. The representative was an utterly enchanting blonde girl in her early twenties; we had nothing of moment to discuss, but in the warmth of her presence I was extremely happy to chat inconsequentially for ten minutes and obviously showed it. When the girl had gone, V. did not conceal that she thought me pathetic. But she also showed genuine pleasure when our first new book during her incumbency, albeit a particularly boring one, was delivered from the printer; and she did organise my office. V. was subject to black moods, which in our confined space were contagious; finally I said that we had better part, to which she agreed, and for about half a day her mood was brighter than it had ever been before.

Her successor was J., a conscientious, quick-witted but easygoing girl of Cockney background. She had not had much education, but was attracted to publishing and had only worked for publishers and, once, for the Publishers Association. Soon afterwards we became a threesome. At the London Book Fair a young man called Antony Mason came up to my table and said that he wanted to learn about publishing; how was he to go about it? I said that if he came to my office we could talk together for a day, and if necessary two days, about the essentials of the business. He came, and at the end of the long tutorial I offered him a job, which he accepted, staying for about eighteen months. J. did the book-keeping, and when she discovered at the end of Antony's first month that as an editor, though one without experience, he was earning slightly more than she was, we had a small explosion and then swiftly equalised their salaries.

Sentimentally attached to hot metal setting as I was, I started around 1976-7 to obtain it from the Tata Press in India; it must have been Maurice Temple Smith, who set up his firm with the help of Tata capital, who turned me in that direction. Tata's setting was cheap and good, and in due course I sent the first set of camera-ready copy to Billings to be turned into a book. I got a phone call back from Chris, my contact at the factory, saying that the Father of the Chapel in the machine room wanted to know where the setting, which did not carry the regulation union sticker, came from – in other words, did it come from a union shop? Because all my setting till very recently had been done by or through Billings, the occasion had never arisen for such a question to be asked. But the mere asking of it raised my hackles and I answered 'Blue Sky Printers, Berwick-on-Tweed'. A day or two later Chris phoned again to say that the Father of the Chapel could not find Blue Sky Printers in his list of union shops, to which I said that this was not surprising since I had invented the name on the spur of the moment. David Hale told me that my unwise bravado had nearly caused all my work to be blacked; but he, being still relatively new in his job, had the authority to calm things down. By now I was also using an electronic typesetting service in a Bloomsbury mews, and its owner – Norma Kitson, a South African political exile – helpfully gave me a collection of spare union stickers to use as I pleased.

Unions, with their closed shops and restrictive practices, were going through a phase of unprecedented confidence, with the collusion of a supine Labour government. The editorial and production departments of publishing houses were affected, which made me all the more thankful to be on my own because submission to union discipline, either as a worker or as a manager forced to sanction it, was something I could never have borne. Thus my heart-beat would race with anger when I had to pass through the strike picket which stood at the entrance to the Economists' Bookshop for nearly a year in 1978-9. It would be no exaggeration to say that I felt burning detestation for the small group of so-called 'Trotskyite' trouble-makers on the staff of the bookshop who, by turning a minor grievance into a major *casus belli*, brought down the existing management. The shop was owned jointly by *The Economist* and the London School of Economics, whose campus bookshop it was as well as being much more. The manager Gerald Bartlett, groomed over many years by Gerti Kvergic, was the model of a new kind of technically competent bookseller, and, unusually early in his career, had been president of the Booksellers Association. His senior colleagues too were excellent people – I remember particularly Tony Comerford, Mark Bone and David Eastman. But Gerald proved ineffective when it came to dealing with particularly ruthless and irresponsible enemies determined to unseat him – some bystanders criticised him for this as if it made him an incompetent manager. The fifty-fifty ownership of the business caused paralysis: *The Economist* did not want to be involved in the dispute, and the L.S.E.'s staff and governors were divided. Tony Benn stoked the fires with a knee-jerk pro-strike speech to the students, most of whom, not surprisingly, backed the strikers anyway. Under the previous normal circumstances the ownership structure had caused no problems and Gerald Bartlett had proved an excellent manager, innovative and able to carry his colleagues with him. I felt that now familiar surge of fury when, at a periodical clients' meeting with my distributors, one client, an avowedly socialist publisher, made the outrageous request that the distributors withhold supplies from the Economists' Bookshop in support of the strikers. These disturbing experiences made me ask Gerald, when the strike was over and he had resigned, to write what had happened, blow by blow, while it was still hot inside him. He did so, and we published it as a 32-page crown 4to pamphlet. Gerald spoke out as I wanted him to, and we both took a certain risk, but nobody sued us. However, he now found his footsteps dogged by sympathisers of his old enemies as he tried to rebuild his bookselling career elsewhere, and he left the trade. At the same time Dillon's University Bookshop in Malet

Street, the Economists' natural counterpart in London, went through similar though less publicised turbulence, which broke up the enlightened, liberal management team led by the inheritor of Una Dillon's mantle, Peter Stockham. Peter, perhaps less wounded than Gerald, found a new bookish identity in the antiquarian field.

Because it had been my old colleague Jack Caspall, Barrie and Rockliff's London rep, who first introduced me to Gerald almost twenty years before, I sent him a copy of the publication. He phoned me and we had a long talk. He had now finally retired and claimed to be not unhappy with his lot. But only a few months later I read in the *Bookseller* that he had died, and immediately shot off a letter to Mrs Caspall. A longish silence followed – then I was phoned by Jack's niece, who thanked me for the letter and explained that she was phoning because Mrs Caspall had died some time before Jack – certainly before he and I had our last conversation – and that he had thereafter neglected himself and faded away. I knew that he and his wife, who had no children, were very close, so he must have felt unable to speak to me of her death.

In 1979 Blackwell, for no apparent reason other than its bullish mood of the moment, took over the head lease of two extra floors of 1-2 Henrietta Street, which gave it control over all the office floors of the building except the top one. I was visited a couple of times by the surveyor advising Blackwell on the organisation of its new property. He told me that if I wanted to stay on at anything like the reasonable rent I had been paying hitherto I would have to vacate the two rooms on Billings's corridor and move into a single room, on the other side of a fire door and overlooking the back staircase. I was left with no practical choice, and so made plans to move. Antony Mason had left, and there was no reason why J. and I could not work happily in the same room.

J. was present the first time the surveyor called. He was a former regular officer in the Gloster Regiment, a keen mountaineer, and married with two children of his own and two step-children. It was a measure of how relaxed we were that he divulged all this information at our first meeting, but I would have forgotten it long ago but for one thing. As the interview came to an end he gave us his address, which was 'Gay Street, Queen Square, Bath'. J. and I did not dare to look at eachother, and I would like to be able to say that I replied 'If you put my rent up, *I* shall be in Queer Street', but I only thought of that after he had left. I would have forgotten that too, or at least not thought it worth recording, if I had not opened *The Times* about two years later and seen a half-remembered face looking out of the 'Home News' page. It was the surveyor.

On Christmas Day his wife had given him a bottle of sherry as
a present, to which he evidently reacted with insufficient enthusiasm.
She went out of the room, returned with his sporting gun, and shot
his head off. At the murder trial his former commanding officer
testified in such glowing terms to her sterling character that she
got off with only one year's imprisonment. I could see that sneering
at the bottle of sherry might have called forth less drastic punishment
if he had not provoked her before in certain other ways, but I still
through that she had got off rather lightly.

Early in 1980 David Hale phoned me to say that he had just
been given the boot. I do not understand the ways of large companies,
but even so I still find this astonishing. He had established 'Bookplan'
at Worcester and brought a lot of new business to the group. It
was said in extenuation by Ted Millett, the long-serving sales director
who never got on with him, that David had not made the operation
profitable enough, but even if that was true it seemed a harsh as
well as inefficient way to deal with what might have been a temporary
and easily surmountable difficulty. I complained by letter to Richard
Blackwell, who asked me to go and see him in Oxford. We had
not met before and I was interested to note, in someone renowned
for his hard-driving ways, the softness of his manner. He unctuously
said 'Bless you' several times during our interview, and I had not
sneezed. I said that for me David had been an ideal printer – enabling
me to improve the efficiency of my business and, especially important,
always prepared to take personal action over any problem. The best
example of this (except for the 1,400-page book on African boundaries
mentioned earlier) was when Billings produced for me a 600-page
book on the East European economies, the ms. of which had literally
been handed to me when I called, with twelve hours' advance notice,
at the federal institute for '*Ostwissenschaft*' (broadly, the study of
the 'Eastern bloc' as then constituted) in Cologne on my way home
from the Frankfurt book fair. It was a splendid book and I looked
upon it as heightening the profile of my firm with one stroke. So
I took great care over it and eagerly awaited the moment of holding
a finished copy in my hands – so much so that I called at the bindery
near London Bridge to receive and cherish the first fruits. For me
it is always a tense moment opening a newly produced book, but
this time I already felt a sick anxiety before I looked at the four-page
contents list, where somehow I and the editors had failed to notice
that all the page numbers of the chapters were missing. It only
took me a few seconds to realise that the fault was wholly mine
and there was no way out, like an errata slip (California were taking
1,500); so I at once phoned David, and his priority then became

getting a fresh four-page section printed and tipped in. It was all done within a few days and at no great cost. I quoted this to Richard Blackwell as an example of David's obvious concern for the welfare of his customers, which for me made dealing with his firm a pleasure. He shrugged his shoulders, saying that he could not involve himself personally in everything that came within his purview and he had to accept the word of lower managers.

One morning in the spring of 1980 I wandered out from Henrietta Street on an impulse – the isolation of my back room was getting me down – and went across the square to the Africa Centre in King Street. The director Alastair Niven, whom I did not know, was in and I asked him if he had any office space to let. He did not. We chatted for a while; then, as we passed through the entrance hall on the way out, I noticed that the shop space there was in darkness and asked Alastair if I might have that. It was true, he explained, that it had no tenant, but the Centre's policy had long been to start a bookshop there. I said without a moment's reflection that I would start that bookshop. Alastair's committee approved, and thus the Africa Book Centre was born. Rachel and I gave a party and David Steel came and cut the tape.

The act of selling books – taking them off the shelf and receiving the money – is something I acutely enjoy, but as a publisher; I am not a bookseller, which is altogether different. So for five years I was a publisher who played at bookselling, and carried on my publishing business in one corner of a bookshop. Fortunately there was a large shop-window, which gave me the opportunity, beyond the dreams of many larger publishers, of displaying my wares to the public in this much-frequented Central London street. I quickly installed shelving, and obtained from the most important publishers of low-priced, 'popular' Africana – Heinemann and Longman, and some smaller houses – agreement to rent shelf-space and operate a consignment system whereby I would account periodically for sales already executed rather than buying stock on spec. This is something that no publisher will do except in special circumstances, but I managed to convince some of my fellow-publishers that the opening of a bookshop dealing only in books on Africa and the Caribbean, and in a location that was both attractive in itself and appropriate because it was at the Africa Centre, was a special circumstance. I bought, outright, stock from the Black publishers in London – mainly the two established firms, New Beacon and Bogle L'Ouverture, but also some very small ones – and I made a few small purchases from African publishing houses, including my old author Arthur Nwankwo's

Fourth Dimension in Enugu. Books from Africa usually arrived with ludicrously inadequate packing.

J. (and, after her time, Susanna Clarke and Joy Ozobia) sat at the front and dealt with the customers. Once she told me that she had just sold a book to Claire Bloom – how I repined at having missed the opportunity to see that beautiful woman at close quarters and declare myself her devoted fan. Of course I often had to deal with customers myself, interrupting whatever I was doing. I enjoyed it, but did not have the necessary patience or self-control. Young parents might come in with a pair of offspring, one in a push-chair but quite able to reach the books on the lower shelves, and the other sucking an ice-cream but no less eager to handle the books. One outraged father accused me, as he bundled his family out, of being an enemy of the young. Then there was a middle-class woman whom I am sure I saw drop a paperback into her large shopping bag – yet I did not feel quite sure enough to challenge her. And there was another woman who asked me a question with her back turned. Such things must be the everyday experience of a bookseller, though the better organised ones have rules about small children and oblige shoppers to leave their bags by the entrance. I could only stand it in the knowledge that it would not be for ever, and that sooner or later I would pass the business on to other hands.

The enthusiasm of the large publishers who rented space, with such benefit to my cash flow, lasted in full only for one year and expired altogether after two; they then wanted to put our trading on a normal basis, with which of course I had to agree. It seemed like a blow when, soon after Alastair Niven left, I was asked to vacate the shop space; it could be let much more lucratively to a business selling African artifacts – 'airport art', as Alastair called it – and I was offered in lieu the back part of the second floor at an attractive rent. In principle I had always liked the idea of a specialist bookseller operating from premises away from the street – I had seen it with the orientalists on the European continent (e.g. Harrassowitz in Wiesbaden and Brill in Cologne) and in New York (Paragon) – but it was almost unknown in England except among antiquarians. The Africa Book Centre's days in my hands were now numbered, and in 1986 I sold it to Joy Ozobia, a highly intelligent Ibo girl who had worked with me for a few months.[*]

[*] Of the later history of the Africa Book Centre suffice it to say that Joy repented of her decision and sold it to Third World Publications, a radical wholesale importer based in Birmingham, run as a cooperative. When this concern folded, one of the cooperators, Tony Zurbrugg, acquired it himself and has run it ever since in a way that I consider ideal: he produces regular catalogues, and the shop is always looked after by well-trained

From Hamburg to Sri Lanka

Hamburg, home of my father's forebears, played its part in nurturing my business, partly by design on my part and partly by chance. Seeing a favourable review in the *Times Literary Supplement* in 1978 of a history (in German) of M.M. Warburg & Co., the famous bank in that city, I wrote to the reviewer who put me in touch with the two authors: Eduard Rosenbaum, a former employee of the bank, living in London since the 1930s, and a much younger American scholar, Joshua Sherman. The book was not particularly long, and because Sherman had written his part in English and already translated that of his co-author, translation was not a problem. This Jewish family bank, founded in the 18th century, became powerful and influential in the early part of the 20th, but it could not survive under the Nazis without ceding control to an 'Aryan' partner. The managing partner for many years up to this parting of the ways was Max Warburg (one of five brothers, the eldest of whom, Aby, founded the Warburg Institute). He is very much the hero of the book, and the farewell address he made to the staff before leaving for America in 1938, never to return, is most moving. My interest stemmed largely from my own family's history, but also from the chance that I knew a member of the Warburg family. I was determined to produce the book with as much panache as possible.

Eric Warburg, Max's only son, by then an old man and virtually retired, took an active interest in the project and bought more than enough copies to cover my outlay; Max Holmes co-published it in America. I used to go occasionally to Hamburg, mainly because I did business with the Institute of Asian Affairs, and while I was on one of these visits, shortly before the book appeared, Eric invited me to lunch in the partners' dining room on the top floor of the bank. There we sat alone together until the coffee was served, when another elderly man was ushered in. This was a notary named Hans W. Hertz. Eric had already told me that, because of my background, he had summoned this friend and co-founder with him of the Institut für die Geschichte der Deutschen Juden, but not invited him for the meal 'because he talks too much'. His family, like mine, had

---

and motivated people. It is still (in 1997) at 38 King Street.

ceased to practise the Jewish religion early in the nineteenth century, but during the Nazi period loyalty to his roots had driven him to hide great quantities of Jewish archives and even some historic grave-stones to save them from destruction – in a place so obvious, Eric said, that the Nazis never thought of looking there. He made my jaw drop by bringing out of his brief-case a collection of Hertz family trees – written out by him in old-fashioned and (for me) in-decipherable German *Schrift* – of which the English branch petered out with my father's generation, but going back further, and providing more detail, than my Uncle Gerald, our chief family archvist, ever knew of. My kinship with this admirable old man was extremely distant, and he had many tables that did not concern me. But in the following months he transcribed those nearest to me into Roman script. In return he asked me to furnish him with details of my immigrant great-grandfather Martin Hertz's descendants. This I could easily do, but when he also asked for such arcane facts as baptism and marriage dates of great-aunts who had married Germans and died before I was born, I drew a blank. My inability to satisfy all his wishes inhibited me from asking for more information from him, and so our correspondence came to an end.

Just as Humphrey Fisher raised the question of publishing his translation of Nachtigal on the back of his own small book, Joshua Sherman, whom I soon got to know a little (Eduard Rosenbaum had meanwhile died in his nineties), asked me if I would be interested in the memoirs of Felix Somary (1881-1956), which he had translated for that worthy man's family. The German edition was published in Switzerland in the 1960s and was out of print. Sherman, after working long on the translation, had become rather jaded; a man as invariably right in his actions and predictions as Somary tends to leave lesser mortals feeling enervated. So who was Somary? In short, he was a Viennese economist whose brilliance led to his being regarded as an oracle, consulted by leading European statesmen and bankers while still in his twenties. As a banker himself he was deeply involved in the affair of the Sanjak railway in Bosnia which helped to precipitate the final crisis in 1914; he served with honour in a bad cause as financial administration of Belgium when it was occupied by the Germans; and warned the German military (and Luden-dorff personally) against the folly of unrestricted submarine warfare, which would inevitably bring America into the war and lead to the defeat of the Central Powers. In 1919 he moved to Zurich, where he acquired a small private bank, and in the Second World War lived in Washington, unofficially representing the Swiss government. Just as some special individuals acquire the power of healing, Somary acquired the power of political and economic prophecy, the price of which was rigorous self-discipline. I found him fascinating, and he told the extraordinary story of his life with spirit and many interesting human touches about the eminences he had met, like the Emperor Franz Joseph. One of his recurrent themes, his fanatical determination to retain his independence (he accepted no salary or contribution to his expenses for his work in Washington), naturally appealed to me. I encouraged Sherman not to give up, and offered to publish the book if Somary's family would pay the bill; thereafter they could appropriate as many copies as they wanted, and I would pay them half my receipts from sales. It might be said that to publish under such conditions is the denial of independence. On the other hand I would only publish on a profit-sharing basis a book which, if the economic prospects were brighter, I would publish anyway. Also, I would never accept unusual conditions about how the book was to be edited or produced. It would have to fit into the 'family' of its fellows in the list. As with the Warburg history, I gave Somary's memoirs, which we called *The Raven of Zurich* (1986), a spankingly smart livery. When Somary's son Wolfgang offered to ask Otto von Habsburg, with whom (and with Empress Zita) he was on visiting terms, to write a foreword, I could not resist this added *cachet*. This led to my having a brief correspondence with the erstwhile Austro-Hungarian crown prince, in the course of which I dared to encourage him, as an established writer, to turn to his memoirs; although his reply was courtesy itself, he made it clear that this was something he would never be free to do – as the repository of many confidences due to his unique position. This, of course, is admirable, but could it not be slightly misconceived? It must be possible for a man to write interestingly about his life, if it has been a remarkable one, without betraying any confidences. And while Otto was certainly alluding to the burden he bears as 'king over the water', the object of much nostalgic loyalty ('*Unser Motto*: *Kaiser Otto*'), the story of his early life, hustled from the glories of Schonbrunn into wandering exile and poverty, and his first emergence as a political figure, could surely be told without prejudice to anyone. But this is by the way.

Hamburg was the home of Germany's principal institute for the study of modern Asia, headed by a young and ambitious Indianist, Dr Werner Draguhn. On my first visit there in about 1975, Draguhn offered me a collection of articles called *Sri Lanka: A Survey*, entirely by Sri Lankan authors and edited by K.M. de Silva, professor of history at Peradeniya University in Kandy. It was bulky, running to some 500 pages, yet it was one of those rather nice publications that turns to money in one's hands. There was no royalty to be paid, yet the University of Hawaii Press bought 1,000 copies, and our edition sold out. Gratifyingly, too, the rich Lake House newspaper group in Colombo, also publishers and booksellers, came in as co-publishers.

I naturally corresponded with de Silva, but not at length since the ms. was virtually edited when it came into my hands. But suddenly out of the blue the book produced a fresh bonanza. De Silva came to see me and said that ten years earlier he had gone to Oxford University Press in England and offered to write for them the first complete and comprehensive history of his country since Sir James Emerson Tennent's history of 1859. O.U.P. accepted the proposal, and when de Silva asked the editor in charge (a well-known O.U.P. figure) whether he should go back to the island's prehistory or start with the first European colonisation, he was told to pursue the first alternative. When he returned ten years later with his large finished ms., a new editor told him that it would be better if he lopped off the earlier part and took it from the colonial period onwards. In a state of subdued anger he came straight and offered the book to me as the publisher of the *Survey*. I accepted it 'sight unseen', and it was indeed a model of its kind.

Such a book requires superior production, but this one had to be produced at a price that a publisher in the Indian subcontinent could afford. This meant printing in India – a course strongly urged by Ravi Dayal, the manager of O.U.P.'s Indian branch. But if normal Indian book printing was anything to go by, the standard would be unacceptable to an American co-publishing partner – a simultaneous and financially more urgent necessity. I went to Ely House, O.U.P.'s London headquarters, and looked at the Indian section in its house library of the Press's publications all around the world, and there the books produced by one printer in particular stood out. These books were set in Monotype and printed letterpress by a firm in Calcutta called Eastend Printers, owned by one S.K. Ghosh. Their standard of presswork was indistinguishable from that of a traditional high-quality printer in Britain. O.U.P. India were at first unwilling to send this book to Eastend; its capacity was limited, by both its small size and its liability to power cuts, and O.U.P. wanted to guard its own quota. But for once I was in a position to insist – O.U.P. India wanted the book – and finally they agreed. Probably this alone enabled us to sell 750 copies to the University of California Press. (The other Indian co-publication with them that has already been mentioned came slightly later.)

So the long production process began, and the first remarkable thing was the care with which the proofs were read by Eastend in-house before being sent to us. The firm still employed a 'reader', a personage once found in all self-respecting British printing houses, but by then approaching extinction like the Tasmanian Aboriginals. When J.M. Dent's old printing works at Letchworth was about to close, I was allowed to look around it, and found my way into the reader's little cubicle, richly accoutred with the two colossal blue volumes of the 1933 (first) edition of the Oxford *Shorter English Dictionary* and many other reference books, the tools of his trade. I developed feelings close to reverence for Eastend's reader. He was familiar with Sanskrit, of course, of which plenty was quoted in de Silva's early chapters, but he permitted himself occasionally to suggest improvements to the English phraseology; and, the sure master-touch, he spotted stylistic inconsistencies more than a hundred galleys apart.

The last thing to be finished by the author was the preface, and in consequence I naturally asked Eastend not to proceed with machining until we knew exactly the number of preliminary pages, numbered in Roman figures, that we would have, so we could aim at an 'even working' (an exact multiple of 32 or 16 pages, or slightly under). To my utter amazement Eastend replied that so valuable was their machine time, because of the ever-present fear of power cuts, that they had gone ahead already, numbering the sections from page 1 (Arabic numerals), and would fit in the prelims later, however they fell out.

The 'reader' just referred to was a strange institution, almost redolent of an 'old Spanish custom' of the trade in that his presence was not strictly necessary. Compositors traditionally do not edit their copy but compose exactly what is placed before them, right or wrong. An inexperienced editor might be tempted to say to a typesetter, 'Just correct any error that you notice which may have slipped through', but if typesetters once started doing that, and thus second-guessing publishers and authors, there would be no end to it. The reader's job was to correct the very first set of proofs, which was never sent to the publisher, and to highlight any insoluble queries. Nobody could deny that he might catch errors that would otherwise slip through; yet the publisher could not blame him for those which did. My contents list without page numbers could not for a moment have escaped the notice of a 'reader'; if it had, I suspect that the reader would have been in trouble with his employers. But although publisher and reader were both on the same side in the game of eliminating errors (I like to call this our 'invisible art', because nobody notices if it is properly done), the publisher bore the ultimate responsibility for the integrity of a text – as he still does, single-handed since the demise of the reader. That responsibility can never legitimately be shifted by the publisher on to the shoulders of an author.

I have already mentioned that we went on a family holiday to Sri Lanka in the summer of 1981, the prime justification being that it enabled me to translate Jean Suret-Canale's *Essays on African History*, but the trip was timed to coincide with de Silva's *History of Sri Lanka* being delivered from the printers. Our stay was to last five weeks, and from long beforehand it had seemed certain that we could launch the book in Colombo within a day or two of our arrival, and then relax in various places, including Kandy, for the rest of the time. This was not to be, and it was only after unaccustomed exertions by everyone in the production chain that we managed to have a handful of advance copies in our hands for the launch, which finally took place on the very last day of our stay. After it was over, we drove straight to the airport.

President Jayewardene himself came, which encouraged assorted ministers, ambassadors and other bigwigs to follow suit. He, like a number of other notables, was dressed entirely in white, and as he entered, repeatedly making the *namaste,* he had an ethereal air. He also seemed at first sight sweet and fatherly – an impression dispelled in the few moments of conversation I had with him afterwards. After we had gone through the ceremony of lighting the lamp, the President, the author, O.U.P.'s Madras manager Mr Parthasarathy and I sat down at a table on a dais facing the audience and spoke in turn. Kingsley de Silva made the only memorable statement: that if he had worked on his book in Europe or America it would have taken him two years to write, whereas in Sri Lanka it had taken ten. This was perhaps a pointed reference to the fact that many of his ablest colleagues emigrated to greener pastures; Kingsley's refusal to follow them has benefited his country, but the personal price he had to pay was considerable. A further price has been pressure to turn his great ability, industry and literary gift to work which, in an airier climate, he might have regarded as beneath him.

Kingsley was a non-executive director of the Bank of Ceylon – which he said was a perk resulting from his having stayed in the island, and a reason for his expanding waist-line. As such he invited us to join a company of local notables, to watch the procession on the final night of the great Buddhist Perahera festival in Kandy from the upper windows of the bank's office, which directly overlooked the processional route. The climax was the passing of a troupe of caparisoned elephants, the most gigantic of which carried the Buddha's Tooth Relic, the cynosure of the whole performance, but before this came countless acrobats and men cracking huge whips. It was as richly accoutred, and as long, as any state procession in England and incomparably more sensuous.

The international reviews of the *History* were respectful, but one review in a local periodical accused the author of plagiarising his own earlier published writings – an odd form of plagiarism, the mere suggestion of which I would have expected to rebound in ridicule upon the accuser. Kingsley did not think so and took the reviewer to court. I implored him not to, thinking that this would only further publicise the absurd slur, but he persisted and was vindicated. Verbal assassination, often of life-long friends behind their backs, is a sport many Sri Lankan intellectuals seem unable to resist.

The first offshoot of my connection with Kingsley de Silva, itself stemming from the Asian Institute in Hamburg, was a *Festschrift* presented to the veteran student of Indian politics, W.H. Morris-Jones, called *The States of South Asia*. The editor was A. Jeyaratnam Wilson, a contributor to the Hamburg-sponsored *Survey*, and professor of political science at the University of New Brunswick in Canada. He is a Tamil, son-in-law of the leading moderate Tamil politician of the post-independence period (S.J.V. Chelvanayakam), and for some years was a personal adviser to President Jayewardene on 'Tamil affairs'. This was unlike many *Festschriften* in that the first, expensive hardcover edition sold out and a second, paperback one followed. My partner for both was the Unuversity of Hawaii Press. No royalty had to be paid.

On Jeyaratnam Wilson's recommendation, I was approached by Yasmine Gooneratne, a professor of English literature at Macquarie University, Sydney. She is a poet, author of books for students on Jane Austen and Alexander Pope, winner of various awards and prizes, and a disarmingly indefatigable publicist of her own works – which have recently expanded to include a novel about being a Sri Lankan in Australia, published by Penguin. She offered me a spicy group portrait of the large and influential Dias Bandaranaike clan, to which she belongs, in the heyday of their wealth and power early in the twentieth century. It includes the moving love-story of her paternal grandparents and a wonderful close-up study of her father, their spoilt youngest child. I went to town on *Relative Merits*, and made it look as beautiful as possible. The only way to reproduce the tentacular family tree, which had to be included, was for me to transcribe it myself on to six pages. Having procrastinated and done it rather late in the day, I omitted to send my work to Australia for final checking, which proved to be yet another cautionary experience, because one or two names were fractionally mis-spelt. Of course we rushed out an errata slip. The author was particularly apprehensive about how one of her relations, whose name, by the displacement of one letter, could now be read as meaning a humble laundryman, would react; as she remarked, he could afford to take us all to the cleaners. I love *Relative Merits* and its author, and am sorry that we did not do better with it; but she had approached some eminent publishers before coming to me, and they rejected it.

A double spin-off from Hamburg came when Jeyaratnam Wilson offered me his account of the ethnic polarisation of his country, which we published as *The Break-up of Sri Lanka*. He referred to the country throughout the book by its old name, Ceylon, which by being of European etymology was ethnically neutral unlike the Sinhala word 'Lanka'. We did not try to sell it direct into Sri Lanka, but opted to make a co-publishing deal with Orient Longman in India. This proved a great headache for all of us, because the 500 copies of the book that docked at Bombay in August 1988 stayed there till February 1990. A zealous and eagle-eyed customs official, on taking a copy out for routine inspection, scented a possible cause of offence to the Government of India (and no doubt a possible cause of promotion for himself) and despatched it to Delhi. The proofs had been seen by Orient Longman, who felt no unease; and whenever I asked what kind of censorship regulations existed in India, I was always assured that there were none – except that maps of India had to show the disputed zone of Kashmir as belonging to India. The author thought that the problem had been caused by a passing reference to the training of Sri Lanka Tamil guerrillas in South India – something which, though embarrassing to the government, had been repeatedly ventilated in the Indian press. My first reaction – a foolish one as it turned out – was not to involve the British High Commission. Instead I tried the Indian High Commission in London, which was quite useless, and then enlisted the help of the Publishers Association's international department and the chairman of its Freedom to Publish Committee (of which I was a member). Their representations achieved nothing, and as the months passed Orient Longman were seeing the book slowly lose its up-to-dateness; they were forbidden to pay for the books while they were embargoed, and if the stand-off went on much longer the consignment might be put on a vessel back to the U.K., which of all things I wanted to avoid. In the .end I wrote to the British High Commissioner in Delhi. He sent me a personal reply by return, saying that he had passed the matter to his Deputy in Bombay, and in under a month the books were cleared and I received my payment. I felt rather proud of being British.

I had experienced this curious doubling of functions among Indian customs officials before. Early in 1975 I shipped 1,500 sets of unbound sheets of a book called *The Last Days of United Pakistan*, by a Bengali ex-minister in Yahya Khan's cabinet, G.W. Choudhury, to Mohan Chawla's Vikas Publishers, and while they were on the high seas Indira Gandhi declared her state of emergency. Although Z.A. Bhutto was the chief villain of the book, Indira too did not come off unscathed, and the 1,500 books were definitively impounded. Chawla told me that he had appealed without success, and that this was the end of the matter. I could not even get them shipped back to me.

We commissioned a second book from Jeyaratnam Wilson – a political biography of his father-in-law, Chelvanayakam. After a difficult gestation it emerged in a form which persuaded Hawaii to order 1,000 copies and Lake House in Colombo 750 (at a good price). Here indeed was vindication of our esoteric interests.

In his 'keynote' address to a conference of academic and college textbook publishers in the mid-1980s I heard a colleague – David Evans of Associated Book Publishers, a medium-sized conglomerate – say that one thing a commissioning editor had to be very definite about was not allowing authors to over-run the date written into the contract for delivery of their mss. At the end of the speech I immediately made the first intervention of the conference, to some laughter, expressing my profound doubts about this narrow-minded doctrine. Some authors work better when they have a deadline, others worse; but that is not the point. I have already mentioned an author who twice managed to get a very big and labour-intensive ms., sent by ordinary airmail from Australia, on to my desk on the very day it was due. I could almost say that I felt threatened rather than reassured by such superhuman punctiliousness. But surely the psychological moment for completing a ms. may become apparent after the contract is signed, and it behoves the publisher to be adaptable so that the auspices at the completion of the ms., the passing of the proofs for press and the issuing of the book itself are as favourable as possible.

Changes of circumstances can sometimes make for a better book than anyone previously thought possible. Soon after the fall of Idi Amin I wanted to find a native Ugandan intellectual who would look not at the horrors of Amin's regime, which were well known, but at what it had done to the basic fabric of the state – legal, administrative, educational, ecclesiastical and so on. After many inquiries I was referred to a professor of history at Makerere University, a Baganda named Phares Mutibwa, and in April 1980, after a synopsis had been duly submitted and approved, we signed a contract and a not inconsiderable advance was paid. What no one could have foreseen was that Milton Obote's second regime, which replaced Amin's anarchy, would be as bloodthirsty as its predecessor. As Mutibwa stated laconically in his preface, many of his closest kin, including his mother and brother, were murdered. For a time he was beyond reach, then he reappeared in a relatively humble teaching post in Swaziland. But after the end of arbitrary rule and the installation of Museveni's National Resistance Front, his fortunes brightened, and when the book finally appeared in 1992 he was a member of Uganda's constitutional commission and a leading citizen. The delay caused what I am sure is a far better book to be written (called *Uganda since Independence: A Story of Unfulfilled Hopes*), and I made co-publication arrangements, both in the United States and in Uganda, with firms that had not existed a few years earlier, when the book might have appeared under its original guise. Here again I had cause to be grateful to British diplomats, because when it was otherwise impossible to communicate with the author, and especially when proofs had to be sent to and fro, the High Commission in Kampala cheerfully agreed to act as a post-office.

At the time when I was congratulating myself on this seeming proof that fexibility paid off, I was confident that another long-running project for which I signed a contract and paid an advance in the early 1980s would also yield to the same devilish arts. This was to have been a much-trumpeted study of a Latin American republic – one of the important ones in world terms – since a military coup in the 1960s. Out of curiosity I had attended a seminar at the Publishers Association on the book market in that country, and the economic and other information about it was expounded by a young redbrick lecturer, F.C. I thought him so intelligent and good at expressing himself that I pursued him and we signed a contract. W.W. Norton in New York – a publisher I have long aspired to do business with – were interested in this book, alone of all our futures. We must have announced it three or four times on cast-iron assurances from F.C. that he only needed to make one more visit to Latin America or rewrite the last chapter before I could have the ms. It was every bit as necessary for his academic advancement, he said, as it was for me that the book should come out, and all his friends in Latin America were impatient to see it. In the end my hopes turned to cynicism and we cancelled the contract – eleven years after it was signed. F.C. offered no resistance, but one day I may yet phone and ask him how the book is coming on.

One reason why I was reluctant to let F.C. go was the paucity of our offerings on Latin America. It is a field where British publishers have to tread with caution, but I was determined that we should make some contribution. Our involvement started when I met Andrew Graham-Yooll, an Argentine-Scottish journalist, who had to flee for his life from his job on the *Buenos Aires Herald* when the military junta was in power in the 1970s, and then worked on the *Guardian* and the *Daily Telegraph* in London. He offered me a ms. about the British colony in Argentina, but although I was attracted by the subject, I did not think it would sell; Hutchinson published it just at the time of the South Atlantic war and it sold rather well. But Andrew introduced me to another exiled bilingual journalist, Eduardo Crawley, who had a finished ms. on Nicaragua. It was journalistic and dramatic, but meticulous in its reconstruction of the career of Sandino and the rise of the Somozas. I seized on it, but in this case subsequent events did not help us; the book, called *Dictators Never Die*, came out just as the Somoza regime fell and the Sandinistas took over. Crawley then asked if I would commission him to write about his own country, Argentina, and the result – *A House Divided: Argentina 1880-1980*, with the story of Juan Peron at its heart – is a vintage work of a scholarly journalist.

Before going to St. Martin's Press with *A House Divided* I offered it to Stanford University Press, which then had the most brilliant editor I have ever dealt with, Jess Bell. An abrasive man, he never praised unsparingly, but he said that he was unable to put Crawley's ms. down – only there was not a chance that his press would take it because the author was a journalist. Such academic snobbery is common in America. When we decided to look for someone to write on Venezuela, we were led inevitably to an American academic, Judith Ewell. Stanford, a fastidious press, did take her book.

I Take an Interest in Trade Politics

My firm first joined the Publishers Association (P.A.) at the beginning of the 1970s. Then I did not pay the subscription for a year or two, but finally rejoined in 1976 as a more conscious act. I knew none of the publishers who were active in the Association, and was at first content to watch from afar with a feeling of pre-destined impotence. The first thing that happened which disturbed my quietism was the announcement at one annual general meeting that a former president had been elected unopposed as treasurer. The time-honoured practice had always been that the offices of treasurer, vice-president and president were held in that order, and that the retiring president would become vice-president for another year before retiring from all offices. I had never opened my mouth at an A.G.M. and did not on this occasion. The then president, Graham C. Greene, apologised disarmingly for what, he said, might seem to members like a 'recycling of the magic circle', but that was just how it did seem to me, and I felt rebellion stirring in my blood. The Association belonged to its small and insignificant members as well as to the large ones.

Soon after this it suddenly struck me as both eccentric and regrettable that the P.A. did not hold an annual conference, unlike almost every other professional and trade association, and in 1980 I wrote a short article which the *Bookseller* published on its first page, recommending that it should. As far as I could discover, every publishers' association in continental Europe holds one, and these are convivial as well as occasions for talking shop and transacting Association business. Of course, in Britain we have the Booksellers Association conference, a great social landmark in the book trade calendar, assiduously attended by senior directors and sales staff from the more prominent general publishers. But this is only in a very small and partial way a conference for publishers, who have many concerns not shared by the home retail trade, and it is good for these sometimes to be aired not only in closed committees of the P.A. but in public discussions open to all. The snag is that it is for middle-ranking staff of large firms, especially in departments other than sales, that attending a publishers' conference would be most valuable – to listen to speakers and both listen to and participate in panel discussions about matters both central and peripheral to their individual concerns, and to meet their peers in other houses. However, they can only do so by the grace of their managers, who may think the advantages not commensurate with the expense and loss of work time.

Donald Sutherland, the director of McGill-Queen's University Press with whom I did so much profitable business in the 1970s, urged me to attend the annual meeting of the Association of American University Presses (A.A.U.P.), which is held in June each year in different places. In 1981, when I first went, it was in San Francisco. I had never been to the West coast before, and this gave me the chance to visit the Berkeley campus of the University of California, the University Press, Stanford University at Palo Alto, the Centre for Independent Living on Telegraph Avenue, Berkeley,* and above

---

* This pioneering self-help organisation for disabled people was visited two years later

all my sister Pam who then had a house in Marin County on the far side of the Golden Gate. (My first sight of the bridge, from the fort on the city side, with fog shrouding the upper half of the towers, a warning klaxon sounding every few seconds and the water grey and choppy, left me with a persistent feeling that it has a sinister aura, a life of its own – perhaps it is something to do with the numerous people who have thrown themselves off it. Yet I know of no modern structure more beautiful, its closest rival being the Chrysler Building in New York.) When the conference was over I moved in with Pam for a few days, which was an enjoyable experience – we talked a lot, she was ultra-considerate, and I met various of her friends. We have had very little contact over the years, and do not really relax in eachother's company, but we came as near to it on this visit as we shall ever do. The vicissitudes of the war and oppressive over-protection by our parents because of her health when she was young seemed to blight any chances she might have had of pursuing a worthwhile career. It saddened me that she seemed in some way to envy the hectic kind of life I was leading.

Since 1981 I have been to seven more A.A.U.P. meetings. The transactions mostly get forgotten and the places remain lodged in the memory – like the Netherland Plaza Hotel in Cincinnati a *locus classicus* of Art Deco, completed in 1931; the pathetic Indian reservation near Tucson, Arizona, the U.S.A.'s Third World; and the many glories of Chicago. In 1982 at Spring Lake, New Jersey, I was one of three British publishers, John Spiers and John Naylor being the others, who spoke in a session called 'How Others See Us' at the invitation of John Gallman. Fred Praeger, a regular attender of A.A.U.P. meetings, was in the audience and told me afterwards that I had spoken better than he expected.

I liked everything about these gatherings which lasted two days and three nights. There are optional excursions to interesting places – on the Sunday before the proceedings begin – but no special programme for 'accompanying persons' (usually the wives of senior delegates), which are a prominent feature of International Publishers Association

---

by Rachel herself, who took the idea back to the U.K. and helped to found a similar organisation in Greenwich. A girl in a manually operated wheelchair, which she propelled herself, showed me round, and as we were crossing an open space I followed my conventional instinct and took the handles of her chair and gave it a push. She quietly said to me 'You're invading my living space', I disengaged, and we went on talking. This phrase has never ceased to be repeated, on appropriate occasions, in our family.

The independent spirit of disabled people in the Bay Area was brought home by another incident. I got off a bus with a blind man and, again obeying an atavistic instinct, offered to give him a hand across the street. He accepted, but when we reached the other side, he said 'Now can I show *you* the way somewhere?'

(I.P.A.) congresses and even the U.K. Booksellers Association conference; to the A.A.U.P.'s credit, accompanying persons who are not themselves publishers are considered integral to the whole scene, not just the social part. Hundreds of people attend, not only press directors (and these vary in the size of their presses and hence their clout) but an assortment of editorial, sales, production and even warehouse people for whom a few days off among confreres, possibly two or three time zones away from home, make a substantial treat. There is thus a palpable *esprit de corps*, enhanced by the homely ceremonial of awarding medals to retiring press directors; the eulogies vary in quality, but the unforced warmth of feeling does not. On one famous occasion the eulogist, even after diligent research, had not been able to find anything good to say about the retiree, who was not present, and the whole assembly dissolved in laughter.

The first time I went to the A.A.U.P. meeting, in 1981, only one other equally obscure British publisher was present. Not surprisingly the committee of the P.A. division dealing with 'scholarly' and 'professional' (i.e. medical, legal and 'business') publishing, of which I had just become a member at the invitation of Norman Franklin (then still the head of his family business, Routledge & Kegan Paul), thought the A.A.U.P. meeting so unimportant that it held its own periodical meeting in the same week in 1981 and, despite my protests, again in 1982, but after that the message filtered through. When Giles de la Mare of Faber was chairman, this division boldly held its own conference at Wadham College, Oxford, and when the question arose of who would organise the next one, I volunteered, and thus organised the next three, all at Oxford colleges. I followed as closely as possible the A.A.U.P. plan, even down to having a 'How Others See Us' session, chaired by me, at which Fred Praeger was one of the speakers. I only failed in my effort to find a choir to sing at the dinner. The conferences lasted two days and one could stay one or two nights according to how sociable one felt. It was acknowledged to have worked well, but in successive years the event became more and more curtailed. My indispensable ally in all this was John Davies, the P.A.'s permanent officer in charge of the educational and scholarly aspects of its work. He was not only a Labour councilor, but Labour parliamentary candidate for Finchley, Mrs Thatcher's constituency; and when, one night, I sat down at the piano in the college bar, he astounded us all with his vast repertoire of songs, including one in Welsh. I became vice-chairman of U.C.P.P.C., but resigned in pique the first time I stood for the P.A. Council and failed in the election. John wrote a handsome short 'obituary' of me in the U.C.P.P.C. newsletter, which touched me.

I have been to two quadrennial I.P.A. meetings, in London (1988) and New Delhi (1992). The recreational or inspirational activities accompanying these events can be memorable. The London conference opened with a poetry reading in Westminister Abbey by four actors including John Gielgud and Peggy Ashcroft. Both Rachel, who was there, and I are keenly susceptible to the spell of Gielgud's voice and felt almost overcome by his reading of 'Fear no more the heat of the sun' from *Cymbeline,* which ended the reading. One day of the congress week is devoted to an excursion, and I could not think why such an undistinguished, botched-up place as Hever Castle should have been shown off to our visitors as a typical English country mansion in preference to, say, Syon, Knole or Woburn. In Delhi the excursion was, of course, to the Taj Mahal, and having seen it twice before and being unable to get the thought of Dr Aziz and the picnic at the Malabar caves out of my head, decided not to go. In the event it rained, and the coaches, which left at dawn, got separated from eachother and returned at 11 p.m. with everyone exhausted and in a bad temper. The 'Freedom to Publish' session at these congresses has a symbolic importance, like honouring the war dead on Remembrance Day; it is left to the end and is followed only by the passing of resolutions and the farewells. In London the readings included an especially moving one from the writings of the Chilean Ariel Dorfman. In Delhi the Dalai Lama made an appearance. Clearly he finds it hard to get into his stride, because he spent many precious minutes uttering banalities and giggling; he did not address 'freedom to publish' but he recommended his hearers to fight injustice with anger but not hatred. At an earlier session the same day, a placeman from China had protested through an interpreter at the presence of the Dalai Lama who, he said, represented nobody. I immediately walked out – alone, unfortunately – making as much commotion as possible. The organisers of I.P.A. congresses allow too much time for the orotundities of V.I.P.s.; in London we had Giovanni Agnelli and in Delhi Mario Soares, one-time hero of the Portuguese left, and neither had anything of interest to say. But in Delhi a small literary publisher from Poland told how his compatriots, who now condemned everything that had originated under communism, 'have allowed our market to be flooded with translations of bad books, especially American ones, which contribute nothing to our culture'. He provided a rare and precious moment of undiplomatic truth.

Many months in advance of the congresses, the word goes out, via member associations, to publishers throughout the world urging them to attend and inviting individuals to read papers. Before the

Delhi congress I replied that I wanted to read a paper on the role of small publishers in the great world of publishing, such a thing had certainly never been done before, and I did not expect a reply, nor did I get one. But just before the congress opened, I asked Andrew H. Neilly, the president (chief executive of John Wiley), if I might be fitted in somewhere. I am sure he would have been glad to forget about it, but being a compassionate man without pomposity or side, he was cooperative and friendly, and showed no irritation at my repeated reminders. I planned to have my say, whether invited or not, but in the end he said that if I spoke for us more than five minutes, I could have a slot in the closing plenary session – considerably more than I had expected. The text owed much to a handwritten memo given me by Ravi Dayal (former manager of O.U.P. in India, now a small independent), whom I had asked for some ideas. The Indian publishers (not the big ones meshed in with the multinationals) seemed to like it, which was not surprising since many of them who are medium-sized in Indian terms are small in Western terms; of all the accredited Western delegates I was by far the smallest. The 1996 congress in Barcelona did have a session on small publishers.

One consequence of my I.P.A. foray that I could not have foreseen came through a party I attended during the week at the house of the British Council representative, Robert Arbuthnott. I fell into conversation with Hasan Suroor, Muslim intellectual and parliamentary correspondent of the great family-owned Madras broadsheet newspaper *The Hindu*, and when I mentioned my little to-do about the speech on small publishers, he asked me to send him the text. It appeared in the paper the following Sunday. A year later Hasan was in England and invited me to contribute a regular monthly article to *The Hindu's* Sunday Magazine. I agreed and have been doing so ever since.

Interlude: A Knock on the Door

Late in 1985 I lost the services of my assistant Joy Ozobia; as already mentioned, she bought the Africa Book Centre from me. But before we lose sight of her, I must pay tribute to a purely commercial service she rendered to the firm. We had just published Jacob Landau's book on Pan-Turkism, and the Greek embassy phoned to say it wanted to buy 200 copies. I was out, and when the person at the embassy asked Joy if there would be any discount on the cover price, she replied that she would have to ask me, but thought I might agree to 10%. I phoned the embassy back with some apprehension, and when the person there asked me if 10% would be acceptable, I hastily said yes. If I had answered the first call instead of Joy, I would have offered at least 30% and expected to be beaten down. On her departure, I advertised as usual in the *Bookseller* for a secretary/ book-keeper, but this time the first applicant was someone who was neither a secretary nor a book-keeper but who none the less offered his services in those capacities. He had, he said, been treasurer of his student union and reckoned he had acquired the necessary skills. But he did not conceal that his real wish was to join me as a publisher. I quickly decided to recruit him and for once my instinct was the right one. At twenty-four, he was thirty-one years my junior.

This was Michael Dwyer who, more than eleven years later, is still with the firm. His earlier career in the book trade had been short but significant – a year in the oriental and African department of Heffer's, where he became acquainted with our books. Before that he took a degree in African history at S.O.A.S. He had thus made a deliberate move in the direction of the firm to do the kind of publishing he felt drawn to.

For several years up till the time of writing the firm has been as much his as mine, insofar as people automatically associate it with him and him with it. We have our own (geographical) area specialisations, and our own functional ones. Editing and designing come mainly within my orbit, sales and publicity within his; list-building and wheeling and dealing with potential co-publisher and partners for right sales are shared responsibilities. But we are as one in wanting the firm to continue, very much as it is, growing not in the numbers of books published or of people employed but only in fame, and above all retaining its independence. Ray Noonan once said to me, when we were working together, 'If you don't grow you die.' I have seen this disproved in various ways again and again. My definition of 'death' in business terms is obviously worlds apart from his; in a phrase, it would be losing the freedom to publish the books that Michael and I agree we want to publish, and for me in particular the freedom to operate independently in the world of trade politics. Growing rich would be pleasant, but not by the terminal act of selling out; without the business I would become like the Flying Dutchman. If I had no successor I would prefer to wind C. Hurst & Co. down and slowly cease publishing new books; continuing to sell the old ones and having no production bills except for the occasional reprint would ensure an adequate income for several years. I remain convinced that if I had gone out and deliberately sought a successor, I.would never have found one.

Journalism and More Trade Politics

I fell into the habit of book trade journalism in the 1980s without any premeditation. Almost everything that I wrote appeared in the *Bookseller* and because I found doing it enjoyable, I owe its editor, Louis Baum, a great debt for his encouragement. The first piece to appear was on the desirability of a full-blown P.A. conference, as already mentioned. Then in the spring of 1981 I was on a delegation to Hungary, and wrote about that. Early in 1982 I asked Louis if he would like me to investigate Black British publishing and bookselling and he agreed, so I went around outer London meeting and interviewing these colleagues of whom the mainline publishing scene knows virtually nothing and I knew nothing before embarking on it. I did not include Allison and Busby, in spite of its important role in publishing C.L.R. James and many of the best Caribbean creative writers, because they had acquired a sophisticated metropolitan air, with an office in central London and their books smart-looking and well designed; besides, they had made it into the media scene, and would have needed, if anything, a separate article to themselves. My main focus – inevitably, so it seemed to me – had to be on the two fully-formed literary publishers of Caribbean origin (Clive Allison is English and Margaret Busby Ghanaian). One of these was New Beacon in North London, of which the poet and intellectual John La Rose was the founder and inspiration. Perforce a bookshop, run by his wife Sarah White, was the main element of the business, because, as he explained, he could only publish books when there was cash available; several accepted mss. were awaiting their turn, the authors willing to be patient for the sake of being published by New Beacon. The other was Bogle L'Ouverture in West London run by Jessica Huntley and also consisting of a bookshop and a publishing operation. It had published Walter Rodney's *How the West Underdeveloped Africa*, which became a bestseller with mythic status after its young author was assassinated by political enemies in his native Guyana. I felt a strong sense of identification with both publishers, since they were of my age and also started their businesses in the late 1960s (Bogle is no longer active and Rodney's book now appears under another imprint). I was also excited by the phenomenon of an intellectual like John La Rose becoming a publisher, with uncompromising objectives which had nothing to do with making (serious) money and for that reason were more likely to be realised. I had met a similar case in Ireland with Liam Miller's Dolmen Press, and on my visit to Prague in 1991 I met several.

Shortly after this, having smelt gunpowder, I went off in search of the country's oriental booksellers. This took me round the old-established firms near the British Museum, then enlarged to four with the migration from Leiden of E.J. Brill's bookshop, a specialist in Arabica and Hebraica. I came to appreciate the warm if shy character of Walter Sheringham* of Probsthain. My most intriguing encounters were with R.A. Gooch, once manager of the oriental department at Heffer's, who had taken off to the south coast and set up a mail-order bookselling business in his house, and J.S.D. Thornton of Broad Street, Oxford. I had visited Gooch in the late 1960s soon after the founding of his firm Ad Orientem, and even then was impressed by the amount of stock he held. By the 1980s not only the floor of every room in the house but the staircase and landings seemed congested with books. John Thornton was the fifth and last of his line, and before his death he sold the business to Willem Meeuws, originally a Russian and East European specialist, but now upholding Thornton's polymathic tradition, and offering new and 'secondhand' books under the same roof as it has always done – and as Blackwell's and Heffer's used to do. But Meeuws has, not unnaturally, divested himself of John Thornton's pride and joy – Ottoman Turkish and Amharic ˙collections, for which he was world-famous among cognoscenti. Thornton was leading me up the steep staircase to his locked sanctum at the top of the house where he kept his treasures, when a young student accosted him and asked whether he had any books on the Kazakh language. Gruff and courteous, he replied that he had not but added, 'Are you interested in Uzbek?' I used the question as the title of the article. After it was published, Thomas Joy, one-time manager of Hatchards in Piccadilly and one of the trade's great characters, wrote me a long letter about his fifteen years at Thornton's, five as an apprentice, of which I had known

---

* He was also a man of noble character. When in his mid-eighties, he was sitting indoors at home alone when a deranged young man broke in and attacked him. To escape, he tried to get out of the window but broke both his legs in the attempt. In response to the get-well card Michael Dwyer and I sent him, he wrote: 'I am now out of hospital and able to walk with the help of a stick. The original cause of the "accident" is long forgotten.' I hope I could take that attitude to someone who had tried to kill me.

nothing. He actually founded its oriental department, but left when it was plain that there was not room in the firm for both him and John.

The *Bookseller* must have published at least twenty of my articles or special reports throughout the 1980s but at the end of the decade the association quietly came to an end.* One or two of the pieces I would rather forget; most are forgettable anyway. But three or four were of rather more consequence. One was on Sir Stanley Unwin. Despite finding his personal character rather unappealing, I looked to him as the foremost British publisher of the twentieth century: starting as a boy in a shipping office, serving a long appreticeship to his uncle T. Fisher Unwin whom he vainly hoped to succeed in business, and finally striking out with the purchase of the moribund firm of George Allen and so founding one of the most admirable and successful imprints of the age. If it could be said to be just one thing, Allen & Unwin was a scholarly general publishing house, highly serious according to the lights of its founder (pacifist, internationalist, puritan, politically liberal, secular). I shrink from slogans like the one he adopted – 'Books that Matter' – since it is for others and not for the publisher to decide which of his books do 'matter', but Unwin succeeded in combining his exemplary aims and standards with great commercial acumen. Thus he could afford time to serve the trade (some of its paladins, like Sir Frederick Macmillian, treated him as an upstart) and the money to found a substantial charity directed entirely to book-trade ends. I never met him, but having read not only his famous textbook *The Truth about Publishing* (which one can dip into profitably at any stage in one's career) but his autobiography, I felt I knew him a little. Although it was something like a painter producing a portrait of a dead person from a photograph, it must have been fairly true to life because of the response it produced. Rayner Unwin was 'overwhelmed', and Fred Praeger, after characteristically reminding me that he still bore me a grudge for something I had written to him in the 1970s (I never discovered exactly what it was, though it could have been a somewhat bald request for payment of a long-overdue invoice), called the article 'elegant, gracious and warm'. Egil Kristoffersen of Cappelen in Oslo wrote that he had read the piece (before realising it was by me) because he had set aside a few lines for a biography of Stanley Unwin in his firm's

---

* Since then I have only published at long intervals three 'profiles' – of K.V. J. (Justin) de Silva, veteran bookseller of Colombo; S. Bhattacharya, the British Council's hyperenthusiastic Books Officer in Delhi; and Shreeram Vidyarthi, founder of Books from India in Museum Street, Bloomsbury, who rightly took me to task for omitting him from my survey of oriental booksellers in 1982.

10-volume encyclopaedia, adding his regret that there is no mention of him in *Everyman's Encyclopaedia* – 'this probably reflects the difference in standing that publishers enjoy (or do not enjoy) in our two countries'. Finally, most of Christina Foyle's letter deserves to be quoted:

> I think your tribute to Stanley Unwin is the nicest article I have ever read. You described him just as he was, with his brilliance and ability and all his odd ways.
>
> I knew him all my life and had the greatest admiration and respect for him. I can remember many funny occasions – one in 1959 in Vienna when we were with some foreign publishers.... Someone offered him a cigarette and he said 'No thank you, I did try smoking once, and only once, and have never done it since'. He was then offered a glass of wine and refused saying 'I did try a drink as a youth, but only once, and I have not tasted alcohol since'. At that moment Rayner came up and Stanley introduced him to a French publisher, who said 'Your only child, I presume?'

The article was published by design on the ninety-ninth anniversary of the great man's birth in December 1884, and ended with a plea that something suitable should be done to mark the centenary a year later. Only half of the money he had put into his charity had been used – to buy the building in Wandsworth which is now Book House, and by the terms of the endowment the capital could only be used for a project involving the purchase of real estate; thus it was stalled for want of another project similar to Book House. Nevertheless, the trustees decided to devote several thousand pounds each year to finance a Sir Stanley Unwin Memorial Travelling Fellowship, and at its inauguration Rayner Unwin acknowledged the part my article had played in bringing this to pass.

The article I wrote that raised the most dust was about 'Possum'. This was a club of 'leading', 'senior' or influential publishers which Peter Allsop, legal publisher and erstwhile chief executive of the Associated Book Publishers group, founded after he completed his term as president of the Publishers Association in 1977. I had no suspicion of its existence until one evening I took the short walk from my office to the Garrick Club to read a newspaper and have a drink. As I went up the stairs I espied, sitting in the space within the stairwell reserved for members only, two publishers of whom Allsop was one; the other, David Gadsby, I knew and hailed. When I came down again, those two had gone, but in the same space were André Deutsch and Sir John Brown, emeritus Publisher of Oxford University Press, and Andre introduced me to this agreeable but archetypally 'Establishment' publishing figure. He then said to me 'Are you coming in?' When I replied 'Coming in where?', he realised that he had made a gaffe, and added as he went off towards one of the smaller dining rooms, 'Don't kick us in the backside'. I wondered why he should think that I would.

I now headed for the front entrance and there encountered, coming in together, Philip Attenborough, Tim Rix, Tom Rosenthal, Gordon Graham and doubtless 'others that I cannot now remember' (as penitents say of their sins in the confessional). I said to Tim, 'What's this meeting?' to which he replied guardedly, 'There's no meeting'. I put the same question to Gordon Graham and he, breezy as ever, answered 'Oh, just senior management'. I went away with my head buzzing. The next morning I phoned first Christopher Helm, a confrere with whom for some years I used regularly to exchange gossip, who was as baffled as I was, and then a book trade journalist, who said 'That must have been the Possums'. This slightly inaccurate terminology emphasised the connection with the animal of that name, which is more successful than the ostrich in its endeavours to make itself invisible. I am told that it was a triple world-play, incorporating not only the Latin for 'I am able' but also an acronym for 'Publishers Senior Management'. My journalist friend sent me a recent list of Possum (*sic*) members,* from whom no obvious person seemed to be excluded, and among whom only one or two non-obvious ones were included – according to one of them, as a token presence.

I proceeded to phone the few among them whom I knew well enough, and although they were vowed to strict secrecy, enough was let fall to enable me to piece together a picture of an informal grouping who would get together to drink and fraternise before being called to order to discuss a trade topic of current concern. The most eloquent description of Possum by one of its more enthusiastic members was 'people of influence who enjoy eachother's company'. Clive Bradley, the chief executive of the Publishers Association, early in whose tenure of office Possum came into existence (it was Allsop, as president, who appointed him), was not a member and the freedom

---

* Peter Allsop, William Armstrong, Philip Attenborough, Bryan Bennett, Francis Bennett, Alewyn Birch, Charles Black, David Blunt, John Boon, Marion Boyars, Sir John Brown, Nicholas Byam Shaw, Carmen Callil, Hugh Campbell, Mark Collins, Robin Denniston, André Deutsch, Matthew Evans, Christopher Falkus, Michael Foyle, Norman Franklin, David Gadsby, Livia Gollancz, Gordon Graham, Graham C. Greene, Philippa Harrison, David Herbert, Alan Hill, Robin Hyman, Ian Chapman, David Machin, Julia Macrae, Simon Master, Peter Mayer, Alan Miles, Nigel Newton, Dieter Pevsner, Charles Pick, George Richardson, Tim Rix, Tom Rosenthal, Paul Scherer, Christopher Sinclair-Stephenson, Nicolas Thompson, Michael Turner, Rayner Unwin, Patrick Wright, Michael Wymer. I knew two confreres who had resigned: Michael Attenborough and Adrian Higham.

to discuss trade matters without him present was, as more than one of my informants averred, part of its attraction. One could understand that the Possumites did not want Clive's intellectual ascendancy over most of them, his rather electric personality and his professional attachment to particular lines of policy to impose an unwanted restraint on free-ranging discussion. (One relatively influential member assured me that the discussions were largely hot air, with 'old men muttering into their beards'.) But, logical or not, Clive's exclusion was in bad taste. How could these colleagues of mine lend their reputations to this charade of *omertà* and parallel policy-making, both outflanking and influencing the Publishers Association?

The *Bookseller* published my article, and I got a strong letter from Allsop saying that he and several of his fellow Possumites thought I had abused the hospitality of the Garrick by accosting them as they arrived for that meeting; and he threatened to report me to the chairman if I could not give a good explanation of my conduct – which I did by reminding him that the people I had 'accosted' were all colleagues and acquaintances of mine and all but one were my fellow members of the Club. In his letter he also assured me that I had misunderstood Possum's purpose, and that it had no influence. But a number of people told me they had been glad to see my article. As far as I know, Possum has ceased to exist, the precipitating factor in this being Peter Allsop's retirement and the impossibility of finding a suitable successor to him. Although he and I knew eachother only by sight before this happened, we have since conversed more than once – though Possum has never been mentioned.

The occasion for my third 'important' article comes later.

In 1987 I first became engaged in an almost solitary fight against the prevailing view in the Publishers Association over voting rights. I had joined the Association not from any noble motive (although I do believe its representational work is essential to the wellbeing of publishing and therefore worthy of support by all publishers), but because I saw it as a club within which publishers (in both the corporate and personal sense of the word) of all types could meet and even work together on a basis of equality, however unequal the size and power of their firms. (It is because I hold to this rainbow vision of a 'commonwealth' of publishers that I have always wanted to see an annual residential conference, however hard it may be to justify on crude cost-benefit grounds.) Throughout most of its existence since 1896, the P.A. has been heavily influenced in its policy and general thinking by a few dominant firms – Longman, Macmillan, Heinemann, Hodder & Stoughton, the ancient university presses – who, by virtue of their size, also pay the largest subscriptions.

Their heads, and those of a few smaller but prominent companies such as John Murray, Dent, Allen & Unwin, Chatto & Windus and Cape, have repeatedly held the elected offices. Nobody has ever thought of opposing this natural order of things, but when these firms decided to increase their already unchallengeable voting power relative to the smaller member firms, I felt that at least a show of resistance had to be made.

It has to be explained that the tendency to consensus within the P.A. has always been strong – contentious issues have traditionally not been fought out in public – and so there has seldom been a need for voting power to be put to the test. It is only likely to happen if an issue arises which can not be settled by a show of hands and has to be submitted to a general vote, or in the election of Council members and of the vice-president (who automatically succeeds as president after a year in that office). In most years up till 1993 a ballot was held in the Council election – it was generally thought to be rather unhealthy if the number of candidates exactly equalled the number of vacacies and there was no need for a vote. Since I first took an interest in these things there has only been one contested vice-presidential election, in 1984 between two very senior figures, Alewyn Birch (the only candidate in a P.A. election who ever canvassed my vote) and Gordon Graham. Birch was thought to be the 'Establishment' choice, and Graham's victory gave him – in my romantic view – exceptional legitimacy. Such a contest would be much less likely to happen today.

For some years up till 1987, a member house was entitled to 1, 2, 3, 4 or 5 votes according to the size of its turn-over. Below £100,000 a minimum subscription was paid, and those smallest member firms, which for a long time included mine, commanded 1 vote. Those with a turnover between £100,000 and £1 million had 2 votes, and so it went on up the scale until the very largest had 5 votes. Thus the smallest members might seem over-generously enfranchised compared to the largest. Why, say, should C. Hurst & Co. with £120,000 turnover have 2 votes, and Longman or Macmillan 5 votes? This seemed a compellingly logical position until one considered the reality. The large firms are capable of organising themselves effectively, but the small ones are not, and few are interested in the issues; thus it is in practice inconceivable that an important measure proposed to the membership by the Council would be defeated by the votes of small firms. So in 1987 when, under the presidency of Gordon Graham, it was put to the A.G.M. that the voting entitlement, per subscription band, be changed from 1-2-3-4-5 to 1-2-4-6-8, I felt that this was the result of nothing but meanness of spirit. Or was the motive mere paranoia? Did the 'Establishment' really imagine that its plans could be upset by a grassroots revolt, or did it merely want its superior strength to be made more visible?

I am no good as a lobbyist, and so, apart from writing a short letter to the *Bookseller* attempting to rally all possible opponents of the motion, I relied on a fairly long and carefully written speech against the motion. One of my points was that the large firms had so much power outside the Association that they surely needed no additional power inside it, where their position was already assured. When I had finished Philip Attenborough – chairman of Hodder & Stoughton and Gordon Graham's immediate predecessor as president – rose to speak in support of the motion, on the pragmatic basis of 'He who pays the piper should call the tune', and began with the words *'Mr President, we have heard the view from King Street....'* There were 44 votes against the motion (not discreditable) and just over 90 in favour; therefore, having obtained a two-thirds majority, the motion passed. The incoming president Michael Turner startled me when we met in the Garrick a few days later by saying that he had regarded my speech as noble, and voted against the motion on behalf of his company (Associated Book Publishers). On the other hand, an ambitious publisher much nearer to me in size and scope, Frances Pinter, phoned after reading my rallying letter in the *Bookseller* to say that she could not offer me her support.

Also in 1987, a few weeks before the Association's A.G.M., it was briefly announced in its newsletter that the Council had decided to set up a 'Small Firms Forum' and that David Gadsby, a member of the Council, was to be its chairman. All member firms of the P.A. with an annual sales volume below £1 million were declared to be automatically members of the 'Forum'. I was incensed about two aspects of this development. First, whichever small members had been consulted by the president, Gordon Graham, or the chief executive, Clike Bradley, before this plan was made public, I was not one of them and yet I was 'senior' in terms of age and experience and already a vocal advocate for dedicated small publishers of which I was almost an archetypal example. And secondly the publisher chosen to chair the new group was the managing director of A. & C. Black which, whatever David Gadsby's personal virtues, was by the standard of small publishers quite a large one. I felt embarrassed at having to oppose the Establishment over two issues at the A.G.M., which usually consists of little more than ritual votes of thanks and congratulations, and therefore did not raise the question of the forum then. But ironically I was invited to address a conference of librarians and others in York on 'publishing' (I was considered knowledgeable enough for that) on the day of the 'Forum's' inaugural meeting, at which the concept itself was discussed. Thus I missed my only appropriate opportunity to attack the way in which the 'Forum' had been set up and was to be run. After making an attempt to do so at one later meeting, which caused bad feeling, I absented myself from all meetings until Gadsby stood down, which he only did on becoming the Association's treasurer. Publishers should not fall out with eachother over P.A. matters, but this episode wounded both my vanity and my sense of justice.

In 1990 a proposal for a further change in the voting arrangements was put before the A.G.M. It was that instead of firms with turnover between £100,000 and £1 million being entitled to two votes and those below £100,000 to one, all those below £1 million would now be entitled to one vote only. The publishers whose votes were being halved were, with the exception of the very smallest, the members of the 'Small Publishers Forum'. I consulted Clive Bradley, the chief executive, and proposed a simple *quid pro quo*: that, in exchange for its lost second vote, the Small Publishers should be directly represented on the Council of the P.A. by its chairperson having an *ex-officio* seat along with the three other ex-officio members (representing educational publishers, academic and professional publishers, and the international division). This might have seemed a tall order, but Clive, who always speaks the truth, agreed that my proposal was reasonable; the treasurer, Sir Roger Elliott, F.R.S. (chief executive of O.U.P.), whom I accidentally met at a book launching, could see no objection to it; and just before the A.G.M. the president, Robin Hyman, told me to have no fear. So I kept silent while the new voting change went through on the nod. At the next Council meeting, a large majority turned down my proposal. I had thought that one good reason for starting a small publishers' group in the P.A. was to 'raise consciousness' and involve this constituency more closely in the problems and decisions facing the P.A., thus perhaps making it less unappealing to the numerous non-members. How, I felt, could my small-publisher colleagues let this happen without speaking out against it? But this was beside the point because they were not interested.

There was a final turn of the screw in 1992. In December 1991 members of the Association received a letter from the president, Paul Scherer, saying that for the next three years, as an experiment, the candidates in the annual Council election (there were to be seven in 1992, an exceptionally large number) would be presented to the membership as a single slate, uniformly proposed and seconded by the officers, the number of candidates being exactly the same as the number of vacancies. The slate would be assembled by a nominating panel consisting of the officers and two lay Council members. I knew that a nearly identical plan had been put before the Council two years earlier by an internal committee chaired by Sir Roger Elliott, and irrationally hoped that it would never come into being. Throughout the Association's history, candidates for the Council had been individually proposed and seconded by their fellow members, doubtless discreetly prodded at times by the officers who by custom were not themselves empowered to take a direct part in the elections. Paul Scherer's letter said that some eligible people were not coming forward for election, and that a more balanced representation of the entire membership's interests was needed to tackle the increasingly complex and urgent problems facing the trade. So it had been decided to take this step, which the Association of American Publishers had already taken. I hated this idea and thought that the 'historic' or 'traditional' freedoms of members were being taken away. Does a handpicked *nomenklatura* ensure more fruitful discussions and wiser decisions than a council elected by the more traditional method? Clive Bradley, whose views most deserve respect since he has the task of managing Council business, appeared to have no doubt that the change would be beneficial. Paul Scherer for his part assured me that there was no sinister intent behind it. Perhaps not, but the reason for it may have been slightly different from the bland managerial one we were asked to accept.

A former president accosted me in the Garrick at this time and said 'Surely you can understand why all this has happened?' He said that during his presidency he was summoned to a meeting with Kevin Maxwell, Robert Maxwell's son and a director of Pergamon, one of the Association's larger member companies, and presented with three splendidly Maxwellian demands: that his company be permanently represented on the Council, that it should occupy the presidency for one term in every three, and that small firms should be flushed out of the Association altogether. There could clearly be only one answer to this, and Pergamon duly withdrew from membership. However, the P.A. had learned a lesson. Macmillan, the largest privately-owned publishing company in Britain, also resigned about this time because of its un-public-spirited but not illogical conclusion that much of the work of the Association, for which it paid a vast subscription, it either did for itself or did not need. It wanted an '*à la carte*' membership or nothing. A sub-plot, but one with great relevance to the issue of Council elections, was that Nicholas Byam Shaw – the chairman of Macmillan, who had emerged victorious in a power struggle with the titular head of the firm, Alexander, second Earl of Stockton – had been elected to the Council at the bottom of the list of elected candidates, which, by the Byzantine rules then in force, gave him a term of one year instead of three; he had felt this to be an intolerable slight on a publisher of his importance. Macmillan rejoined a few years later, but these two resignations of large members, coming so close together, conveyed the frightening message that if the Association was not to lose other large members and thus be immobilised for lack of cash, it would have to listen very carefully to what they wanted.* The changes in the voting rules that had unfolded by stages since 1987, and to which I had so ineffectively objected, were no more than the outward signs of a consolidation of power by the mega-corporations. These might not always know what they wanted at any particular time, but the mere possibility of their consensus being disturbed by the votes of the numerical majority had to be made even more remote than it was already. They might toss us a 'Small Firms Forum', with no previous consultation and putting a large publisher in charge of it, but ultimately we were expendable. Others have been less slow to perceive this reality than I, which is why so many excellent small and medium-sized publishing firms are not members. One may regret that British publishers are bloody-minded, and cannot accept the idea that all should belong to the only professionally run and effective trade organisation, but that is the way we are.

I was determined that the first Council election at which the candidates were presented as an official 'slate' should not go uncontested and, although Paul Scherer invited me to go on the slate, I asked Ian Chapman, former head of Collins and of all the ex-presidents the one whose style in office I had most admired, to propose me as an independent candidate. I did not get elected, but Paul told me that my vote had been less than a total disgrace. The next year, 1993, I agreed to go on the slate and, at the time of writing, am serving my second three-year term as a Council member. It was a climb-down, but I simply wanted to experience the workings of the Council from the inside rather than go on fighting an unwinnable battle, about which I gradually began to feel doubts, or at least indifference. I would have liked things to be otherwise, and fired a last salvo before sinking below the waves at the A.G.M. in 1995 when the three-year experiment of the slate had to be ratified, but there were – there are – more important things to worry about.

For general publishers the home market is supremely important. This is as true for the fortunate British, who have a seemingly unlimited

---

* Macmillan's '*a la carte*' demands were a partial consequence of a steady expansion of the P.A.'s activities, staffing and accommodation over the years after Clive Bradley's appointment. Its withdrawal prompted a painfully rapid contraction.

export market due to English being so widely used, as it is for nationalities whose languages are understood either not at all or only in small pockets outside their own heartlands. But scholarly publishing in English is a world business, particularly the kind pursued by C. Hurst & Co., where much of the subject-matter is international in character. It has to be, because English is pre-eminently the language (French is the runner-up, some way behind) in which our kind of publishing can be viably conducted, and hence we attract authors from many other countries who have to publish in English in order to be known in the worldwide scholarly community. The North American market, with its ability to absorb co-editions in quantities varying between a few hundred and a few thousand, is C. Hurst & Co.'s lifeline. But markets that we cannot ignore exist all around the world. Therefore we must travel to visit them – as well as to find new authors and visit old ones.

This has been the conventional wisdom of British publishing houses at least during all the time that the Publishers Association has existed. O.U.P., Longman, Macmillan and others established offices overseas from the beginning of the twentieth century. But the P.A. itself became seriously export-minded after the Second World War, and if there is one practical reason that firms sharing my interests can give for belonging, it is that its constant efforts to improve market opportunities, combat piracy and 'market infringement by competing editions' in overseas market, and its promotion of delegations to visit the more promising of those markets with government support, are of tangible value to us. After I joined the Council, there was a move to disband the international department and spread it between the general, educational and academic/professional divisions, but the ferocity of the attack on it my confrere Philip Kogan led to second thoughts. The international department remained intact.

The Strange-World of Trade Delegations

It might be thought that visiting an interesting foreign country in the company of like-minded people and with the Department of Trade and Industry making a sizeable contribution to one's expenses is something no one could resist, but of course the colleagues in whose company one finds oneself are not all like-minded, and there are constraints on one's freedom; some are statutory but others are due to pressure to conform. I have been on four delegation and was able to enjoy each of them in different ways.

My first, to Hungary in the spring of 1981, was unusual in that the impetus for it came from the Hungarians, who paid our expenses in the country while the British Council bought the air tickets. Creative and inventive nationalities with 'difficult' languages – and the Hungarians are among the prime examples – are desperate to make the works of their poets, novelists and playwrights known in the world outside their borders, which means *par excellence* translation into English. It is humbling to be told that more Hungarian works are translated into Finnish or Korean than into our language, which for them holds the key to so much, but British publishers – to generalise not inaccurately – have no taste for this sort of experimentation pursued for its own sake, and when the object is not the pragmatic one of bringing an exceptionally talented writer to wider notice.

Every delegation has a leader, and ours had Andre Deutsch, an eminent and admirable British general publisher of Hungarian birth and deeply Hungarian character who did not leave his native Budapest till his twenties – who could have been more suitable? But André probably inspired us more than he did our hosts. Having only become a publisher after the war, in London, he was completely ignorant of the Hungarian publishing scene – I, with my peculiar world-view and specialised interests, probably knew it better. It was the very last thing he had ever needed to know about and when confronting it could only draw on his own experience in a free, capitalist, cosmopolitan environment. He was plainly feigning interest for most of the time and couldn't wait for it to be all over. As he said to us with feeling in the privacy of a taxi, who could possibly want to be a publisher in Hungary? He spoke Hungarian when he had to, but seemed more at ease speaking English.

We were charmed by the sensitive and sophisticated head of the Hungarian book trade organisation, Dr Ferenc Zöld, and fell in love with our spirited female interpreter (she was middle-aged and very plain). The nadir was briefly plumbed when we all had to sit at a large table facing a deputy minister and his acolytes, going through a ritual of asking questions to which we knew he could not give satisfactory answers – regrettably George Fisher, the British Council representative, an effusive Welshman, showered this self-satisfied mediocrity with flattery, which he lapped up. George had a more difficult assignment simultaneously looking after the great Clifford Curzon, who had come to give a piano recital and a concert with one of the national orchestras, and who phoned him repeatedly to complain about the rehearsal facilities. I went to the concert, and because he was – and looked – old and far from robust I could not help being nervous each time he raised his hands (rather high) just before the end of the orchestral passages in Beethoven's Fourth Piano Concerto in case they did not fall on the right keys; it was a foolish fear. I thought it a good idea that they made the concerto the last item in the programme, so that he could play a couple of solo encores at the end. A nice thing about delegations is that they can lead to new friendships. Till then I hardly knew Richard Bailey, then sales director of Routledge & Kegan Paul, but when we met, late on a Sunday morning, in the departure lounge at Heathrow for the flight to Budapest, he at once said in his deadpan way, 'You look like a member of the Church of England.' I was at the time, and so of course was he, and we had both been to church that morning. And I made an enemy, as is also liable to happen on delegations. This fellow had come into publishing from advertising in mid-career and bought control of one of my favourite publishing houses, then in the doldrums; happily he has long since moved on. I was irritated by everything he said – and particularly by his obsequious and un-colleague-like behaviour towards André, whom we all respected – and he certainly reacted in the same way to me. When my colleagues flew home I took the train to Vienna, which I saw for the first time in the company of my nephew Jolyon Naegele, then stationed there. There must be few cities so grand yet – with nothing obvious amiss, as in divided Berlin – conveying such a sense of dislocation, as an orphaned imperial capital.

In 1989 I applied to join an advertised mission to the Soviet Union, and was surprised when I found that only three of us were travelling – the other two being David Foster, who is with an agency than promotes book exports, and Lynette Owen, the rights director at Longman. It would have been difficult in such a small group if we had not got on, but we did. I was conscious, without any unease, of being a makeweight since I knew nothing of the market, but Lynette knew more than enough for all of us. She is the acknowledged doyenne of rights experts, and it is characteristic of the Longman ethos as I have known it ever since I became a publisher that she gives much of her time to work for the trade as a whole. We were friendly acquaintances before, partly because at the I.P.A. meeting in London I praised her qualities before the entire assembly, but our time together in Russia established one of those close book trade friendships I so relish – we don't actually visit eachother's homes but are always glad to see eachother. It is because of people like Lynette that I tend to feel exaggerated bile towards confreres who are not companionable.

On our first night we found ourselves left to fend for ourselves in a very basic hotel in the wrong part of Moscow, but Lynette campaigned vigorously and effectively – through our inscrutable cicerone Sasha – to get us moved. We were transferred to a building, opposite the vast Hotel Sport built for the Moscow Olympics, reserved for visiting trade union delegations – for me it became Arthur Scargill House. We now each had a large and luxurious suite, but apart from a doorman there was no domestic staff and one could not even get a cup of tea. While we were in town Lynette and I both did as much as we could to promote the interests of our own firms. I met several Africanists and orientalists, and by chance, for the only time in my life, the renowned Ernest Gellner; also, to earn my keep as a member of the delegation, I investigated projects on hand with compatible publishers which in our report could be communicated to the least unlikely takers back home. The dual economy was apparent in the art book publisher Aurora (in Leningrad), which did nothing but co-editions with Western publishers, produced to a far higher standard than anything placed on the regular domestic market. We went one evening to the thrilling and flawless Moscow State Circus, but the ballet, with canned music, was not so good.

We met some extraordinarily charming people, but there was more than an undercurrent of 'dysfunction'. Sasha and others functionaries on whom we relied for transport and general assistance were almost always late, and we often had to wait helplessly as the wasted minutes and sometimes hours ticked by. When Lynette, David and I tried to get dinner one evening at the Hotel Sport, we had to argue at length with the staff before they would agree to admit us, although the dining room was nearly empty, because we could not show that we belonged to a recognisable group. Even then, there was only one main dish on the menu. The one evening I spent alone, I went to the 'Havana' restaurant, near Arthur Scargill House, expecting some creole exoticism, but having battled my way past the suspicious receptionist and head waiter in turn, found sadly that it was so named for political and not for gastronomic reasons. I was put at a table with a former military attaché and his wife; she did not speak English but on learning where I came from was just able to say 'I like Mrs Thatcher'. One evening we were taken out by some people from the Uzbek S.S.R. book trading organisation, who had come all the way to Moscow to meet Lynette, but when we arrived at one of their ethnic restaurants, the owners were there but it had been closed due to threats from protection racketeers. When we had eventually driven in convoy to another one some miles away, we had the best and longest meal of our whole trip. In Leningrad the three of us and our guide were driven around in a bus big enough to carry fifty people. One day I lost my pocket comb, and went with a driver to half a dozen likely shops, large and small, before we could find one; the assistants would not even look up to answer the driver's inquiries. I cannot say whether frustration or a sense of pathos predominated.

We migrated to Leningrad, on to Tallinn and then back to Moscow, each time by night train, and there is little I remember about the business we did in either place except that in Tallinn Lennart Meri, an academic who had just taken over the direction of a new shoe-string national cultural organisation, came to see us off at the station; in 1994 he became President of Estonia. Perhaps my expectations of the reputed glories of Leningrad were exaggerated, but the great squares and vistas and the two former royal palaces we saw did not make my heart beat faster. The pictures in the Hermitage were a different matter, and I even found myself excited by our visit to the British-built (in 1898) cruiser *Aurora*, moored right within the city, from which the shot was fired which gave the signal for the storming of the Winter Palace in October 1917. Tallinn has an unspoilt old city centre through which I wandered with delight, but of all that we saw no sight could equal the Moscow Kremlin. It is wonderful inside and out.

What did we expect from the rather small and not very high-profile mission to Mexico in 1990? As usual there were representatives of the large 'E.L.T.' (English-language teaching) section of the industry, whose markets are world-wide, and who find a poor but populous country like Mexico a particularly stimulating challenge. Medical publishers do too, and our leader, a friendly and hard-working Spanish-speaker, Michael Manson, was one of their number. I would probably never have gone had not a Spanish diplomat, Eduardo de Laiglesia, whom I came to know when he was at the embassy in London, moved on from there to Mexico and said I would always be welcome to stay with him and his wife there. (He is the only person I know who buys several of my firm's recent books each time he comes on a visit – and then reads them. He has a large personal library and can describe the contents of every book in it.) With age I have become prepared to take up invitations such as Eduardo's whenever they are offered, but never thought that either business or pleasure could take me to Mexico until this mission was announced. I therefore stayed in the relaxing comfort of Eduardo and Margarita's house just north of the Bosque de Chapultepec, with maids to wait on me, while my colleagues put up in a more mundane downtown hotel.

This was a government-sponsored and -aided mission of the usual type, in which members have to fulfill certain bureaucratic conditions: filling up a form in advance about one's company's past performance in the market and future expectations, collaborating in the production of a report afterwards, and – escapable only on pain of forfeiting one's share of the government subsidy – attending a briefing by officials of the British embassy, mainly on the local economic conditions. Since I proceed in foreign countries entirely on the basis of information I have gleaned from various sources privately, these sessions are as unimportant to me as morning chapel was in my schooldays. But it was a surprise in Mexico City when the ambassador said to me after the briefing 'I have met you before'. I recognised neither his name nor his face, but he was right – he had added a second barrel to the former and disfigured the latter with an incongruous bushy moustache. (He had been the top scholar in his year at Eton, and I could not but wonder if this was the apex to which he had aspired then.)

I thought that the only thing I could do that would add something of practical interest to the mission's eventual report was to visit publishers and talk with them about the chances of their collaborating with London on translation. This was a somewhat strange proposition to them since their natural anglophone partners are the North Americans, but they seemed to welcome the opening of this new window – we were the first British mission to Mexico for many years. More than one of these firms had originally been Spanish, and had migrated there to escape Franco. As if to emphasise the éliteness of the profession in Mexico, all the publishers I met had European features and colouring; only one had the distinctive look of the *mestizos* (overwhelmingly the majority of the population) and he spontaneously remarked that as such he was unique. His firm, unlike the others, was aggressively modern in style. A serious category of literature in publishing terms was *belles lettres*, or essays. This signified to me that sea-green, uncorrupted intellectualism, extending right across the spectrum from art to politics and economics, has a place in Mexican life similar to many European countries but quite alien to our life in London.

I had decided to pursue a minor research interest: the lines of force in Spanish-language publishing. What was the book trading relationship between Spain and its former empire, when the peseta was so much stronger than the peso (in Mexico, at any rate)? Was it perhaps something like Britain's relationship with, say, India rather than that with North America? Which countries in Central and South America were the best markets for books from Mexico and what were the terms of trade? And where did Puerto Rico come, with the U.S. dollar as its currency? If all this told one nothing of any moment that could be applied to our global anglophone book trade, it reflected cultural phenomena that were interesting in their own right. One of the intellectuals I met urged me to visit the Libreria Gandhi, which a successful businessman in some unrelated field had set up close to the National University with its tens of thousands of impecunious students. It contained a cafe and a small theatre, but its great pull was its practice of offering new books at large discounts – something which the conventional retail book trade viewed with disdain. All the books were in paperback and, by European standards, extremely cheap already. The manager told me that when a new book by Gabriel Garcia Marquez, Umberto Eco or some other eminent figure came out, he would buy 500 copies from the publisher, on firm sale, at a discount of 60% and sell them at a discount of 40%. Similar deals, with less dramatic discounts, would be done for most new books. I became convinced that Libreria Gandhi was creating new readers among the country's budding intellectual and professional class, and it shook my faith in price-fixing. When the British trade started cutting the retail prices of new hardbacks and ignored egghead paperbacks, except for a narrow range of standard classics, I felt that it had got the wrong end of the stick.

The whole of Mexican publishing and printing was tied up in a close corporatist network. For a publisher, not to be a member of the trade organisation was inconceivable (the current president, Gustavo Lewis, was typically a publisher of mass-circulation magazines, beside whom we all felt pretty small – courteous and inscrutable, he exuded power. Belonging was a matter not of conscience but of plain economics because paper and printing services were available at special controlled prices to members only. The association's magazine was beautifully produced, and contained much of solid literary interest related to new books, among which vulgar bestsellers definitely did not figure. All it had in common with our trade periodicals was a swathe of publishers' advertisement. I felt envious.

At the weekend, Eduardo and Margarita had to wait on a visiting Spanish Infanta at Acapulco, and it was decided that Ismail, the driver, could take me the 500 km. to the famous colonial city of Oaxaca and at the same time stay with his father, a goatherd who lived, as he said, nearby '*en el campo*'. This, more than my visits to the Pyramids outside Mexico City or the Zocalo and the Ribera frescoes within it, gave to my journey the essential element of 'travel' – seeing things some way off the beaten track.

I went on a mission to the Southern Cone of South America in November 1995 with more hope of doing business than I ever had in Mexico. This time the profile was higher; we had in our

British Council, the (government) Department
...ustr and the Publishers Association staff and, as
a prominent literary publishing house – who at
powerfully of Toby Gibson (above, pp. 93-7);
...nt velvet-gloved aggression and power-play left
fulfilled his task ably. I flew to Buenos Aires
...order to do my business unfettered
...ayed in a modest downtown hotel (delega-
...p in five-star establishments); at the weekend
...north to two colonial cities (with some agreeable
...our of Oaxaca), Jujuy and Salta, where
...e Andean looks. The delegation crossed
...a few hours in Montevideo; again I went
...romantic but flyblown city for at least
...generation it is where Captain Langsdorff,
...Spee, shot himself after scuttling
...tory in World War II). Then we
...re again I stayed in modest comfort on
...in the western Argentine city of
...a hilltop monument to San Martin
...de Gloria) that is grandiloquent
...s, and a most humane and
...hill, before taking a bus over

...delegation was over, I went
...wntown business district reminiscent
...y, turn-of-the-century elevators that
...nd its grand villas. In these southern
...great days before the opening of
...k with British business enterprise
...and induce sadness as well as aesthetic
...e visible to the uninformed eye of the
...and military dictatorship in the 1970s,
...ointed to a building where enemies
...ded me that some of these
...ft far out in the broad River
...by the proud republican symbols
...a matter of place and history rather
...generally live in divided and unstable
...of much of their history, especially
...the Spanish empire, and they are
...om which we suffer living in
...interesting to grasp suddenly,

as I had not done from afar, that the omnipresent Spanish language has nothing to do, there, with Spain – any more than English in the United States has anything to do with England.

The monument to the Argentine servicemen killed in the South Atlantic war stands at one end of the Plaza San Martin, with the park behind it, facing a tall clock-tower built by the Anglo-Argentine community to commemorate Queen Victoria's diamond jubilee. Like the Vietnam memorial in Washington, it consists of a black marble wall incised with the names of the dead; a perpetual flame burns, two sentries stand guard and the national flag flies at half-mast. While I was in town, some Argentine families flew to Port Stanley to attend the burial of their loved ones and the raising of a small memorial. They were treated with honour by the garrison and hospitality by the islanders. It was the kind of thing the British do well, and everybody was deeply moved. Princess Diana was due to arrive the week after we left, and I could not help wishing that she might, in one of her independent gestures, lay some flowers by the wall of names, but she was probably not told of its existence.

Interlude: A Visit to Germany, 1990

Having been to the Frankfurt book fair almost every year since 1965, I went for the last time in 1990. By a combination of errors, for which I was partly responsible, my books failed to turn up and I had an empty stand. I have seen a disconsolate Nigerian sitting, reading a newspaper, in front of his non-existent national exhibit, but never expected that it would happen to me. This was by far my worst time at Frankfurt, although some degree of paranoia always took hold of me there. Employees of large firms, whom I never envy at any other time, had their full diaries and an engagement every quarter of an hour (they admit that few yield results, but that does not matter; it is the appearance of activity that counts). In the intervals when they are not having meetings with their trading partners they are happily chatting, laughing and sipping sekt among themselves. Then in the late afternoon there are the receptions on the stands, before everyone troops off to a succession of glamorous parties at the Frankfurter Hof, the Hessischer Hof, the Plaza and even real castles in the Taunus mountains. So as not to prolong the agony, I made sure to leave the fair at the end of business on Saturday, and my lodgings at dawn on Sunday – I always took my car and would drive off either to look at Bavarian Rococo, or visit Jurgen Domes in Saarbrucken, or Dr L., the West Irian expert, in Holland, or – on one memorable occasion – Verdun and the Ossuary of Douaumont. But even during my four days confined at the fair I would have to find things to do – there was simply not enough to fill the time. And always, like the lone man in Edvard Munch's painting 'Jealousy', I imagined that all the good things were happening to others and not to me.

In 1990, after four days attached to a bookless stand, I escaped to Berlin to stay with two of my firm's authors. On my arrival I made for the home of Helmut Stoecker, retired professor of history at Humboldt University, who had edited and partly written a history of German colonialism in Africa which I treasure as a model of its kind. Most of the research material was in East Germany, and the book could not have been produced anywhere else. Stoecker lived in an old-fashioned apartment amid drab streets, but told me that he was one of the privileged ones; most of his colleagues lived far more modestly. He was a rarity among scholars in the G.D.R. in speaking and writing perfect English; his father had been a Communist whom the Nazis arrested and murdered in the 1930s and in the nick of time his mother took him to England, where he went to school and university, only returning in 1947. It had then seemed natural to him to settle in the east, and until he retired in the late 1980s his active career ran parallel with that of the state in which he lived, starting and ending at more or less the same time. When we first met in London I found him chilly and uncommunicative; he gave no hint that he was anything but satisfield with his lot and a wholehearted supporter of the regime. The production of the book was trouble-free; it was excellently written, but my few editorial suggestions were accepted, including a request to alter a statement on the last page that the fall of Nazi Germany had been brought about entirely by Soviet arms. An indication of the competence of the negotiators at Deutsche Buch-Export und -Import was their quotation for the book: the price per copy for 2,000 copies was less than half that for 1,000, so it was cheaper in absolute terms to buy 2,000, which I did without pointing out this absurdity.

The book was already published when I stayed with Stoecker and his wife, so it was no more that a friendly visit; but I was also to meet the orientalists and Africanists of note among his old colleagues. On the day of my arrival we went to the historic museums of this part of the city. The strangeness of walking freely about with a visitor from the West, with whom he could talk about anything under the sun, obviously moved him because he made the extraordinary remark for a scholar of his eminence – 'I don't often meet a man like you'. He was now mellower than he had been a few years earlier. When we got back to the apartment, his bitterness at some of the results of re-unification came out: 'We have been taken over', he said; in particular, from his point of view, the learned institutions now had West German directors, who were like foreigners. Every former ambassador in the G.D.R. foreign service had been dismissed. The regimes of Ulbricht and Honecker had been shameful, but was it right to treat them all as a defeated people? I suggested that he write a memoir of his and the G.D.R.'s parallel lives, pulling no punches, and he agreed. It was doubtless a therapeutic exercise, but he did not have a gift for this sort of writing. The resulting ms. was simply not interesting enough to be published. He was still vaguely thinking of altering it when he died in 1994.

Warmly as I felt towards Stoecker, I did not begin to recover from the horrors of my experience in Frankfurt until I moved in on the second day with Werner Meissner, a sinologist on the west side, who had managed to recover a quite large suburban house which had belonged to his father before the war and made it very comfortable. He and his partner Renate Scherer were a generation younger than Stoecker, and we talked, joked, ate, drank and made music in a relaxed atmosphere. They took me to visit the glories of Potsdam. I found the interior of Frederick the Great's Sans-Souci palace, so graceful from the outside, a disappointment, but on Werner's recommendation I inspected the inside of the gents' urinal in the centre of the town, which was a remarkably preserved example of the early 20th-century arts and crafts style.

Distribution – To the Winds

The only one of my articles which the *Bookseller* asked its lawyers to vet for libel – three times, they said – was about the bankruptcy of J.M. Dent & Sons (Distribution) Ltd.* This event did varying degrees of harm to some thirty medium-sized to small publishers, including C. Hurst & Co., and has become a byword in the trade for the vulnerability of publishers unable to handle their own warehousing

---

* It was published on 5 January 1990.

and order fulfilment. This means all but the biggest. We were Dent's clients for the whole range of distribution services – it warehoused our books, invoiced the sales, collected the resulting revenue and, at the end of one period for inland turnover and another for exports, paid the revenue to us minus its commission. The essential fact is that the distributor receives and holds the money owed to the publisher. This puts the publisher wholly in the distributor's hands, and if the distributor fails, the publisher will receive little or possibly none of the money owing to him.

J.M. Dent was once a great name in publishing: solid, unspectacular, the proud creator of *Everyman's Library* and *Everyman's Encyclopaedia*. As soon as I heard, in 1976, that the firm was looking for distribution clients, I wanted at all costs to get in there. It was not necessary to contrast Dent with Noonan Hurst to think it a 'blue chip' concern. For decades Dent owned its own printing works on an industrial site in Letchworth, but it had become under-used and antiquated, and as a major investment the company built a new warehouse and ancillary buildings alongside it on the site. It was modern and efficient, but there was also a good feeling about the place, which may have been because some of the senior staff were old Dent hands who had been with the firm, man and boy, since all its functions were concentrated in a fine Edwardian building in Bedford Street, Covent Garden.

In 1976, when I was accepted as one of Dent Distribution's earliest clients, there was no doubt that it was the offshoot of the publishing house, but slowly the position altered. First, the printing company closed – probably this step was overdue – and the site was taken up with new warehouse space. Then, on Martin Dent's death, there was a management buyout of both the publishing and distribution companies by a triumvirate, of which the unlikely leader was V.J. (Joe) Chamberlain, the chief accountant, a man of the utmost respectability who had spent many years with O.U.P. He now became chairman of the combined operation. I felt worried enough to phone Joe for reassurance, which he gave me, but of course I should have sought more disinterested advice. None of my fellow-clients seemed unduly disturbed. What contributed to our inertia was the unaffectedly good rapport that had grown up between us and the Dent senior management. They held periodical liaison meetings at Letchworth with clients at which information, suggestions and complaints were freely exchanged.

The next stage in the unravelling process was the sale of the publishing company to Weidenfeld and Nicolson, agreed in 1987, leaving (to quote myself in the *Bookseller* article) the tail without the dog; somehow we still managed to convince ourselves that the tail was the dog.' Friendly liaison meetings had by this time ceased; *glasnost* was behind us. One client moved away but the rest of us, like mice under the stare of a rattlesnake, stolidly stayed where we were. If there were problems, we did not want to make them worse. The blow fell on 22 February 1988, when Joe Chamberlain phoned me to say that Dent's bank, Barclays, had called in the receivers. I was as calm and polite as he was, and offered him my sympathy. I immediately calculated that C. Hurst & Co. would be saved by its smallness from being wiped out, though I would personally be obliged to make up the cash loss. (Some of my bigger fellow-clients suffered devastating losses.) That evening Rachel said that if I needed to raise money on our unencumbered and jointly-owned house, I could do so, although this was one thing I had promised never to do. This offer was beyond normal generosity, but I did not accept it. What depressed me most was the thought of how much valuable publishing time would now have to be wasted in lengthy meetings with receivers, lawyers, accountants and even my valued colleagues – avoiding such things is the reason above all others why I value smallness and independence.

Anyone sufficiently interested can look up my article – nothing else has been published on this miserable episode. In retrospect I blame the Dent directors for not taking us, their clients, into their confidence over the firm's cash difficulties at an early stage. We might have been able to work out a compact which would have saved Dent and ourselves. But the role of Barclays Bank in the affair raises some specific questions to which we are unlikely ever to get clear answers. Above all, what was the true nature of its dealings with the Automobile Association, which it knew to be interested in acquiring Dent Distribution well before its collapse,* and which eventually bought Dent from the receivers at a fraction of what it would have cost as a going concern? Both the cash-rich A.A. and the ailing Dent were customers of Barclays – I have been told that they were even customers of the same branch. The key question was whether Dent needed to go into receivership. Hubert Schaafsma of Dragon's World Publishers, who emerged as the most clear-headed and determined of our number, asked Joe Chamberlain some time afterwards how much extra time Dent would have needed to hold back our periodical payments for it to survive. Joe's answer was: thirty or at most sixty days. The company's troubles, be claimed, had been caused by Terry Maher's Dillons group, a major account

---

* Unknown to the clients, Dent Distribution advertised itself for sale in the *Financial Times*.

in the home market, which was delaying its payments far beyond agreed terms (much later, it too collapsed). Longer payment terms between distributors and client publishers are now the norm. To Hubert Schaafsma we owed the final agreement of the receivers to disburse to us 29 per cent of what we were owed, instead of the mere 5 per cent they originally offered.

I particularly remember an information meeting called by the receiver in the conference room at his office some time into the crisis. He was flanked by two junior accountants from his firm, and sitting beside them were a solicitor acting for the bank or the receivers (I forget which), a Mr Crowley, and two of his juniors. This prodigality with manpower was entirely at our expense; the professional fees charged were huge. But most notable was the offensively haughty and severe demeanour with which Mr Crowley answered questions from us, while he smiled knowingly at his associates. Like rape victims in court faced by the defendant's counsel, *we* were somehow to blame for being there. We had, in a manner of speaking, been raped ourselves.

Many publishers, not only small ones, have known the experience of disorder breaking out at their distributors; suddenly what you ask to be done as a matter of the greatest urgency doesn't get done or gets done wrong; things you have not asked for get done, and everyone wonders why; communication is impossible. This was what it was like when A.A. took over at Letchworth. For some time after they had stepped into the breach, the receivers managed distribution for Dent's clients themselves, not using the established procedure but re-inventing an extremely labour-intensive one and charging extra commission for it. The first thing the A.A. did was sack several of Dent's most experienced staff, notably the director in charge of the order department, Reg Lloyd, who had been with the company all his working life, and his assistant Tom Brown; both men were approaching retirement, but we had regarded them as ultra-dependable and as personal friends. Then the A.A.'s service sank into the abyss, to the despair of its new clients and their customers.

We were able to extricate ourselves fairly quickly, and went to Central Books who, like Dent Distribution, had begun as the wholesale arm of another business, the famous Marxist-Leninist bookshop of the same name in Gray's Inn Road, but then became free-standing when the bookshop closed. They gave us an acceptable service, and – more important – we liked and completely trusted them. They were comparatively small, but I always believed that, if they had ever found themselves in a similar position to Dent before it collapsed, they would have been open with us and put our welfare before their own. This I attributed mainly to their political beliefs, which had not changed noticeably since 1989, but they were also unusual characters; if I had met any of the two or three people in charge in another setting, I would never have guessed that they were book distributors. We left them in 1996 for Marston Book Services (owned by the Blackwell organisation), because we needed the services of a larger firm.

But, where our trade creditors are concerned, we are no differently placed now than we were in February 1988. No one has yet devised a form of contract that allows a distributor to function while at the same time guaranteeing to the client publisher that all its accumulated credits will be safe from the hands of debenture-holders or receivers, and will be paid over to it, come what may. The one undisputed bonus from our experience with Dent is that this problem is never far from our consciousness.

Family Business

On 23 July 1979, the centenary of my father's birth, a celebration was held in his honour at the Royal College of Physicians in Regent's Park. It consisted of an afternoon of short lectures on various gastro-enterological and neurological conditions in which he had been interested, with the general theme 'Was Hurst right?' After a break there were two longer talks, one on my father himself by Dr Thomas Hunt and the other by Sir Roger Ormrod, a senior judge who had studied medicine under him at Oxford before going to the bar. Finally there was a banquet at which I gave the main speech. The prime mover of all this was Dr Hunt, a retired gastro-enterologist, late of St Mary's Hospital, who had been associated with my father in founding a gastro-enterological society in the 1930s. He and my father were starkly contrasted types, which is perhaps why I had never met or heard of him before he suddenly phoned me a couple of years earlier. The first thing he said on that occasion was that this society, under his aegis, had published a collection of my father's writings – articles and extracts from his books – in volume form; it was too late to ask for my permission, but he agreed to give me the standard six author's copies. I thought the design appalling and unworthy, but had to admit that its existence so long after all my father's books had gone out of print was useful. Dr Hunt also told me of his plan to commemorate my father in the way mentioned above.

Hunt was an energetic man in his late seventies who had had a distinguished career, but I did not warm to him. He seemed managerial and, above all, smooth; my father had never had a 'bedside manner' but Hunt's was a powerful emanation. He had organised the event down to the last detail and got financial support for it from the Wellcome Foundation. Of course there was an ulterior motive – to raise money for gastro-enterological research – and I was asked to angle my speech in that way. In this object, unfortunately, it was humiliatingly unsuccessful, but it cannot be denied that we had a wonderful time. I invited all my father's nieces and nephews, by then in their sixties and seventies, although the ones I most wanted to come could not because of sudden illnesses. Both my sisters came over from America, and too late I found that Dr Hunt, for whom snobbery was as natural as breathing, had seated them at one of the miscellaneous tables in the hall and not at the top table, at which he had placed my only cousins with titles – Frederic and Eve Seebohm – and his own daughters. When I saw Freddy Seebohm, who stood out among the male guests by wearing a light grey suit and blue shirt, my mind darted back to when he had secured me an interview with Wilkinson Brothers Discount Company in the City and told me to be sure to wear a dark suit and white shirt, and I figured – I am sure not inaccurately – that in his evaluation of public functions, this one rated pretty low. Had he not made plain all those years before that he perfectly understood the semiotics of dress?

Rachel, who needless to say rose perfectly to the occasion, had reason to deplore the fickleness of fate, because 23 July 1979 was her fortieth birthday, which thus had to be subsumed in the medical junketings. Because my father's sixtieth birthday, the day of his official retirement form Guy's Hospital, was a landmark in my childhood, I was thus in the unusual situation of remembering the day on which my wife was born.

I could have wished that my father had been portrayed in a more life-like fashion by Hunt, who gave little more than a recitation of dates and appointments which could have been culled from *Who's Who*, but generally he had been done proud, and we all felt it was a great occasion. My mother received only the most fleeting mention as an item in my father's biography, and it was this that germinated into an intention, somewhere around the mid-point of 1993, to commemorate the centenary of her birth in March 1994 in a way that would hark back deliberately to Hunt's extravaganza in July 1979. There could be no lectures, but a banquet at which

I would give a speech that did justice to her as a human being was a possibility. Such events only come once, and as soon as I had conceived the idea there could never be any question of driving it out of my mind, whatever the logistical difficulties. I wrote to my cousin Celia Fullerton-Smith, daughter of the erstwhile Rosalind Arkwright (above, pp. 23-4) in New Zealand and asked her if she would make the arrangements and send out the invitations. About thirty of us gathered at Taupo – there could have been many more but a limit had to be set. There were cousins of my own generation and two succeeding ones, and my son Andrew, his wife Paloma and children Marcus and Laura came down from Hong Kong where he worked with Reuter. The New Zealanders could not quite believe that I had actually had this idea and gone through with it. In preparing the half-hour speech with which I responded to the toast to my mother's memory from Rosalind, I had to think harder about my mother and come closer to her than ever before.

Of course I did not waste the opportunity of doing my usual scouting in the universities and visiting compatible publishers. There were now several of these, and the one with the acutest sense of New Zealand's position in the world constellation of publishing was undoubtedly Bridget Williams, founder of an eponymous house in Wellington. Needless to say, that position is highly unfavourable. I had always been aware that New Zealand, together with Australia, Canada and South Africa, absorb the literary and scholarly book production of Britain and the United States, but send very little back into the anglophone mainstream. Their native publishing, both literary and scholarly, is largely oriented towards domestic concerns which have almost no interest outside, except when a writer of genius emerges, and this only happens a few times in each century. Bridget is a high-class non-fiction literary – and, to a smaller extent, scholarly – publisher whose publications, if they were published in a British setting, would put her in the same class as firms like John Murray and Constable. Yet she had not only given up any thought of seeking American co-publication, with all the financial and cultural advantages it would bring, but did not even think that anything could be gained by trying to break into the nearest English-language export market, Australia, which appeared to be unreceptive to books from New Zealand. This revelation led me to develop a theory that New Zealand is like Finland: a culturally vigorous country with a population of 3-4 million, but unable to export its books. Having a language which is read round the world instead of one, like Finnish, which no other people understand gives it an apparent advantage but one on which it is unable to capitalise. But is this so great a disaster? Shakespeare and Jane Austen wrote for the people in the society around them – their friends, one could almost say – and so do the best writers in every time and every country. It is well that the wider world should know about them if possible and enjoy them; but, if this is not possible because of barriers to communication, it does not in the end matter too much. What matters is writing and publishing in the first instance.

We had known for a long time beforehand that Rachel would have to attend the conference of Disabled People's International in Sydney in December 1994, and she asked me to go too. So I went to the Antipodes twice in one year, not having been there since 1966. I did business in Brisbane, Canberra and Sydney on the way down before attending the last day of the conference, and we then gave ourselves up to an orgy of visiting with the descendants of my father's only sister, Aunt Jo, who settled in Australia during the the First World War, bought a farm in New South Wales and raised five children. She had rebelled against her strait-laced bourgeois English family, and her children, apart from a few facial resemblances, might have come from totally different stock. They were even more different from my maternal relations, just over the water in New Zealand, who are mostly good, warm-hearted, unintellectual people, tending to go to church and remain married to the original partner, and to be politely embarrassed by any excessive display of enthusiasm or its reverse. The Australians are warm-hearted too, but also warm and unrestrained in their expressions, non- or anti-religious, much married and divorced, and almost without exception left-leaning politically. At least three of the generation junior to mine are gay. We had a succession of huge picnics, barbecues and sit-down dinners in three cities. The older of my two surviving Australian first cousins – Betty Nicholson, who lives in Hobart, Tasmania – is a 'wise woman' with supernatural powers of divination. She told us of several occasions when she had warned distant friends of impending disaster, which they had thus taken steps to avoid – all but one who, having ignored the warning, was murdered by a former lover who, at the time when Betty had her vision, was actually crossing the country to track her down.

Both my New Zealand and Australian families were agog at an extraordinary development in my immediate family the previous year. During the summer of 1945, as readers of a much earlier chapter may remember, I went to stay with a cousin in the Isle of Wight. Although I had no suspicion of it at the time, the invitation was arranged to get me out of the way. My elder sister Pam, who had been in the W.A.A.F. for about three years, was pregnant by an officer on the station, and the time of my absence coincided with the short interval between her coming out of the service and going to live with a family in London before the birth. A boy was born in November and immediately adopted. Pam soon left home to work with the Allied Control Commission in Germany.

I did not learn what had happened till after leaving school two years later. Even then, I gathered, my mother was doubtful whether to tell me, but my Uncle Gerald said I should know. Her instinct was probably the correct one, because with the protected life I lived I knew nothing of what makes people act the way they do out in the real world, and consequently felt vague and undirected indignation – against the vanished boy-friend, of course, but also against Pam and even my mother. I could only vaguely understand what my mother felt on seeing her newly-born first grandchild, knowing that they would never meet again; it was easier to grasp the trauma suffered by Pam. I asked my mother the obvious question: where was the father? She had been to see Pam's station commander and asked him the same question, to which he replied that it had been decided not to tell him, because he had returned to his own country overseas and was engaged to be married.

Taking into account all the personalities involved, adoption alone would meet the need of the moment. My mother, without my father's support for the past year, felt helpless and ashamed. As she said, 'getting into trouble' was the kind of thing which, in the old days, one of the maids might do – certainly not a 'nice' girl.

Pam and I had been friendly during her W.A.A.F. service, but we never felt easy in each other's company after this. She could not mention what had happened even obliquely, so clearly I, a callow schoolboy seven years her junior, was barred from so much as hinting at it. Yet for a long time the thought was often present. She emigrated to America while I was away doing my National Service, and since then we have only met at long intervals.

In July 1993 I was driving past the Registry of Births, Deaths and Marriages with Rachel and said how much I wished that I could know somehow what had become of Pam's son. My mother had told me that he had dark hair, and was adopted by people in Cambridgeshire; apart from that, we knew nothing. I had made similar remarks on rare occasions before, but the thought had become more insistent lately – with the awareness that he was already middle-aged and the chance of there ever being any break in the cloud of ignorance, inconceivably remote as it already was, seeming only to recede with the passing of time. I had once gone into the registry and found an entry for him under the date of his birth, but did not go to the length of ordering a copy of the birth certificate; anyway, it is always from the side of the adopted child that moves towards the 'natural' family come, not the other way round. And such – I knew – were Pam's sensitivities that I could not have done anything on my own initiative, even if there had been a possibility of success. Rachel simply said that I should not upset myself thinking about it. This was on a Saturday, and the next Wednesday the phone rang in my office and a man whose voice I did not recognise asked if I was Christopher Adrian Riddiford Hurst. Something about this question gave me a faint, tingling intimation of what was to come. The caller said he was a cousin of my sister's son through his adoptive family. He told me my nephew's name and said that he was a master at the school where my father was a pupil a hundred years earlier, and was not married. He had been the only child, adopted or natural, of a couple in Cambridge, and received a stable upbringing. He had gone to a famous school and later to university. He was the author of several school textbooks, published by a respectable firm.

L. knew from earliest childhood that he was adopted, but his parents never told him any more about his origins, and out of respect for their sensitivities he never asked. When the second of them died and he had to clear up their house, he came upon a sealed envelope at the bottom of a wardrobe with his name written on it. Inside was his original birth certificate and correspondence between his adoptive parents and S.S.A.F.A., the armed forces' welfare society, which arranged the adoption. It was the first he knew of the name with which his birth was registered. One of these letters mentioned my father's name – to indicate the child's intellectual pedigree. Our Oxford address was on the birth certificate, and that led on to my mother's will where, among the executors, I was named with the style of 'editor'. This in turn led to a search through a directory of publishers, where the firm of C. Hurst & Co. seemed to offer a slender hope. I doubt whether I would have made the leap from such a multi-faceted personal description as 'editor', on a document drawn up in the 1950s, to a publishing house in the 1990s, especially given the volatility of the publishing industry, but L.'s cousin, who did the detective work, clearly has exceptional powers of logical deduction and intuition. There was no other channel though which the connection could have been made. L., who is devoted to his adoptive family, thought hard before letting his cousin pursue his investigation, and even after I had been tracked down he wanted more time to reflect before agreeing to a meeting. We met at Waterloo station, and when we got close to eachother I found that his eyes, wide-set and with characteristic sloping lids, were identical to my sister's. He had my father's sallow complexion, smooth black hair and long, thin fingers. We spent a couple of hours talking in the Festival Hall, where I showed him photographs of Pam and other members of our family. I soon discovered that we were not his family, although he was a very important part of ours. I had prepared for him a family tree which, even though simplified, was quite complex, and wondered if I had been wise to show it to him so soon. I imagined that for him our many ramifications must have been like the stage in a theatre when the curtain rises and a large company of actors or singers, previously hidden, becomes visible, all vigorously performing their parts.

I immediately wrote to my sister, and she responded by phoning L. and having a long talk. They did not meet until a year later, when he travelled to California, meeting my other sister Rosemary and her husband Thomas at Kennedy airport in New York on the way. Like Pam he has not inherited our family's musical gene, but he is a traveller and, like me, has an addiction to architecture, and is especially drawn to St Sophia in Istanbul. He and I now meet about twice a year – he lives too far away for frequent visiting. Whatever else happens to me, I am grateful for this.

Of Prime Ministers and Others

Once, when my stepdaughter Kate Gane was studying at Exeter University, I drove her down there at the beginning of term, and the next morning did some scouting on the campus. I already had one friend there, the historian Malyn Newitt, who had written a commissioned volume for me called *Portugal in Africa* (1981), which Longman co-published in North America and Africa, and was to write another, *A History of Mozambique* (700 pages, 1995), in the preface of which he thanks me for waiting nearly ten years for the manuscript, thus vindicating my usually relaxed attitude to late delivery. This book was co-published by the University presses of Indiana in the United States and Witwatersrand in South Africa, and we also sold gratifying numbers of copies to Mozambique itself and to the department of the Gulbenkian Foundation dealing with Lusophone Africa.

But I struck oil when I called on the head of the political science department, an American called Malcolm Shaw. He had had the idea of asking a number of colleagues in British universities each to write an essay on the relationship between the U.S. President since the time of F.D. Roosevelt (Reagan was then in office) and particular organs of the body politic – in this case the Constitution, his party, Congress, the Executive Branch, his staff, and foreign relations. The ms. was complete and only had to be revised by each of the contributors, because it was now a year or two since they were written. I had published nothing before on the U.S. and seized this opportunity. One of the authors thought that Cass Canfield of Harper and Row was interested in the book, and so it proved, although the conditions they offered were pitiful. Then the problems began. It took much longer than anticipated for Shaw to obtain the updated versions, and when it came to his providing his introduction and concluding article, the delays became so dreadful that I began to contemplate telling him that I could not go on. I had to resort to an undignified amalgam of threats and wheedling because I did want the book. Eventually the mss. came into my hands, and it was plain that Shaw had had some sort of nervous breakdown. But it was not all over, because he had to produce the index, and over this I nearly had a nervous breakdown myself. So when the book came out I was exhausted and it was not for another year or two that it suddenly struck me what a beautiful formula this prime example of an unintentionally difficult author had come up with. Why not apply it to do other polities?

We started with the U.K., and I turned to the versatile Richard Hodder-Williams, professor of politics at Bristol, one of the contributors to the American volume. (He is also the son of a former chairman of Hodder & Stoughton, and was one of the many family shareholders in the company before, regrettably, it was sold in 1993; thus we were able to exchange plenty of publishing gossip.) A contract was signed, with Donald Shell as co-editor, and although this volume took an inordinately long time to complete, the process was not traumatic. Before it appeared, as *Churchill to Major* (1995), there were five others: *Malan to De Klerk* (1993), *Menzies to Keating* (1993), *De Gaulle to Mitterrand* (1993), *Adenauer to Kohl* (1994) and *Nehru to the Nineties* (1995). It was the only time we had ever been involved in a 'series' – something much favoured in the world of textbook publishing, but which in general I think of as constricting. Here it was compelling. The editors of the volumes were all pleased with what they were doing, and the reaction was good. As ever, I had the feeling that a bigger publisher would have done more justice to the books, not editorially but in their promotion. Once I start, I can enjoy editing a book on almost any subject within my range, but these books are rare among C. Hurst offerings in being ones I could also objectively read for pleasure, especially *Churchill to Major*, where the subjectmatter is so familiar.

I had long wanted to publish something about Northern Ireland when a man came to see me in the late 1980s who wanted to write 'something about' the situation in South Africa, where he had recently been teaching. He was Robert Crawford, a minister in the Presbyterian church and a doctor of divinity, but when I asked him if he had a particular angle related to his profession, he said no. I did not think that the book he wanted to write would offer anything new, but noticing that he spoke with an Ulster accent, softened by long absence, I asked if he would write 'something about' the Ulster Protestants, his own people, to help those outside Northern Ireland to understand them better. It was clear that to the *bien pensant* people in mainland Britain they they were generally more odious than the nationalists, an attitude which, whether unfair or not, I felt should be tempered by greater understanding. Crawford accepted my proposal and wrote the book published in 1987 as *Loyal to King Billy*. He included what I thought a convincing comparison between his people and the Afrikaners of South Africa. We were pleased when, a random television interview with a nationalist prisoner in his cell showed a copy of it clearly visible on the shelf behind him.

After this a young Jesuit priest and academic born in the working-class nationalist Turf Lodge area of Belfast, Oliver Plunkett Rafferty, asked us if we would like him to write for us a history of the Ulster Catholics; we encouraged him and the book was written and published. And we published a collection of sociological writings about the South Asian communities in Britain called *Desh Pardesh*, meaning 'home away from home'. So we have gradually become more interested in our own islands.

The Freedom to Publish Committee and I

Paranoia, compounded of different causes, has doubtless played a part in my relations with the Publishers Association. The leading figures in the publishing Establishment have been of my age-group and background since the early 1970s, yet for a long time I felt that I did not belong. I had never worked in one of the major publishing houses, I certainly did not come from a publishing family, and, most important of all, I was a small independent who, with the growing indifference to disapproval that comes with age, sometimes expressed views on controversial issues that were at odds with the Establishment view. I have already given some idea of what these were – mostly matters of procedure and ethos. But I had also come to think that I wanted a little place for myself in the sun.

I became intensely interested when, during the presidency (1981-3) of Tim Rix, head of Longman, an intelligent man whom I admire and like although his performance in the P.A. seemed to me lacklustre, a small working group was set up to prepare a 'code of practice' for publishers in their relations with authors. It had been thought necessary as a pre-emptive strike to pacify the authors' lobby, which was getting increasingly restive at what it considered unfair contracts, high-handed behaviour in publishing houses generally, and sloppy accounting procedures. The chairman of the group was Rayner Unwin, another nice man and, as Sir Stanley Unwin's son, by heredity a senior figure in the industry though never a chip off the old block, and the tenth draft, passed by the Council, was released to the membership for what was assumed to be automatic rubber-stamping. I thought it a feeble and quite unnecessary document, riddled with small anomalies and archaisms, and sent in a list of queries and suggestions. Possibly my agitation in some way led to a special general meeting being called to debate it; anyway, the 'code' came out to a muted fanfare and was immediately forgotten. My reaction to it was prompted partly by no more than a desire to be involved in something about which I felt my ideas were clear and knowledge adequate; but also an unfashionable willingness to defend the prerogatives of publishers *vis-à-vis* their authors. This came rushing to the surface when Faber and Faber announced a new 'minimum terms' agreement, allegedly inspired by the 'code of practice', which seemed to me a surrender of a publisher's legitimate interests and therefore not ultimately in its authors' interests. The superior airs of that firm had long got up my nose, and I thought this a cynically calculated stunt designed to make it look good in the eyes of the uninstructed, but at the same time naive. I wrote a rude and personal article in the *Bookseller* ('Mandarins and Applecarts', 21 July 1984), which was studiously ignored here but drew forth a comment from my friend Grant Barnes, then director of Stanford University Press: 'I sent a copy . . . to my old friend and mentor, August Frugé [former director of the University of California Press] [...] Of the content of your article Fruge comments: "I not only agree with what he says and with his way of thinking, but I almost felt as if I were reading myself, so much like me did he sound at times.'"

Tim Rix was followed as P.A. president by Philip Attenborough, the last holder of that office born in the purple. Philip became chairman of his family's firm Hodder & Stoughton in 1973 while still in his thirties, and was the third P.A. president the firm had supplied since the 1950s, doubtless from a sense of *noblesse oblige* as well as genuine public spirit. Philip took his task seriously, and this showed in his public performance – the only part I was in a position to judge. During his time in office I read in the P.A. newsletter that a small 'Freedom to Publish' (F.T.P.) committee had been set up, chaired by André Deutsch, in pursuance of a request by the International Publishers Association (I.P.A.) to all national associations. I immediately decided that I wanted to join it – believing incidentally that my long acquaintance with André would help. My first approach was made through the P.A. committee concerned with academic and professional publishing, to which I belonged, suggesting that I should represent it. It seemed obvious that issues of intellectual and academic freedom are as prevalent in this kind of publishing as they are in the literary field. The answer was that the group was small and informal, and no formal representation of special interests could be considered. I wrote twice to Philip pressing the point and saying that my interest was personal, though coloured by the kind of publishing in which I engaged, which I thought should be represented anyway as a matter of course. Each time I got an evasive but negative answer, and when Gordon Graham succeeded Philip in 1975 I wrote to him repeating my request and saying, almost though not quite *en clair*, that I would resign from the Association if it was refused again. He wrote back that he could not see what the problem was, and so I became a member.

André is not a committee man and did not direct the proceedings. However, on the question of freedom to publish he is a fundamentalist – and the fact that I am only one (as far as my courage allows) where *political* censorship is at issue and had a secret desire to play the devil's advocate was one of the reasons which had driven me on. Two people ran the committee: Charles Clark, a lawyer and former publisher, also author of the standard manual on copyright, who has been the F.T.P. committee's secretary and factotum from its foundation to the time of writting, and Graham C. Greene, the industry's most accomplished committee man and lobbyist, ambitious and determined. The well-known quatrain written about George Nathaniel Curzon when he was an undergraduate at Oxford requires very little modification when applied to Graham. Yet he is not grand all the time, and is incapable of unkindness or malice, which was far from being true of his uncle and namesake; and anyone born, as it were, bearing someone else's famous name undoubtedly deserves some sympathy.

At the end of the first meeting I attended, André announced that he was standing down – 'nothing to do with Christopher joining', he added with his engaging want of tact. But I believe he had made his main point, which was to give the F.T.P. committee his blessing, merely by presiding over it for a short time. He was succeeded by George Richardson, an Oxford economics don who was chief executive of O.U.P. and later became Warden of Keble College; I liked him instinctively, and used occasionally to write to him asking for his opinion about one thing or another. He left in due course and at his last meeting – we only met twice a year – asked us whom we would like as his successor. This simple act of courtesy was astonishing since the P.A.'s elected officers tend to be suffocatingly hierarchical in their instincts (Gordon Graham has been the most obvious exception in my time), and the executive, in the person of Clive Bradley, unusually certain of what is wanted all the time. We gave George some ideas, but our words were wasted. Soon the announcement came forth that our new chairman was to be none other than Philip Attenborough. I wrote to Michael Turner, the president, protesting that none of us had asked for him; Michael's reply was that we needed an experienced chairman, which Philip undoubtedly was. However, I wondered whether that was the most important qualification for the job (one that he may have possessed in his own eyes was an involvement in I.P.A. affairs).

Certainly Philip kept a steady hand on the tiller during his four-year tenure, but I would be hard-pressed to say that he contributed any ideas or initiatives of his own. Did I contribute anything? Not much but I wrote the fifth and final clause of our quasi-constitution, which set forth a concern for international developments, even if unconnected with the affairs of British publishers, and pressed successfully for the editor of *Index on Censorship* to be co-opted, to reinforce it. Giles de la Mare succeeded Philip and took a more vigorous and pro-active line, and I also claim the credit for bringing him on to the committee.

The F.T.P. committee was thrown back on its heels during Philip's time there by the *Satanic Verses* affair, which raised the subtle, difficult and fascinating issue of what constitutes blasphemy in a book, and whether there should be any legal sanction against it. But this issue was soon overlaid and subsumed by the stark and straightfoward issue of Ayatollah Khomeini's *fatwa,* after which it was permanently lost from view. The *fatwa* was now everything, and from then on became the concern of governments, but it was also taken to justify a liberal-fundamentalist approach to blasphemy in literature, which was said to be an outdated concept. There were calls for the admittedly partial and inadequate English blasphemy legislation to be repealed and not replaced. British Muslims, on the other hand, wanted it extended, and were in despair at the obliviousness to their sensitivities shown by the dominant, post-Christian liberal Establishment, whose line the F.T.P. committee uncritically followed. I could not help asking Philip Attenborough what he, as head of a firm known for its religious publishing, thought about blasphemy, but it was hitting below the belt and I did not press the question.

But what about the continuation, discontinuation or replacement of the old blasphemy law? Visiting Bergen in the late spring of 1993 I found what seemed to me the answer. In Oslo, as always, I spent some time with Hans Butenschön, and he told me that while in Bergen – my next stop – I should make a point of visiting Atle Grahl-Madsen, an eminent professor of international law (one of his books had been published by Praeger) and in particular an expert on the legal problems of refugees. He was known to be writing a summation of his life's work – in a race against time because he was dying of stomach cancer. I have not met many people when they have known they were staring certain death in the face – my mother was perhaps the only one – and viewed such a meeting with nervousness. None the less I phoned Grahl-Madsen when I reached Bergen and in a robust voice he invited me to his house the next afternoon. He said to me after my arrival that, as a last resort, he was receiving treatment from a shaman, and she would come while I was there; he would then retire with her for the treatment, at the end of which we would have dinner.

It would be difficult to say the number of reasons why this was an interesting visit. The house was a few miles outside the city overlooking a fjord, and they had not been there long; he was in his late sixties – a large and handsome man, though now haggard and with bowed shoulders. Only a few years earlier he had left his wife of many years and remarried – a middle-aged Danish woman who matched him in looks and intelligence. He had had a massive operation the year before our meeting, and then earlier this spring they found that the cancer had come back and was getting worse. No medical remedy could now save him.

We talked for some time, and it soon became clear that he did not have any attractive publishing proposition to make. He could immediately offer me two things: one was a book that had already been published by an international organisation, and which could be reprinted with a new short introduction; and the other was a collection of his articles. If I would accept these, he could promise me the book he was working on (with a co-author) – if he had time to complete it, which he did not think likely.

The time was past when the shaman was due to arrive – her time-keeping was notoriously uncertain – and Mrs Grahl-Madsen proposed that we should dine straight away. So we went to a table in the window looking out on. the fjord, over which the evening sun on the water was turning to gold. The food and wine were as splendid as the view outside. When finally the shaman did arrive, she and the professor withdrew, leaving us in the company of a lady of about sixty who had driven her here; whenever the shaman came to town it was her custom to house and look after her continuously, in gratitude because the shaman had cured her own supposedly inoperable cancer.

There was a second session of supper for the two visitors, and the rest of us sat with them and talked. The shaman was a Sami (Lapp), from the far north of Norway, who worked for certain months of the year as a healer in Oslo and Bergen, but returned to the north periodically to 're-charge her batteries'. She would stay in her father's encampment: he was a much more famous shaman, from whom she had acquired her skills, but he never came south or mixed in urban society. She herself was in her late forties, but looked younger – short and wiry, with a small, round, open face and straight dark hair that hung below her shoulders. At supper she mentioned that of her two sons one had inherited her skills to a remarkable degree – but both were dead, the 'unskilled' one in a motor-cycle crash, and the other.... She did not say the cause, but when I asked if it had been a murder, she answered yes. In the car returning to the city, she said that she lived in the world of the spirits – the source of all her skills. She had a young Canadian girl disciple, she said, whose familiar spirit with which she was never out of contact was a man who died in the early seventeenth century. She told me that she was writing a doctoral thesis about her father – I wrote to her afterwards expressing interest in it, but she did not reply, and we have not so far been in touch again.

I looked at Grahl-Madsen's collection of articles, but was not tempted. However I felt thankful for the evening I had spent in his house. He soon died with the new work uncompleted. But while we were talking in his study I asked him whether Norway had a law against blasphemy. He took down a fat volume containing the

Norwegian civil penal code, and read to me the following (paragraph 142):

> Any person who by word or deed publicly insults or in an offensive or injurious manner shows contempt for any creed whose practice is permitted in the realm, or for the doctrines or worship of any religious community lawfully existing here, or who is an accessory thereto, shall be liable to fines or to imprisonment for a term not exceeding six months. A prosection will only be instituted when the public interest so requires.

I thought this admirable, and would like to see the same formula adopted in Britain, even if the Church of England loses its established status and we become a purely secular state.

The F.T.P. committee has many other concerns besides blasphemy, but this is not the place to dwell on item.

A Temporary Victory for the Dinosaurs

Much will be written in the future about the ending of the Net Book Agreement (N.B.A.) in 1995, its causes and effects, and various theories will no doubt be developed about how it happened. The N.B.A. was brought into existence at the very end of the 19th century through the concerted efforts of leading publishers of the time, among whom Sir Frederick Macmillan was pre-eminent, with the purpose of bringing order primarily into retail bookselling but thence into publishing too. It was the bedrock of both trade associations, particularly the Publishers Association (P.A.). Publishers fixed the prices of books, and booksellers had to stick to them. The N.B.A. was challenged in the early 1960s in the wake of the abolition of Retail Price Maintenance by the Conservative government under Harold Macmillan; but an epic defence in the Restrictive Practices Court resulted in its being declared not to be against the public interest, and thus it was preserved for a further three decades. It was vindicated again in the 1980s, but the decision of the Office of Fair Trading to refer it to that Court again in 1994 was a mighty blow, and there was no unanimous will to resist it. Both Terry Maher's retail empire (Dillon's) and the Reed publishing group had already tried to destroy it. It was generally felt to be in a fragile state, and that one more serious push would cause its last defences to buckle.

None the less, the P.A. Council with the vigorous support of Eddie Bell, the head of HarperCollins and a man with a fierce protective loyalty towards his company which sometimes leads him to lash out and break heads in its defence,* resolved at its meeting in September 1994 to defend the N.B.A., which meant undertaking to accept legal costs which could run to £1 million. Such is the clout of HarperCollins under Eddie's dynamic leadership that his support was considered the next thing to a cast-iron guarantee that the defence would be carried through with utmost vigour. Immediately after the result of the P.A. 'Council of War' was publicly announced, the head of Hodder Headline** announced that it would be ceasing to observe the N.B.A. regulations at the end of the year; that firm was then still a member of the P.A. but later resigned. I was the only Council member at that meeting who advised against defending the N.B.A. My reason was that it needed only one P.A. member with sufficient clout to decide, in its own short-term interests, that it would no longer observe the N.B.A. for the defence to collapse, however much money had hitherto been spent in legal fees. I had a shrewd suspicion which member this would be.

The N.B.A.'s collapse became definitive a year later when Eddie Bell and Simon Master (managing director of Random House in London, and president-elect of the P.A.) agreed with W.H. Smith that they would henceforth do deals with it, and inevitably with the other major bookselling chains as well, enabling the current best-sellers to be sold to the public, new, at a discount. The P.A. president, Nicholas Chapman, stated publicly, after a discussion with Eddie Bell, that he considered the N.B.A to be a millstone around the neck of the trade. Eddie remarked that the P.A. should in future concern itself with 'what it is really for' rather that with the N.B.A. All this happened less than a week before a P.A. Council meeting,

---

* One instance, reported in the *Bookseller*, can suffice. The Booksellers Association (B.A.) publishes an annual Christmas catalogue of top sellers, and publishers pay considerable sums to have their titles included. However the decision over which titles to include rests with an independent jury. In 1994 several of HarperCollins's submissions were accepted, but one – a retelling of the Christmas story by Jeffrey Archer – was turned down. Eddie was upset and asked for it to be reconsidered. It was again turned down, and he promptly ordered that all HarperCollins's titles in the catalogue be pulled out, thus depriving the B.A. of revenue in the region of £28,000. The innocent excuse given was that HC particularly wanted to keep Archer sweet, and expected the B.A.'s jurors – whose concern did not extend beyond the quality of the books it was considering – to understand this.

** The 125-year-old Hodder & Stoughton was sold to the seven-year-old Headline Books, ending Philip Attenborough's career and resulting in the creation of this new conglomerate.

at which, in the growing atmosphere of crisis over the N.B.A., a decision was expected on whether to continue the defence or not. The P.A. Council's freedom to decide had been pre-empted.

The *Bookseller* canvassed Council members for their views, and mine was that Chapman had acted inconsistently with his supposedly impartial role as P.A. president with his indiscreet 'millstone' remark, and should resign. At the start of the fateful Council meeting, the officers themselves brought up the question of possible resignation. Simon Master, who I did not think had acted, and certainly had not spoken, inconsistently with his status as vice-president, offered to resign in a decent and straightforward fashion which compelled my respect. Chapman made an unconvincing defence of his position. One member present, Iain Burns of Macmillan, did quietly resign afterwards in protest at Chapman's action, but at the meeting itself the moment was allowed to pass and both officers remained *in situ*. But the worst thing of all was that word had gone around that if we forced Nicholas Chapman to resign, Eddie Bell would remove HarperCollins from membership of the P.A., with disastrous results for its solvency. I now regret that I did not mention this supposed threat at the meeting and ask for comments – Bell himself was ill and unable to attend – or persist in my contention that Chapman should resign. If the threat was real, a serious scandal would have come to light, and better so; if it was a fabrication, we could have asked how the rumour came about.

Having a tendency for contrariness in trade affairs, I tried for years to find reasons why the N.B.A. was not a good thing; I thought particularly that if serious paperbacks could be offered at reductions, there would be a beneficial cultural effect (I am an unashamed élitist). Terry Maher's early efforts at price-cutting showed a reverse type of élitist thinking; the books affected were hardback bestsellers, mainly fiction. I still do not know who buys these books, except as gifts, but obviously there are people who do. This is how things have gone on since the N.B.A. ended. As the moment of truth approached, I realised that I had to take a position if only to satisfy myself, since my views affected no one else. C. Hurst & Co. would not be greatly affected whatever happened, which made it seem all the more important not to wash my hands of the affair. I became convinced that, overall and considering the public good, the advantages of having the N.B.A. in being greatly outweighed the disadvantages. In the days before what was to have been the crucial Council meeting, Council members received a stream of letters and faxes from booksellers of all sizes, begging us to save it. A letter from the eminent Edinburgh bookseller Ainslie Thin pointed out a crucial point I had not understood before. Those hardback bestsellers, about which a self-confessed élitist can feel superior, are the staple stock item of every bookshop, small ones in small places as well as large ones in cities. And these are the books which were now, above all, to be subject to discounting. Only the big bookselling chains can afford to negotiate deals with publishers on such favourable terms to themselves that they can offer deeply discounted prices; the small bookshops cannot, and thus they are liable to lose an essential part of their business. Who will buy a big book at full price from a small shop, however good the service it offers, if it is available for several pounds less from the nearest big one? Some quixotic souls may do, but not many.

It was an ugly and a sad business. The P.A. intends to monitor the results of the N.B.A.'s collapse as they unfold. I hope that one day it will be restored.

A Tornado Hits Bedford Square

A ripple of curiosity tinged with mild consternation went round the publishing world in 1988[*] when, on the retirement of George Richardson as Secretary to the Delegates and chief executive of Oxford University Press, his place was taken by Sir Roger Elliott, F.R.S., Wykeham Professor of Physics in the University. He was already sixty, and the appointment was for five years.

Who heads O.U.P. always excites some general interest, but having an eminent physicist in charge was something new, not to say portentous. The Secretary to the Delegates – they are the academic overseers of the Press – has always (till 1993) been a don, but for most of the twentieth century the world at large would not have known or cared who filled that post. The person who mattered was the Publisher, thus titled, who since early in the century had his office in London (till the 1970s, when it was demolished, at Amen House in the shadow of St Paul's Cathedral), and whose name appeared on the title page or verso of the Press's publications; thus you could not own an Oxford Bible or dictionary or a volume of the World's

---

[*] There was more than a ripple inside the Press. Richard Charkin, a 'Young Turk' for whom a bright future there had been expected, left in disgust and joined the Reed group as the person in charge of 'Consumer Books' (who coined this peculiarly odious phrase?). In that role he was responsible for pulling the group out of the P.A., and did his utmost – some time before its final collapse – to undermine the Net Book Agreement.

Classics without being subliminally aware of Humphrey Milford, Geoffrey Cumberlege or John Brown. Although technically a 'player' while the Delegates to whom he reported were the 'gentlemen', he was a great figure – until the Press was repatriated to Oxford and the sole 'Publisher' was replaced by a number of senior publishing executives. The Secretary emerged for the first time in living memory as the dominant figure in public perception as well as in fact.

Richardson had kept a low profile, but Elliott quickly imposed his authority on the whole trade. The Publisher or, under the new dispensation, the Chief Executive at O.U.P. has almost always found his way on to the P.A. Council, and three have become president. With Elliott this process was speeded up, partly no doubt because of the short time in which he would be available, but also because Clive Bradley, with a sure instinct, targeted him as someone who could be of great use and with whom he could work in harmony. A man of great brainpower, energetic and independent, he was of a quite different species from the average 'senior publisher'. Courteous without being very warm, and good-humoured without having a sense of humour, he was aloof by nature and not by cultivation; indeed he seemed completely natural and without any artifices.

The first task allotted to him – and who more suitable than an Oxbridge professor, for whom this would be familiar territory? – was to chair a small committee to devise a formula for targeting and inducting new Council members that would replace the traditional 'live' method of election. He came up with the idea, already mentioned, of having a slate of candidates to be proposed and seconded by the officers. A document detailing the first draft of such a scheme was leaked to me early in 1992 by a friend who rightly thought that I would appreciate this (as he put it) 'Stalinist' plan. I was about to leave for the International Publishers Association congress in Delhi and, fired by a quotation from Gibbon ('The principles of a free constitution are irrecoverably lost when the legislative power is nominated by the executive') at the masthead of the *Times of India*, sent from there a letter protesting against it to the *Bookseller*. This forced Paul Scherer, then P.A. president, to admit its existence and defend it. It became law in 1995, in a slightly less draconian form than that proposed in the draft. Elliott took over the presidency in 1993 from Scherer, a man I liked and admired.[*]

Elliott, having already revolutionised the Council recruitment system,

---

[*] When Scherer, under the rules, stood down as a P.A. officer in 1994, I asked and was allowed to sing his praises in a brief speech at the A.G.M. When I had finished, Elliott, his neighbour on the platform, turned to him and remarked *sotto voce*: 'That was nice of Christopher, but wasn't it a bit over the top?'

was instrumental in introducing another radical change. Up till 1993, every president since the P.A. was founded had been elected to serve for two years. But Elliott was due to retire from his post at O.U.P. within less than one year from the beginning of his term, and therefore agreed to serve as president for that year only. Unprecedented it may have been, but his reasons were ones of the utmost propriety. Perhaps no run-of-the-mill publisher could have set such a condition and got away with it, but Elliott, quietly and I am sure unintentionally, had accumulated great prestige within the P.A., and the departure from custom was accepted without question. But this proved to be the stone which started a landslide. It soon became clear that what Elliott had done on his own account for honourable reasons would be seized on as the norm for the future: among the whole (narrow) range of 'senior publishers' eligible for the presidency it appeared that most would not agree to serve at all, or would do so, at the most, for one year. The pressure on company chief executives is indeed severe,* and one could understand this; but I did not sympathise with it, because Paul Scherer, a successful chief executive (of Transworld), served as president for two years in 1991-3 without complaint and in a way that won him only plaudits. I also felt sure that it needed two years for a president to 'get into the saddle', and that he could only truly give of his best in the second year; I said this at a special general meeting called to pass the innovation into law, but when I asked for a vote Elliott told me from the chair that this would not be in order because I had not given advance notice. Damn technicalities! The pressure on the P.A.'s chief executive is acute for most of the time, and a one-year presidency was not going to make his task easier, as Clive Bradley admitted. Elliott managed the little affair with his usual vigour and gave no sign that he thought the reform other than desirable.

It was ironical that the first president to be elected for a one-year term, Nicholas Chapman, actually served for two years. This was because the president-elect – Paula Kahn, chief executive of Longman – resigned her post in reaction to the dismemberment of that great publishing house (founded in 1724 and sold by the Longman family to the Pearson group in the late 1960s) by its owners. I pleaded with my fellow members at the first Council meeting after the an-

---

* Not least from *their* ultimate bosses. This was vividly brought home to me when Trevor Glover, then U.K. managing director of Penguin, was proposed as vice-president in 1996. Nicholas Chapman, when putting the matter before Council, unctuously said that we would all be pleased to know that Peter Mayer (international boss of Penguin) had given Trevor's candidature his blessing. I thought this terribly *infra dig*.

nouncement to give Paula 'cover' so that she could go on to serve as president (incidentally, the first woman to do so) with a non-executive position in a substantial publishing house, even if only temporarily. I 'started the bidding' then and there by offering her a non-executive, unpaid directorship of C. Hurst & Co., which lightened the proceedings somewhat, but when I said that it was unthinkable for the P.A. to 'dump' Paula, Nicholas Chapman, the president, reacted with horror, at which I modified the expression to 'letting her go'. In the event she was 'let go' and did not become president, and because it was too late to find a new 'live' vice-president, i.e. one who would succeed as president, a 'dummy' one was nominated in the person of my fellow small publisher (though one with a long history in 'big' publishing), Colin Whurr – it was never intended that he should be in the succession for the presidency – and Chapman remained for an extra year. One can only speculate whether, with Paula as president, the exit from the N.B.A. would have been less messy than it was with Chapman. Elliott by this time was no longer around in 19 Bedford Square, but if he had been, it is inconceivable that he would not have led the Association through the crisis in deed as well as in name; with his unquestionable integrity and authority he might have been able to bang the parties' heads together to ensure an orderly outcome, whatever that might have been. Even after retiring form O.U.P. he continued to chair a P.A. committee on the knotty subject of photocopying.

When Elliott took office as president I could not avoid feeling that the Association should never have as its titular head someone other than a professional publisher, which he never had been and never could be. I also resented the way he had come in, an outsider to the trade, and initiated, one after the other, two major changes in the ecology of our Association. I disliked the changes themselves, but I disliked much more the fact that Elliott, a physicist whose professional centre of gravity was a world away from the *souk* of commercial publishing, had engineered them. Tony Benn brought about two great innovations in the British constitution – the right to renounce peerages and the referendum – but at least he was a politician, whose duty was to be political. Elliott was an apparatchik and instinctively in tune with the corporatist nature of modern 'big' publishing. But what did it all really mean to him other than as a few interesting little problems to solve? I wished that this physicist's hobby had been chamber music instead of administration.

In the early summer of 1996 I found that he was sitting behind me at a meeting. It was more than two years since he had stood down as president and much had happened since, little of it good.

Seeing him there, I felt a sudden and unexpected surge of warmth. My words to him were: 'Roger, you probably never expected to hear me say this, but I miss you.' He seemed not displeased with the compliment.

It may seem strange to my colleagues, even those among them who are most loyal to the Publishers Association, that this body arouses in me such interest and attachment, in which the fury of a jealous lover is occasionally mixed. They may think that I blind myself to the Association as it actually is, and see only what I would like it to be, or how I imagine it once was in a mythical Arcadian past. This must be partly true, but it is one with my belief that the Association would be a really fine thing if all publishers belonged to it – even if they were compelled to do so by law, as in Germany. Here most of the largest firms are prepared to blackmail the other members by threatening to withdraw and thus bankrupt the Association, if they do not get what they currently want. Smaller ones casually decide either to withdraw – or not to join, having never done so – merely because they think it is not cost-effective for them. Some will say that they are entitled to do this if it is how they feel, but I say that they are not.

Members' interests – in the narrow sense of what we publish and whom we sell to – differ, but in the sense of creating or preserving a tolerable environment in which we can all prosper, they are the same. What motivates us is also essentially the same, and because it contains an element of idealism, it should extend to making the small sacrifice – proportionately the same for every member – of paying dues to the Association. The sacrifice, needless to say, can be many times outweighed by the satisfactions of membership, which members can help to create for themselves if they do not find them ready-made.

End and Beginning

To my father probably, and to my Uncle Gerald certainly, publishing would have meant a partnership in a reputable firm,[*] and they might

---

[*] In 1995 I caught a glimpse of how this might work. Gerald had had two books published by Constable, then as now highly reputable, and on the strength of this Ralph Arnold, then a power in the firm, agreed to see me. Evidently putting the cart before the horse,

even have thought it a suitable occupation for me since I was apparently suitable for no other; 'publishing' was a less opprobrious version of being sent to the colonies for those of indoor rather that outdoor inclinations and a smattering of literary education, but no over-riding aptitude. But publishing chose me rather than the other way round. When I applied for a job with the unpromising-sounding firm of Barrie and Rockliff I had no idea of what was about to happen. And it did not truly happen till I met John MacCallum Scott and Fred Praeger and saw a kind of publishing that would suit my interests and capabilities as no other could; but my two years with Barrie had shown the way. They vastly enlarged the experience I had first gleaned at the Architectural Press and even at Rolls-Royce; then Pall Mall and Praeger enlarged it in other directions. So, when I started on my own, I was more or less a fully formed journeyman, capable of producing a decently edited and produced book from start to finish. And it is as a journeyman, resolutely determined never to become corporatised, that I have continued.

I have found my home in what has to be called a specialised area of publishing, but it is one that seems to me to give enough play to the spirit to satisfy any idealistic urges. I would not enjoy being any more specialised than I am – say, a publisher of school texts or legal, medical or reference works, lucrative as these branches of the trade can be. On the other hand, although the greatest works of the human spirit are seldom to be found in my field but rather in poetry, drama, novels, *belles lettres,* science, philosophy, biography, 'big' history and religion, I could never feel easy publishing such works. At odd times publishers of genius arise who can identify and encourage the great writers of their time. But although I read for preference novels, biographies and essays, I do not believe I could ever have possessed that flair which gives assurance that one is publishing the best. There is also the danger that, because of either defective judgement or lack of adequate finance, I would have had to be content with publishing the secondrate and unexciting. Publishers are under an obligation to trumpet the virtues of their publications, and I cannot think of anything worse than having to trumpet virtues in a work which one actually knows it to lack. In my field, fortunately, trumpets can never be blown to their full volume.

---

he said that I might be able to become a partner if I could produce £7,000 but before I could explore this possibility he wrote to say there was nothing doing.

Index

Notes 1. Nobody referred to in the book by a pseudonym is included in the Index. 2. An asterisk (*) indicates authorship of a book published by C. Hurst & Co.